# AMERICAN PHILOSOPHIES

*Also Available from Bloomsbury*

*American Philosophy*, Erin McKenna and Scott L. Pratt
*The Continuum Companion to Pragmatism*, ed. Sami Pihlström
*Classical American Philosophy*, Rebecca L. Farinas

# AMERICAN PHILOSOPHIES

## FROM WOUNDED KNEE TO THE PRESENT

*Erin McKenna and Scott L. Pratt*

BLOOMSBURY ACADEMIC
LONDON • NEW YORK • OXFORD • NEW DELHI • SYDNEY

BLOOMSBURY ACADEMIC
Bloomsbury Publishing Plc, 50 Bedford Square, London, WC1B 3DP, UK
Bloomsbury Publishing Inc, 1385 Broadway, New York, NY 10018, USA
Bloomsbury Publishing Ireland, 29 Earlsfort Terrace, Dublin 2, D02 AY28, Ireland

BLOOMSBURY, BLOOMSBURY ACADEMIC and the Diana logo are trademarks of Bloomsbury Publishing Plc

First published in Great Britain 2025

Copyright © Erin McKenna and Scott L. Pratt, 2025

Erin McKenna and Scott L. Pratt have asserted their right under the Copyright, Designs and Patents Act, 1988, to be identified as Authors of this work.

For legal purposes the Acknowledgments on p. ix constitute an extension of this copyright page.

Cover image © Flag #1890 by Alexander B. Pratt

All rights reserved. No part of this publication may be: i) reproduced or transmitted in any form, electronic or mechanical, including photocopying, recording or by means of any information storage or retrieval system without prior permission in writing from the publishers; or ii) used or reproduced in any way for the training, development or operation of artificial intelligence (AI) technologies, including generative AI technologies. The rights holders expressly reserve this publication from the text and data mining exception as per Article 4(3) of the Digital Single Market Directive (EU) 2019/790.

Bloomsbury Publishing Plc does not have any control over, or responsibility for, any third-party websites referred to or in this book. All internet addresses given in this book were correct at the time of going to press. The author and publisher regret any inconvenience caused if addresses have changed or sites have ceased to exist, but can accept no responsibility for any such changes.

A catalogue record for this book is available from the British Library.

ISBN: HB: 978-1-3503-4275-0
PB: 978-1-3503-4274-3
ePDF: 978-1-3503-4276-7
eBook: 978-1-3503-4277-4

Typeset by Deanta Global Publishing Services, Chennai, India
Printed and bound in Great Britain

For product safety related questions contact productsafety@bloomsbury.com.

To find out more about our authors and books visit www.bloomsbury.com and sign up for our newsletters.

*In memory of*
*Roger Sayers Pratt*
*(May 23, 1962–February 25, 2009)*
*Betty Jean Sayers Pratt*
*(July 26, 1932–December 17, 2022)*
*and*
*W. Waugh Smith*
*(June 13, 1917–August 27, 2010)*

# CONTENTS

| | |
|---|---|
| Acknowledgments | ix |
| Prologue | x |
| **Part I   American Philosophies of Resistance** | 1 |
| 1   Introduction | 3 |
| 2   Defining Pluralism: Simon Pokagon, Ida B. Wells-Barnett, and T. Thomas Fortune | 13 |
| 3   Evolution and American Indian Philosophy | 21 |
| 4   Feminist Resistance: Margaret Fuller, Anna Julia Cooper, Jane Addams, and Charlotte Perkins Gilman | 29 |
| 5   Transcendental Origins: Ralph Waldo Emerson and Henry David Thoreau | 41 |
| 6   Labor, Empire, Populism, and the Social Gospel: Washington Gladden, Walter Rauschenbusch, and Jane Addams | 53 |
| 7   A New Name for an Old Way of Thinking: William James | 69 |
| 8   Making Ideas Clear: Charles Sanders Peirce | 77 |
| 9   The Beloved Community and Its Discontents: Josiah Royce and the Realists | 85 |
| 10   War, Anarchism, and Sex: Emma Goldman and Margaret Sanger | 93 |
| 11   Democracy and Social Ethics: John Dewey | 101 |
| **Part II   Resistance and Transition** | 115 |
| 12   Naturalism and Idealism, Fear and Conventionality: Mary Whiton Calkins and Elsie Clews Parsons | 117 |
| 13   Race Riots and the Color Line: W. E. B. Du Bois | 131 |
| 14   Creative Experience: Mary Parker Follett | 141 |

15  Cultural Pluralism: Horace Kallen and Alain Leroy Locke ... 153

16  War and the Rise of Logical Positivism ... 163

17  Analytic Philosophy and the Pluralist Revolt ... 181

Part III  Social Revolutions ... 197

18  Civil Rights: Martin Luther King, Jr., Richard Wright, and James Baldwin ... 199

19  Black Power: Malcolm X, James Cone, Audre Lorde, Bell Hooks, Angela Davis, and Cornel West ... 211

20  Latin America ... 227

21  Red Power, Indigenous Philosophy: Vine Deloria, Jr., and Contemporary American Indian Thought ... 247

22  Feminist Philosophy and Practice ... 267

23  Engaged Philosophy and the Environment: John Muir, Aldo Leopold, Joseph Wood Krutch, Rachel Carson, and Contemporary Environmental Pragmatism ... 289

Part IV  Democratic Futures? ... 309

24  Recovery and Revitalization of the American Tradition ... 311

25  American Philosophy and "the Culture Wars" ... 335

26  American Philosophy for the Future ... 349

Epilogue ... 373
Bibliography ... 381
Index ... 407

# ACKNOWLEDGMENTS

This book, and now this revised edition, is the result of many years of study, writing, and conversation. We cannot hope to thank everyone who has influenced and contributed to our thinking. So we start with thanks to the community of American philosophers, and special thanks to those who are members of the Society for the Advancement of American Philosophy. In particular, we would like to thank those who have provided specific guidance and support: Charlene Haddock Seigfried, John J. McDermott, Marilyn Fischer, Doug Anderson, Leonard Harris, John Lysaker, Mark Johnson, Jerry Rosiek, Douglas Lewis, Lee McBride, John Kaag, Kim Garchar, Trevor Pearce, and Chris Voparil. We would also like to thank our many graduate and undergraduate students in the Department of Philosophy at the University of Oregon who have read and commented on the first edition. They have helped to make clear its value for understanding the history of American philosophy and for understanding the present world and the potential for philosophy to address its problems. We hope you, and all our new readers, will find this both a useful teaching tool and a resource for understanding the American philosophical tradition.

We would like to thank those who reviewed the first edition in preparation for this revision. Their comments and suggestions were very helpful. Even though we were not able to follow through on all the recommended changes and additions—especially those that called for making this long work longer—we appreciate the thoughtful reading and comments. We would like to thank the editors at Bloomsbury who supported this new edition.

We offer special thanks to Aaron Pratt Shepherd and Mary Breiter. Aaron provided invaluable editing and reference work, along with good humor, for the original edition of the book. Mary served as the primary editor for the revised edition, not only carefully editing the text but also providing comments that helped us to improve the clarity and quality of the entire work. Finally, we would like to offer special thanks to Alexander Pratt for the use of his painting, Flag #1890.

Portions of Chapter 3 were taken from Pratt, Scott L., "Agency and Sovereignty in American Indian Philosophy," *Pragmatism Today*, 10 (2) Winter 2019, 16–23. Several paragraphs of Chapter 5 previously appeared in Pratt, Scott L., "Native American Thought and the Origins of Pragmatism," *Ayaangwaamizin: The International Journal of Indigenous Philosophy* 1 (1) 1997, 55–80. Portions of Chapter 26 were published in McKenna, Erin and Scott L. Pratt, "The Present Place and Purpose of American Philosophy," COGNITIO: Revista de Filosofia, 15 (1) 2015.

# PROLOGUE

On New Year's Day, 1891, Dr. Charles Eastman, a Dartmouth-trained physician and Dakota Indian, led a group of one hundred civilians from the Pine Ridge Reservation to a snow-covered field on the bank of Wounded Knee Creek. Three days before, elements of the Seventh US Cavalry—the same unit that had been virtually eliminated by a coalition of American Indian warriors at the Little Bighorn River in Montana fourteen years earlier—killed more than 300 Miniconjou and Hunkpapa Lakota men, women, and children after surrounding and disarming them. "Fully three miles from the scene of the massacre," Eastman wrote in his autobiography, "we found a body of a woman completely covered with a blanket of snow, and from this point on we found them scattered along as they had been relentlessly hunted down and slaughtered while fleeing for their lives" (1916, p. 111).

The massacre that cold December morning marked a response framed by fear and a certainty that in the end the land would be rid of those who would challenge the supremacy of a European America. Writing in the *Aberdeen Saturday Pioneer* newspaper five days after the massacre, L. Frank Baum, later author of *The Wizard of Oz*, summarized:

> The *Pioneer* has before declared that our only safety depends upon the total extermination of the Indians. Having wronged them for centuries, we had better, in order to protect our civilization, follow it up by one more wrong and wipe these untamed and untamable creatures from the face of the earth. In this lies future safety for our settlers and the soldiers who are under incompetent commands. Otherwise, we may expect future years to be as full of trouble with the redskins as those have been in the past. (1891)

At stake in this confrontation was the struggle for American pluralism and what it means to live in the context of difference.

In the larger context, the massacre on the banks of Wounded Knee Creek might seem to be a small matter. The United States was only twenty-five years away from the Civil War, in which more than 620,000 Americans were killed by combat or disease. In 1871, Congress passed the Indian Appropriations Act, ending the practice of negotiating treaties with Indigenous tribes within the United States. In 1876, Reconstruction ended in the Southern states with the withdrawal of federal troops, and in 1890, Mississippi had established the first poll taxes and literacy rules that served to block African Americans from voting. In 1887, the US Congress passed the General Allotment Act (the "Dawes Act") that redistributed parcels of American Indian lands to individual tribal members. The US government claimed the leftover land and sold or gave most of it to White settlers, as well as to railroad, lumber, and mining companies.

By 1890, industrialization was well underway; in an effort to stop the growth of monopolies, Congress passed the Sherman Anti-Trust laws that year. In November, after the collapse of banks in England, panic hit the New York Stock Exchange, beginning a period of decline that would culminate in the financial panic of 1893. In the census of 1890, nearly 15 percent of the

## Prologue

US population was identified as "foreign born" (the highest percentage in any census, although the 2010 census reported 12.9 percent, the highest level since 1910), and about 12 percent of the population was identified as Black. The census also reported that US territory included about 248,000 American Indians, a decrease of 38 percent in just 40 years. The 1890 census also declared, as part of its report, that the United States no longer had a "frontier" (Porter, 1892).

In the midst of all this, White America began to follow news of a new "religious" movement among Western American Indians. In the spring of 1890, an Oglala Lakota named Kicking Bear addressed a Lakota council. In his address, Kicking Bear described a journey to the Great Spirit, who entrusted him with a message for all Native American peoples that, with sufficient faith and the practice of a ceremony called the Ghost Dance, White people would be covered over with earth, Indigenous plants and animals would be restored to the land, and Native peoples would again "eat and drink, hunt, and rejoice" (Kicking Bear, 1890).

Despite initial reports of the Dance as unimportant, White Americans quickly changed their assessment and came to the conclusion that the Ghost Dance was in fact a threat. On November 23, 1890, the *New York Times* published a long report under the headline "It Looks Like War." The article led with a statement from Little Wound, a Lakota from the Pine Ridge reservation, explaining that the people would not cease their dancing at the request of the Indian Agent, Daniel F. Royer. Little Wound was reported as saying:

> I understand that the soldiers have come on the reservation. What have they come for? We have done nothing. Our dance is a religious dance, and we are going to dance until spring. If we find then that the Christ does not appear, we will stop dancing, but, in the meantime, troops or no troops, we shall start our dance on this creek in the morning. (*New York Times*, 1890)

The reporter concluded: "This letter is an open defiance to the troops [now stationed at Pine Ridge]. The ghost dancers have been warned to stop their revolting orgies and this is their answer." Agent Royer was then quoted: "The [Lakota] mean war. They have been ordered to stop their dancing. They have refused to do so. It now remains for the soldiers to enforce their orders" (*New York Times*, 1890).

Within several months, the Ghost Dance had gone from a curiosity and a "craze," as some called it, to fanaticism, and finally to a certain cause of war despite Native appeals to the contrary and pleas for peace. In order to preempt the expected Indian attacks, the US military mobilized troops throughout the West, sending 600 to 700 troops to the Pine Ridge Agency in October 1890. The troops were commanded by General Nelson Miles (1839–1925), who had led the troops who captured Chief Joseph and the Nez Perce in 1877. Miles would later lead the troops who put down the Pullman Strike in 1894, lead the invasion of Puerto Rico in 1898, and run for president of the United States in 1904. [Citations]

On December 28, 1890, Chief Big Foot's band of Lakota encountered Major Whiteside and elements of the Seventh Cavalry and agreed to be escorted peacefully to an established camp along Wounded Knee Creek on the way to Pine Ridge. There, the Lakota spent the night surrounded by US troops, who celebrated the "capture" of Big Foot and his people. The next morning, now under the command of Major Forsyth, the Seventh Cavalry separated the Lakota into two groups of 106 men and approximately 250 women and children and demanded that the Lakota surrender their weapons. When nearly all the weapons had been surrendered, someone—probably a deaf-mute Lakota man—fired his weapon as some soldiers tried to take it away.

The soldiers quickly retreated to the perimeter of the Indian camp, and then the Seventh Cavalry, arrayed in a square around the camp, opened fire. Within an hour, as most of the Lakota lay dead or dying, a blizzard moved in. Survivors that could be found by the army were loaded into wagons and taken to the Pine Ridge Agency along with thirty-nine wounded soldiers. When the blizzard ended, 146 Lakota men, women, and children were unceremoniously buried in a mass grave. It is likely that many more were killed and their bodies removed by relatives during the blizzard before the burial party arrived from Pine Ridge. Still others were wounded as they fled the carnage and later died of their wounds. Some estimate that more than 300 of the 356 members of Big Foot's group were killed at the creek. Twenty-five soldiers were also killed, most as a result of friendly fire from across the square.

Newspapers declared that a great battle had been fought and the "Sioux Rebellion" had been quelled. To confirm the valor of the Seventh Cavalry in its action against the Lakota, eighteen Congressional Medals of Honor were granted to soldiers involved in the massacre, more than in any other single US military action before or since. While the commanding general and others claimed that the Ghost Dance was part of a plot to attack White settlements, no evidence was found then or since to verify the claim. The "preemptive" strike effectively ended most of the efforts of the Plains Indians to live life free of reservations and the US Office of Indian Affairs. Although the military forces remained ready to fight for some months after, over the next few years the military turned its interests elsewhere—first to suppressing labor actions and then to the Spanish-American War.

While the Ghost Dance offered hope to Native peoples, it posed deep questions for Whites. How were they to understand the claims of renewal by prophets like Kicking Bear? What did the prophecy portend for relations along the borders in the West? Was it possible to coexist with people who held such beliefs?

Most Whites, it appears, concluded that the Ghost Dance was a threat that must be ended. While some favored a policy of aggressive assimilation where Native beliefs and cultures were set aside in favor of Christianity, property ownership, and farming, others claimed that such a policy was too slow and ineffective. According to them, the "awful" action at Wounded Knee was a necessary, even humanitarian, response because it brought a quick end to a "craze" that was good for neither Whites nor Indians. *The Word Carrier* concluded in January 1891, "Taking [the slaughter of a whole tribe of Indians] in its bearings on the whole condition of things among the rebellious [Teton] Sioux it was a blessing. It was needful that these people should feel in some sharp terrible way the just consequences of their actions, and be held in wholesome fear from further folly" (DeMallie, 1982, p. 397).

These assessments of the situation, however, did not stand on their own. Beneath the proclamations of those who favored assimilation and those who favored war, there operated a certain way of thinking—about knowledge and the nature of the world—through which non-Native people heard the prophets and their message. In retrospect, the Ghost Dance and the action at Wounded Knee can be seen not only as historical events but also as a signal moment in the development of a set of philosophical commitments that gave meaning and direction to those in the dominant society who took up arms against the Lakota. Such commitments—still active in American society—mark a logic in which incompatible ways of thinking can only be resolved through assimilation or exclusion. In resisting the alternatives, the Ghost Dancers in effect left the dominant society no choice but the destruction of Native people.

After Wounded Knee, however, thinkers, Native and non-Native, came forward to offer an alternative set of philosophical commitments that could lead to a broader conception of pluralism and a wider range of responses to conflicts in a divided world. Against the demands for progress, wealth, unification, and certainty, diverse thinkers offered critical challenges—diverse philosophies of resistance.

The classical pragmatists, Charles S. Peirce, William James, and John Dewey, tried to show the limits of established philosophies by reconceiving the practice of inquiry, the idea of self, and the nature of democracy. American Indian thinkers, including Charles Eastman (Santee Sioux), Arthur Parker (Seneca), Gertrude Bonnin (Yankton Dakota), and Luther Standing Bear (Oglala Lakota), challenged extermination and assimilation by proposing ideas of community and place that drew on North American Indigenous traditions. W. E. B. Du Bois and Jane Addams challenged industrial capitalism and aimed to reconceive communities around an idea that Addams called "lateral progress." Josiah Royce, Alain LeRoy Locke, and Horace Kallen offered a notion of community around a logic of borders that could inform experience in the context of lived diversity. These philosophies of resistance have rarely found a place in academic discussions of American philosophy either as they are practiced today or as they were developed over the past century and a half. Reasons for this neglect are probably connected with the interests of these philosophers of resistance who, in their most critical work, aimed to make the complacent uncomfortable and the dogmatic doubtful.

On September 11, 2001, Islamic fundamentalists hijacked four commercial airliners and successfully used three of them in an attack on the World Trade Center in New York City and the Pentagon in Washington, D.C. Innocent lives were taken and, in the wake of the attack, as in the wake of Wounded Knee, Americans asked how they could go forward in a world still framed by apparently incommensurable differences. From one angle, the others who seemed to threaten the American vision were "religious fanatics"—not the particular men who carried out the attacks, but peoples who find themselves living in a world not wholly compatible with Western science and global capitalism.

In the aftermath, the United States took upon itself the task of reducing the "incommensurable differences" through war. It is estimated that more than 149,000 civilians died as a result of the US invasions of Afghanistan and Iraq. In Afghanistan, over 3,400 members of the military (United States and coalition) died, while more than 46,000 Afghan civilians and 50,000 opposition fighters died during the US invasion and occupation from 2001 until 2022 (United States Institute of Peace, 2024). In Iraq, 4,804 US and coalition troops died, while it is estimated that between 186,000 and 210,000 Iraqi civilians were killed by the United States, the Iraqi military and police, and their allies since the US invasion in 2003 (the United States withdrew its military in 2011 but continues to support the Iraqi government and military) (Watson Institute, 2022). In both cases, these invasions (motivated by the events of 9/11) resulted in a catastrophic loss of innocent lives that was many times greater than the initial attack.

After September 11, 2001, everyone faced choices about how to respond. Were the attacks acts of terrorism or acts of war? Were they attacks on US freedoms or attacks on US power? There were disagreements both about how to see the attacks and how to respond to them. At the time, however, one particular understanding became dominant and overshadowed the alternatives. The mentality that governed much of the immediate response—the invasion of Afghanistan and the subsequent invasion of Iraq—was one that relied on simplistic dichotomies to assert absolute moral certainty. In a speech just five days after the attacks, President George W. Bush proclaimed: "My administration has a job to do and we're going to do it. We will rid the world of the evil-doers" (Perez-Rivas, 2001). And a few days later in an address before Congress, Bush (2001) made clear the absolute choices to be made: "Every nation, in every region, now has a decision to make. Either you are with us, or you are with the terrorists."

In his book *The Abuse of Evil*, American philosopher Richard J. Bernstein argued that the dominance of this kind of mentality is a threat to democracy. In its place, he suggested an approach that "questions the appeal to absolutes in politics, that argues that we must not confuse subjective moral *certitude* with objective moral *certainty*, and that is skeptical of an uncritical rigid dichotomy between the forces of evil and the forces of good" (2005, p. vii). He called this pragmatic fallibilism: that is, an attitude that allows for the possibility of being wrong. Bernstein found this mentality in the tradition of American philosophy and turned to Peirce, James, and Dewey—thinkers who offered philosophical resistance through a call for pluralism and fallibilism.

An important part of pragmatic fallibilism is the belief that ideas develop in a particular environment and context and are necessarily provisional.

> When the pragmatists critically attacked absolutes, when they sought to expose the quest for certainty, when they argued for an open universe in which chance and contingency are irreducible, they were not concerned exclusively with abstract metaphysical and epistemological issues. They were addressing ethics, politics, and practical questions that ordinary people confront in their ordinary lives. (Bernstein, 2005, p. 23)

The alternative strand of American philosophy—American philosophies of resistance—is one that helps to challenge the desire to respond to difference with fear, demonization, and distancing. As two sorts of philosophical commitments framed the circumstances of 1890, 2001 marked another signal moment in which versions of these two philosophical perspectives were shown again in sharp contrast.

March 2020 marked a new set of signal events that at once showed the importance of fallibilism and its limits. When the pandemic shut down much of the world, systematic, fact-based responses seemed important. In the midst of the political polarization that emerged around the 2016 elections, responses to Covid-19 were often met with skepticism and a claim that the "facts" in question were really dogma bent on undermining certain groups and their claims to freedom and power. On May 25, 2020, George Floyd, an African American man who had been arrested for allegedly passing a counterfeit $20 bill, was killed by a police officer in Minneapolis. The murder set off a summer of protests around the country demanding the end of police violence against Blacks. In the shadow of the Black Lives Matter movement, the incumbent president lost the November election. He and his supporters claimed without evidence that the election was rigged. From their perspective, the alleged facts about the election could be mistaken or forged and so justice demanded that the former president be restored to office. Efforts to settle the conflict by an appeal to evidence had no effect. For many, once facts are recognized as fallible, they can no longer settle disputes. These people claim that since a fact might be false, alternative facts are just as acceptable. When both sides have their own facts, disputes persist and other principles—like the commitment to a defeated president or to justice for one group or another—become sufficient to ground action and settle differences.

American philosophies of resistance emerge at the boundary between a commitment to pluralism and principles that exceed the moment and serve as guides to the actions that emerge there. On January 6, 2021, when supporters of the defeated president attacked the US Capitol and demanded the election be overturned, they were surely committed to principles that exceeded the moment and that, for them, made the claims true. But unlike philosophies of resistance, they also rejected outright a commitment to pluralism. Resistance of the sort we see as central to this strand of the American tradition embraces the paradox of pluralism and emergent principles, for better or worse.

In the wake of Wounded Knee, a struggle was waged over the character of life in America between those committed to both pluralism and principles that guide solutions and those committed to a vision of a singular nation and world. The 9/11 renewed that struggle. The divided nation of the 2020s marked another iteration of the conflict, where philosophies of resistance met an opposition that brought together fallibilism and the suppression of differences. This book is an effort to clarify the first of these strands in a way that both illuminates the history of philosophies of resistance in America and their potential to make a contribution to the future.

# PART I
## AMERICAN PHILOSOPHIES OF RESISTANCE

# CHAPTER 1
# INTRODUCTION

The title of the history you are reading names our subject "American Philosophies," though we have not yet said what that means. If you are like most students of the formal discipline of philosophy, you will ask first about the moniker "American." You might say, "I thought that philosophy was something that is not fixed to a geography or owned by a people." Those close to the idea that there is a distinctive American philosophy will respond that what is American is a particular kind or way of doing philosophy "indigenous" to the American intellectual scene and called "pragmatism." In the story you are reading, however, that term and its associated stable of thinkers are only part of the field.

In the context of this history, the meaning of the name "America" has at least four dimensions. It is, first, a geographic term marking a place, so that "American philosophy" means philosophy of that place, philosophy done by people there and influenced by it. When Europeans determined that their future lay in a continent "discovered" and consequently "owned" by them, they became strangers in an already peopled world. They imported their ideas and aspirations and, with them, framed their engagement with the land and its people. In the fifteenth century, a series of decrees by the Roman Catholic pope, Alexander VI, and by King Henry VIII of England established what became known as the Doctrine of Discovery. The 1493 declaration by Alexander granted to Columbus and his heirs

> all the islands and mainlands found and to be found, discovered and to be discovered, in the west and south, with all of their dominions, cities, castles, towns and villages, and all rights, jurisdictions and domains, and make, appoint and regard you and said heirs and successors as their lords with full, free and all-encompassing power, authority and jurisdiction. (Modrow and Smith, nd.)

The doctrine affected the entire Western Hemisphere, including what became the United States, where, in 1823, the Supreme Court under Chief Justice John Marshall created a new body of law that made the doctrine of discovery the founding principle of property ownership. America, as geography, marks a philosophy that responds to the place that became the "American" hemisphere through the process of colonization. Our story here focuses on one version of that invasion of the Northern part of the Western Hemisphere and its later consequences after the Europeans had settled in this place for more than 400 years. A larger "hemispheric" history of philosophy is yet to be told. When it is, it will likewise connect the thought of Native American peoples and European thought in a history of struggle more than 500 years long.

The story of philosophy in a place also requires consideration of life in that place. In this second sense, "America" also names a shared experience of coexistence, conflict, oppression, and liberation. Living in America has never been a one-sided experience. At every turn, people lived together in good situations and bad as they responded to changing environments geographically and culturally, the demands of power, and the consequences of oppression. "What is crucial here, from the philosophical side," says John McDermott, "is that the press of the environment as a decisive formulator of thought about the basic structures of the world became the outstanding characteristic of the American temperament" (2007, p. 68). American philosophy, in effect, begins from the experience of living in America.

The third sense of "America" is that it names a history that itself emerges from the experience of the place. There are many ways to tell a story—from outside and above, as if the times and places do not matter, as if only some set of thinkers or issues matter. Our American history of philosophy intends to tell the story on the terms provided by the tradition in relation to the events and experiences to which the praxis of philosophy responds. The history of philosophy, in this sense, is not a matter of abstract contemplation or ruminations that transcend all time and space.

Finally, "America" here is taken as a prospective term that marks a particular kind of future (placed, plural, and bounded, in the process of overcoming its past). Writing in *The Darkened Light of Faith*, Melvin Rogers observes that "The meaning of the past is forever being revised in light of an unsettled future" (2023, p. 6). The future matters because it is in relation to different possible futures that philosophy is carried out and its story is told. In fact, the struggle for different futures is central to this story. In the wake of the Civil War and during the rise of industrial capitalism, Indigenous people sought to reclaim their place on the ground of the continent, workers sought to be freed from the exploitation of their bosses, women sought to have a voice and vote, alternative visions of freedom were proposed and fought for, and the ruling conceptions of life and truth received from Europe in the process of colonization were challenged and transformed. In the story we choose to tell, the vision represented by "America" is one that is fundamentally pluralistic, democratic, and framed by the quest for equity, opportunity, and the ability of individuals and communities to flourish in relation to each other and the places where they live.

Some have argued that adopting the name "American" for any philosophy is a mistake because it associates the endeavor with industrial capitalism, militarism, the creation of grinding poverty and extreme wealth, exploitation based on gender and race, and global domination. Better, they say, to treat philosophy as having no borders at all. We say that such an approach mirrors the very single-minded domination it decries. Instead, we must see the work of philosophy—and philosophy in America in particular—as inexorably bound to a history of domination and the struggle for liberation. Those who would set aside the American name while considering the tradition or working within it, in effect, fail to take responsibility for these histories.

John Lysaker, in his paper "Essaying America," challenged the use of "American" we propose here, declaring, in the end, his independence from the term. His reasons—the association of "America" with the United States and its imperial and capitalist history—aim to take up philosophy outside such history in order to resist it. "American," he says, "names a certain kind of situatedness, but not one with which philosophy should identify." As a result, he concludes,

> My venture thus both eschews and retains the word American in the realm of philosophical conduct, which is to say, I hereby declare my independence from "America" in the name

of a philosophy that would be, or rather, that would enable, as best it can, something more. (2012, p. 548)

Lysaker goes on to explain that this form of resistance involves recognizing the implications of America for Indigenous peoples, the ancestors of African slaves, mestizo peoples of South and Central America, the environment, and the global economy, ultimately seeking a mode of reflection that is forward-looking—a vision of life that does not require the oppression of so many to support the advantages of a few. That Lysaker engages in debate about the meaning of America in order to resist its history is itself a response to American circumstances. The situation calls for a philosophical practice that is bound to those circumstances and returns to them with a declaration of independence. As he observes, "for the time being 'America' remains a condition for the possibility of that declaration and the independence to which it aspires" (2012, p. 548). There are few things more characteristic of the philosophies of resistance traced in this book than the effort to declare independence from a dominant culture that has brought both pain and loss. Such independence is not possible, but the declaration and the reasons for it, grounded in American circumstances, mark his philosophical investigation as a part of the tradition of resistance we describe in this book.

In *Genealogical Pragmatism: Philosophy, Experience, and Community*, John J. Stuhr offered an alternative characterization of the American philosophical tradition by presenting three senses of American philosophy: national, philosophical, and cultural. The "national" category is not interesting because its only meaning is to identify those philosophers who happen to live and work in the United States. The "philosophical" sense of "American philosophy" is more interesting as it suggests that one can engage in a philosophy that has "common attitudes, purposes, procedures, problems, terminology, and beliefs" (1997, p. 23). He addressed what this might be by examining the work of John Lachs, who stresses the primacy of action and will; John J. McDermott, who stresses the primacy of experience; and John E. Smith, who discusses how purpose and interest "help shape the importance and direction of reflection" (1997, p. 24). That purpose and interest can shape reflection is in part why the third sense of American philosophy—the cultural sense—is also important. The "cultural" sense means that an American philosopher is marked "by a particular relation to a distinctly American culture, or, more accurately, to plural American cultures" (1997, p. 25). He rejected the idea that philosophers can be transcultural or non-genealogical and pointed to Dewey, James, Santayana, and others to support his claim. Stuhr concluded that "Here, and more generally in all philosophy that is philosophically and culturally American in character, philosophy regularly and critically addresses the pressing problems of its time and place" (1997, p. 38).

Stuhr's conception of American philosophy recalls Dewey's in his essay "Philosophy and Civilization." For Dewey, "the life of all thought is to effect a junction at some point of the new and the old" in the context of "some conflict with newly emerging directions of activities." In this case, "philosophy is not just a passive reflex" of a culture, "it is itself change; the patterns formed in this junction of the new and old are prophecies rather than records; ... they proclaim ... that such and such *should* be the significant value" (Boydston, 1981–90, Volume 3, LW 3, p. 7).[1] Philosophy, in short, "marks a change of culture"; for better or worse, it is bound to a land, seeking to find its better side.

This quest for a "better side" might lead you to believe that the story you are about to read is a sort of pseudo-narrative, bringing together the authors' favorite philosophers who happen to have lived in America and have the "right" ontology, politics, and pluralistic agenda. How can this be a "history" at all? It is a history because it is an approach based upon the central problems of the American philosophical tradition. Du Bois once declared that the problem of the twentieth century is the problem of the color line—the problem of the coexistence of differences that figure in our experience as members of communities. The formative problem of American philosophy continues to be the coexistence of difference. The thinkers who are part of the American tradition we examine take up that problem in a variety of ways, from the racialist philosophy of T. Thomas Fortune to the analytic philosophy of May Brodbeck to the pragmatism of Richard J. Bernstein. Rather than offering a narrow account of an internal philosophical debate, we will examine the American philosophical tradition of debate as it is bound up with the lived circumstances that stretch from the massacre at Wounded Knee Creek in 1890 to the present day.

Despite the discipline's present narrow vision of who is part of the American tradition, even those philosophers who have been canonized held views that would challenge the canon as it was formed. This is, in part, because the so-called classical pragmatists began their own philosophical reflections by affirming the centrality of experience. For Peirce, James, and Dewey, philosophy worth the name began in response to experienced problems—situations marked by confusion, doubt, indeterminacy—and then returned to these problems, aiming to transform and reconstruct them in ways that allowed the inquirer to go forward, to encounter still more experience. Philosophy, then, should be understood as an activity that arises from experience. Since experience is framed by language, culture, and history, philosophy is not a transcendental practice engaged with the really real and truly true. Instead, as Dewey wrote in "Philosophy and Civilization," the practice is "approached with the antecedent idea that philosophy, like politics, literature, and the plastic arts, is itself a phenomenon of human culture." As a work within culture, within experience, he continues,

> Philosophy thus sustains the closest connection with the history of culture, with the succession of changes in civilization. It is fed by the streams of tradition, traced at critical moments to their sources in order that the current may receive a new direction. . . . But philosophy is not just a passive reflex of civilization that persists through changes. . . . [P]hilosophy marks a change of culture. In forming patterns to be conformed to in future thought and action, it is additive and transforming in its role in the history of civilization. (LW 3, p. 7)

Philosophy, then, at least from the perspective of one of America's canonical figures, can be understood as a mode of inquiry into widely held beliefs and methods of solving problems that begins when established beliefs and methods fail.

Put another way, questions of meaning and how problems are solved are part of what is called culture—the habits, relations, practices, and values that frame daily experience. When elements of culture break down and no longer provide meaning or reliable ways of addressing problems, people call established ways and beliefs into question and find new ways to bring meaning to their lives. This work of seeking new ways of making things and actions meaningful is the work of philosophy. Political campaigns, voting rights, anti-Black and gun violence, wars, abortion rights, nationalism, and more mark a time when established methods of addressing shared problems seem unable to generate meaningful solutions. If philosophy is a form of inquiry aiming to find new ways to address the apparently unsolvable problems of the wider community, then the need for philosophy is ongoing.

Grace Lee and James Boggs, philosophers in the American tradition whose work spanned the range of political movements from the 1960s until the twenty-first century, saw the importance of philosophy in responding to race violence, poverty, and the trials and limits of American politics. They called for revolutionary philosophy in their 1974 book, *Revolution and Evolution*. In an America faced with violent responses to the demand for plural and equitable communities in the 1960s and 1970s, they concluded, "[t]he very purpose of life is now in question" and for "great numbers of people," life has "become purposeless." This loss of meaning, they declare, "is why philosophy is so necessary. It is the essence of philosophy," they continue, "to provide a concept of the relationship between ideas and reality (past, present, and future) and the critical bearing which each has on the other. Philosophy begins when individuals question reality" (1974/2008, p. 197–8).

Our approach to telling the story of American philosophy, our historical method, also begins in Dewey's philosophy of history. In *Logic: The Theory of Inquiry*, he writes:

> The slightest reflection shows that the conceptual material employed in writing history is that of the period in which a history is written. There is no material available for leading principles and hypotheses save that of the historic present. As culture changes, the conceptions that are dominant in a culture change. Of necessity, new standpoints for viewing, appraising and ordering data arise. History is then rewritten. Material that had formerly been passed by, offers itself as data because the new conceptions propose new problems for solution, requiring new factual material for statement and test. (LW 12, pp. 232–3)

History, on this account, is the product of a particular place and time. And it is a practice that is grounded in a commitment to a particular kind of world. "There are no absolute originations or initiations or absolute finalities and terminations in nature," Dewey concludes. "The 'from which' and 'to which' that determine the subject-matter of any particular narration-description are strictly relative to the objective intent set to inquiry by the problematic quality of a given situation" (LW 12, p. 221). Dewey uses the phrase "narration-description" to represent the idea that no description can be meaningful without a context provided by a narration—one that acknowledges a past from which it proceeds and a future toward which it trends. In this way, histories are not "objective" descriptions of some given reality but ongoing and dynamic interactions in the present that reconstruct the past and in so doing provide a context for the future. As Dewey puts it,

> There is accordingly, a double process. On the one hand, changes going on in the present, giving a new turn to social problems, throw the significance of what happened in the past into a new perspective. They set new issues from the standpoint of which to rewrite the story of the past. On the other hand, as judgment of the significance of past events is changed, we gain new instruments for estimating the force of present conditions as potentialities of the future. (LW 12, p. 238)

Our approach to the present American philosophy is through a history of the tradition framed by the philosophical tradition itself and the commitment to a dynamic, pluralistic world of experience in which knowledge is a product of ongoing investigation, always limited in resources and scope, subject to failure, and liable to be overturned as the problems of the world change. The question of which philosophers are "real" American philosophers (or even which are "real" philosophers) is not some question answered by consulting the transcendent categories of "American" or "philosophy"; such questions are answered in light of the concerns at hand. From this perspective, the story told here is not the final story of American philosophy, but to the extent that the problems of difference are experienced here and now, it is a story that ought to be heard and engaged.

Our work follows in important respects other efforts to rethink the American philosophical tradition. John J. McDermott, in his 1965 essay, "The American Angle of Vision," helped to set the stage for our history when he wrote, "No longer do we hold to radical breaks in historical continuity or hold to the absolute novelty of positions taken by individual thinkers" (2007, p. 43). Instead, history takes its lead from the experience at hand. The "American angle of vision" and its expression as American philosophy

> is not so much a question as to whether the American tradition is radically different from other cultures but whether, in its emphases, concerns, and blindspots, as generated by its historical situation, such a tradition doesn't offer options of a profound kind for the immediate human future. (2007, p. 63)

Cornel West, while making a case for Ralph Waldo Emerson as "the appropriate starting point for the pragmatist tradition," also made a case for expanding those who counted as pragmatists—adding W. E. B. Du Bois, C. Wright Mills, and Lionel Trilling to the story—and their impact on the trajectory of American philosophy. West's *The American Evasion of Philosophy: A Genealogy of Pragmatism* (1989) stands as a key moment in transforming American philosophy from the story of a few early twentieth-century thinkers to a broad movement deeply connected to the experience of those living in North America.

Charlene Haddock Seigfried's 1996 *Pragmatism and Feminism: Reweaving the Social Fabric* further contributed to the process of understanding American philosophy by reintroducing the role of women thinkers. In the process of arguing for a place for pragmatist feminists in contemporary philosophy, she made her case in part by showing the central place of feminist thinkers in the development and basic commitments of pragmatism. And Scott L. Pratt's 2002 *Native Pragmatism* argued that many of the same philosophical commitments that marked classical pragmatism were also part of Native American thought and that interaction between Native and European Americans can also be seen as part of the origin of the distinctive tradition of American philosophy.

Louis Menand, in his popular history of classical pragmatism, *The Metaphysical Club: A Story of Ideas in America* (2001), presents the story of American thought focused on the work of Peirce, James, Dewey, and Oliver Wendell Holmes, a Civil War veteran, lawyer, philosopher, and eventually an associate justice of the US Supreme Court. For Menand, the Civil War was the defining event that gave rise to what he argued is the common idea shared by all four thinkers. Ideas, Menand wrote, "are not 'out there' waiting to be discovered, but are tools—

like forks and knives and microchips—that people devise to cope with the world in which they find themselves" (2001, p. xi). Such ideas are not the product of individuals but are the work of "groups of individuals . . . [and] are entirely dependent, like germs, on their human carriers and the environment." As circumstances change, ideas will necessarily change, and to hold on to ideas of the past as though they are the last word can only lead to disaster. "The belief that ideas should never become ideologies—either justifying the status quo, or dictating some transcendent imperative for renouncing it—was the essence of what they taught" (2001, p. xii). From these basic commitments, Menand concludes, pragmatism laid the ground for a conception of society that "permitted a greater . . . margin for difference" and so "create[d] more social room for error [in order to] give good outcomes a better chance to emerge" (2001, p. 440). The resulting theory of democracy, he argued, is the enduring legacy where "Democratic participation isn't the means to an end . . .; it is the end. The purpose of the experiment is to keep the experiment going" (2001, p. 442). Menand's history is narrowly focused but opens the way to consider a still broader conception of American philosophy that—like the pragmatists—aimed to resist the establishment of a single dominant culture in the United States.

American philosophy has taken a variety of forms as it emerged in the encounter with the people and lands of North America. One strand sought to tame the Americas and institute a particular vision of human life drawn from the European Enlightenment and bound to a conception of a single humanity governed by fixed and certain principles. The other strand grew in resistance to the invasion and sought pluralism with the recognition that fixed principles and certainty are not available options—and that seeking them leads to disaster. The first strand included the Jacksonian democrat described by James Fenimore Cooper, the Social Darwinism of William Graham Sumner, the authoritarian democracy of Walter Lippmann, and the antidemocratic visions of Sidney Hook.

Our interest here is in the philosophical effort that stands on the other side of assimilation and exclusion: the transformative thinking that rejects settled truth, fixed goals, and endless progress. Instead, thought is situated, fallible, and committed to the idea that liberation is a placed and shared experience. This view bears a commitment to a metaphysics of change and the idea that individuals and communities have the ability to act with a purpose. It has its own fallible conception of knowledge (epistemology) and consequently has a particular approach to ethics and politics. This book leaves it to others to describe in detail the dominant and dominating strand of American thought; our interest here—and our belief in the power of philosophy—is in the resistant strand of philosophy in America. Despite its general invisibility in philosophy as a discipline, this strand of American philosophy nevertheless offers examples of the way philosophy can challenge domination, and of a living philosophy whose practice is still available and perhaps never more important.

What then is a philosophy of resistance? First, it is one that challenges dogma and settled belief from a perspective that recognizes the pluralism of experience and the value of growth and change. It is resistance in an expected way because it takes on systems of domination as a necessary step in a process of liberation. At the same time, American philosophies of resistance do not rest with criticism but actively work to establish alternative ways of thinking and living. It is a philosophy of the sort offered by the Lakota prophet, Kicking Bear, for example, that begins outside the philosophical commitments of the dominant culture. As such, the philosophies of resistance are commonly (but not universally) marked by apparently contradictory commitments to both pluralism and continuity.

Philosophies of resistance can generally be understood as having four characteristics. First, philosophy in general, like other forms of inquiry, begins in the context of an indeterminate situation; in this case, a situation framed by conflicts among widely held beliefs experienced as disruption, dislocation, or confusion. The widely held or dominant beliefs are viewed as the problem. In philosophies of resistance, these dominant beliefs include not only the categories used to order and understand the world but also the resources available to solve problems that emerge, assumptions about the institutions that govern daily life, and the futures that people envision for themselves and others. Philosophies of resistance challenge these dominant beliefs and propose alternatives.

Second, in order to do this work, philosophies of resistance seek "grounds" upon which to stand against the dominant order. "Grounds" in this sense involve the recognition of actual ground—of places that frame and sustain communities—as well as visions of the future toward which transformation (both of concepts and action) will move. The Boggs's work explicitly responds to the conditions faced by people in the United States and, more particularly, in their local Detroit community. And even Lysaker, who seeks to be free of the American name and the specificity of its history, nevertheless responds to the circumstances of that history and place.

Third, philosophies of resistance, in making a stand, also create a place at the edges between the dominant order, the oppressive past, and the future sought (see Pratt, 2022). This position at the edge is crucial in the work of those we see as resistance philosophers because it is from this place that the resistance creates paths toward new possibilities. Resistance philosophers in the American tradition—most anyway—take up positions at the edge so that they stand between the dominant order and other orders (actual and possible). They are both outside the systems they challenge and inside them. For instance, the original situation of colonists and Indigenous Americans created this space between, and its legacy continues to define the tradition we consider. Much like Gloria Anzaldúa's conception of the border (see Chapter 20) and what she will call mestiza consciousness, resistance is paradoxical, and in the resulting indeterminate space between, it may develop the resources both to critique the system and imagine new possibilities.

Fourth, the efforts of philosophers of resistance, as Dewey expected of philosophy in general, return to the situations that gave rise to the philosophical effort. Philosophy directs action toward specific futures using the resources produced in the places between communities, cultures, and ways of thinking. The return to experience by philosophies of resistance, in most cases, attempts to be, in Dewey's words, both critical and constructive. It is important not only to show the problems with the dominant system but also to point the way to alternative visions and the hope of a new place, with new relations among its people—human and other—and new ways of thinking about others. There is no guarantee of the outcome of a philosophical resistance, and the results can lead to a failure to flourish or can discover that the efforts to resist only reinstate the system challenged. When this happens, the process can begin again.

Resistance philosophies emerge across American traditions with similar characteristics. Robin D. G. Kelley, writing about youth resistance in the Black community, echoes the concept of philosophical resistance we propose: "Resistance is not just about getting people organized, getting people to protest. It's also always about thinking. One big weakness in scholarship on youth resistance is that it rarely takes into consideration theorizing going on among young people, especially young people who are organized" (2013, p. 87). Eve Tuck (Unangax̂) and K. Wayne Yang, writing from an Indigenous perspective, see resistance as parallel to the process of decolonization. There can be, they say, "no generalized theory of decolonization, because decolonization is always local and specific." Likewise, theories of resistance cannot be generalized. They continue:

> Resistance is always in context, in a place, between real people—even when some of those people embody the state. Resistance is always in real time too, and what is possible in one time and context is unthinkable in another time and context. (2013, p. 8)

American philosophies of resistance echo these conceptions of resistance in a way that responds to the particularity of American experiences in order to realize better futures.

Like Kicking Bear, philosophers of resistance recognize difference, but do not assume that difference is merely appearance, reducible to sameness, or explainable using universal truths. They reject the ideas that experience is divisible into realms of knowledge and being, public and private, that action can be separated from language or theory, and that facts and values are distinct. To manage the tension between these ideas, most of these thinkers also adopt a robust conception of boundaries that are sites of contradiction, possibility, and a relational ontology. The resulting philosophies are centrally concerned with questions of agency and sovereignty, power and purpose, the continuity of knowledge and action, and a cluster of ideas related to place, culture, and embodiment.

This story of American philosophy, framed by its interest in philosophies of resistance, is, like any history, perspectival and therefore incomplete. Further, the work of the thinkers who are discussed here is not presented completely, nor are the parts we introduce fully discussed. This book is focused on a story of American philosophy told in response to the experience of coexisting in a context of pluralism on a land largely taken from its Indigenous peoples and built by the labor of the poor and enslaved. America, the place, is now overlaid with imported concepts and institutions meant to preserve a particular vision of the future, including who does and doesn't belong within its borders.

Consistent with the work of McDermott, West, and Seigfried, we have embedded our discussions of the philosophical work within some historical context; then again, many significant historical moments are left out. We have rather selected some signal events to help readers gain an understanding of the social and political context in which the various philosophers we discuss were writing. We encourage readers to expand this history as they consider the present world and the issues that define their moments and places.

This book is one that seeks the active engagement of the reader.[2] It makes room for a plurality of approaches to philosophy, a range of philosophical interests, and the study of multiple figures. We hope it is useful to those encountering these thinkers for the first time. We also hope that by presenting philosophical thought alongside historical events, those long familiar with these figures in American philosophy will find new ways to think about their work. Furthermore, we have been able to draw some interesting connections between various thinkers that may cause the reader to rethink the history of the tradition as well as the import of particular ideas. Our overall goal has been to enable readers to critically engage with the philosophical ideas and concepts presented here, but also to see how these philosophical ideas and concepts have been put to work in the world. Our hope is that students of philosophy, and students of American thought and history, will continue to build upon this story.

## Notes

1. Most Dewey citations are to Boydston, 1967–1990, which includes three series: Early Works (EW), Middle Works (MW), and Later Works (LW). These citations will be indicated by the series, volume, and page number, for example, "LW 3, p. 7."
2. This book is introductory and should be paired with further reading of the primary texts and considered in light of secondary literature (most of which we do not discuss here). Our purpose is to provide an outline of American philosophy and illustrate how the discussion of philosophy interacts with events in the wider world. We hope that this will enable those reading and teaching the text to tailor their courses and reading by selecting some particular figures to explore in more depth, or by choosing one or two themes to follow throughout the history.

# CHAPTER 2
## DEFINING PLURALISM
### SIMON POKAGON, IDA B. WELLS-BARNETT, AND T. THOMAS FORTUNE

The World Columbian Exposition in Chicago (also known as the Chicago World's Fair) opened on October 9, 1893, a day set aside to remember the Chicago Fire of 1871. According to the official guide to the fair, its stated purpose was to "exhibit material progress . . . and to portray the wonderful achievements of the new age in science, literature, education, government, jurisprudence, morals, charity, religion . . . as the most effective means of increasing the fraternity, progress, prosperity and peace of mankind" (Flinn, 1893, p. 29).

The day's celebration began with an opening fanfare performed by musicians sent by General Nelson Miles from Fort Sheridan. On the West plaza of the Fair's Administration Building, surrounded by thousands of visitors, Simon Pokagon, a leader of the Pottawattamie Indians, was introduced to the crowd by Emma Sickles, administrator of the Indian boarding school at Pine Ridge during the Wounded Knee Massacre three years earlier. As the introduction concluded, Pokagon rang a replica of the Liberty Bell and addressed the expectant crowd. "What can be done for the best good of the remnant of our race?" he asked. "[W]e [Indigenous North Americans] *must* give up the pursuits of our fathers. . . . We *must* teach our children to give up the bow and arrow that is born in their hearts; and, in place of the gun, we must take up the plow, and live as white men do." Whites had eliminated the game animals that had sustained his people and so it was, he said, "vain to talk about support from game and fish." He concluded: "Our children *must* learn that they owe no allegiance to any clan or power on earth except the United States" (Pokagon, 1899, p. 21).

Pokagon's greeting in the wake of Wounded Knee, printed in the "Publisher's Notes" of Pokagon's novel, *O-Gî-Mäw-Kwe Mit-I-Gwä-Kî (Queen of the Woods)*, marks what appears to be a concession to the assimilation of Native people into the dominant culture. But it was not the whole story.

Even as Pokagon declared, "in my infancy I was taught to love my chief and tribe, but since then the great west has been swallowed up by the white man, and by adoption we are the children of this great Republic" (1899, p. 23), friends were distributing to the crowd a second address by Pokagon printed on birch bark that began, "In behalf of my people, 'the American Indians,' I hereby declare to you the pale-faced race that has usurped our lands and homes, that we have no spirit to celebrate with you the great Columbian fair now being held in this Chicago city, the wonder of the world" (2001, p. 31).

In his birch bark address, sometimes called "The Red Man's Rebuke," Pokagon went on to identify the impact of the European invasion. "The cyclone of civilization rolled westward, the forests of untold centuries were wiped away, streams dried up, lakes fell back from ancient bounds, and all our fathers once loved to gaze upon was destroyed, defaced, or marred" (2001,

p. 33). Pokagon joined the prophets of the Ghost Dance in describing a contrast between the dominant world and the world of Indigenous America.

> You say of us that we are treacherous, vindictive and cruel; in answer to the charge, we declare to all the world with our hands uplifted before high heaven, that before the white man came we were kind, outspoken, and forgiving. Our real character has been misunderstood because we have resented the breaking of treaties made with the United States. (2001, p. 34)

At issue in Pokagon's two messages was the ongoing question of how people in America, in their ordinary lives, in their education, politics, business, and law would understand and act in a context of diversity. The tension between assimilation and maintaining Indigenous character and culture despite "the cyclone of civilization" in Pokagon's messages both defined a distinct kind of pluralism and a particular form of resistance.

On its surface, the Columbian Exposition of 1893 was a celebration of the triumph of Europeans in America. The Civil War and the end of Reconstruction had re-unified the United States as a political and economic power dominated by White men. But the resources of economic growth that had been provided by Western expansion (timber, mining, agriculture, and land speculation) were vanishing. The 1890 census noted: "Up to and including 1880 the country had a frontier of settlement, but at present the unsettled area has been so broken into by isolated bodies of settlement that there can hardly be said to be a frontier line" (US Census Bureau, 1890, §4). Growth had to be redefined. Now the fuel of economic power would be labor, technology, and industry. The Chicago World's Fair brought together new economic forces and the vision of a unified America.

The Civil War had ended 28 years earlier and Reconstruction and the military occupation of the former Confederate States had ended only 17 years before. Although the War's impact on the character of American society and its pattern of industrialization had been significant, the only overt acknowledgment of the War at the Exposition was "Grand Army Day," celebrated by an encampment and parade by members of the Grand Army of the Republic (a fraternal organization of veterans of the Union army that served as an arm of the Republican Party). In light of the success of Grand Army Day, the director of the Fair proposed a Confederate Army Day, but protests from the Grand Army of the Republic prevented it, demonstrating that tensions were not far below the surface (Kingsbury, 1915, p. 393).

Pokagon had been invited to participate in the Exposition in a visible way. Participation by other American Indians was limited to a display of tribal people living in the "traditional" way in the anthropology exhibit. On the "Midway Plaisance"—a wide boulevard stretching one mile from the entrance to the Fair—Native people and others were arranged in a series of zoo-like villages in order of progress from "savagery" to the modern civilization of the Columbian Exposition itself. Here, each state along with a variety of nations (including Germany and France, Guatemala and Costa Rica, for example) were invited to prepare an exhibit. Major industries were also invited so that in addition to the New York, Kentucky, Sweden, and Spain buildings, the Exposition also featured the Electrical, Merchant Tailors, and Shoe and Leather Trades buildings. Though designed by well-known architects, most of the buildings were temporary (one exception was the Palace of Fine Arts, which became the home of the Chicago Museum of Science and Industry). To capture the look of permanence, each building was covered in a layer of white gypsum plaster to look like stone. The main grounds of the Exposition became known as The White City. Perhaps not surprisingly, there were no invitations to African American groups to prepare an exhibit (see White and Igleheart, 1893).

Ida B. Wells-Barnett (1862–1931) and Frederick Douglass (1818–95), among others, protested this exclusion. In a pamphlet published near the end of the Exposition, *The Reason Why the Colored American Is Not in the World's Exposition*, Douglass wrote, "There are many good things concerning our country and countrymen of which we would be glad to tell in this pamphlet, if we could do so, and at the same time tell the truth" (Douglass, 1894). Douglass then listed some of the falsely claimed accomplishments, including improvement of "material civilization," that "260 years of progress and enlightenment have banished barbarism and race hate from the United States," and the idea that "American law is now the shield alike of black and white" (Douglass, 1894). Douglass's bitter irony set the stage for the pamphlet that argued that the exclusion of Blacks from the Exposition was only a symptom of the systematic exclusion of African Americans from economic opportunity, adequate housing, property ownership, the political process, and the justice system.

In her essay on lynch laws in the Exposition pamphlet, Wells-Barnett argued that lynching was originally defended as a response to Blacks who sought "to rule white people." When public opinion rejected that rationale, anti-Black violence and lynch laws were justified as legitimate punishment for Black men who raped White women. "The men who make these charges encourage or lead the mobs which do the lynching," she wrote.

> They belong to the race which holds Negro life cheap, which owns the telegraph wires, newspapers, and all other communication with the outside world. They write the reports which justify lynching by painting the Negro as black as possible, and those reports are accepted by the press associations and the world without question or investigation. (Wells-Barnett, 1894)

Wells-Barnett rejected both the justification for lynch laws and the criticisms of the laws made on racial grounds alone. For her, the actions of the mobs and their legal defense formalized both racism and sexism as intersecting oppressions holding Blacks and women, White and Black, in a system of fear and domination.

Wells-Barnett was born into slavery in Holly Springs, Mississippi, at the beginning of the Civil War. She attended Shaw University until her parents died in the 1878 yellow fever epidemic. She became, at sixteen, a teacher in a rural school and, in 1883, moved to Memphis, where she continued to teach and also took classes at Fisk University to establish her teaching credentials. While on a train home from her teaching job in 1884, Wells-Barnett chose to sit in the front of the "Ladies" car. When the conductor demanded that she move to the rear, she objected, and an altercation ensued. Three men finally forced her from the car while the White passengers cheered. In the aftermath, Wells-Barnett sued and was awarded $500 in damages, though the Tennessee Supreme Court eventually overturned the ruling (see Wells, 1970).

She continued to teach in Memphis until 1892 when three of her friends, owners of a newly opened small grocery store, were lynched by a mob encouraged by the White owners of what had been the only grocery store in the area. The Black grocers armed themselves and wounded three White men who helped to storm the grocery. The Black men were arrested, and the White-owned press portrayed the men as the aggressors and demanded justice. The following day, a White mob forced its way into the jail and killed the three Black men. Over the next few days, thousands of African Americans fled Memphis, and Wells-Barnett took up the cause of opposing violence against Blacks, especially violence justified by state lynch laws. She began to write a series of scathing editorials in the Black Memphis newspaper, the *Free Press*, and started a lecture tour to present facts about the Memphis lynching. While she was away, another mob destroyed the *Free Press* office in search of Wells-Barnett. She realized that she could not return to Memphis, and so when she completed her lecture tour, she settled in Chicago. Beginning in 1892, Wells-Barnett wrote a series of books to document lynching throughout the United States, analyze the circumstances, and present an assessment of the ideas and actions that led to the violence (see Wells, 1970).

Central to Wells-Barnett's method was a process that began in the experiences of Black and White Americans living side by side. Despite analyses offered by others that the behavior of mobs and the press were in service of broad notions of racial superiority, Wells-Barnett argued that race hatred and male dominance joined to restructure race in gendered terms and restructure gender in ways that could preserve both White dominance and female subservience. As Patricia Hill Collins observed, Wells-Barnett was among the first social theorists to explicitly analyze social conflict as the product of intersecting oppressions (Hill Collins, 2002, p. 21). In particular, she argued that lynching was a form of "sexual violence against African American men via lynching and African American women via rape" so that concepts of gender difference "are in fact deeply racialized constructs" (p. 21). Understanding—and resisting—lynching required attention to the ways in which race and gender were practiced and a recognition that "African Americans' interpretations of their own experience were of special value" (p. 22) in the fight.

The direction of Wells-Barnett's analyses did not stop with her essays but were intended to direct action meant to transform the situation. At the end of her 1894 report, *The Red Record*, published around the time of the Columbia Exposition pamphlet, she wrote, "It is a well-established principle of law that every wrong has a remedy" (Wells-Barnett, 2002, p. 147). Her remedy for the oppression she saw was the dissemination of information, encouraging community groups—White and Black—to "pass resolutions of condemnation and protest every time a lynching takes place" (p. 148), boycott communities and states where mob violence held sway, and support anti-lynching legislation. Perhaps most significant was the injunction to "think and act on independent lines in this behalf" (p. 149), by taking up reflective or intelligent action in light of the cause to stop violence and in light of the principles people already claimed to value. "[A]fter all," she continued, echoing Pokagon, "it is the white man's civilization and the white man's government which are on trial" (p. 149).

Despite her efforts, no federal anti-lynching law was passed in Wells-Barnett's lifetime, or even in the twentieth century. The Emmett Till Antilynching Act was passed by Congress and signed by the President in 2018. Pluralism, for Wells-Barnett, was necessarily multidimensional, and resistance required shared knowledge of intersecting experiences and, for better or worse, reliance on the structures of the dominant system to bring about change.

Wells-Barnett's assessment of racial violence and ability to reach a wide audience was thanks in part to the support she received from T. Thomas Fortune (1856–1928), a journalist, editor, and publisher who was also born a slave. After the Civil War, Fortune attended Howard University and then worked for several Black newspapers. In 1881, he became the owner and editor of the *New York Globe* (later called the *New York Age*). He met Wells-Barnett during her 1892 lecture tour and, when she settled in Chicago, began to publish her editorials and reports in the *Age*. Fortune was already known as an important voice on race relations in the United States.

In 1884, he wrote and published *Black and White: Land, Labor and Politics in the South*. While Wells-Barnett developed a conception of contact between races framed by the intersection of race and gender oppression, Fortune understood race conflict in terms of the demands of labor and land against the backdrop of deep racial difference. Fortune held, as Tommy Curry observed, that "[c]hange comes from conscious and deliberate action against tyrannical forces of white supremacy, not through rhetoric(s), but the manipulation of the historical forces of social change" (2002, p. 468). This is accomplished by agitation. According to Fortune:

> There is no halfway ground between right and wrong. The one or the other must obtain, and prevail. Mental inertia is death. Indifferent acquiescence in wrong is death. Tame submission to outrage is death. Agitation, constant protesting, always standing up to be counted, to be heard, or to be knocked down—this spirit breeds respect and dulls the edge of tyranny. (Fortune and Alexander, 2008, p. 115)

In *Black and White*, he declared that it is his "purpose to show that the American Government has always construed people of African parentage to be aliens" (Fortune, 2007, p. 6) and that, even in the wake of the Civil War, "the newspapers, voicing the wishes of the rabble and the cormorants of trade" proclaimed "that each State is '*sovereign*,' and that its citizens have a *perfect right* to terrorize and murder one another, if they so desire" (pp. 7–8). This conclusion, the permissibility of terror and violence, did not simply represent politics for Fortune but "Caucasian human nature as well—that nature which seldom rises above self-interest in business or politics" (p. 8). In Fortune's analysis of race difference, Whites—Caucasians—had a distinct "nature" committed to self-interest and manifested in a system of private land ownership and economic exploitation of non-Whites. In contrast, Fortune claimed, "Colored people are naturally sociable, and intensely religious in their disposition. Their excellent social qualities make them the best of companions . . . musical and generous to a fault" (pp. 8, 42). While Fortune emphasized what would come to be seen as stereotypical "traits" of African Americans (traits that were used to further justify the exclusion of Blacks from access to educational and economic opportunity), Fortune's point was rather that Black individuals and communities framed their lives and actions in ways that were not first a matter of economic self-interest as they were for Whites. In this way, Fortune introduced a critical conception of Whiteness.

Whether one attributes the differences to biology or culture or a combination of the two, Fortune identified race differences as manifesting in practices and organizing values. Following his review of the exploitation of African Americans under slavery, he asserted that the people of this Nation who enslaved the black man, who robbed him of more than a hundred years of toil, who perverted his moral nature, and all but extinguished in him the Divine spark of intelligence, are morally bound to do all that is in their power to build up his shattered manhood, to put him on his feet, as it were, to fit him to enjoy . . . freedom. (p. 36)

Despite the differences in systems of value, Fortune held that Whites nevertheless incurred a moral obligation to make things "right." At the same time, what constitutes relevant differences for Fortune appears to be, in contrast with Wells-Barnett, a matter of race and class but not gender. Even as Wells-Barnett recognized the ways that conceptions of gender are central to the system of oppression of Blacks, Fortune did not. Despite the gap in his analysis, however, Fortune still argued for a new set of values that should apply to Whites as well as Blacks. The "greatness" of a people, he concluded, "is to be found in the general diffusion of wealth, the comparative contentment and competency of the masses, and the general virtue and patriotism of the whole people" (p. 37)—a value commitment that Jane Addams would later call "lateral progress," the process of sharing more and more widely the benefits of a flourishing society.

In order to realize change, however, the policies of Reconstruction were, as Fortune observed, "how not to do it" (p. 56). Rather than acknowledging the fact of deep racial differences, the "originators" of Reconstruction presumed that "the master class would accept cordially the conditions forced upon them, or that the [newly] enfranchised class would prove equal to the burden . . . forced upon them" (p. 58). Change, if it were to occur at all, would happen only when the underlying structures of wealth and land were addressed. Blacks, he argued, must "learn to take care of [themselves] . . . read, listen, think, reform [their] own ideas of affairs in [their] own locality" (p. 79). Even as "black and white citizens of the South . . . are, essentially, one people, and should be mutual aids instead of mutual hindrances," they must "alter" but not eliminate "the lines that divide them" (p. 84).

According to Fortune, however, the transformation of society cannot be accomplished from above: "Society is not corrupted from the apex but from the base." In Fortune's analysis of the means by which society can be repaired from the base, he made two arguments: one framed by an analysis of labor and the other by an analysis of land. Neither argument rejected the reality of race difference, but both affirmed a concurrent common humanity. Fortune argued, following socialist analyses of the day, that "capital can produce nothing." Consequently, the wealth of the "master class" is taken from "producing agents" "without which there could be no wealth, without which the landlord could exact no rent and capital could draw no interest" (p. 91). In this system "the producing agency alone receives an inadequate proportion of the wealth it produces." While African Americans as slaves and then as industrial workers produced significant wealth, Fortune argued that White industrial workers had also been exploited as producing agents. He concluded "the condition of the Black and the White laborer is the same, and that consequently their cause is common; they should unite under one banner and work upon the same platform of principles for uplifting labor, the more equal distribution of the products of labor and capital." Despite visible and historical differences between Black and White and the reality of race hatred, Fortune claimed "thus with the so-called 'war of races:' it will pass away and not leave a trace behind" (p. 112).

Fortune offered a similar analysis of land where tenants living on the land produce wealth for the landlord who merely owns it. "Land is, in its very nature," he said, "the common property of the people"; like air and water it is necessary for life and access to it cannot be denied. "Individual ownership in the land," he continued, "is a transgression of the common right of man, and a usurpation which produces nearly, if not all, the evils which result upon our civilization" (p. 136). The "ground" of slavery was literally the system of property ownership that guaranteed that the wealth of land was denied to its producers. After the Civil War, property was restored to its former owners so that freed slaves who now worked the land as tenant farmers were once again denied the wealth they produced. Those who could not survive as farmers moved to cities and became laborers in industry so that "the thing that gave birth to *chattel slavery* . . . is now fast giving birth to *industrial slavery*" (p. 150). Tenant farmers, however, were both Black and White, and so, just as capital exploited Black and White laborers, landlords exploited both Black and White farmers. Pluralism, for Fortune, recognized the coexistence of race and class differences. Resistance was a matter of the laboring classes setting aside race as an obstacle to cooperation and taking up arms—intellectual and otherwise—against the system of property that arose in the context of American slavery.

In the end, Fortune concluded that "the future struggle in the South will be, not between white men and black men, but between capital and labor, landlord and tenant." Fortune saw the system of capital and land ownership as a system of "whiteness," less a "race" in the embodied sense, but instead a system of intersecting economic oppressions upon both Black and White people. Fortune explained, "The white man having asserted his superiority in the matters of assassination and robbery, has settled down upon a barrel of dynamite, as he did in the days of slavery, and will await the explosion with the same fatuity and self-satisfaction true of him in other days" (p. 153). Instead of a contradiction, the tension between the system of Whiteness and the lived experience of White people marked a central tension in the effort to resist the new economic, political, and epistemic orders represented at the World's Fair.

## Primary Texts

Fortune, T. Thomas (2007). *Black and White: Land, Labor, and Politics in the South*, with an introduction by Seth Moglen. New York: Washington Square Press.

Pokagon, Simon (2011). *Ogimawkwe Mitigwaki*, with foreword by Philip J. Deloria and essays by John N. Low, Margaret Noori, and Kiara M. Vigil. East Lansing: Michigan State Press.

Wells-Barnett, Ida B. (2002). *On Lynching*, with an introduction by Patricia Hill Collins. Amherst, NY: Humanity Books.

# CHAPTER 3
# EVOLUTION AND AMERICAN INDIAN PHILOSOPHY

Underlying the Columbian Exposition was a conception of human progress framed by evolution theory. Charles Darwin (1809–1882) published *On the Origin of Species* in 1859, and Herbert Spencer (1820–1903) published his influential version of evolution theory in 1862 in *First Principles*. While Darwin's book was somewhat technical (and not widely popular), Spencer's multi-volume *Synthetic Philosophy* sold more than 360,000 copies worldwide between 1860 and 1903. As Richard Hofstadter observed, "Spencer and his philosophy were products of English industrialism . . . a system conceived in and dedicated to an age of steel and steam engines, competition, exploitation, and struggle" (1955, p. 35). Spencer coined the phrase "survival of the fittest" and in so doing found a way to make Darwin's evolution theory based on natural selection compatible with the mainstream ideas of industrializing America. Despite the seemingly inherent tension between the creation of the world by chance and survival and the creation of the world by the god of the Bible, Spencer connected the two by arguing that the very social and moral principles that were implied by (Protestant) Christianity were likewise implied by the principle of evolution.

The idea of evolutionary development became a central way of understanding the development of human society. Various theories of evolution had been around for some time. An earlier theory of evolution developed by Jean-Baptiste Lamarck (1744–1829) also argued for species change but held that change was not the product of random mutation but rather the result of changing habits that could be inherited. The publication of Darwin's *Origin of Species* initiated a new interest in explaining human development in terms of species change as a consequence of random mutation and natural selection. Darwin's work struck a blow against many of the central commitments of European philosophy that had come to organize American society in the nineteenth century. Christian creation stories, the concept of sin, and the separation of body and soul were called into question, and the categories that had been developed to codify the worlds of plants and animals, the organizing distinctions of good and evil, right and wrong, and justice and injustice all had to be reinterpreted in light of the idea that their present forms were the product of history and not the givens of God or Nature. The impact was at once destabilizing and potentially revolutionary.

Thomas Huxley (1825–95), a follower of Darwin, popularized the idea that competition was the major mechanism of evolution, and Spencer presented a broader conception of evolution theory to explain not just the development of organisms, but also the development of social systems, mechanical systems, geological systems, and even astronomical systems. Spencer famously defined a general principle of evolution as "an integration of matter and concomitant dissipation of motion; during which the matter passes from an indefinite, incoherent homogeneity to a definite, coherent heterogeneity," in short, the movement of things from "incoherent" simplicity to "coherent" complexity (Spencer, 1862, p. 358).

Spencer's general principle provided a starting point for his effort to unify the sciences (an effort that would be made again in the mid-twentieth century). His theory of human development, presented first in the first volume of his *Principles of Sociology* in 1876, was foundational for the generation of philosophers who would respond to the world after the Columbian Exposition closed its doors and disassembled its monumental white buildings. There are two threads in Spencer's sociology that emerge in and structure the philosophies of the late nineteenth and early twentieth centuries. The first, well-examined by Trevor Pearce (2020), is the role of the organism-environment relationship. Spencer calls these elements extrinsic and intrinsic factors. The former include climate, "surface" or geography, and the flora and fauna of the region. The latter are characterized as physical, emotional, and intellectual. Other factors that combine the extrinsic and intrinsic include the presence and size of surrounding communities, "complex co-operations, governmental and industrial," and "sundry developed forms of activity both predatory and peaceful . . . made practicable only by the power which large masses of men furnish" (Spencer, 1900–91, p. 11). The environment also involves a range of "derived factors" that include technology, language, knowledge, and art (pp. 12–13).

The second thread is the assumption that the original state of humanity is rightly characterized as primitive or savage and that human development is to be understood as progress from the original state to civilization. Spencer puts it this way: "since the commencement of history, there has been going on a continuous differentiation of races, a continuous over-running of the less powerful or less adapted by the more powerful or more adapted, a driving of the inferior varieties into undesirable habitats, and, occasionally, an extermination of inferior varieties" (1900–1, pp. 40). Significantly, progress means the progressive ability to "subjugate" the environment and bring it into greater and greater control. The two keys to Spencer's theory are likewise bound together in much of the American philosophical tradition. The environment sustains and challenges the organism and its community. Civilization requires more resources and safety from the environment, and a more and more controlled environment means human progress is occurring.

With respect to the physical aspects of human beings, Spencer concludes that the most general factor is when individuals arrive at maturity. "Other things being equal, the less evolved types of organisms take shorter times to reach their complete forms than do the more evolved" (1900–1, p. 52). The "less evolved" arrive at maturity more quickly and so are less adaptable. Such inflexibility, Spencer says, increases "obstacles to progress" and leads to the primary primitive emotional trait "fixity of habit" (p. 71). "The primitive man," he says, "is conservative in an extreme degree" (p. 71). At the same time, primitive traits include "Impulsiveness which, pervading the conduct of primitive men, so greatly impedes co-operation," which, of course, "makes it 'impossible to put any dependence on their promises'" (p. 72). Consequently, "sociality, strong in civilized man, is less strong in the savage man" (p. 72). Intellectual traits follow predictably. "The savage lacks *abstract ideas*," such as the concepts of property (or quality) and of causes (p. 76). "Absence of the idea of natural causation, implies absence of rational surprise" (p. 87). As a result, Spencer concludes, "The intellectual traits of the uncivilized, thus made specially difficult to change, . . . are traits recurring in the children of the civilized" (p. 91). While the details of Spencer's version of "savagism" are rarely mentioned in detail by later thinkers, the deposit of his conception is enduring and often orders the efforts to think through problems and their solutions. The influence of the savage/civilized distinction is considerable, long-lasting, and disastrous for the people of North America, Indigenous, settler, and enslaved.

The emergence of state-funded science in the 1860s provided an opportunity to further develop evolution theory and popularize it. The federal Morrill Act of 1862 established "land grant" universities by redistributing land, taken by treaty and force from Native peoples, to the states. The new universities were to be dedicated to the study of agriculture, science, and engineering. In 1863, President Lincoln established the National Academy of Sciences to advise on federal science policy and eventually to recommend funding support for scientific research. The US Geological Survey was established in 1879 to survey the Western United States, map coastlines and waterways, and support a wide range of geographic and geological investigations. The same year, the federal government established the Bureau of Ethnology to collect archeological, linguistic, and ethnographic information about North American Indigenous peoples. In 1883, the Smithsonian Institution (founded in 1846) established a department of anthropology to systematically collect cultural artifacts, American Indian human remains, and archeological materials.

The importance of evolution to science was made clear at the Columbian Exposition in its Congress on Evolution, which featured Herbert Spencer as a speaker. His talk, titled "Social Evolution and Social Duty," reinforced his general theory of evolution:

the concentration of nebulae into stars and the formation of solar systems are determined entirely by certain properties of the matter previously diffused. Planets that were once gaseous, then liquid, and finally covered by their crusts, gradually undergo geological transformation in virtue of mechanical and chemical processes. Similarly, too, when we pass to organic bodies—plant and animal. (1894, p. 1190)

Other papers included "Constructive Evolution," "Evolutionary Psychology as Related to Education," and "The Beastliness of Modern Civilization—Evolution the Only Remedy." In this last paper, Mary A. Dodge (1833-96), who also published essays advocating for equal education and employment opportunities for women under the name Gail Hamilton, asserted that "Science is the true interpreter of salvation" for the human race (Dodge, 1894, p. 1189). The Congress explored the relevance and import of this new scientific lens to grave social and economic problems.

The new theories of evolution supported the view that there was a single human species differentiated by stages of development. This conception of evolution was on display at the Exposition in at least two forms. In the anthropology building, Franz Boas (1858-1942) and his director, Frederick Ward Putnam (1839-1915), designed a display of Indigenous people recruited from the Kwakiutl, Navajo, and Arawak peoples, who dressed in "traditional" clothes, ate "traditional" food, and performed "traditional" ceremonies for the passing crowds. At the same time, in the Midway Plaisance, showmen like Buffalo Bill Cody and others recruited Indigenous people from the Americas and Africa to live in "authentic" villages and thrill the crowds with dancing and risqué displays. Some have argued that the Midway itself displayed human evolution directly. When people entered the Midway from the main Exposition site and its vast white-washed buildings, "The White City," they would first see a German village, then an Irish one, and pass a series of more "barbarous" villages until they reached the "most primitive," including the American Indians and Africans. Handicrafts and photographs of "savages" were available for purchase (see Domash, 2002; White and Igleheart, 1893).

The depiction of the different levels of development of the racial groups included in the displays was based upon a concept of individual growth as well. On this account, tribal groups characterized primitive humanity, but as the species developed, tribes of indistinguishable individuals gave way to autonomous individuals bound to society by self-interest. Human individuals were taken to follow the same course, beginning as dependent children and developing into autonomous rational adults. Growth depended on gaining independence from one's social groups and particular places and asserting one's self as an individual.

G. Stanley Hall (1844–1924), who founded experimental psychology first at Johns Hopkins University and then at Clark, followed Spencer's recommendation that present science "study existing races of men which, as judged by their visible characters and implements, approach most nearly to primitive man" (Spencer, 1900–1, p. 40). The result was the application of Spencer's view as a resource for studying the growth of individuals. In his work *Adolescence* (1916), Hall proposed what he called the "recapitulation theory" of human development in which individual lives recapitulate the evolutionary development of humanity. The process of development for individual Indians at the Columbian Exposition, for example, culminated in the display prepared by the Carlisle Indian Boarding School, where American Indian students wore short hair and Western clothes while demonstrating vocational skills like sewing and carpentry (Commissioner of Indian Affairs, 1893).

This conception of individualistic human development was both a product of and a guide for the development of what can be called a second phase of the genocide of Indigenous Americans. The centrality of the individual and the disdain for Native communities and culture provided a rationale for the Indian boarding school system, the General Allotment Act of 1887, the American Indian Citizenship Act of 1924, and the Termination Acts of 1953. Boarding schools (first instituted in the eighteenth century in the American Northeast) removed Native children from their homes, forced them to wear Western clothes, and prevented them from using their first language. Inspired by the Reconstruction era Freedman schools, the boarding schools emphasized vocational training and discouraged interest in literature, arts, law, and science. Once separated from their communities, the education process was meant to "assist" Native children in becoming "true individuals."

The Allotment Act federally mandated the redistribution of reservation lands to individual tribal members, thereby eliminating commonly held property. The Act also had the benefit of transferring by sale undistributed land to non-Indigenous settlers, since the tracts of land were large, and the number of Indians small. By providing property to individuals, the Act intended to provide resources for individual economic achievement and independence from the tribe. Later, the 1924 Indian Citizenship Act granted US citizenship to all Indians born after the Act came into effect, whether they chose it or not. Termination marked the last stage of the process in which sovereign tribes were outlawed by the federal government. This last phase was overturned in the 1970s, and some federally recognized tribes that had been terminated were restored (though lands sold in the process of termination were not returned).

Resistance to this program of genocide came in a variety of forms, beginning with speeches like the one distributed by Simon Pokagon at the Columbian Exposition. Within twenty years, Native American intellectuals, many trained at Indian boarding schools, joined together to form the Society of American Indians (SAI), founded in 1911, to provide leadership in challenging the program of de-tribalization and dispossession adopted by the federal government. The SAI was founded just two years after the National Association for the Advancement of Colored People (NAACP) and counted among its "associate" (non-Indian) founding members W. E. B. Du Bois, the cofounder of the NAACP, Social Gospel movement leader Lyman Abbott (1835–1922), and Cornell University philosopher Frank Thilly (1865–1934). The shared language enforced by the boarding school system and the shared oppression faced by nearly all North American tribes led the SAI to adopt a "Pan-Indian" perspective. Despite their many differences, the SAI held that Indigenous North American cultures shared a more or less common philosophical framework and a wide range of similar needs.

The leading intellectuals of the SAI shared four central philosophical commitments: first, that Indigenous peoples held that all things are relational—that is, things exist only in and through relations with other things that are also relational; second, such relationality gives rise to the importance of place—that is, the particular relations that characterize individuals and their groups; third, placed relations were not given or static but imbued with what is often called "power"—power as an individuating and connecting motive that seeks to fulfill purposes; and fourth, as a consequence of the resulting diversity of powers marked by different relational locations, Indigenous philosophies are committed to ontological, epistemic, and phenomenological pluralism. Taken together, these commitments formed a philosophy of resistance that can be found in the speeches of Kicking Bear in 1890. He emphasized a concept of place where the people were who they were by the relationships that sustained them. The Ghost Dance he called for amounted to a constructive act, the assertion of indigeneity and community against displacement and genocide. Such conceptual resistance, of course, was met by military force along Wounded Knee Creek.

Twenty-one years after Kicking Bear described his vision to a council of Hunkpapa Sioux, Ohiyesa (1858–1939), called Charles Eastman in settler society, published a volume, *The Soul of the Indian*, whose title recalled Du Bois's book published a few years earlier, *Souls of Black Folk*. Ohiyesa (Eastman) was a Boston University-trained physician who had grown up with his Dakota grandparents on the Northern plains after his mother died and his father fled to Canada in the aftermath of the "Great Sioux Uprising" in 1862. In 1873, his father returned and urged his son to become Western educated. After attending Beloit, Knox, and Dartmouth Colleges, Eastman received his medical degree in 1890 in time to be assigned by the Indian Bureau as the physician at the Pine Ridge Reservation. On December 31, 1890, Eastman led a group of civilians—Indian and White—to the site of the Wounded Knee Massacre to look for survivors. In his autobiography, he wrote, "It took all of my nerve to keep my composure in the face of this spectacle, and of the excitement and grief of my Indian companions, nearly every one of whom was crying aloud or singing his death song." It was, he said, "a severe ordeal," especially "for one who has so lately put all his faith in the Christian love and lofty ideals of the white man" (Eastman, 1977, pp. 112, 114).

*The Soul of the Indian* was presented as an account of American Indian religion, but like Kicking Bear's address, it also offered a philosophical framework attributed by Eastman to North American Indigenous people. Central to this framework was the conviction that "every creature possesses a soul in some degree, though not necessarily a soul conscious of itself. The tree, the waterfall, the grizzly bear, each is an embodied Force, and as such an object of reverence." In a world in which every creature, that is, every created thing, has a "soul," Eastman argued that people behave differently and with respect. Framing the resulting way of life as "religious," Eastman explained, "Every act of [an Indian's] life is, in a very real sense, a religious act. He recognizes the spirit in all creation, and believes that he draws from it spiritual power" (1911, p. 15). Thanks are due to the creatures with whom one interacts, and freely giving back to those creatures makes reciprocal relations also mutually constructive.

This ontological view of relational beings also provided a critical perspective on settler society. "As a child," Eastman said,

> I understood how to give; I have forgotten that grace since I became civilized. I lived the natural life, whereas I now live the artificial. Any pretty pebble was valuable to me then; every growing tree an object of reverence. Now I worship with the white man before a painted landscape whose value is estimated in dollars! Thus the Indian is reconstructed, as the natural rocks are ground to powder, and made into artificial blocks which may be built into the walls of modern society. (1911, p. 88)

Eastman's account adopted the evolutionary commitment to "savagism," but revised it, accepting the difference between savagism and civilization, but calling the hierarchy into question. Even as he framed a conception of Indigenous life, he also challenged "civilized" religion by harnessing both indigeneity and Christianity as critical tools. "There is no such thing as 'Christian civilization,'" he concluded. "I believe that Christianity and modern civilization are opposed and irreconcilable, and that the spirit of Christianity and of our ancient religion is essentially the same" (1911, p. 24).

Arthur C. Parker (1881–1955), Seneca, who also served as the editor of the SAI journal, both affirmed the need for American Indians to "assimilate" to the dominant economy and at the same time made a case for sustaining aspects of Indian culture as a means of combating the evils of industrial capitalism. In his first address to the SAI on education, Parker concluded, "The true aim of educational effort should not be to make the Indian a white man, but simply a man normal to his environment" (1912, p. 75). Here, standing against "commercial greed" and the "sordid . . . conventional ideas of white civilization" required that Indians "should use [their] revitalized influence and more advantageous position in asserting and developing the great ideals of [their] race for the good of . . . all [hu]mankind" (1912, p. 76).

Parker, like Eastman, also accepted both the commitment to the importance of the environment in development and the original state of "savagism" set out by Spencer. In his paper, The Problem of Race Assimilation in America, published in the SAI *American Indian Magazine* in 1916, Parker argued that assimilation into the "civilization" of North America happened at different rates according to racial difference. The reason for the differences, however, was not racial difference but unequal ethnic and cultural conditions. European immigrants, he argued, found assimilation easiest because their home cultural conditions were closely aligned with the dominant "Anglo-Saxon" civilization. The descendants of enslaved African peoples faced much greater obstacles. While European immigrants chose to come to America, as Parker sees it, African people were forced to America and learned the habits and culture of enslaved people once they arrived. Rather than assimilating, African Americans learned only to imitate civilization. Since, he continued, civilization is an "inward growth during the process of which, there is much of the old nature eliminated" (1916b, p. 291), formerly enslaved people adapt slowly if at all. The result, he thought, is that African Americans are rightly segregated until the slow process can be accomplished.

Native Americans, in contrast to the other groups, are Indigenous to the land and so come to civilization by choice. Even as he frames his account in evolutionary terms, Parker argues that Native peoples are conservative by nature (in the sense of being disposed to conserve or retain their cultural forms, ceremonies, and practices). "*Indians,*" he writes, "*are proud of their racial extraction and count it no virtue to imitate other races.*" The decision not to join civilization had consequences, however. "[T]he Indians," Parker says, "made the fatal mistake of thinking that because they loved a certain environment, they could retain it and continue the habits that characterized the old life. The new life had surrounded them in their segregated localities. Its forces had engulfed them without absorbing them." Echoing Pokagon, he concludes, "They reluctantly accepted the white man's methods and did so, usually, as a matter of economic necessity" (1916b, p. 296). For Parker, evolution was at once a frame for understanding difference in America and, for Native Americans, a resource for understanding resistance to the dominant culture even as they sought to assimilate to that culture.

Parker's case for revitalizing Native communities in the context of assimilation stood against the new system of genocide that developed in the late nineteenth century. "[T]here was an endeavor to occupy the land forcibly and by various means to exterminate its barbaric owners.... The idea of extermination persisted for a long time,... but there was enough sentiment to bring about a new course—that of segregation" (1916a, p. 252). For Parker, segregation was not a program designed to foster tribes but was rather a continuation of the system of genocide that began with the process of displacement and removal. "Segregation," he concluded, "did more to exterminate the Indians than did bullets" (1916a, p. 252). The practices carried out, Parker charged, "[have] permitted the soul of a race ... to sink beneath the evils of civilization into misery, ignorance, disease, and despondency" (1916a, pp. 252–3). The response, Parker argued, was to demand that settler society "return" certain stolen or destroyed aspects of Indigenous life that could support the renewal of tribal cultures and the possibility of reciprocity with other cultures. These included Indigenous intellectual and community life and economic independence (1916a, pp. 258–9).

Laura Cornelius Kellogg (1880–1947), Oneida, served as secretary for the SAI and argued, like Parker, for the restoration of Native communities. In her first address to the society, she challenged the culture that had come to surround Native people by identifying its failures. "The development of intense individualism and the age of unprecedented prosperity no doubt are largely responsible for the selfishness of the American people." To this overarching charge, she added specific "evils" like child labor, industrial accidents, unemployment, and unsanitary living conditions (1912, p. 47). Against these consequences of empire, Cornelius Kellogg maintained that "the line of least resistance to the greatest possible good under our present circumstances is to citizenize the possibilities and to reorganize the opportunities of the Indian *at home*; to organize the Indians' holdings into a system of economic advantages" (1912, p. 45). As a response to the reservation system and its isolation and poverty, Cornelius Kellogg proposed in her book, *Our Democracy and the American Indian*, published in 1920, the development of small-scale local economies that could sustain individual tribes and participate in the wider industrial economy.

Outside the SAI, other Native thinkers also challenged settler society. Luther Standing Bear (1868–1939), Oglala Lakota, was among the first students taken to the Carlisle Boarding

School in Pennsylvania, where he was trained as a tinsmith. His brother, Henry Standing Bear (c. 1874–1953), was one of the founding members of the SAI (and was apparently a resident of Hull House in Chicago around 1891 to 1892). When Luther returned from Carlisle, he worked for a time as a teacher and a shopkeeper at the Pine Ridge reservation. In 1905, he was elected chief of the Oglala and, after much controversy and conflict with the Bureau of Indian Affairs, left South Dakota in 1912 to become an actor, first with the Buffalo Bill Wild West Show and then in Hollywood movies. Late in life, he became an activist against the conditions imposed on the Lakota and wrote four books. In his last, *Land of the Spotted Eagle*, published in 1933, Standing Bear diagnosed the failure of White society. "The White man," he said, "does not understand the Indian for the same reason he does not understand America. He is far too removed from its formative processes. The roots of his tree of his life have not yet grasped the rock and soil." In contrast, "in the Indian the spirit of the land is still vested; it will be until other men are able to divine and meet its rhythm" (1933, p. 248). Like Kicking Bear, Standing Bear was clear about the future of life in North America and what kind of thinking would create such a future: "[It] is now time for the destructive order to be reversed. . . . [In] denying the Indian his ancestral rights and heritages the white race is but robbing itself. But America can be revived, rejuvenated, by recognizing a nature school of thought. The Indian can save America" (1933, p. 255).

Evolution theory was at once the ground of resistance against the savagism imposed by settlers on Indigenous peoples and the ground for resistance against the imposition of fixed categories of all sorts. American philosophies set themselves against understanding life separately from the environments in which it flourished. The result was a revolution in education, conceptions of knowledge, conceptions of what is, and of the ways in which many came to resist the inheritances of European philosophy. As Dewey observes in his 1909 article, The Influence of Darwinism on Philosophy, "In laying hands upon the sacred ark of absolute permanency, in treating forms that had been regarded as types of fixity and perfection as originating and passing away, the 'Origin of Species' introduced a mode of thinking that in the end was bound to transform the logic of knowledge, and hence the treatment of morals, politics, and religion" (MW 4, p. 2).

## Primary Texts

Eastman, Charles (Ohiyesa) (1980). *The Soul of the Indian*. Lincoln, NE: University of Nebraska Press.
Kellogg, Laura Cornelius (2002). *Our Democracy and the American Indian*, excerpt in *American Philosophies: An Anthology*, eds. Leonard Harris, Scott L. Pratt, and Anne Waters. London: Blackwell Publishing.
Parker, Arthur C. (1968). *Parker on the Iroquois*, ed. an introduction by William N. Fenton. Syracuse: Syracuse University Press.
Pearce, Trevor (2020). *Pragmatism's Evolution : Organism and Environment in American Philosophy*. Chicago: The University of Chicago Press.
Standing Bear, Luther (1978). *Land of the Spotted Eagle*. Lincoln: University of Nebraska Press.

# CHAPTER 4
# FEMINIST RESISTANCE
## MARGARET FULLER, ANNA JULIA COOPER, JANE ADDAMS, AND CHARLOTTE PERKINS GILMAN

Even as American Indians were included in problematic ways at the Chicago Columbian Exposition, women, like African Americans, were initially left out entirely. Unlike the case of African Americans, after extensive lobbying, a "Board of Lady Managers" composed mainly of wealthy Chicago women, was appointed to organize the Woman's Building and display at the Exposition. One of the most important results was that a woman architect, Sophie Hayden (1868–1953), was selected to design the building. Even though the building received more visitors than any other at the Fair, it remained controversial. Initially, the Board had intended to place women's exhibits in all of the other buildings to demonstrate women's accomplishments. Long delays in receiving approvals meant that nearly all of the space was gone in the other buildings, and so most of the women's displays were left to the Woman's Building. Such exclusion had become the general approach to dealing with women's demands for a place in the leadership of American society.

While Ida B. Wells-Barnett protested such exclusion, six African American women did speak at the Columbian Exposition. Among them was Anna Julia Cooper (1858–1964), the author of *A Voice from the South* (1892). Cooper was born in slavery to an enslaved mother and her White master. In the course of her 105-year life, she became a prominent writer and speaker and, for much of her career, a teacher in the Washington, D.C., public school system. From 1901 until 1906, Cooper served as principal of the prominent M Street High School. After she called for changes in the curriculum, White members of the school board, possibly with the encouragement of allies of Booker T. Washington (then viewed as the leading spokesperson for African Americans), began a campaign to oust her from the school district. The resulting controversy became public and her contract was not renewed for 1907–8. She taught in St. Louis, Missouri for five years, then returned to M Street High School as a teacher until 1930. She had received her undergraduate education at St. Augustine's College in Raleigh, North Carolina, and received her BA in 1884 and MA in 1887 from Oberlin College in Ohio. At age sixty-six, she completed her PhD at the Sorbonne in Paris. In 1930, she became the president of Frelinghuysen University, a program that offered a wide range of courses, mostly in private homes and in a house in the African American Shaw neighborhood of Washington, D.C. Eventually, the University lost its building and Cooper offered her house to serve as the University's office and main classroom building. In 1937, the University lost its accreditation and was restructured as Frelinghuysen Group of Schools for Colored Working People led by Cooper until it disbanded in the 1950s (May 2007, p. 13, 18, 21, 25, 35).

Cooper stood at odds with both the race advocates who argued for separation between Blacks and Whites such as Washington and Martin Delaney (1812–85), and those who advocated for suffrage and used racial arguments against Blacks to make the case. In *A Voice from the South*, for example, she challenged Delaney, who advocated "colonization," that is, asking Blacks in America to "return" to Africa. Cooper charged that Delaney saw his view as *the* view of African Americans, so that "when he entered the council of kings the black race entered with him" (1998, p. 63). She replied that such "eminent" men did not represent oppressed African Americans. "We must point to homes, average homes, homes of the rank and file . . . (where the masses are) . . .—then and not till then will the whole plateau be lifted into the sunlight" (p. 63). For Cooper, the recognition of ordinary lives centered in homes and communities was the key to "uplift" and the struggle for Black liberation. It was not when men rose in respect and power, but when those most oppressed, the women of the community, had a voice and opportunity that freedom could be achieved. As a result, she proclaimed, "Only the BLACK WOMAN [sic] can say, 'when and where I enter, in the quiet, undisputed dignity of my womanhood, without violence and without suing or special patronage, then and there the whole *Negro race enters with me*'" (p. 63).

Cooper argued that what the world most needed at the time was a "feminine flavor" (1998, p. 76). This included "ready sympathy, loving appreciation and unfaltering friendship" and the realization of "woman as an equal, as a helper, as a friend" (1998, p. 57). For Cooper, the hope for the country rests "chiefly on the homelife and on the influence of good women in their homes" (p. 55) and "the race cannot be effectually lifted up till its women are truly elevated" (p. 69). Like Jane Addams, Cooper noted the many young college-educated women were "quick to see and eager to help the needs of the needy world—women who can think as well as feel, and who feel none the less because they think" (p. 73). The world needs this feminine sensibility to complement the long-dominant masculine approach of grasping selfishness, but "the feminine factor can have its proper effect only through woman's development and education" (p. 78).

While one way this feminine influence could be made manifest would be through voting, Cooper split with White advocates for suffrage who argued that "[t]he great burly black man, ignorant and gross and depraved, is allowed to vote; while the franchise is withheld from the intelligent and refined, the pure-minded and lofty souled white woman." Cooper thought that the case for women's suffrage ought to be based on the recognition that "*the world needs to hear her voice*" (1998, p. 107). She called on women to reject the place of racial distinctions in the struggle against their exclusion from opportunity and their need to be heard. "Why should woman become plaintiff in a suit versus the Indian, or the Negro or any other race or class who have been crushed under the iron heel of Anglo-Saxon power and selfishness?" (p. 108). She concluded in her address at the Exposition:

> Let woman's claim be as broad in the concrete as in the abstract. . . . The colored woman feels that woman's cause is one and universal; . . . not till the universal title of humanity to life, liberty, and the pursuit of happiness is conceded to be inalienable to all; not till then is woman's lesson taught and woman's cause won—not the white woman's, nor the black woman's, not the red woman's, but the cause of every man and of every woman who has writhed silently under a mighty wrong. (1894, p. 715)

Yet she also believed in the importance of race as defining communities. "What the dark man wants then is merely to live his own life, in his own world, with his own chosen companions" (1998, p. 102).

While Cooper underscored her analysis with appeals to Christianity and universal humanity, the core of her view nevertheless recognized the reality of the contradictions in her position. Describing a stop at a train station in the South, she said, "I see two dingy little rooms with 'FOR LADIES' swinging over one and 'FOR COLORED PEOPLE' over the other" and wondered "under which head I come" (1998, p. 95). "The colored woman of to-day . . . is confronted by both a woman question and a race problem, and is as yet an unknown or an unacknowledged factor in both" (p. 112). Rather than resolving the contradiction, Cooper saw her position as an "ambiguous middle, as the logicians would call it" (p. 101). From here, at the intersection of oppressions, she was able to both affirm and challenge differences as a means for gaining a voice and finding ways to acknowledge that "[t]he cause of freedom is not the cause of race or a sect, a party or a class,—it is the cause of humankind" (p. 106). This approach, however, did not characterize the early "women's movement."

It is hard to point to a specific moment when the "women's movement" began in the United States. Women agitated for equal rights even at the founding of the country. In the 1820s, Lydia Maria Child (1802–80) began a tradition of women writers in the United States who argued in essays and fiction for and against women's rights. Child became a practical advocate of women's rights when she published *The Frugal Housewife* in 1829. In addition to providing women with recipes and instructions for laundry and soap making, the volume also encouraged women to acquire their own money and employable skills for independent living.

The women's movement became organized and recognized as a movement when women, working in abolitionist groups, began to act politically against slavery while also arguing for the right of women to vote. In 1840, women delegates to the London Anti-Slavery Convention who had been vocal opponents of slavery were not allowed to speak. Lucretia Mott (1793–1880) and Elizabeth Cady Stanton (1815–1902) returned to the United States with plans for a women's rights convention. They were in part inspired by the work and example of Margaret Fuller (1810–1850).

Born in Massachusetts in 1810, Fuller became an important part of the Transcendentalist movement, inspiring the likes of Ralph Waldo Emerson, Henry David Thoreau, Nathaniel Hawthorne, and Walt Whitman. Her father's disappointment in her not being born a boy was channeled into her education. He instructed her as he would have a boy, so she learned Greek and Latin and read widely. Later, she taught herself German and Italian. This kind of education enabled her to be a teacher, and she taught at Bronson Alcott's school for a year, in addition to teaching privately to earn a living. She became well known as an informed and lively conversationalist, and she began a series of conversations among women in Boston. These conversations also attracted the attention of prominent men. Her reputation resulted in invitations to visit Emerson, and she was a frequent visitor to Brook Farm, a utopian community near Boston founded by Sophia and George Ripley. Emerson had first met Fuller in 1835 and was much impressed. In 1839, he asked her to edit the Transcendentalist journal *The Dial*, and she accepted.

Fuller's life was unconventional for the time. Never paid for her work at *The Dial*, she went on to work for Horace Greeley at the *New York Tribune*. She became their first female editor. In 1846, the *Tribune* sent her to Europe as their first female foreign correspondent. She became especially interested in the work of several Italian revolutionaries and fell in love with one in particular. She lived with, and had a son with, Giovanni Angelo Ossoli (ten years younger than she), but they never married. In 1850, the family set sail for the United States. The ship ran aground just off Fire Island in New York. The body of her son was found. Thoreau went to New

York to search for Fuller, but Ossoli's and Fuller's bodies were never recovered. This loss was felt keenly by many, including those active in the women's movement. For them, Fuller's life and work had been important ("Margaret Fuller").

In 1845, Fuller had published *Woman in the Nineteenth Century*, setting the stage for the development of an explicitly feminist theory. She used history, religion, mythology, and science to present centuries-old debates about the nature and status of women. She argued that the male/female dualism common in Western culture was damaging for everyone, but especially for women. Fuller argued that all human beings had two "sides," the masculine side characterized by "energy, power and intellect," and the feminine side characterized by "harmony, beauty and love." "These two sides are supposed to be expressed in Man and Woman, that is, as the more and the less, for the faculties have not been given pure to either, but only in preponderance" (1860, p. 169). To be fully human, a woman must recognize and develop both sides. Femininity was only disabling when it was separated from masculinity. Humans should express their whole nature rather than be artificially pushed to either extreme. "Male and female represent the two sides of the great radical dualism. But, in fact, they are perpetually passing into one another. Fluid hardens to solid, solid rushes to fluid. There is no wholly masculine man, no purely feminine woman" (pp. 155–6).

Like many thinkers of her day, Fuller was also concerned about the treatment of American Indians. After a series of wars with Native peoples in the West and the 1838–9 removal of American Indians from the Southeastern United States by force, Fuller decided to travel West to understand the issues better. In 1844, she published a volume recounting her travels along the Western frontier in Illinois, Wisconsin, and Michigan. In addition to reading all of the recognized Native and non-Native sources on Native culture she could find, Fuller spent a great deal of time with the Indigenous people she encountered on her way. Her summary presented a mixed impression: "Although I have little to tell, I feel that I have learnt a great deal of the Indians, from observing them even in this broken and degraded condition. There is a language of eye and motion which cannot be put into words, and which teaches what words never can. I feel acquainted with the soul of this race" (1994, p. 223). On one hand, Fuller shared the post-revolutionary view that the end of Native culture was inevitable. On the other hand, it seems that she found new insights and perspectives that, according to commentator Christina Zwarg, were crucial in the development of her feminism (1995, pp. 97–124).

At least three insights served to further Fuller's own philosophical development. First, she recognized the centrality of character in the production of meaning. Reporting a Native story about Mackinaw Island, Fuller observed that a "simple creed . . . forms the basis of all this mythology." At the center of the creed, she claimed, is a "moral code" which is "clear and noble in the stress it laid upon truth and fidelity" where the moral ideal is one of virtue, "if virtue be allowed to consist in a man's acting up to his own ideas of right" (1994, p. 197). As in Indigenous American traditions and in classical pragmatism later, character and meaning are intertwined.

Second, Fuller's encounter with Native cultures helped her to develop an understanding of the role of culture in the process of making and using meaning. She identified the relevance of culture in the construction of knowledge, for example, in claiming that the "historian of the Indians should be one of their own race, as able to sympathize with them, and possessing a mind as enlarged and cultivated as John Ross [a contemporary Cherokee leader]" (1994, p. 212). She identified the relevance of culture to the meaning of individual lives by taking up an analysis of the status of women proposed by Jane Schoolcraft (1800–1842), an Ojibwa. Schoolcraft argued that women were better off in Native cultures than in European ones on the grounds that in Native cultures women had more "power." Fuller modified the conclusion:

> The power is good for nothing, unless the women be wise to use it aright. Has the Indian [woman], has the white woman, as noble a feeling of life and its uses, as religious a self-respect, as worthy a field of thought and action as man? If not, the white woman, the Indian woman, occupies an inferior position to that of man. It is not so much a question of power, as of privilege. (1994, p. 181)

Here, by drawing parallels between Native and European women, Fuller located the meanings of women's lives in a larger cultural context. Such a claim recognized the connections between culture and oppression.

Finally, Fuller recognized that while difference is valuable and ought to be preserved, significant ways of thinking about the world grow together. Writing about the variety of origin stories she encountered in her travels, she concluded: "Soon, soon [the] tales of the origin of things [told by European immigrants], and the Providence which rules them, will be so mingled with those of the Indian, that the very oak trees will not know them apart,—will not know whether itself be a Runic, a Druid, or a Winnebago oak" (1994, p. 171). Fuller's plural-but-unified perspective marks it as an American philosophy of resistance. Her interest and engagement with Native American thought and culture played a crucial role in the development of her conceptions of gender and the place of women in American society and her commitment to feminist reform.

The first women's rights convention was convened in 1848 by Mott, Cady Stanton, and Matilda Joslyn Gage (1826–1898). All three women had been inspired by the model of women's leadership in the Haudenosaunee (Iroquois) nations that lived in New York, and all three frequently visited friends at the Haudenosaunee villages near the first convention site in Seneca Falls. Mott and Cady Stanton both noted the importance of the Haudenosaunee model in making a case for women's suffrage, and Gage, after her arrest for attempting to vote in a school board election, was adopted into the Wolf Clan of the Mohawk nation (Wagner, 1992).

In 1851 at the Ohio Women's Rights Convention, Sojourner Truth (c. 1797–1883) delivered her famous "And Ain't I a Woman" speech and forced the suffrage movement to begin to face issues of race and class. At the end of the Civil War, in an effort to affect Reconstruction policies, the American Equal Rights Association was founded to work for a constitutional amendment that would guarantee equal rights for all regardless of race, color, or sex. The Fifteenth Amendment that was ratified in 1870 nevertheless left women out. Many suffrage activists objected to the amendment because it granted the vote to African American men but not to women and, as a result, passage of the amendment split the women's rights groups into two camps. In 1869, the National Woman Suffrage Association (NWSA) was founded with Cady Stanton as president. The association, which did not let men serve in leadership positions, opposed the Fifteenth Amendment because it did not include women. The American Woman Suffrage Association (AWSA), on the other hand, was founded with Henry Ward Beecher (1813–1887) as president and was willing to accept the Fifteenth Amendment while working for passage of women's suffrage in the individual states. Further, both groups presented a clear tension between the views of the more privileged and educated White women who led the groups and the views of working women—poor White women, Black women, and immigrant women. While this tension carries over into the women's movement in the present day, there were, even at the time, some who spoke up and challenged the idea of a universal woman's experience. This would not, however, become a prominent idea until late in the twentieth century.

By 1890, the NWSA and the AWSA merged to form the National American Woman Suffrage Association with Cady Stanton, Susan B. Anthony (1820–1906), and Lucy Stone (1818–1893) as officers. Other countries, and even some states, had already begun granting women the right to vote, but it was not until August 1920 that the Nineteenth Amendment was passed, granting women the right to vote in national elections in the United States. The right to vote, however, was not the only issue facing women, and the passage of the Nineteenth Amendment was only one step in a wider effort to improve women's circumstances through the reformation of property rights, marriage laws, and access to birth control.

Jane Addams (1860–1935) was a good example of a woman who worked to achieve a place for women in public and political affairs but did not think the right to vote alone would be enough. Addams was born in Cedarville, Illinois, the daughter of a successful miller who became a cofounder of the Republican Party in Illinois, a state senator, and a friend of Abraham Lincoln. Her mother died in childbirth when Addams was two years old. Addams attended Rockford Female Seminary, a four-year college for women, and there faced what she later called the "snare of preparation," using a phrase of the Russian author Leo Tolstoy. She studied Greek, read Emerson (and Tolstoy among many others), learned science and math, and led the debate team. As she completed her study at Rockford (later receiving a BA when the women's college became accredited), she found herself at once committed to high ideals and at the same time unsure what she should do about them. After a brief enrollment at the Woman's Medical College of Philadelphia (followed by severe depression), she joined other affluent young college-educated women by taking what some called a "grand tour" of Europe (Knight 2010).

Society expected Addams to take up the position it had set for such women: to serve as a wife and mother while keeping her ideals abstract and her demeanor pleasant. Addams would later write in *Twenty Years at Hull House* (1990) that, in the years after college, she "was absolutely at sea so far as any moral purpose was concerned, clinging only to the desire to live in a really living world and refusing to be content with a shadowy intellectual or aesthetic reflection of it" (1990, p. 39). Unlike many "grand tours" of Europe, Addams's travel took her to the worst parts of the cities she visited. In London, she visited Toynbee Hall in the impoverished East End. Toynbee Hall was opened in 1884 to provide support for the poor of London. The young staff, mostly students from Oxford and Cambridge, lived at the Hall and, although many worked in the city during the day, they provided assistance to the neighborhood in the evenings and on weekends. Reporting on her visit, Addams wrote to a friend in 1888, "It is a community for University men who live there, have their recreation and clubs and society all among the poor people, yet in the same style they would live in their own circle." Even as they brought literature and culture to the neighborhood, they did so "free from 'professional doing good'" and were "so unaffectedly sincere and so productive of good results" in the classes they offered and the library they provided, that it seemed to her "perfectly ideal" (quoted in Crunden, 1984, p. 25). "I gradually became convinced," she wrote, that it would be a good thing to rent a house in a part of the city [Chicago] where many primitive and actual needs are found, in which young women who had been given over too exclusively to study, might restore a balance of activity along the traditional lines and learn of life from life itself; where they might try out some of the things they had been taught and put truth to "the ultimate test of the conduct it dictates or inspires." (1990, p. 51)

The result of her plan was to establish a "Settlement," as Toynbee Hall was called. "The Settlement," she wrote, "is an experimental effort to aid in the solution of the social and industrial problems which are engendered by the modern conditions of life in a great city" (p. 75). She and her friend Ellen Gates Starr returned to the United States, found an old house on Halsted Street on the South side of Chicago, and founded Hull House. The neighborhood was poor, and the living conditions were unhealthy. Most of the residents were recently arrived European immigrants who had come to Chicago in search of good jobs and often to escape even worse economic and social conditions in their home countries.

What made Addams and Starr's efforts distinctive among the many settlement houses founded in the United States in the late nineteenth century was that they took seriously the experimental element of their mission. Many settlements came to a neighborhood with a set of established ideas about what the community needed; Hull House began that way, but it quickly became apparent to Addams and her colleagues that they should first listen to their neighbors. After the experience of trying to establish a coffee house as an alternative to the many saloons in the neighborhood, Addams said that the experience "taught us not to hold preconceived ideas of what the neighborhood ought to have, but to keep ourselves in readiness to modify and adapt our undertakings" (1990, p. 79). This openness to hearing the concerns of the community became a central component of the work of Hull House so that it became "valuable as an information and interpretation bureau," acting "between the various institutions of the city and the people for whose benefit these institutions were erected" (p. 99).

While Addams was particularly concerned with the circumstances faced by women in the neighborhood, she recognized that women's issues were intertwined with issues faced by men, children, and the elderly, including learning English, adapting to new types of food and cooking, managing money, and getting access to schools and child care. Faced with pressing local needs, Addams did not take the larger question of women's suffrage as a high priority. In 1897, however, after unsuccessful efforts to change Chicago and state policies around child labor and workplace laws, she realized that such issues were also related to the infrastructure of the neighborhood (things as local as garbage collection and as sweeping as legal protections for women and children at work). Writing in *Newer Ideals of Peace* (2007), Addams argued that enfranchisement—the vote—was now a necessity for women. Working conditions, especially those in clothing manufacturing "sweat shops," were imposed by bosses more interested in profit than safety, and there was little the workers could do. Unionization provided some relief, but the owners could take advantage of laws written by the men of the legislature to limit the scope of union activism. "Women directly controlled the surroundings of their work as long as their arrangements were domestic," she wrote, "but they cannot do this now unless they have the franchise, as yet the only mechanism devised by which . . . a number of persons are able to embody their collective will in legislation" (2007, p. 106). In Addams's work and the work of the other residents of Hull House (many of them women), the "women's movement" transformed from one primarily focused on getting the vote to broader concerns that would join with the work of others such as Cooper and Wells-Barnett to see the problems faced by women as complex and multilayered, involving racism, sexism, poverty, education, politics, and culture.

As Hull House addressed Addams's "snare of preparation," it also provided a place for young women in particular to respond to the familial and societal expectations that they return home after college to marry, raise a family, and care for their parents. Settlement houses such as Hull House provided an alternative place for these women where they could work for the public good and be generally free from domestic duties. The domestic work at Hull House was shared among the residents and so everyone had time to dedicate to their public work. This option, however, was not generally available to women—especially married women.

Another response to women's desire for a greater role in public life was the cooperative housekeeping movement. Melusina Fay Peirce (1836–1923), the first wife of Charles Sanders Peirce, one of the founders of the "school" of pragmatism, was a leader in this movement. The idea behind this movement was to organize neighborhood women to collectively clean houses on a rotating basis. This allowed them to share equipment and labor, which in turn made the work go faster, leaving them more time for other activities. It also provided a means of forming a community among the women and organizing around causes. It did not, however, challenge the notion that this domestic work should be unpaid "women's work."

Charlotte Perkins Gilman (1860–1935) offered a more radical understanding of the problem this public/private split posed for women, and she proposed a more radical solution. She was a well-known writer, speaker, and publisher of the magazine the *Forerunner*. Her own life reflected the tensions women faced at this time. Her best-known work, *The Yellow Wallpaper*, is a loosely autobiographical story that followed a young woman who became depressed after marrying and having children. She wanted to write, but the medical advice at the time was that women with symptoms of depression should rest and do nothing but be with their children. Both Addams and Gilman were treated by the leading advocate for this treatment, Dr. S. Weir Mitchell (1829–1914). This "rest cure" drove the character in *The Yellow Wallpaper* to a complete mental breakdown, mirroring the one Gilman experienced in 1885. The woman in the story finally went mad, while Gilman divorced her husband, left her daughter to be raised by the child's father and his new wife, and created a professional life for herself in which she worked to change the possibilities for women and thus for society as a whole.

At issue for Gilman, Addams, and others was a response to the increasingly dominant ideal that individuals achieved their potential by freeing themselves from the entanglements of home and community. At the same time, the practical concerns of food, housing, and care of children meant that only some individuals could pursue the ideal, while others, women in particular, would be barred by biology, religion, or economic necessity from achieving the autonomous ideal. Rather than simply demanding access to the industrial capitalist system that came to dominate America at the beginning of the twentieth century, feminist philosophers argued for an alternate model of human nature grounded in the idea of "social individuals." Housework and childcare should be seen as a collective responsibility, even as each individual ought to be free to make their own distinctive contribution to the community. This philosophical starting point demanded both an underlying theory and a practical outcome. Gilman offered a version of both.

Gilman understood the division of labor as a habit left over from an earlier organization of human society. Influenced by the evolutionary theories of the day and especially the "gynaecocentric" view of human evolution developed by Lester F. Ward (1841–1913), she acknowledged that the current division of labor, and the accompanying ideas of femininity and masculinity, may have made evolutionary sense at some point, but times and circumstances had changed and new ideas were necessary.

Ward's social theory attempted to bring together Lamarck, Darwin, and Spencer. Lamarck's "principle of exercise"—the idea that inheritable characteristics could be developed by repeated activity—and Darwin's principle of natural selection—the combination of random mutation and survival—should be understood as "dynamic" principles united under Spencer's "static" concept of "equilibration." Exercise and natural selection characterize the process of species change, and equilibration serves as the organizing frame for the dynamic system. Ward called the organizing principle "synergy" because the term combines the "two-fold character of *energy* and *mutuality*, or the systematic and organic *working together* of the antithetical forces of nature" (Ward, 1907, p. 171). He summarizes: "It is primarily and essentially . . . a process of equilibration" where different "forces" begin "in collision, conflict, antagonism, and opposition," changing into ameliorative "phases of antithesis, competition, and interaction . . . ending in collaboration and coöperation" (1907, p. 175). The forces that are at work in human development are ontogenetic, that is, responses to pleasure and pain that promote survival, and phylogenetic, or the processes of selection that lead to reproduction and the evolution of a species (pp. 261–2).

It is the phylogenetic forces that lead to the gynaecocentric theory since females have "the power of selection" (1907, p. 376). Thanks to accidental circumstances, for example, the various requirements of food collection and conflict among groups, males advanced in physical ability and authority, leading to "a profound social revolution" that "overthrew the authority of woman, destroyed her power of selection, and finally reduced her to the condition of a mere slave of the stronger sex, although that strength had been conferred by her" (p. 376). Ward argued that in contrast to androcentric models of humanity in which men are viewed as dominant, women ought to be seen as the dominant sex. His view is that the "female sex is primary and the male secondary" and "that originally and normally all things center . . . about the female, and that the male, though not necessary in carrying out the scheme, was developed under the operation of the principle of advantage to secure organic progress through the crossing of strains" (p. 296).

For Gilman, Ward's identification of the rise of androcentrism helped to explain the history of domestic labor. Prior to the Industrial Revolution, families worked together as extended units. While work was generally divided along gender lines, the family worked as an extended cooperative unit. Everyone might work together to get a harvest in, to get a barn built, or to put up food for winter. Further, no task fell to a single individual, as there were usually multiple generations to help with various tasks. The problem emerged when the organization of labor and families shifted with the Industrial Revolution. Gilman argued that society had become stuck in an arrangement that no longer served the development and growth of the human species. This arrangement, which reflected a particular stage of human development and the economic structure that sustained it, was one in which women were dependent on men for economic support. She argued that humans are the only species in which the female is not "economically" independent—that is, the only one in which females depend on males for food and shelter.

While Gilman's main focus was on middle- and upper-class women, her point still held for the many poor women who were working to help support their families. According to Louise Knight, most married women in this period did not work. "In 1900 only 5.6 percent of married women worked, while 44 percent of single women worked, as did 30 percent of those who were widowed (or abandoned) or divorced" (Knight, 2005, p. 130). The legal doctrine of coverture (that the money married women earned belonged to their husbands and that they could not own property on their own) was the norm in the United States throughout the nineteenth century, even after many states passed Women's Property Acts in the 1840s and 1850s. Gilman also noted that the idea that women earned their living by the work they did in the home did not make sense, since the women who worked the hardest—poor women—"earned" the least. Wealthy women "earned" the most but did the least work; the economic status of women was tied to the economic status of the men they married, not their labor. Because of this, it made sense for women to compete, to "marry up," and focus on being attractive to men of wealth. Gilman again appealed to other species to say that generally males compete for females who, in turn, select the "fittest" mate. Humans reversed this order so that men selected mates based on appearance without concern for the "fitness" of intelligence and ability. As a result of this shift, Gilman concluded, the females of the human species were generally weaker and more passive than the males. "She gets her living by getting a husband. He gets his wife by getting a living." (Gilman, 1889, p. 99) This results in individualistic competition that frustrates the evolution in cooperative effort that she sees emerging. The relation between males and females was thus contrary to the process of evolutionary development and so, if the species were to grow and thrive, the relationship must be changed so both can contribute positive social service.

Gilman sought to change the nature of women (and the human species generally) by changing how they lived. She wanted to eliminate the distinction between private and public realms of work; rather than shut individual women up to do the cooking, cleaning, sewing, nursing, and childcare in private, these tasks should become paid professions that attracted those who were most qualified. It is important to remember that in 1898 it was not yet generally possible to buy ready-made clothes, prepared foods, or safe and effective medicines. Women had to know how to preserve and prepare food without the convenience of refrigeration, how to keep the fires in stoves burning without endangering the family, and how to clean and do laundry in the face of the soot in the house and in the air generally. The house entailed full-time and difficult labor. Gilman proposed professionally staffed kitchens instead. Qualified experts who could judge the quality of ingredients and oversee the safe preparation of nutritious food would run these kitchens. Further, people would come together to eat and so help end the increasing isolation of the family unit from the larger society. Women would be able to engage in political discussions while they ate with people outside their immediate family. By restructuring how domestic work was accomplished, women would be freed up to participate in public life. Like Cooper, Gilman thought that as active wage earners not bound to private, unpaid labor, women could begin to transform the relationships between men and women into relationships that would foster the growth of humankind.

Women in the home tended to focus on the needs of their husbands and their children (especially their sons) because they were the means to achieve economic security and advancement. This put women in competition with each other and placed the burden of economic support on men. As a result, men worked in jobs that paid well, whether or not they suited their individual talents or society's greatest need. Gilman's conclusion was that something as simple as removing the kitchen from the home could release the full potential of men and women for the service of society as a whole.

This move from individualism to a social ethic was central to the view offered by Gilman, Addams, and later by John Dewey and other twentieth-century social philosophers. "The time has come," Gilman wrote in her 1899 *Women and Economics*, "when we are open to deeper and wider impulses than the sex-instinct; the social instincts are strong enough to come into full use at last. This is shown by the twin struggle . . . in sex and economics,—the 'women's movement' and the 'labor movement'" (1899, p. 138). She argues that social evolution is tending toward "the gradual subordination of individual effort for individual good to the collective effort for the collective good" and this "increasing interdependence of the component parts" benefits "the individual as well as the social body" (p. 95). This sort of increased "social consciousness" was displayed by workers in Chicago the year after the Columbian Exposition closed when their response to economic depression erupted in the infamous Pullman Strike of 1894.

## Primary Texts

Addams, Jane (1990). *Twenty Years at Hull House*, introduction with notes by James Hurt. Urbana: University of Illinois Press.
Cooper, Anna Julia (1998). *The Voice of Anna Julia Cooper*, eds. Charles Lemert and Esme Bhan. Lanham, MD: Rowman and Littlefield Publishers, Inc.
Gilman, Charlotte Perkins (1989). *The Yellow Wallpaper and Other Writings*, with an introduction by Lynn Sharon Schwartz. New York: Bantam Classic, Random House Publishers.

# CHAPTER 5
## TRANSCENDENTAL ORIGINS
### RALPH WALDO EMERSON AND HENRY DAVID THOREAU

Gilman's project developed alongside a rising movement of women's activism whose character was determined in part by its leadership—people like Julia Ward Howe and Josephine Shaw Lowell—who had first become activists as abolitionists. Many, like Howe and Lowell, became part of the US Sanitary Commission during the Civil War and found their work in that organization to be valuable not only in the context of the war, but also as a framework for defining a particular kind of assistance to others. The Congressionally chartered but privately managed Commission helped to pave the way for collective action that emphasized order over responses to individual need, laying the groundwork for turn-of-the-century social service institutions that at once provided help against the worst conditions of industrialization and maintained the hegemony of wealthy and White Americans (see Fredrickson, 1965). Gilman identified the genealogy and importance of this movement in *Women and Economics*. "When it became possible to work together for other than religious ends,—when larger social service was made possible to women, as in our sanitary commission during the last war—women everywhere rose to meet the need" (1899, p. 165). The resulting organizations, the General Federation of Women's Clubs and the Charity Organization Society, became models of collective social action, a (nonvoting) political force, and means for advancing women's causes from the 1890s well into the twentieth century.

The ideals and work of these organizations emerged as a kind of transformation of what had become the dominant "philosophical" movement in the Northeast in the decade before the Civil War. That perspective, called Transcendentalism, was outlined in the work of Ralph Waldo Emerson and his close friends, Margaret Fuller (discussed in Chapter 4) and Henry David Thoreau. In the period of the Transcendentalists, as they are collectively known, philosophy had not yet become a formal field of study in America. Instead, it was often discussed only in the context of religion; when it was taught as a separate subject matter in colleges and universities, it usually took the form of moral philosophy, taught by the college president as a final course in how graduates ought to act (see Kuklick, 1979). Apart from a few textbook authors such as Noah Porter (also president of Yale) and Francis Bowen, who sought to summarize the prominent schools of philosophy in Europe, philosophical practice was found outside the academy in the context of public lectures aimed at the improvement of life in America. This work coincided with a rising interest in narrative histories of the United States and the call for a distinctively American literature.

This generation of thinkers included novelists and essayists such as Washington Irving, James Fenimore Cooper, Lydia Maria Child, Lydia Sigourney, Catharine Maria Sedgwick, and Nathaniel Hawthorne; historians such as George Bancroft and Francis Parkman; and popular lecturers such as Frances "Fanny" Wright, Henry Ward Beecher, Wendell Phillips, and Emerson. Many of these same authors gained popular audiences at meetings sponsored by the American Lyceum movement. Begun by Josiah Holbrook in 1826 in Millbury,

Massachusetts, lyceums were a form of adult education sponsored by local societies. A town lyceum, as Holbrook wrote in his 1829 instruction manual, *American Lyceum*, or *Society for the Improvement of Schools and Diffusion of Useful Knowledge*, was "a voluntary association of individuals disposed to improve *each other* in useful knowledge, and to advance the interests of their schools" (1829, p. 3). By the end of the 1830s, there were more than 3,000 lyceums across the United States. Popular speakers like Wright and Emerson were in constant demand. These writers and lecturers, despite widely divergent views, were united in trying to make sense of the American experience in a rapidly expanding society that fostered both extreme poverty and increasing wealth, slavery and Christianity, and a sense of the "manifest destiny" of westward expansion that was carried out in overt wars of conquest against the Indigenous peoples already occupying the land.

Emerson's Transcendentalism emerged from the same roots as classical pragmatism: romantic idealism filtered through Samuel Taylor Coleridge and English interpreters of Immanuel Kant and post-Kantian idealism, tempered by the pluralistic character of American experience, and framed by the need to coexist in a context of diversity. The resulting view involved two intertwined strands of thought: one focused on the individual as the site of coexistence, the place where differences are manifested and overcome; and the other focused on what George Fredrickson called Emerson's "anti-institutionalism," that is, Emerson's rejection of institutions as obstacles to the project of cultivating such individuals (Fredrickson, 1965).

In his 1837 address, "The American Scholar," Emerson made a case for the ideal individual as one who resists established dogma and unquestioned inheritance of the past and becomes, "in the right state, . . . *Man Thinking*. In his degenerate state, when the victim of society, he tends to become a mere thinker, or, still worse, the parrot of other men's thinking" (1983, p. 54). "We have," he concluded, "listened too long to the courtly muses of Europe" (1983, p. 70). Instead, "We will walk on our own feet; we will work with our own hands; we will speak our own minds" (1983, p. 71). In his 1841 essay, "Self-Reliance," Emerson added to his vision of *man thinking* by holding that "imitation is suicide" (1983, p. 259), that "Whoso would be a man must be a nonconformist" (1983, p. 261), and that "A man is to carry himself in the presence of all opposition, as if every thing were titular and ephemeral but he" (1983, p. 262). "If you maintain a dead church," he wrote affirming a principle akin to the pragmatist maxim, "contribute to a dead Bible-society, vote with a great party either for the government or against it, spread your table like base housekeepers,—under all these screens I have difficulty to detect the precise man you are. But do your work, and I shall know you. Do your work, and you shall reinforce yourself" (1983, pp. 263–4).

At the same time, Emerson recognized that individuals were not independent of others—rather, their ability to achieve their own selves was a matter of their striving in the context of others, benighted others, and true individuals. As John Lysaker explains, "the self of self-culture neither stands nor proceeds alone, but only with the support of others" (2008, p. 38). The power of an individual, Emerson wrote, "consists in the multitude of his affinities, in the fact that his life is intertwined with the whole of organic and inorganic being" (quoted in Lysaker, p. 26). Here, affinities mark connections that serve the double purpose of supporting and sustaining the individual and separating the individual from nature, the "non-me." The Latin root, *affinis*, Lysaker observes, "means not only 'relation by marriage,' but 'bordering upon,' thus underscoring the difference that persists in the bond" (2008, p. 36).

The tension between the inward *man thinking*, the self not lost in external institutions and given dogma, and the public "man" who is seen in his relations to others results in what Emerson called double consciousness. "A man must ride alternately on the horses of his private and his public nature, as the equestrians in the circus throw themselves nimbly from horse to horse, or plant one foot on the back of one, and the other foot on the back of the other" (1983, p. 966). At work in this idea of the self is the commitment, on the one hand, to the Soul which, as he observed in the essay "Nature," "knows no persons," seeing all things but existing as a "transparent eye-ball." On the other hand, what he called understanding, a practical knowing that allows one to get around but always risks becoming too narrow and parochial, excludes the Soul in favor of present and minor concerns. "The worst feature of this double consciousness," Emerson wrote, "is, that the two lives . . . really show very little relation to each other; one prevails for now, all buzz and din; and the other prevails then, all infinitude and paradise; and with the progress of life, the two discover no greater disposition to reconcile themselves" (1983, p. 206). The double consciousness of the self entails a precarious life lived between one's immanent commitments in daily life and one's potential for radical, spontaneous and transcendent freedom.

Since the Soul is to be valued and cultivated, those aspects of life that narrow consciousness, insist on adherence to dogma, and commit a person to worldly goals like business success or popularity are to be avoided. In his famous address to the Harvard Divinity School in 1838 (as he prepared to leave his career in ministry), Emerson declared that the church itself is an obstacle, not a route, to salvation. Rather than preaching adherence, ministers really concerned with the salvation of souls ought to preach self-cultivation and leave the organized church behind. The structures of government, institutional reform, education, and business were all obstacles to the fostering of individual souls. "Let me admonish you, first of all, to go alone," he charged the seminarians, "to refuse the good models, even those which are sacred in the imagination of men, and dare to love God without mediator or veil" (1983, p. 89).

Emerson's resistance to the character of American society as it developed in the 1830s, 1840s, and 1850s was part of a larger movement of Northeastern intellectuals who sought to challenge the Calvinism that dominated both public and private life. This Calvinism held, among other things, that human beings were fundamentally limited, sinful, depraved beings who could be saved only by the act of a god who stood separate from the world of experience. Since salvation could only come from "above," and since God, as omniscient, already knew the outcome of each person's life, such Calvinists also held that human effort could make no difference in one's salvation. Emerson and the other members of the philosophical resistance to these tenets held that, rather than being separate from God, divinity was present in the world. Rejecting Calvinism's Trinitarian view of divinity (that God is three beings in one), they affirmed the unity of God with the world (and hence called themselves Unitarians). As part of God, human effort could be transformative and could make a difference.

In 1836, two years before Emerson delivered his Divinity School address and ended his career as a minister, he and a handful of others began to meet regularly in Boston. Initially called the Hedge group after Henry Hedge, a Unitarian minister in Maine who proposed regular meetings during his visits to Boston, the group included Emerson, George Ripley, Bronson Alcott, Orestes Bronson, Convers Francis, Margaret Fuller, and Elizabeth Peabody, among others. Initially dedicated to the study of idealism, Kantian and post-Kantian, the group eventually was dubbed the "Transcendentalist Club" and served to promote collective inquiry and provide a publication venue for their thought (*The Dial*, edited by Margaret Fuller). They even established a short-lived utopian community called Brook Farm, where participants sought to practice self-cultivation together.

The same year he took counsel with the Transcendentalist Club, Emerson also acknowledged a list of public issues that required attention, including "slavery, temperance, antimasonry, bank policy, executive power, . . . 'the treatment of Indians,' war, elections, Sunday schools, charitable societies, and the 'crisis of trade'" (quoted in Buell, 2003, p. 244). Within two years, Emerson took up the treatment of American Indians. He had probably become familiar with the issue through the extensive news coverage of a series of wars in the West against various tribes (the Winnebago War in 1827 in what is now Wisconsin, and the Black Hawk War of 1832 in Illinois and Wisconsin). He would also have known about these issues through his brother Charles, who was an activist in support of Indian land rights. As a student at Harvard in 1819 (just six years after the Shawnee leader Tecumseh helped defeat the US Army at Detroit in the early days of the War of 1812), Emerson publicly debated the questions "Whether the conduct of the U. S. towards the Indians can be reconciled to the principles of justice and humanity?" and "In which state of society, the civilized or the savage, is the greatest degree of happiness to be found?" Unfortunately, his positions in these debates are not recorded (Emerson, 1939, vol. I, p. 85n.). Later on, at the encouragement of his brother, Emerson attended speeches by Native orators who frequented Boston in the 1830s to protest government policies. In 1832, for example, Emerson wrote his brother: "Your friends the Cherokees are in town[.] Mr. Walker-on-the-Mountains addressed a great meeting the other [evening] at Federal St. Ch. and put to shame our orators A. H. Everett and Mr. Hoar and Dr. Beecher who spoke on the same occasion" (Emerson, 1939, vol. I, p. 346). The speaker, the Cherokee leader known as John Ridge in settler society, "said he wd. speak like an Indian, plain, right on, & fine Indian eloquence it was," according to Emerson. He continued: "What is most strange he fully understood the oratorical advantages of his situation—the romance—and availed himself to the full thereof" (p. 346). Elias Boudinot, another Cherokee leader, also spoke that evening.

In late 1835, in the wake of the 1830 passage of the Indian Removal Act under the leadership of Andrew Jackson, the United States signed a treaty with a small faction of the Cherokee people in Georgia. This faction, led by John Ridge, decided that removal was inevitable and agreed to trade the Cherokee lands in Georgia for land in Indian Territory (now Oklahoma) along with a cash settlement of $5 million. In the winter months of 1838 and 1839, the army executed the treaty by marching 15,000 Cherokee men, women, and children more than 1,000 miles in what came to be called the Trail of Tears. Over 4,000 people died during the journey. The Cherokee removal followed the removal of the Muscogee, Seminole, Chickasaw, and Choctaw peoples. In response to word of the impending removal, groups of concerned Whites in the Northeast met and many protested. Emerson attended one such meeting in April 1838 and was drafted by the group to prepare an open letter to President Martin Van Buren.

The letter is significant in that it both frames opposition to the Removal in terms related to his developing philosophical vision and because it reveals the limits of that vision. As a statement of resistance, Emerson acknowledged the "worth and civility" of the Cherokee thanks to their efforts to "borrow and domesticate in the tribe the arts and customs of the Caucasian race" (2012, p. 94). The Cherokee, Emerson observed, had developed a written language, were more literate than the surrounding White population, and had protested the treaty in an 1835 petition signed by 15,000 tribal members condemning the agreement and declaring that a nonrepresentative faction had signed it. The appeal had no effect.

In his letter to Van Buren, Emerson declared that the policy of Removal errs both in terms of practical understanding and principles of justice. The action, he wrote, "confounds our understanding by its magnitude, a crime that really deprives us as well as the Cherokees of a country." Even if there were immediate practical economic concerns that seemed to demand the removal (a response to "hard times," he says), such a practical reason

> is the chirping of grasshoppers beside the immortal question whether justice shall be done by the race of civilized to the race of savage man, whether all the attributes of reason, of civility, of justice, and even of mercy, shall be put off by the American people, and so vast an outrage upon the Cherokee Nation and upon human nature shall be consummated. (2012, p. 98)

It was the recognition of "the outrage" through the sentiment of "brotherly love" that led to the resistance against the government action. The resistance was first a matter of individual souls standing against felt injustice, even as it disregarded the value and contributions of the tribal community (excepting those standards of civility and "social arts" adopted from the surrounding culture). The protest against Indian Removal set the stage for the fundamental tension between affirming the individual (which would be central to the development of post-Civil War America) and the pluralism of communities and culture (which meant resistance to liberalism in all of its various forms).

Following the publication of his open letter to Van Buren, Emerson noted in his journal what Buell called Emerson's "internal revulsion" to the letter: "I fully sympathize, be sure, with the sentiment I write," [Emerson] told his journal, but because he did it at the urging of his friends rather than from an impulse to speak out, "therefore my genius deserts me, no muse befriends, no music of thought or of word accompanies, Bah!" (quoted in Buell, 2003, p. 245). Apparently deciding that the resistance was not of his own making, he concluded in his journal to "let the republic alone until the republic comes to me" (quoted in Buell, 2003, p. 45).

Emerson's support for abolitionism, however, presents a contrasting case. Early in his life, he noted his opposition to slavery in his journals and his first public sermon in 1826. In 1844, in an address on the tenth anniversary of the end of slavery in the British Empire, Emerson, as he had with the case of Indian Removal, distilled his case against slavery down to a sympathetic response: "I am heart-sick when I read how [slaves] came there, and how they are kept there" (1883, p. 134). In contrast to the benefits that were "there for all, but not for them,"

> [f]or the Negro, was the slave-ship to begin with, in whose filthy hold he sat in irons, unable to lie down; bad food . . .; disenfranchisement; no property . . .; no marriage . . . no right to the children of his body; no security from [illness], crimes, none from the appetites of his master: toil, famine, insult and flogging. (1883, pp. 134–5)

Slavery, Emerson concluded, perverted experience itself: "The blood is moral: the blood is anti-slavery: it runs cold in the veins: the stomach rises in disgust and curses slavery" (1883, p. 136).

The end of slavery in the British Empire, on Emerson's account, was partially earned by "the powers and native endowments" of the slaves themselves. "When at last in a race, a new principle appears, an idea,—*that* conserves it; ideas only save races" (1883, pp. 171–2). If a race is "feeble," he declared, its members "must serve, and be exterminated." "But if the black man carries in his bosom an indispensable element of a new and coming civilization; for the sake of that element, no wrong, nor strength nor circumstance can hurt him; he will survive and play his part" (1883, p. 172). In effect, if a race has a contribution or gift to make to humanity as a whole, it ought to be fostered and not enslaved. W. E. B. Du Bois would make a similar argument in his address, "On the Conservation of Races," to the American Negro Academy in 1897.

Yet despite the "powers and endowments" of Blacks, in the end, emancipation in Britain was ultimately the result of "the masters revolting from their mastery. . . . The end was noble and the means were pure" (1883, p. 164). The lesson was one he thought applied to the United States as well. "There is a blessed necessity by which the interest of men is always driving them to the right. . . . The genius of the Saxon race, friendly to liberty; the enterprise, the very muscular vigor of this nation, are inconsistent with slavery" (1883, p. 175). It was the "sentiment of Right," Emerson argued, "the voice of the universe, [that] pronounces Freedom" (1883, p. 175). Emerson's case against slavery, like his case against Removal, recognized the felt opposition experienced by individuals, and, in contrast to his case against removal, he also recognized that the group—the race—itself had worth. The institution of slavery, as Emerson suggests in his 1862 address, "American Civilization," stood in the way both of self-cultivation and of the cultivation of affinities that could contribute to self-cultivation (1883, p. 279).

Eventually, he came to see that the inequality faced by women also stood in the way of self-cultivation and the cultivation of American civilization. Emerson's views on slavery led many in the women's movement to seek him as an ally for their cause. He resisted such invitations for many years and then, in 1855, accepted an invitation to speak to a gathering of suffragists. In that address, published as "Woman," he granted that if women wanted these rights, he would not stand in their way, but he hoped they would not avail themselves of all that such equality might offer. For instance, he hoped they would not hold political office as this could make them less womanly. For Emerson, women had sentiment and men had will, and if women were to enter public life they would lose their capacity to soften and civilize men. He did not speak on the issue again until 1867, and by then his position had changed. At that point, he acknowledged that men and women both share in intelligence and affection and that women had full right to the equality they were seeking. In fact, to stand in the way of that equality would be harmful to the Republic as men and women educate and influence each other in their daily lives. Women continued to draw on Emerson in support of their abolitionist work. For women such as Katherine Prescott Wormeley, Julia Ward Howe, and Josephine Shaw Lowell, Emerson also helped to frame their commitment to the idea of collective support for self-cultivation in the context of the US Sanitary Commission during the Civil War.

After the passage of the Fugitive Slave Act in 1850 (which required residents of Northern states to return escaped slaves to their owners if caught), Emerson was fully caught up in the abolitionist movement. When John Brown failed in his attempt to start a slave rebellion by raiding the US military armory in Harpers Ferry, Virginia, supported by a small group of Black and White militants, Emerson spoke on his behalf. As if embodying Emerson's own case against slavery, Emerson concluded that Brown's commitment to the cause of abolition was not a matter of understanding but of sentiment. After witnessing a slave he knew being beaten with a shovel, Emerson explained, Brown became so indignant "that he swore an oath of resistance to Slavery as long as he lived" (1883, p. 260). The right response to slavery exemplified by Brown was not a calculation or the consequence of some moral principle, but a felt response to the practices and persons of slavery, a felt sense of commitment to resist regardless of the consequences.

Perhaps the best exemplar of Transcendentalism was Emerson's young friend, Henry David Thoreau. Fourteen years younger than Emerson, Thoreau, who graduated from Harvard in 1837, was also from Concord and met Emerson in 1838 after a brief career as a teacher. He lived with the Emerson family from 1841 until 1843. In 1845, Thoreau built a small cabin beside Walden Pond on some property owned by Emerson. Here he produced his famous journal, *Walden* (published in 1854). "I went to the woods," he wrote, "because I wished to live deliberately, to front only the essential facts of life, and see if I could not learn what it had to teach, and not, when I came to die, discover that I had not lived" (1975, p. 343). Although Thoreau viewed himself as a writer, he worked in a variety of jobs, as an occasional teacher and farmhand, most often as a surveyor. At every turn, however, his interest was one of self-cultivation. More than just Emerson's notion of "man thinking," Thoreau was *man living*, reflecting but also actively engaging his surroundings. "The mass of men," he wrote, "lead lives of quiet desperation . . . [while] it is a characteristic of wisdom not to do desperate things" (1975, p. 263). Instead, Thoreau sought to deliberately engage life, not as an abstraction but as a present experience.

> If you stand right fronting and face to face to a fact, you will see the sun glimmer on both its surfaces, as if it were a cimetar [*sic*], and feel its sweet edge dividing you through the heart and marrow, and so you will happily conclude your mortal career. Be it life or death, we crave only reality. (1975, p. 351)

Such reality emerged in Nature on one hand and in culture on the other. The process of self-cultivation benefited from both sources, but was bound to neither. In his late essay, "Walking," he began, "I wish to speak a word for Nature, for absolute freedom and wildness, as contrasted with freedom and culture merely civil" (1975, p. 592). At the same time, Thoreau wrote, "I feel that with regard to Nature I live a sort of border life, on the confines of a world into which I make occasional and transient forays only" (1975, p. 625). It is at the border that towns emerge with the potential for insight. "A town is saved, not more by the righteous men in it than by the woods and swamps that surround it." Here, life can be sustained, as a fit place "to raise not only corn and potatoes, but poets and philosophers for the coming ages" (1975, p. 613). The result is a kind of progressive human development on the border between Nature and culture (in the form of towns and cities). Such development ought to compel one to "walk toward Oregon and not toward Europe. And that way the nation is moving, and I may say that mankind progress from east to west" (1975, p. 604). In this westward progress, succession reconfigures the land, "the farmer displaces the Indian even because he redeems the meadow, and so makes himself stronger and in some respects more natural" (1975, p. 614).

This transition, however, risks losing the experience of nature and so must cautiously cultivate ignorance as well. "We have heard," he said, "of a Society for the Diffusion of

Useful Knowledge. . . . Methinks there is equal need for a Society for the Diffusion of Useful Ignorance, what we will call Beautiful Knowledge" (1975, p. 622). Useful knowledge, Thoreau argued, is at once "positive," giving people a sense of confidence, while obscuring what one does not or cannot know. Useful ignorance, on the other hand, marks an opening to the Nature beyond human control that makes place for "higher knowledge," what he calls "Sympathy with Intelligence" (1975, p. 623). In the end, such knowledge is cultivated through a process of coming and going between Nature and civilization that, in turn, fosters human progress in this border region.

Like Emerson and Fuller, Thoreau also became interested in American Indian issues as a means of understanding self-culture. But where Fuller's engagement was largely a result of her travels in the summer of 1844 and Emerson's was superseded by his interest in abolitionism, Thoreau's interest led to a planned book about Native cultures (that was never completed) and descriptions of his encounters with Native people in his travels in the Northeast. One of the most extensive was *The Maine Woods*, which gave an account of three journeys in 1846, 1853, and 1857. The story of the first trip to Maine discussed Native culture from afar because Thoreau was unable to hire an Indian guide for his trip. Without guidance, Thoreau described himself as at odds with nature, so that, at one point, he rushed back to more familiar civilized surroundings. On his second journey, he successfully found a guide but viewed him as a primitive, as one from whom nothing important could be learned.

On Thoreau's third venture into the woods, however, he hired a guide, Joe Polis, a Penobscot Indian, from whom he was ready to learn. He wrote: "I should like to go to school [with Polis] to learn his language, living on the Indian island for a while . . . I would like to tell [him] all I know and he should tell me all he knew, to which he readily agreed" (1988, p. 229). Despite his willingness to learn, Thoreau's narrative reveals his limitations. On one hand, he was able to adopt a philosophy of place that emerged directly from his experiences with American Indians. On the other hand, he overtly set aside the Native conception of relational agency in favor of a romantic conception of individuals over against both nature and civilization.

The tension between Thoreau's interest in Native culture and his rejection of it was illustrated in his response to a story told by Polis. On a different hunt with another White hunter, Polis and the hunter tracked a moose back and forth through the woods. After they successfully killed the moose, Polis told the hunter to go directly back to camp without following the wandering path they had cut earlier in the day. The hunter admitted that he could not. Polis led them back. When Thoreau asked Polis how he found his way, Polis replied: "O, I can't tell you. . . . [there is a] Great difference between me and white man" (p. 253). "It appeared," Thoreau said, "as if the sources of information were so various that he did not give a distinct, conscious attention to any one, and so could not readily refer any when questioned about it . . . but he found his way very much as an animal does. . . . He does not carry things in his head, nor remember the route exactly like a white man, but relies on [his Indian instinct]" (1988, p. 253). The assessment reflected the tension in Thoreau's view of Native Americans. He hypothesized that Polis related differently to the place. At the same time, he diminished Polis's relationship as something animal-like, unreflective, and unlike the agency of Whites.

In "Walking," an essay published a few years after his last Maine sojourn, Thoreau made a similar division between himself and civilization. "Give me a wildness whose glance no civilization can endure" (1975, p. 610), he said. Like most thinkers responding to the emergence of evolution theory, Thoreau assumed savagism as distinct from and preliminary to civilization.

The self-cultivated individual stands at the boundary between them, taking advantage of both and desiring the end of neither. "I feel that with regard to Nature I live a sort of border life," he wrote in *Walking*, "on the confines of a world into which I make occasional and transient forays only" (1975, p. 625). Here, the border is not a place but a line that he crosses on occasion to free himself of too much civilization.

Thoreau embodied the distancing of American Indian thought from the mainstream of American philosophy. In spite of his admiration for American Indians and the ways he brought Native American ideas into conversation with Transcendentalism, Thoreau's inability to move beyond an individualistic concept of agency places him in line with the policy of the United States toward Indians that Pokagon, Eastman, and Standing Bear all resisted.

Despite this limitation, Thoreau's Transcendentalism, like Emerson's, was nevertheless a philosophy of resistance that came to inform more than a century of protest movements in the United States and around the world. In 1849, Thoreau was jailed for refusing to pay his taxes. He spent a night in jail and was released the next day when a friend paid his taxes. The incident provided an occasion for his essay, "Civil Disobedience." The essay begins with the motto, "That government is best which governs least," quickly modified to read "That government is best which governs not all" (1975, p. 109). While the motto seems to set a tone of sharp separation between individuals and government, the essay as a whole recalls both the importance of self-cultivation and the recognition that the Transcendentalist project can only take place within a context of "affinities."

Individuals, for Thoreau, are not only separate from the government but are also intimately connected to one another, so much so that one is responsible for knowing what the government does. In light of that knowledge, each person is then responsible for either affirming these actions or actively separating themselves from the government. Thoreau asked, "How does it become a man to behave toward this American government today?" He answered, "he cannot without disgrace be associated with it . . . cannot for an instant recognize that political organization as *my* government which is the *slave's* government" (1975, p. 113).

How ought one resist a government that permits slavery? Perhaps surprisingly, Thoreau first observed that "it is not man's duty, as a matter of course, to devote himself to the eradication of any, even the most enormous wrong" because "he may still properly have other concerns to engage him." It is, however, one's duty, "at least, to wash his hands of it, and if he gives it no thought longer, not to give it practically his support" (1975, p. 117). While following laws and community norms is a matter of course, one who lives deliberately must attend to the constraints and opportunities one faces. If a law "is of such a nature that it requires you to be the agent of injustice to another, then, I say, break the law. Let your life be a counter-friction to stop the machine" (1975, p. 120). In short, one's affinities, connections with others, and dependencies that make life possible and worthwhile are central to Thoreau's motivation for resistance.

In the face of slavery, he wrote, "those who call themselves Abolitionists should at once effectually withdraw their support, both in person and property, from the government" (1975, p. 120). By refusing to return escaped slaves (despite the demands of the 1850 Fugitive Slave Law) and to pay taxes, the minority gains power and becomes "irresistible when it clogs by its whole weight" (1975, p. 122). If enough people refused to support State efforts "to commit violence and shed innocent blood," such resistance would be, Thoreau observed, "the definition of a peaceable revolution" (1975, p. 123). In response to injustice and in light of the transcendental conception of self, Thoreau "quietly declared war with the State," not as an anarchist or someone who was, in principle, anti-government, but because, in the end, he recognized the importance of others in the project of self-cultivation. He concluded, "I please myself with imagining a State at last which can afford to be just to all men, and to treat the individual with respect as a neighbor" (1975, p. 137). Such a state, he thought, would even support people like him who would "live aloof from it, not meddling with it, not embraced by it" so long as he "fulfilled all the duties of neighbors and fellow men" (1975, p. 137).

Thoreau's vision of a new state brought about through civil disobedience, so characteristic of the Transcendentalist movement as a whole, was rocked by the outbreak of the Civil War in 1860. Emerson, who had been a leading figure in the abolitionist movement for ten years at that point, was forced to rearticulate his position in terms of this new historical context. Consistent with his early recognition of the importance of others for self-cultivation, since it was clear that the "masters" were not going to revolt against slavery, Emerson concluded that it would take a collective organized force to emancipate both the masters and slaves. In an address given in Washington, D.C., in January 1861 to an audience that included Abraham Lincoln, Emerson declared that

> a man coins himself into his labor; turns his day, his strength, his thought, his affection into some product which remains as the visible sign of his power; and to protect that, to secure that to him, to secure his past self to his future self, is the object of all government. (1883, p. 278)

So important is the function of securing the context in which self-culture occurs, that "[g]overnment must not be a parish clerk, a justice of the peace. It has, of necessity, in any crisis of state, the absolute powers of a Dictator" (1883, p. 282). And if the leadership of the government should fail, then inspired people will "leave the government behind and create on the moment the means and executors it wanted" (1883, p. 282). Expanding the central issue from slavery alone to the project of bringing "civility up to the height at which it is best," Emerson affirmed that "Emancipation is the demand of civilization. This is a principle; everything else is an intrigue" (1883, p. 283). Later in the same address, Emerson denied that politics was merely concerned with "free institutions" or a republic or democracy—these are only "the means" of politics. Rather, "Morality is the object of government" (1883, p. 288).

The Civil War marked a shift in Emerson's Transcendentalist vision of self-culture—or perhaps it made its elements more concrete. In his commencement address to Harvard in 1865, just after the end of the Civil War, Emerson framed the war as a revolution that "gave back integrity to this erring and immoral nation" (1883, p. 320). Rather than continuing to declare the need to be suspicious of institutions and to stand—with Thoreau—"aloof" from the State, Emerson increasingly saw the state as essential to the project. Individuals are capable of "feeling moral distinctions," but the government is responsible for helping them do so; this is a process accomplished by "organization," establishing a proper order in which the "largest thought and the widest love are born to prevail" (1883, p. 412).

It is not surprising that many who were Transcendentalists when the war began followed Emerson in this shift to a belief in the necessity of institutions. In the early days of the war, it became readily apparent that the North was not prepared to receive the massive casualties that the war was to bring. The response came from the Women's Central Association of Relief for the Sick and Wounded of the army, established in 1861 in New York. The organization set out to care for the sick and wounded and to establish an orderly system for doing so. In May 1861, the association asked Congress for a charter to provide support for all of the Federal Armies, and the following month the US Sanitary Commission was established. Among the leaders of the commission were Henry W. Bellows, a graduate of the Harvard Divinity School and a Unitarian minister in New York City, and Samuel Gridley Howe, a Harvard-trained physician and abolitionist (who was later appointed head of the US Freedman's Bureau). Others included Katherine Prescott Wormeley (who published a study of the Commission in 1863 and was later the primary English translator of Balzac's work), Julia Ward Howe, and Josephine Shaw Lowell.

The Sanitary Commission and the organizations that followed after it was closed in 1865 shared an Emersonian vision of the value of individuals and of the need for organized support of individual improvement. Howe, in her 1880 essay, "Modern Society," concluded, "Humanity is . . . a thing of oppositions, and of oppositions which are polar and substantial. Its contradictions do not exclude, but, on the contrary, complement each other, and the action and reaction of these contradictions result in . . . the intense sympathies and antipathies which bind or sunder individuals" (1881, p. 9). Lowell, in her 1884 handbook, *Public Relief and Private Charity*, challenged those who, after the Civil War, demanded an end to public charity as undermining private ambition. She concluded that "they forget, apparently, that there are in every community, persons who cannot maintain themselves, and who have no friends upon whom they have a claim." Supporting such individuals benefited not only those receiving support who might be "driven to desperation by the absolute pressure of want," but others in the community as well. As a result, "public relief is a benefit to the whole people, acting as a preventive of violence" (1884, p. 2). The emergence, in the 1880s of settlement houses and the work of the Social Gospel movement grew in part from the intellectual framework established by Emerson and the Transcendentalists, as well as the administrative infrastructure that was established by the Sanitary Commission.

The poet, Walt Whitman, who shared the contradictory commitments of Transcendentalism to individual self-culture and the need for affinities that bind and support the project of self-culture, worked during the Civil War as a medic for the Sanitary Commission. His poem, "By Blue Ontario's Shore," written originally in 1856 and revised in 1867 and 1881, can be seen as a restatement of what the dominant culture saw as the problems and hopes of the United States after the Civil War.

> AS I sat alone, by blue Ontario's shore,
> As I mused of these mighty days, and of peace return'd, and the dead that return no more,
> A Phantom, gigantic, superb, with stern visage, accosted me;
> *Chant me the poem, it said, that comes from the soul of America—chant me the carol of victory;*
> *And strike up the marches of Libertad—marches more powerful yet;*
> *And sing me before you go, the song of the throes of Democracy.*
> . . .
> A Nation announcing itself,
> I myself make the only growth by which I can be appreciated,

## American Philosophies

> I reject none, accept all, then reproduce all in my own forms.
> A breed whose proof is in time and deeds;
> What we are, we are—nativity is answer enough to objections;
> We wield ourselves as a weapon is wielded,
> We are powerful and tremendous in ourselves,
> We are executive in ourselves—We are sufficient in the variety of ourselves,
> We are the most beautiful to ourselves, and in ourselves;
> We stand self-pois'd in the middle, branching thence over the world;
> From Missouri, Nebraska, or Kansas, laughing attacks to scorn.
> . . .
> Nothing is sinful to us outside of ourselves,
> Have you thought there could be but a single Supreme?
> There can be any number of Supremes—One does not countervail another, any more than one eyesight countervails another, or one life countervails another.
> All is eligible to all,
> All is for individuals—All is for you,
> No condition is prohibited—not God's, or any.
> All comes by the body—only health puts you [in] rapport with the universe.
> Produce great persons, the rest follows.

Whitman's hopeful vision captured both the commitment to individual flourishing central to Emerson's vision and the vision of a national culture that would be pluralist in character and would serve to "produce great persons."

But Whitman published his final revision of "On Blue Ontario's Shore" in 1881 during a brief respite between the long economic recession that began in 1876 and the deeper economic recession that began the following year. Two more recessions would follow and serve as a prelude to the Panic of 1893, the same year the Columbia Exposition declared the victory of Western civilization. Institutional responses to the economic crisis were limited. The Pullman Strike in 1894 shut down the nation's railroads. The US Army was called up to end the strike. Despite the end of legal slavery and the commitment of the Transcendentalists and the activists dedicated to the advancement of individuals in a context of collective support, three years after the economic disaster of 1893, the US Supreme Court issued its decision in Plessy v. Ferguson, making Jim Crow and apartheid the law of the land. New forms of philosophical resistance began to emerge for the new century.

### Primary Texts

Atkinson, Brooks, ed. (2000). *Essential Writings of Ralph Waldo Emerson*, introduction by Mary Oliver. New York: Random House.

Cramer, Jeffrey S., ed. (2014). *The Portable Thoreau*. New York: Penguin Classics.

# CHAPTER 6
# LABOR, EMPIRE, POPULISM, AND THE SOCIAL GOSPEL
## WASHINGTON GLADDEN, WALTER RAUSCHENBUSCH, AND JANE ADDAMS

The Panic of 1893 started in May, the same month as the Columbian Exposition in Chicago, but the depression that followed lasted much longer than the Exposition. It continued for four more years, leaving hundreds of thousands unemployed, over 500 banks and other financial institutions closed, more than 15,000 failed mercantile businesses, over 70 railroads in receivership, currency devalued, and the stock market at record lows (Carlson, 2013). The Fair came as a distraction from the crisis and a chance to think about a brighter future even as thousands no longer had the means to buy a ticket. As summer gave way to fall, the Exposition prepared to close. The Panic was always close at hand, and the anxiety was increased when, the evening before the final day of the Fair, the popular mayor of Chicago was assassinated. The Exposition's closing ceremony transformed from a celebration to a funeral. As the Fair was taken down over the next few weeks, thousands more lost their jobs in Chicago.

In 1880, George M. Pullman (1831–1897), owner of the Pullman Car Company, built a factory town on the Southwest side of Chicago in which the workers at his railway car company lived and paid rent. The town had many amenities not available elsewhere in the Chicago area—water, paved streets, garbage collection, a sewer system, a library, a mall, and a school with a playground. The amenities (and employment in Pullman's factories) came at a cost, however. In addition to imposing strict moral rules in the town, the rents were higher than in the surrounding areas. In order to continue to provide profit to himself and his investors when the Panic began, Pullman laid off some workers and gave the workers who remained pay cuts of as much as 25 percent. At the same time, in order to ensure sufficient profit, Pullman also continued to demand the same rent from his employees as he had before the Panic. After unsuccessful negotiations with Pullman, workers voted to strike in May 1894. The Pullman Company refused to negotiate with the union that represented the workers, the American Railway Union, and so the union voted to stop handling trains with Pullman cars. Since Pullman cars were attached to nearly every passenger train in the United States, train service was affected nationwide (Riggs, 2015). By July there was a federal injunction against the union to prevent them from interfering with the operation of the railroads since the railroads carried US mail. Federal troops were sent in to take control of the railroads and put down the strike, under the leadership of General Miles (Morolo, 2011).

Just three years after his "triumph" at Wounded Knee, General Miles was the Commander of the US Army Department of the Missouri stationed in Chicago. Miles was a Civil War hero, he had been in charge of the troops at Wounded Knee, he would go on to be involved in the invasions of the Philippines and Cuba, and he led the invasion of Puerto Rico. Commenting on the Pullman Strike, Miles said, "Some unimportant question arose, a strike was ordered in the Pullman works, with the result that several thousand men left their occupation" (1911, p. 252). The "unimportant question" that arose was one of corporate control and profit versus individual living wages and social welfare.

At the start of the conflict, Miles had argued against the use of federal troops but then changed his mind. In Washington, D.C., at the time, he met with President Cleveland and argued that sending the proposed 200 troops would not be sufficient. Since the government and US mail needed protection, he was ordered to return to Chicago with 3,000 troops assembled and the full support of the federal government to "do what was needed to restore law and order" (1911, p. 254). He referred to the labor action as an "industrial rebellion." Even though he came to acknowledge that the labor question was a serious question facing the nation, he nonetheless had no tolerance for such "rebellion" and felt that all means of response were permissible.

In justifying the use of force, he used the same kind of thinking he had employed to justify his actions against the Lakota: prosperity and growth require defense against disruption. Miles would later employ similar thinking and action in Cuba and Puerto Rico. Writing about Puerto Rico, he said:

> The chief object of the American military forces will be to overthrow the armed authority of Spain and to give to the people of your beautiful island the largest measure of liberty consistent with the military occupation. We have not come to make war upon the peaceful people of a country that for centuries has been oppressed, but, on the contrary, to bring protection, not only to yourselves but to your property, to promote your prosperity and bestow upon you the immunities and blessings of the liberal institutions of our government. (1911, p. 307)

Similarly, in 1890, he published "Our Unwatered Empire" in which he distinguished among the types of citizens deserving help and protection. He described the loyal, upright, and industrious people who helped build the nation as its proper citizens and contrasted them with recent immigrants who had "sought this country either for a place of refuge or asylum, crowding our cities and towns, inhabiting the alleys, breathing foul air, their idea of life contaminated" (1911, p. 316). Miles justified contempt, armed conflict, the occupation of Native American lands and Puerto Rico, and the suppression of labor protests using the same hierarchical logic of progress and civilization that had informed the Columbian Exposition.

The view Miles presented was a widely shared one among industrialists, educational reformers, and mainstream philosophers. Against this view, there arose a variety of philosophies of resistance. Among the most significant in its impact was the Social Gospel movement, founded by a broad group of Christian preachers and theologians in the decades following the Civil War. The movement was in part a response to the new demands of evolution theory and the work of people such as William Graham Sumner (1840–1910), who argued that, in light of evolution, the struggle for existence was the supreme moral principle. On one hand, evolution called into question the conception of human nature offered in the Bible and so raised doubts about the proper ends of human life. On the other hand, evolution seemed to offer an alternative purpose that could both account for human development and provide a guide for social life. For Sumner, this last implication of evolution led to the concept of social Darwinism that justified laissez-faire social and economic policies that would permit individuals to flourish or fail "naturally."

Sumner's most widely known essay is "The Forgotten Man." The essay, first published as a pair of essays in 1883 in the collection *What Social Classes Owe to Each Other*, sets the stage for both the laissez-faire demands of those seeking to limit government control and for those who will demand government intervention in industrial, agricultural, and financial monopolies. "The forgotten man," Sumner concluded, is at the foundation of American society. "He is the simple, honest laborer, ready to earn his living by productive work" (1918, p. 476). Such a person "only wants to make a contract and fulfill it, with respect on both sides and favor on neither." The government ignores the interests of these stalwart citizens and nevertheless uses them to address problems like crime and the regulation of industry by imposing taxes and laws meant for others. They are "mulcted a percentage of [their] day's earnings to hire a policeman to save the drunkard from himself." For Sumner, "a drunkard in a gutter is just where he ought to be"—in a place where, as Spencer might claim, "Nature is working away at him to get him out of the way" (p. 476).

"The whole system of social regulation by boards, commissioners, and inspectors," Sumner concludes, "consists in relieving negligent people of the consequences of their negligence and so leaving them to continue negligent without correction" (p. 482). Sumner does not argue that there is no place for government; rather, he believes that it should be in the business of ensuring "true liberty" that "lies in the equilibrium of rights and duties, producing peace, order, and harmony." For Sumner, this "means that a man's right to take power and wealth out of the social product is measured by the energy and wisdom which he has contributed to the social effort" (p. 473). It also means that "there can be no civil liberty anywhere unless rights are guaranteed against all abuses, as well as from proletarians as from generals, aristocrats, and ecclesiastics" (p. 470). Such rights include those shared by both men and women "for it is time to remember that the Forgotten Man is not seldom a woman." "It is plain enough," he summarizes, "that the Forgotten Man and the Forgotten Woman are the very life and substance of society. They are the ones who ought to be first and always remembered" (pp. 492–3) as policies are set and rewards are distributed.

In December 1890, as the US Army gathered in the Dakotas to put an end to the Ghost Dance, the leadership of the National Farmers' Alliance and Industrial Union—a group founded in Texas in 1877 and by 1890 listed more than 1.2 million members—gathered in Ocala, Florida, to develop a platform for changing the lives of America's farmers. The resulting movement, now called Populism, emerged as a complex response to a range of problems of the day and culminated in the formation of the People's Party in 1892. The People's Party, as Charles Postel described it, was a "confederation of industrial organizations generally consisting of farmer's associations, labor organizations, women's groups; and an array of non-conformists, including urban radicals, tax and currency reformers, prohibitionists, middle class utopians, spiritual innovators, and miscellaneous iconoclasts" (2009, p. 13). The meeting in Florida established a platform that called for monetary reform, adherence to the principle of equal rights under the law in economic matters, state and national control over communication and transportation, and direct election of senators to the US Congress. Two years later, when the group met in Omaha, Nebraska, the delegates adopted elements of the Ocala platform and incorporated it into a larger declaration that the participants adopted on July 4, 1892, and named the Second Declaration of Independence (200, p. 158).

The Omaha Platform described the circumstances that faced farmers and workers just the year before the Columbia Exposition opened. "The conditions which surround us best justify our co-operation; we meet in the midst of a nation brought to the verge of moral, political, and material ruin. Corruption dominates the ballot-box, the Legislatures, the Congress, and touches even the ermine of the bench" (People's Party, 1892). Recalling Sumner's conclusion, they declared that they "seek to restore the government of the Republic to the hands of 'the plain people,' with which class it originated" and, anticipating twenty-first-century resistance, declared that the rich and powerful "propose to sacrifice our homes, lives, and children on the altar of mammon; to destroy the multitude in order to secure corruption funds from the millionaires." The People's Party solution to the situation was to demand, among other things, the nationalization of the railroads and means of communication, establishing a progressive income tax, reforming US monetary policy (restoring silver as coinage), reforming elections to require secret ballots, establishing the direct election of senators by the people, and a one-term limit for president and vice president.

The platform was also explicit in its recognition "that the civil war is over, and that every passion and resentment which grew out of it must die with it, and that we must be in fact, as we are in name, one united brotherhood of free men" (People's Party, 1892). Unspoken in the platform was the deep commitment to the idea that races would remain segregated and that the one united brotherhood would be a brotherhood of White men. Such commitments were present in the demand that "alien" ownership of United States land be banned—preventing non-citizens from owning land (ironic in a world where the Native inhabitants of the land were, by law in 1892, not citizens). Despite efforts by some of the People's Party leaders to establish ties with the Black farmers' alliances, populism remained racially divided.

The populist movement's paradoxical stand on human rights was at once a philosophy of resistance against the treatment of workers and the poor and, at the same time, a movement that affirmed the dominant conceptions of race and gender. Later iterations of populism during the 1930s and in the early 2010s in the Occupy movement, and again in the late 2010s as a nationalist movement, illustrate the same ambivalence of its purpose and calls to action. There is probably no better example of this ambivalence than in the work of Mary Elizabeth Lease (1850–1933), called, among other things, "Queen of the Populists," the "Wichita Cyclone," "Kansas Pythoness," and Mary "Yellin" Lease (Lovett, 2007, p. 19). Lease was a renowned speaker and agitator. Born in Wisconsin but eventually a Kansas farmer, she read law and passed the Kansas bar exam, becoming one of the few women lawyers of the time. She argued that the benefits of equality should extend to women without question. "In an organization founded upon the eternal principles of truth and right, based upon the broad and philanthropic principle, 'Injury to one is the concern of all,' having for its motto, 'Exact justice to all, special privileges to none,'—the farmers and laborers could not well exclude their mothers, wives and daughters, the patient burden bearers of the home" (Lease, 1890, para. 5.). The key to exact justice was to respond to the economic circumstances that exploited labor in the cities and drove farmers into bankruptcy through monetary policy and corrupt loan practices. She declared in one of her stump speeches, "Wall Street owns the country. It is no longer a government of the people, by the people, and for the people, but a government of Wall

Street, by Wall Street, and for Wall Street. The great common people of this country are slaves, and monopoly is the master" (Lease, 1890b). But her sympathies were narrow at best.

For Lease, populism was an evolutionary stage meant to advance White supremacy. "Through all the vicissitudes of time," she writes, "the Caucasian has arisen to the moral and intellectual supremacy of the world, until now this favoured race is fitted for the *Stewardship of the Earth* and *Emancipation from Manual Labor*" (1895, p. 17). In 1895, she published her first and only book, *The Problem of Civilization Solved*, to develop this view and propose a concrete strategy for establishing supremacy. The book brought together the platform of the populists alongside deep racism and nationalism. In conjunction with the populist policies she supported, she argued for autocratic leadership, racial segregation, and the ultimate exclusion of people of color, the poor, and dissenters from North America through what she labeled "tropical colonization" (p. 18). On this plan, the United States would deport "poor [and] homeless people," most from "our overcrowded centres of population." Dissenters would also be deported:

By transferring the moody and dangerous Communist, the dark plotting, sinister Anarchist to a tropical plantation, where he may be busied in planting his own vine, olive, date, or bread fruit, where he becomes transformed from the Foe of Peace to the Pillar of Society in contemplating his own importance as a tropical planter of comparative prosperity. (p. 27)

Those deported would be sent to Latin American countries that would join a federation of American nations led by the United States. The cost of deportation would be paid by the receiving countries.

White deportees, regardless of background, would be appointed as "guardians" of the deported people of color—the Whites to serve as the "planters" and the others as tenant farmers (p. 203). People of color, for Lease, would be essential to the success of the plan. "Without their aid tropical colonization by the Caucasian would fail, for the northern white man is unable to perform manual labor in the tropics" (p. 220). By the second generation, "the inferior classes cannot fail to have been elevated to intelligent citizenship and material prosperity while the planter class ... will have become acclimated to the tropics, with their homes highly improved and will have attained a high standard of intelligence" (p. 224). To achieve her ambitious plan, Lease wrote, "We need a Napoleon in the industrial world who, by agitation and education, will lead the people to a realizing sense of their condition and the remedies, and teach them that by wise legislation and access to the land they can attain such majesty and happiness as will fulfill the hopes of humanity and the promise of the ages" (p. 6).

Lease's book was widely criticized for poor writing and lack of argument (see Lovett, 2007). It is nevertheless representative of the fundamental tension in populism between support for farmers and laborers and a deep commitment to racism and nationalism.

Shortly after the founding of the Farmers' Alliance by mostly White Texans, Black Texans founded the Colored Farmers' Alliance and Co-Operative Union in 1886. The Colored Alliance was the first of many Black farmers' unions that developed in the South. Even as White populists actively excluded Blacks from their efforts and sought to maintain segregation, a few White and Black members of the movement looked for ways to promote unity around their shared interests.

Thomas Watson, a Georgia attorney and journalist who advocated for the People's Party, spoke to both Black and White farmers: "You are kept apart that you may be separately fleeced of your earnings. You are made to hate each other because upon that hatred is rested the keystone of the arch of financial despotism which enslaves you both. You are deceived and blinded that you may not see how this race antagonism perpetuates a monetary system which beggars both" (Watson, 1892, p. 18). Instead, farmers should pursue a unified political agenda in order to achieve "political independence; . . . a fair return on [their] work; a better chance to buy a home and keep it; a better chance to educate [their] children and see them profitably employed; a better chance to have public life freed from race collisions; a better chance for every citizen to be considered as a citizen regardless of color in the making and enforcing of laws" (p. 19). If political unity could be achieved, Watson concluded, "the race question at the South will have settled itself through the evolution of a political movement in which both whites and blacks recognize their surest way out of wretchedness into comfort and independence" (p. 19).

Watson's efforts were aided in the Black community by the efforts of Rev. Henry Sebastian Doyle, a Black pastor of the Trinity Christian Methodist Episcopal Church in Augusta, Georgia. As recreated in W. E. B. Du Bois's novel, *The Ordeal of Mansart*, Doyle helped Watson see that the key to the success of populism was an alliance with Black farmers and laborers. "[Watson's] inherited reaction was to despise if not hate Negroes," Doyle says in the novel, "But knowing too well what poverty and ignorance had done to the white world, he had the courage to ask earnestly if the Negro was not only suffering from the same oppression, which re-inforced white degradation" (Du Bois, 1957, p. 166). When Watson took up a role in the new Peoples' Party, Doyle joined him and, in the fall 1892, during Watson's campaign for reelection to the US Congress, Doyle was attacked by an angry mob of White citizens for his commitment to including Black labor and farmers in the populist alliance. He was saved by taking refuge in Watson's home, but after Watson's loss in the election, Doyle retreated from politics. The story was common. Even as African Americans took up the populist cause in a quest for fair treatment, land ownership, and opportunities for wealth, their leaders were attacked by the populist Whites with whom they shared common interests.

Despite his recognition of shared concerns, Watson also made it clear that social equality did not "enter into the calculation at all. That is a thing each citizen decides for himself. No statute ever yet drew the latch of the humblest home—or ever will. Each citizen regulates his own visiting list—and always will" (Du Bois, 1957, p. 20). It was also clear that social inequality was not a barrier to sharing the values of "civilization." "If we were dealing with a few tribes of red men or a few sporadic Chinese, the question would be easily disposed of. The Anglo-Saxon would probably do just as he pleased, whether right or wrong, and the weaker man would go under" (p. 13). But Blacks in America numbered 8,000,000 and "They are interwoven with our business, political, and labor systems. They assimilate with our customs, our religion, our civilization. They meet us at every turn,—in the fields, the shops, the mines. They are a part of our system, and they are here to stay" (p. 14). Where Indigenous people, for example, are viewed as vanishing, Black Americans are part of the success of the American colonial project and so, for Watson, should join in the Populist movement to secure the results of that history.

The effort to unite farmers across racial differences in the South failed. The populist movement remained divided and its mainstream continued to advocate for White supremacy even as the movement continued to challenge capitalism and the class of elite landowners that controlled their lives. Eventually, Watson gave up his program for racial unity, and in a speech in North Carolina in 1904 he declared, "However widely we may differ on other things, on this we are together: we are all white men and we would die for white man's supremacy" (Watson, 1908, p. 301).

The White supremacy of Watson and others in the populist movement was often reinforced by their general commitment to science as a key resource in bringing about changes to protect farmers from the abuses of capitalists, bankers, and landlords. As Postel observed, "Only by the 'light of science' could the people find their way to salvation" (2009. p. 266). Counter to many assessments of populism that claimed farmers actively rejected science, Thomas Cator, a California populist and lawyer speaking in 1890, declared that "The minds of the masses . . . must be trained to solve by reason the questions before us [wherever] it will lead" (quoted in Postel, 2009, p. 266). This led, for populist leaders, to where the mass of White citizens already was. M. G. Elzey, an editor at the *National Economist* (an agrarian journal edited by Charles W. Macune, a founder of the Farmers' Alliance), for example, wrote "Mr. Darwin to the contrary . . . mixed races are as a rule inferior" (quoted in Postel, 2009, p. 177). Evolution science, but also physical, biological, and chemical sciences were viewed as essential to successful farming, and journals sprung up across the country to convey the latest findings in plain language. Such science informed the Farmers' Alliance's efforts both to increase crop yields and to establish segregation laws that formed the social order of the Jim Crow apartheid.

At the same time, the populist commitment to science was always tempered by its commitment to following the "will" of the people. When three-time populist presidential candidate William Jennings Bryan spoke against evolution theory in the 1925 "Scopes Monkey Trial," he did so on the grounds that, despite the claims of science, education policy should be the choice of local communities (Maddux, 2013). When teacher John Scopes was fired for violating the Butler Act, a new state law banning the teaching of evolution, Bryan volunteered to testify in the case. His argument in favor of the Butler Act, summarized in his lecture "The Menace of Darwinism," has as its "chief concern . . . protecting man from the demoralization involved in accepting a brute ancestry" (1925, p. 31). Darwinism, despite the successes of science, should be rejected because it seeks to replace the "law of love" with the "law of hate" by understanding human development in terms of survival of the fittest. Science was, for the populists, both a source of salvation in responding to the economic and agricultural problems that kept the people in poverty and a source of antidemocratic danger in that its findings were not subject to the interests of the people.

Even as the populists attempted to respond to Darwinism and new science, especially in relation to farmers, many Christians sought to interpret the message of Christianity into a framework for present social action to help workers in the rapidly industrializing cities of the North. They argued that rather than working toward rewards in heaven, human communities should work collectively to address human needs in the current world and so also work toward realizing the Kingdom of God on earth. The United Presbyterians adopted a classic statement of the central principle of the Social Gospel in 1910:

> The great ends of the church are the proclamation of the gospel for the salvation of humankind; the shelter, nurture, and spiritual fellowship of the children of God; the maintenance of divine worship; the preservation of the truth; the promotion of social

righteousness; and the exhibition of the Kingdom of Heaven to the world. (Presbyterian Church [USA], 2011, § F-1.0304)

Theologians such as Washington Gladden (1836–1918) and later Walter Rauschenbusch (1861–1918) offered a program of action in terms of these "Great Ends" that recognized human beings as fundamentally relational beings, dependent on and responsible for others.

Against the demand for individuals to develop beyond the confines of their families and communities, the Social Gospel offered a live alternative. "[T]he social structure which our unbridled egoism has been building is not in all respects well-built," wrote Gladden in his 1894 book, *Tools and the Man*. "That its foundations are insecure, and that its walls are full of inflammable and explosive material; that unless something is done, and . . . speedily, to protect and preserve it, the catastrophe may be sudden and terrible." The Social Gospel response was to challenge "fierce greed" and "conscienceless purpose" with a commitment to the Christian principle that one ought to "love your neighbor as yourself." Since "in a highly organized society like ours, economic relations are found underlying and conditioning almost everything we do," the implications of the Christian principle must also be economic (1894, p. 26). The result is a call for a systematic reconstruction of the American economy as Christian and socialist.

Rauschenbusch (grandfather of Richard Rorty, who emerges much later in this story), in his *Christianity and the Social Crisis* (first published in 1907), offered an even bolder model when he argued that "the spirit of Christianity has more affinity for a social system based on solidarity and human fraternity than for one based on selfishness and mutual antagonism" (1913, p. 397). The former, communism, ought to be the goal of the social change sought by churches, while the latter, capitalism or "competitive" society, ought to be actively challenged. "In competitive society," he wrote, "each man strives for himself and his family only, and the sense of larger duties is attenuated and feeble." In "communistic society," people are united in a "great organization" and know that each person "owes it duty and loyalty." In a time of rapid capitalist industrialization, Rauschenbusch declared that "[t]he moral and wholesome influences in society to-day proceed from the communistic organizations within it." Individualism and competition, he claimed, marked the "divisive, anarchic, and destructive influences" that "racked the social body" (p. 397). The Social Gospel reconceived Christianity as an effort to bring about the "kingdom of God" on earth, to "perfect" humanity. For Rauschenbusch, the means of perfection involved the transformation of society from one framed by competition and self-interest to one framed by cooperation and other-interest.

The Social Gospel movement acquired many followers as a means to respond to the increasing ills of industrialization and the growing gap between rich and poor. The movement (also called "Mutualism" in its more secular manifestations, such as the economic policies of Theodore Roosevelt and the temperance movement) worked to establish labor laws, juvenile courts, temperance laws, and anti-trust laws. While some activists in the movement came to adopt overtly racist programs aimed at fostering an "Anglo-Saxon" America (Josiah Strong was one of the most prominent), others such as Gladden and Rauschenbusch challenged racist policies to varying degrees and advocated for access to education and employment opportunities for non-Whites, especially African Americans.

Even as the Social Gospel theorists supported, for example, the right of workers to organize and bargain collectively, many of these same thinkers joined Miles in advocating for a larger vision of a single humanity and a single set of values. The same values expressed by Miles in his case for the invasion of Puerto Rico were also expressed by Gladden in his 1898 pamphlet, *Our Nation and Her Neighbors*. "We are acting not as avengers of blood [for the sinking of the USS Maine], but as the executor of righteousness." He concluded that we are acting to "put an end to savagery in our neighborhoods. If anyone shall say that this is a new kind of war, be it so; perchance it is a holier and more justifiable kind of war than has hitherto been undertaken" (1898, p. 10). The Social Gospel became both an intellectual foundation for a program of assimilation and imperialism even as it provided a vision of social individuals, the need for a "social ethic," and a new social science committed to inquiry in service of social reconstruction. The latter vision influenced a wide range of philosophers, including Dewey, Addams, and Du Bois, who saw their work as an attempt to understand the world and to change it.

In July 1894, Dewey was headed to Chicago as the Pullman Strike began. He had been at the University of Michigan and was now on his way to begin teaching at the University of Chicago. While at Michigan, Dewey began to take an interest in the application of philosophy to problems of society. This was in large part due to the influence of his wife, Alice Chipman (1858–1927), who was a feminist and educator. Dewey had arrived at Michigan after finishing his PhD at Johns Hopkins University in 1881. His move to the newly founded university in Chicago was in part recognition of his promise as a philosopher. He had already written on a wide variety of topics and, at the end of his long career, he wrote on even more—leaving thirty-seven volumes of collected books and papers. Best known for his work on education, democracy, and theories of knowledge and inquiry, he became one of the central figures of American Pragmatism. Dewey's decision to move to Chicago was encouraged by Addams, whom Dewey and Chipman had met during an earlier visit. Dewey and Chipman became good friends of Addams's over the next few years (Dewey and Chipman even named one of their daughters "Jane" in honor of Addams) and both were frequent visitors at Hull House.

While teaching at Chicago, Dewey became head of the philosophy, psychology, and teaching programs, and founded a "laboratory" school to experiment with curriculum development and teaching methods. Chipman became the principal of the school. In 1904, after the University of Chicago President William Rainey Harper decided to fire Chipman from her position under pressure from faculty members who said that Dewey had too much power, Dewey resigned his position in protest. He moved to Columbia University, where he stayed until his retirement in 1925. He continued to write until he died in 1952 at the age of ninety-two.

On July 1, 1894, on a train headed to Chicago, Dewey wrote to his wife Alice about a conversation he had with a Pullman Strike organizer that demonstrated the unity among the strikers and their concern for the social good.

> I only talked with him 10 or 15 minutes, but when I got through my nerves were more thrilled than they had been in years; I felt as if I had better resign my job teaching & follow him around till I got into life. (Dewey, 2005, no. 00152)

In a letter a few days later, Dewey reported that the strike had begun and assured Alice that the city was much calmer than the newspapers reported it to be. He said that, except for seeing soldiers, one wouldn't know there was a strike at all. He went on to worry about the government's military response to the strike.

> [President] Cleveland seems getting ready to declare martial law for Chicago! . . . Of course, the [government] can't put up with actual rioting, but a more sympathetic attitude, a discrimination between the strikers and the looting rioting crowds of bums, and the attempt to bring a little pressure to bear on Pullman instead of all on the strikers [would] have made a vast amount of difference. It is impossible that all the wrong should be on the side of the men, when they are willing to do as they do in standing by each other. (2005, no. 00156)

By July 14, the strike had been put down, but Dewey saw that progress had been made in changing how people think.

> The business made a tremendous impression . . . the exhibition of what the unions might accomplish, if organized and working together, has not only sobered [the "upper classes"], but given the public mind an object lesson that it won't soon forget. (2005, no. 00159)

In his philosophical writings, Dewey would reevaluate the liberal individual that lay behind theories of capitalism, propose a theory of democracy that rested on the idea of a social individual, propose an approach to education that would help develop the capacities of critical thinking required by a democracy, and rethink the role of experience in philosophy. Here in Chicago, we see his growing connection with real life as he began to experience the life and work going on at Hull House and in the city.

In September 1894, Dewey was invited to Hull House to give a talk on Epictetus, a Greek Stoic philosopher born in the first century CE. In a conversation following his address, he and Addams had a disagreement about the role of antagonism in argument. "I asked her if she didn't think that besides the personal antagonisms, there was that of ideas & institutions, as [Christianity] & Judaism, & Labor & Capital . . . & she said no. The antagonism of institutions was always unreal." Addams continued to argue that such antagonism was the result of putting one's personal attitudes and ego in the mix. Dewey reported that he was convinced both by her argument and the calm manner in which she made her case. While he was impressed that she not only believed this as a philosophical point but also "believes it in all her senses & muscles," he admitted that he was not deeply convinced: "She converted me internally, but not really, I fear. At least I can't [see] what all this conflict & warring of history means if it's [perfectly] meaningless. . . . my pride of intellect, I suppose it is, revolts at thinking its [sic] all <u>merely</u> negative, & has no functional value." The conversation, Dewey thought, called into question his understanding of and commitment to Hegel's dialectic. "[T]he only reality is unity, but we assume there is antagonism & then it all goes wrong." "I can [see] that I have always been interpreting the [Hegelian] dialectic wrong end up," he wrote to Chipman, "the unity as the reconciliation of opposites, instead of the opposites as the unity in its growth, and thus translated physical tension into a moral thing" (2005, no. 00206). By seeing the tension of action as opposition, he missed the fact that such oppositions were actually not opposed but continuous with growth and development.

This conversation with Addams marked a key moment in the development of Dewey's thought. He replaced the antagonism of dialectic with a view that inquiry begins in indeterminate situations, goes through a process of transition, and leads to a new situation in which the problem is resolved and the situation is unified. Any resolved situation can become indeterminate again and call for new inquiry. This encounter with Addams helped Dewey to think of difference and division in new ways.

Addams did much to influence the thinking of people like Dewey and James. She also did much to transform the world. In her work at Hull House, Addams illustrated her conception of social change through cooperation and not antagonism. When the Pullman Strike began, and despite criticism from some of Hull House's donors, she was already very much involved in labor relations in the city. Hull House residents often hosted meetings on unionization and encouraged discussion groups about how to solve local labor issues. Even before the Columbian Exhibition opened and the Pullman Strike took place, Addams saw the conflict as one between an individualist ethic that society was outgrowing and a social ethic that needed to be developed. Pullman's approach of moralistic benevolence toward "his" workers, combined with an individualistic ethic that blinded him to the ways in which his own well-being was tied to the well-being of the working class in general, was the source of the conflict. Like Miles, Pullman was set on improving and civilizing the "less fortunate." This was exactly the approach to charity that Addams and Hull House rejected. Rather than doing good "for" people, she believed you had to do good "with" people. The people who were in need of some help or improvement in their lives had to be involved in naming and working for that improvement. Democracy had to be at work in all social relations. This kind of progress was slower but more secure. In *Democracy and Social Ethics* (2002a) she wrote:

> The man who insists upon consent, who moves with the people, is bound to consult the "feasible right" as well as the absolute right. . . . He has to discover what people really want, and then "provide the channels in which the growing moral force of their lives shall flow." What he does attain, however, is not the result of his individual striving, . . . but it is sustained and upheld by the sentiments and aspirations of many others. Progress has been slower perpendicularly, but incomparably greater because lateral. (2002a, p. 69)

Pullman's mistake was in deciding for the people what was good for them. He also failed to see how his own interests were connected to the interests of others. Failing to recognize that his refusal to share in the austerity of the economic downturn could endanger his own economic benefit, he embarked on a course that put at risk the well-being of the entire nation in the name of his individual profit. On the other hand, many union members were able to see that they shared the plight of the Pullman workers. This sympathy caused them to sacrifice their safety and security on behalf of the social welfare of all. The violence that resulted from the use of US Marshals and federal troops made many individuals afraid for the stability and security of their own individual interests and led many to condemn the strikers. But over time, Addams believed, most would come to see that the strikers had demonstrated the very kind of social ethics that everyone should adopt.

Addams gave an address in 1895 called "A Modern Lear," in which she presented an analysis of the Pullman Strike in terms of family relations. While others had addressed the strike in political and economic terms, Addams's approach considered the felt relations between the parties. She introduced the method of sympathetic interpretation in order to solve real problems of life and theory. With this method, one must really engage the people involved in the problematic situation at hand and work to construct a narrative that gives meaning to the experience and proposes ways of making the situation better. One example of this can be found in her 1915 book *Long Road of Woman's Memory*. Here she used narrative accounts to make the lives of women in her community meaningful and to point the way to the possibility of reconstructing the community. Underlying Addams's notion of sympathetic interpretation was a metaphysical conception of individuals and communities as relational beings and a conception of knowledge that depended upon ongoing collective inquiry.

Addams believed that the social point of view could come to dominate ethics and help individuals to continue to enlarge the circle of those they considered. As young women were beginning to see that the love and support they provided for their families could be extended to other children and other parents, they began to want to work on behalf of society. Many concluded that rather than working only to feed their own children, they ought to work to remove all children from poverty. Rather than work only to achieve peace in their country, they ought to work to achieve peace in the world. She believed that abolishing poverty and disease would do more for world peace and human well-being than any number of armed conflicts. Peace is not the absence of war, for Addams, but the nurturing of life. "To join in this determined effort" to abolish "poverty, disease and intellectual weakness," she wrote in *Newer Ideals of Peace*, "is to break through national bonds to unlock the latent fellowship between man and man" (2007, p. 236). If people all learned to think as world citizens, rather than giving their energies to national patriotism alone, there could be real progress on real issues facing real people.

Despite the efforts of Addams and many others to reject war as a method of national development, the United States declared war on Spain in 1897 after the USS Maine was sunk in Havana harbor and US officials and the hawkish press determined that the sinking was an act of war (though those responsible for the sinking were never identified). The war ended the following year with a peace treaty and the US occupation of former Spanish colonies, including Puerto Rico, Guam, and the Philippines (Cuba was occupied temporarily), making the United States a new imperial power. The Anti-Imperialist League, formed in 1898, challenged the new imperial policy and was popular among intellectual leaders and included among its members Jane Addams, Andrew Carnegie, Mark Twain, William Graham Sumner, William James, and John Dewey. Over the next decade and a half, anti-imperialist activism gave rise to a growing peace movement that provided an opportunity for philosophers to reconsider conceptions of human nature and knowledge and to seek ways of applying these ideas to the circumstances of industrial America. On the evening of October 7, 1904, at a banquet meeting of the Universal Peace Congress held in Boston, Booker T. Washington (1858–1915), Addams, and James (among others) gave short addresses taking up ideas of human nature and its relation to war.

Washington, by this time the acknowledged (and controversial) leader of the African American community from the perspective of White America, argued in part that "my race in one respect can teach the white races a lesson" (Rose and Trueblood, 1904, p. 260) in relation to questions of peace and war. While other "races" are given to "right wrongs" by violence, the "negro race," "the most patient, the most God-fearing, the most law-abiding of them all, has depended for the righting of wrongs upon his midnight groans, his prayers, and upon an inherent faith in the justice of his cause" (1904, p. 259). Washington accepted the idea, also proposed by Fortune, of substantial differences in the "human nature" of different races and that these race differences masked lessons that could be shared.

For Washington, the "nature" of his race was that it was fundamentally capable of making a significant contribution to other races both in attitudes toward adversity and by providing essential economic services. In 1895, at the Cotton States and International Exposition in Atlanta, in a famous address that helped to raise him to prominence, Washington developed the implication of his notion of racial natures. He offered what people called the "Atlanta Compromise," proposing that Blacks in America work to make an economic contribution to the nation through vocational and industrial work while they set aside their claims to political power and demands for access to education and employment areas dominated by Whites. "Cast down your bucket where you are," Washington famously proclaimed to African Americans across the country (1895). Rather than demanding new places in American society, they should be patient, avoid conflict and violence, and prove the value of their race. During his address to the Peace Congress, Washington was repeatedly interrupted by applause. Those interested in peace seemed to applaud the patience of Blacks, while others seemed to applaud the willingness of Blacks to "stay in their place."

Washington's address was followed by an address given by Addams, her third of the Congress that had begun several days before. Addams's address identified two human natures: one that held that human beings are fundamentally volatile, aggressive, and childlike, the other holding that human beings are fundamentally peaceful, thoughtful, and adult. Addams argued that the two natures were continuous, one capturing the character of the youth of humanity and the other its maturity. In order to move from one to the other, Addams argued for a kind of practice that trained youthful energies into a more productive and social self-commitment to helping others and the wider community. Where children were taken as individuals driven by passions and self-interest, adults recognized their dependence on others and took the resulting obligations seriously. She cited the example of men joining philanthropic groups that took on the outward trappings of the military but also took on the work of helping the poor—illustrated by the Salvation Army. "It is in this direction," she concluded, "that much of our hope lies. It is in persuading our fellow men that they are grown up" (Rose and Trueblood, 1904, p. 262). Consistent with the conceptions of the individual and community in her major works, Addams's address pointed forward to both a version of pacifism and a method of change.

William James followed Addams on the program. Like Washington and Addams, James also presented a conception of human nature. In this case, human nature was taken as fundamentally warlike. "Our permanent enemy," James said, "is the rooted bellicosity of human nature" (Rose and Trueblood, 1904, p. 267). "The plain truth is that people *want* war. They want it anyhow for itself, and apart from each and every possible consequence" (1904, p. 268). Even as war is desired by human beings, human desire is itself conditioned by human experience. "Man lives *by* habits indeed," he said, but these habits can be modified because "what a [human] lives for is thrills and excitement." Human nature, from this perspective, is not a fixed essence but a dynamic character that can be altered under the right conditions. Such conditions, however, should be ones that involve "preventative medicine" rather than a "radical cure." As James argued earlier in his 1890 two-volume work, *Principles of Psychology*, habits are both inherited from one's environment and in response to unformulated desires that seek "thrills and excitement" and seek to avoid fear and pain.

Eventually, James came to adopt a view like the one offered by Addams that night in 1904. In his 1910 essay, "The Moral Equivalent of War," he argued that the "military virtues" of "hardihood and discipline," for example, could be put to work bettering society by first making people aware of "man's relation to the globe he lives on, and to the permanently sour and hard foundation of his higher life" (1977, p. 669). Such awareness would have concrete effects on how one lives. Using a metaphor perhaps more violent than Addams would use but making a similar point, James concluded that by drafting youth to work in "coal and iron mines," "freight trains," "fishing fleets," dishwashing, clothes washing, road building and so on, they "get the childness knocked out of them and come back into society with healthier sympathies and soberer ideas" (1977, p. 669).

A comparison can be made between the Social Gospel movement and populism. The Social Gospel and its secular progeny, the Progressive Movement, were led by prominent intellectuals and activists who framed their work in terms of reconstructing the ideas that framed the possibilities of American society in a way that would promote better lives in the present for working men and women. The populist movement was led largely by activists who took for granted the founding ideas that framed the present world and sought to make them real. Freedom, equality, and the right to land and the fruits of one's labor were viewed as past ideals to be restored. The same ideas that Pokagon and Fortune viewed as cover for the acquisition of lands and resources at the expense of Native and enslaved people were viewed by the populists as the rightful possessions of ordinary citizens, the "forgotten men and women" Sumner described. The first wave of populism had brought the election of Andrew Jackson as president in 1828 and with it the passage of the Indian Removal Act in 1830, the forced removal of Indigenous peoples of the Southeast on the Trail of Tears, numerous wars against Indigenous peoples in the Midwest, and the rapid expansion of White settlement. In a time when the "frontier" was closed and land could no longer be easily taken, the populism of the 1890s sought to free farmers, artisans, and merchants from the limitations imposed by government, capital, and the so-called elites. Populism aimed to restore the imagined American past when individuals could benefit from their hard work and be rewarded with their own piece of land, economic security, and wealth that could be passed to their children. Such ideals had appeal to Black and White, women and men, farmers and workers. The emergence of Black alliances and efforts to unite alliances across racial differences speaks both to the importance of the "American" ideals and as a reminder that the colonial project was not restricted to the actions of White people. The failure of the alliances across differences also speaks to the fact that the project was fundamentally connected with the attitudes and hierarchies of White supremacy.

Jan-Werner Müller (2016) defines populism as critical of elites (as against "ordinary people"), anti-pluralist (in demanding that the populist commitments are the only acceptable ones), and a form of identity politics (committed to the idea that there is only one homogenous people). Even as the populists of the 1890s demanded the nationalization of the railroads and significant government financial support for farmers, such "socialist" measures were proposed strictly to advance the goals of fostering the success of ordinary people and undercutting the ability of the rich elites to take advantage. While philosophies of resistance like those developed by Pokagon, Fortune, Fuller, Addams, and others sought to challenge the commitments of the American colonial project, populism worked for the project—securing more lands, excluding those who were viewed as different, and narrowing the notion of success to a select group. Rather than offering a philosophy of resistance that aimed to reconstruct ideas to bring about new futures, populism was a conservative movement that aimed to conserve a way of life and a set of "American" ideals taken as foundational and superior to those that had come to dominate the post-Civil War world. In this sense, the populists of the 1890s sought to make America great again.

## Primary Texts

Addams, Jane (2007). *Newer Ideals of Peace*, introd. Bernice A. Carroll and Clinton F. Fink. Urbana: University of Illinois Press.
Gladden, Washington (1894). *Tools and the Man: Property and Industry under the Christian Law*. Boston: Houghton, Mifflin.
Postel, Charles (2009). *The Populist Vision*. Oxford: Oxford University Press.
Rauschenbusch, Walter (1907). *Christianity and the Social Crisis*. London: The Macmillan Company.
Washington, Booker T. (1995). *Up from Slavery*, ed. William L. Andrews. New York: Oxford University Press.

# CHAPTER 7
# A NEW NAME FOR AN OLD WAY OF THINKING
## WILLIAM JAMES

William James was born in 1842, a "gilded youth," son of a famous mystic with a strong philosophical bent, Henry James, Sr. (1811–1882), who had inherited a significant fortune from his father, who made his money in real estate (Myers, 2001). He was also the brother of the renowned author Henry James, Jr. (1843–1916) and of Alice James (born 1848), who died of breast cancer in 1892 after suffering from diagnoses of "hysteria" and long periods of "the rest cure." William was educated at home and at fine schools in the United States and Europe. At first, he pursued training in art as an apprentice to William Morris Hunt (1824–79), a well-regarded painter, but in 1861 gave up art training and entered Harvard University's Lawrence Scientific School. The Civil War began in April of that year and William James's two younger brothers, Garth Wilkinson ("Wilky") (1845–1883) and Robertson ("Bob") (1846–1910), both enlisted. Wilky became an officer in the 54th Regiment, the first regiment in Massachusetts to include African American troops (led by White officers). He was seriously wounded in the assault on Fort Wagner in North Carolina and spent much of the war recovering with William at his bedside. Bob enlisted in the 55th Massachusetts, the second Black regiment in Massachusetts, but saw no significant military action.

At Henry Sr.'s insistence, William and Henry Jr. did not enlist and instead continued their education. William entered Harvard Medical School in 1864. He graduated with an MD in 1869 but fell into a deep depression and began to consider suicide. On February 1, 1870, he wrote in his diary: "Today I about touched bottom, and perceive plainly that I must face the choice with open eyes: shall I frankly throw the moral business overboard, . . . or shall I follow it, and it alone" (1977, p. xxviii). After a long struggle with questions of meaning and purpose, James's entry suggests that he gave up the attempt to find a larger principle to settle the questions. Instead, when faced with the question of taking up the "moral business" of affirming and following meaningful values, James decided to give such business a "fair trial": that is, to act not in light of previous principles, but as a consequence of his decision. In an April letter, James affirmed the continuity of choice, action, and purpose.

> Not in maxims . . . not in [contemplation], but in accumulated acts of thought lies salvation. . . . Hitherto, when I have felt like taking a free initiative, like daring to act originally, without carefully waiting for contemplation of the external world to determine all for me, suicide seemed the most manly form to put my daring into; now I will go a step further with my will, not only act with it, but believe as well; believe in my individual reality and creative power. (1920, p. 148)

The decision to choose to act and so find purpose became a general framework that James combined with versions of a principle proposed by his friend Charles Sanders Peirce in the years following James's depression, in the context of a philosophical discussion group sometimes called the Metaphysical Club.

James presented a version of Peirce's principle in a paper he wrote in the wake of his depression and recovery and published in 1879 as "The Sentiment of Rationality." In the paper, James proposed that the work of philosophy was to find "conceptions" that made sense of the world. But a conception, he declared, "is a *teleological instrument*. It is a partial aspect of a thing which *for our purpose* we regard as its essential aspect, as the representative of the entire thing" (1879, p. 319). The idea that the meanings of things are to be understood as directive (teleological) and that their "working" is a matter of believing the conception and acting on it points toward what would become the famous "pragmatic" principle given by James in 1898 during a lecture at the University of California. Attributing the idea to Peirce, James wrote:

> To attain perfect clearness in our thoughts of an object . . . we need only consider what effects of a conceivably practical kind the object may involve. . . . Our conception of these effects, then, is for us the whole of our conception of the object, so far as that conception has positive significance at all. (1977, p. 348)

Expressed more broadly, James said, "The ultimate test for us of what a truth means is indeed the conduct it dictates or inspires" (1977, p. 348). Instead of establishing an independent reality to provide meaning or some set of transcendent ideals, James proposed a view in which purpose, action, ideas, and the "real" intersect to produce truth and the reality of lived experience. In his 1907 volume *Pragmatism*, James wrote, "Any idea that helps us to *deal*, whether practically or intellectually, with either the reality or its belongings, . . . that *fits*, in fact, and adapts our life to the reality's whole setting, . . . will hold true of that reality" (1977, p. 435).

Against his own desperation and sense of aimlessness, James carried his commitment to give life a "fair trial" into a philosophical principle he called "pragmatism" that mirrored a set of commitments already present in the efforts of American Indian thinkers such as Eastman, Parker, and Standing Bear; feminists such as Addams, Gilman, and Cooper, and social reformers including Fortune and Wells-Barnett (Pratt, 2002). As these thinkers sought to affirm purposes and ways of life that stood outside the demands of dominant culture, they also needed to reframe meaning in a way that recognized differences, acknowledged limits, directed action, and provided means to inspire. They also sought critical tools that could examine the products of modern industrialized America and identify both its goods and its evils. Peirce's principle, in James's hands, provided a more or less formal version of a central commitment of this larger philosophical project.

The philosophical disposition identified by James in 1898 as "pragmatism" he called a "new name for an old way of thinking." In the history of philosophy, this philosophical "school" or "method" proposed by James and taken up by others also became identified as "pragmatism," so that the "founder," Peirce, along with Dewey, George Herbert Mead (1863–1931), Addison Moore, and others became known as the "classical" pragmatists. In the late twentieth century, as practitioners of the dominant analytic mode of philosophy realized that they had lost touch with historical roots and lived experience, they began to return to these classical academic thinkers and reappropriated the label "pragmatism." Their work would be called neo- or new pragmatism. The degree to which these later thinkers are pragmatic in spirit remains to be decided and will be discussed later in the book.

Yet, even as the label "pragmatist" was taken up into new discussions and reconstructions, the new use also served to obscure the larger tradition out of which classical pragmatism emerged. James and his colleagues did not write or live in an academic vacuum. The pragmatism that emerged against a background of philosophical despair for James also emerged from the same wider cultural background that stood by as medals were awarded to the Seventh Cavalry for their "bravery" at Wounded Knee, "inspired" the Columbian Exposition to feature displays of living American Indians, and enabled crowds to cheer General Miles as he deployed the US military against striking workers seeking food and shelter.

Pragmatism in its broadest sense is a philosophy of resistance that is part of a wider shared philosophical disposition that recognizes limits, and with them, the reality of boundaries and differences. It is a way of engaging questions and problems from the perspective of lived experience and realizing that the ideas that frame experience anticipate and direct action. American philosophy, as it is understood here, is wider than pragmatism but shares with pragmatism the idea that the work of philosophy in understanding and criticizing ideas is work that transforms life. Pragmatism also shares with the wider American tradition the idea that philosophy is a way of doing and understanding things that is not confined to professional philosophers, members of the academy, or men with the proper degrees. The pragmatism named by James and representing the work of a handful of academic philosophers is but one aspect of an American philosophical tradition born of resistance against the dominant social, economic, and philosophical structure that sought to unify, commodify, and militarize the world of the twentieth century.

As a child of privilege, James might have joined others of his class and seen the world as a unity: borderless to those with the means to travel, ordered in an economic hierarchy, destined to evolve into a brighter future in which only the fittest have survived. Recall William Graham Sumner's popularized version of evolution theory as an economic system in which the best able rose to wealth while those less capable were deservedly poor. "The millionaires," Sumner wrote in a 1902 essay, "are a product of natural selection, acting on the whole body of men to pick out those who can meet the requirement of certain work to be done." Such men, he held, "may fairly be regarded as the naturally selected agents of society for certain work," and while they receive high salaries and "live in luxury," "the bargain is a good one for society" (1992, p. 155). The poor and the weak, who benefit from charity and taxes, are what they are by nature, and providing them with support ultimately only hampers the honest laborer who is forced to carry the burden. While the Social Gospel movement argued for the support of the poor, Sumner had a harsh reply. "[T]he weak who constantly arouse the pity of humanitarians and philanthropists," he wrote, "are the shiftless, the imprudent, the negligent, the impractical, and the inefficient." Charity, in such cases, is a cost without benefits: "Whatever capital you divert to support the shiftless and good-for-nothing person is so much diverted from some other employment, and that means from somebody else" (p. 208).

James, however, experienced the limits and boundaries of the world as a pluralism that had implications for how one lives, what one knows, and what the "real" world is. In "On a Certain Blindness in Human Beings," he noted that we are often blind to the feelings and sensibilities of others if they are different from our own. We cannot see what others value or understand why they value it—we become hardened to the joy of others. This lack of attention narrows our lives, and this gives us reason to work to become sensitive to how others see and experience the world. The blindness James identified effectively blocks access to the perspective of others, but realizing this limit also provides a starting point for other forms of engagement that require tolerance and an alternative conception of knowledge that expects uncertainty. "Hands off," James wrote; "neither the whole of truth nor the whole of good is revealed to any single observer, although each observer gains a partial superiority of insight from the peculiar position in which he stands" (1977, p. 644). The result for James is the recognition of value pluralism (different conceptions of what is good) on one hand and epistemic pluralism (different ways of knowing and what is known) on the other. In response to the homogenous system of value necessary for Sumner's model of human development, James recognized a diversity of systems (each person is "faithful to his own opportunities") and a diversity of knowledge systems (based on a diversity of "peculiar positions").

Similarly, James proposed a pluralistic ontology: that is, the view that finds the world "a pluralism." Western philosophy had long been engaged in a debate about whether the nature of reality is one (monistic) or many (pluralistic). The debate focused on the question: Are the differences and separations we experience just illusions and fundamentally reality is all one, or are the differences and separations themselves real? James acknowledged that the question cannot now be settled and so we are in a position to believe the proposition that helps us navigate our lives more successfully. Monism, James claimed, required that everything (every thing, every thought, value, desire, and action) must be connected in a single whole. As a result, it had serious problems: it did not account for our finite human consciousness, it created a problem of evil, it contradicted reality as we perceive it, and it was fatalistic. The view could, for example, lead people to accept and justify all sorts of evil, since whatever happens must happen necessarily because it is connected with everything that came before and everything that comes after.

Monists, as James said in his last book, *The Pluralistic Universe*, claim that there are no disconnections. Pluralism, he said, is the "negation of monism," that is, the claim that "it is not the case that there are no disconnections." The alternative to monism is not seeing everything as separate from everything else (and so simply many). Rather, James's pluralism recognized that some things are connected and some things are not. A pluralistic world is one that supports the possibility of novelty, incommensurability (of some things not having a common ground), and the possibility of making things better (meliorism). Science, whose work is to provide systematic descriptions of the world in relation to particular interests (where psychology and physics, for example, represent distinct interests), is more compatible with a pluralistic universe that allows for alternative accounts of the world (pp. 267–9). In the end, the pragmatist is neither an absolute monist nor an absolute pluralist. The world is *both* one and many: "One just so far as its parts hang together by any definite connexion. It is many just so far as any definite connexion fails to obtain. And finally it is growing more and more unified by those systems of connexion" (p. 415). Monism, then, tends to be dogmatic since it insists that everything is one and so can acknowledge no alternatives, while pluralism has the potential to tolerate difference and reject dogmatism.

Given this pluralistic take, James does not try to reduce all experience to one. Consequently, he writes in "What Makes Life Significant" that the first rule of human interaction is "non-interference with [others'] peculiar ways of being happy, provided those ways do not assume to interfere by violence with ours. No one has insight into all the ideals." He goes on to say that being dogmatic about ideals "is the root of most human injustices and cruelties" (p.

645). Although blindness to others' interests is permanent, one can recognize its effects and work to reduce intolerance and cruelty and balance sympathy, insight, and goodwill. Even something so small as asking how much tolerance and sympathy one can extend to another moves us from our inherited, stuck positions. "Your imagination is extended," James observed, and "[y]ou divine in the world about you matter for a little more humility on your own part, and tolerance, reverence, and love for others; and you gain a certain inner joyfulness at the increased importance of our common life" (p. 658).

The blindness of individuals is repeated in the outlook of classes, as James illustrated in his discussion of the "labor question," which he takes to refer to "all sorts of anarchistic discontents and socialistic projects and the conservative resistances they provoke" (p. 658). For James, it is not that there is conflict between these positions, "the unhealthiness consists solely in the fact that one-half of our fellow-countrymen remain entirely blind to the internal significance of the lives of the other half" (pp. 658–9). In the resulting conflict between rich and poor, the poor see the rich as greedy and the rich see the poor as envious. "Each, in short, ignores the fact that happiness and unhappiness and significance are a vital mystery; each pins them absolutely on some ridiculous feature of the external situation; and everybody remains outside of everybody else's sight" (p. 659). While James does think a more equal distribution of wealth is necessary in the future, to think that that alone will remove the felt differences between people is naïve. However, by recognizing limits and looking to points of intersecting concerns—such as the economic character of the community or the ways in which tolerance is practiced or ignored—it is possible for different groups, viewpoints, and even "worlds" to coexist.

At the same time, pluralism potentially raises the specter of relativism, another long-recognized problem in Western philosophy. Although relativism comes in many forms, the term typically marks a view that holds that standards of evaluation (of truth or goodness or usefulness) are determined relative to the view, person, or community making a claim or proposing a solution. "The rich," in James's example, might hold that low taxes are good or that the poor have earned their social position. Given other commitments shared by the group, one might conclude that these claims about the world are "true for that group" but not true for "the poor" in the same example. Inevitably, a relativistic view will lead to the conclusion that, for example, it is both true and not true that the poor earned their poverty. Any view that leads to a contradiction would appear to be problematic, and James's appears to be such a view.

It is possible to see the situation that emerges from plural points of view to be more like the situation one faces in cases of making a choice. One response is to retreat into authority and dogma and consult some larger set of rules that can settle the matter. While at times, from a pluralist perspective, there may be some common frame of reference that will provide guidance about which claim to accept, it is also possible that there is no such frame. In this case, James observed, those who face a choice must choose but also recognize that whatever choice is made, it can be mistaken. "Objective evidence and certitude are doubtless very fine ideals to play with," James said in "The Will to Believe," "[b]ut where on this moonlit and dream-visited planet are they found?" What remains in a world without "objective certitude" is "the practical faith that we must go on experiencing and thinking over our experience, for only thus can our opinions grow more true." However, to take any single opinion to be universally and unchangeably so "I believe to be a tremendously mistaken attitude, and I think that the whole history of philosophy will bear me out" (p. 725). At the same time, James grants that there is nevertheless "one indefectibly certain truth[:] that the present phenomenon of consciousness exists. That, however, is the bare starting-point of knowledge, the mere admission of a stuff to be philosophized about" (p. 725). The truth is that there is nevertheless an agent or person who makes a decision, whose decision can be in error, but who, despite this, is able to affect the world.

Do pluralism and its apparent relativism mean we can believe anything we want? No. When faced with the choice of believing and acting on the claim that the poor have earned their poverty or its contrary, pluralism sets up the conflict but does not resolve it. The alternatives seem to exhaust the options so it would appear that a person faced with the two claims must choose. Can one simply ignore or set aside the competing claims? In a sense, one can make precisely that choice, but the choice is not neutral. Different courses of action are at stake in the two claims, but a third claim—indifference—is also available and it has its consequences as well. To choose not to choose is, in effect, to make a choice nevertheless. In "The Will to Believe," James famously concludes that "In either case we *act*, taking our life in our hands" (p. 734). Pluralism leads to a kind of relativism, but not one in which anything goes; it instead sets up a context for tolerance and engagement that recognizes the role of oneself and others in the work of deciding what to believe and how to proceed.

Yet such a conclusion again seems to account for pluralism but not for cases in which truth is at issue. In *Pragmatism*, James proposed what has come to be regarded as his controversial "pragmatic theory of truth" in order to answer the concerns of relativism. The theory, however, has generated at least as many objections as it has addressed. True ideas, James argued, "*are those that we can assimilate, validate, corroborate and verify. False ideas are those that we cannot*" (p. 430). To which he added, "You can say of [an idea] either that 'it is useful because it is true' or that 'it is true because it is useful.' Both these phrases mean exactly the same thing, namely that here is an idea that can be verified" (p. 431). He added that verification is "the function of agreeable leading." From this perspective, a given claim serves as a kind of guide to further action (a leading) that gains its character as true *if* the leading is "successful." A simple claim about the amount of money in one's wallet is something that leads to further action (buying a newspaper). It is an "agreeable leading" if one has the amount of money claimed and can pay for the newspaper. The claim fails or is false if I think I have $5 and find, when I try to buy a paper, that I have only $1.

Bertrand Russell (1872–1970), among others, objected to the pragmatist theory of truth by arguing that the theory appears to return to the relativism that allows anything to be true (Russell, 1910). If an idea is true because it is useful, then surely if one tells lies that advance one's business prospects or political career, they are true since they are useful. If "the rich" claim that "the poor" earn their poverty and this "truth" supports a reduction of social services to people in poverty and so reduces taxes, the claim is a useful one to those who benefit from reduced taxes and so also true. On the pragmatist theory, it is easy to find many things true that simply are not. James's response to this criticism was to argue that some claims, often narrow in scope, may operate precisely this way (James, 1977). Others are claims on parts of the world that are shared and so to be "useful" cannot be just a matter of how they work for one person. Instead, claims, expectations, and dispositions are subject to being reinforced or undermined by the experience of others and by the world that they engage.

A politician's lies might be useful in an election and even treated as true by her supporters and staff, but they may fail to be useful, to be assimilated, validated, corroborated, and verified by the voters, by independent election observers, by "facts" collected by researchers, or by observant members of the public. And if the "facts" are themselves claims about the world, then they too are subject to standing or being overturned as they come to be used. The simple objections of Russell and later philosophers are better understood as a misreading or oversimplification of James's view. But they also point to a final key component of pragmatism as envisioned by James. If claims about the world "agree" with it in some way, what is it that they agree with?

In his 1904 paper "A World of Pure Experience," James proposed a view he called "radical empiricism." The general notion of empiricism developed in the tradition of English philosophy in which knowledge is a product of experience understood as a set of sensory inputs. The idea that knowledge began in experience became a widely accepted view, in contrast with rationalism, which attributed knowledge to the operations of minds in a way that could leave sensory inputs—experience—behind. For James, rationalism was also associated with monism and an interest in wholes, while empiricism was "a philosophy of plural facts." "To be radical," he argued, "an empiricism must neither admit into its constructions any element that is not directly experienced, nor exclude from them any element that is directly experienced" (1977, p. 195).

In other words, radical empiricism was a view that "admitted" (recognized or took into account) everything that was part of experience, from the sight of trees on a summer afternoon, to the measurements taken of the diameter of the tree trunks, to the experience of the trees as living beings with their own purposes and interests. Such experiences, of course, are not just images of trees or measurements of growth but are rather *relational experiences*. The trees stand somewhere and are seen from a particular angle by particular beings. The measurements taken are relational—they mark a relation between a measurement device and the actual trunks of trees. The experience of a tree as living is the experience of a tree over time and in relation to an observer who has a concept of growth and understands how it relates trees to people, for example. "For such a philosophy, *the relations that connect experiences must themselves be experienced relations, and any kind of relation experienced must be accounted as 'real' as anything else in the system*" (p. 195). "Reality" is then a vast field of experienced relations whose particular character is a matter of how a relation experiences and how it is experienced. As a result, there are no fixed entities, and instead only things in relation that are themselves in a process of interaction with still other things. "Taken as it does appear," James said, "our universe is to a large extent chaotic" (p. 197). The actions of persons or agents, the generation of knowledge claims and value judgments bring some order to the world. "In radical empiricism there is no bedding; it is as if the pieces clung together by their edges, the transitions experienced between them forming their cement" (p. 212).

Although James concluded in the Preface to *Pragmatism* that "there is no logical connexion between pragmatism . . . and . . . radical empiricism," it seems clear that radical empiricism provides the ontology for the vision of inquiry and action that is expressed in the doctrines of *Pragmatism*. The connection is important because pragmatism, as James proposed it, is not only an account of meaning within a given or dominant system, but rather is one inherently open at the edges to encountering its limits and being influenced by what stands outside and, because of our "blindness," unseen. The result is an account of how it is that "Experience itself, taken at large, can grow by the edges" (p. 212).

## American Philosophies

Despite his deep connections to privilege in Victorian America, James joined the intellectuals who sought to distance themselves from what they took to be the limiting philosophical views inherited from Europe. Where Social Darwinist thinkers sought fixed principles of survival as providing the standards in terms of which American life would develop, and the populist movement held tight to the values of an earlier agrarian society sustained by hierarchical social relations and the free labor of enslaved people, James—and those who adopted his "old way of thinking"—resisted the constraints and, perhaps most importantly, recognized and sought to compensate for the blindness inherent in human understanding of each other and the world. His psychological theory, developed alongside his pragmatism in the 1890s, likewise resisted the inheritance of the idea that the faculties of mind were given in advance and served as rigid organizers of life and values. Instead, human minds are organized through interactions with their environments. Souls or selves, rather than givens, are in fact like ocean waves, distinct in their shape and course but individual, material beings continuous with other beings. Souls are distinctive energies moving through the environment, relational in character, and responsive to change. Such a view would influence theorists such as John Dewey and activists such as Jane Addams to rethink individualism and community and apply these concepts anew to efforts to respond to the problems of people. James did not join Fortune, Pokagon, Addams, Gilman, or Goldman in their efforts to bring about social change. James's pragmatism was nevertheless an effort to respond to how the world thought about change and how activist philosophers imagined new futures.

## Primary Text

James, William (1977). *The Writings of William James: A Comprehensive Edition*, ed. with an introduction and new preface, by John J. McDermott. Chicago and London: University of Chicago Press.

# CHAPTER 8
# MAKING IDEAS CLEAR
## CHARLES SANDERS PEIRCE

Much of the philosophical work of James was inspired by the work of Charles Sanders Peirce (1839–1914). Peirce's father, Benjamin (1809–80), was a respected professor of mathematics at Harvard and a cofounder of the American Academy of Sciences. Considered a prodigy in his youth, Peirce's own academic career did not go far, but his philosophical influence did. Unable to secure a permanent academic position, Peirce worked for the US Coast and Geodetic Survey. From 1879 until 1884, Peirce also taught mathematics and logic at Johns Hopkins University in Baltimore, where his students included Christine Ladd Franklin (a well-regarded logician) and Dewey (who took advanced logic and a course on philosophical terminology from Peirce in fall 1883). In 1884, the university president, Daniel Coit Gilman, dismissed Peirce from his position. In 1891, after pressure from the US Congress over large expenditures on a series of pendulum experiments conducted by Peirce, he was asked to resign from the Coast Survey. He moved to a farm in Milford, Pennsylvania, hoping to continue his philosophic investigations. Without a steady job, his friend William James lent him financial and academic support over the years. James asked Peirce to lecture at Harvard and other venues in Cambridge several times. Peirce's writings were intellectually dense and often not fully comprehended by his audiences. In one invitation to lecture, James, aware of this, asked Peirce to direct his upcoming talk to "matters of vital importance." Peirce responded with a highly technical paper that ridiculed James's request and further alienated him from the Harvard community. From his privileged youth, his circumstances declined over the years to such poverty that he lived without heat during the Pennsylvania winters.

His personal life did not fare much better. His first marriage to Melusina Fay, who was already mentioned as one of the leaders of the cooperative housekeeping movement, ended in divorce after twenty-one years. Just months after the decree was issued, Peirce married Juliette Pourtalai (d. 1934), a young woman twenty-seven years his junior. Letters and journals indicate that Peirce's relationship with Pourtalai was probably abusive. Unfortunately for Peirce, the affair with Pourtalai before they married became public while he taught at Johns Hopkins, and rumors around the affair played a significant role in Gilman's decision to fire Peirce, despite an earlier promise to make his position permanent. His dismissal from Johns Hopkins and his reputation as a difficult person probably also related to medical problems Peirce had throughout his life, for which he regularly took morphine, laudanum, alcohol, caffeine, and nicotine. Despite his personal and professional difficulties, he produced a large body of work that is still being assembled and studied by scholars. The reasons for this ongoing scholarly interest in his work are many and include the scope of his work, which ranged from mathematics, geometry, and the physical sciences to logic, semiotics, and metaphysics. As with the other thinkers discussed in this book, we cannot pretend to do justice to his wide-ranging and complex work. Instead, we present some of the central ideas and interesting features of his writings as they relate to this story of American philosophies of resistance.

Just before the World Columbian Exposition was to open in 1893, Peirce published an article in *The Monist* entitled "Evolutionary Love" (1992). This piece presented a different view of evolution theory than the one that framed the Columbian Exposition and offered a critique of the emerging focus on individualism that accompanied the economic theories of capitalism and the moral theories of Social Darwinism. Coming just before the economic crises of 1893 and increased labor activism (as exemplified by the Pullman Strike), Peirce's article takes on an increased significance. Peirce developed his strong critique of the fundamental commitments of the dominant conception of economics and morality by considering three competing views on evolution.

The three competing views on evolution Peirce discussed in his article rely on different ways of understanding how change occurs. One (which he aligned with Darwin) relies on "fortuitous variation" or chance; another (which he aligned with a list of naturalists including Spencer) relies on some mechanical necessity that follows from heredity and/or events in the environment; the third (which he aligned with Lamarck) relies on the transmission of acquired characteristics (or habits). He found flaws with approaches that relied strictly on chance or strictly on necessity and noted that the third approach bridges the tensions between the first two. He called this view "agapastic evolution," as it is based on the Greek term *agape*—love or sympathetic understanding. This mode of evolution is not heedless or blind, but recognizes the intelligibility of the cosmos and the continuity of "minds" (what Peirce called *synechism*) and the participation of these "minds" in the processes of change. If we think about evolution within the confines of human history, as an example, then we would see the following structure: "Minds" generate new ideas and then habits begin to emerge and shape new activities and things in ways compatible with what already is. For example, in art history, impressionism became a cultural habit of French painting. Then Cezanne introduced modifications of impressionism that led to new ways and new habits of painting.

If we think more generally of biological evolution, Peirce said that habit, combined with chance or contingency, both pushes plants and animals into new activities and then helps the new come into harmony with the old. Peirce illustrated the process by considering the relation of a parent to a child. To help the child grow or develop, the parent needs to provide both structured necessities and the opportunities for spontaneous activities. To rely either on necessity or pure chance in raising a child often leads to a maladjusted child. For Peirce, love is "the ardent impulse to fulfill another's highest impulse" (1992, p. 354). Love is what makes growth possible—for plants, animals, ideas, or humans. As Peirce put it, "It is not by dealing out cold justice to the circle of my ideas that I can help them grow, but by cherishing and tending them as I would the flowers in my garden" (1992, p. 354). This process is what Peirce labeled *agape* or evolutionary love.

Aside from his general interest in science, Peirce was also concerned with evolution theory because it was being put to use in social, economic, and political theories that were used to justify a range of new policies and practices. The fortuitous and mechanistic views were being used to lend support to the economic and social competition that capitalism was to encourage. He described this view ironically: "Intelligence in the service of greed ensures the justest prices, the fairest contracts, the most enlightened conduct of all the dealing between men, and leads to the *summum bonum*, food in plenty and perfect comfort." But Peirce asked, "[f]ood for whom?" and answered, "for the greedy master of intelligence" (1992, p. 354). Peirce argued that such conclusions did not necessarily follow, even from the arguments of Darwin and Spencer, but concluded that this was one prominent way in which they were actually taken up by the society and many other theorists.

> What I say, then, is that the great attention paid to economical questions during our century has induced an exaggeration of the beneficial effects of greed and of the unfortunate results of sentiment, until there has resulted a philosophy which comes unwittingly to this, that greed is the great agent in the elevation of the human race and in the evolution of the universe. (1992, p. 354)

Peirce cited a political theory text of the time as an example. The author gave the first motive for action as "The love of self," the second as love of "a limited class having common interests and feelings" and the third, "Love of mankind" (1992, p. 355). The first motive, love of self, Peirce rejected as not genuine love, claiming that love always involves others. But he rejected the third as well because "love of mankind" is too abstract and so was an ineffective "tutor of love" and led to demands to prevent the poor or "the vicious" from reproducing (a form of eugenics) or to decide that "'no measure of repression would be too severe,' in the case of criminals" (1992, p. 355). Peirce affirmed the second sort of love—of others—but in order for it to be genuine love, it must grow out of kinship and interaction with other persons. This kind of love can become sympathy.

Further, this view that underwrites abstract "love of mankind" also suggests that generosity itself could be a problem.

> So a miser is a beneficent power in a community, is he? With the same reason precisely, only in a much higher degree, you might pronounce the Wall Street sharp to be a good angel, who takes money from heedless persons not likely to guard it properly, who wrecks feeble enterprises better stopped, . . . and who by a thousand wiles puts money at the service of intelligent greed, in his own person. (1992, pp. 356–7)

Peirce suggested that Darwin's *Origin of Species* simply extends to the realm of plants and animals the political and economic analysis that sees misers as good because they make the economic system more successful. "As Darwin put it on his title page, it is the struggle for existence; and he should have added for his motto: Every individual for himself, and the Devil take the Hindmost!" (1992, p. 357). The problem with this Darwinian view is that progress "takes place by virtue of every individual's striving for himself with all his might and trampling his neighbor under foot whenever he gets a chance to do so. This may accurately be called the Gospel of Greed" (1992, p. 357). As we have seen, Peirce argued that greed does not benefit society. Even more important, Peirce held, the idea that there could even be individual, unconnected agents was mistaken. Individual achievements are not the work of isolated individuals but the product of the history of the world and the spirit of any given age. In contrast to the Darwinian ideal was the Christian idea "that progress comes from every individual merging his individuality in sympathy with his neighbors" (1992, p. 357). "Sympathy" marks an attitude that bridges individual differences and connects their activities through larger purposes.

The focus of his contemporaries on greed raised concerns for Peirce because greed had obvious social, political, and economic implications. These are brought into sharper relief in the context of his metaphysical views. For Peirce, all things have a tendency to take habits and "[t]he existence of things consists in their regular behavior" (1992, p. 278). Peirce argued that in the "infinite past," the universe was indeterminate and filled with chance. Through time and evolution, the universe became more determinate and habituated—that is, regularities or laws emerged. He posited that in a possible "infinite future," there would be no chance, only law. But this world is not the one in which we live. We live in an intermediate stage with regularity (law) *and* chance. In this world, theories and practices that rely on fixed absolutes are not justified. "We must therefore be guided by the rule of hope, and consequently we must reject every philosophy or general conception of the universe, which could ever lead to the conclusion that any given general fact is an ultimate one" (1992, p. 275).

The caution against fixed absolutes is supported by Peirce's examination of how we come to hold beliefs. In "The Fixation of Belief," Peirce delineated four ways humans come to hold and "settle" beliefs. The first, the method of tenacity, is simply to defend whatever beliefs an individual holds come hell or high water. The tenacious believer does not ask where his or her beliefs came from. The second method Peirce called the method of authority. In this method, one simply accepts and uses beliefs as given by cultural authorities such as churches, state institutions, fashion experts, politicians, and so forth. In these first two methods, believers seldom or never question their beliefs and hold them despite contradictions in their own experience. Rather than reexamining beliefs, they stubbornly stick with them whether "they work" or not.

A third method of holding beliefs is the a priori method, which involves relying on what seems reasonable or intuitively true; that is, something is true "before" or prior to experience. This method, for Peirce, has an air of intellectual reasonableness; the problem is that when two a priori beliefs conflict, there is no way to settle the conflict by way of reason. In the face of two claims justified a priori, one must default to one of the other methods to solve the dilemma. All three of these methods have their place, but any one (or combination) of the above leaves believers vulnerable to trying to negotiate the world with beliefs that do not match experience or are not connected with the beliefs of others. They do not, in James's terms, "get into satisfactory relations with other parts of our experience" (1907, p. 34).

If we settle our beliefs too quickly or too firmly, we are likely to find ourselves out of sync with the world around us. This can happen as things around us—physical, social, or moral—change. It can happen as *we* change or grow as well. Given the evolutionary nature of the universe and the beings in it, we need a way for beliefs to change as well. Peirce introduced the method of science as the fourth method of arriving at beliefs. By this, he meant that one should take up the attitude and general approach of holding beliefs as hypotheses to be used and tested, rather than as final beliefs. As experience exposes problems with specific beliefs, believers can revise the hypothesis or belief. This means holding beliefs as tentative and revisable so that beliefs can be corrected and improved. For Peirce, this process of arriving at and revising beliefs required a community of inquirers with various perspectives who help correct the views of others. This is an ongoing, self-correcting process that acknowledges human fallibility—the potential to be in error—and should make believers cautious about proclamations of absolute or final truths.

Part of what humans do in the process of social inquiry is look for regularity and fixed laws. Peirce argued that human individuals form habits, but so too do social groups, other plant and animal beings, and the universe itself. This is, again, part of what he called the continuity of reality, or synechism. All parts of the universe are continuous with one another. There are no sharp divides, only continuous blendings. Consider the border between any two colors: for Peirce, the border is always a mixture of the two; there is no sharp dividing line. In a social or political context, this continuity allows for the recognition of individuality (as we are able to distinguish each of the two colors) and of community (as the various combinations and blendings of the colors). For Peirce, the fact that we are individuals *but also* essentially communal helps us develop sympathy with other beings.

Peirce's metaphysical categories of firstness, secondness, and thirdness also support the claim that humans are not isolated knowers of the world. According to Peirce, we know the world through mediated experience. We encounter the world in direct experience—he called this firstness. Firstness cannot be articulated or described until it meets with secondness—something different or other that makes awareness possible and provides resources to help articulate the experience. But to be able to interpret and understand an experience, for it to be meaningful, thirdness—an interpretant or mediating representation—is also required. Attention to experience on its own does not equal thinking about the experience; firstness is just presence. Awareness increases with secondness—something that stands in relation to the first and reveals a contrast or distinction. It is not until we get the idea of the relation of the first to the second that we can begin to interpret and make arguments. So, the first simply is itself, the second is what it is in virtue of the first, and the third owes what it is to the mediation that brings the first and second into relation (1992, p. 245ff.).

Peirce's metaphysical categories also provided a framework for his theory of signs or what he sometimes called "semiotic." Semiotic is often understood as a theory of language meaning that begins by looking at words, gestures, and physical objects like street signs and billboards. For Peirce, semiotics meant "the doctrine of the essential nature and fundamental varieties of possible semiosis" (1998, p. 413). The latter term, "semiosis," Peirce defined as "an action, or influence, which is, or involves, a cooperation of *three* subjects, such as a sign, its object, and its interpretant" (1998, p. 411). The "three subjects," Peirce argued, are to be understood in terms of the three categories so that a sign has the character of a first, the object the character of a second, and the interpretant the third. For anything to have meaning, that is, for it to have an interpretant, it can stand neither alone nor in a simple two-term or dyadic relation. For a claim to be meaningful, for example, the utterance (or expression in print) must stand in relation to an object. The relation as an active process of mediation is the interpretant, the meaning of the claim. The claim "the ocean is calm today" is meaningful because the expression and its object, the ocean at hand in this case, are connected by an active looking, a movement from claim to scene. This three-fold or triadic result (the meaningful claim about the ocean at hand), then becomes a new sign that in turn connects with another object, this time it might be a prediction about sailing or the weather to expect, as well as another interpretant.

Peirce did not stop with the meaning of language, however. Since the process of language meaning is framed by the most general categories of first, second, and third, he could also claim that the meaning of things, actions, and events is also triadic. To know the meaning of a rose, a bicycle race, or a death is to take the thing, action, or event as a sign related to some object (the love of another, a bicycling triumph, or an unmeasured loss) by means of an interpretant, a mediating relation connecting the first and the second. Meaning from this perspective is an ongoing process in which no object is ever encountered on its own (objects are seconds) and in which no sign can have meaning (even formal meaning) without a process of interpretation.

Peirce's semiotic stands in sharp contrast with the work of Ferdinand Saussure (1857–1913), whose volume *Course in General Linguistics* (1916) proposed a theory of signs that recognized only two terms: the *sign* and the *signified*. For Saussure, the relation of signs to the signified was a matter of arbitrary assignment (though once the assignments were made, no individuals or even the community could change the assignments). Since things signified are arbitrary, meaning is not first a matter of objects but a matter of the system of signs that provides a structure for meaning even before assignments are made. Saussure's work served as one of the starting points for twentieth-century structuralism and the rebellion against it in the work of Jacques Derrida (1930–2004). Peirce's semiotic—though it has received far less attention than Saussure's—opposed the concept of a dyadic understanding of meaning. As John Sheriff explained, "What Saussure's definition of a sign does not account for is that which determines the sign's meaning, the relation of the sign's object or signified to its interpretant" (1989, p. 57). While Saussure's view suggests that "language is something arbitrarily added to preexisting objects" (Sheriff, 1989, p. 71), Peirce's view rejects the notion of "preexisting objects" in favor of the idea that language shapes experience even as it is also shaped by it.

So, even in his more technical metaphysics and epistemology, we find that Peirce's philosophy assumed the reality of social individuals in a process of interpreting a world that can only be known in its relations. This process requires encountering differences *and* finding things that demonstrate commonalities. This returns us to the damaging habit of greed and self-interest; these are not just bad social habits, but they demonstrate a failure of inquiry and lead to bad ways of fixing beliefs.

Peirce began his philosophical work in the 1850s as a self-described "passionate devotee of Kant" (Peirce, 1931, Vol. 4, para. 2; henceforth, CP 4.2). As a practicing scientist and philosopher, he became critical of the limitations he found in Kant's theory of knowing (cognition) and of the rationalism of Rene Descartes. In his 1868 essay, "On a New List of Categories," Peirce sought to address Kant's limits by proposing an alternative set of categories to frame questions of knowledge and being. He also applied the new list to a critique of Cartesian philosophy, rejecting, among other doctrines, the idea that philosophy must begin in complete doubt. "We must," he wrote, "begin with all the prejudices which we actually have when we enter upon the study" but we ought to be open to overturning our prejudices because there emerges "some positive reason" to do so in the course of the study (CP 5.265). In the back of these challenges was the conviction that philosophy matters; that theories of cognition, metaphysics, and logic all have concrete implications for human life and community. About the "question of realism and nominalism"[1] that characterizes the theories of Kant and Descartes, he wrote that while "its roots [are] in the technicalities of logic, its branches reach about our life. The question whether *genus homo* has any existence except as individuals, is the question of whether there is anything of any more dignity, worth, and importance than individual happiness, individual aspiration, and individual life" (CP 8.38). It is this question, whether humans "have anything in community, so that *community* is to be considered an end in itself [that] is the most fundamental practical question in regard to every public institution the constitution of which we have it in our power to influence" (CP 8.38).

In answer to the challenge, Peirce develops his theory of signs and reconsiders the process of knowing as a fallible, ongoing practice. Until this point, philosophers usually conceived of reason as the processes of induction—reasoning from particular experiences and examples and so error-prone and lacking in validity—and deduction—knowing from fixed principles and facts to conclusions in a way that preserves truth and guarantees the certainty of the result. Peirce overturned the standard model, arguing that reason properly includes a third process he called abduction or retroduction, which serves as the only source of novelty and new ideas. Abductive reasoning is guesswork framed by circumstances and hypothesis generation, and, he argued, a valid argument form that provides the framework for testing—for induction— which in turn is framed by the standards set by deduction, or reasoning from general claims justified by experience, or supposed in order to imagine outcomes and possibilities. For Peirce, the processes of reasoning as he understands them provide a context for "the rule of hope," for challenging the philosophy of greed, and for seeking a better future. While Peirce himself cannot be seen as a political activist or an advocate for the just causes of his day such as abolition, women's suffrage, and Indigenous rights, his work nevertheless helped to establish a conceptual ground for those who would seek to resist slavery and oppression. His work echoed, even if it did not inform, the epistemic and ontological commitments of theorists including Pokagon, Fortune, Addams, Gladden, and others who sought an end to the policies of exclusion and removal central to industrial capitalism. In this sense, Peirce was a central figure in the tradition of American philosophies of resistance.

## Note

1   "Realism" and "nominalism" refer to two ways of understanding general categories. Realists hold that a general category, such as the category of human being, is real so that there is a real essence, and having that essence makes a thing human. Nominalists hold that categories are made by assigning a name to things. What is common, then, is not an essence, but the name attached. For a nominalist, humanity is the set of individuals that share the name.

## Primary Texts

Peirce, Charles S. (1992). *The Essential Peirce*, vol. 1, eds. Nathan Houser, and Christian Kloesel. Bloomington: Indiana University Press.

Peirce, Charles S. (1998). *The Essential Peirce*, vol. 2, ed. Peirce Edition Project. Bloomington: Indiana University Press.

# CHAPTER 9
# THE BELOVED COMMUNITY AND ITS DISCONTENTS
## JOSIAH ROYCE AND THE REALISTS

In January 1900, Josiah Royce (1855–1916) addressed the Aberdeen Philosophical Society. A few months before, the British Empire had been drawn into a second war with the South African Boers over ownership of the Transvaal gold fields. By the time of Royce's address, the British had suffered a series of military defeats, and the press raised general alarm about the future of the Empire. Royce, who was in Scotland to give his second set of Gifford lectures at the University of Edinburgh (he gave the first in 1899), gave an address focused on characteristics of American civilization as a means of offering hope to the beleaguered British imperialists for the future of their Empire. Royce proposed that America's "peculiar and most characteristic tendency" was "assimilation," a term that applied "not only to the assimilation of alien races, but to the organization into one close-knit nationality of the diverse types and regions of our country" (2009, p. 227). The British, he thought, had yet to learn this characteristic. He concluded his address by offering his audience a set of recommendations to improve the "spiritual fortunes of your Empire." Standing before the Aberdeen Philosophical Society, Royce could hardly be expected to be considered a part of the developing tradition of philosophical resistance emerging in the United States in the work of Fortune, Cooper, Eastman, or even James.

In 1900, Royce was at the height of his career. He had joined the Harvard faculty in 1883 after receiving his doctorate at Johns Hopkins University and teaching at the new University of California in Berkeley. Following the publication of his books *The Religious Aspect of Philosophy* in 1885 and *The Spirit of Modern Philosophy* in 1892, Royce was acknowledged by those interested in academic philosophy as America's most prominent philosopher. He was best known as an Absolute Idealist, a view identified with the monism James criticized and which held that all of the experienced world was a fully determined part of "The Absolute," or "God." James called the resulting view a "block universe" and rejected it as a view that failed to capture the world's pluralistic nature. As the chief spokesperson of a view that sought to unify every bit of the universe in the being of one Absolute, Royce's address on assimilation easily appears as a practical application of the process of reinforcing a system of imperialism and control.

Such appearances, however, do not capture the central commitments of Royce's philosophy and overlook its place in the tradition of resistance. Royce was born in 1855 in California, the son of a schoolteacher and a gold miner. As the "Forty-Niners" gold rush began to leave thousands of would-be miners without prospects, Royce's father quickly gave up mining and worked at times as a farmer, a grocer, and a traveling salesperson. His mother and sisters largely handled Royce's early education. When he was eleven, Royce entered school in San Francisco and eventually enrolled at the University of California (see Clendenning, 1999).

Near the end of his life, in December 1915, Royce gave a brief autobiographical address at a dinner in his honor at the Walton Hotel in Philadelphia. His earliest memories, he reported, "include a very frequent wonder as to what my elders meant when they said that [his hometown, the mining town of Grass Valley] was a new community" (2005, vol. 1, p. 31). When he finally entered school "redheaded, freckled, countrified, quaint, and unable to play boys' games" (2005, vol. 1, p. 33), the idea of community was present there too, albeit in a different way. His fellow students introduced him to "the majesty of the community," apparently through "disciplinary and persisting" bullying that "on the whole . . . seemed to me 'not joyous but grievous'" (2005, vol. 1, p. 33). Regardless of the good and bad of the communities he experienced, he concluded that throughout his career, "I feel that my deepest motives and problems have centered about the Idea of the Community" (2005, vol. 1, p. 34). His arrival at Harvard as a beginning instructor thrust Royce into another new community in which he once again felt "countrified [and] quaint," and throughout the remainder of his life at Harvard, it seems that he always saw himself as struggling to become part of that community.

What made Royce part of the American tradition of resistance was that his passionate, almost desperate desire to become part of the community of elite and wealthy intellectuals that he encountered in Cambridge and Boston. This desire also led him to seek to understand how individuals were related to communities in general. As Royce developed a philosophical perspective that could offer a conception of what is important to unifying a community, people, or region, he also offered a conception of how one could dissent and rebel against a dominant community and establish new communities. It is no wonder that despite the caricature of his philosophy as a block universe in which freedom is not a possibility, later philosophers used key elements of Royce's work to establish overtly resistant views that informed such movements of liberation as the racialist movement of Du Bois, elements of Addams's settlement house work, the cultural pluralism movement led by Horace Kallen (1882–1974) and Alain LeRoy Locke (1886–1954), and the Civil Rights Movement led by Martin Luther King, Jr. (1929–1968).

Royce's earlier philosophy is easy to take as a kind of monolithic absolutism, but his Gifford lectures (later published as *The World and the Individual*) marked a change. Rather than focusing on static relations to understand the relationship of individuals to the whole or Absolute, Royce explicitly took up the idea that beings are to be understood as things with a purpose. In a review of Royce's Gifford Lectures, Peirce observed that this conception of purposive beings was in fact an expression of a maxim proposed by "another writer, a quarter of a century ago," that is, the "pragmatic maxim" proposed by Peirce himself. Although Peirce criticized significant aspects of Royce's account, he seemed to approve of the direction Royce had taken. Yet despite Peirce's apparent approval of Royce's view as a version of pragmatism, Royce returned to the United States to face growing criticism of his views that culminated, in 1909, with a series of papers highly critical of his work given at the annual meeting of the American Philosophical Association. The papers and subsequent support for them, some by his own former students calling themselves "The New Realists," eventually ended the dominant role Royce and philosophical idealism played in American academic philosophy.

As criticism of his view grew, Royce seems to have been in the process of taking more and more seriously the task of making his philosophy address the problems of human experience. In the second series of Gifford Lectures (given just after the Aberdeen address), Royce sought to turn his attention from the "grand metaphysics" of the first series of lectures to an account of what it was to live in a world of finite, error-prone individuals in search of meaning and community. In the fall of 1903, this direction in his work led him to call together a group of students and friends to directly address the question of how to ensure that philosophy was relevant to life. The group met in a series of what Royce called "philosophical conferences" at his home to discuss each other's work and its practical import. On the first evening they met, Royce explained his purpose: "A group of students and teachers . . . all at least acquainted with the business of sowing the seed of wisdom, and with the task of trying to make it grow may . . . meet together and hold conference with regard to the questions which serve to connect philosophy and life" (1903, pp. 8–9).

Present at the first meeting were three wealthy philanthropists, Reginald C. Robbins (1871–1955), Elizabeth Glendower Evans (1856–1937), and George Dorr (1855–1944), and a number of Royce's present and former students. The students included Ella Lyman Cabot (1866–1934), the wealthy author of several books on ethics; Richard Cabot (1868–1939), Ella's husband and a wealthy and prominent physician who later established the short-lived department of social ethics at Harvard; William Ernest Hocking (1873–1966), later a well-known philosopher in his own right and professor at Harvard; and Mary Whiton Calkins (1863–1930), a professor of philosophy at Wellesley for most of her career. The presence of four women among the nine participants reflects Royce's ongoing teaching commitment first at the Harvard Annex and then at Radcliffe, both programs set up to allow women to pursue advanced study when Harvard rigidly denied women access to the "regular" program.

As some of the participants in the philosophical conferences worked to apply philosophy (particularly Ella and Richard Cabot), Royce also tried to find a way to make more explicit the connection between philosophy and life that he had long recognized. In his 1896 *The Spirit of Modern Philosophy*, Royce explained,

> You philosophize when you reflect critically upon what you are actually doing in the world. What you are doing of course is, in the first place, living. And life involves passions, faiths, doubts, and courage. The critical inquiry into what all these things mean and imply is philosophy. (1896, p. 2)

After hearing Peirce's 1898 Harvard lectures, Royce began a systematic study of the logic of formal relations between wholes and their parts in relation to the Absolute. In 1907, he offered what he called the "philosophy of loyalty" as a practical application of his logic to the problems of daily life. The publication of *The Philosophy of Loyalty* was followed in less than a year by a collection of essays, *Race Questions, Provincialism, and Other American Problems*, that tried to show how his conception of loyalty could be used to address particular problems in the American context.

*The Philosophy of Loyalty* was part of an attempt to reinterpret the Absolute in terms that applied to the experience of finite human beings by considering the relation of individuals to their communities (parts to wholes). The resulting framework established the independence of purposive individuals and the communities that gave them meaning, but also the independence of communities from the individuals on which they depend. For Royce, the key idea was loyalty, defined as "the willing and practical and thoroughgoing devotion of a person to a cause" (1995, p. 9). Human individuals developed self-consciousness in the context of others whom they learned to imitate at an early age. Imitation at first meant that children adopted the purposes and behaviors of others. As they come to realize that they are distinct from others, however, individuals become aware of themselves as independent, in need of purpose and support, and also subject to failure, loss, and error. "Since no [person] can find a plan of life by merely looking within [her] own chaotic nature, [she] has to look without, to the world of social conventions, deeds, and causes" (1995, p. 21). To make sense of such situations, individuals adopt causes or loyalties to provide purpose and support. Causes themselves are not just statements of belief or platforms to guide action but are ongoing collectives that could act such that the cause, in a real sense, could adopt the individual, just as the individual could take up the cause.

Belonging, as Royce came to use the term, was a reciprocal relation in which individuals are loyal to a cause or community, and the community welcomes the individual through the operation of what Royce called "grace." As a result, communities or causes are not reducible to a specific set of individuals. Causes are characterized as collectives that persist beyond any particular group. Members can come and go, live and die, and the cause can live on. Causes can include specific endeavors (such as the cause of saving an endangered species) or can be complex, long-standing organizations such as universities, religious traditions, communities of scientists, and nations. The relation of belonging is not a static relation in which an individual is simply a part of a larger whole; rather, belonging is a kind of activity in which individuals advance the group through their actions but do so in a unique way. The relation of belonging provides a means for individuals to become individuals. At the same time, the community as a whole benefits from the work of individuals while providing a sense of purpose, companionship, and a context in which the efforts of its members can be judged. Royce's logic, developed at the same time he developed his conceptions of loyalty and grace, argued that meaning (truth or error) finally depended on a three-fold or triadic relation. For a claim to hold or fail, it must stand in relation to some object, event, or state of affairs, and do so in light of some framing purpose in terms of which it can succeed or fail. Likewise, in the relation between individuals and their communities: the individual is a part of a community in terms of the causes that frame the relationship. Belonging, like meaning, is a triadic relation.

In his 1911 *Sources of Religious Insight*, Royce proposed that to understand the character of human life, one can "postulate that [humankind] needs to be saved. And religious insight should for us mean insight into the way of salvation" (2001, pp. 8–9). Perhaps recalling his own life, he proposed that people seek "some genuine home land of the spirit, some place or experience" where one's efforts and desires are "justified—and fulfilled" (2001, p. 30). Such fulfillment or salvation emerges only as part of an "object," an ever-wider cause that serves as a unifying end and marks a process in which each individual plays a role. "[If] we are to learn of such an object of insight," he wrote, "we must indeed come into touch with a Power or a Spirit that is in some true sense not-Ourselves. And so we must be able to somehow transcend the boundaries of any *merely* individual experience" (2001, p. 32). James's claims about Royce to the contrary, Royce's view rejected the notion of a block universe and instead recognized the universe, as it is lived, as necessarily plural, composed of diverse individuals and communities that, in their interactions, provided the possibility of salvation, the possibility of making experience meaningful.

This notion of salvation—of making things meaningful—at once shows the risks of Royce's view and its possibilities. It seems to be the case that what people most need is to belong to a larger cause or community. But if that community is one that aims to oppress classes of people through exclusion in some cases and assimilation in others, can such a community really provide salvation? Royce himself talks about the ways in which loyalty to the cause of the Southern Confederacy in the Civil War offered an opportunity for individuals to be loyal and to distinguish themselves in service of a larger cause that depended on them and even loved them. The Confederacy, however, explicitly affirmed the institution of slavery: could loyalty to the Confederacy bring salvation? In Royce's own life, he cultivated close friendships with the wealthiest members of the Cambridge community and sought acceptance and privilege among its elite class. Even as members of the Boston elite debated US imperialism, Royce remained ambivalent. In his work on "race questions," he seemed to avoid challenging the presumption of racial hierarchy and explicitly affirmed policies that were intended to maintain an oppressed class of people. Royce's response to these concerns came at the intersection of logic and loyalty: his conception of community.

In his last major work, *The Problem of Christianity*, Royce sought to answer the broad question of whether one could still be religious in the modern world by examining the idea of a Christian community. To answer his question, he borrowed from Peirce's semiotic theory, his "theory of signs," the idea of interpretation. On this account, a community of interpretation is one in which some past, present, or future shared experience or goal is "interpreted" relative to the community. When confronted with an event or action, the present community "makes sense" of the event or action by judging it in terms of the commitments that form the community. From this perspective, Royce seems to be proposing a view that affirmed the value of any community and its cause, regardless of its consequences. A community would simply judge actions, individuals, and other causes in terms of its own established interests. If it does so, however, then the community itself must be an isolated group that stands in no further relations. Its judgments, lacking any critical standards but those already accepted within the community, could never be wrong. But human communities are not infallible. Like individual human beings, communities can also make mistakes. In order for a community to be wrong, Royce argued, that community must stand in some larger context in which another, broader community can also interpret the action and conclude, from this larger perspective, that the original assessment is an error.

Any given community, on this account, if it is a finite human community subject to error and limitation, must necessarily belong to a larger collective: but what serves as the loyalty that can connect a given community with a larger one, even one that is not yet known? Royce's answer is that every community, as a community formed by loyalty to a cause, shares at least one thing with any other "genuine" community—it recognizes the value of loyalty. Put another way, if a community seeks meaning in its history and has hope for its future, it is also necessarily committed to the process of meaning-making in general. If this is so, a given community in its present loyalties is already implicitly bound up in a larger system of loyalties that will, over time, make the present world with all its limitations meaningful—finding some commitments and actions in error and others in the right.

The evils of the Confederacy are, in effect, judged by a wider community that places it in relation to others. This process of ongoing interpretation, therefore, moves constantly toward a wider and wider perspective. The widest perspective of all, the one not achievable in any limited time frame or by any finite community, is what Royce called the Beloved Community. This infinitely distant community, like the Absolute of his early work, serves to organize and motivate ongoing interpretation. What the Beloved Community (he sometimes called it the

"Great Community") adds is not a final judge (as the Absolute was sometimes understood) but a set of conditions in terms of which communities grow and die.

Beginning with a long essay at the end of the first series of *The World and the Individual*, Royce tried to understand the quest for belonging as a system of order—a logical system—founded on the logical relations established by the actions of willing agents. The process of interpretation that made communities is, in the end, a logical process that formed, for Royce, the fabric of the universe. It is an inherently unstable fabric, assuring members of every community that they must be ready to give up their strongest commitments in light of wider and wider perspectives. Royce's logic, even as it affirmed the potential value of causes of all sorts, also had the potential to undermine the dominant system by showing the dominant system's limitations. Royce's logic and theory of community were left to others to develop formally and informally as the tradition of resistance developed in the twentieth century.

Royce's own resistance never stood against dominant society in its particulars—at least not systematically so. Instead, it was a resistance that laid bare a particular vision of individual agents and the communities they were a part of in order to see that, despite their present righteousness, their deepest convictions could be mistaken. For his students, including Du Bois, Locke, and Kallen, the same notion that accounted for a community's ability to assimilate and exclude also showed what was required to resist: the wider perspective of outsiders, the presence of not-Ourselves, and alternative causes and communities that could challenge and speak truth to power.

Yet by the time *The Problem of Christianity* was published in 1912, his idealism (or as Royce called it, "Absolute Pragmatism") was already vanishing from the scene. At the center of the attacks raised by his former students was the rejection of Royce's conception of reality. Idealism held that things of the world, including material objects, thoughts, moral principles, scientific laws, and so on are all connected by ideas, so that reality itself is necessarily a matter of ideas alone. Realists, in contrast, held that things are independent of ideas and so can be found in experience in a way that the "finding" or knowing has no effect on the things found. Some of Royce's students argued that by rejecting this conception of reality, his idealism was simply incompatible with science, which discovered real things in the world.

Ralph Barton Perry (1876–1957), a student of Royce and James and later a philosopher at Harvard, charged that idealism suffered from what he called the "egocentric predicament." The idealist claimed, Perry argued, that human beings could only interact with the world through the knowledge relation. This means that to encounter anything at all required that one know something. There was, according to Perry, no way for an idealist to encounter something directly, whether it was a thing of ordinary experience like an apple or a table or things in a specialized experience like chemical compounds or biological species. Instead, things are encountered through ideas and, thanks to this mediation, ideas always intervene between the knower and what's real. The problem with the idealist view, Perry argued, was that, on the contrary, ordinary knowing and science encounter the world directly. "The realist," Perry explained in 1902, "believes reality to be a *datum, a somewhat that is given independently of whatever ideas may be formed about it*" (in Auxier, 2000, vol. 2, p. 97). William Pepperell Montague (1873–1953) described a position like Perry's in 1907 as the view that "things do not depend for their existence upon the fact that we know them, and that consequently, they can continue in what is called existence during those intervals of time in which no subject [knower] is aware of them" (quoted in Werkmeister, 1949, p. 373).

In July 1910, Perry and Montague, along with Edwin B. Holt (1873–1946), Walter T. Marvin (1872–1944), Walter B. Pitkin (1878–1953), and Edward Gleason Spaulding (1873–1940), joined together to form a philosophical movement to challenge the dominance of idealism and published "The Program and First Platform of Six Realists." The group called their emerging philosophical view "The New Realism," and in 1912 the six realists published a volume of essays they called "Cooperative Studies in Philosophy" aimed at clarifying and advancing their view. They aimed to replace idealism and its emphasis on the knower as part of the knowing process with the view that "the knower himself may, in a great majority of cases, be disregarded and the object explained in its own terms" (Holt et al., 1912, p. 41). Realism "may afford a basis for a more profitable intercourse [of philosophy] with the special sciences" (p. 36). Rather than locating science within a larger philosophical system, realism would establish philosophy as a special science: "Philosophers will be looked to for breadth of generalization, for refinement of criticism, and for the solution of such problems as are peculiarly connected with the limits of generalization and criticism" (p. 42). By 1915, New Realism had displaced idealism as the dominant view in the American academy.

In 1914, as the New Realists celebrated their prominence in academic philosophy, the First World War began when the heir to the throne of the Austro-Hungarian empire was assassinated while riding in a car through the streets of Sarajevo, Bosnia. On May 7, 1915, a German U-boat sank the RMS Lusitania. Royce had long held Great Britain and Germany as examples of enlightened communities committed to the largest cause of meaning-making—of being loyal to loyalty—and so somehow above the base practices of war and destruction. The killing of 1,198 people, including several of Royce's current and former students, made Royce realize the potential for evil that should have been visible since Royce first visited Germany or stood before the philosophers at Aberdeen. In the wake of this very present disaster, it was suddenly clear that the world of ongoing interpretation gave no insurance against violence, oppression, and war.

Royce struggled in his work over the next year, writing and rewriting discussions of loyalty and interpretation to find a way that the conditions of meaning-making could also provide salvation in the face of the chaos of world war. On the dais at the Walton Hotel in December 1915, he concluded his autobiographical address by asking,

> But why should you give so kind an attention to me at a moment when the deepest, the most vital, and the most practical interest[s] of the whole community of mankind are indeed imperiled, when the spirit of mankind is overwhelmed with a cruel and undeserved sorrow, when the enemies of mankind often seem as if they were about to triumph? (2005, p. 35)

In the end, Royce realized the need for active resistance, but it was too late. It was only later that the resistance inherent in Royce's understanding of communities, agents, and purposes would begin to be realized. He died the following September as the Battle of Verdun entered its ninth month and the United States debated entering a war that would eventually take 16.5 million military and civilian lives.

## Primary Text

Royce, J. (2005). *The Basic Writings of Josiah Royce*, vols. 2, ed. with a new introduction by John McDermott. New York: Fordham University Press.

# CHAPTER 10
# WAR, ANARCHISM, AND SEX
## EMMA GOLDMAN AND MARGARET SANGER

Twelve days before Royce died in his Cambridge home in 1916, Woodrow Wilson (1856–1924) received the official notification of his nomination for president. In his acceptance speech, Wilson reaffirmed his policy of neutrality in the war in Europe. He said,

> We have been neutral not only because it was the fixed and traditional policy of the United States to stand aloof from the politics of Europe . . . but also because it was manifestly our duty to prevent, if it were possible, the indefinite extension of the fires of hate and desolation kindled by that terrible conflict. (Wilson, 1918, pp. 308–9)

While Wilson's policy was never strict and permanent neutrality in the European conflict, his campaign was founded on the slogan "He kept us out of war!" The claim, specific policies aside, and his support for progressive labor legislation, including child labor laws and the eight-hour workday, led him to reelection in November. He was inaugurated on March 5, 1917, and just one month later, on April 12, he spoke to a joint meeting of Congress and asked for a declaration of war against Germany and its allies.

The beginning of the war marked the end of a long period of labor struggle and of a unified political opposition to the domination of industry and financial institutions. The changing American society led to changes in higher education including space for more students, greater specialization in study, the increase of science and business-related work, and the professionalization of the study of philosophy. The American Philosophical Association (APA) was founded in 1900 to provide a framework for professional philosophy as a discipline in colleges and universities. Speaking in May 1919, just after the war ended, the president of the APA, Hartley Burr Alexander, observed, "The world has changed since 1914 . . . Then we believed, with all our ostensible souls, . . . in our superiority over all that was humanly past and in our ability to insure progress through the future" (quoted in Campbell, 2006, p. 201).

Once war was declared, the government and the system of higher education united in their support of the war. In his commencement address in June 1917, Nicholas Murray Butler, president of Columbia University, said that once war was declared, "What had been tolerated before became intolerable now. What had been wrongheadedness was now sedition. What had been folly was now treason." The implications of this new situation were clear:

> In your presence, I speak by authority for the whole University . . . when I say with all possible emphasis that there is and will be no place in Columbia University either on the rolls of its faculties or on the rolls of its students for any person who opposes or who counsels opposition to the effective enforcement of the laws of the United States, or who acts, speaks or writes treason. (Butler, 1922, p. 451)

In October, Butler dismissed James McKean Cattell, a well-known psychologist at Columbia, for speaking against sending US soldiers to fight in Europe.

In May 1917, Congress reestablished the Selective Service and began to draft young men for military service in the war against Germany and its allies. A few days after Butler's address, the United States enacted the Espionage Act, making it illegal to aid declared enemies of the United States, "to cause insubordination, disloyalty, mutiny or refusal of duty in the military," or to interfere with recruiting or enlistment in the military. In May 1918, the act was extended by the Sedition Act, making it illegal to utter, print, write or publish "any disloyal, profane, scurrilous, or abusive language or language intended to cause contempt, scorn, contumacy, or disrepute as regards the form of government of the United States." It also became illegal to advocate, teach or defend such speech or other actions intended to undermine the government (Chafee, 1920, pp. 42–5). The law was quickly put to use when Eugene Debs, who was a leader in the Chicago, Burlington, & Quincy Railroad and Pullman Strikes and founder of the international union Industrial Workers of the World, was arrested in Ohio for speaking against the draft. Debs was convicted and sentenced to ten years in prison and denied the right to vote or run for office.

In the fall of 1918, as James Campbell observed, "the American system of higher education became fully involved with the war when it was virtually nationalized" (2006, p. 209). A memo from the War Department made this clear: "During the war you are no longer degree-giving institutions, but rather short-course training schools for the specific purpose of preparing officers for the army and navy" (quoted in Campbell, 2006, p. 210). The Sedition Act and parts of the Espionage Act were repealed in 1921, though elements of the Espionage Act remain in effect today. President Harding commuted Debs's sentence after the Sedition Act was repealed, also in 1921, but Debs received no official pardon.

While these laws and broad governmental reach could be seen as innovations in wartime, they can also be seen as a continuation of policies and practices established at the turn of the century in response to labor activism, demands for equality and justice for racial minorities and immigrants, demands for rights (including voting rights for women), and activism for social support for those faced with poverty, old age, and illness. While some of this activism was haphazard, some was organized explicitly around the principles of communism, socialism, and anarchism.

The twentieth century began with the assassination of President McKinley in 1901 by an assassin who claimed to be an anarchist. In response, anarchists and socialists around the country were arrested, including the Russian immigrant, writer, and activist Emma Goldman. In the public's mind, socialists and anarchists were the same people, though in reality they each represented different approaches to the economic and social tensions of the time. For instance, some anarchists approved of the use of violence, while others did not. Similarly, some socialists believed that economic redistribution was all that was needed, while others did not. What both groups shared at the time was membership from the working class and recent immigrants. This made them suspect and vulnerable.

After McKinley's assassination by an anarchist, the United States passed the Anarchist Exclusion Act in 1903. After the First World War, anarchist activities again gained public attention, and J. Edgar Hoover, the new director of the General Intelligence Division of what would become the FBI, began looking for potential anarchists. At the same time, Jane Addams emerged as one of a handful of people willing to defend people arrested as anarchists. People Addams knew, and knew to be nonviolent, were arrested without warrants and held without representation. Addams raised their bail and, in a speech in Chicago, declared, "An attempt is being made to deport an entire political party." All "these radicals" sought, she said, was "the right of free speech and free thought, nothing more than is guaranteed to them under the Constitution of the United States" (quoted in Davis, 1973, p. 260). Rather than jailing "hundreds of poor laboring men and women," they should be allowed the chance to voice their positions. "Free speech is the greatest safety valve of our United States. Let us give these people a chance to explain their beliefs and desires. Let us end this suppression and spirit of intolerance which is making of America another autocracy" (quoted in Davis, 1973, p. 261). The next day, the Chicago newspapers carried the headlines, "Reds Upheld by Jane Addams as Good Americans" and "Jane Addams Favors the Reds" (p. 261).

Someone more central to the history of anarchism in the United States, though, was Emma Goldman (1869–1940). Born in Lithuania, she came to the United States in 1885 at the age of sixteen to escape the prospect of an arranged marriage. Joining a sister already in Rochester, New York, she found US industrialization particularly brutal as it glorified profit and removed any sense of community from the workers. She was attracted to the socialists but found them less inspiring than the anarchists. Both groups were active in the changing social, political, and economic landscape. "Between 1881 and 1906 more than thirty thousand strikes and lockouts took place in America alone, involving over nine and a half million workers, and affecting thousands of businesses of every sort. Hundreds of these confrontations ended with state or federal troops being called in" (Gornick, 2011, p. 14). The Haymarket Riot crystallized Goldman's path. In Chicago on May 4, 1886, eight years before the Pullman Strike, a rally was held in Haymarket Square to support striking workers. A pipe bomb was thrown at the police who opened fire and the result was eighteen dead. Four labor leaders—all anarchists—were accused, tried, and hung in 1887. The four were not generally thought to be guilty and so the case gained worldwide attention. Rather than bringing justice, the trial and executions were viewed as an effort to silence labor.

By 1889, Goldman was in New York City in the middle of would-be revolutionary immigrants. In the years before the First World War, according to Gornick, "there were more than three hundred socialist publications . . . originating in every part of the country" while "between 1902 and 1912 the Socialist Party's membership swelled to well over a hundred thousand and socialists were able to deliver nearly a million votes to Eugene Debs when he ran for president in 1912" (2011, p. 19). In the end, most of this energy focused on reform and participation in social democracy to change, rather than destroy, existing structures. The anarchists were less accommodating of capitalism, though, and saw the need for an armed struggle. Given the mood of the country, by 1893 Goldman became a popular and effective speaker. She began a speech at Union Square in New York: "Men and women, do you not realize that the State is the worst enemy you have? It is a machine that crushes you in order to sustain the ruling class, your masters. . . . The state is the pillar of capitalism, and it is ridiculous to expect any redress from it." Unless workers demanded their rights, the rich "will go on robbing." She urged the crowd to "Demonstrate before the palaces of the rich. Demand work. If they do not give you work, demand bread. If they deny you both, take bread. It is your sacred right!" (1931, vol. 1, p. 122). Later, the speech was used to justify her arrest for inciting people to commit illegal acts (i.e., stealing bread). Confirming her effectiveness, J. Edgar Hoover is said to have declared her "the most dangerous woman in America"—something he is also supposed to have said of Jane Addams.

In 1892, the Carnegie Steel Company (under the management of Henry Clay Frick) and the Amalgamated Association of Iron and Steel Workers clashed in Homestead, Pennsylvania, over Andrew Carnegie's attempt to eliminate collective bargaining. Pinkerton guards were called in to disperse the strikers. With as many as sixteen dead, there was general condemnation of the use of the Pinkertons. In response, Goldman and her partner Alexander (Sasha) Berkman (1870–1936) decided to assassinate Frick. Berkman shot and stabbed Frick, but Frick survived, and Berkman went to jail. Goldman disavowed violence after the assassination attempt but would not condemn others who felt compelled to use it. She did think violence, though problematic, was less dangerous than passivity.

In and out of jail, including an arrest after McKinley's assassination in 1901, Goldman continued to speak, write, and organize. She worked to stop the deportation of anarchists after the Anarchist Exclusion Act was passed in 1903. She founded the anarchist magazine *Mother Earth* in 1906. It ceased publication in 1917 when fear of promoting communism led the US Post Office to refuse to deliver it. She spoke and wrote about anarchism, free love, jealousy, the limits of monogamy, homosexuality, birth control, and Friedrich Nietzsche (1844–1900). The economic problems were not the whole of the issue for her. She read Nietzsche, Henri Bergson (1859–1941), Sigmund Freud (1856–1939), James, and Dewey. She mingled with suffragists, unionists, and settlement workers. These influences helped her see the complexity of the economic and social issues and helped her form her view that within collective action, there needed to be support for individual development and expression. This understanding of the individual would prove to be an important modification of her anarchist views.

Goldman was important for the feminist movement as well, even as she was in tension with many of the main figures of that movement. While many found common cause in birth control, Goldman rejected the efforts for legal reform and equal rights as she thought that the legal system and the government ought to be abolished. She also argued, despite her own example, that women's primary focus should be on motherhood. She preferred a focus on the right to love and sex over equal political rights. Women's freedom and independence will come, Goldman argued, "first by asserting herself as a personality, and not as a sex commodity. Second by refusing the right to anyone over her body; by refusing to be a servant to God, the State, society, the husband, the family" (1969, p. 211). Women also need to free themselves "from the fear of public opinion and public condemnation. Only that, and not the ballot, will set woman free, will make her a force hitherto unknown in the world, a force for real love, for peace, for harmony" (1969, p. 211). Rather than seeking the right to vote, Goldman was interested in women's right to love and be with whomever they chose without state sanction, including the possibility of multiple partners at one time or over time. She challenged both governmental restrictions and cultural limits to the expression of love. State marriage laws, laws criminalizing adultery and homosexuality, as well as the social habits that inhibit individual behavior, were all to be overturned. Just as the individual cannot be contained, love cannot be contained.

A partner in Goldman's call for free love and access to birth control was Margaret Sanger (1879–1966). Born to a socialist father and married to a socialist, Sanger found her calling in the cause of birth control. By 1911, Sanger and Goldman associated with the same circles and influenced one another. Sanger saw no way to address poverty as long as women were expected to be perpetually pregnant. Frequent and multiple births harmed the health of women, produced less healthy children, and meant large families with little support for each family member. Larger families with few economic opportunities also led to a cycle of poverty where the next generation would suffer from the same conditions. Birth control meant smaller families and also made it possible for women to pursue professions or even real love (for children or husbands). In addition to working to make birth control available for women (since men were not inclined to use condoms), she started naturalization classes for recent immigrants and taught English to some of her fellow prisoners when she was in jail.

Sanger's fight for birth control brought her up against the Comstock Law of 1873, which was enacted to prevent the publication of articles on venereal disease and to keep obscene, lurid, lascivious materials out of the US mail. This same law was used against Goldman's *Mother Earth*, Max Eastman's *The Masses*, and Sanger's newsletter *The Woman Rebel*. Anthony Comstock (1844–1915), the most visible advocate of the act that carried his name, also went after art and store mannequins as providing too much sexual temptation. He sent women to doctors' offices as decoys and arrested doctors who supplied information on contraception. By discouraging doctors and threatening to humiliate women, Comstock helped to force women to seek help outside legitimate health care. As a midwife, Sanger saw the effects of attempts at self-induced abortions and the work of disreputable doctors. Not only were women maids and sex slaves of their husbands, they often died as a result. While others, including Goldman, were speaking on birth control (and getting arrested), Sanger went further. In addition to giving actual advice on how to achieve "family limitation" in pamphlets, she started birth control leagues and opened clinics. With the help of the physician and activist Havelock Ellis (1859–1939), Sanger researched various methods of birth control and promoted the use of diaphragms by smuggling them into the country from Europe.

Critics of Sanger sometimes accused her of basing her cause on classism and racism. While it was true that she argued for limiting population growth, she advocated that all classes and races limit their reproduction. However, after the 1927 Supreme Court decision finding involuntary sterilization constitutional under some circumstances, Sanger also became "an outspoken advocate" of the practice (Baker, 2011, p. 223). The court decision, written by Oliver Wendell Holmes, Jr. (1841–1935), concluded, "[i]t is better for all the world, if instead of waiting to execute the degenerate offspring for a crime or to let them starve from imbecility, societies can prevent the genetically unfit from continuing their own kind" (quoted in Baker, 2011, p. 223). Given the popularity of various eugenicist views at this time it is not surprising that Sanger also endorsed an argument that birth control—voluntary or not—could help humanity.

In her 1922 book, *The Pivot of Civilization*, Sanger proposed the American Birth Control League (the predecessor of Planned Parenthood). The founding principles illustrated the tensions in Sanger's view. The League was to provide "instruction by the Medical profession to mothers and potential mothers in harmless and reliable methods of Birth Control" (Sanger, 1922, p. 282) as a means of improving women's and children's health. Birth control allowed a family to have fewer children spaced further apart. She believed that less frequent pregnancies would result in healthier babies as the mother had more time for her body to recover and so nurture another fetus. It also allowed for the family to provide better food, health care, and education for each child. At the same time, the League would also support "[s]terilization of the insane and feeble-minded and the encouragement of this operation upon those afflicted with inherited or transmissible diseases" (p. 282). With these practical resources, women deciding when to bear children and not "bringing forth the unfit," Sanger was convinced that birth control would foster what she called "racial progress," also to be promoted by the League (pp. 282–3). "We shall see that it will save the precious metals of racial culture," she said in *Women and the New Race* in 1920, "fused into an amalgam of physical perfection, mental strength and spiritual progress. Such an American race [would contain] the best of all racial elements" (1920, p. 46). For Sanger, like others in the feminist movement before her, the cause of other oppressed groups came into conflict with the cause of improving the circumstances of women.

While birth control placed women at the center of human development, her vision of progress also involved involuntarily sterilizing those whom society found unfit, despite the difficulty of establishing just who counts as unfit (a problem she acknowledged in *The Pivot of Civilization* (1922, p. 181ff.)). Her vision of a kind of genetic "melting pot" (1920, p. 46) also overrode the value of cultural differences manifested in race and ethnicity and so denied the value of distinct peoples as it mixed future generations into a single "American race." By connecting cultural traits and physiology, Sanger thought that "breeding" would not only foster "better" physically fit humans, but a better culture as well. Sanger's vision was not unique. José Vasconcelos (1882–1959), a Mexican philosopher who lectured at Harvard in the 1920s, also advocated for an American race formed of the amalgamation of Indigenous and European peoples. He called this the "Cosmic Race." In both cases, however, the visions marked the conflict of oppressions and resolved the conflict in favor of a particular set of concerns.

The subtleties of different views of eugenics became less clear with the passage of time and in light of the experience of Nazi Germany. Sanger herself condemned the example of Nazi Germany and argued that involuntary sterilization should never be practiced on a targeted group. Other American advocates of eugenics, such as Madison Grant (1865–1937), argued for the conservation of the "white race" through the practices of eugenics to foster "those hereditary traits through which the principles of our religious, political and social foundations were laid down [while preventing] their insidious replacement by traits of less noble character" (1922, p. ix). Sanger in fact supported a complex approach to eugenics but courted the support of those who advocated involuntary sterilization and spoke of "race suicide" as White middle- and upper-class families began having fewer children. She realized these associations could interfere with her work to improve conditions for the poor, immigrants, and African Americans. She noted this concern when she recruited leading African American pastors to help assure the African American community that "race extermination" was not her purpose when she opened a clinic in Harlem in 1930. This mixed picture of her work remains today and separates Sanger from her more radical friends, such as Goldman. Her willingness to compromise allowed her to continue her birth control activism, even as some of her supporters advocated for and carried out racially targeted forced sterilization, while Goldman's revolutionary approach led to her deportation.

Goldman's radicalism, while rooted in concerns shared by many in the late 1800s and early 1900s, became less tolerated as tensions around the world entered into overt conflict. As the United States entered war in Europe in 1917, Goldman was tried for sedition, served two years in jail, and then was deported. Goldman was just one example of the many who fell prey to repressive laws like the Espionage Act and the Sedition Act. Those who voiced dissent could face fines of 10,000 dollars or a prison term of twenty years. While many were arrested on charges of disloyalty, only a few of the cases were upheld in court. Nonetheless, the laws served the purpose of stifling criticism of the war. Goldman criticized this shift in US policy when she spoke at her trial. She stated that the conscientious objector played an important role in a free society. At times, good people must stand against the law. She went on to give examples from world history as well as the recent work of abolitionists in the United States. She warned that the eyes of the world were upon the United States now, "not because of sympathy for us or agreement with Anarchism. They are upon you because it must be decided sooner or later whether we are justified in telling people that we will give them democracy in Europe when we have no democracy here" (1917, p. 65). She demonstrated the sincerity of her views when, upon her deportation, she ended up in the Soviet Union. Eventually, she left the Soviet Union more than disappointed. She regarded it as a "colossal fraud wrapped in the Red mantle of 'October'" (1931, p. 928). She alienated her remaining radical friends with her critique of the Soviet Union and the rest of her life was lonely and difficult.

The liberal intellectuals of the time were not exempt from social pressure as they too got caught up in the call for "patriotism" and the demand to support government policy against dissenters and, in 1917, to support Wilson's call to arms. While some, like Randolph Bourne (1886–1918), were critical of this capitulation, others, like Dewey and Du Bois, seemed to shift their positions. Jane Addams did not.

Like the loneliness suffered by Goldman, Jane Addams found herself deserted by friends and labeled a traitor after the United States entered the First World War. She could not support the war and instead actively worked for peace. She was elected the first president of the Women's Peace Party (WPP) in 1915 and went to a meeting of women at The Hague to help make the voices of women heard in opposition to the escalating conflict. This effort resulted in the formation of the International Committee of Women for Permanent Peace (ICWPP) and Addams was elected president of this association as well. "Our protest may be feeble," she stated, "but the world progresses . . . only in proportion to the moral energy exerted by the men and women living in it; social advance must be pushed forward by the human will and understanding united for conscious ends" (2005, p. 7).

Addams's peace work took on a whole new meaning after the Germans sank the Lusitania in May 1915. On July 5, Addams returned from her efforts in Europe and four days later delivered a report on her journey to a crowd at Carnegie Hall. In the last minutes of her talk, she reported that soldiers with whom she had spoken said that they received alcohol and drugs from their officers before they were ordered to charge across "no-man's land" into the enemy's entrenched positions. The following day she was attacked in the press. For many, her description had called into question the bravery of the soldiers she interviewed because they had carried out their attack under the influence. Given the mood of the country, the criticism spread. Theodore Roosevelt called for the country to enter the war and criticized Addams and the other women who had gone to The Hague, saying that they were "actively engaged in exciting contempt and derision for themselves and their own country by crying for peace without justice and without redress of wrongs." They were, he said, "amiable peace prattlers" who "utter[ed] silly platitudes which were of comfort to the wrongdoers" (1916, pp. 174–5). All pacifists came under attack.

Nonetheless, Addams remained active. Speaking before the House Committee on Military Affairs in 1916, she said: "I do not want to say that men are more emotional than women," but they are "much more likely to catch this war spirit and respond to this panic. They think they must prepare to defend the country, even when there is no enemy to prepare against. . . . Women are not quite so easily excited" (2005, pp. 123–4). One year later, the United States entered the war, passed the Conscription Act and the Espionage Act, and President Wilson called on war critics to stop their critique out of a sense of patriotism. Many of Addams's friends did just that, and she was left isolated and dispirited.

Despite her increasing isolation, Addams worked on behalf of men jailed for being conscientious objectors, helped found the National Civil Liberties Bureau (later the ACLU), and worked to provide food relief to the citizens of the warring nations. In the end, the platforms for peace she had worked so hard to formulate with the WPP and the ICWPP came to influence President Wilson's Fourteen Points, though these were not included in the final treaties. As the war ended, Addams remained suspect in the eyes of many. In January 1919, her name topped a list of sixty-two radicals prepared by Archibald Stevenson, a member of the US Military Intelligence Service. According to the *New York Times* on January 24, 1919, the list included other such "radicals" as Charles Beard, a historian at Columbia University; Addams's Hull House colleague, Emily Green Balch; Quaker mystic Rufus Jones; Social Gospel leader Vida Scudder; peace activist Lillian Wald; socialist labor leader Eugene Debs; and philosopher and sociologist Elsie Clews Parsons. The list became part of the Lusk Report commissioned by the New York legislature and used to make a case for new laws requiring, among other things, that teachers certify their loyalty to the United States. Governor Al Smith, later a Democratic candidate for president, vetoed the laws.

Despite her isolation and ongoing criticism of her views, she persisted in international activism on behalf of peace. As already mentioned, she defended many who were accused of being anarchists and continually defended free speech. While being investigated by J. Edgar Hoover for her work with the ACLU in 1920, Addams celebrated the passing of the Nineteenth Amendment, granting women the right to vote. Her life's work was recognized when she was awarded the Nobel Peace Prize in 1931, the first American woman to receive the prize. She died in 1935 at the age of seventy-four.

### Primary Texts

Addams, Jane (2002). *Peace and Bread in Time of War*, intro. Katherine Joslin. Urbana: University of Chicago Press.

Goldman, Emma (1969). *Anarchism and Other Essays*, intro. Richard Drinnon. New York: Dover Publications.

# CHAPTER 11
# DEMOCRACY AND SOCIAL ETHICS
## JOHN DEWEY

Jane Addams was at John Dewey's seventieth birthday celebration in 1930 and spoke with admiration of his work despite their disagreements over the First World War. In reply, Dewey said,

> I have learned many things from Jane Addams. I notice that with her usual modesty she attributed to me some of the things in Chicago which she and her colleagues in Hull House did. One of the things that I have learned from her is the enormous value of mental non-resistance, of tearing away the armor-plate of prejudice, of convention, isolation that keeps one from sharing to the full in the larger and even the more unfamiliar and alien ranges of the possibilities of human life and experience. (Boydston, 1967–90, vol. 5, p. 421, hereafter LW 5, p. 421)

The relationship between Addams and Dewey was long and mutually transformative. But their responses to the issue of the war pointed to some of their differences.

While Dewey had reservations about entering the war, he eventually came to support such action, disappointing many of his friends and former students. In "Democracy and Loyalty in the Schools," written in 1917, Dewey explained that "[e]ver since President Wilson asked for a breaking of relations with Germany, and afterwards for war against that country," he had been a "complete sympathizer with the part played by this country in this war." The war, he said, "is not merely a war of armies," it was "a war of peoples." In his judgment, "we ought not to be neutral when the war comes home in one form or another and to talk about being neutral is to talk foolishness" (MW 10, p. 158).

On the same page, however, he lamented the wastefulness of people "running about and making irresponsible accusations against opinions of people they do not happen to agree with." Speaking in defense of teachers who had been dismissed on charges so vague that no defense would be possible, he continued, "I do not think that to defeat Prussianism abroad it is necessary to establish Prussianism at home" (p. 159) and likened the treatment of the teachers to the Inquisition (p. 161). Those who prosecuted the case against the teachers, he observed, did not charge them with "overt disloyalty; they were charged with a lack of active or aggressive loyalty which [the prosecutors claimed] the state has the right to demand, in wartime particularly, from its paid servants" (p. 173). From the perspective of education, Dewey thought that what was needed was a demonstration of independent thinking as an example for students to follow. Dewey also opposed universal military service as a kind of education that would help assimilate recent immigrants. He gave two reasons. First, military service did not result in the kind of independence of thought he sought from education. Second, he objected to the idea of the melting pot. One of the strengths of the United States is its multicultural character. He argued that if America "is not to be a cross-fertilization of our various strains, it had better be a juxtaposition of alien elements than an amalgam of the barracks, an amalgam whose uniformity would hardly go deeper than the uniforms of the soldiers." He worried about using fear of "enemies" as a way to attain unity. "To stir up fear and dislike of home countries as a means of securing love of an adopted country does not seem a promising procedure" (p. 185).

Instead, Dewey thought that education aimed at critical thinking could unite the American people. "I can . . . imagine the American people arming universally to put an end to war. I cannot imagine them doing it to defend themselves against a possible and remote danger. The American people is more idealistic and more high-spirited than its critics" (p. 190). Even as Dewey supported the war, he sought peace and critiqued the effects of war. He saw how emotions were used to create an unthinking partisanship that interfered with the use of intelligence. Under these conditions, fair and impartial thinking became suspect. "Impartiality and detachment of mind are suspicious traits. A loyal and serious soul, so it seems, does not weight evidence too closely or reach conclusions too scrupulously when his country's fate hangs in the balance" (p. 216). What attracted many to this kind of simplistic partisanship was "a sweetly complete sense" of certainty that accompanied it. Such partisanship is "so undivided as to leave room for but one kind of thinking and one form of belief. . . . In it the discriminations and doubts which always accompany the efforts of a critical intelligence are submerged" (p. 216). Nonetheless, he remained hopeful that freedom was not in real jeopardy since history demonstrated that restricting freedom was self-defeating.

In addition to defending domestic liberties, Dewey defended Addams's approach to peace even as he was publicly critical of pacifists as the United States entered the war.

> The best statement which I have seen made of the pacifist position since we entered the war is that of Miss Addams. . . . She holds that the popular impression that pacifism meant abstinence and just keeping out of trouble is wrong; that it stood for a positive international polity. . . . In short, the pacifists "urge upon the United States not indifference to moral issues and to the fate of liberty and democracy, but a strenuous endeavor to lead all nations of the earth into an organized international life." (p. 266)

So, even while he supported the war and critiqued some pacifists, he affirmed the work of constructive pacifists, who sought to create the conditions for peace and guard against those who sought to stir up discord. Unfortunately, many put the ability to destroy other nations above the ability to cooperate with them. "[M]any influential and well-meaning persons attempt to foster the growth of an inclusive nationalism by appeal to our fears, our suspicions, our jealousies and our latent hatreds" (pp. 203–4).

Despite these responses, many saw Dewey's support of the war as a compromise that revealed a weakness in his philosophical outlook. Randolph Bourne, a former student who had become a popular editorial writer, was disappointed that Dewey sensed "so little the sinister forces," was more concerned about the "excesses" of the pacifists than "the excesses of military policy," and could "feel only amusement at the idea that anyone should try to conscript thought, and assume[d] that the war-technique can be used without trailing along with it the mob fanaticisms, the injustices and hatred, that are organically bound up with it" (2002, p. 105). Bourne argued that while Dewey's philosophy might be fine in a time of peace, it was inadequate when faced with serious conflict. He saw Dewey as an advocate of an instrumentalism without values and so as dangerous. Bourne acknowledged that this was not a fault with Dewey's thought itself, which had values guiding growth, but it was a danger for Dewey and those who took up his philosophy without remaining committed to those values. Bourne's critique resulted in many young radicals becoming disillusioned with Dewey's pragmatism, which, as a result, began to lose favor as a philosophy of resistance. Yet Bourne's assessment may not have been fair.

While being critiqued by people like Bourne for "selling out," Dewey did his share of critiquing and in so doing asserted a set of values that cut against the ways the war was conducted. He worried about those liberals who tolerated limitations on free speech, as this could create the very conditions they sought to protest.

> [I]t behooves liberals who believe in the war to be more aggressive than they have been in their opposition to those reactionaries who also believe in war—and who believe that loud denunciation of treason on sight is the best way to regain a political prestige of late badly discredited. (MW 10, p. 295)

Dewey's position before and during the war was clearly complicated. While Addams was defending anarchists in Chicago, Dewey was publicly critical of unthinking responses to anarchist protests. "Having witnessed the spectacle of continuous wholesale bombing," Dewey wrote, "can we henceforth reprimand the sporadic and private bombing of the anarchist without putting our tongues in our cheeks?" In the case of anarchist violence, "How are we to decide whether this willingness to resort to the threat of force is a pledge of the final loyalty to ideals, or an evidence of growing contempt for the precious fruits of human labor, the only things which stand between us and the brutes?" (p. 211). Questions about the use of force and the means and ends of the war led to further questions about the use of force by anarchists and by those who tried to suppress them, and thereby extended such questions to all aspects of current social conditions.

"From the barracks it is but a step to the police court and the jail," Dewey wrote in the *New Republic* in 1916.

> Behind the prison rises the smoke of the factory, and from the factory the road lead [*sic*] to the counting-house and the bank. Is our civic life other than a disguised struggle of brute force? Are the policemen and the jailer the true guardians and representatives of the social order? Is our industrial life other than a continued combat to sift the strong from the weak, a war where only external arms and armor are changed? Is the state itself anything but organized force? (pp. 211–12)

From this perspective, "force" took on two different characters. When "harnessed to the accomplishment of ends," force becomes the "power of doing work." On the other hand, "[e]xactly the same force running wild is called violence" and, he concluded, the objection to violence is not that it involves the use of force, but that it is a waste of force; it uses force "idly or destructively" (p. 212). Dewey sought to challenge the idea that force is necessarily violent and that uses of force are always evil. Law, from this perspective, is one way of "harnessing" force in a way that would accomplish work.

While Bourne was concerned that Dewey did not provide a means of determining values that would prevent the "work" accomplished from becoming simple conquest, Dewey argued that values needed to be determined in light of the circumstances using "intelligence," critical thinking that sought to promote growth and enrich experience. It was the chaos of force unguided by law that led to destruction of the sort that had enveloped Europe and became more than just a waste of energy. Intervention in the war in Europe was a way of restoring order and directing force toward the ongoing benefit of humanity. Pacifists who rejected intervention risked advocating still more chaos and destruction. Pacifists, it seemed, were unwilling to look at force within a context and did little or nothing to create the conditions where it was not a likely means to be employed. Dewey concluded, "Until pacifism puts its faith in constructive, inventive intelligence instead of an appeal to emotions and in exhortation, the disparate unorganized forces of the world will continue to develop outbreaks of violence" (p. 214).

Dewey and Addams both opposed the conscription of the youth, especially without exceptions for conscientious objectors. While Addams opposed the Conscription Act (the military draft) and worked on behalf of jailed objectors, she did not stop Hull House from hosting a draft registration station. Dewey supported efforts to try to provide noncombat options for conscientious objectors. He noted that the youth were in a difficult position given the rapid shift from peace activism to war patriotism they were witnessing in the country. President Wilson had provided a bridge by arguing that the defeat of Germany was the way to secure peace. Dewey found it unfortunate that many of the youth quickly moved from "thou shalt not kill" to "obey the law" without thinking for themselves (p. 263).

Dewey's position was made even more complex by his support for teachers who were fired for being "unpatriotic" and his testimony against military training in schools on the grounds that it frustrated the development of critical thinking, even as he criticized pacifists for their resistance. He had seen the kind of violence and repression that can occur when fear rules people's lives, and he focused on education as a way to foster a more thoughtful and critical approach to the issue of war (p. 20). By the time the United States faced the decision to enter the Second World War, he more clearly argued that democratic ends required democratic means—not military intervention or fascist governments.

When the First World War ended on November 11, 1918, Dewey's hope that force would bring peace seemed to be fulfilled. By the following June, however, Dewey saw his hopes dashed by the Treaty of Versailles that ended hostilities with Germany and then imposed severe economic sanctions on Germany's future. The victors sought to punish Germany rather than set conditions for a lasting peace. After the war, Dewey turned his support to an international effort to outlaw war through the development of national and international legal structures. Ironically, this entailed arguing against the League of Nations and the Court of International Justice because, as he saw it, they were not proposed in a way to set realistic conditions for peace, but to provide further power and advantage to imperialistic nations. His support for the effort was in part because he thought that if war was made illegal, while it may not be effective at stopping war, it would nevertheless change moral discourse around war and so affect people's behavior.

In addition to the list of practical intercessions in which he was involved, Dewey also became louder in his call for philosophy to "reconstruct" along the lines of the pragmatism developed by Peirce, James, Addams, himself, and others. In his view, part of what had caused the war was devotion to philosophical principles that separate knowing from doing and to philosophical ideas that support ideals as fixed and unchanging. Instead, he appealed to advances in science to argue that truth, knowledge, and ethics were a matter of ongoing change and process. What was needed was philosophy that responded to the real problems of real people when they are experienced. Philosophy, he said, "is fed by the streams of tradition, traced at critical moments to their sources in order that the current may receive a new direction; it is fertilized by the ferment of new inventions in industry, new explorations of the globe, new discoveries in science" (LW 3, p. 7). In short, it responds to the "problems of men" as they emerge in the context of human culture and in relation to the constantly changing conditions. Philosophy, in this sense, "marks a change in culture" that establishes new patterns of thought that lead to new ways of action; "it is additive and transforming in its role in the history of civilization" (p. 7).

When he wrote a revised introduction to *Reconstruction in Philosophy* in 1948, he was only more adamant that hanging on to old ways of thinking was dangerous. The capacity for growth is what is needed (MW 12, p. 262). If philosophy does not embrace the process of growth as the guide to knowledge, truth, and ethics, it will fall into "the apathy of irrelevance" (p. 273) and continue to separate means from ends. Joining means and ends, however, and recognizing that boundaries are not sharp does not mean "uniformity and unanimity in culture," which Dewey found "rather repellant." Instead, Dewey argued for a robust pluralism: "Variety *is* the spice of life, and the richness and the attractiveness of social institutions depend upon cultural diversity among separate units. In so far as people are all alike there is no give and take among them" (MW 10, 288). While some have challenged Dewey's apparent reduction of pluralism to a "spice," Dewey seems to follow more closely Royce's argument that real pluralism is closely tied to unity. "The same feeling that leads us . . . to respect individuality between person and person," he wrote, "also leads us to respect those elements of diversification in cultural traits which differentiate our national life" (p. 289). The result is a concept of communities and cultures that foster distinctive characteristics while they unify in relation to shared circumstances and problems to be solved.

In his 1926 book *The Public and Its Problems*, this pluralism of communities emerged as an ongoing process of inquiry into shared problems among individuals and among groups or "publics." The emphasis on the process of inquiry and the shifting emphasis on pluralism and unity suggested in the 1910s anticipated later developments in his work during his long philosophical career. While he did not give up the commitments to pluralism, democracy, and education, the experience of the war pushed him to develop a more nuanced framework for the approach Bourne criticized and many called "instrumentalism," so that it would not be confused with an expedient pursuit of fixed ends.

The legacy of his conversation with Jane Addams during the 1894 Pullman Strike can be seen in this development of his philosophy as well. By the time he wrote *Liberalism and Social Action* in 1934, he said, "[e]very problem that arises, personal or collective, simple or complex, is solved only by selecting material from the store of knowledge amassed in past experience and by bringing into play habits already formed" (LW 11, p. 37). Yet, in order to be successful, this "store" needs to be "modified to meet the new conditions that have arisen"; in the context of problems faced by groups, the habits and knowledge of the past take the form of "traditions and institutions." The danger of attempts to solve problems (a danger Dewey thought routinely ignored in both philosophy and daily life) "is either that they will be acted upon implicitly, without reconstruction to meet new conditions, or else that there will be an impatient and blind rush forward, directed only by some dogma rigidly adhered to" (p. 37).

He specifically noted that the dogma of using force had the power of habit; we see it as inevitable and so do not consult intelligence for alternatives. But he also critiqued Hegelian and Marxist accounts as they rely on antagonism and the inevitability of force to motivate historical "progress." As Addams had earlier, Dewey rejected the idea that antagonism was required and argued instead that "progress" began in indeterminate or confused situations. In response to such confusion, the "method of intelligence" responded to the situation by first deciding what sort of problem the indeterminacy marked, and then engaged in a process of hypothesis and testing to convert the indeterminate situation into a determinate or "unified" situation in which the problem was (at least for the present) "solved." The idea that every problematic situation in social life, for example, inevitably demanded the use of "violent force" is the "fruit of dogma" and blocks the use of intelligence. In situations where alternative forms of action might serve to transform the problematic situation into a settled one, a dogmatic framing of problems that presumes "the inevitability of violence tends to produce the use of violence in cases where peaceful methods might otherwise avail" (p. 55).

Democracy, according to Dewey, is the "rule" of intelligence and the rejection of dogmatic uses of antagonism and violence as a means of solving shared problems. The means one uses to achieve an end in turn affect the end; so violent means leave their residue on anything achieved. Joining the critics of his own position in 1917, Dewey wrote in *Liberalism and Social Action*, "I know of no greater fallacy than the claim of those who hold to the dogma of the necessity of brute force that this use will be the method of calling genuine democracy into existence. . . . Force breeds counterforce" (p. 60). When a nation or people declare their commitment to democracy and suppress democracy as a means of achieving it, that does not mark a commitment to liberation and growth, but rather "signifies desire for possession and retention of power by a class, whether that class be called Fascist or Proletarian" (p. 60). For Dewey, the only means available to secure democracy is the widespread use of "intelligence," the process of inquiry.

While Dewey had certainly given voice to a similar position before the First World War (the idea that force controlled by inquiry was necessary to address the war), his later expressions were informed by a wider experience gained after the war, both by the American public and by Dewey himself. As the war ended, Dewey and his wife Alice Chipman prepared for what would be a more than two-year trip to Japan and China. In late 1918, he delivered a series of lectures at Stanford University that would be revised during his time away and become *Human Nature and Conduct: An Introduction to Social Psychology* (published in 1922). In this book, Dewey presented a view of the social nature of the human individual who is characterized by the formation of habits in relation to the environment, social and natural, in which they live. These habits become the "conduct" or ways of acting that mark individual humans and the shared character of groups. But conduct is not a one-sided affair. "[A]ll conduct," he said, "is *interaction* between elements of human nature and the environment, natural and social" (MW 14, p. 9). As a result, "freedom is found in that kind of interaction which maintains an environment in which human desire and choice count for something" (p. 9). Habits, though developed in ongoing response to the environment, are also subject to adjustment and control using intelligence. Just as dogma derails intelligence in the realm of social action, dogma in the life of an individual blocks the use of intelligence to adjust habits and respond to changing circumstances. And in philosophy, dogma emerges as "the supposition that whatever is found true under certain conditions may forthwith be asserted universally or without limits and conditions," a situation Dewey called "*the* philosophical fallacy" (p. 123).

The need to challenge dogma and foster the development of what Dewey called "flexible habits" (LW 2, p. 106)—habits that respond to problems by initiating the process of inquiry rather than automatically taking action—meant that the process of education is central to human development. A "truly humane education," Dewey wrote, "consists in an intelligent direction of native activities in the light of the possibilities and necessities of the social situation" (MW 14, p. 70). It is, in effect, the use of the method of intelligence to produce *the habits* of the method of intelligence in a new generation. "[A]mong the native activities of the young, are some that work towards accommodation, assimilation, reproduction and others that work toward exploration, discovery and creation" (p. 70). Oppressive education—mis-education—emphasizes the former to the exclusion of the latter. Liberatory education, on the other hand, aims to foster the development of habits that meet confusion with questions, mystery with curiosity, and problems with imagination. "The only freedom that is of enduring importance," Dewey concluded in his 1938 *Experience and Education*, "is the freedom of intelligence, that is to say, freedom of observation and of judgment exercised in behalf of purposes that are intrinsically worth while" (LW 13, p. 40). This gives education an important role in developing democratic citizens who are capable of resisting dogma, force, and intolerance as their main means of response to problems.

Education's primary task, then, is to create the habit of inquiry as the primary means of response. Though Dewey expressed it somewhat differently, the process is clearly similar to Peirce's account of inquiry in "Fixation of Belief" (1992). Like Peirce, Dewey made it clear that inquiry is always context-specific and informed by empirical facts. Also, like Peirce, inquiry begins when one encounters a situation in which old habits do not "work," and so one experiences "doubt," not as a private "mental state" but as the quality of the situation as a whole. An inquirer then diagnoses the problem, deliberates about possible solutions, and tries them out in what Dewey calls "dramatic rehearsals." These imaginative tests are essential because they allow an inquirer to consider the consequences of certain outcomes even before putting new habits into action. This is an ongoing cycle because there is no guarantee that an inquiry will be successful and still more inquiry may be necessary to address a situation as it develops. It is also ongoing because every "solution" gives rise to new problems that are then subject to inquiry themselves. Such thinking is active and informed; it makes a difference in the world. For Dewey, it is the ground of individual and social freedom.

This account was quickly joined by the publication of *Experience and Nature* (1925), *The Public and Its Problems* (1927), *The Quest for Certainty* (1928), *Art as Experience* (1934), and *Logic: The Theory of Inquiry* (1938). In these books, Dewey reiterated that the world is contingent and changing, not certain and fixed. An open universe calls for humans to take an experimental approach rather than a dogmatic or absolutistic approach. This makes possible the intelligent use of the pluralism found in the world rather than responding to it with fear. "The growth of the experimental as distinct from the dogmatic habit of mind is due to increased ability to utilize variations for constructive ends instead of suppressing them" (LW 1, p. 7). Dewey argued that the fear of difference and uncertainty is one of the main obstacles to using intelligence to improve, that is, ameliorate, individual and social circumstances. But amelioration is never permanent or certain.

> The distinctive characteristic of practical activity, one which is so inherent that it cannot be eliminated, is the uncertainty which attends it. Of it we are compelled to say: Act, but act at your peril. Judgment and belief regarding actions to be performed can never attain more than a precarious probability. (LW 4, pp. 5–6)

Dewey's claims about the nature of knowledge and action are underlined by his further conclusion that existence itself is both precarious and stable. As a result, "[m]an finds himself living in an aleatory [contingent] world; his existence involves, to put it baldly, a gamble. The world is a scene of risk; it is uncertain, unstable, uncannily unstable" (LW 1, pp. 42–3). Experience, on this account, is the process of negotiating an unstable world with uncertain knowledge, framed by purposes, and informed by successful and unsuccessful actions. It is a process of "[d]oing and suffering, experimenting and putting ourselves in the way of having our sense and nervous system acted upon in ways that yield material for reflection" (p. 29).

In *Art as Experience*, Dewey further developed the idea of experience to recognize the character of different experiences marked by distinctive, unifying qualities. For example, the experience of a frightening thunderstorm is not an assembly of rain, wind, and lightning. It is at first a whole—a unique and distinct experience marked by a "pervasive quality" that is not merely subjective but characterizes the whole. To be frightened is not to have a random feeling, but rather to be part of a situation in which the wind really blows and the thunder is deafening. Similarly, when inquiry begins, it is because the situation at hand is indeterminate, doubtful, or confusing. As he observed in *Logic: The Theory of Inquiry*, "It is the *situation* that has these traits. *We* are doubtful because the situation is inherently doubtful" (LW 12, p. 109). Likewise, a fearful experience or a satisfying experience is "inherently" so. Some such experiences are what Dewey called "*an* experience," that is, an experience that is not merely a passing moment, but one that runs its course to fulfillment. Such "consummatory experiences" range from the experience of a storm, to the experience of a work of art, to an excellent meal. In each case, the experience is unified and unique, memorable, and fulfilling. Such experiences mark the end of inquiry as well as the character of art—the satisfied experience of solving a problem and the experience of an extraordinary concert. In each case, the experience is not mine or yours alone, but is rather an interaction of the environment and a subject (a person or agent). Taken together, Dewey's view included an ontology (of a precarious and stable world), an epistemology (of the process of inquiry), a conception of education (developing the flexible habits of inquiry or "intelligence"), a conception of freedom (to act with intelligence), and a conception of democracy (a community of inquirers perpetuated by a process of education in a precarious world).

From this perspective, Dewey also diagnosed what he saw as the growing individualism that made intelligent social action hard to achieve. Just before the economic crash of 1929, Dewey published *Individualism Old and New*, in which he pointed to the many ways money interests had come to dominate individual lives, corporate businesses, and government concerns. The surrender of the individual to economic forces erases liberty and encourages conformity. His response to the idea of rugged—or as Dewey said, "ragged"—individualism was to create the conditions for a new integrated individual. This integrated individual can productively live through the changing and increasingly interconnected world. Such an individual can intelligently examine the past in relation to present conditions and act in a way to achieve some consciously chosen possible future goal—what Dewey called an end-in-view. For Dewey, education, of course, played a large role in creating the possibility for such integrated individuals. But so did work.

As long as education and industry treat individuals as means to some end in which they do not participate, and as long as education and industry continue to accept the dualism that separates mind from body, Dewey believed that self-interested individualism would continue to dominate, rather than genuine individualism with integrated individuals capable of intelligent foresight. Without such integrated individuals, society is likely to get either apathy or militant fundamentalism. Both are signs of what Dewey called the "lost individual" and both are dangerous as they block intelligent response to present problems.

This prescient diagnosis was followed by further analysis in the 1932 book *Ethics*, which he coauthored with James Hayden Tufts. This book, a substantial revision of their 1908 *Ethics*, was situated in the realities of the Great Depression and the emerging tensions with Italian fascism, Russian communism, and German Nazism. In this book, they traced a history of moral views and pointed to a pattern that moves from ethical responses to situations based on impulse, to responses based on habit, to responses based on intelligence. In other words, they present an account of ethics that moves from needs to customs to the reconstruction of the conditions that contribute to the "problem." Dewey and Tufts made the case that morality is not about particular rules but is about intelligent response to present problems. True freedom, the possibility of genuine individuality, and the possibility of making things better rest on this shift from seeking fixed rules to the use of intelligence to reconstruct conditions. They then used this perspective to analyze contemporary issues. Most of those issues concern the ways that industrial relations work against the emergence of the integrated individual who understands the changing and increasingly social nature of the problems humans face. Changes in technology change social and economic relations and make old habits ineffective or even damaging. For instance, the old habit of employers and employees negotiating the conditions of work—hours, wages, and decision-making—makes no sense when industry no longer needs the skills of individuals, but merely bodies to perform a function. Since individuals in this circumstance have nothing with which to bargain, the balance of power is destroyed and replaced with a situation in which the employer has all the power to set the conditions of work. To continue to try to address this at the point of individual employees is futile; collective bargaining emerged as a way to address the new circumstances.

Throughout the 1930s, Dewey wrote about the importance of addressing economic conditions and issued a call for radical political action. In "Steps to Economic Recovery" (LW 9), he offered a picture that is familiar today when he noted the "appalling existence of want in the midst of plenty" (LW 9, p. 61). He said, "millionaires and tramps multiply together" and pointed again to the need to realize that this is a consequence of the myth of the rugged individual and a failure to embrace the social nature of the individual. It is also the result of a failure to approach social situations in an open and experimental way. In "The Future of Radical Political Action" (LW 9) and "Imperative Need: A New Radical Party" (LW 9), he again pointed to the changing nature of social conditions and called for a response that was partial, tentative, and experimental—not rigid or doctrinaire. He worried about the willingness "to use the methods of coercion, intimidation, suppression . . . that were used in war-time. Just as happened after the war, the methods will continue and will be ready to suppress free discussion and to mislead opinion." (pp. 79–80).

As though anticipating the concerns raised after the 2010 Supreme Court decision in Citizens United v. Federal Election Commission, Dewey observed that "[w]hen business interests dominate political and social discourse freedom is at risk." He claimed that it is "a significant and sinister fact" that advocates of business who call for "'liberty' with the greatest vehemence" are members of "the class that is most responsible . . . for the loss of actual liberty by the mass of our citizens." He continued,

> They loudly profess adherence to the glory of the Constitution as the protector of human liberties. But when the guaranteed freedom of speech and public assembly are violently interfered with by organized gangs, these men are strangely—or not so strangely—silent. They rather devote themselves to asserting that the Civil Liberties Union and others interested in maintaining the civil rights guaranteed by the Constitution are subversive of Americanism and are even financed from Moscow. (p. 87)

If we do not adopt the method of intelligence, Dewey worried that all we have is "[d]ogmatism, reinforced by the weight of unquestioned custom and tradition, the disguised or open play of class interests, dependence upon brute force and violence" (p. 108). These views were brought together in his 1934 *Liberalism and Social Action* mentioned earlier.

These concerns about economics and politics were not just aimed at internal or domestic US issues. Dewey was aware of the growing tensions in Europe and the impending decision the United States would face about entering another war. In taking up the investigation into the actions of Leon Trotsky (1879–1940) in 1937, he again emphasized the need to employ democratic means to achieve democratic ends. Trotsky had been accused by Joseph Stalin (1878–1953) of fomenting an internal conflict in the Soviet Union and arranging for the assassination of key government officials. In response to the charges, Trotsky was sentenced to death with no trial and so fled to Mexico. A group of progressives from the United States took up Trotsky's cause and called for an impartial commission to determine Trotsky's guilt or innocence. Dewey was asked to chair the commission. He went to Mexico to carry out the hearings, not because he agreed with Trotsky (he did not), but because he felt not to participate would have been to betray his whole life's work. In the introductory statement of the report that ultimately found Trotsky not guilty of the charges against him, Dewey explained that he had hoped the commission could find a chair "whose experience better fitted him for the difficult and delicate task to be performed." He then observed "I have given my life to the work of education, which I have conceived to be that of public enlightenment in the interests of society," concluding that he finally accepted the role "because I realized that to act otherwise would be to be false to my life work" (LW 11, p. 309).

Dewey was critical of liberals and fascists alike for their unwillingness to use the method of intelligence and engage in democratic methods. He chastised liberals for not wanting to examine the possible excessive force used by leaders in the Soviet Union and noted that, in the impending war, the United States would probably be asked to ally with the Soviets against Hitler's Germany. He pointed out that it would not do much good to fight fascism with an ally who used the same tactics. What real difference, he asked, was there between Hitler and Stalin?

Worse yet, he noted, if the war was delayed, the Soviet Union and Germany might become allies. Dewey warned his readers to fear this possibility. The fear was well founded when, in 1939, the two nations signed a nonaggression treaty, enabling Germany and the Soviet Union to invade Poland. Dewey argued that both cases should be seen as failed social experiments that put in sharp relief the imperative need to rely on democratic processes—even in the defense of those with whom we disagree.

On the evening of December 7, 1941, just hours after the US Naval base at Pearl Harbor, Hawaii, had been attacked by Japanese naval forces, Dewey gave a talk in New York City. He began by saying, "I have nothing, had nothing, and have nothing now, to say directly about the war" (LW 14, pp. 325–6). But when his talk actually began, that turned out not to be the case. He said:

> If the present state of the civilized world with its clash of arms, social policies, forms of institutions, ideas and ideals is capable of teaching anything to future philosophy, then the past of philosophy must have had something to do with forming the conditions that culminate in the present catastrophe. If so, adequate discussion of the present would require a critical survey of the main trends of thought for at least the last two or three centuries. (p. 312)

He went on to note that when philosophy and education become too separated from emotions and action, it "creates an intolerable vacuum" and becomes ineffective, leaving a hole in people that they want filled. But they must be careful about how it is filled. The "abounding zeal" found in the youth of totalitarian nations allows one to infer that "there was a vacuum of this sort, and that totalitarian philosophies alike in Germany and Russia, somehow succeeded in uniting intellectual beliefs and the well-springs of emotion in a way that filled . . . a deep-felt want" (p. 323). Dewey was clear that philosophy is not neutral in its impact on the world and continued to speak and write to encourage people to adopt a more pluralistic, democratic, and critical perspective.

In the afterword to a new edition of *The Public and Its Problems*, Dewey wrote again about these concerns. Originally published in 1927, this book was just as relevant when it was reissued in 1946 in the aftermath of the Second World War. In the years between the editions, Dewey thought that humanity had learned something. After the First World War, the League of Nations was established (in part through the efforts of people like Addams), but the United States did not join. After the Second World War, however, the United States joined the United Nations; Dewey attributed this shift to a decline in the individualistic and isolationist way of thinking. Part of the reason for this change was the emerging view of nations as publics that needed political organization, and an emerging sense that the absolute sovereignty of a nation did not work in an increasingly interconnected world. Changes in technology had increased the contact between peoples and raised the possibility for more conflict. This situation had to be handled in positive and peaceful ways.

He hoped that this war had removed any remnants of the idea that war was an effective or necessary means to settle disputes or achieve progress. The new technologies (including the atomic bomb) had made war so destructive that there was no way to argue that such conflict was a positive good. A central idea of *The Public and Its Problems* was to bring people with different views together around a common problem. This would help them see beyond their differences and work together to use the method of intelligence to address the issues they faced. Dewey worried it would be hard to find a common interest with the Soviet Union given its commitment to a fixed truth but argued that trying to engage with them in a process of open inquiry around a common interest was the best hope for peace. But this hope entailed giving up *the quest for certainty* that Dewey challenged in his 1927 book of that title.

Inquiry around a problem was our best hope, he argued, because thinking *is* experimental inquiry in the same way directed activity called out by a problem is experimental. Such thinking results in beliefs (warranted assertions), but not infallible knowledge, so that any belief is open to further inquiry. Further, such inquiry has to be applied to the means one uses as well as to the ends-in-view one seeks to achieve. Love of certainty results in rigid dogmas and frustrates thinking. Thinking is a way of acting in the world. The thinking organism is part of the natural world, and the results of such inquiry are additive to the world; thinking makes a difference—for good or ill. When thinking is tied to the hope for finality, however, it is dangerous. In *The Quest for Certainty*, Dewey wrote that an important change would result from introducing the experimental method used in physics to social inquiry. Standards, principles, and rules "would lose all pretense to finality—the ulterior source of dogmatism." For Dewey, it is "both astonishing and depressing that so much of the energy of mankind has gone into fighting for (with weapons of the flesh as well as of the spirit) the truth of creeds, religions, moral and political" rather than testing them by "acting upon them" (LW 4, p. 221). If the latter approach of testing and modifying were widely accepted, it would "do away with the intolerance and fanaticism that attend the notion that beliefs and judgments are capable of inherent truth and authority." A belief is important as a guide to action, but "as such is tentative, hypothetical; it is not just to be acted upon, but is to be *framed* with reference to its office as a guide to action. Consequently, it should be the last thing in the world to be picked up casually and then clung to rigidly" (p. 221).

Knowledge, according to Dewey, is framed by the problems it is developed to address. This qualifies knowledge in an important way and should help people not cling to outmoded or irrelevant knowledge as new conditions emerge. Further, knowledge framed by the problem it is addressing is instrumental, but not in a reductive sense. He wrote,

> [T]he purport of our whole discussion has been in praise of tools, instrumentalities, means, putting them on a level equal in value to ends and consequences, since without them the latter are merely accidental, sporadic and unstable. To call known objects, in their capacity of being objects of knowledge, means is to appreciate them not to depreciate them. (p. 238)

On this view, means and ends are, again, equally important and both must be subject to inquiry. The charge of instrumentalism is usually associated (as it was in Bourne's critique) with the idea that the means are independent of the ends. On this understanding, pragmatism simply stresses a choice of means to achieve the ends at hand. In *Theory of Valuation* (1939), Dewey called this conception of inquiry a fallacy that simply picks out means for some arbitrary (or dogmatic) end without ever considering the full range of consequences that follow from the means (LW 13, pp. 228–9). Both means and ends must, on this account, be evaluated in light of outcomes in relation to the problem or problems at hand. The result leads to a process of means and ends that can be tried and, in light of the result, maintained, modified, or abandoned.

Since human inquiry and action are always framed this way, human beings should be able to find common cause "in the inevitable uncertainties of existence [that] would be coeval with a sense of common effort and shared destiny. Men will never love their enemies until they cease to have enmities" (LW 4, p. 246).

Dewey's emphasis on the need to rely on the results of past inquiries and his claim that change only emerges in the wake of the breakdown of established habits and institutions may suggest that his pragmatism is fundamentally conservative. Since it aims to preserve as much of what has worked as possible (potentially for good or ill), one might conclude that it is not an instance of a philosophy of resistance. On the contrary, Dewey's work is largely and explicitly meant to challenge the philosophies inherited from the European tradition—*Reconstruction in Philosophy* and *The Quest for Certainty* are direct criticisms of the tradition that call for new ways of thinking in light of new circumstances. While not resistance in the mode of Pokagon, Fortune, or even Addams, it is nevertheless a form of resistance, against received ways of thinking and forward-looking toward new futures. In a way, Dewey's work is the best example of a philosophy of resistance in the context of academic philosophy in that it takes seriously the past and how past ways of thinking have made the present moments, while it also remains committed to the need to freely and creatively imagine futures beyond the context built by the past. Overturning the status quo is not simply negation of the past but a reconstruction that critically engages the present circumstances in all its complexity and builds something new. One might say, borrowing from James, that resistance is at the edges, between the past and present, between communities and cultures, between alternative visions of the future. James argued that "Experience itself, taken at large, can grow by the edges" (1977, p. 212). James did not say, but Dewey might have, that resistance at the edges makes that growth possible.

## Primary Texts

Dewey, John (1998). *The Essential Dewey, Volume 1: Pragmatism, Education, Democracy*, eds. Larry Hickman and Thomas M. Alexander. Indianapolis: Indiana University Press.

Dewey, John (2009). *The Essential Dewey, Volume 2: Ethics, Logic, Psychology*, eds. Larry Hickman and Thomas M. Alexander. Indianapolis: Indiana University Press.

# PART II
RESISTANCE AND TRANSITION

# CHAPTER 12
# NATURALISM AND IDEALISM, FEAR AND CONVENTIONALITY
## MARY WHITON CALKINS AND ELSIE CLEWS PARSONS

In 1944, as the Second World War continued, Yervant H. Krikorian (1892–1977) published a collection of essays, *Naturalism and the Human Spirit*. Krikorian was an Armenian born in Turkey who fled in advance of the 1915–16 Armenian genocide by the Turks. With the help of friends, Krikorian completed, first, a degree at the Yale Divinity School and then later, in 1933, his PhD at Harvard. The volume included essays by Dewey and his students John Herman Randall Jr., Sidney Hook, and Ernest Nagel, as well as Harry Costello and Harold A. Larrabee, both students of Royce. In *Logic: The Theory of Inquiry*, Dewey proposed that naturalism began with the "primary postulate" of the "continuity of the lower (less complex) and the higher (more complex) activities and forms." Although he granted that the meaning of "continuity" was not "self-explanatory," "its meaning excludes complete rupture on one side and mere repetition of identities on the other" and "precludes reduction of the 'higher' to the 'lower' just as it precludes complete breaks and gaps" (LW 12, p. 30). Put another way, "the postulate of continuity [excludes] the appearance upon the scene of a totally new outside force as a cause of changes that occur" (p. 31).

In his contribution to the volume, "Naturalism in America," Larrabee proposed that "naturalism" was "a major unreflective assumption of everyday existence in America," though, until recently, it had only a minor place in what was recognized as American philosophy. For Larrabee, "[t]hose who have come to share the naturalistic outlook . . . tend to begin with whatever confronts the human observer in his complete daily living and to endeavor to frame a satisfactory account of it in its own terms" (quoted in Krikorian, 1944, p. 319). Given either Dewey's or Larrabee's characterization, naturalists were those who rejected all forms of "supernaturalism" and so, Larrabee concluded, ran "the whole gamut of popularity from execration to acclaim . . . as the feared and detested party of opposition to the entrenched theology of the academic world" (quoted in Krikorian, 1944, p. 324). He contended that there was a clear line of development in the American tradition, from the colonial period to the 1940s, of American thinkers struggling to establish a naturalistic philosophy against an often-dominant theology and philosophical idealism. "Just as the Civil War killed transcendentalism [represented by Emerson and Thoreau]," Larrabee asserted, "so the first World War and its disillusioning aftermath precipitated the downfall of the feebler Roycean idealism which had succeed it" (quoted in Krikorian, 1944, p. 251).

While Dewey's notion of naturalism began with continuity, another version emerged in the work of Roy Wood Sellars (1880–1973), a member of a group called the Critical Realists. By the end of the First World War, the argument between idealists and the New Realists seemed resolved in favor of realism. Realism's ability at once to take seriously the work of science without idealist complications and the ability to stand outside the politics of the day made realism a potent option for academic philosophers who had just emerged from the political environment of the war and its demands for loyalty and constraints on academic freedom. As if to confirm the increasing narrowness of the field, the only effective criticism of New Realism came from a group of philosophers led by George Santayana (1863–1952), who had joined the Harvard faculty after completing his doctorate there in 1889. Santayana, born Jorge Agustín Nicolás Ruiz Santayana in Madrid, moved with his mother Josefina Borrás Sturgis to Boston when he was eight, and there he studied first at Boston Latin and then at Harvard. Renowned as a philosopher and writer, Santayana published many books including *Scepticism and Animal Faith* (1923), *The Realms of Being* (four volumes, published 1927–40), and *The Last Puritan* (1935), his "autobiography in the form of a novel." Though he resigned from Harvard in 1912 and spent the rest of his life in Europe, he remained active in the American philosophical conversation.

In 1920, he and six other realist philosophers, including Sellars, published a collection of essays challenging New Realism. Critical Realism set aside the old debate with idealism and focused on correcting the mistakes of New Realism. As Durant Drake (1878–1933) observed, the New Realists had "attempted too much" by reducing "the cognitive relation to two categories, the knower . . . and the object known" (Drake, 1930, p. 284). The result was a view with a variety of problems: it could not account for error or hallucinations, it seemed to argue that awareness of a thing proved its existence, and it seemed to claim that knowing something was to grasp the thing itself. Critical Realism, in contrast, proposed "three categories to describe the cognitive situation, the knower (or self, or organism), the object of knowledge (which in the case of knowledge of an existent has its own independent existence), and the datum of experience, that of which we are aware" (p. 284).

For Sellars, Critical Realism led to naturalism that "takes the common world, in which we find ourselves immersed, as the real and only world." As a result, "it is skeptical of those religious and philosophical traditions which want to reduce it to illusion or to dependence upon something more real back of it all in some mysterious sense" (1932, p. 12). "To the naturalist," he concluded, "the physical universe is self-sufficient and substantial" (p. 12). For Sellars, Dewey was a "half-reformed idealist" who rejected "frank physical realism" and denied "any reference to antecedent existence," such as objects and categories, that exist before inquiry begins (pp. 9, 10). As naturalism became a key way of describing (and polarizing) American academic philosophy, two strands developed: those like Sellars who began with some form of physicalism and a strong reliance on physical sciences, and those who began with the recognition of continuity. Emerging from the first strand were the logical positivists and their successors, including W. V. O. Quine, Roy Wood Sellars's son Wilfred Sellars, and Donald Davidson. Emerging from the other was a broad range of naturalists including Randall, Hook, and Justus Buchler.

"Idealists," including Royce, were generally taken to be, as Sellars claimed, "anti-naturalistic and favorable to what—for lack of a better term—may be called a religious view of the world" (p. 11). Yet Royce clearly subscribed to the postulate of continuity, saw knowledge as a response to "daily life," and argued against the separation of the Absolute and nature. Krikorian recognized this in his contribution to the *Naturalism* volume (1944, p. 247) as did George Boas in his contribution (p. 134). What ruled out Royce from the perspective of these naturalists was his affirmation of the constructive role of purpose in nature. A closely related view—and so, arguably, another naturalism—was developed by Royce's student Mary Whiton Calkins.

## Naturalism and Idealism, Fear and Conventionality

Sharing many of the commitments Dewey and Addams held in their later work, Calkins anticipated their work by at least a decade. In July 1888, as a young college teacher, Calkins published a short book titled *Sharing the Profits*. Raised in Buffalo, New York, the daughter of a Presbyterian minister, Wolcott Calkins, she and her family moved to Newton, Massachusetts in 1880, and in 1885, she graduated from nearby Smith College. The following year, she traveled to Europe where she studied the economic conditions of workers in France and Geneva, Switzerland, along with classical languages and history in Greece. On her return, she was hired as an instructor at the newly founded Wellesley College to teach Greek. That first year, Calkins also gave a series of lectures on the principles and practice of profit-sharing that served as the basis for her book. Like Addams, who would found Hull House the next year, Calkins saw the conditions faced by workers in America to be a crucial social problem.

Where Fortune addressed the problem of labor in terms of land ownership and race, and others like Goldman understood the problem in terms of undoing the system of capital and government, Calkins saw the problem faced by workers as one of sharing in the value produced by their labor. "A material value," she wrote, "belongs to those who have created it" (1888, p. 9). Unlike those who challenged the right of capitalists to any share of the produced wealth, Calkins argued that "the creators of definite value are many," including those "who supply the necessary money, . . . the necessary intellect, and finally . . . who supply the necessary physical factor, the muscular power" (p. 10). The problem as she saw it was that "wages in no sense adequately represent the share of the laborer in the value produced" (p. 10). Rather than sharing in the value, employers paid for time and effort as if it were a commodity, not as if it amounted to a share of the value. Profit-sharing would transform the system, she thought, by making workers part owners of the value produced and so would share in upturns in value and downturns as well.

Calkins's proposal came just months after a second great railroad strike in America began in the Midwest. In February 1888, the Chicago, Burlington, and Quincy Railroad (C, B, and Q) was struck by members of three "craft" unions: the Brotherhoods of Locomotive Engineers and Locomotive Firemen, and the Switchmen's Mutual Aid Association of North America. The protests involved working conditions on the railroad and depressed wages that the workers believed had been kept low to pay investors. The strike continued most of the year, but by April, trains were running again largely using non-union labor. Eugene Debs participated in the strike organizing but concluded that its failure was the result of the role of "craft" unions that tended to have narrow membership and disconnected locals. The rise of unions that included all workers in a particular industry became the standard in the wake of the Great C, B, and Q Strike.

Calkins took the strike as a reason to propose ways of transforming the present economic system. "A strike like that on the Chicago, Burlington and Quincy Railroad," she concluded, "which delayed the traffic of a continent, and involved an incalculable loss, is a proof of the need for some reform, which shall remove the very principle of the discord between capital and labor" (1888, p. 4). Profit-sharing, she thought, provided both an ethical and economic justification. "The demands of justice for re-division of the wealth already produced may be slighted," but creating new wealth by "coining the dormant industry economy, and intelligence of our working men into gold" would be too compelling to reject. At the center of Calkins's moral justification for profit-sharing was the idea that apparently opposed classes of people can be united when individuals commit to a larger shared interest. Though a "glittering generality," the claim that "the interests of capital and labor are the same" was nevertheless true, she held (p. 12). Labor struggles like that on the C, B, and Q were the consequence of the "abnormal state of affairs, in which a man's foes are of his own household" (p. 13), a view also developed by Addams in her address "A Modern Lear." Profit-sharing, Calkins concluded, "claims to put an end to all those evils by rewarding care, fidelity, and energy with a part of what [the workers] have helped to produce" (p. 14).

The central justification for her profit-sharing system became the center of her thinking as well. When Wellesley sought to create a philosophy and psychology department, Calkins was interested in becoming part of the new program. Knowing her interest in the fields, the Wellesley president invited her to join the department on the condition that she seek further study first. She decided that she would attend Harvard University, where James had just published his two-volume *Principles of Psychology*, transforming the field. Unfortunately, Harvard did not admit women. Still, Calkins was committed to her plan of study, and after an appeal by her father assuring the University that her attendance would not be an "embarrassing precedent" since she was already a faculty member at Wellesley, she was permitted to begin classes in fall 1890 in a seminar with James (Furumoto, 1980, p. 59). She reported that within a few weeks, all of the other students registered for the class dropped out, and so "James and I were left quite literally at either side of a library fire. *The Principles of Psychology* was warm from the press, and my absorbed study of those brilliant, erudite, and provocative volumes as interpreted by their writer, was my introduction to psychology" (quoted in Furumoto, 1980, p. 59). She also attended courses with Royce, whom she described later as "my great teacher" (1930, p. 212n.) and, after 1892, with the German psychologist Hugo Münsterberg (1863–1916), who had just joined the Harvard faculty.

As she neared completion of her program, Münsterberg requested that Calkins be admitted to the doctoral program, concluding that "she is the strongest student of all who have worked in the [psychology] laboratory [and her] publications and her work here do not let any doubt to me that she is superior also to all candidates of the philosophy Ph.D. during the last years" (quoted in Furumoto, 1980, p. 61). The president of Harvard denied the request. Nevertheless, on May 28, 1895, Calkins defended her dissertation before the Harvard philosophy and psychology faculty, including James, Münsterberg, and Royce. She passed the examination but received no degree. In 1902, the trustees of Harvard established Radcliffe College and offered to grant Calkins her degree retroactively from Radcliffe. Calkins refused.

As a professor at Wellesley, Calkins published several books, including *The Persistent Problems of Philosophy* (first edition, 1907, fifth revised edition, 1925) and *The Good Man and the Good* (1918) and over one hundred articles. In 1905, she was elected the first woman president of the American Psychological Association, and in 1918, the first woman president of the American Philosophical Association. Again in 1929, upon her retirement from Wellesley, a group of leading philosophers and psychologists, all Harvard graduates, petitioned Harvard to award her a doctorate in light of her work at Harvard and "her subsequent achievements as a constructive psychologist and philosopher of outstanding international reputation" (quoted in Furumoto, 1980, p. 63). Harvard denied the request, saying that "there was no adequate reason" for the degree (Furumoto, 1980, p. 64). Calkins died the next year of cancer.

The central commitment of Calkins's earliest work emerged as the central commitment of her moral theory in *The Good Man and the Good*. She identified two ways of understanding human action that she thought framed most moral theories. One, self-assertion, is the idea that "I subordinate my object to myself," and is exemplified in egoistic moral theories that begin with some principle of self-interest. The other, loyalty or altruism, is the idea that "I subordinate myself to my object" (1918, p. 28). In contrast to both of these alternatives, Calkins proposed a third option: "the good, or object of supreme volition, is all inclusive: it excludes no one, shuts no one out, embraces me with my fellows, is concerned for every family, and group, and class, and country" (pp. 48–9). While the egoist and altruist views can both be challenged for their narrowness, Calkins's alternative requires inclusion at every turn. The very principle of shared interest that served as her answer to the oppression of labor and as a principle that would address her own exclusion and that of other women from educational, economic, and professional opportunities also served as the foundation of the good. The principle of inclusion led Calkins to claim that the "object of supreme volition" is "the Great Society" "from which no sentient being could be excluded and to which the good man himself would belong" (p. 50). A person is thus altruistic because of her commitment to others in the community, and at the same time egoistic because the community is integral to the self. As a result, one is at once altruistic in one's commitment to others necessarily included in one's community and egoistic since one's community is formative of oneself. "Individuality" is confirmed because it "means not separateness but uniqueness" (p. 64). At the same time, individuals are nevertheless "inextricable, bound up with other people, a complex of personal relationships and attitudes—a son, a citizen, a party man, a church member, and always a citizen of the Great Society" (p. 64).

As a philosophy of resistance, Calkins's view supports particular forms of activity as legitimate resistance. Rebellion, she said, "is never justified when it is mere egotistical assertion of one's own individual desires" or when it is only on behalf of "the wishes of those one loves" (1918, p. 157). It is "only when [one's] conformity to a law entails his disloyalty to the supreme purpose"—the Great Society—that one has "the right and duty to refuse obedience to recognized authority" (p. 157). Later, in her short paper "Militant Pacifism," Calkins argued that this notion of the good in relation to the Great Society also provides a means to reframe the "instinct" that supports the widespread commitment to war in human society. She explained that *militant* pacifism is a process of harnessing the "natural instinct of pugnacity" in order to change human habits to support social goods. "And the people for whom this new war is fought will be no longer the tribe, or state, or nation, but the great world-self, the universal community of sentient beings" (1917, p. 79). The resulting view directs resistance against militarism and war but also social structures that deny opportunities to individuals or groups.

The idea of the good does not stand alone, however. Calkins's conception turns on adopting a particular metaphysical view that she called "monistic personalism." The philosophical view called personalism was widely recognized in the early twentieth century through the formative work of Borden Parker Bowne (1847–1910), who taught at Boston University. According to Bowne, personalism is a philosophical perspective founded on three "common sense" postulates. First, he claimed that "It is a personal and social world in which we live, and with which all speculation must begin" (1908, p. 20). Second, he stated that the community of persons is bound by a "law of reason"; and third, that "there is a world of common experience, actual or possible, where we meet in mutual understanding" (pp. 20–1). Rather than seeing persons as emergent in history (or as a product of evolution), their very existence is the starting point and amounts to a metaphysical foundation for all of experience. Bowne argued that the existence of finite persons, since they could not emerge from the "impersonal" or material, must, therefore, depend on "the living will and purpose of the Creator" or "Supreme Person" who "produces and maintains" them (pp. 255–6). Bowne's views were developed in theology within the doctrine of the Methodist Church and the work of theologian Albert C. Knudson (1873–1953), and in philosophy through the work of George Howison (1834–1916), Edgar Sheffield Brightman (1884–1953), and Ralph T. Flewelling (1871–1960), among others.

James and Royce held views similar to personalism, and Calkins explicitly adopted the name and developed a version of personalism based on Royce's metaphysics, in contrast to the "pluralistic personal idealism" that she attributed to James, Dewey, and the other pragmatists. The latter view claimed a universe of disparate persons only partially unified, according to Calkins: a "community or kingdom of selves [not] a Self" (1919a, p. 418). Calkins's view conceived "ultimate reality" as "consisting in one underlying, all-inclusive self, manifested or expressed in all the many selves" (p. 418). The all-inclusive Self, the Absolute, is a person composed of relations with an infinite array of finite persons and capable of having purposes, reasoning, and the capacity to experience emotions. "An absolute self," she concluded, "is a complete, a consistent, not self-contradictory consciousness" (p. 430). She offered a view that linked metaphysics, epistemology, ethics, and social theory together in a single account framed by a universe of persons.

The metaphysical position, as Calkins described it in the personal statement she wrote for *Contemporary American Philosophy* (1930) was one that anticipated in important ways the view that came to be called material feminism in the twenty-first century and has been associated with Donna Haraway, Karen Barad, and Susan Hekman, among others. Calkins's view, she said, was "unambiguously idealistic" and so renamed it "mentalism." She held "not only that the universe whatever else it contains includes mental realities, but that the universe is through and through mental in character, that all that is real is ultimately mental, and accordingly personal in nature" (1930, p. 203). In an earlier paper, "A Personalistic Conception of Nature," she explained her view as "the doctrine that any reality—electron, brain, protoplasm, as well as self or purpose—is mental" (1919b, p. 123), that is, *personal*, based on the argument that the only "unchallengeable assertions about alleged material, i.e. non-mental reality are assertions of somebody's way of being conscious" (p. 123). "The world," she concluded, "is . . . made up . . . of selves" (p. 125). When Calkins argued that the shared purpose of the Great Society includes "all sentient beings," she was making the claim not just that human beings or humans and "higher" animals are part of such a society of persons, but that such a society includes other persons as well—trees and flowers, buildings and waterfalls, communities and planets. At the same time, she observed that "the conception of the world of nature as a world of genuine selves does not . . . preclude the possibility or probability that these selves differ vastly from human selves and from each other." While it is easy to recognize persons with whom we communicate, "the world of nature is accordingly in great part . . . an uncommunicative world" (p. 129). From the perspective of continuity and experience discussed earlier, Calkins's view, like Royce's, stands as a distinctive part of the naturalist tradition even as it rejects the physicalist model of Sellars and the Critical Realists.

One approach by women working in philosophy is to address philosophical problems of the day, and another is to take up the problems faced by women and other oppressed groups using philosophical resources. Calkins took the first approach as a philosophy professor and writer and adopted a distinctive naturalism. Elsie Clews Parsons (1875–1941) took the other path; she still adopted a recognizable naturalism but took it up outside of academic philosophy with an eye toward the process of transformation.

As the United States entered the First World War, Parsons, a feminist social theorist, diagnosed the cascading support for involvement in the European conflict. She noted that the Zuni people of New Mexico observed a sacred day each fall called *ahoppa awan tewa*, "the day of their dead." In discussing the ceremony with her, several Zunis explained that this sacred day had been part of their lives "since they came up," since the Zuni people arrived in the present world. Despite the Zuni claim, Parsons concluded that the rituals of the day were, in fact, imported and based on the Catholic "All Souls Day." How such a European sacred day could become central to the Zuni ceremonial calendar, she thought, called for an explanation. She argued that before "All Souls Day" was practiced, Zuni culture already involved ceremonial practices and "that borrowing is facilitated by a certain degree of preexistent resemblance; by the presence of cultural pegs, so to speak, on which the cultural novelty may be readily hung" (1917, p. 229).

In a similar way, the militarization of the United States in the run-up to its entry into the European War could be explained as the adoption of modified patterns thanks to the prior presence of other patterns—"cultural pegs"—on which the new patterns could hang. She argued that the military mobilization and associated suppression of dissent emerged as a result of certain "preexistent resemblances." "Certain features of American life do give color to this theory," she wrote. "Negro disfranchisement, segregation and lynching suggest that racial discrimination is not altogether alien to American practice," along with anti-Semitism and "certain attitudes towards immigrants" (1917, p. 230). Americanization, she continued, "where conscious or unconscious ... insists on homogeneity, and the homogeneity or like-mindedness it demands permits of so little variation that we are led to question whether respect or tolerance for minorities in general is a notable American trait" (p. 231). In short, war patterns lived by Americans at the opening of the First World War were a consequence of American practices of racism and other forms of oppression that were established in the nineteenth century.

Worse, by Parsons's estimation, was that identifying these patterns—the work of researchers and theorists—was itself suppressed by patterns surrounding the "heterodox," that is, those who dissent from orthodox beliefs and practices. Such people, she said, "are not always banned, for they are not always taken seriously" (1917, p. 231). As long as those who resist dominant ways of thinking and acting are viewed as "infertile or inconsequential they are tolerated." "But let the innovating theorist forget [her] place by any chance ... and [she] may count on quick suppression ... the price of existence is remaining ornamental" (p. 231).

Parsons was born in 1875 in New York City, one of three children of Henry Clews, an English immigrant and banker who became wealthy by selling federal war bonds during the Civil War, and Lucy Madison Worthington, a direct descendant of President James Madison and a member of New York's high society. On completion of her college degree at Barnard College, Parsons enrolled in Columbia University's School of Philosophy and, in 1899, completed a doctoral degree with sociologist Franklin Giddings (1855–1931), with minors in sociology, philosophy, and religion. In 1900, she married Herbert Parsons (1869–1925), a lawyer, who also served as a New York City alderman, and friend of Theodore Roosevelt (US president from 1901 to 1909). In 1904, Herbert Parsons was elected to the US Congress and served for three terms. After receiving her degree, Parsons taught sociology at Barnard and, while lecturing, wrote her first book, *The Family*, to serve as a textbook for her classes.

The book was, on the whole, a dry presentation of current research on the nature of human families. In the concluding section, however, Parsons presented a short discussion of ethical issues related to the family. Among her conclusions was one that followed an analysis of the place of prostitution in modern society. She argued, in part, that if prostitution were eliminated, then

> It would . . . seem well from this point of view, to encourage early *trial* marriage, the relation to be entered into with a view to permanency, but with the privilege of breaking it if proved unsuccessful . . . without suffering any great degree of public condemnation. (1906, p. 349)

The advocacy of trial marriage generated a cyclone of criticism of her and her husband, newly elected to Congress. The *New York Herald*, for example, claimed that Parsons's ethical arguments were "the morality of the barnyard" and that "The idea of men and women living like animals, separating at will and contracting new alliances . . . is barbarism and nothing else" (quoted in Deacon, 1997, pp. 68–9). Her critics were not only bothered by her views; most also expressed shock that a woman of her "social position" should take such a stand. Parsons's response, permitted by her wealth and position, was to leave her regular position at Barnard and to take up writing and research full time to systematically critique American society, its treatment of women, and its wider culture of oppression. Parsons sought to become more than an "ornamental radical."

Underlying her work, Parsons drew on two key sources. The first was developing French and American psychology grounded in the work of Gabriel de Tarde (1843–1904). Parsons had spent the summer of 1896 in Paris translating Tarde's book, *The Laws of Imitation*, and published the translation in 1903. The book (both in French and English) made a significant impact on a wide range of American thinkers, including James, Royce, Calkins, and James Mark Baldwin (1861–1934), a well-known philosopher and experimental psychologist (known for proposing the "Baldwin effect," the idea that long-sustained cultural practices have an impact on evolution). The model of society developed by Emil Durkheim (1858–1917) that came to dominate much of social science emphasized a conception of societies as unified wholes that could serve as a ground for explaining the behavior, knowledge, and experience of individual human beings. In contrast, Tarde argued that society, as Bruno Latour explained, was a

> principle of connections; that there was no reason to separate "the social" from other associations like biological organisms or even atoms; [and] that no break with philosophy, and especially metaphysics, was necessary in order to become a social science. (Latour, 2005, p. 13)

Tarde (in Parsons's translation) wrote, "society is a group of people who display many resemblances produced either by imitation or counter imitation" (1903, p. xvii). Society is an array of connections marked by particular patterns of imitation, and social change is a consequence of "invention," that is, the products of individual insights or abilities that are then imitated and become part of the pattern. "Progress, then, is a kind of collective thinking, which lacks a brain of its own," said Tarde, "but which is made possible, thanks to imitation, by the solidarity of the brains of numerous scholars and inventors who interchange their successive discoveries" (pp. 148–9). The study of human society considers inventions and discoveries alongside the patterns of thought and action that unify "brainless" society and in terms of which society develops.

In 1906, Parsons became a member of a reading group started by Alexander Goldenweiser (1880–1940), Robert Lowie (1883–1957), and Paul Radin (1883–1959), all then graduate students of Franz Boas (1858–1942) in anthropology at Columbia and all soon to become leaders in their field. The group also included Horace M. Kallen (1892–1974) and Morris Cohen (1880–1947), who had both completed philosophy degrees studying with James and Royce at Harvard. Called the "Pearson Circle" by its founders, the group began by studying *The Grammar of Science* by Karl Pearson, a British mathematician who had made significant contributions to statistics (including coining the term "standard deviation"). Pearson argued that ethical questions were better answered by empirical science than by philosophy. "*Modern science*," he said, "*as training the mind to an exact and impartial analysis of facts, is an education specially fitted to promote sound citizenship*" (1900, p. 9). The scope of such science was broad so that no subject was out of bounds (including the subject matter of philosophy). Such science also had direct implications for society. Pearson wrote,

> If society is to shape its own future, if we are to replace the stern processes of natural law . . . by milder methods of eliminating the unfit—then we must be peculiarly cautious that in following our strong social instincts we do not at the same time weaken society by rendering the propagation of bad stock more and more easy. (p. 27)

Pearson, like Sanger, Theodore Roosevelt, and others, was an advocate of eugenics, and this program, from his perspective, had the potential not only to improve society but to make philosophy obsolete. "The 'philosophical' method can never lead us back to a real theory of morals. Strange as it may seem, the laboratory experiments of a biologist may have greater weight than the theories of the state from Plato to Hegel!" (p. 28). The Pearson Circle also read work by Ernst Mach, a physicist whose work profoundly influenced a group of philosophers just beginning to meet in Vienna (later called the Vienna Circle), as well as James in his books *Pragmatism* and *A Pluralistic Universe*.

Boas's influence extended well beyond the circle of his students. Born in the Westphalia region of Germany, Boas immigrated to the United States in 1886 to work as an ethnographer in Massachusetts (even though his doctorate earned in Germany was in physics). In 1890, as the Ghost Dance spread among the Native people in the West, many commentators, including General Nelson Miles writing in the *New York Times*, called the movement the "Messiah Craze" and concluded that the participants were being manipulated by other interests. Boas, speaking at a conference of the American Folk-Lore Society in November 1890 (and quoted in the *Times*), disagreed and argued that the movement was better understood as a "nervous disease" (see Pratt, 2005). For Miles and Boas, the Ghost Dance could be fully explained in terms provided by one Western science or another: either as political manipulation or as a psychological disease, and not as a response to colonization and removal within an Indigenous world that could not be explained in Western terms.

In 1892, Boas was hired as an assistant to Frederic Ward Putnam (1839–1915), who organized the anthropology exhibitions at the Columbia Exposition. In 1896, Boas was hired by Columbia University as a lecturer and in 1899 as a professor of anthropology, where he taught until 1939.

The dominant view of Indigenous people at the time was that they were living examples of earlier human development coexisting with later ("civilized") products of human evolution. With G. Stanley Hall, most theorists held that adult Indigenous people were developmentally the same as the children of "civilized" people, an idea called "recapitulation theory." As discussed in Chapter 3, the idea is that the evolution of human societies is recapitulated in the development of individual humans. Education should consequently be framed in a way that brings children through the various stages of development in order that they become successful adults. Indigenous people (along with Black Americans and other non-White peoples around the world) must be understood as children who could be taught to give up their childish (culture-bound) ways to become civilized.

Boas rejected this theory. Based on his critical analysis of ethnographic and other evidence generated in support of recapitulation, Boas argued that the evidence was not valid. While most arguments in favor of recapitulation identified similarities across societies and then constructed rules to account for their development, Boas argued that such societies were more different than similar and that the "shared" characteristics were selected in order to advance the theories they supported. For Boas, so-called "primitive" peoples should be seen as distinctive products of history and circumstance. That some peoples did not develop certain technologies or social organizations was not a sign of a lack of development. Instead, it marked a successful use of resources made available through a particular history and in a particular place that did not lead to those technologies or social forms. The resulting theory rejected scientific theories of race and stage theories of human evolution (where certain forms of human society—hunter societies, agriculture societies—preceded other "more advanced" forms). Boas's work and the work of his students are generally taken to be a decisive response to the racism and racist policies developed in the wake of Reconstruction and set the stage for the Civil Rights Movement that began after the Second World War.

The stance taken by Boas toward the Ghost Dance prefigured his later work. In his response, Boas argued that individual Indigenous people were led by their circumstances and their histories to believe that dancing would lead to the elimination of White people and the restoration of Native ways of life. Since such beliefs distracted Native people from more valuable work to sustain their communities, a reasonable response was to teach the believers to believe otherwise—to cure them of the disease. On this account, the standards for which beliefs are best are established in relation to the dominant society. Documenting distinctive beliefs, the work of ethnography, was an important step in understanding differences and in devising practical responses to the problems that Indigenous and other communities faced. While Boas's project and those carried out by his students, including Zora Neale Hurston and Ella Deloria, are often seen as a kind of resistance to efforts to exclude and undermine Black and Indigenous cultures, others have argued that Boas's program was also effectively used by educators and policy makers to further the larger settler colonial project of eliminating Indigenous peoples and controlling other groups by prioritizing the values of the dominant culture.

Boas's theory was grounded in the development of a general conception of culture that influenced generations of thinkers in every field of study, including philosophy. Dewey, for example, who knew Boas and some of his students when he was a professor at Columbia, adopted the idea of culture as a way of understanding shared habits. The influence was so strong that when Dewey planned a revised edition of *Experience and Nature* (he wrote a new first chapter in 1948), the title of the revised edition would be "Nature and Culture." Explaining the new title, Dewey wrote, "I would substitute the term 'culture' [for 'experience'] because with its meanings now firmly established it can fully and freely carry my philosophy of experience" (LW 1, p. 361).

"Culture," Boas wrote in the 1938 revised edition of *The Mind of Primitive Man*,

> may be defined as the totality of the mental and physical reactions and activities that characterize the behavior of the individual composing a social group collectively and individual in relation to their nature environment, to other groups, and to members of the group itself. It also included the products of these activities and their role in the life of the groups. (1938, p. 159)

Such "reactions and activities" include language, food preservation and preparation, shelter and clothing, manufacturing, methods of locomotion and more (p. 159). Dewey echoes and expands Boas's idea: "The facts named by 'culture' . . . include the whole body of beliefs, attitudes, dispositions which are scientific and 'moral' and which as a matter of cultural fact decide the specific uses to which the 'material' constituents of culture are put . . . ." Dewey concludes, "It is a prime philosophical consideration that 'culture' includes the material and the ideal in their reciprocal interrelationships and . . . designates that immense diversity of human affairs, interests, concerns, values which compartmentalists pigeonhole under 'religion' 'morals' 'aesthetics' 'politics' 'economics' etc." (LW 1, pp. 362–3). Parsons likewise adopts Boas's idea of culture in order to understand and challenge not other cultures, but her own.

Parsons's participation in the Pearson Circle provided new insight into the critical examination of contemporary American society using the methods of ethnography. While Tarde provided an ontological starting point (the idea that societies were patterns of connection and individuals were the product of imitation and invention), ethnography provided Parsons a means to be what her biographer, Desley Deacon, called a "native informant" of her own culture. While ethnographers had long collected information about other cultures by finding "informers" who could explain stories and practices to the outsider, Parsons turned this method on her own culture and became an informer, seeking to identify problematic practices and ideas and reform them. From this perspective, Parsons took up the position of a cultural observer whose work could engage key practices and "catchwords" or "ideals" and not only show their meanings, but (to borrow a later term) deconstruct them. Terms such as "liberty" and "equality" were applied "uncritically to fresh conditions—like the present war" (1917, p. 231). Once the war is so labeled, questions could be set aside and US involvement would "pass unquestioned." The ability to be an "impartial" observer is supported by using a comparative method—for example, Zuni ceremonials serve as points of comparison that can highlight aspects of her own culture.

This internal cultural perspective served as the starting point for Parsons's feminism as well. Her close examination of the family in American and other cultures provided a framework for her to examine governmental policies and personal experience. Her investigations led her, as we already mentioned, to propose trial marriages as a means of addressing other problems in

American society. She quickly became an advocate of birth control and free love. Thanks to her wealth, she was able not only to publish her observations and analyses, but she was also able to provide financial support to causes related to family planning and suffrage.

In her journal (published posthumously as *The Journal of a Feminist*), Parsons recounted an exchange with her mother:

> "What is feminism?" [her mother asked], "do tell me." "I have been telling you all my life." I answered. "When I would play with the little boys in Bryant Park although you said it was rough and unladylike, that was feminism. When I took off my veil or gloves whenever your back was turned or when I stayed in my room for two days rather than put on stays, that was feminism. When I got out of paying calls to go riding or sailing, that was feminism. When I kept to regular hours of work in spite of protests that I was 'selfish', that was feminism. When I had a baby when I wanted one, in spite of protest that I was not selfish enough, that was feminism." (1994, p. 86)

Her mother replied that this only proved that she was "rebellious." But it also proved that her mother missed the point; in the end, feminism was a critical and constructive engagement with the social constructions that determined sex and gender in American society. Like later feminist theorists, Parsons argued that sex and gender were performed by characteristic activities that served to enable and constrain individuals and groups. The results of a critical analysis could lead, she thought, to liberatory conceptions of gender that would not be imposed but adopted when and how each individual wished. "There will be no common measure. This morning perhaps I may feel like a male; let me act like one. This afternoon I may feel like a female, let me act like one. At midday or at midnight I may feel sexless; let me therefore act sexlessly" (p. 91).

Parsons applied a similar strategy of analysis to class hierarchies in American society in a series of books in the 1910s. Taken together, the books document a range of social practices that serve to determine classes of the young and old, women, men, servant, criminal, host and guest, worker and manager, and so on. In *Fear and Conventionality*, Parsons tried "to indicate some of the ways in which dread of novelty, of the unlike or the unusual, has entered into our social life; how much fear of having to change our habits has affected them" (1915, p. vi). In order to consider the ways in which fear and conventionality have worked in American culture and contrasting cultures, Parsons rejected the assumption of social progress and instead assumed, following Boas, that "human nature has changed little if at all" (p. xi). This starting point was in stark contrast to social theory of the time that presumed—citing Darwin—that human nature not only had changed but had progressed from worse to better. By adopting what was for the time an alternative conception of human nature, Parsons was able to proceed by setting aside the dominant notion of a hierarchical relation between so-called savage people and so-called civilization. In a paper published in 1915 in *The Journal of Philosophy*, Parsons directly challenged the idea of social progress through a process of "survival of the fittest." The argument for social progress, she concluded, "is an argument that backs any oppression of the weak by the strong, any claim to special privileges, any spirit of exclusiveness, and intolerance or brutality" (1915, p. 611).

In the final chapter of *Fear and Conventionality*, "The Unconventional Society," Parsons offered a vision of a society that has responded to a critical analysis of itself: "In this society, the viability of the world will be taken advantage of.... We shall live at large, truly mobilized, going where it is best for us to be, unperturbed by novel experience and not safeguarded against it" (1915, p. 210). Yet even as she offered this conception of a new world where individuals are free to pass in and out of various relations, seeking the places where they are "best," America was still sharply divided by race and class, and not everyone who considered this situation agreed that the answer was to "live at large."

## Primary Texts

Calkins, Mary Whiton (1918). *The Good Man and the Good.* New York: Macmillan.

Calkins, Mary Whiton (March 1919). "The Personalistic Conception of Nature." *The Philosophical Review* 28 (2): 115–46.

Parsons, Elsie Clews (1994). *The Journal of a Feminist*, intro. Margaret C. Jones. Bristol: Thoemmes Press.

Parsons, Elsie Clews (1997). *Fear and Conventionality*, intro. Desley Deacon. Chicago: University of Chicago Press.

# CHAPTER 13
# RACE RIOTS AND THE COLOR LINE
## W. E. B. DU BOIS

The First World War ended on November 11, 1918, with over thirty-five million casualties, including more than sixteen million dead. Innovations that contributed to the slaughter and destruction included the use of tanks and aircraft, increasingly accurate weapons, and poison gas. The scope of the war included battles in Europe, Asia, Africa, and the Middle East, as well as significant naval operations in the Atlantic, Mediterranean, and Pacific Oceans. Treaties after the war disbanded the Ottoman and Austro-Hungarian Empires, placed Germany under severe economic and political restrictions, and reshaped European control of colonial territories, including those in Africa and Asia. In February 1917, while Allied and Central powers froze in trenches to the West, workers and peasants in Russia revolted against the government of Tsar Nicholas II and, in October, the Bolshevik party led by Vladimir Lenin (1870–1924) took over the government. In early 1918, Bolshevik Russia signed the Treaty of Brest-Litovsk with Germany and withdrew from the European War.

After the November ceasefire, representatives of the warring governments (not including Russia) met in France and in June 1919 officially ended the war with Germany by signing the Treaty of Versailles. Following the vision of Woodrow Wilson (largely based on work done by Addams and others), the Paris Peace Conference also founded the League of Nations. The League was a body intended to promote peace and international cooperation that included most of the combatants in the war, with the noticeable exception of the United States, which never joined the League.

By mid-1919, many of the five million US troops (including 350,000 African American soldiers) who had entered the military to fight in Europe were mustered out of service to find a changed world. The military draft had left a need for workers, especially in the major industrial centers in the North. With little European immigration during the war, African American workers who fled the poverty of tenant farming in the South filled many jobs. The return of the soldiers, Black and White, meant increased competition for jobs and greater racial tension both North and South.

Beginning in May 1919, race riots broke out in cities across the United States, first in Georgia and South Carolina and then, in June and early July, in Northern cities including New London, Connecticut, Annapolis, Maryland, and Scranton, Pennsylvania. On July 19, a group of off-duty White soldiers and sailors entered a Black neighborhood in Washington, D.C., as a reprisal for an alleged assault on a White woman by two Black men the evening before. The soldiers beat Black residents, looted stores, and burned buildings. By the third night of the riot, Blacks organized and began to fight back, driving the White rioters from the area and attacking police. The US Army sent in troops to stop what was seen as the Black "uprising." The violence finally ended when a heavy thunderstorm broke up the crowds and helped to put out the fires, but not before four people were killed (according to official records) (see Krugler, 2015).

Several days later in Chicago, another vastly larger riot broke out after a White man killed an African American youth at a swimming beach on Lake Michigan. When a police officer at the scene refused to arrest the White man (and instead arrested one of the African Americans at the scene), word spread quickly in the Black community, and many people assembled to protest. In response, crowds of Whites gathered and attacked the Black protesters. Thirty-eight people, including twenty-three African Americans and fifteen Whites, were killed over the next several days. Carl Sandburg (1878–1964), the well-known poet and then a journalist in Chicago, published a short volume on the riots tracking its causes, especially the combination of the Great Migration (the movement of African Americans to Chicago from the South), the attendant poverty in the city in the wake of the war, and the return of unemployed soldiers. For Sandburg, the riot illustrated both the problems of a pluralistic city and the promise of workers uniting across racial lines. "Thousands of white men and thousands of colored men," he wrote, "stood together during the riots, and through the public statements of white and colored officials of the Stockyards Labor Council, asked the public to witness that they were shaking hands as 'brothers' and could not be counted on for any share in the mob shouts and ravages." Sandburg noted that "This was the first time in any similar crisis in an American community that a large body of mixed nationalities and races . . . proclaimed that they were organized and opposed to violence between white union men and colored union men" (Sandburg, 1919, p. 3).

Sandburg's assessment of the Chicago riots marked hope but not an end to the violence. The final riots of the summer did not occur until September in Elaine, Arkansas. Ida B. Wells-Barnett produced a report published in 1920 detailing the riot and its aftermath. Following the return of some African American soldiers from Europe, many of the local tenant farmers decided to band together to form a farm cooperative to try to increase the price for their cotton, to buy the land they farmed, and to hire a lawyer to help settle their accounts with the White landlords. Wells-Barnett wrote:

> The colored men who went to war for this democracy returned home determined to emancipate themselves from the slavery which took all a man and his family could earn, left him in debt, gave him no freedom of action, no protection for his life or property, no education for his children, but did give him Jim Crow cars, lynching and disfranchisement. (1920, p. 8)

The system of tenant farming, which bound Black farmers to landlord farms through debt and control of local economies, combined with other labor practices to become another form of slavery, peonage, or debt servitude. In many states, African American men were routinely arrested—for loitering, spitting, looking at a White woman, violating segregation laws—and, after conviction, were "leased" to White farmers and mining and manufacturing companies as cheap labor. The practice of leasing prisoners to hard labor, which began after the Thirteenth Amendment ending slavery, continued in the years after the First World War and was not eliminated in the United States until 1927. Tenant farming continued long after.

On the evening of September 30, 1919, members of the Elaine farm cooperative were gathered at a church, when around 11:00 p.m., the church was attacked with gunfire by a group of White men, killing several members of the cooperative. One White man was also killed, probably by the Black armed guards who had been posted outside during the meeting. The next day, the church was burned to destroy evidence of the attack, and a call went out to

White communities in the area that a Black insurrection was underway. Between 500 and 1,000 vigilantes answered the call, and over the next few days, 100 (or as many as 200 according to some sources) African Americans were killed, along with 5 Whites. Federal troops were deployed to end the bloodshed and help arrest those guilty of starting the riots. While no Whites were arrested, 285 African Americans were arrested and 122 were charged by a grand jury for participating in the violence. The first twelve, tried by all-White juries, were convicted of murder and sentenced to death. Sixty-five more pled guilty to second-degree murder and were sentenced to jail. Wells-Barnett and the NAACP produced reports on the riots and supported appeals of the "Elaine Twelve." By the end of the long summer, riots had occurred in at least thirty-four cities, hundreds had been killed or wounded, and the hope expressed by Sandburg and others for peaceful and cooperative coexistence among racial communities ended in violence.

Observing all of this from his position as the editor of the NAACP magazine, *The Crisis*, W. E. B. Du Bois presented a philosophical conception of race conflict by proposing a distinctive epistemic position. "High in a tower," he wrote, "where I sit above the loud complaining of the human sea, but none there are that intrigue me more than the Souls of White Folk." He goes on:

> Of them I am singularly clairvoyant. I see in and through them. . . . Not as a foreigner do I come, for I am native, not foreign, born of their thought and flesh of their language . . . I see these souls undressed and from the back and side. I see the working of their entrails. I know their thoughts and they know that I know. This knowledge makes them now embarrassed, now furious! (1920, p. 29)

The essay, titled "The Souls of White Folk," is a kind of reprise of his 1903 classic volume *The Souls of Black Folk*. In this earlier work, Du Bois had taken a more hopeful view of race conflict. In the first essay of the 1903 volume, after offering a critique of racism, Du Bois concluded:

> Work, culture, liberty,—all these we need, not singly but together, not successively but together, each growing and aiding each, and all striving toward that vaster ideal . . . the ideal of fostering and developing the traits and talents of the Negro, not in opposition to or contempt for other races . . . in order that some day on American soil two world-races may give each to each those characteristics both so sadly lack. (1903, p. 8)

In 1910, Du Bois and a group of young African American leaders called the "Niagara Movement" joined with a group of leading White intellectuals and activists, including Addams and Dewey, to found the NAACP. After serving as a professor of history and sociology, first at Wilberforce University and then, from 1897 until 1910, at Atlanta University, Du Bois left the academy to serve as editor of *The Crisis*. Drawing on his earlier work, he continued to develop a conception of race, race difference, and the coexistence of diverse racial communities. The outbreak of the First World War posed a challenge to Du Bois's position; to resist supporting the United States in its efforts, first to stay out of the war and then to enter it, risked making the African American community seem unpatriotic, separate, and in some ways confirming the idea of Black inferiority in the eyes of the dominant White society. Du Bois remained skeptical about Black involvement in war efforts but recognized the value for Blacks of serving in the military.

In 1917, encouraged by his White friend and president of the NAACP, Joel Spingarn, Du Bois decided that the Black community should—despite racism and exclusion from White society—"close ranks" with President Wilson and join the war effort. Du Bois wrote: "Let us, while this war lasts, forget our special grievances and close our ranks shoulder to shoulder with our own white fellow citizens and the allied nations that are fighting for democracy" (1917, p. 111). Despite overt racism in the military, the assignment of most Blacks to service rather than combat roles, and even despite accusations against Black soldiers of cowardice and incompetence, Du Bois called for a united front. Though his support was and is controversial, at issue in his decision to support the war effort was an attempt to work out a practical notion of racial difference founded on two conceptions developed in his earlier work: the conceptions of race and identity.

William Edward Burghardt Du Bois was born in Great Barrington, Massachusetts, in 1868, a descendant of both Africans brought to America as slaves and French ancestors who settled in the Caribbean. The African American community in Great Barrington was small, and Du Bois found himself the only Black student in his class during much of his education. He was talented and enjoyed surpassing his fellow students. Recognition of racial difference, he said, came early. As a child, "in a wee wooden schoolhouse," he and the other students exchanged "visiting cards." When a new student "peremptorily, with a glance" refused his card, "it dawned on me with a certain suddenness that I was different from the others; or like, mayhap, in heart and life and longing, but shut out from their world by a vast veil" (1903, p. 2). This recognition of his own racial identity through the eyes of another helped him to frame a conflicting sense of self.

> After the Egyptian and Indian, the Greek and Roman, the Teuton and Mongolian, the Negro is a sort of seventh son, born with a veil, and gifted with second-sight in this American world—a world which yields him no true self-consciousness, but only lets him see himself through the revelation of the other world. It is a peculiar sensation, this double-consciousness, this sense of always looking at one's self through the eyes of others, of measuring one's soul by the tape of a world that looks on in amused contempt and pity. One ever feels his twoness—an American, a Negro; two souls, two thoughts, two unreconciled strivings; two warring ideals in one dark body, whose dogged strength alone keeps it from being torn asunder. (p. 3)

The double consciousness, as a product of a history of racial difference and oppression, was at once an opportunity and a curse. In one sense, it placed Du Bois and others who shared a similar identity at a border—a boundary—between races where he was both a part of distinctive groups ("an American, a Negro") and, in a real sense, different from them both ("one dark body"), so that he could see the world differently and add his particular vision back to the communities of which he was a part. In another sense, such double consciousness left him outside both communities, Black and White, and demanded that he choose between them.

This view is reminiscent of the conception of self and community formulated by Du Bois's teachers, James and Royce. Following his high school graduation, Du Bois wanted to enter

Harvard, but when he was not admitted, he enrolled at Fisk University in Nashville, Tennessee. The experience of attending a Black college in the legally segregated South reinforced for Du Bois both the reality of racial differences and the character of double consciousness. On completing his degree at Fisk, Du Bois applied to Harvard to pursue a graduate degree, and this time was accepted but as an undergraduate junior. At Harvard, he continued to be a successful student, taking a range of courses, especially in philosophy, psychology, and history. It was here that he met and worked with James and Royce and considered a career in philosophy. "I hoped to pursue philosophy as my life career," he wrote, "with teaching for support." And while he studied with Santayana and Royce, "it was James with his pragmatism and Albert Bushnell Hart [in History] with his research method, that turned me back from the lovely but sterile land of philosophic speculation, to the social sciences as the field for gathering and interpreting that body of fact which would apply to my program for the Negro" (1968, pp. 133, 148). James discouraged Du Bois from continuing in his chosen field after he finished his undergraduate degree because there was "not much chance for anyone earning a living as a philosopher." Du Bois continued at Harvard in the graduate history program. At the encouragement of his professors, he studied for two years in Germany. On his return in 1894, Du Bois accepted a position at Wilberforce University, a Black university in Ohio, and the next year completed his doctoral degree, the first African American to do so at Harvard.

Du Bois's work with James and Hart had convinced him that real social problems, like those faced by African Americans, could only be addressed by relying on carefully collected facts that defined the situation and helped to define alternative solutions. After two years at Wilberforce, Du Bois accepted a one-year appointment as a research assistant at the University of Pennsylvania, where he completed a study of the lives and circumstances of the Black community in Philadelphia. The result, a volume titled *The Philadelphia Negro* published in 1899, used an approach very much like the one used by Addams and other researchers at Hull House in their work *Hull House Maps and Papers*, published in 1895. The problem Du Bois sought to address in his work was the problem of segregation: "Here is a large group of people . . . who do not form an integral part of the larger social group," where

> the segregation is more conspicuous, more patent to the eye, and so intertwined with a long historic evolution, with peculiarly pressing social problems of poverty, ignorance, crime and labor, that the Negro problem far surpasses in scientific interest and social gravity most of the other race or class questions. (1899, p. 5)

The work initiated in Philadelphia became the core of Du Bois's research efforts, backed by ongoing examination of the notions of race and identity in general.

While Du Bois presented a conception of identity that was framed by race and its boundaries, what constituted a race also demanded his attention. His initial answer to the question came as part of his support for the American Negro Academy, founded by Alexander Crummell (1819–1898), a leader of the antislavery movement in the North who took a position as a professor of English and Moral Philosophy at Liberia College in Monrovia before returning to the United States after the Civil War to participate in the intellectual efforts of the Reconstruction period.

At the first meeting of the Academy in March 1897, Du Bois presented an address titled "On the Conservation of Races." Rejecting conceptions of race based on biology or lineage alone, Du Bois offered this definition:

> A vast family of human beings, generally of common blood and language, always of common history, tradition and impulse, who are both voluntarily and involuntarily striving together for the accomplishment of certain more or less vividly conceived ideals of life. (2007, p. 8)

In short, races are cultures distinguished from one another by "blood" and language ("generally" not always), but also history, cultural practices, and ideals ("always"). The central argument was that there are distinct races (or what might be called racial cultures) that, thanks to their histories and character, have the potential to make a contribution to the larger whole of humankind. If this is so, races need to be "conserved"—that is, maintained and developed—for the benefit of all. This view is sometimes called *racialism* since it affirms both the reality of races and their inherent value. Racism, or prejudice on the basis of race, is an obstacle to the conservation of races both because it blocks the development of races through oppression and blocks the exchange of contributions that races can make to one another. In the present debate, some argue that racialism necessarily leads to racism and so argue that racialism must be rejected in order to eliminate racism. Du Bois held that racialism was justified by experience and history and that racism is not a necessary consequence but a problem to be addressed in order to promote the conservation of races.

In 1920, when Du Bois published his essay "Souls of White Folk" in a volume titled *Darkwater: Voices from Within the Veil*, he saw his hopes for a more tolerant America defeated by race riots, virulent prejudice against Black veterans, lynching, and increasing rural and urban poverty among African Americans. *Darkwater* begins with a prayer of sorts, called a "Credo [Creed]," in which Du Bois declared, "I believe that all men, black and brown and white are brothers, varying through time and opportunity, in form and gift and feature, but differing in no essential particular." He then declared, "Especially do I believe in the Negro Race: in the beauty of its genius, the sweetness of its soul, and its strength in that meekness which shall yet inherit this turbulent earth." He went on to assert his belief "in Pride of race and lineage and self" (1920, p. 1). Though consistent from the perspective of his notions of race and self, the declarations also capture the tensions that emerged in the wake of the war. Humanity in some sense is one, even as it is divided among races in which individuals can have pride in their race over other races. But the Credo also implied a problem, a kind of paradox of conservation. If races were real and valuable and so ought to be conserved, does it follow that the "White" race, which seemed to be founded on exploitation and violence against African Americans, also should be conserved? Was the case for an African-descended race in America that was valuable to all humanity also a case for the conservation of Whiteness? In "The Souls of White Folk," Du Bois rejected the idea that Whiteness ought to be conserved through a radical analysis of the meaning of that particular so-called race.

Whiteness, he concluded, is not a racial culture but rather a system of ideas and practices that are bound to destroy racial cultures in service of an economic system of greed and power. "The discovery of personal whiteness among the world's people," he wrote, "is a very modern thing" (p. 21). This discovery was accompanied by the confidence that whoever is White is "by that token wonderful" because "of all the hues of God, whiteness alone is inherently and obviously better than brownness or tan." But the character of Whiteness is not merely self-appreciation, it is a range of practices and attitudes that amount to the claim that "whiteness is the ownership of the earth forever and ever, Amen!" In the present world, religion bound to particular histories and peoples was rapidly replaced with "White" religion that found its expression in economic terms. "The world today is trade. The world has turned shopkeeper; history is economic history; living is earning a living" (p. 26). In the wake of the war, Du Bois claimed, "our chiefest industry" has become fighting. We find "machine-guns against [spears]; conquest sugared with religion; mutilation and rape masquerading as culture—all of this, with vast applause at the superiority of white over black soldiers" (p. 27). From this perspective, "Whiteness" overrides the value of diverse races and in so doing undermines the potential of humankind taken as a whole. Rather than being a race to be conserved, Whiteness emerges as an anti-race and so, as antithetical to human flourishing, can be taken as a form of antihumanism.

Incorporating papers he had written in the early days of the war, Du Bois argued that the demand for labor to serve the needs of European economic development led to the colonization and exploitation of what he called the "darker races" in Africa and Asia. War in Europe became inevitable, not because of a complex network of treaty commitments, as is sometimes suggested, but because colonial labor and resources were limited, and the need for more forced the European powers to attack each other. "The World War was primarily the jealous and avaricious struggle for the largest share in exploiting darker races." On this analysis, "Whiteness," or the economic system that had come to dominate the Western world and its related cultural framework, overrode the diversity of colonized lands and even the interests of some White folk in order to advance the cause of ownership and wealth production. Writing about the horrors of the Belgian war in the Congo, Du Bois said that "This is not Europe gone mad; this is not aberration nor insanity; this *is* Europe; this seeming terrible is the real soul of white culture—back of all culture—stripped and visible today" (p. 28).

Anticipating the sophisticated philosophical, social, and economic analyses of "Whiteness" that emerged in the late twentieth century, Du Bois addressed the paradox of the conservation of races with the rejection of the idea that the practices and attitudes of Whiteness could be understood as a race at all. Under the guise of race, European-descended colonial practices marked systematic efforts to rid the world of racial difference and, by extension, distinctive identities, by converting ethnicities and races into sources of laborers, consumers, and capitalists. Visible race differences became a convenient badge not of a particular history and perspective, but of who was or was not exploitable. In response, Du Bois reasserted the value of conservation. In a claim that seems to mirror the claim of Luther Standing Bear in the 1930s, Du Bois concluded, "A belief in humanity is a belief in colored men. If the uplift of mankind must be done by men, then the destinies of this world will rest ultimately in the hands of darker nations" (p. 35). Du Bois continued,

> What then is the dark world thinking? It is thinking that as wild and awful as this shameful war was, *it is nothing to compare with that fight for freedom which black and brown and yellow men must and will make unless their oppression and humiliation and insult at the hands of the White World ceases. The Dark World is going to submit to its present treatment just as long as it must and not one moment longer.* (p. 35)

This radical analysis caused many to reject *Darkwater* as a representative voice of the African American community.

Du Bois's work, even in *Darkwater*, was not solely critical. In the essays "Of Work and Wealth" and "Of the Ruling of Men," he developed his general commitment to cultural pluralism into a more concrete pluralism that argued for recognition of distinctive human groups formed by history, circumstance, and biology, as well as for the necessity of their inclusion in the wider process of governing societies. He argued that races had been taken up into the dominant economic system and it was this system that must be addressed.

> There are no races, in the sense of great, separate, pure breeds of men, differing in attainment, development and capacity; . . . the world today consists, not of races, but of the imperial group of master capitalists, international and predominantly white; the national middle classes of several nations, white, yellow and brown with strong blood bonds and common languages and common history; the international laboring classes of all colors; [and] the backward, oppressed groups of nature-folk, predominantly yellow, brown and black. (p. 75)

In response to this hierarchical system framed by industrial capitalism, Du Bois claimed a higher ideal: "We must envisage the wants of humanity. We must want the wants of all men. We must get rid of the fascination with exclusiveness" (p. 78). But does rejecting exclusion require the acceptance of "a world where everybody looks like his neighbor, and thinks like his neighbor and is like his neighbor?" (pp. 119–20). In fact, he concluded, "there are differences between men and groups of men and there will ever be," but the differences will be the gifts that individuals and groups will be able to give to humanity as a whole: "they will be differences of beauty and genius and of interests" (p. 78). The path toward the goal is one in which "the disinherited darker people must either share in the future of industrial democracy or overturn the world," (p. 78) where democracy is taken as "a method of realizing the broadest measure of justice to all human beings" (p. 110).

The key to achieving democracy is in part an epistemic matter, a matter of what and how knowledge is produced. Such knowledge will direct the actions of individuals and groups. Even though we might be tempted to "ask only for the wisdom of citizens of a certain grade or . . . recognized worth" (p. 111), a functioning democracy—the method of realizing the broadest measure of justice—requires inquiry that involves every part of the community. For example, those involved in the effort to determine what will benefit the women of the community recognized that "in the last analysis only the sufferer knows his sufferings and that no state can be strong which excludes from its expressed wisdom the knowledge possessed by mothers, wives, and daughters" (p. 112). "The same arguments apply to other excluded groups," he claimed. "If a race . . . is excluded, then so far as that race is a part of the economic and social organization of the land, the feeling and experience of that race are absolutely necessary to the realization of the broadest justice for all citizens" (p. 112). For Du Bois, the inclusion of diverse wisdom in the method of governing is the first step to sharing the goods of society widely, the first step to the "lateral progress" proposed by Addams. In such a context, the "tyranny of the majority" that "demands that all people be alike or that they be ostracized" (p. 119) is thwarted by the participation of more and more diverse groups. The result is "government by temporary coalition of small diverse groups" (p. 118) that recognizes that "no nation, race or sex has a monopoly of ability or ideas; that no human group is so small as to deserve to be ignored as a part ... of the mass of [humankind]" (p. 119).

Du Bois's conception of race and identity is a philosophy of resistance. It emerges from a world framed by the failure of post-Civil War Reconstruction and the establishment of legal apartheid through new forms of racial exclusion and exploitation. Rather than accepting the approach taken by some theorists to reduce the meaning of racial groups to the product of oppression, Du Bois sought to establish a positive ground for the separate value of race, particularly of Blacks in America. Contrary to racial eliminativism, which argues against the reality of race and might be seen as accepting the structures and standards of some universal (and European) conception of humanity, Du Bois sought to recognize racial difference as organic, cultural, and irreducible. Such a conception was not only a retrospective view of race that recognized the role of physical differences and the structures imposed by the system of human enslavement but proposed a vision of distinctive futures that would contribute to the collective benefit of a heterogenous humanity. Like other philosophers of resistance, Du Bois saw his efforts as both critical and constructive and not as efforts that would reinforce, even unintentionally, the structures of the dominant system. By creating concepts in the space between the White world and the "darker world," Du Bois attempted to challenge the separation by undermining the central laws of division and generating new possibilities in an uncertain world. In the end, however, he thought that his efforts failed. In 1963, the US refused to renew his passport. He became a citizen of Ghana and died there shortly after.

## Primary Text

Du Bois, W. E. B. (1986). *Writings*. New York: The Library of America, Penguin Books.

# CHAPTER 14
## CREATIVE EXPERIENCE
### MARY PARKER FOLLETT

In December 1918, just after the armistice was signed ending the fighting in Europe, Hartley Burr Alexander (1873–1939) gave an address titled "Wrath and Ruth" at the American Philosophical Association comparing the philosophical perspective of 1918 with that of 1914. Echoing Du Bois's diagnosis of the war published first in *The Crisis* and then in *Darkwater* as "The Souls of White Folk," Alexander concluded: "we trusted unblushingly in the white man's capacity to calculate and get the Good" (1919, p. 253). But the war "shattered [the world of self-illusion], pricked our bubble of conceit, and has shown us, not Man as he is, which God alone can know, but the civilized twentieth century man of Europe and America, blown with pride, as both worse and better than he had dreamed" (p. 254).

Alexander was born in 1873 in Lincoln, Nebraska, the son of a Methodist minister. His mother died when he was three. When his father bought and published the newspaper in Syracuse, Nebraska, he learned the trade of typesetting, and despite a lack of formal education, he entered high school and then the University of Nebraska. After graduate study at Johns Hopkins University and the University of Pennsylvania, he graduated from Columbia University in 1901. Unique among White academic philosophers of his day, Alexander became deeply interested in Native American thought, publishing several volumes on Native culture, and incorporating Indigenous insights into his own philosophical views. For Alexander, every human group, "which has developed a sense of its own solidarity and its own collective power and fate has brought to expression its appraisal of its own humanity, and this we call its culture or, in its more reflective manifestation, its philosophy" (1999, p. xxix). Native thought had the advantage of providing a philosophy developed "by a unique people in a unique continent" while also shedding light on how others experience their places. In his 1918 address, he concluded with a reference to a Wikeno story about the introduction of mortality into the world. "So it was decreed that men must die, and the immortals returned to heaven, whence they looked down and beheld men mourning their dead; whereupon mortal souls were transformed into drops of the blood of life" (1919, p. 258). The lesson of the story is that the presence of death on such a scale as that of the war just ended should serve as a starting point for new reflection.

Over the next six months, negotiations continued over a treaty to formally end the Great War and to establish the League of Nations. The League, strongly advocated by President Wilson as a means of preventing future wars, came into existence on January 10, 1920, but without the United States as a member. At issue in both the treaty discussions and the founding of the League was the nature of communities—local, ethnic, national, and international. At the 1918 meeting of the APA, the membership adopted as the theme for discussion at its 1919 meeting the topic "The Nature of Community." Those appointed to present papers and lead the discussion included Morris Raphael Cohen (1880–1947) and Mary Parker Follett (1868–1933), whose contrasting views of the aim of philosophy became a central conflict about the purpose of philosophy in the context of American communities.

Cohen was a professor at City College of New York from 1912 until 1938. He was born in Minsk, Russia, but spent his first decade in the small town of Nesviesh, where his love of wisdom "was awakened by [his] grandfather, a poor tailor . . . [who] never learned to write and had only a moderate reading knowledge of Hebrew [but] had become the master of an extraordinary amount of knowledge and wisdom" (1930, p. 221). In 1890, Cohen was taken to live in Minsk and then in 1892 to New York City. In 1895, he entered City College to study mathematics and science. He came to the study of philosophy through his involvement with the Socialist Labor Party. In order to prepare "for more active and intelligent propaganda," he and several other young college students began reading Marx. When the ideas of Marx seemed at odds with the ideas of J. S. Mill, Cohen widened his reading and enrolled at Columbia University and then, in 1904, entered Harvard University, where he was a student of James and Royce. He finished his doctoral degree with Royce in 1906. "To philosophize," he wrote, "has always seemed as natural and desirable in itself as to sing, to dance, to paint, or mould, or to commune with those we love" (p. 222).

Cohen's address at the 1919 APA meeting represented well the tensions faced by philosophers in the aftermath of the war. While his paper was a discussion of community framed explicitly against the background of current events, he began by arguing that the practice of philosophy is one that is necessarily disconnected from present problems. He said, "pure philosophy" is "the true love and fearless pursuit of fundamental truth for its own sake" and "is in itself one of the greatest blessings of human life, and, therefore, never to be entirely subordinated to the solution of social problems—whatever the words solution and social may mean" (1919, p. 674). In this light, he wrote,

> When I read [Alexander's] paper on "Wrath and Ruth" with a mental picture before me of the spirit in which a mathematician, physicist, biologist or scientific historian reads the announcement of a new discovery in his field, I find myself entirely outside of what Professor Alexander must regard as the standard of philosophic truth. (p. 676)

Rather than submitting his claims to critical consideration, Alexander simply embraced them. "Doubtless," Cohen said, "the last conflict exceeded all previous ones as regards the number of combatants, but is that the most significant philosophic test? . . . Why should a philosophy be any the worse because it has nothing to learn from the war?" (p. 676).

Cohen's point was that philosophy ought to be an "intellectual antiseptic" and "the philosopher should not undertake to cure the ills of humanity before he has learned to disinfect himself and his instruments" (1919, p. 675). For Cohen, "the work of the philosopher, like that of the scientist, [is] part of humanity's organized search for universally ascertainable truth, a truth that can withstand partisan contention and critical doubt" (1929, p. 128). Even as Alexander took what appeared to be a partisan stance, demanding that philosophy as a discipline address the problems of peace and war, Cohen's conception of philosophy took a position focused on questions of logic and metaphysics that he saw as necessary conditions for the possibility of any debate.

According to Cohen, Dewey's conception of philosophy "must be dominated by a sense of social responsibility." Such a view demands that

Even the physicist and the biologist may pursue their work only if they emerge from their laboratories with some results that bear on human destiny. Philosophic ethics then, according to this view, must endeavor to help us to solve the problems that distress mankind, how to obtain better political representation, better administration of justice, better milk for babies and the like. (1929, p. 147)

In contrast, Cohen held that

Reflection on human good is not worthy to be called philosophy unless it is scientifically neutral about the various ethical or moral issues, i.e., unless it regards its own thoroughly logical procedure as more important than any of the results of such a critical study. (p. 148)

Significantly, Cohen made the case for neutrality by arguing that philosophy can do better work for humankind's problems, claiming that "philosophy can best aid those actually engaged in the more concrete human problems by vigorously maintaining just that spirit of impartiality and aloofness so frequently and thoughtlessly condemned by those whose business it is to think" (1919, p. 674).

Cohen's conception of philosophy helped to set the stage for a kind of counter-resistance in American philosophy. While some sought to resist the dominant culture by focusing philosophical inquiry on experienced problems—for example, Goldman, Gilman, and Addams on the problems of the poor, Du Bois on the problems of the color line, Dewey on the problems of fostering democracy—Cohen criticized such inquiry and advocated for a separation between conceptual critique and practical problem-solving. Just as the Counter-Reformation sought to stop the efforts of the Reformation in sixteenth-century Europe by offering a different model of change that conserved elements of the past, the philosophy of the American counter-resistance conserved the questions and some of the character of the systems of philosophy inherited from Europe even as it sought to change them. Both conceptions of philosophy responded to present problems, but they chose different strategies of resistance. The counter-resistance begun by Cohen would continue in the work of the Critical Realists, the work of the logical positivists, and eventually in some of the work of the new and neo-pragmatists.

When Cohen challenged Alexander's claims about the implications of the Great War, he did so by asking whether the claims themselves were clear and whether they also admitted other meanings. As a philosopher, Alexander could contribute to the work of social scientists, lawyers, and diplomats by critiquing the formal aspects of their claims, identifying ambiguities and alternatives, and helping to define the nature of communities that might be relevant to the question of responsibility.

Acknowledging the need for local communities, Cohen nevertheless cautioned against adopting the idea of communities as persons or agents by pointing to two dangers. The first was that "small groups or communities may be far more oppressive to the individual than larger ones" (1927, p. 687). Foreshadowing the later work of Iris Marion Young, Cohen argued that cities provide more freedom because the community is more diffuse and as such less like a person and more like a collection of diverse individuals. The second danger is that, on the view of communities as separable and sovereign persons (who join together perhaps in a federation of communities as proposed by Harold Laski [1893–1950]), "there will be nothing to prevent that group from oppressing" other communities. "In the presence of the obvious conflict between the principle of individual responsibility and that of collective responsibility, the philosopher is tempted to decide for one or the other of these principles" (1931, p. 393). But people accept and reject each notion at various times.

> If I tell my neighbor that the coal he uses is soaked with the blood of miners and brakemen killed in the mines . . ., he may see the truth of my contention, but he would resent my statement that by using coal he is participating in these killings and that the blood of these men is on his head. In any case he will go on using coal. (p. 393)

For Cohen, philosophers are adept at identifying these tensions but are not charged with resolving them. What is to be resisted is the position of dogmatism—of placing philosophers in the position of prophets or kings. The world does not need more kings, but rather more people who can see dogma for what it is and whose critical engagement opens the way for new construction.

It is in this light, or perhaps, this light shaded by the presence of an un-credentialed woman philosopher, that Cohen reserves special condemnation for Mary Parker Follett (1868–1933). Follett was a writer and social activist unaffiliated with any university and who had not received an advanced college degree. She received a BA from Radcliffe, where she studied with James and Royce, and briefly attended Cambridge University and studied with philosopher Henry Sedgwick (1838–1900). Her recently published book, *The New State*, had emerged from her community organizing work and offered a vision of pluralistic communities that sought to manage conflict through local collaborative action. In his address, Cohen declared that the "failure to maintain a critical attitude seems to me exemplified in almost every page of Miss Follett's book on *The New State*" (1919, p. 676). Though it may be judged by "philosophic standards," it is clear that it is rather

> a work of exhortation, pleading on behalf of what she regards as the solution to a practical problem. It is certainly not written in the style of the scientist or philosopher, . . . but rather in the inspired style and absolute confidence of the prophet such as Buddha or Mohammed. (p. 676)

In fact, while Cohen believed that philosophy must adopt a narrow stand on the claims it makes, Follett adopted something akin to Cohen's own concept of "twilight zones" that stand between opposing camps. From this position, she provided insight not only into abstract matters but also into the implications of principles of order for individuals as agents in relation to others, as well as a conception of power that provided a normative framework for the development of new modes of agency.

Follett's response to Cohen at the 1919 meeting was generous. Setting aside his remarks about her writing in the voice of a prophet, she affirmed the importance of a critical attitude. She continued, "I too deplore the jargon of much of our political science which accepts without analysis time-consecrated phrases and notions, which treats as fundamental ideas the crude, primitive attempts to get at democracy by rule of thumb" (quoted in Tonn, 2003, p. 320). The basic idea of democracy, she claimed, was "integration," the process of "evolving" a collective purpose upon which to act. Understanding this process required "the study of community" as "modes of association." Her conception of community required participation by all members in decision-making, not simply the use of the machinery of voting. Cohen charged she had rejected voting without an argument; however, her position reflected not a lack of evidence but—as Cohen himself may have recognized—a new set of assumptions about the nature of human communities. Follett's claim in *The New State* was not that neighborhoods and labor unions should become states (as Cohen understood her argument), but that human life in community should be a process of community building of the kind found in local organizations.

Follett's *The New State* was written in a few months as the United States entered the Great War. Unlike Du Bois and Dewey, who ultimately came out in support of the US intervention, and Addams, who opposed it, Follett challenged the fundamental questions at issue. She said the "peace propaganda urges us to choose peace rather than war. But the decision between 'war' or 'peace' never lies within our power. These are mere words to gather up in convenient form of expression an enormous amount that is underneath." What lies beneath the choice, she claimed, is a process of competing interests and ideas: "peace or war has come, by other decisions, long before the question of peace or war ever arises" (1998, p. 356). Follett would certainly have agreed with Du Bois when he said that "the preparation for war is the cause of war," since war is not a simple yes or no decision, but the product of many decisions aimed in general at the idea that conflict can only be resolved by some form of domination. In *The New State*, Follett made a case for a different framework for conflict in which participants sought the integration of their interests in unifying purposes. *The New State* begins: "Our political life is stagnating, capital and labor are virtually at war, the nations of Europe are at one another's throats—because we have not yet learned how to live together. The twentieth century must find a new principle of association" (p. 3). The new principle she proposed emerged out of her own experience as a worker in the settlement and community center movements in Boston.

Follett was born in 1868 in Quincy, Massachusetts, into a middle-class family. Her father, an alcoholic, left for a few years, leaving her and her mother to take in boarders. Eventually, her father returned sober and supported the family until his death in 1885, leaving Follett responsible for her now-invalid mother. Follett's maternal grandfather had left her a small trust fund so she was able to graduate from Thayer Academy in 1884 where she took classes from Anna Boynton Thompson (1848–1923), a history teacher who published work on the German idealist philosopher, Johann Gottlieb Fichte. The year following the death of her father, Follett began taking courses from the Society to Encourage Studies at Home, founded by Anna Eliot Ticknor (1823–96). Four years later, Follett began study at the newly opened Harvard Annex, a non-degree academic program established for women who were not permitted to attend Harvard. Here Follett met Hart, the Harvard historian who was one of Du Bois's most influential teachers. Follett also studied with Wendell Barrett, a literature professor at Harvard (also one of Du Bois's teachers), who strongly opposed admitting women to college (Tonn, 2003, pp. 50–1). Follett spent the next year studying at Newnham College, the women's college of Cambridge University.

On her return to the United States, Follett began to teach at Mrs. Shaw's School in Boston. Here she met Isabella Briggs (1848–1926), who was the principal of the school. Briggs, twenty years Follett's senior, soon became Follett's closest mentor and editor and eventually her life partner, living with Follett until her death in 1926. While teaching at Mrs. Shaw's School, Follett returned to the Harvard Annex and began a thesis project with Hart in which she studied the office of the Speaker of the House of Representatives. She based her study on analysis of textual evidence about the office and interviews and other forms of investigation that today we would call "qualitative research." The approach was revolutionary for its time and it remains a classic study on the topic. In 1894, Harvard Annex became Radcliffe College and in 1898 Follett graduated with a BA degree (along with her teacher, Thompson, and Gertrude Stein (1874–1946), who would become a famous modernist author).

Just as Addams had completed her college study only to find few career opportunities and so became a leader in the settlement movement, Follett also turned to settlement work as a means of both practicing her interests in political theory and serving the community. Working first at Boston's South End Settlement, Follett saw a need to establish programs that would attract men to the opportunities that a settlement could provide. In 1902, she founded the Highland Union, a debating club for young men. By the next year, the program expanded to include lectures, theater, and athletic programs. The following year, another association sought to expand opportunities for local communities by "extending the use" of public school buildings. Since schools were generally not used in the evening, the "extended use" association sought to open the buildings for meetings, adult education classes, and athletics. Another committee, later called the Roxbury League, wanted to address the problem of alcohol abuse among men in the Roxbury neighborhood by offering alternative forms of fellowship and entertainment. Rather than closing saloons (which also served a recognizable community function), the League, working with local community members, established sports leagues, night school classes, and political forums. As a result of her involvement in neighborhood matters, Follett also began to participate in labor mediation, and the centers provided space for union organizing and labor education.

In 1905, Follett closed the Highland Union to focus her attention on the growing "community centers" movement, as the "extended use" projects became known. Eventually, Follett would serve as the vice president of the National Community Centers Association, which helped to establish centers in schools and other public buildings across the country. Her experience working with neighborhood groups led her, in a 1913 address to the Ford Hall Forum, to formulate a conception of democracy founded on the practices of neighborhood and labor associations. "Democracy is not the glorification of the individual in any form, but the subordination of the individual to the well-being of all," she claimed. "It is not the liberty of the individual, but the restraint of the individual by himself, for the good of all.... We must emphasize unity rather than equality, brotherhood rather than liberty" (quoted in Tonn, 2003, p. 328). The key to democracy, then, is not an abstract idea of harmony nor simply a process of voting, but rather an "effective" process. "What we want is to make our democracy effective, telling, an actual fact. Association ought to mean action for common ends" (quoted in Tonn, 2003, p. 239). Adopting a view suggested by Royce in *The Philosophy of Loyalty*, Follett argued that common ends are a product of a process

> where the wishes of the individual must be constantly sacrificed to the needs and interests of the group, where the loyalty developed will be group loyalty, where every one will feel that he as part of the group is something bigger and finer than just one man all alone by himself, that he partakes of the strength and power and potentiality of the whole. (quoted in Tonn, 2003, p. 239)

In the context of industrial capitalism, the nature of daily work at machines and in offices meant that people were isolated and had little opportunity to develop common ends to organize and improve their lives. Community centers, open at night, could provide a place for meeting and "self-expression" and the opportunity to develop "initiative and will-power" (quoted in Tonn, 2003, p. 239). To achieve these goals, such centers, she concluded, "must be community affairs, organized by community initiative, for community ends" (quoted in Tonn, 2003, p. 240).

*The New State* emerged from this experience and, in a sense, from the need to address a problem suggested by her Ford Hall address. Her emphasis in that speech was that democracy turned on the sacrifice of the individual to the group. The conception of the individual that she developed in *The New State*, however, challenged this very idea. Describing the work of a neighborhood group she wrote, "We sit around the council table not blank pages but made up of all our past experiences. Then we evolve a so-called common will, then we take it into the concrete world to see if it will work" (1998, p. 50). How is the "common will" evolved? When people sit at the council table, they each bring ideas about the issues at hand. "[W]e cannot add all of these ideas to find the group idea," Follett observed. The ideas will "not add any more than apples and chairs will add. But we gradually find that our problem can be solved, not indeed by mechanical aggregation, but by the subtle process of the intermingling of all the different ideas of the group" (pp. 24–5). In the course of the conversation, listening to the ideas around the table, a common idea evolves and it becomes what "we" want together—our common purpose that can then organize our actions for testing.

> [W]e have learned to do that most wonderful thing, to say "I" representing a whole instead of "I" represented in one of our separate selves. The course of action decided upon is what we all together want, and I see that it is better than what I had wanted all along. It is what *I* now want. (p. 25)

The process, Follett concludes, is "integration," and it is distinct from either compromise (in which someone agrees to sacrifice some purpose) or domination (in which someone's purpose is rejected or overwhelmed).

One example of integration is a dispute between management and workers over wages. After the discussion of their purposes, it emerges that both management and labor want to make sure that the production facility survives. As a result, the original goals of management and labor vis-à-vis wages are "transvalued" to become the shared goal of ongoing production at the present site. Both sides have united with a single purpose without compromise or domination. Further negotiations will then try different ways of carrying out the purpose determined. The process is also different from simple majority rule because, again, when the majority imposes its will (through the ballot or by other means), its triumph amounts to either compromise on the part of the minority or domination of the minority. Loyalty, then, is a product of these interactions when our original commitments evolve into ones that unify us and commit us to further action and evaluation. Democracy can be understood as "the rule of an interacting, interpenetrating whole" where everyone builds a "single life, not my life and others, not the individual and the state, but my life bound up with others, the individual which *is* the state, the state which *is* the individual" (1998, p. 156).

In part, *The New State* aimed at challenging the increasingly dominant view that states are composed of smaller groups who themselves have rights as groups. A central advocate for this position, Harold Laski, then a political scientist at Harvard, argued that groups (churches, cities, states, corporations, and the like) are often in a position to legally overrule the claims of the federal government. Federalism, in this sense, affirms a kind of rigid pluralism in which persons (of whatever size) are wholly independent of each other and so can make and resist claims of others. Follett argued against this view on the grounds that he had misunderstood the meaning of pluralism. Recalling James's argument for the "compounding of consciousness," she argued that individuals (whether individual human beings or neighborhoods or unions) are both wholes and parts and as such are both independent in the sense proposed by the pluralists and united as parts of a larger whole. Follett quoted James, saying, "states of consciousness can separate and combine themselves freely and keep their own identity unchanged while forming parts of simultaneous fields of experience of wider scope" (1998, p. 264).

The key to "true federalism" is that the "all-form" (the whole) and the "each-form" (parts) are not incompatible. "If we ... live James's philosophy of the compounding of consciousness, if we obey the true doctrine, that each individual is not only himself but the state ... then will the perfect form of federalism appear and express itself" (1998, p. 265). The particular principle is an instance of a larger recognition of the relation between the one and the many. "[T]he Many and the One are creating each other," Follett asserted. This is not a speculative claim, either: she concluded that "we shall actually see the Many and One emerging at the same time" in the community process. Follett's view then represented what she called a "third alternative" in which human communities are at once becoming one and at the same time becoming many. If sovereignty is the ability of groups to act with a purpose, then it is, on this account, the process of unification. "The fact is that local units must grow sovereignty, that we want to revivify local life not for the purpose of breaking up sovereignty [as the pluralists would argue] but for the purpose of creating a real sovereignty" (p. 284).

The circumstances of the First World War were not far from her concern as she finished *The New State*. She asked, "When I find that my loyalty to my group and my loyalty to the state conflict (if I am a Quaker and my country is at war, [for example]), how do I act?" "First," she said, "as a matter of immediate action, [I must] decide between these loyalties." But this does not end the matter: "I must, if my disapproval of war is to be neither abandoned nor remain a mere particularist conviction, seek to change the policy of my state in regard to its foreign relations" (1998, p. 313). Far from resolving in advance conflicts of this sort, Follett argued that these are the conflicts that make the state. The state "is neither an external force nor an unchanging force. Rooted in our most intimate daily lives, in those bonds which are at the same time the strongest and most pliant, the 'absolutism' of the true state always depends on our activity" (p. 313).

Follett's postulate that individuals are not isolated beings but rather are constituted by their associations was one inherited in part from James, but also from Royce in his version of pragmatism. This view was also adopted by Edwin Holt (1873–1946), a student of both James and Royce who returned to Harvard as a professor of philosophy and psychology after completing his degree there in 1901. Holt read and commented on Follett's work in 1919 and made his lecture notes available to her. He was also one of the first American psychologists to engage the work of Freud, and Holt's 1915 book, *The Freudian Wish*, provided an important resource for Follett as she took on objections to *The New State*. Working at first with coauthor Eduard Lindeman (1885–1953), a sociologist sympathetic to Follett's method and political theory, Follett envisioned a new book that would examine the nature of experience as a ground for the theory she offered in *The New State*. Hampered by health problems and then the dissolution of her plan for a coauthored book, Follett finally managed to complete the planned book, *Creative Experience*, and publish it in 1924. The book added three key ideas to the discussion of community in *The New State*.

The first idea responded to the objection voiced by Cohen when he challenged Follett's analysis of human nature. "Doubtless," Cohen wrote, "every mind is made what it is by interaction with others, but such interaction surely does not disprove the existence of the separate minds which do interact" (1919, p. 678). In *Creative Experience*, Follett clarified her position by affirming a distinctive ontological starting point in which "reality is in the relating, in the activity-between" (1924, p. 54). Holt, she wrote, "shows us how in the 'behavior-process' subject and object are equally important and that reality is in the relating of these, is in the endless evolving of these relatings" (pp. 54–5). In response to Cohen, Follett's claim was that if reality is relational, then the challenge is not to disprove the existence of separate minds, but rather to prove that separate minds can exist. Holt (along with James and Royce) rejected the assumption that separate minds are possible.

By focusing on the "activity-between," Follett affirmed that the subjects and objects are processes and not static entities, and that their particular character is always at an intersection between still other relations. The intersection is also not static, but a reaction: "the most fundamental thought about all this is that reaction is always reaction to a relating" (1924, p. 62). "In human relations," she continued,

> I never react to you but to you-plus-me; or to be more accurate, it is I-plus-you reacting to you-plus-me. "I" can never influence "you" because you have already influenced me; that is, in the very process of meeting, by the very process of meeting, we both become something different. (pp. 62–3)

This "interweaving" process, as she called it, occurs not only between individuals but between individuals and the environment in which they find themselves. She summarized three principles that, given this ontological starting point,

> guide us in our study of social situations: (1) that my response is not to a rigid static environment, but to a changing environment; (2) to an environment which is changing because of the activity between it and me; (3) that function may be continuously modified by itself, that is, the activity of the boy going to school may change the activity of the boy going to school. (p. 73)

Such "betweenness" is not simply the addition of an individual with a fixed past and a discrete environment. It is rather the generation of a "plus-value," the novelty in the situation, the source of something new. These intersections, when they are genuine intersections, are what Follett meant by creative experience. When they are not "genuine," when one factor or another obscures or eliminates the other factors in the meeting, creativity is thwarted and experience becomes redundant and unchanging. Echoing James, she concluded that "Creative experience is a federalistic growth" (p. 101).

The second key idea is that creative experience is a normative standard, that is, a kind of experience to be sought and promoted, that also provides a means to understand the alternative ways in which diverse agents unify their different purposes. As in *The New State*, Follett proposed that unification could occur in three different ways: as domination, compromise, or integration. The first two options are oppressive; only the third (integration) is creative. It is important to note as well that the process of evolving purposes is not simply a conversation between the two parties. It also involves interaction with the environment in which the conversation is conducted. Follett stressed the importance of the "total situation" in the process of evolving purposes. From this perspective, all of the processes of interaction interact with each other to form the total situation in which the agents operate. "What the psychologist [or sociologist or community leader] must do . . . is to study the whole a-making; this involves study of the whole and parts in their active and continuous relation to each other," that is, their activities. "When we are watching an activity we are watching not parts in relation to a whole or whole in relation to parts, we are watching a whole a-making" (1924, p. 102). Further, "environment too is a whole a-making, and the interknitting of these two wholes a-making create the total situation—also a-making" (p. 102). If one accepts the idea that it is the nature of organisms to grow—that this is an acceptable normative standard—then activities (unifications) that result from integrations are in general better than those that result from compromise or domination.

The third idea Follett developed in *Creative Experience* is raised in the introduction. "What," she asked, "is the central problem of social relations? It is the question of power" (1924, p. xii). Nearly alone among the American philosophers of the first half of the twentieth century, Follett not only recognized the centrality of power as a social and ontological issue, she recognized it by name and offered a theory. While her treatment of power vanished from consideration by the 1940s, it is likely that many of the discussions in the second half of the twentieth century owed something to her early framing of the issue. Power, Follett said, is not a single process but rather has two forms: power-over and power-with. In a series of lectures Follett gave in 1925, she explained, "Whereas power usually means power-over, the power of some person or group over some other person or group, it is possible to develop the conception of power-with, a jointly developed power, a co-active, not a coercive power" (1924, p. 101). On this account, "genuine" power, like genuine unifications, "can only be grown" (1924, p. xiii). Integration, not surprisingly, marks the use of power-with. Domination and compromise are both forms of power-over in that they override the purposes of some of the agents involved.

Further, Follett claimed, "the only genuine power is that over the self—whatever that self may be" (1924, p. 186). This claim seems puzzling at first because presumably power-with can be carried out only with others. Recall, however, that selves are individuals or groups who have a common purpose—that is, they are in their unification selves or agents who can act with a purpose. "When you and I decide on a course of action together and do that thing, you have no power over me nor I over you, but we have power over ourselves together" (p. 186). From this perspective, "there is no power-over in a single [i.e. whole] situation" (p. 188). Power-over marks the failure of integration and the triumph of domination. One situation has been created by the imposition of power, but without integration, it is fragile and risks falling apart. Such an exercise of power, Follett called "pseudo-power."

Follett's conception of power provides a framework for the critical evaluation of how conflict is understood and resolved on one hand, and a guideline for how conflict ought to be engaged and resolved in light of the nature of purposive activity on the other. Taken together, the account of community in *The New State* and the account of purposive activity in *Creative Experience* offer a theoretical framework for taking up questions of power and pluralism. Follett spent eight years advocating her ideas as a business management consultant before her death from cancer in December 1933. Her ideas found little audience among philosophers in the decades to come, even as questions of power became more significant in the field. But her work did find an audience among business management theorists and community activists such as Saul Alinsky in the 1960s and may have served as the inspiration for the book *Getting to Yes* (2012).

Follett, like many of the other philosophers of resistance in the American tradition (and unlike the philosophers of the counter-resistance), rejected fundamental structures of the dominant society by recognizing the reality of betweenness and relationality. Contrary to later theorists of power (such as Michel Foucault), Follett argued that power, accurately understood, made it possible to resist from outside systems of domination, or better, from the edges. On her account, resistance was not simply a process that sustained domination—as resistance is literally required for some systems to function. Power as "integration" can break a system, undercut its dominion and compromises, and replace it with something new. For Follett, such resistance is not some special process originating in the clouds or in the minds of some special elite, but rather it is already present in ordinary practices that are blocked and covered over by systems that seek to sustain their domination. By recognizing the potential of genuine power, Follett held, people can gain control of their collective lives and transform them toward new futures.

Follett, however, was not naïve about the risks and cost of such resistance. In *Creative Experience*, she concludes: "In my emphasis on integration, it must not be supposed, however, that I ignore the part of disintegration in the creative process. . . . We should always see the relation between disruptive and creative forces; disruption may be a real moment in integration. . . . [D]isruption is only a part of that total life process to which, in its more comprehensive aspect, we may give the name integration" (1924, p. 178). Resistance, for Follett, is not simply integration—the use of power-with—but also requires disruption, disintegration, even the use of power over to make creativity possible.

## Primary Texts

Alexander, Hartley Burr (1999). *The World's Rim: Great Mysteries of the North American Indians*, intro. Thomas M. Alexander. Mineola, NY: Dover Publications.

Cohen, Morris R. (1931). *Reason and Nature: An Essay on the Meaning of Scientific Method*. Glencoe, IL: The Free Press.

Follett, Mary Parker (1924). *Creative Experience*. New York: Longmans, Green and Company.

Follett, Mary Parker (1998). *The New State*, with forewords by Benjamin R. Barber and Jane Mansbridge and an introduction by Kevin Mattson. University Park, PA: Pennsylvania State University Press.

# CHAPTER 15
## CULTURAL PLURALISM
### HORACE KALLEN AND ALAIN LEROY LOCKE

While Follett published *Creative Experience* as a means of addressing issues of pluralism in 1924, that same year Horace Kallen (1882–1974) published *Culture and Democracy in the United States*. This book was a collection of essays written since 1915, attempting to analyze the conflicts between culture in the United States before and after the Great War. Like Morris Cohen, Kallen was a Jewish immigrant and also a student of James and Royce at Harvard. Unlike Cohen, he saw philosophy as both capable of analyzing pluralism and offering a model for how America ought to be pluralistic. Where Cohen remained neutral on the question of group and individual agency, Kallen argued that individuals were the relevant agents, and cultural difference marked different environments in which individuals were raised and educated. The volume opened with an essay titled "Postscript—To be read First: Culture and the Ku Klux Klan." In the years before the Great War, racist organizations had experienced a resurgence, especially the Ku Klux Klan, which had been featured in the immensely popular 1915 film by D. W. Griffith, *Birth of a Nation*. The film, famously screened in the White House and praised by Woodrow Wilson, depicted the Klan as an organization committed to defending America from "dangerous" African Americans in the wake of the Civil War. The Klan's actual program was not restricted to anti-Black racism but extended to "defending" America from immigrants, Jews, and Catholics as well.

Kallen, born in 1882 in Germany, the son of a Jewish Orthodox rabbi, came to the United States as a child in 1887 and completed his PhD in 1908 at Harvard, where he taught until 1911. From 1911 to 1918, he taught at the University of Wisconsin in Madison, and in 1918 became one of the founding faculty members of the New School for Social Research in New York City. Even though Kallen set aside the Jewish religious faith early in his life, he nevertheless continued to identify himself ethnically as a Jew and came to believe that this "cultural" identification was important to his self-identity.

Following his teacher James, Kallen held the view that human beings were complex combinations of what James called "material, social, and spiritual" selves. The material self, James argued, included one's body as well as one's family and friends and whatever aspects of the material world one saw as one's own. The social self was the self one had as a result of one's place in society. It was, James thought, how others see you as a friend, a teacher, a student, a danger, or an enemy. The spiritual self was the "aspirational self," the self as expressed by goals and ideals (see James 1907/1984, chapter XII). Drawing on the work of Boas at Columbia and his conversations with his friends in the Pearson Circle, including Parsons, Goldenweiser, and Lowie, Kallen saw individuals working in cultural complexes made up of learned habits, built environments, patterns of social interaction, and ritual practices. Cultures were not optional additions to otherwise complete persons, nor were they fixed aspects of individuals unable to change or grow. At the core, human beings were the same—human beings. But in their daily lives, as products of their environment, they were much more.

Consistent with this view, Kallen and his friend, future Supreme Court Justice Felix Frankfurter (1882–1965), cofounded the Menorah Society at Harvard. The Society worked to encourage Jewish students to maintain connections with their cultural heritage in the context of a university that included anti-Semitic students and faculty and, at times, adopted overtly anti-Semitic policies. Later, Kallen became a member of the Zionist Organization of America, a group committed to the founding of a Jewish homeland in Palestine, not because of his commitment to the theology of a Chosen People, but because a homeland would help to sustain the cultural distinctiveness of Jewish people.

In his essay on the Ku Klux Klan, Kallen argued in part that the program of groups like the Klan, under the guise of "Americanism," was in fact bent on undermining America by eliminating the diverse cultures that made America the distinctive place it was. "On the record," he wrote, "the Klan seeks social and intellectual conformity and economic and political rascality. Unopposed, it would render culture impossible in the United States" (1998, p. 33). America had, on the contrary, served as a place that "permitted the spontaneous self-rooting and automatic growth of differentiated communities" (p. 34). Such diversity, Kallen claimed, was "the indispensable prerequisite to the existence and growth of culture in the United States. In manyness, variety, differentiation, lies the vitality of such oneness as they may compose." He proposed that the possibility for the growth of culture is based in pluralism, and that that pluralism "is possible only in a democratic society whose institutions encourage individuality in groups, in persons, in temperaments, whose program liberates these individualities and guides them into a fellowship of freedom and cooperation" (p. 35). Ironically, despite the Klan's overt and well-known attacks on Blacks and the diversity represented, Kallen never mentioned African American culture or its place in American society in his essay.

*Culture and Democracy in the United States* also included the essay, "Democracy versus the Melting Pot." This essay was first published in 1915 in *The Nation* as a response to the idea of America as a "melting pot." This idea had been popularized by Israel Zangwill's 1905 play by that name and an increasing number of books like E. A. Ross's *The Old World in the New*, which argued that immigrants should either assimilate to the common "American" culture or leave. "What troubles Mr. Ross and so many other American citizens of British stock," Kallen contended, "is not really inequality; what troubles them is difference" (1998, p. 107). What Ross and others failed to notice was that the success of the American economy, that is, the successful functioning of "greed," required immigration. By introducing more workers who brought with them diverse cultural practices and products, the US economy was able to grow.

> Democratism and the federal principle have worked together with economic greed and ethnic snobbishness to people the land with all the nationalities of Europe, and to convert the early American nationality into the present American nation. For the United States are in the process of becoming a federal state not merely as a union of geographical and administrative unities, but also as a cooperation of cultural diversities, as a federation or commonwealth of national cultures. (p. 108)

Rather than a melting pot, America had the opportunity to become an orchestra, a

> perfection of the cooperative harmonies of European Civilization. As in an orchestra every type of instrument has its specific timbre and tonality, founded in its substance and

form ... so each ethnic group may be the natural instrument, its temper and culture may be its theme and melody and the harmony and dissonances and discords of them all may make the symphony of civilization. (pp. 117–18)

Kallen's vision of an "American orchestra" was inspirational to many, including Randolph Bourne, who cited it as a source for his vision of a transnational America.

Yet, the limits of the view are also apparent. Even as Kallen affirmed the value and place of European cultures, he once again did not mention the culture of African Americans who had been living in the aftermath of enslavement since the Civil War or the Native peoples of America who were victims of an ongoing program of genocide. Cultural pluralism became a key term in the United States between the world wars, but it remained limited in its scope and vision.

When Kallen revisited cultural pluralism in a 1956 essay, however, he revised his view of what cultures could be part of the "orchestra." Acknowledging the rejection of Native Americans from "American" cultural pluralism, Kallen offered a qualified inclusion: "Only long after the turn of the new century was the Indian's cultural economy seen ... and a new program devised which envisaged his cultural survival and growth as a different and equal fellow citizen amid the diverse formations of white enterprise" (1956, p. 76). African Americans, through distinctive cultural development (particularly in the arts), had likewise come to be a part of the American Idea.

Yet the orchestra metaphor captured, in the end, only one aspect of Kallen's conception of pluralism. As a result of developments in cultural anthropology ("culturology," he called it), "The group culture will seem to have a nature independent of [the individuals who make it up], to be a whole different from its parts, with ways and works evincing its own different laws of persistence, struggle and growth" (1998, p. 45). The group culture is capable of determining its own future. Such cultures can play in the orchestra of America as independent agents in themselves, recalling Royce's and Follett's conceptions of communities.

At the same time, Kallen offered another, possibly contradictory notion of pluralism. In this case, the boundaries of diverse cultures are recognized as artifacts of contingent history. In a multicultural world (renamed an "intercultural" world in his 1956 essay), individuals learn to cross boundaries freely so that the more they cross, the better their education and the more aware they are of the values of others—"freer are [their] powers to avail [themselves] of them." The "equipment" of such a person "renders him, mind and body, a cosmopolitan, literally a citizen of the world. Without ever losing his commitment to his home base, his citizenship, and his original culture, he is now also not a stranger in any different country and culture" (p. 53). Kallen's cosmopolitanism—at odds with the constraints placed by cultures that set sharp boundaries—approximated the later cosmopolitanism of Martha Nussbaum and the idea of World Traveling proposed by Maria Lugones in her book, *Pilgrimages/Peregrinajes* (2003).

At the heart of Kallen's conception of culture were two key notions, one marking a kind of metaphysical starting point and the other marking a practical one. The metaphysical point was framed in his 1918 essay "The Original Form and Philosophical Leanings of Job." Drawn from the Jewish tradition, Kallen argued that the Book of Job should be seen as a Jewish tragedy modeled on ancient Greek tragedies and roughly contemporary to them in their composition. What is significant about this framing of Job is that the force of the narrative is transformed from one that is primarily religious in character to one that captures the character of finite human life in general. Human beings are, because of their limitations, beings whose lives are always tragic in the end. It is in this context that human cultures develop as distinctive responses to the human condition. While Job appeared to have a distinctively Jewish attitude, Kallen took up the attitude as universally human. As William Toll concluded, "The drama of [Job's] unfolding tragedy, [Kallen] believed, would better depict the Jew as one who could face the uncertainty of the Jamesian universe with intelligence and dignity" (Toll, 1997, p. 63). Jewish character, that is, a character framed by a distinctive culture, became a model for human character in general.

The practical thread of Kallen's work emerged in his study of art. Practical tools, foods, furniture, and decorations are made in the context of daily life and are located in a specific place and time. With use and reflection, practice and interaction with others, art evolves into fine arts of diverse styles that come to make new aesthetic experiences. Cultural pluralism, as he suggested in his 1956 essay, is a means of developing new art and meaning through the cultivation of "the different" and its intersections with others. American democracy is predicated on the aesthetically laden pluralism that, by the 1950s, was in jeopardy as the forces of assimilation again ruled. Writing in his 1942 book, *Art and Freedom*, Kallen argued that aesthetic experience—the experience of beauty that brings both joy and the potential for meaning—"happens as readily in factories and office-buildings as in museums and concert halls; in elevators and subways, on highways and streets, as among the mountains or on the sea; . . . on dumps, by slagpiles and dungheaps, as in landscaped gardens or well-ordered groves" (1942, p. 949). These diverse sites of meaningful experience give rise to different "styles," patterns of expression, and habits of experience. These styles, framed as art or other cultural elements,

> All live and move and have their being in the democratic process whereby men's ways and works, each different from the other, come together with each other, and by searching and seeking, adjusting and readjusting, come finally to a common sentiment in a common way of life. (p. 934)

Kallen's notion of cultural pluralism eventually came to be known as multiculturalism. He noted that the idea was generated in discussions with Alain LeRoy Locke (1885–1954), a student of his at Harvard. In a letter to his former professor and friend Barrett Wendell, Kallen wrote of his interaction with Locke.

> It was in 1905 that I began to formulate the notion of cultural pluralism. I had a Negro student named Alain Locke, a very remarkable young man—very sensitive, very easily hurt—who insisted that he was a human being and that his color ought not to make any difference. And, of course, it was a mistaken insistence. It had to make a difference and it had to be accepted and respected and enjoyed for what it was.
> Two years later when I arrived at Oxford on a fellowship he was there as a Rhodes scholar, and we had a race problem because the Rhodes scholars from the South were bastards. So they had a Thanksgiving dinner which I refused to attend because they refused to have Locke.
> And he said, "I am a human being," just as I had said it earlier. What difference does the difference make? We are all alike Americans. And we had to argue out the question of how the differences made differences, and in arguing out those questions the formulae,

then phrases, developed—"cultural pluralism," "the right to be different." (Quoted in Harris and Molesworth, 2008, p. 69)

In other accounts by Kallen, though, he took credit for the idea and the terms and suggested he was responsible for Locke coming to the idea of pluralism. Kallen was also conflicted in his personal feelings. In the 1907 exchange of letters with Wendell, Kallen had written to ask for support for Locke, "despite" Locke being a Negro. Wendell was overt in his racism, and Kallen agreed with his friend's assessment of the Negro race, though noting Locke as an exception. This may have been done in hopes of gaining Wendell's favor, but it points to a tension within Kallen himself. That Kallen was one of Locke's most important supporters tells us much about the world Locke had to navigate as one of the first African American philosophers.

Influenced by racial conflict and two world wars, Locke worked to retain a robust individuality while acknowledging the thoroughly social project of democracy. Supportive of Black participation in both world wars, he also witnessed the race riots in Washington, D.C., that occurred at the close of the First World War. Living through the Depression also made him conscious of the contributions of capitalism to various forms of oppression. Locke was born in Philadelphia in 1885. Locke's parents were both educated and worked outside the home, and both stressed the importance of education as a responsibility to the individual and the community. Having suffered from rheumatic fever when he was young, Locke was only about five feet tall. His stature, combined with his race, made plain his minority status, and his somewhat covert homosexuality complicated his social position even further. His strict upbringing by his mother resulted in behavior that gained him a reputation for being aloof and a snob.

Part of his response was to excel in school. Locke attended Harvard, was elected to Phi Beta Kappa, and was the first African American Rhodes scholar, and among the first to receive a PhD in philosophy. He taught for nearly forty years at Howard University and served as a visiting professor at Fisk University, University of Wisconsin, City College of New York, and, with the help of Kallen, the New School for Social Research. All of this required working through how others saw him. Even as a Rhodes scholar, he was denied entrance to many of the Oxford colleges. This, combined with the slights of his fellow Americans described above, did much to bring issues of race more forcefully to Locke's attention.

Perhaps best remembered for his work supporting African American literature and the arts (*The New Negro*, 1925), Locke was also concerned with the concept of race and with issues of value more generally. As a student at Harvard, Locke became centrally interested in developing a theory of value. Drawing on James's pragmatism, Locke argued that human behavior was "selectively preferential, and not always in terms of outer adjustments and concrete results." When experiencing a situation, human beings not only calculate results but also react emotionally, preferring some things to others.

> Value reactions guided by emotional preferences and affinities are as potent in the determination of attitudes as pragmatic consequences are in the determination of actions. In the generic and best sense of the term "pragmatic," it is as important to take stock of one as the other. (1925, p. 37)

These emotional preferences represented the presence of diverse feeling-modes that helped to categorize experience. Some feeling- or "value-modes" framed awe and fear (the "religious mode"), others a moment of choice (the "ethical mode"), others framed acceptance or rejection (truth and falsity: the "logical mode"), and still other value-modes framed repose and disruption (the "aesthetic mode"). Just what events or situations would generate a certain emotional response and just how that response would emerge in the attitudes of individuals was a product of culture and history. As a result, different cultural groups came to value different things as awesome, as morally right, as true, and as beautiful. But all cultural groups, as human organisms, lived through their emotions, through value-modes, and, as a result, Locke could posit common functions—ways of ordering life—that served as the source of "value ultimates" in terms of which cultures could be encountered and differences engaged.

While different cultural groups may not share the same truths, they could recognize, even across differences, that the other held some things as true and false. Thanks to the common function—Locke called this "cultural equivalence"—objects experienced as beautiful in one culture could be recognized as equivalent to certain other objects in another. These same objects, as objects of beauty, could become candidates for beauty in another culture, though not in exactly the same way. Locke called this "limited cultural convertibility." These sorts of exchanges across cultural boundaries mark the potential for interaction and mutual change—that is, "cultural reciprocity." From this perspective, the values of any culture, while they may fill a common function, are nevertheless relative to particular histories and circumstances and so are not absolute.

With regard to racial groups, Locke took up Du Bois's idea of the "talented tenth," which called upon educated members of the Black race to be representatives to the White race and role models for other Blacks. At the same time, however, he questioned the very category of race and regularly pointed to the long history of people mixing—biologically and culturally. Locke rejected the idea that race is solely biological. Instead, race is the development of habits and preferences within a culture—a matter of "social heredity." "Instead . . . of regarding culture as expressive of race, race is . . . regarded as itself a culture product" (1989, p. 193). Physical aspects of race (skin color, hair texture, etc.) are incorporated into cultural practices so that, from an ethnological point of view, "Race . . . seems to lie in that peculiar selective preference for certain culture-traits and resistance to certain others which is characteristic of all types and levels of social organization" (p. 195). Preferences, racial and otherwise, "are themselves factors in the process of culture making, and account primarily for the persistence and resistance of culture-traits" (p. 194). In order to avoid the difficulties caused by the so-called scientific conception of race, Locke suggested that "the best procedure would be to substitute for the term *race* the term *culture-group*" (p. 194).

As products of ongoing experience, races are also constantly subject to change. In a coauthored work, *When Peoples Meet*, Locke wrote:

> It should . . . be noted that cultural exchange passes in reciprocal streams from conquerors to the conquered and from the conquered to the dominant groups. It is not always the dominant stock or the upper classes who are the carriers or importers of culture. Societies have just as frequently received infiltrations of alien culture from the bottom through the absorption of conquered and subject groups. (1946, p. 10)

Despite the inevitability of contact and influence, however, Locke also affirmed "the fact of the distinctive character of individual cultures" and that such sharply different groups are vital to cultural growth and development. "Variation is at the root of cultural change, and cultural diversity is conducive to it" (p. 11). Locke's active promotion of the art and literature of the Harlem Renaissance—his promotion of "Negro art"—is not an affirmation of inherent race differences, but the affirmation of a process of fostering cultural development through cultural difference.

Related to this pluralism, and influenced by James, Locke sought to capture the constructive possibilities of James's pluralism but to add methods for critiquing values. "Ever since William James's ardent and creative advocacy of it, pluralism has involved, explicitly or by implication, an antiauthoritarian principle" (1946, p. 96). "It is not sufficient," however, "merely to disestablish authoritarianism and its absolutes." It is also necessary to develop "effective mediating principles for situations of basic value divergence and conflict" (p. 96). There is a need both for a theory of value that identifies "commonality" and "a profound and nonaggressive respect for difference and the right to differ" (p. 100). This kind of respect is important if we hope to work through conflict in ways that do not rely on violence.

> If pluralism and relativism can nip in the psychological bud the passion for arbitrary unity and conformity, they already have functioned effectively as ideological peacemakers.... For with greater mutual understanding, there can only be less motivation for forced unification. Just as in the democratic philosophy, the obvious limit of one's personal rights is where they begin to infringe similar rights of others, so in this value domain mutual respect and reciprocity, based on nonaggression and nondisparagement, can alone be regarded as justifiable. (p. 101)

Locke further identified the limits of such respect: reciprocity, tolerance, and parity.

He argued that once we understand that cultures are the consequence of the mixing of peoples, we lose the logical framework that understands cultures as sharply divided and as superior and inferior, or dominant and backward. "Civilization, for all its claims of distinctiveness, is a vast amalgam of cultures. The difficulties of our social creeds and practices have arisen in great measure from our refusal to recognize this fact" (1989, p. 203). This context of reciprocity helps us learn tolerance rather than dismissal and subjugation. Those who do not extend a "parity of respect," that is, equal respect, fall back on absolutist views and seek to force a kind of uniformity; they try to dominate and use those peoples and cultures deemed inferior. It is this attitude that we do not have to respect, according to Locke, as it fails to be open to difference and instead relies on various forms of absolutism. Beginning with the work of James and Kallen, Locke promoted pluralism, but he tried to improve on what he saw as James's anarchic pluralism by demonstrating that there are values humans hold in common and by pointing to the limits of tolerance. "For if once this broader relativistic approach could discover beneath the expected culture differentials of time and place such functional 'universals' as actually may be there, these common-denominator values would stand out as pragmatically confirmed by common human experience" (p. 56).

In 1943, Locke traveled to Haiti as an Inter-American professor, where he delivered six lectures under the general theme of "The Negro's Contribution to the Culture of the Americas." He began by stressing the importance of mutual, two-way sympathy between the United States and Haiti: "The new order of the new day in human relations is reciprocity, not aggression, mutual assistance not overlordship, fraternity, in short, not paternalism" (Carter, 2016, p. 9). Locke argued that "just and enduring group relations" could foster solidarity among nations if we could "lift the fog of chauvinism" that promotes notions of racial or cultural purity and superiority. He cautioned against blaming Nazi racialists alone for thinking that "civilization was both the sole product and property of those classes, nations or ethnic groups that have sat in the seat of political and economic power." Many have made that error and ignored the fact that "[s]ome of the richest growths of culture have been transplanted crops not native to the land in which they flowered; . . . a great deal of what is best in culture derives not from pure but from crossed and hybrid strains" (pp. 11–12). He argued that the common denominator among the various nations and cultures of the Americas is the dominant presence of transplanted and reimagined Negro art forms and traditions (a case of an oppressed minority becoming "a dominant cultural force" (p. 15)). The very mixing of cultures that resulted from the institution of slavery in the Americas gives them the chance to be "pioneers of that cosmopolitan culture typical of complete democracy and of an increasingly international world" (pp. 13, 90).

For Locke, "cultural pluralism" is the only "fully democratic notion of culture and the only realistic and safe concept of nationality. For the majority factions, it imposes modesty, tolerance and a fraternal spirit; for the minority groups it is a boon of protection, self-respect and reciprocity" (Carter, 2016, p. 14). Put in a more radical way, Locke says that cultural influence is "a double reciprocal process that is not only top down, but also bottom up. If the master has an influence on the slave, the slave in some respect has an influence on the master" (p. 29). While he thinks this is self-evident in culture (understood as music, painting, literature), he thinks it also is the case politically. Because the treatment of minority groups is an "index by which the practical efficiency and integrity of that particular country's democracy can readily be gaged [sic] and judged," the "Negro has thus become a basic part and conspicuous symbol of the cause of democracy in our Western hemisphere." And given the international tensions of the time (Second World War) there is a need for "sounder and more consistently democratic practices of race at home" (p. 92). Without more consistently democratic practices, there is a real risk that "fascism and its attendant racism should gain firm rootage in American soil" (p. 93). This caused Locke to reject not only the color caste that accompanied the institution of slavery but also the idea of a "racial elite split off, largely on the basis of a color class, from the race proletariat" (p. 101). Here, Locke rejects ideas such as Du Bois's talented tenth as enforcing a division that can promote absolutism and dogmatism and block reciprocity and a critically engaged tolerance.

Locke's version of pluralism thus tried to capture the Jamesian spirit that disallowed absolutism and dogmatism, while promoting the evaluation of values and helping to see values as tentative and subject to revision. The commonality of value formation provides resources for the critique of values and justification for the critical aspects of a functioning democracy.

> We know, of course, that we cannot get tolerance from a fanatic or reciprocity from a fundamentalist of any stripe, religious, philosophical, cultural, political or ideological. But what is often overlooked is that we cannot, soundly and safely at least, preach liberalism and at the same time abet and condone bigotry, condemn uniformitarianism and placate orthodoxy, promote tolerance and harbor the seeds of intolerance. (1989, p. 57)

Writing in 1942, shortly after the United States entered the Second World War, he suggested "that our duty to democracy on the plane of ideas, especially in time of crisis, is the analysis of just this problem and some consideration of its possible solution" (p. 57). Most of us are unaware of the ways absolutism holds in our beliefs and habits. Many loyalties are held in this way and have more in common with a totalitarian temperament than with the demands of democracy. "We are all sadly acquainted with how [tolerance] may blow away in time of crises or break when challenged by self-interest," Locke wrote, "how under stress we find ourselves, after all, unreasonably biased in favor of 'our own,' whether it be the mores, ideas, faiths or merely 'our crowd'" (p. 58). This kind of bias is evidence that "value bigotry is somehow still deep-rooted there. Under the surface of such frail tolerance some unreconstructed dogmatisms lie, the latent source of the emerging intolerance" (p. 58). Some examples of this process of developing intolerance have already been noted in this book: the Anarchist Exclusion Act, the Sedition Act, the Allotment Act, and lynch laws, to name a few.

Locke believed that if we come to see the real commonalities among humans that underlie the differences, we can strengthen our tolerance and build bridges. This is important for democracy as "it puts the premium upon equivalence not upon identity, calls for co-operation rather than for conformity and promotes reciprocity instead of factional antagonism. Authoritarianism, dogmatism and bigotry just cannot take root and grow in such intellectual soil." He called this a "more pragmatic and progressive rationale for democratic thought and action." (1989, p. 60). The resulting approach to democracy would call for "the enlargement of the democratic life," including real tolerance for, and integration of, minority groups and nonconformist ideas. Such inclusion would both "temper the quality of patriotism and sub-group loyalties" (p. 61) and foster direct participation in the process of decision-making and culture-building. The dual emphasis on difference and inclusion would also require a "realistic world mindedness," the ability to see the world from the perspective of other cultures, eschewing bigotry and dogmatism. Such an approach, Locke argued, would make the conditions of peace more possible by requiring the integration of the interests of both the "victors and vanquished alike" (p. 62). In Follett's terms, democracy required power-with not power-over. Like other philosophers of resistance, Locke further believed that challenging ideas and constructing new ones—the work of philosophers—is a necessary condition for democracy to flourish.

> Broadening our cultural values and tempering our orthodoxies is of infinitely more service to enlarged democracy than direct praise and advocacy of democracy itself. For until broadened by relativism and reconstructed accordingly, our current democratic traditions and practice are not ready for world-wide application. (p. 63)

There were, of course, serious obstacles to achieving the goal. "Political and cultural dogmatism, in the form of culture bias, nation worship, and racism, still stands in the way and must first be invalidated and abandoned." However, the risk of not carrying out such work, that is, failure "to orient ourselves courageously and intelligently to a universe of peoples and cultures" would leave "little or no hope for stable world order of any kind—democratic or otherwise" (p. 63).

But Locke had hope. Pluralism, he said, is the "intellectual antidote" to authoritarianism. He cautioned that we "should not be stampeded into pluralism" as a response to totalitarianism (the ideological enemy the allies were fighting in the Second World War). Pluralism is "our handiest intellectual weapon against the totalitarian challenge." He went on to say that "if, as we have seen, it can also make a constructive contribution to the internal fortification of democracy, then it is even more permanently justified and should on that score be doubly welcomed" (1989, p. 64). The pluralism advocated by Locke and sought by others in the philosophical resistance, including Du Bois, Follett, Kallen, and their predecessors, struggled to find a place in the American academy and in American culture. The coming of the Second World War, however, transformed society and pushed pluralism and its version of democracy further out of reach.

## Primary Texts

Carter, Jacoby Adeshei (2016). *African American Contributions to the Americas' Cultures: A Critical Edition of Lectures by Alain Locke*. New York: Palgrave Macmillan.

Kallen, Horace (1956). *Cultural Pluralism and the American Idea: An Essay in Social Philosophy*. Philadelphia: University of Pennsylvania Press.

Locke, Alain (1989). *The Philosophy of Alain Locke: The Harlem Renaissance and Beyond*, ed. Leonard Harris. Philadelphia: Temple University Press.

# CHAPTER 16
# WAR AND THE RISE OF LOGICAL POSITIVISM

On April 13, 1931, John Dewey delivered an address on the nationwide NBC radio network. He described high unemployment and the increasing number of people without adequate food, clothing, and housing. He called for the federal government, under President Herbert Hoover, to respond by raising taxes on the wealthiest Americans. The problem was not a *lack* of food and clothing, he said, but that the collapse of the economy had made it impossible for ordinary Americans to buy food and clothes. "[Grain] elevators," he said, "are crammed with grain; the government has millions of bushels on hand, and thousands of persons are starving and being fed from soup kitchens in the midst of plenty" (Dewey in Boydston, LW 6, p. 341). As the winter of 1930–1 ended, he said, "Coal mines shut down because they can't sell coal, and thousands have shivered through the winter for lack of heat. Warehouses are stuffed with shoes and cloth, and men and women are going ragged and out at the toes and heels" (p. 341).

The Great Depression, brought on by a host of factors including widespread financial speculation using unsecured loans, began in earnest on October 28 and 29, 1929, when the New York Stock Exchange lost nearly one-quarter of its value. Though there was a brief recovery, the trend continued downward until July 1932, when the market closed at 41.22, down from its high of 381.17 at the beginning of September 1929—a decrease in value of 89 percent. The crash cut wages and threw millions out of work. The response by the Hoover administration was to encourage producers to refuse to sell their products until the prices rose again. The result, as Dewey observed, was full warehouses, plentiful coal, and significant grain stores, even as poor Americans starved. A group called "The People's Lobby" sponsored Dewey's radio address. The People's Lobby was founded after the First World War to support the labor movement by providing information about working conditions and related issues to the larger public. In 1929, Dewey was asked to serve as the Lobby's president. At the same time, Dewey was also the national chair of the League for Political Action. Both groups worked to found a third political party committed to socialist principles as a means of reconstructing the American economy.

In response to the lack of work and the increasing poverty of the working class, riots broke out in major cities; some associated with labor action and others simply the result of the worsening economy. Veterans of the First World War, for example, had been given "bonus certificates" in 1924 that they could redeem in 1945 as extra compensation for their military service. In response to the depression, the veterans demanded that the government redeem their certificates immediately so that the veterans could support themselves and their families during the hard economic times. The Hoover administration refused and, in the summer of 1932, the veterans formed the "Bonus Army" and marched on Washington, D.C. Over 40,000 people, mostly veterans (sometimes with their families), slept in tents and vacant buildings along the Washington Mall until Hoover ordered the army to remove them. General Douglas MacArthur, later commander of the Second World War effort against Japan and the leader of the United Nations forces that intervened in Korea in 1950, led the military force. MacArthur's aide in the action was Dwight D. Eisenhower, later supreme commander of the Allied forces in Europe during the Second World War and President of the United States from 1953 until 1961. On MacArthur's orders, infantry, cavalry, and tanks drove the veterans out of the city using tear gas, burning the veterans' camp as they went. Eventually, the Bonus Army received its bonuses when Congress, in 1936, passed the Adjusted Compensation Payment Act over a presidential veto.

The protest of the Bonus Army, and other protests and riots around the country for food and work, helped to seal Hoover's defeat in the 1932 election. After Franklin Delano Roosevelt took office as president in 1933, the federal government reversed the Hoover administration's strict economic hands-off policy and began to implement a series of measures called "The New Deal" aimed, as Howard Zinn later observed, "mainly at stabilizing the economy, and secondly at giving enough help to the lower classes to keep them from turning a rebellion into a real revolution" (1995, p. 384). The recovery was slow.

In October 1933, after Roosevelt had begun to put his economic recovery plan in place, Dewey gave an address in which he challenged the assumptions of the New Deal. He had been asked to talk about the need for a new political party, but he instead wanted to talk about the need for a "new conception of politics, a new conception of government, and of the relation of the government to the people in this country" (LW 11, p. 274). He observed that those in power made it a regular practice to declare that "all of our great industrial advance" and all that came with it, from new technologies to improved agricultural productivity, "is the product of our competitive economic system and that . . . even if there are break-downs and injustices and sufferings, we have got to give all that to the credit of the economic system we have been living under" (p. 278). To which he responded, "Well, now, . . . it is *not true*" (p. 279).

The economic system for Dewey was an obstacle rather than an engine of growth. "And it is," he declared, "*that* which demands not a 'patching' here and there but some fundamental re-thinking of our social and political relations" (p. 280). What the Great Depression called for was "a new conception" of the purpose of government. It is to be "an instrument in the service of the people and not, as under the system of competition for power and competition for command of power, the tool and instrument of selfish acquisitive interest" (p. 280). In the face of the ongoing Depression, Dewey and other philosophers advocated for the use of careful inquiry aimed at the problems faced by ordinary Americans as a means of transformation. The importance of science—for Dewey the practice of careful inquiry—became central in the philosophical resistance to the circumstances that maintained industrial capitalism as the heart of American life. The Great Depression would continue until the next world war began. In anticipation of the coming conflict, Roosevelt and Congress began to re-militarize the United States. The resulting investment in industry and labor began to change the economic situation in 1939.

Worry about the rise of totalitarianism was not confined to politics. During the Fifth International Congress for the Unity of Science held at Harvard in September 1939, Horace Kallen challenged the assembled philosophers and scientists. "We are living in totalitarian times," he announced. "In free countries, representatives of Big Business, so habituated in the language of laissez faire as to be practically incapacitated from speaking any other, nevertheless stretch it to cover extensions of their authoritarian hierarchies of trust and monopoly to the national economic order" (1940, p. 82). Unification, he observed, is identified with "nobility and reverence," while the many are taken with vulgarity and scorn. "Not philosophers alone," he continued, "but churchmen, statesmen, businessmen and scientists have been, and continue to be, against the Many" (p. 81). According to Kallen, the unity of science movement—the movement the philosophers at the meeting had gathered to support—was dangerous. It required that all science (knowledge) be expressed in a single language and that any knowledge that cannot be so expressed be rejected as meaningless (or at least not meaningful as knowledge). The result was that the movement excluded particular knowledges from what Kallen called the "orchestra of science."

In contrast to the idea of unification that involved a single scientific language in which all knowledge could be expressed, Kallen argued that "unity here signifies the ways in which individualities, be they thoughts or things or people, who are different from each other can live together with each other and not sacrifice their integrities as individuals" (p. 89). Rejecting the program of the movement gathered at Harvard, Kallen proposed that unity be understood as "orchestration" "with its implication of diversities of instruments and parts, of movements and pauses, of dissonances and discords as well as harmonies, of sequences whose every new item suffuses without deindividualizing all that have gone before" (1940, p. 96). "Orchestrations," he concluded, "would sustain and enhance the right to be different" (p. 97).

Two days before the conference opened, the armies of Nazi Germany had begun their invasion of Poland. On the day the conference began, the Allied nations of Europe declared war on Germany. As an advocate of Zionism and a view he called Hebraism (secular Judaism), Kallen had strong connections with Jewish leaders in the United States, including Louis Brandeis (an associate justice of the Supreme Court) and Rabbi Stephen S. Wise, a founder of the American Jewish Congress in 1920 (and one of the founders, with Du Bois, Addams, Dewey, and others, of the NAACP). After Adolf Hitler was appointed chancellor of Germany in January 1933, systematic attacks on German Jews became government policy. Wise helped organize anti-Nazi protests and boycotts of German-produced goods in the United States.

In 1933, speaking as the honorary president of the American Jewish Congress, Wise declared, "The time for prudence and caution is past. We must speak up like men. How can we ask our Christian friends to lift their voices in protest against the wrongs suffered by Jews if we keep silent?" He went on to caution that "What is happening in Germany today may happen tomorrow in any other land on earth unless it is challenged and rebuked" (Wise, 2014). In response to the protests, the US Secretary of State, Cordell Hull chose only to issue a letter to the German government "regretting" the events in Germany. Suppression of and violence against Jews, homosexuals, Romani people, and others viewed as dissenters and outsiders continued mostly without challenge by the US government.

In June 1939, activists in the United States helped to convince Congress to consider a bill permitting the immigration of 20,000 Jewish children from Germany over a two-year period. The bill failed to pass. That same month, the SS St. Louis, a passenger ship, left Hamburg, Germany, with nearly 1,000 German Jews onboard. The ship had planned to land in Cuba but was turned away. As the St. Louis sailed slowly along the US coast, President Roosevelt ordered the Coast Guard to ensure that no passengers were allowed to leave the ship and enter the United States. In mid-June, the St. Louis finally landed in Belgium, and Belgium, the Netherlands, France, and Great Britain took in its passengers. Most of the refugees not taken by Great Britain were eventually captured and killed when the Nazis invaded their host countries. When Kallen stepped to the podium at Harvard in 1939, it was with an awareness of this persecution and the knowledge that totalitarianism and its demands for unification and conformity had brought the world to war.

When Kallen addressed the Fifth International Congress for the Unity of Science, he joined sixty philosophers, scientists, mathematicians, and social scientists to discuss the promise of science as a means of addressing the ills of the world. The model of science discussed was one that argued for the unification of science in a way that would preserve its independence from the politics and power struggles that led to war in Europe. At the center of this movement was the work of a group of philosophers who first gathered in Vienna, Austria, and consequently called themselves the Vienna Circle. The acknowledged leaders of the Circle were Otto Neurath (1882–1945), a sociologist, and philosophers Moritz Schlick (1882–1936) and Rudolf Carnap (1891–1970). Neurath studied political science and statistics at the University of Vienna. The group also included Herbert Feigl, Friedrich Waismann, Kurt Gödel, and Gustav Bergmann.

Many of the members of the group were Jews and in the 1930s were increasingly subject to anti-Semitism both in their academic work and in their daily lives. In 1936, a former student assassinated Schlick as he came down a staircase in the central hall of the University of Vienna. While the student confessed to the murder, the case drew wide public attention because, according to the press, it highlighted the growing "problem" of Jews in the Austrian academy (though neither Schlick nor his assassin was a Jew). For the other members of the Circle, as opportunities to leave continental Europe developed, most chose to leave, many for positions at major American universities. Feigl left in 1931 and taught at the University of Iowa. He moved to the University of Minnesota in 1940 and was replaced at Iowa by Bergmann, who arrived in the United States in 1938 as the German army occupied Austria. Neurath left Austria in 1934 for Holland and then fled Holland on a motorized lifeboat as the Nazis invaded in 1940. He was picked up by a British destroyer and, after eight months in prison, spent the rest of the war in Great Britain. Carnap left Austria in 1935 and became a professor at the University of Chicago and later, in 1954, at the University of California, Los Angeles (UCLA) (Uebel, 2011; Murzi, 2001; Neurath, 1946a; Edmonds, 2020). The newly arrived philosophers quickly came to be the recognized leaders of American academic philosophy.

The Vienna Circle was officially formed in 1928 as the *Verein Ernst Mach* [Ernst Mach Club]. In 1929, Carnap, Hans Hahn, and Neurath published an informal manifesto representing the general program of the group. The *Wissenschaftliche Weltauffassung: Der Wiener Kreis* [*Scientific Conception of the World: The Vienna Circle*], as summarized by Jørgen Jørgensen, announced the central commitment of the group to develop "a unified science comprising all knowledge of reality accessible to man without dividing it into separate, unconnected special disciplines, such as physics and psychology, natural science and letters, philosophy and the special sciences" (Jørgensen, 1951, p. 4). The means of achieving this unified science was "the logical method of analysis," credited to Giuseppe Peano, Gottlob Frege, Alfred North Whitehead, and Bertrand Russell, which was "to eliminate metaphysical problems and assertions as meaningless as well as to clarify the meaning of concepts and sentences of empirical science by showing their immediately observable content" (p. 4). As a result, "a framework [was] created for the work of the Vienna Circle; its negative task [was] an expurgation of metaphysical-speculative statements as meaningless, while its positive task [was] to define ever more precisely and fully the meaning of scientifically tenable statements" (p. 4).

One type of "tenable" statement about the world is "empirical." The meaning of such claims "can be determined by logical analysis, or, more precisely, by reduction to simple sentences about the empirically given," especially in the context of controlled experiments (p. 5). These simple sentences are often called "observation statements" or "atomic propositions." Other statements are sentences that, while they appear to have the same structure as empirical claims, are not observations but have to do with emotions. To claim that there is a God, for example, is not properly a claim about experience but rather expresses (in misleading terms) fear of death, hope for the future, or love for others. On this view, "metaphysicians and theologians, misinterpreting their own sentences, believe that their sentences assert something, represent some state of affairs" when really, they do not. The "adequate means for [expression of these feelings] is, for example, lyric poetry or music," and "not theory, information or cognition" (p. 5).

The resulting approach seemed to address the worries of this group of philosophers who, during the First World War and its aftermath, had seen philosophy implicated in global war, the virtual destruction of the German and Austrian economies, violence against Jews, communists, homosexuals, and other minorities, and the breakup of the Austro-Hungarian Empire. Claims of special knowledge of God or human purpose simply could not count as knowledge for the empiricists of Vienna. Even as they argued against metaphysics and speculative philosophy, they simultaneously made the case for a kind of critical thinking that is grounded in the need to clarify the meaning of terms, and the demand that broad claims about the world be grounded in facts accessible to all. The project, from this angle, was deeply political and called for a reconstruction of philosophy and of social knowledge in general.

Although the Vienna Circle is often remembered as a monolithic movement (and usually labeled "Logical Positivism" or "Logical Empiricism"), the group and the movement that emerged had at least two strands. One strand, led by Neurath, emphasized a form of pluralism, a strong relativism, and an overtly political agenda. The other, most closely connected with Carnap, accepted a very limited pluralism and rejected both Neurath's relativism and his politics. As suggested by Carl Hempel (a member of a similar group of philosophers in Berlin and an occasional visitor to the Vienna Circle) and supported by recent research by Thomas Uebel, "there were two quite different schools of logical empiricism, namely the one of Carnap and Schlick and so on and then the quite different one of Otto Neurath, who advocated a completely pragmatic conception of the philosophy of science" (Uebel, 2011).

After the war in 1945, Neurath, writing from England, returned to the criticisms leveled by Kallen in 1939 against the Unity of Science movement and argued that the movement was committed to pluralism and not to the totalitarian monism Kallen claimed. Kallen's 1939 criticism, voiced again in 1946 in an issue of *Philosophy and Phenomenological Research*, was that the unity sought by the movement was founded on a common language in which all knowledge would be expressed. It must, he said, "select, fix, insulate against change, and impose one language as against many others, with immutable terms and immutable denotations for all its terms, and one exclusive logic pattern for any and all arrangements of its terms" (Kallen, 1946a, p. 494). To be successful in this effort, Kallen concluded, the movement would need to "exact conformity and to control education" (p. 494); thus, the movement was inevitably totalitarian in its program.

Neurath, who had responded to Kallen indirectly several times over the intervening years between Kallen's 1939 lecture and his 1946 restatement, argued that, while such a result was a risk, the movement was nevertheless fundamentally committed to tolerance and inclusiveness, and that this very goal would be aided by the generation of a universal language. Borrowing Kallen's own metaphor for science, Neurath wrote that the universal language—he called it the "universal jargon"—"will always be in the making." Neurath did not think it would be possible to dictate how this language would be formed: "The Universal Jargon will rather be achieved by successive adaptations and compromises, by a kind of 'orchestration,' as Horace Kallen called it" (Neurath, 1940, p. 129).

What Neurath proposed was a language founded on "observation statements." Such statements were to be aggregates that included three components: "a protocol," or a statement of what happened at a particular moment, a statement of "word-thinking," or the idea that was generated at the given moment, and the object at issue in relation to the one perceiving the object. His cumbersome example of such a statement was "Otto's protocol at 3:17 [Otto was word-thinking at 3:16 (in the room at 3:15 was a table perceived by Otto)]" (p. 136). Setting aside some of the problematic details of the example, Neurath aimed to develop a language that would describe what diverse observers would take as uncontroversially shared. The sample statement would simply record that at a certain time, Otto had the thought of perceiving a table. Here, the description is of the "physical" state of thinking and perceiving and not of a subjective mental state. Whether one is an idealist or a realist, a Christian or a Jew, a capitalist or a communist, the statement should accurately note what diverse observers could take as a starting point. Knowledge that could be reduced to or translated into such a language would then be accessible to all and provide for common understanding.

In his 1946 response to Kallen, Neurath explained, "My thesis is that this start [everyday language 'after dropping some expressions, derived from magical, theological, or metaphysical speculations'] is common to human beings, past and present, all over the world." He continued by asserting that

> We are not presenting them with some new unity; not at all, we only want to say that wherever people speak to one another, for example, marooned men on an island coming from different parts of the world about fishes and trees, drink and sleep, pain and pleasure, they will have no particular difficulties in communicating through gestures, pictures, and words. (Neurath, 1946b, p. 499)

"Difficulties arise," however, when conversations take up "'causality,' 'inner experience,' or something like that" (p. 503). Knowledge of the world—in every science—should finally find its meaning in uncontroversial observation statements. Other claims, particularly metaphysical claims about causes and transcendence, cannot find their meaning in observation and so should be set aside.

"Logical empiricism is fighting 'metaphysical idealism' along the whole line," Neurath said. "It is just this set of phantasmagoria, allowing terrible means to lofty ends, which very often reduces the preparedness of people to object to the mercilessness of totalitarianism" (p. 503). It was in Plato's *Republic*, for example, that the "Nazis found fine argument for persecution, for destruction of mentally or bodily weak people and for teaching children to be cruel" (p. 503). Likewise, "Fichte's lofty so-called idealism . . . permitted him to ask for the degradation and expulsion of the Jews" (p. 504).

For Neurath, the Unity of Science movement had two central commitments: first, the establishment (over time and in a revisable way) of a universal language of science, and second, an anti-metaphysics program that would lead to a systematic elimination of claims that could not be reduced to the universal language. He concluded that "Pluralism is the aura of this scientific world community of the common man," and that "The encyclopedism of logical empiricism ... [and] the unified science encyclopedia are the children of the tolerant approach of democratic cooperation. It competes with no philosophy and is antitotalitarian through and through" (p. 508).

Kallen responded to Neurath's assessment with two arguments. First, the model that seeks complete cooperation demonstrated its efficiency and its danger in the war. "The fabrication of the [nuclear] bomb provides us with a supremely momentous instance of one mode of the unity of science—the military or totalitarian mode" (Kallen, 1946b, p. 516). By organizing scholars in diverse disciplines around a single purpose, suppressing dissent and concern, and providing vast funds to accomplish the goal, the Manhattan Project produced bombs with sufficient power to end the war.

> They and their doings were fitted to one another and to the machines they tended like so many equally inanimate bits of matter shaped into machine-parts fitted so as to compose a unified whole whose unity did come to fruition. (p. 516)

This model of unified science so impressed "the authorities and experts" that they sought to carry over the methods of wartime inquiry "to the ways and aims of peace." "What better method," Kallen asked, "to gain understanding, and win knowledge-which-is-power than to map the body thereof, define the gaps therein, and then plan to fill them?" (pp. 516–17). The method marked the way to antidemocratic authoritarian structures of the sort found in "the realistic Soviets" and "Big Business."

Second, Kallen claimed that the reduction of meaning to observation statements works only by excluding from consideration much of what makes up experience. To illustrate the value of observation statements, Neurath had proposed a hypothetical lunch with Kallen and someone from a South Pacific island. Kallen accepted the invitation and proposed to also invite "a Brahmin Hindu, an observant Orthodox Jew, a Buddhist Chinese, and [a Native American]." He continued, "What is edible and inedible to these guests will, I am afraid, depend far less on the sensory data ... than on attitudes, feelings, and judgments which may be meaningless illusions and superstitions vis-à-vis Neurath's [observation statements]" (pp. 521–2). The "unity" would not be achieved by ignoring the differences at the table, but by engaging them— "the unity of different fares consumed by different people eating together" (p. 522).

In his use of Kallen's orchestra metaphor, Neurath had argued that, just as in the process of performing a symphony, the diverse players would rely on a common system of notation to foster harmony and perform the piece. Kallen concluded his reply by transforming his orchestra example into a jazz ensemble. Science in Kallen's metaphor does not depend upon a common system of notation, but a common experience of listening and responding to the other players.

> In terms of orchestration, scientists do not make up a concert-band repeating already-existing compositions under the baton of a conductor; they compose a swing orchestra

> with a fellow player for a leader. . . . Their playing is the same as their composing, a new and yet unheard music being created by the spontaneous harmonizing of the musicians. Their orchestration is self-orchestration from within, not directed from without. (Kallen, 1946b, pp. 524–5)

If logical positivism sought, as Neurath insisted, to promote democracy and tolerance, it had chosen the wrong model. "For among the tools of thought," Kallen noted, "the idea of unity is the one which gives itself most readily to idolization. Business and war have extended its potential to the entire political and industrial economy of the modern world" (p. 526).

When Neurath died suddenly in 1945 before the exchange with Kallen was published, Carnap (and American, Charles Morris) inherited editorship of the *International Encyclopedia* and helped to solidify the second strand of the logical positivist movement in the United States. Neurath's vision of logical positivism (he called it "logical empiricism" to avoid what he took to be negative connotations associated with "positivism") was overtly political in its aim to promote democratic cooperation both in science and daily life. In contrast, Carnap's vision of logical positivism (the name he accepted) was of a method whose political purpose was to remove philosophy from politics and social issues and cultivate neutrality to match the supposed neutrality of science.

Founded as a philosophy of resistance in Europe in response to the rise of totalitarianism, the unity of science movement and its offspring in logical empiricism and positivism became, as they immigrated to the United States, a kind of counter-resistance that aimed to transform philosophy in a way that set aside the resistance philosophies of Dewey and Kallen, feminist philosophies, and philosophies responding to the experience of race and class oppression in favor of a philosophy whose "neutrality" served as its central disposition.

The war against Germany and its allies officially ended on May 8, 1945, and the war against Japan ended with the signing of the Japanese surrender on September 2, 1945. Almost immediately, territories captured from the Axis powers were placed under the administration of the Allied powers—the United States, Great Britain, France, and the Soviet Union. While the Western nations worked to establish national governments modeled on Western representative democracy, the Soviet Union worked to establish Soviet-style governments that would carry out a Stalinist form of communism. The nations that had been allies, quickly divided into the Eastern and Western "blocks" and, in the United States, the fear of communism that had resulted in charges of disloyalty in the 1920s returned.

In 1947, President Truman instituted "loyalty reviews" for federal employees. Within four years of the end of the war, the University of California instituted a requirement that all faculty sign loyalty oaths as a condition of employment. Similar laws were passed in other states. In 1950, Julius and Ethel Rosenberg were arrested for giving secret information about nuclear weapons production to Soviet spies. In February 1950, Senator Joseph McCarthy (1908–1957) of Wisconsin gave a speech at a Republican Women's Club in West Virginia in which he declared that he had "in his hand" a list of 205 employees of the US State Department who were members of the Communist Party. The FBI, long active in investigating dissenters like Goldman, Addams, and Sanger, took on the task of investigating a new, supposedly antipatriotic, generation.

Not long after McCarthy began his hunt for communists, on June 25, 1950, forces of recently partitioned North Korea invaded South Korea in an attempt to eliminate the Southern Western-allied regime and unite Korea under a single government sponsored in large part by the Soviet Union and China. The attack was devastating. The North Korean army overwhelmed the Southern army and within a few days, the forces of South Korea occupied only a small corner in the Southeast. Like Germany and the nations of Eastern Europe, Korea (which had been occupied by Japan during the Second World War) had been split roughly in half when the allies divided up the territories they had taken during the war. The United States had assisted South Korea in establishing a government and military and saw the nation as part of the Western nations opposed to communism. The invasion was quickly viewed as the first "hot" phase of the "Cold War" that had begun in the days after the Second World War and would continue until 1990.

Two days after the invasion of South Korea, the Security Council of the United Nations, founded just four years earlier, passed a resolution calling for military intervention in Korea by its member states. The Soviet Union and China protested the decision, but by July 5, US troops who had been stationed in Japan joined the South Korean army. In September, the United Nations (with mostly US troops and under the command of General MacArthur) landed a large, well-equipped force on the West side of the Korean peninsula and within a month had routed the North Korean army and stood ready to invade China. On October 25, 1950, China entered the war and pushed the UN force back to the original border between North and South. A stalemate ensued and, on July 27, 1953, after three years of war, the UN and North Korea agreed on a permanent ceasefire (see Halberstam, 2007).

On July 9, 1950, Sidney Hook (1902–1989), who had been one of Dewey's students at Columbia (sometimes called "Dewey's Bulldog" for his often-vehement defense of his mentor's views), published a short article in the *New York Times Magazine* in response to the "hot" war that had just begun in Korea. The article, "Heresy, Yes—But Conspiracy, No," argued that liberals of the postwar age needed to clarify the meaning of liberalism because "communism invokes the freedom of a liberal society in order to destroy that society" (1950, p. 154). For Hook, heresy should be understood as "a set of unpopular ideas or opinions on matters of grave concern to the community" (p. 154). He argued that the "right to profess and advocate heresy of any character, including communism, is an essential element of a liberal society" (p. 154).

Conspiracy, in contrast, was "a secret or underground movement which seeks to attain its ends not by normal political or educational process but by playing outside the rules of the game" (p. 154). Communism, for Hook, was not primarily a critical philosophy openly calling the present system to task and publicly seeking change; that is, communism, on examination, was not heresy. It was a doctrine predicated on secrecy and subterfuge. "Under present conditions of political and military warfare," he wrote, "it is not hard to see what immense dangers to the security of liberal institutions [are] implicit in this strategy of infiltration and deceit" (p. 154). In Hook's view, liberals needed to take communism seriously and support efforts to expose conspirators and protect the institutions of democracy. "This is a matter of ethical hygiene," he declared, "not of politics or of persecution" (p. 167).

Hook's first book was a version of his dissertation written under Dewey and titled *The Metaphysics of Pragmatism* (1927). He was best known, however, for several books on Marxism, *Towards the Understanding of Karl Marx: A Revolutionary Interpretation* (1933) and *From*

*Hegel to Marx* (1936). Often an activist in support of socialist causes, in 1937, Hook helped to lead the group of liberal intellectuals that convened the Trotsky hearings in Mexico, chaired by Dewey. Yet, despite his early commitment to Marxism and sympathy with the communist movement, by the end of the Second World War, Hook became an energetic anti-communist who supported efforts by schools and universities to demand loyalty of their faculty. He concluded in his 1950 article, "Liberalism must defend the free market in ideas against the racists, the professional patrioteer, and those spokesmen of the status quo who would freeze the existing inequalities of opportunity and economic power by choking off criticism" (p. 167). But, for Hook, the free market of ideas "may be checked wherever their likely effects constitute a clear and present danger to public peace or the security of the country" (p. 154). In his work after the Second World War, Hook exemplified a position that has continued to the present day, that "ethical hygiene" in service of nationhood is often necessary. In 1985, Hook was awarded the Presidential Medal of Freedom by President Ronald Reagan.

In October 1953, in the midst of McCarthy's hunt for communists in education and government, the House Un-American Activities Committee (HUAC) received an internal report naming Carnap as a person of interest. Carnap had, among other things, signed a petition in favor of the repeal of the McCarran-Walter Immigration Act passed earlier that year. The law aimed to restrict immigration, particularly from Eastern Europe, in order to guard against the immigration of communists. Carnap and some ninety-eight others, organized by a group called the American Committee for the Protection of Foreign Born, agreed that the law was too restrictive and signed a petition published in the *Daily Worker* (a newspaper often associated with the American Communist Party). Carnap was also listed as a participant in the Committee for Peaceful Alternatives to the Atlantic Pact (i.e., alternatives to NATO), a member of the National Council of the Arts, Sciences and Professions, and an endorser of the World Peace Appeal (which petitioned the UN to seat Communist China and protested the arrest without bail of non-citizens under the McCarran-Walter Act). Carnap was also a longtime associate of Phillip Frank, who was falsely accused of coming "to the United States for the purpose of organizing high level Communist Party activities" (quoted in Reisch, 2005, p. 268).

On August 14, 1953, a secret memorandum was sent to J. Edgar Hoover reporting on Carnap's activities. Though most of the names of those who gave statements were redacted when the report was made public years later, it was clear that the FBI interviewed many of Carnap's academic and social acquaintances. Typical of the findings, one interviewee "advised that the subject [Carnap] appeared to be completely wrapped up in his capacity as professor at the University and very rarely deviated from his study habits." John von Neumann (a mathematician, one of the Manhattan Project leaders, and the Atomic Energy Commissioner) was interviewed by the FBI and reported that he knew Carnap both in Prague and in the United States. Von Neumann assured the agent that he had seen "nothing which would indicate that the subject is sympathetic towards Communism [and] that the subject is interested '99% in scholastic matters and has little or no interest in politics of any kind'" (FBI File, 2014, pp. 13, 11).

The investigation of Carnap reinforced the idea that academics—philosophers included— now worked in an environment where their political views and activities were under close scrutiny. For philosophers like Carnap who had escaped Europe on the eve of world war, the scrutiny must have been eerily familiar. While Hook responded to the new circumstances by becoming an activist in the service of ethical hygiene, many other philosophers, including Carnap, stepped back from political issues and activism and instead attempted to frame a new standpoint from which a certain kind of peace could still be obtained. Still others rejected both paths and remained committed to the view that philosophy was neither a matter of patriotism nor a matter of knowing separate from the work of political and social change.

In the spring of 1950, the University of California Board of Regents fired Jacob Loewenberg (1882–1969), a senior professor in the philosophy department at Berkeley, because he refused to sign the required loyalty oath. Born in 1882 in Latvia, then a state in the Russian Empire, he became an office worker in the capital, Riga. In 1903, as Russia militarized to deal with its own inner unrest (which culminated in the 1905 Revolution), Loewenberg fled the military draft and, in 1904, arrived in Boston after sailing from Europe in steerage with other refugees from Russia. Within a day, probably thanks to Latvian contacts in Boston, he received a loan from Harvard University president, Charles Eliot, to make his initial tuition payment and become a student at Harvard. He received his undergraduate degree in 1908 and completed his doctoral degree with Royce in 1911. After serving as an assistant to Royce, he became an instructor at Berkeley in 1915. After Royce's death in 1916, Royce's wife, Katherine, asked Loewenberg to edit Royce's papers. His work led to the publication of two posthumous works, *Fugitive Essays* (a collection of early essays by Royce, 1925) and *Lectures on Modern Idealism* (1919).

In his 1930 essay in *Contemporary American Philosophy*, Loewenberg called his own view "problematic realism," in contrast with the multiple popular realisms of the day. He rejected some central aspects of Royce's idealism but remained committed to the view that human knowledge was instrumental in determining what is real, even as it was limited and subject to error.

This view allowed Loewenberg to challenge the rapidly growing philosophical commitment among logical empiricists to the idea that knowledge claims can be traced to some empirical "given." "I find the 'given,'" he wrote, "bewildering" (p. 60). While most philosophers take the "given" as already something—the point at which inquiry should end—he argued that the term "the given" has two different uses: "pre-analytic" and "post-analytic." As pre-analytic, "[t]he given in science signifies any fact, event, situation, or circumstance capable of enticing inquiry and eliciting the operation of the scientific method" (p. 60). As such, the pre-analytic given is "democratic and accommodating" since it does not insist on finality and recognizes the fallibility of inquiry. "Post-analytic" givens are the results of analysis and serve not as the source of analysis but as the limit where "analysis is obliged to halt" (p. 60). As a result, they are "aristocratic"; "they are privileged beings of an exclusive order" (p. 61). Freed from the aristocracy of "givens," science (or inquiry in general) can be seen as the process by which reality inspires questions.

Loewenberg's commitment to democratic fallibilism and his opposition to views that demanded conformity perhaps made his firing inevitable in the anti-communist hysteria that developed in postwar America. In spring 1949, the Board of Regents of the University of California, reacting to increasing fear of communism, determined to protect the University and its students by requiring all faculty members to take a loyalty oath that included the pledge "I am not a member of the Communist Party, or under any oath, or a party to any agreement, or under any commitment that is in conflict with my obligations under this oath." After a year of protests, the Board rejected the appeals of the faculty to eliminate the oath requirement and announced an August 1950 deadline for faculty to sign it. Loewenberg and thirty-seven other faculty in the University of California system refused and were fired. In the philosophy department that included Alfred Tarski (whose theory of truth was central to Carnap's logical positivist program), Loewenberg was the only philosopher to take such a stand.

In 1952, the California Supreme Court overruled the action of the Board of Regents and Loewenberg was reinstated. After the two-year suspension (during which he taught at Columbia), he elected instead to retire. The following year, he was invited to give the American Philosophical Association's Carus Lecture, later published in 1959 as *Reason and the Nature of Things*. The lecture was an extended consideration of the nature of the philosophical method and a case for pluralism. It is unclear what impact it had in the discipline, especially as a treatise by a philosopher who had been summarily dismissed from his post. The year the oath requirement was instituted, Carnap had turned down a job offer in the University of California system. The year Loewenberg's lecture was published, and two years after the Supreme Court invalidated the oath requirement, Carnap accepted an offer at UCLA, giving California two leading positivist departments. In his 1930 essay, Loewenberg affirmed that, from James and Dewey, he had "imbibed, indeed, the spirit of rebellion against the pretensions of absolutism" (1930, p. 80). By the end of his career, however, he seemed to be nearly alone in that spirit (see Stewart 1950).

The anti-communism of the California system joined a nationwide trend. Two years earlier, Melvin Rader, a philosopher at the University of Washington, was fired for allegedly being a member of the Communist Party. Although he had supported the communists in the Spanish Civil War, in fact, he was never a member of the Communist Party, and he was eventually reinstated. Just a few months before Loewenberg was fired in California, Herbert Phillips, another philosopher at the University of Washington, was also fired. Phillips was an admitted member of the Communist Party, and his dismissal became a central case in redefining the rules of academic freedom. The question at issue was whether those who held views that opposed the government could be teachers and scholars. The answer (eventually) was that one's views (conservative or liberal) could not by themselves lead to dismissal.

In 1951, Forrest O. Wiggins was fired after giving a talk titled "The Ideology of Interest" at a student forum at the University of Minnesota. In his talk, Wiggins challenged what he took to be a widely shared assumption that the Cold War and the Korean War were battles between political systems. Instead, he argued, they were in fact conflicts between economic systems (capitalism and communism) waged between powerful White nations over the lands and resources of the non-White world. Those caught in the violence of the Korean War were not the aggressors but rather were victims of the conflict. "Who is it, then, that wants war?" he asked. "The Koreans? Their towns and villages and cities and hospitals and schools and huts are reduced to rubble. More than three-fourths of Korea is destroyed.... The Koreans do not want war" (1951, p. 1). The Chinese, he said, just ended their own civil war and since the 1930s had lost more than ten million people. The Germans and Russians, likewise, he claimed, were not interested in war. "The answer," he declared, "is that it is the capitalists and the militarists in the United States who want war" (p. 2). He argued that the present task was to see that self-interest does not remain "a principle upon which we organize human society" (p. 7). Instead, "[o]ur task is to find another, more suitable, principle... before all of us are blown to oblivion"

(p. 7). Self-interest, Wiggins concluded, should be replaced by the simple principle that "goods, things, and property shall be used only as instruments in the service of humanity" (p. 7). The talk was distributed to members of the Minnesota state legislature who immediately called for his dismissal. Wiggins was the first African American hired to teach in the Philosophy Department at Minnesota, which by then was well-established as a leading logical positivist department. Wiggins was not reinstated.

On February 16, 1951, W. E. B. Du Bois, now eighty-two years old, author of many volumes on the issues of race and the status of Blacks around the world, was arraigned in federal court on the charge of being a "foreign agent." He was searched, fingerprinted, and handcuffed. Hours later he was released on $1,000 bail and was forced to surrender his passport. In 1950, Du Bois had become the chair of the Peace Information Center (PIC) in New York City. The small organization was founded to disseminate information about the Stockholm Peace Appeal, a petition prepared by the World Peace Council that called for a complete ban on the development and use of nuclear weapons. Just after the Korean War began, the PIC issued a *"Peacegram"* reporting that the petition had collected 1.5 million signatures and that the PIC was preparing a mass rally in New York City. At about the same time, the US Secretary of State, Dean Acheson, announced that the Appeal was "a propaganda trick in the spurious 'peace offensive' of the Soviet Union" (quoted in Lewis, 2000, p. 547). A few days later, Du Bois issued his own statement accusing Acheson of having "no desire for peace, or a realization of the horror of another world war or of sympathy with the crippled, impoverished and dead who pay for [the] fighting" (quoted in Lewis, 2000, p. 547).

The following month, apparently in response to his public accusations, the US Department of Justice demanded that Du Bois, as chair of the PIC, register "as an agent of a foreign principal within the United States," in effect, that he register as an agent of the Soviet Union. Du Bois declined and in August traveled to Prague to deliver an address. When he returned, he found he had been nominated to run for the US Senate as a candidate for the American Labor Party. He accepted the nomination and received more than 200,000 votes in the November election (about four percent of the votes cast). He also received word that the PIC had decided to disband—a decision apparently ignored by the Department of Justice when it again demanded that Du Bois register as a foreign agent. Du Bois was indicted in February and the trial was finally held in November 1951. The charges were dismissed, but the trial had an effect on Du Bois. "I have faced during my life many unpleasant experiences," he wrote in his last autobiography, "the growl of a mob; the personal threat of murder; the scowling distaste of an audience. But nothing ever so cowed me as that day, . . . when I took my seat in a Washington courtroom as an indicted criminal. I was not a criminal" (1968, p. 395).

Despite the dismissal, the Justice Department kept Du Bois's passport and so prevented him from traveling outside the country. "It was a bitter experience and I bowed before the storm," he wrote (p. 395). Though he continued to write and travel within the United States, he became increasingly frustrated with his apparent inability to make a positive difference. He sued the federal government for the return of his passport. Finally, in 1958, a few weeks after his ninetieth birthday, the Supreme Court ruled that the State Department could not deny passports to citizens for political reasons. In August, Du Bois left the United States. He returned for brief stays but seemed ready to leave for good. On October 1, 1961, he applied for membership in the Communist Party of the United States. He wrote to the chair of the party, "Today, I have reached a firm conclusion. Capitalism cannot reform itself; it is doomed to self-destruction" (quoted in Lewis, 2000, p. 567). After this final signal to "his country" that had, he said, sold "its birthright" and betrayed "its mighty destiny" (1968, p. 419), he left the United States for the last time to live in the Republic of Ghana. On his ninety-fifth birthday, he became a Ghanaian citizen. He died in his new country on August 27, 1963, on the eve of the March on Washington led by Martin Luther King, Jr. Word of Du Bois's death reached King as he prepared to deliver his famous address, "I Have a Dream."

Du Bois was one of a wide array of writers, actors, and activists who were subject to suppression and exclusion in the wake of the Second World War. Wiggins, Rader, Phillips, and Loewenberg, and at least nine other philosophers at Michigan, Temple, Johns Hopkins, Pittsburgh, Colorado, Hunter College, and even the famously liberal Reed College, were dismissed for resisting demands to submit to oaths or change what they taught (or how they thought). As John McCumber has argued in *Time in the Ditch: American Philosophy and the McCarthy Era* (2001), certain philosophical commitments (even ones as central to the American tradition as those held and taught by Loewenberg) became risky views. By the mid-1950s, only a few American philosophers continued to struggle against the new climate of academia. Most members of the discipline came to accept views that reinforced the sharp separation between "the problems of men," described by Dewey as the central philosophical concern, and the problems of philosophy that promoted debate only inside the profession, safe from legislatures and regents. Ironically, even as some students and followers of James and Royce—Du Bois, Loewenberg, Kallen, and Locke—maintained a commitment to pluralism and the relevance of philosophy to ordinary life, other Royce students—Henry Sheffer and C. I. Lewis in particular—were instrumental in shifting philosophical inquiry to a narrower focus on language meaning.

Part of the effort to bring academic philosophy into line with the analytic project of philosophy as a neutral science was a critical reexamination of philosophical pragmatism, especially Dewey's work. In her 1952 study, *Philosophy in America—1900–1950*, May Brodbeck took the lead in this critical work when she offered a new vision of philosophy in America that culminated in the linguistic turn. Her challenge to American philosophies of resistance represents the dominant view of the tradition embraced by American academic philosophy from the 1950s to the present day. Remarkably, Brodbeck gets much of the tradition, especially pragmatism, right in the details, but reads the implications of the tradition from the perspective of the analytic counter-resistance. The very aspects of the tradition that mark its resistance to dominant systems are the elements that make it dangerous.

Brodbeck was born in New Jersey in 1917 as May Schachter and was raised in a Jewish household. She went to a vocational high school and put herself through college by taking night courses at New York University and finished a bachelor's degree in chemistry in 1941. She married Arthur Brodbeck in 1941 (they divorced in 1949) and became a researcher on the Manhattan Project. In 1944, she left the Project and enrolled at the University of Iowa. Her primary interest was in the philosophy of science, but her adviser (Bergmann) directed her toward the philosophy of social science and assigned her to take up the twofold task of recasting the history of American philosophy and challenging (and undermining) classical pragmatism. In 1948, after completing her degree, she became a professor at the University of Minnesota. In 1974, she became the vice president for Academic Affairs at the University of

Iowa, at the time one of the highest-ranking women in the American academy. She retired in 1983 to California where she was to become a member of the prestigious Institute for Social Science Research. She committed suicide that fall without leaving an explanation.

In Brodbeck's account, before 1900 American philosophy "was the handmaiden of theology" (1952, p. 4). In the wake of the Civil War and the rising popularity of evolution theory, philosophy turned to idealism, largely imported from Germany. These philosophers "expounded Absolute Idealism, the last, boldest, and most grandiose systematic defense of God, immortality, and eternal values" (p. 4). Idealism, she concluded, "was a transitional philosophy," "a compromise, and like all compromises it satisfied nobody" (p. 9). Brodbeck described the resulting view (represented as much by the British idealist Francis Herbert Bradley as it was by Royce) as "inherently absurd," claiming that it "disparage[d] scientific knowledge" while echoing "the poet's claim that his knowledge is of a different and higher kind" (pp. 8–9). She observed that idealism began with a recognition of the "precariousness of the human condition" that was a reaction against "a crass, industrial world that overvalued getting and spending and the knowledge of things at the expense of that of man and human relationships" (p. 9). Despite this, idealism claimed that "from our hopes and fears, expectations and suspicions, we form our own worlds," "thus mistaking 'the inner landscape for the outer'" (p. 9). The "break" from idealism took two forms: pragmatism and realism. Brodbeck continued, "Not until hostilities were over and the common enemy routed, however, did it become clear that the conquering allies had incongruous ideologies, resulting in a cold war whose chill breezes can still be felt along academic halls" (p. 11).

New and Critical realism helped to shift philosophy from concern for purpose and emotion toward "very real intellectual if not very practical problems" around questions of scientific knowledge that "the pragmatists would have abandoned . . . as outmoded, artificial and even politically suspect" (p. 65). Just as important, she claimed (and ironically, too, given her historical project), the realists "also had to insist, and fortunately they did insist, on separating philosophy from its history" (p. 65). The pragmatist idea that reflecting on the past can shed light on any problem "is a superstition" (p. 66). The "prejudice against analysis" held by both the idealists and the pragmatists needed to be abandoned. "We do *not*," she declared, "'murder to dissect.' Wholes must be intellectually broken into parts . . . in order to better understand the way in which the parts were indeed related to form a whole. Analysis, to be sure, is not an end in itself but an access to reality" (p. 66). On her account, the proper successors to the realists were those who accepted this "analytical turn."

The central commitment of analytic philosophy was linguistic analysis. To those who held that the resulting philosophy was trivial since it was merely verbal, she said, "the underlying assumption, without which the concern with language would indeed philosophically be trivial, is that the structure and logic of our ordinary language is significant and not arbitrary." Brodbeck concluded, "We use the language we do use because it fits, in some sense, the world in which we live" (p. 73). This assertion led her to a conclusion about the nature of metaphysics: "Whether or not a particular philosophical system or linguistic structure is adequate or true, an exhaustive map of reality can only be determined by each individual for himself in terms of his own experience" (p. 76).

Pragmatism, especially Dewey's version, violated Brodbeck's expectations from the start. In her 1959 paper on Dewey's philosophy, she set out a critique that helped to show what was at stake for both analytic and pragmatist philosophy. Dewey, she began, never "executed the linguistic turn" described by her mentor Bergmann and made famous by Richard Rorty (1931–2007) in his collection of that name. She claimed that by failing to grasp the new logic of Russell and Whitehead, Dewey focused on criticism of the quest for certainty and the use of dualisms and he "never relented in his battle against the linguistic philosophers" (1963, p. 190). While the logical positivists shared Dewey's general humanistic attitude and faith in science, he remained "hostile" and found "the analytical, formal method . . . offensive and viciously abstractive" (p. 190). Instead of a focus on language, Dewey focused on the concept of continuity. For example, he held that meaning is contextual so that any particular claim is continuous with the inquiry of which it is a part. Furthermore, every inquiry is itself part of a larger "continuum of inquiry." The problem, for Brodbeck, was that "since the context forever expands—inquiry is, by its nature, unending—the situation is . . . inexhaustible" (p. 200). To specify any meaning would seem to require an inquiry whose meaning requires still another inquiry, until "we are faced with an infinite regress" (p. 202).

Brodbeck also challenged Dewey's use of continuity to address dualisms. For Dewey, dualisms, at best, are the product of efforts to order a situation: that is, they are both tools and results of inquiry. Consequently, dualisms like body/mind and subject/object are not "real": they are not "discovered in the world," but rather are divisions established in a purposive inquiry that are useful to the process of solving a particular problem. Consider the dualism of analytic and synthetic (between claims that are true in virtue of the meaning of their words and those that are true in virtue of the meaning of their words *and* something experienced). The distinction was central to the logical positivist separation of philosophy (as a producer of analytic claims) and science (as a producer of synthetic ones). Dewey rejected the distinction as anything but the product of a certain philosophical history, illustrated by the recognition that there is no sharp divide between analytic and synthetic statements—that is, they are continuous. The problem, according to Brodbeck, was that Dewey's rejection of such dualisms also dismissed the project of logical positivism.

Continuity also emerged in Dewey's rejection of the fact/value distinction. For Brodbeck, facts and values are distinct categories of statements, originating from different processes and having different sorts of implications. Dewey's "mistake" was to claim that such statements are not distinct because there are no "pure" facts or values. For Dewey, a factual claim is the product of a purposive process in which selections are made as a result of the values that control the process. Similarly, the claim that something is a value requires a situation (including facts about what is at stake) in order to be made. Put another way, facts are value-laden and values are fact-laden (or rather, they are part of the experienced world and not just inner states). Worse, according to Brodbeck, Dewey held that values were "felt" qualities of approval, pleasure, and satisfaction. In order for inquiry to end, it must be marked by a value, that is, a feeling of consummation or fulfillment. To find the truth about gravity or the speed of light, on this model, no matter how much data has been collected, scientists would still need to "feel" that they had reached a true conclusion. "Here," Brodbeck declared, "we have the roots of a fundamental anti-intellectualism" (1963, p. 212). By making values necessary to even science, Dewey accepted "The supremacy of the 'enjoyed', of the 'had', over the known" and so "subjectifies" both fact and value (p. 212). In order to eliminate "dreaded" dualisms, Dewey had to link fact and value, object and subject, known and knower by prioritizing value, subject, and knower.

For Brodbeck, the result is a philosophy born out of a certain politics that demanded social reform and "the promotion of group effort and state planning." Dewey's philosophy "provided a theoretical rationale and justification for the social idealism of the reformers. Through his philosophy, their goals received welcome 'scientific' sanction" (p. 214). Despite his "forever reiterated denunciation of ethical absolutism, his philosophy is not," Brodbeck concluded, "just another brand of ethical relativism" (p. 214). It is rather an instrumental philosophy that serves as a "method of changing the world" (p. 215). And this was its greatest danger.

> Some hard facts must be faced. A great power does not go away just because we do not officially recognize it. What is and what ought to be remain asunder. Only by facing the former, can we act intelligently about the latter. By casting everything into the process, [Dewey's pragmatism] at once denies the very notion of "fact" and of personal responsibility for moral decision. Can any reflective person who has survived the past quarter of a century lightly embrace such an ontology? Thus it is in a sobered America [pragmatism] is now on the wane. (p. 215)

Pragmatism was on the wane in the academy, framed by the project of separating philosophy from the problems of the day, protecting it from the attention of people like McCarthy, and making a safe space for philosophers to work without apparent risk. Dewey anticipated this objection in *The Quest for Certainty*. People, he said,

> have longed to find a realm in which there is an activity which is not overt and which has no external consequences. "Safety first" has played a large role in effecting a preference for knowing over doing and making. With those to whom the process of pure thinking is congenial and who have the leisure and the aptitude to pursue their preference, the happiness attending knowing is unalloyed; it is not entangled in the risks which overt action cannot escape. (LW4, 6–7)

But for Dewey and many in the American philosophical tradition, safety was not—could not—be the goal. Instead, they sought to respond to the problems of daily experience critically and constructively to make things better. And this work did not come without risk.

## Primary Texts

Hook, Sidney (2002). *Sidney Hook on Pragmatism, Democracy, and Freedom: The Essential Essays*, eds. Robert B. Talisse and Robert Tempio. Amherst, NY: Prometheus Books.

Kallen, Horace Meyer (1956). *Cultural Pluralism and the American Idea : An Essay in Social Philosophy*. Philadelphia: University of Pennsylvania Press.

Neurath, Otto (April 1937). "Unified Science and Its Encyclopaedia." *Philosophy of Science* 4 (2): 265–77.

Brodbeck, May (1952). Philosophy in America, 1900–1950, *American Non-Fiction, 1900–1950*, eds. May Brodbeck, James Gray, and Walter Metzger. Chicago: Henry Regnery Company.

# CHAPTER 17
# ANALYTIC PHILOSOPHY AND
# THE PLURALIST REVOLT

When Brodbeck published her critique of Dewey in 1963, the brief reign of logical positivism was already ending. At the 1950 meeting of the American Philosophical Association, three philosophers were asked to address recent trends in philosophy. William Frankena (1908–1994), a student of Lewis, Perry, and Whitehead at Harvard, discussed recent work in ethics. His review reported a rise in metaethics (the study of the meaning of terms such as "good" and "right") and a need for normative ethics (a study that asks what things or actions are good and right). Grace de Laguna (1878–1978) received her PhD from Cornell University in 1901 and was asked to address current trends in speculative philosophy. Her paper identified phenomenology and the work of Peirce and Whitehead as primary trends (though Peirce died in 1914 and Whitehead in 1947).

Whitehead (1861–1947) joined the Harvard philosophy department in 1924. He began his career at Trinity College, Cambridge, England, where he met Bertrand Russell. Both published well-regarded works in the philosophy of mathematics (*A Treatise on Universal Algebra* by Whitehead in 1898 and *The Principles of Mathematics* by Russell in 1903), and both shared a commitment to logicism, the view that mathematics could be reduced to logic. The result of their collaboration was the three-volume work *Principia Mathematica* (1963), that provided key resources used to build the logical positivist program.

Although Whitehead continued to work on the logicist project (producing a second edition of *Principia* in 1927), his interest turned to metaphysics and, in 1925, he published a series of lectures, *Science and the Modern World*, that "sketched an alternative philosophy of science in which *organism* takes the place of *matter*" (1925, pp. 193–4). Organisms, as active "realizations" of value, emerge in the context of nature understood as "a structure of evolving process. The reality is the process" (p. 72). A few years later, in his Gifford lectures published as *Process and Reality* (1929), Whitehead identified the central philosophical problem as the effort to understand the "first vague generalization" that "all things flow" (1929, p. 208). "Without doubt," he concluded, "if we are to go back to that ultimate, integral experience whose elucidation is the final aim of philosophy, the flux of things is one ultimate generalization around which we must weave our philosophical system" (p. 208).

Whitehead's focus on the idea of process became the starting point for another strand of American philosophy in the second half of the twentieth century that is generally labeled "process philosophy" and developed most visibly by Whitehead's student, Charles Hartshorne (1897–2000). Whitehead also influenced the development of American environmental philosophy. Of Whitehead's place in philosophy in 1950, de Laguna wrote that he "belongs to the present age in his emphasis on the dependence of thought on its symbolic formulation." However, his work differs from the positivists and their emphasis on language "in holding, as does Dewey, that the precision of formulation is relative to a systematic context not itself explicitly formulated" (1951, p. 15). This wider context, de Laguna observed, is one characterized finally by the principle of creativity, which Whitehead described as "the universal of universals characterizing ultimate matter of fact" (Whitehead, 1929, p. 25). Creativity at once unifies the universe, Whitehead said, and ensures its constant change.

The third paper on the program at the 1950 APA meeting, alongside the papers by Frankena and de Laguna, was by Willard Van Orman Quine (1908–2000) and titled "Two Dogmas of Empiricism." The paper was published the next year. Quine was born in 1908 and grew up in Akron, Ohio. He received his BA from Oberlin College, studied at Harvard with Lewis, Perry, and Sheffer, and finished his PhD with Whitehead. He was immediately asked to join the faculty and given funds to spend time in Europe. There he met the leading Polish logician, Alfred Tarski, members of the Vienna Circle, including Carnap, and A. J. Ayer in England. He remained at Harvard his entire career, and his students included Donald Davidson, David Lewis, Daniel Dennett, Gilbert Harman, and Hao Wang. During the Second World War, Quine served in Naval Intelligence and rose to the rank of Lieutenant Commander. Although Quine "executed the linguistic turn" and was viewed as a leader among linguistic philosophers, he also maintained his connection with pragmatism. While logical positivists like Brodbeck challenged holism and required the analytic/synthetic distinction, Quine embraced the former and challenged the latter.

Quine's "Two Dogmas" essay was aimed at logical positivism. Although published as positivism was still rising in prominence, the paper is now generally credited with marking the beginning of positivism's end. However, it also provided the means to preserve the linguistic turn in the post-positivist philosophical world. The first dogma Quine challenged was "the belief in some fundamental cleavage between truths which are *analytic*, or grounded in meanings independently of matters of fact, and truths which are *synthetic*, or grounded in fact." The second was "*reductionism*: the belief that each meaningful statement is equivalent to some logical construct upon terms which refer to immediate experience" (1980, p. 20).

The belief in a "fundamental cleavage" between analytic and synthetic statements, Quine argued, required a sharp and specifiable division. Since analytic statements could not depend upon any contingent matters of fact, the division needed to be a matter of language meaning alone. Since analytic statements are to be true strictly in virtue of the meaning of the terms, it is easy to see that "No unmarried men are married" is an analytic truth. Since "bachelor" means "unmarried man," "No bachelors are married" should also be analytic. However, Quine demonstrated that the ways in which terms like "bachelor" and "unmarried men" get their meanings are contingent—there is no necessary method of meaning-making. So, in a given language, it may be that the meaning of terms is determined by assigning (e.g., by conventional use) their "extensions," the objects that they point out. So, while "No unmarried men are married" is true and analytic in virtue of the terms (and the logical operators of "no," "un-," and "are"), "No bachelors are married" could be true only because those men assigned to the class of bachelors happen to be unmarried. If it only "happens" that the assignments confirm the claim, it might also happen that the assignments do not confirm it. What if the community routinely assigns a man to the category of bachelor when he is not married to a woman? If the man is gay and committed to another man for life, then (at least for some in the community), at least one bachelor is nevertheless married. In this light, "No bachelors are married" is not analytic but only a contingent truth. One might say that this is simply a confusion of terms—

the man was mistakenly called a bachelor, or the category of marriage is misunderstood. The objection makes Quine's point. Analyticity depends upon contingent features of the language in their use in context. The analytic/synthetic distinction is not meaningless, but it is contingent and so the first dogma of logical positivism fails.

The dogma of reductionism is closely connected to the first dogma because analyticity simply represents the "limit case" of verification. The point of reductionism is that every claim can "be reduced" to "sense-data" or at least to statements that emerge through sense experience ("there's a yellow dog" or "the brick is on the table"). Analytic statements are simply statements that require no particular sense experience at all and so are "vacuously confirmed, *ipso facto*, come what may" (p. 41). But such limited cases do not exist (because the first dogma must be rejected), and so the belief in reductionism is also mistaken. Quine concluded, "in general the truth of statements does obviously depend both upon language and upon extralinguistic fact," and the failure of the distinction between analytic and synthetic also means that statements about experience are no more based on fact alone than analytic statements are based on meaning alone.

The lesson Quine drew from the failure of the dogmas is that "[t]aken collectively, science has its double dependence upon language and experience, but this duality is not traceable into statements of science taken one by one" (p. 42). Claims get their meaning from the whole system of which they are a part. The language used provides a framework and the sense experience of the "corporate body" provides the "tribunal" that confirms and rejects claims. Quine concluded that "The unit of empirical significance is the whole of science" (p. 42). The resulting model of language meaning, including the "totality of our so-called knowledge or beliefs, from . . . matters of geography and history to the profoundest laws of atomic physics or even of pure mathematics and logic, is a man-made fabric which impinges on experience only along the edges" (p. 42). In such a "web of belief," as he called it later, claims from experience (observation sentences again) reinforce different parts of the system. At times, claims from experience find no place in the web and these are either lost or added by making adjustments to the web as a whole. Adjustments are relatively easy among beliefs that make up the periphery. Core beliefs, in contrast, such as beliefs about math, logic, and physics, are relatively difficult to change. Whether easy or difficult to change, however, Quine maintained that "no statement is immune to revision," even logical laws (p. 43).

For Quine, once the dogmas are set aside, the "formal" aspect of language can be seen as a system of concepts that serves to organize experience and provide a viewpoint from which to consider further experience. A "conceptual scheme," Quine argued, can be seen "as a tool for predicting future experience in the light of past experience" (p. 44). Observations that provide the "content" of science can be seen as "[p]hysical objects [that] are conceptually imported into the situation as convenient intermediaries[,] . . . as irreducible posits comparable, epistemologically, to the gods of Homer" (p. 44). Both physical objects and Homer's gods "enter our conception only as cultural posits" (p. 44). That the "myths of physical objects" are taken as superior to Homer's gods is because the former have proven "more efficacious than other myths as a device for working a manageable structure into the flux of experience" (p. 44). The resulting view combines concepts and experience in a conception of meaning holism that rejects the sharp dualisms that Brodbeck found key. Quine concluded his argument by observing that Lewis and Carnap both took "a pragmatist stand on the question of choosing between language forms, scientific frameworks; but their pragmatism [left] off at the imagined boundary between analytic and the synthetic" (p. 46). By rejecting this boundary, Quine "espouse[d] a more thorough pragmatism" (p. 46).

In order to illustrate meaning holism and its ability to adapt, Quine proposed a thought experiment. "Imagine," he wrote, "a newly discovered tribe whose language is without known affinities" (1969, p. 1). In such a case, a linguist, sent to learn the language, must do so "directly by observing what the natives say under observed circumstances, encountered or contrived" (p. 1). The only method open to the linguist is their observations of the people in relation to the utterance of the words in question. "A rabbit scurries by, the native says 'Gavagai', and the linguist notes down the sentence 'Rabbit'" (p. 29). The problem, for Quine, is that while "Gavagai" is uttered in the presence of the rabbit, it is not clear how best to translate it. It could, for example, mean "rabbit," but it also could plausibly be translated as some other concept: "rabbithood" or (famously) "undetached rabbit parts," or some other phrase compatible with the sense experience. Each alternative, Quine argued, represented a different categorization of the things associated with "Gavagai," and each intersected differently with the system of English meaning. In this way, one can recognize the principle of the indeterminacy of translation.

At the same time, even as the translation may be indeterminate, the extension of the term—the things it points to—is also indeterminate or "inscrutable" (p. 38). When pointing, does the Native speaker point to the rabbit or the color or the location relative to other objects? In order to know, the linguist must also know the relevant principle of individuation (p. 31), that is, how to pick the rabbit out of the scene. And yet, despite the obstacles to translation and reference, Quine argued that ongoing interaction between the linguist and the Native speakers will yield a more and more accurate understanding of the foreign language. Quine asserted that this process of "radical translation" shows that "we are bound to adapt any alien pattern to our own" (p. 1). The process is like the process of translating from any other language. "The case of the linguist and his newly discovered heathen," Quine wrote, "finally differs simply in that the linguist has to grope for a general sentence-to-sentence correlation that will make the public circumstances of the heathen's affirmations and denials match up tolerably with the circumstances of the linguist's own" (p. 5).

Meaning holism, it seems, is a process of incorporating the languages of others—the "heathens"—into one's own. The thought experiment itself assumes a kind of imperial perspective. The translation presented is strictly one way, and the characterization of the Native speaker incorporates the long-standing savage/civilized distinction that was used to frame the relations between Western and Indigenous cultures. The linguistic turn provided what African American and Native American philosophers would later challenge, a theoretical means of bridging differences by inclusion in terms of the linguist's language, the language of the dominant culture. Such inclusion is made still more compelling and problematic for later thinkers when Quine placed ontology inside language, and so set aside questions of being that may be crucial to defining cultural difference. His slogan, "To be is to be the value of a variable," is a formula that is not intended to explain what there is, but rather "what a remark or doctrine, ours or someone else's, *says* there is" (p. 15). Questions of being become questions about what is said. Experience can still "impinge" on one's talk, but the sense it makes is a matter of the language one speaks.

Quine transformed the linguistic turn from one bound to the positivist framework of ideal languages and observation statements that emerged unproblematically from experience into a question of language systems and cultural posits. Observation statements remained central to Quine's view, but as part of the language used and not neutral "inputs." Quine's transformation pointed the way for American philosophers to leave the narrow agenda of positivism behind and take up a wider range of questions while still remaining firmly linguistic in method. His meaning holism became a starting point for a variety of philosophical developments including the work of Donald Davidson and Richard Rorty on one hand, and feminist philosophers including Lynn Hankinson Nelson, Sharyn Clough, and Nancy Tuana on the other.

Nelson, in her book, *Who Knows? From Quine to a Feminist Empiricism* (1990), argued that Quine's holism provided a means of recognizing the continuity of science and politics. As a result, the research in feminist science studies (including work by Sandra Harding, Evelyn Fox Keller, and Susan Hekman) identified ways in which science was male-dominated and actively excluded both women and women's concerns from investigation and theory. This exclusion could be seen as part of a wide cultural system of science, political interests, and daily practices. If Quine was right, Nelson argued, the answer to the question "Who knows?" is the "corporate body," the community as a whole. "What constitutes evidence for a claim is not determined by individuals, but by the standards a community accepts concomitantly with constructing, adopting, and refining theories" (1990, p. 277). But if it becomes clear that some parts of the community are excluded from the process (or, as a result of dominant interests, the community systematically excludes concepts and observations), then the system of beliefs can and should be altered.

Science, according to Quine, is "our best theory" at present. When it is clear that this best theory is not taking into account of the full range of experience available, it must be changed as needed (even at its core) to accommodate additional insights. Just as physics adjusted at a fundamental level when Newtonian physics replaced Aristotelian physics, so can the community (science and the wider culture) adjust to undermine masculinist exclusions and take seriously the need for the community to examine the values present in the process of knowing. "Once we abandon the view that science, values, and politics are forever disparate," Nelson wrote, "we can expect our science, our values, and our politics to evolve, and each to inform the others and, perhaps, ultimately to become indistinguishable" (p. 317). Here Quine's meaning holism becomes the framework for a new feminist empiricism.

However, Quine himself was uninterested in such social applications of his work. In a 1979 comment published in *Newsday* (and in a revised form in *Theories and Things* (1981)), Quine made clear that philosophy in the wake of the advances of science and disciplinary specialization focused on questions that may not matter to those outside philosophy. Traditional "introspective" notions, "of meaning, idea, concept, essence, all undisciplined and undefined" had proven to "afford a hopelessly flabby and unmanageable foundation for a theory of the world" (1981, p. 192). Traditional reasons for studying philosophy were no longer valid. "The student who majors in philosophy primarily for spiritual comfort is misguided and is probably not a very good student anyway, since intellectual curiosity is not what moves him" (p. 193). Work intended to "inspire and edify" should, Quine concluded, be left to novelists, poets, and pastors. "Philosophers in the professional sense have no peculiar fitness for it. Neither have they any peculiar fitness for helping to get society on an even keel, though we should do all we can. What might just fill these perpetually crying needs is wisdom: *Sophia* yes, philosophia not necessarily" (p. 193).

Even as feminist empiricism developed by drawing on meaning holism, another line developed in response to the rejection of the analytic/synthetic distinction. Thanks to the idea of a conceptual scheme, language meaning can be seen not as a matter of the meaning of individual terms or sentences, but as a matter of the language system as a whole. Science can be seen as a portion of a larger conceptual scheme whose work involves encountering new experience and adding to and modifying knowledge, strengthening it, and expanding its scope. The trouble with this picture, according to Davidson (1917–2003), is that it requires accepting a third dogma of empiricism. In his 1974 paper, "On the Very Idea of a Conceptual Scheme," Davidson argued that, while Quine rejected the analytic/synthetic distinction, he instituted "the dualism of scheme and content, of organizing system and something waiting to be organized" (1974, p. 11). Yet this third dogma, Davidson concluded, "cannot be made intelligible and defensible" (p. 11).

Davidson approached the problem by asking what can be expected when translations fail either completely or partially. If a conceptual scheme organizes the materials of experience in distinctive ways, then two conceptual schemes (if they are as distinct as Quine proposed in the case of radical translation) must be two different ways of organizing what could be the same materials of experience. If they are two distinct schemes, then translation between them should be difficult, if not impossible. But if translation is impossible, it is unclear how the speakers of one language could ever know that they have the translation of the other language wrong. One could, in principle, generate an entire dictionary for a "heathen" language that gives meanings in English that correlate with the actions and objects engaged as the "heathens" speak. If the translation were a complete failure, it would presumably never be noticed since it nevertheless correlates with all of the expressions and actions of the native speakers. If, on the other hand, the translation is a partial failure, noticing the failure would prove that there were at least some elements of the two languages that provided a "background of common beliefs and a going method of translation" (p. 18).

When speakers attempt to understand each other, Quine affirmed (following Neil Wilson) the "principle of charity" where the speakers select as their object "that individual [thing] which will make the largest possible number of statements true" (1960, p. 59, no. 2). In order to have even partial failures of translation, Davidson argued, "[c]harity is forced on us; whether we like it or not, if we want to understand others, we must count them right in most matters" (Davidson, 1974, p. 19). Even more than Wilson's principle, which amounts to selecting a common object, Davidson granted that speakers must also count others as correct. But to do this, it is necessary to recognize that there are no radical differences among speakers of different languages. What this meant for Davidson is that there is "no intelligible basis on which it can be said that schemes are different" or that schemes are one (p. 20). The indeterminacy of schemes led Davidson to conclude that the dualism of "scheme and reality" must be given up. In doing so, "we do not give up the world, but re-establish unmediated touch with the familiar objects whose antics make our sentences true or false" (p. 20). Davidson began his argument by saying that the third dogma of empiricism would also be its last, "for if we give it up, it is not clear that there is anything distinctive left to call empiricism" (p. 11). And so, Davidson rejected Quine's version of the linguistic turn, but also concluded by offering a new, perhaps even more linguistic turn, no longer bound to empirical concerns.

Six years after Quine offered his assessment of empiricism, Wilfrid Sellars (1912–1989) offered his own critique of another central idea in the developing analytic philosophy of the 1950s. In an address given at the University of London, Sellars called into question the philosophical idea of "the given." The function of the given, he said, is to provide a foundation for knowledge claims. Candidates for what is given have included (from various philosophical perspectives) sense data, material objects, universals, relations, first principles, and so on. In logical positivism, observation statements served as the given. In C. I. Lewis's "conceptualistic pragmatism" as developed in *Mind and the World Order* (1929), the given was the "content of experience" that was then interpreted using concepts. In each case, the meaning of claims about the world could be traced back (or forward) to meaningful immediate experience. The claim "there is a yellow dog" counts as knowledge if I can verify the claim with a sense experience: "I see a yellow dog" or better "A canoid patch of yellow there." Sellars rejected such grounds. "There is no 'sky hook' of *given* meanings to serve as a fulcrum for moving the world of ideas" (1967, p. 28).

Sellars was born in 1912 and grew up in Ann Arbor, where his father, Roy Wood Sellars, taught philosophy at the University of Michigan. Young Sellars graduated from Michigan in 1933 and completed an MA at the University of Buffalo in 1934. In the same year, Sellars was selected as a Rhodes Scholar, enrolled at Oriel College, Oxford, and, in 1936, began work on a doctorate in philosophy at Oxford. He left the program in 1937 (receiving a second MA) and enrolled at Harvard, where he briefly studied with Lewis, Quine, Sheffer, and others. The following year, he left Harvard hoping to complete his dissertation while teaching at the University of Iowa, where he became a close friend of Feigl. He never completed his degree. During the Second World War, Sellars entered naval intelligence and, after the war, moved to the University of Minnesota, where Feigl had become chair of the philosophy department. In 1957, he moved to Yale and, in 1963, moved again to the University of Pittsburgh. Here he (along with Nicolas Rescher, John McDowell, and Robert Brandom) helped to build a philosophical center that would lead one version of the pragmatist revitalization in the 1980s.

In important ways, Sellars's critique of the given emerged from his understanding of his father's critical realism. Roy Wood Sellars had argued that knowledge depended on the physical world, but that it was not caused by the physical world. His son observed that in the "Moore-Russell line" of thinking, for example, knowledge is grounded in one's "acquaintance" with the objects known; to be acquainted with an object is to know that it is a "*such-and-such*" (1967, p. 13). The problem with this view is that it equates "*aboutness*," in which a thought is about a such-and-such, with "*awareness*," in which one is aware that something is there that has color and extension (p. 13). When I see a yellow dog, to borrow Russell's example (Russell, 1963, p. 40), I am first "aware" of a certain sense experience. When I claim that it is a yellow dog, I make a claim about the object, in effect, suggested by my awareness. The first part of the process that discriminates the object from my field of vision is a physical response to the environment. The second part, saying something about a yellow dog, is a linguistic process that depends on my knowing the language at hand. The difference is illustrated in the difference between a thermostat that can sense changes in temperature and a person who complains "It is getting hot in here." The device is, in a simple sense, "aware" of the changes in temperature. The person is both aware of the change (felt sensations on the skin, for example) but *says*, "It's getting hot." The latter, the report on temperature, is a "proposition," "not a mental or subjective entity" but rather "[i]t is, in effect, a possible state of affairs" (Sellars, 1963, p. 16).

In his critique of the "myth of the given," after showing that different forms of the given do not stand up to close examination, Wilfrid Sellars argued that knowing is a process. One is aware of some experience and makes a claim. The claim counts as knowledge not because some mental entity confirms it (or because it has been encountered as known), but because the linguistic community at hand accepts it. "A report can be correct as being an instance of a general mode of behavior which, in a given linguistic community, it is reasonable to sanction and support" (1991, pp. 167–8). The community accepts a claim because "we are not giving an empirical description of that episode [of knowing] . . .; we are placing it in the logical space of reasons, of justifying and being able to justify what one says" (p. 169). The myth of the given accepts the idea that "observation . . . is constituted by certain self-authenticating nonverbal episodes, the authority of which is transmitted to verbal and quasi-verbal performances" made in ways that conform to "the semantical rules of the language" (p. 169). While recognizing the connection of experience to reality, Sellars shifts the weight of knowing to the justification of claims by reasons acceptable to one's community of speakers. In the wake of Sellars's critique, the "given" rapidly became a subject of criticism in philosophy, further undermining the empiricism of the positivists. It simultaneously had the effect of strengthening the linguistic turn and focusing increased attention on the nature and practice of language as the primary philosophical subject matter. It gave less reason for philosophers to worry about action and application and more reason to worry about the details of language.

As the linguistic turn was completed in analytic philosophy, other philosophical perspectives struggled for a place in the discipline. Among the philosophers whose work fell outside the developing philosophical mainstream were those whose work—now called "continental philosophy"—emerged from the phenomenological tradition as it developed in the United States, from existentialist philosophy in the post–Second World War years, and from post-structuralism as it emerged after the Vietnam War. Its development was the result of the work of a handful of American philosophers who began in the 1920s to connect French and German philosophy with philosophies of resistance in the United States. With the rise of analytic philosophy in the years following the Second World War, American continental philosophy became one of the few alternatives in academic philosophy.

Leading the work of connecting philosophical traditions was Marvin Farber (1901–1980). He completed his doctoral degree at Harvard in 1922 and studied for a year in Germany with Edmund Husserl (1859–1938), whose work was in the developing field of phenomenology. Farber's first book, *Phenomenology as a Method and as a Philosophical Discipline* (1928), introduced philosophers in North America to Husserl's work and philosophical method. "In the phenomenological method," Farber wrote in 1966, "one begins with an individual and his stream of experiences" (p. 13). Begun in support of the empirical psychology of the sort advanced by James, Baldwin, Münsterberg, and Hall in the United States, phenomenology sought to clarify the "essential structures of experience" by carefully analyzing the character of experience as it is had by a subject. The resulting philosophy would not only support psychology but would also function as a critique of knowledge, account for "the part played by the mind in experience," unify philosophy and science, and "help realize the ideal of a complete descriptive philosophy" (p. 14).

Farber's interest in phenomenology was shared by others at Harvard. One of his teachers, William Ernest Hocking, who was a student of Josiah Royce, studied with Husserl in 1902 and 1903. As interest grew in the field, others followed the same path. Charles Hartshorne (1897–2000), also a student of Hocking, completed his PhD in 1923 and spent two years after his graduation in Germany where he studied with Husserl and Martin Heidegger (1889–1976). In 1928, Hartshorne, who with Paul Weiss edited the *Collected Papers of C. S. Peirce*, joined the faculty at the University of Chicago where he was central in the development of what came to be known as process theology. In 1955, he moved to Emory University and in 1962 to the University of Texas at Austin. Thanks to study with key figures in phenomenology, Hartshorne and others made a place in American academic philosophy for new generations of philosophers who would take the work of Husserl and Heidegger seriously even as the discipline as a whole set them aside. While Hartshorne himself ultimately found that philosophers closer to the American tradition were better sources of insight, he recognized that the work of Husserl and Heidegger could find a place in the ongoing American philosophical tradition. Writing in 1983, Hartshorne concluded, "when I find truth in what Husserl or Heidegger say, I think Peirce, Dewey, James, Bergson, [or] Whitehead . . . can teach us that truth as well or better. Obviously, many think differently" (1983, p. 374).

Two other key philosophers in the development of phenomenology and existentialism in the United States also began their work at Harvard. Dorion Cairns (1901–1973) studied with Husserl and completed his PhD in 1933 with a dissertation titled *The Philosophy of Edmund Husserl*. He then taught at Rockford College (Jane Addams's alma mater) until 1952 and then at the New School for Social Research until 1971, where he encouraged the study of phenomenology.

Six years before Cairns completed his studies, John Daniel Wild (1902–1972) completed his PhD at Harvard. He joined the Harvard philosophy department the following year and in 1931 received a fellowship for study at the University of Freiburg, where he attended lectures by both Husserl and Heidegger. After publishing books on the history of Western philosophy and realism, Wild published *The Challenge of Existentialism* in 1955. The book began with a stinging critique of academic philosophy in the United States. "At a time when there is a desperate need for the wide dissemination of sound and appealing cultural aims, academic philosophy at least seems bankrupt" (1955, p. 3). Acknowledging the "need for general education in the humanities and in those subjects dealing with what are now commonly referred to as 'values,'" he concluded that "philosophy has so far contributed very little towards the meeting of the need" (p. 3).

Existentialism, though often regarded at this time as relevant only to theology (in the work of Martin Buber and Paul Tillich, for example), had yet to be taken up as philosophical. Wild's book aimed to introduce academic philosophers to existentialism. Though Wild did not seek (at least in this volume) to supplant other philosophical doctrines and approaches, "[b]ecause of the decay into which philosophy has fallen in many parts of the world, it is," he said, "a joy to learn that philosophy in the great classical sense of the word is now reviving in Western Europe" (p. 7). Existentialism, as a development of the phenomenological tradition, took seriously the very questions of being and meaning that had been left out of the mainstream in the face of McCarthyism and Cold War politics. Wild was part of the resistance to that trend.

A few years later, Wild further challenged the developing status quo by showing how philosophy born in the phenomenological tradition could intersect with the new ordinary language philosophy that aimed to make no metaphysical claims. In his paper, "Is There a World of Ordinary Language?" Wild argued that ordinary language philosophy required a conception of a world in order to understand the operation of language. Efforts to capture this world in scientific terms alone were insufficient. The idea of a life-world—*lebenswelt*—as proposed by Husserl provided precisely the context necessary. Analytic philosophy's commitment to understanding the world in narrow empirical terms forced it to set aside questions of meaning and value in favor of description using only terms of science. Phenomenology and existentialism provided an alternative empiricism, which, he said, "philosophers alone can perform" (Wild, 1958, p. 462).

While at Harvard, Wild had developed a reputation as a realist, but *The Challenge of Existentialism* marked him as dissenting from the dominant conversation. In 1961, he accepted the position of department chair at Northwestern, where he hosted the first meeting of the Society for Phenomenology and Existential Philosophy (SPEP). In 1963, he became chair of philosophy at Yale. His last book, *The Radical Empiricism of William James*, was published in 1969 and marked the beginning of a revival of James's philosophy over the next several decades. In this volume, Wild argued in part that James should be primarily considered a phenomenologist whose work could make a present contribution to philosophy and psychology.

Wild's treatment of James helped to confirm the claim made in 1964 by James Edie that phenomenology was welcomed to American philosophy because James had set the stage. Writing about the reception of the work of Maurice Merleau-Ponty, Edie wrote, "it is not surprising that the rapprochement between Western European and American philosophy has begun in the form of a reevaluation of the philosophy of William James" (1964, p. 120). The reevaluation, he continued, was made necessary by the fact that "the real, historical William James" had been lost in the work of his later interpreters (including Dewey, Hook, and Kallen). Rather than being "*the* American philosopher par excellence, the founder of a pragmatic American-frontier style of philosophy," James's philosophy, "like Husserl's, is a return to *the things themselves*, to *the primary phenomena of consciousness*, to the existential life-world as the ultimate foundation of all philosophical theories or abstractions, of all the 'sub-universes' of language" (p. 121). For Wild and Edie, phenomenology and existentialism were as much part of "American" philosophy as they were of German and French philosophy.

In October 1968, Yale University hosted a meeting of the SPEP. The conference—held months after the assassinations of Martin Luther King Jr. and Robert Kennedy and in the midst of increasing unrest on college campuses—featured an address by Jacques Derrida (1930–2004). The previous year, Derrida had published three works destined to challenge and change philosophy in Europe and America: *Writing and Difference, Voice and Phenomenon*, and *Of Grammatology*. Born in Algeria and a Sephardic Jew, Derrida studied at the École Normale Supérieure in Paris, focused on the work of Edmund Husserl, and spent a year at Harvard. His studies were interrupted by the Algerian War of Independence when he served as a language teacher. Following the war, he secured a teaching position at the Sorbonne in Paris and began to write and publish.

While he had presented a paper on Husserl at SPEP two years earlier (on a program that also featured Richard Rorty and Paul Ricoeur), his 1968 address, "The End of Man," took on greater significance as he began with the assassination of King. His talk served as a sort of formal introduction to the philosophical method of deconstruction and the idea of post-structuralism. Derrida began by acknowledging that the circumstances represented by the international meeting of SPEP were a confirmation that "philosophical nationalities have been formed" (1969, p. 31). The occasion of the meeting marked both the affirmation of differences and the presupposed presence of a "common element: . . . the so-called universality of philosophical discourse" (p. 32). He aimed to call into question the confidence of his audience in the possibility of such a universal discourse.

In order to carry out this deconstruction, Derrida observed that his audience at SPEP had the freedom not to "identify with the official political policy of their country . . . in certain areas of the world, notably Vietnam" (p. 33). However, one would be "naïve" if one let "oneself be reassured by the appearance of such freedom" (p. 33). He observed that "a statement opposing some official policy [that] is authorized by the authorities, indicates that it does not upset the social order; it *does not disturb*" (p. 33). What did disturb—what could upset the social order—was the assassination of King and, as he began to work on his SPEP lecture while in Paris, the occupation of the Paris universities by "forces of social order" to quell student protests.

Almost as an answer to Wild's concern about the lack of engagement in philosophy, Derrida opened his 1968 SPEP lecture with a proclamation of present unrest. What followed—using the work of Heidegger and Nietzsche—was an examination of the idea of the end or *telos* of humanity and the realization that there was no one organizing end. As a challenge to structuralism—the view that human activity was framed by basic ordering structures that were universal and could be discovered and analyzed—Derrida argued that the attempt to find such structures is always already bound up with the structures themselves and so can never reveal structures that existed outside the processes of discovery and analysis. The arrival of post-structuralism in the midst of social revolutions in America and Europe added to continental philosophy and helped to reinforce its place as an alternative to analytic philosophy.

While many of the leaders of continental philosophy in the late twentieth and early twenty-first centuries were European, Walter Brogan and James Risser, in their 2000 anthology *American Continental Philosophy*, argued that there was also a distinctive strand of continental philosophy properly called American. In their introduction, they acknowledged that American philosophers in the tradition had come to speak "with a distinctive voice and a unique contemporary perspective" (2000, p. 6). It was, they declared, "an original appropriation" that "assimilated and reinterpreted" European philosophy and then developed its distinctive character by "crossing back and forth over the ocean that separates and connects the European and American experience" (p. 7). Agreeing with Gilles Deleuze that continental philosophy is "a kind of transformational thinking, . . . a thinking that occurs through its repetition" (p. 7), "American continental philosophers do not merely re-present what has been created in Europe" (p. 7). Brogan and Risser see this philosophical approach as "[l]ike America itself, . . . [as] 'transitional,' at the crossroads of culture, dismantling classical structures by establishing new connections between past and future" (p. 7). Recalling much of the American tradition we have discussed here, Brogan and Risser concluded, "Continental philosophy has provided a way of thinking and speaking that addresses and affirms multiculturalism in America." "[T]his commitment to pluralism," they said, "speaks directly out of an American need and an American experience" (pp. 8–9).

From this perspective, continental philosophy seems to be another element in the larger story of the philosophies of resistance we have discussed. While this is surely the case for many of the philosophers in this tradition (we discuss a number of those influenced by this approach, including Richard Bernstein and Judith Butler), Brogan and Risser also suggest an aspect of this thought that stands at odds with much of the tradition here. "The American experience, because of its immigrant roots, has always been imbued with a sense of the foreign" (p. 8). The result is a philosophical practice that philosophizes "in the face of the foreign, of what is not one's own" in a place that is "a siteless site, a place for experience and thinking whose boundaries are not sedimented but open to the recovery of the foreign sites that define us" (p. 8). It is the claim of ongoing foreignness that stands in at least some contrast to the work of many of the philosophers we have considered. The struggle—for Pokagon and Standing Bear, James and Follett, Dewey and Addams—was not about recovering "the foreign sites that define us," but rather about becoming part of the place at hand. Brogan and Risser aptly describe American experience as one "of belonging and not belonging, of being at home and yet not at home" (p. 8). The difference is how philosophy responds to such experience. One strategy is disposed to seek answers elsewhere, often without much regard for the histories and circumstances at hand. Another strategy is to seek answers closer to home, engaging the history of the place, and seeking answers in the indeterminate situation that frames the experience. Standing Bear's conclusion that "men must be born and reborn to belong. Their bodies must be formed of the dust of their forefathers' bones" (1933, p. 248) emphasizes this point. Belonging, in this sense, is a matter of living in the place of one's ancestors, those whom one honors and depends upon for a sense of self. The resources of other lands may be useful, but they are, for Standing Bear, no substitute for being an embodied part of a place.

The dominance of academic American philosophy by analytic philosophers committed more or less to the priority of language philosophy and the separation of philosophy from social issues was fostered by a handful of prominent graduate programs and the primary professional organization in the United States—the American Philosophical Association. While the prominent graduate schools preserved a narrow philosophical focus, making it harder for new philosophers to take up work outside the mainstream, the APA, as the place to present new work (and to look for jobs in philosophy), also sought to remain narrow in the work it fostered. As John Lachs (1934–2023) observed in *Freedom and Limits* (2014),

> In the [American Philosophical] Association's dominant Eastern Division, disciplinary exclusivity was wedded to institutional nepotism in such a way that it became nearly impossible for philosophers who were not analytic in orientation and who did not serve in Eastern seaboard graduate schools to break into the power circle or even into the program. (Lachs, 2014, p. 292)

Faculty at "leading" graduate schools saw themselves as maintaining the standards of philosophy and so, with the help of their students also taking positions in these same schools, held the leadership positions and decided who would be permitted to present their work at the annual conference. As a response to the launch of the Sputnik satellite by the Soviet Union, the National Defense Education Act was passed in 1958 and provided funding that helped to increase the number of philosophy graduate programs around the nation. Faculty at the new graduate programs and graduates who found positions at universities and colleges outside the confines of the "best" programs suffered what Lachs called "haughty neglect."

By the late 1970s, philosophers interested in continental philosophy, feminist philosophy, idealism, and pragmatism became frustrated by their routine exclusion from elected positions in the APA and from the program of presenters at the annual meetings. Shortly after the 1978 meeting of the Association, members of the Society for the Advancement of American Philosophy (SAAP), founded in 1972, together with members of the SPEP, met and decided to change the APA. This group included John McDermott (1932–2018) and Lachs, who had helped found SAAP, and Bruce Wilshire (1932–2013), who recorded the events in his criticism of analytic philosophy, *A Fashionable* Nihilism (2002). They sought to change the makeup of the leadership committees in charge of deciding who was allowed to present work at the annual meetings. In December 1978, this group of insurgent philosophers, now called "The Committee on Pluralism," met and decided to encourage others attending the next annual meeting to participate in the election of officers. Usually, this business meeting was a small, quiet affair in which a few participants voted for a predetermined slate of candidates. At the 1979 meeting, the room was full, and when the hand-picked slate of candidates was nominated, members nominated an alternative slate from the floor including John E. Smith (1921–2009) for President, Quentin Lauer (1917–1997) and John McDermott for the Executive Committee, and John Lachs for Secretary. Smith, Lauer, and McDermott were all elected. "A strange, stunned pandemonium ensued," wrote Wilshire. "To use a vulgar locution—but a more telling one I cannot find—the shit had hit the fan" (2002, p. 57). Immediately, Ruth Marcus (1921–2012), part of the APA leadership, observed that there were students and other participants not eligible to vote in the room who may have voted. She called for a ruling by the Eastern Division APA president who was chairing the meeting, Richard Rorty.

A few months earlier in 1979, Rorty had published *Philosophy and the Mirror of Nature*. Although viewed as a prominent analytic philosopher (despite his introduction to *The Linguistic Turn*, which suggested a critical stance toward philosophy in the analytic style), Rorty's new book was a systematic challenge to the central commitments of analytic philosophy. "The aim of this book," he wrote,

> is to undermine the reader's confidence in "the mind" as something about which one should have a "philosophical" view, in "knowledge" as something about which there ought to be a "theory" and which has "foundations," and in "philosophy" as it has been conceived since Kant. (p. 7)

At issue throughout the text were the very dualisms that Dewey had challenged, and the holisms proposed by Quine and Sellars as an antidote. Contrary to the standard rejection of history and social context as relevant to philosophical analysis, Rorty took a historicist approach to understanding the rise and failure of the dominant philosophical tradition. He concluded, "I present Wittgenstein, Heidegger, and Dewey as philosophers whose aim is to edify—to help their readers, or society as a whole, break free from outworn vocabularies and attitudes, rather than to provide 'grounding' for the intuitions and customs of the present" (1979, p. 12). The work was, for many, the beginning of a new era in American academic philosophy that made the way clear again for philosophy that arose in response to the problems of society, its history, and its hopes for the future.

In response to the appeal from the APA executive committee to invalidate the 1979 election of officers, Rorty decided to let the results stand. By the following November, a group of prominent philosophers (including Quine) wrote a letter of protest:

> The Committee on Pluralism seeks to obtain, through political means, a position of influence which its members have not been able to obtain through their philosophical work. We believe that the Committee favors the suppression of serious scholarly and intellectual standards under the false banner of open-mindedness. (Quoted in Wilshire, 2002, p. 60)

Quine, according to Wilshire, was asked if it was true that no pluralists had done quality work. He allowed that some might have, but that "he did not know their work" (Wilshire, 2002, p. 61). The rejection was a familiar one: first dismissing the work of outsiders, and then accusing them in turn of what the dominant group had practiced for decades. The results of the "pluralist revolt," as the episode is still called at meetings of the APA, changed election procedures and expanded the program to include work by diverse (nonanalytic) philosophers. But much of the profession remained the same. As Wilshire concluded, "Faced with declining student enrollments and massive public indifference, academic philosophy has become increasingly technical, 'analytic,' defensive, insular, and too often a Mandarin pastime" (p. 62).

Lachs, however, offered a positive assessment: "The revolt aimed not at defeating or eliminating analytic philosophy but at establishing the legitimacy of alternative methods. It wanted to introduce a wholesome pluralism into the profession, and a look at philosophical activity today shows that in this it clearly succeeded" (2014, p. 300). The presence of diverse philosophical issues and methods at the annual APA meetings has grown dramatically since 1979. New venues for publication have emerged, and a wide range of new philosophical resources (including new histories of American philosophy) have continued to transform the discipline. Yet, perhaps strangely, most philosophy departments around the country continued on their course within the larger philosophical agenda still set by an elite committed to "protecting" the discipline. Despite the changing APA and new work by individuals inside and outside the academy, philosophy departments remained marked by what Lachs called "the tendency to exclude the different" (p. 297). An explanation for the continued narrowness of the academic field might be found in the declaration of Ruth Marcus after the election in 1979: "You keep the conventions! We'll keep the graduate schools" (quoted in Wilshire, 2002, p. 62).

American analytic philosophy gained its prominence in the wake of world war in part by adopting a politics of neutrality and non-involvement. It was a philosophy of counter-resistance that turned its work away from the pressing problems faced by the wider community in order to avoid the mistakes of the past. May Brodbeck's question for pragmatism can stand as a question for the tradition of American philosophies of resistance. She asked, "Can any reflective person who has survived the past quarter of a century lightly embrace such [philosophies]?" (1963, p. 215). Her answer and that of her colleagues was "no," and their efforts in the discipline helped to ensure that their answer was widely shared. Through its focus on language and technical problems, academic philosophy on the whole separated itself from the politics it hoped to avoid. In so doing, it separated itself from the students who sought to make sense of a world of sexism and racial unrest, poverty, environmental destruction, and war. The work of American philosophies of resistance went on, as we will show, but, for the most part, it did not go on primarily in the philosophy classrooms of American colleges and universities.

## Primary Texts

Nelson, Lynn Hankinson (1990). *Who Knows? From Quine to a Feminist Empiricism.* Philadelphia: Temple University Press.
Quine, Willard Van Orman (1980). "Two Dogmas of Logical Empiricism." In *From a Logical Point of View*, 2nd edn, Revised, 20–46. Cambridge: Harvard University Press.
Whitehead, Alfred North (1997). *Science and the Modern World.* New York: Free Press.
Farber, Marvin (1959). *Naturalism and Subjectivism.* Albany: SUNY Press.
Sellars, Wilfrid (1963). *Science, Perception and Reality.* New York: Routledge & Kegan Paul Ltd; London, and The Humanities Press, reissued in 1991 by Atascadero, CA: Ridgeview Publishing Co.

# PART III
## SOCIAL REVOLUTIONS

# CHAPTER 18
# CIVIL RIGHTS
## MARTIN LUTHER KING, JR., RICHARD WRIGHT, AND JAMES BALDWIN

On May 2, 1963, more than one thousand African American youths gathered at the Sixteenth Street Baptist Church in Birmingham, Alabama. Most had skipped classes in order to join civil rights leaders from the Southern Christian Leadership Conference (SCLC) in their effort to desegregate the city. Trained in the practice of nonviolent protest advocated by the SCLC, the protesters began their march through the center of the city where they were met by the Birmingham police. Even after hundreds of the protesters were arrested and taken to jail in police vans and school buses, the students assembled again the next day. In response to the first day of protest, Eugene "Bull" Connor, the commissioner of public safety and a segregationist, ordered the police and city firefighters to meet the next day's protest with force. With television news cameras and dozens of reporters on hand, the students were beaten, attacked by police dogs, and hit by water from fire hoses. Hundreds more protesters were arrested, and many were injured.

The protest, called the Children's Crusade, was part of a larger strategy begun by the SCLC in April. The first stage of the protest had been a boycott of White-owned Birmingham businesses. With broad support from the African American community (which accounted for nearly half the city's population), along with other "direct action" such as mass meetings, sit-ins, and marches, local merchants quickly felt the impact. In response, the city appealed to the state circuit court and received an injunction to halt the protests. SCLC and local Black religious leaders met and decided to violate the injunction, and on April 12, Good Friday, the protesters marched through downtown, and many, including Martin Luther King, Jr., were arrested. That same day, eight Alabama clergymen published an open letter urging "our own Negro community to withdraw support from these demonstrations, and to unite locally in working peacefully for a better Birmingham." The call for protesters to obey the court injunction and the claim that unity should be a local matter were direct indictments of the SCLC's presence in Birmingham; the clergy—not to mention Bull Connor and most of the Birmingham business community—wanted things to return to "normal." "When rights are consistently denied," the clergy reasoned, "a cause should be pressed in the courts and in negotiations among local leaders, not in the streets" (Carpenter et al., 1963).

While in jail, King began a letter on the margins of the newspaper that carried the open letter and continued it on pieces of paper provided by another prisoner. Published later as the "Letter from Birmingham Jail," the response provided a philosophical framework for King's vision of the Civil Rights Movement. At the center was King's belief that the movement was an attempt to bring justice to the oppressed. "Injustice anywhere is a threat to justice everywhere," he wrote. "We are caught in an inescapable network of mutuality tied in a single garment of destiny. Whatever affects one directly, affects all indirectly" (1964, p. 77). The passage places justice at the center of the movement. It also recalls the Social Gospel movement and its secular collaborators (the "mutualists") and the conception of community developed by Addams, Royce, and Dewey, among others. Individuals are individuals, both as dependent and independent, only in light of their sociality, their relations with others. Such interconnectedness made the civil rights revolution necessary since African Americans and Whites were, whether they liked it or not, members of the same whole, clothed with the same "garment of destiny." On this ground, King rejected the claims by his challengers that he was an outsider in Birmingham. There were no outsiders "anywhere within [the] bounds" of the United States.

King's response to the clergymen's letter rejected what he called their "narrow provincialism" (and their apparent unwillingness to fight for justice) and called instead for a renewed and expanded movement. While the clergy letter called for the protesters to respect the law, King argued that there were, in fact, two sorts of laws: just and unjust. Following a long Christian tradition, King observed that just laws are those consistent with "moral law" or "the law of God," while unjust laws are not. He further qualified his definition in terms that recalled his background in the American philosophical tradition. "Any law that uplifts human personality is just," he wrote. "Any law that degrades human personality is unjust" (1964, p. 82).

As a graduate student, King studied at Boston University with faculty members who accepted versions of personalism, the view developed by Borden Parker Bowne and Mary Whiton Calkins, that emphasized the ontological priority of persons. From this perspective, human persons are themselves members of larger and larger communities that are finally all members of what King called, following Royce, "the Beloved Community." Writing in 1956 about his conception of nonviolent resistance, he concluded that a boycott, for example, is not an end: "it is merely a means to awaken a sense of shame within the oppressor." The end, he continued, "is reconciliation; the end is redemption; the end is the creation of the beloved community" (1986, p. 140). The apartheid practiced in the American South blocked reconciliation and redemption. "All segregation statutes," he wrote in his 1963 "Letter," "are unjust because segregation distorts the soul and damages the personality. It gives the segregator a false sense of superiority and the segregated a false sense of inferiority" (1964, p. 82).

King cited Martin Buber (1878–1965) as well, an Austrian-born Jewish philosopher who fled to Palestine from Germany in 1937 and spent the rest of his career in Jerusalem. Buber argued that the model relation between humans and between humans and God was the "I-thou" relation. According to King, segregation adopted instead an "I-it" relation that treated Blacks and the poor as objects, as "its" rather than as people. The liberal theologian Paul Tillich (1886–1965), who left Germany in 1933 and taught at Union Theological Seminary in New York City, took a related position by arguing that "sin is separation." King concluded that legal segregation consequently amounted to legalized sinfulness.

King offered more concrete examples as well. "An unjust law is a code that a . . . power majority group compels a minority group to obey but does not make binding on itself. This," he concluded, "is *difference* made legal" (1964, p. 83). Implicit in such unequal laws is the recognition that minority persons are denied access to some goods available to the "power majority" or are made to suffer some evils that the "power majority" can avoid. As a result, the law degrades persons. In contrast, a just law is "a code that a majority compels a minority to follow and that it is willing to follow itself" (p. 83). A just law is "*sameness* made legal" (p. 83). King's second example was voting laws that suppress or deny members of a minority group the opportunity to vote. Here again, persons are degraded, in this case by being denied access to participation in the process of self-governance. Just laws—and systems of government—are by implication those that provide for universal suffrage and shared governance. Each person has both a voice and a stake in the consequences of the laws established, and decisions made.

Finally, King argued that some laws appear just but fail to be just in their application. For example, while the requirement that parades have permits does not appear problematic, when it is applied in order to help maintain the unjust laws of segregation, that requirement becomes unjust. Civil disobedience, willfully violating an unjust law, is itself a just act because it is one that seeks to foster "personalities" and the communities upon which they depend. Such disobedience, King said, must be done "openly, lovingly, and with a willingness to accept the penalty" (p. 83).

King viewed his position, at least in the "Letter," as one that stood between two factions of the African American community. One faction, he said, was complacent, who, "as a result of long years of oppression, are so drained of self-respect and a sense of 'somebodiness' that they have adjusted to segregation" (1964, p. 86). This faction included "a few middle-class Negroes" who, thanks to their "education and economic security," profited by segregation (p. 87). The other faction was one of "bitterness and hatred" and came "perilously close to advocating violence" (p. 87). These alternatives, King implied, equally fail to address injustice, the first by sustaining segregation and the second by undermining persons. "I have tried to stand between these two forces," he concluded, by "saying that we need emulate neither the 'do-nothingism' of the complacent nor the hatred and despair of the black nationalist" (p. 87).

The "Letter" was widely distributed and helped to solidify a particular vision of the Civil Rights Movement. It was reprinted in King's book, *Why We Can't Wait* (1964) alongside an account of the civil rights struggle. In the wider account, however, King made it clear that the civil rights revolution extended further than just desegregation. Echoing Du Bois's economic critique in *Darkwater*, King also argued that the revolution must address the unjust economic system of America. While Blacks, he said, represented a "majority" of the disadvantaged in America, there were also "millions of white poor" who were "the derivative victims of slavery" (1964, p. 138). By depressing wages through the use of human slaves, Whites were also exploited by those who controlled the economy. In order to respond to the situation faced by Blacks and poor Whites—both women and men—as a result of the history of slavery, King advocated the development of a "Bill of Rights for the Disadvantaged." Beyond equality, such a bill of rights would provide differential opportunity to those who suffered a history of oppression and exclusion. "For it is obvious that if a man is entered at the starting line in a race three hundred years after another man, the first would have to perform some impossible feat in order to catch up with his fellow runner" (p. 134). To advantage only Blacks would lead to a new inequality and Blacks "will not long permit themselves to be pitted against white workers for an ever decreasing supply of jobs" (p. 139). Instead, in King's vision, labor and government would collaborate by taking what he (and the administration of President Johnson) would later call "affirmative action" (1967, p. 189) to increase opportunities for the poor and provide a "social work apparatus" to support all persons. The result, he concluded, was that the "Negro in winning rights for himself produces substantial benefits for the nation" (1964, p. 151).

On May 8, after images of beaten and arrested Black students circulated through the national news media, SCLC and the city of Birmingham agreed (with the help of Robert Kennedy, then serving as the US Attorney General) to end the protests and end segregation in Birmingham. On May 10, King and other leaders announced the agreement, and that the city would establish a biracial commission to monitor the agreement. That night, a bomb went off near the hotel where the SCLC leadership was staying. The next day, President Kennedy ordered 3,000 federal troops to a camp near Birmingham. Even though the protests had ended, the Birmingham public schools suspended the students who had missed school to march in the Children's Crusade. The federal district court reversed the decision on May 22 and the public school system was reprimanded.

On June 10, 1963, in nearby Tuscaloosa, the effort to end segregation in colleges and universities was blocked when Alabama Governor George Wallace lived up to his promise to "stand in the schoolhouse door" if Blacks tried to integrate the University of Alabama. In response, President Kennedy ordered the troops he had stationed near Birmingham to intervene and "federalized" the Alabama National Guard to support the action. The next day, Governor Wallace backed down, allowing two Black students, Vivian Malone and James A. Hood, to enroll.

Even as the protests in Birmingham were coming to an end, A. Philip Randolph, president of the Brotherhood of Sleeping Car Porters, proposed a March on Washington to demand a comprehensive civil rights bill that would address segregation in public facilities, protection of voting rights, and the integration of public schools. Randolph's union, formed in 1925, had organized the Black porters who worked for the Pullman Company (which, after the 1894 strike, had become the largest producer of railroad sleeping cars). In 1941, Randolph had proposed a similar march on Washington. In response to the threat of that march, President Roosevelt had agreed to establish a commission to end discrimination in the defense industry. Randolph's proposal for a march in 1963 was eventually taken up by the leaders of the SCLC, the Student Nonviolent Coordinating Committee (SNCC), the Congress on Racial Equality (CORE), the Urban League, and the NAACP. As the planning continued, the Kennedy administration became concerned about the size and potential message of the march, especially in light of its desire to introduce what they thought would be an unpopular civil rights bill in Congress. On August 23, 1963, an estimated 250,000 people joined in the "March on Washington for Jobs and Freedom" from the Washington Monument to the Lincoln Memorial.

The program for the march included an address by King (his famous "I Have a Dream" speech), as well as speeches by Randolph, James Farmer (president of CORE), and Roy Wilkins (president of the NAACP). It also included a speech by John Lewis, the young leader of SNCC (who would later become a member of Congress). Lewis's speech included a strong criticism of the Kennedy administration's civil rights record and their proposed legislation. In his original draft, Lewis proclaimed, "The revolution is at hand and we must free ourselves of the chains of political and economic slavery.... We will not wait for the President and the Justice Department, nor Congress, but we will take matters into our own hands and create a source of power outside of any national structure." He went on to state, "we will march through the South, through the heart of Dixie, the way Sherman did, leaving a scorched earth with our nonviolence" (Lewis and Orso, 1998). At the last minute, under pressure from Archbishop Patrick O'Boyle and Randolph, Lewis edited his speech to present a less critical view. Lewis's speech remained the most radical of the day, but it is King's speech that is best remembered for its hopeful vision of American race relations. The March was a visible sign of change in at least part of American culture. But the change it marked was limited, and it marked an ongoing struggle as well. Less than a month after the March, on the night of September 15, members of the Ku Klux Klan set off a bomb at the Sixteenth Street Baptist Church in Birmingham, killing four African American girls and injuring twenty-two others. Despite eyewitnesses who identified at least one of the terrorists, no one was arrested for the crime until 1977 (three White men were eventually convicted).

In 1954, nine years before the March on Washington, the US Supreme Court handed down its unanimous decision in Brown v. Board of Education of Topeka, Kansas. The case (one of five decided together) challenged the principle established by the court in 1896 in Plessy v. Ferguson that it was legal to establish separate public facilities (schools, public transportation, even water fountains and bathrooms) for White and Black citizens. The 1896 decision made American apartheid laws ("Jim Crow laws") legal; in the 1954 decision, however, Chief Justice Earl Warren concluded that "in the field of public education the doctrine of 'separate but equal' has no place. Separate educational facilities are inherently unequal" (Supreme Court, 1954). Warren explained that even if schools were equal in terms of funding, facilities, and curricula, separate schools nevertheless had the potential to do permanent damage to minority students. "To separate [minority students] from others of similar age and qualifications solely because of their race generates a feeling of inferiority as to their status in the community that may affect their hearts and minds in a way unlikely ever to be undone" (Supreme Court, 1954). The following year, the school board of Prince Edward County in Virginia asked the Supreme Court to allow them to desegregate their schools over a period of time. The court responded by requiring schools to desegregate "with all deliberate speed," a requirement that was so vague that many schools took no action at all.

Many African Americans welcomed the Brown decision as a victory against the oppression that was part of the legally segregated South. Its requirement for integration became a central justification for the protests against segregation that began in earnest in 1955 with the bus boycott in Montgomery, Alabama. At the same time, Du Bois, among others, expressed doubt about the decision and its implications for African Americans. The decision, Du Bois thought, was necessary for liberation, but it also created a "cruel dilemma" (1970, p. 283) for African Americans. On one hand, Blacks wanted their children educated—"a must, else they continue in semislavery." On the other hand, "with successfully mixed schools they know what their children must suffer for years from southern white teachers, from white hoodlums who sit beside them and under school authorities from janitors to superintendents, who hate and despise them" (p. 283). At issue was Du Bois's idea that identity was, in significant part, the ability to organize one's life as part of a larger community with shared ideals. Integration presumed that such shared ideals would emerge in the context of Black and White relations to sustain and enrich each individual. Du Bois, however, feared that Black children would lose their connection with their own communities of shared ideals and histories by becoming part of the White community in which they were viewed as inferior in spite of the new legal requirements for equality. He predicted that the "best of Negro teachers" would leave teaching because "they will not and cannot teach what many white folks will long want taught" (p. 283). He also thought that the "teaching of Negro history will leave the school and with it that brave story of Negro resistance" (p. 283). In the end, Blacks in America had little choice. "They must eventually surrender race 'solidarity' and the idea of American Negro culture to the concept of world humanity, above race and nation." The surrender, he concluded, was both "the price of liberty" and the "cost of oppression" (p. 283). Despite this apparent challenge to the community in the long run, Du Bois still held that "we Negroes will stand fast and pull through ... we will survive" (p. 284).

The tension Du Bois saw in the prospects of integration was widely shared. Even as civil rights advocates demanded integration, others argued instead for the very Black solidarity that integration put at risk. On April 19, 1967, during a speech at Garfield High School in Seattle, Stokely Carmichael (1941–1998), then president of SNCC and a close friend of King, declared, "Black Power is the coming together of black people to fight for their liberation by any means necessary" (Carmichael, 1967). Although Carmichael, who changed his name to Kwame Ture in 1968, had earlier been committed to King's vision of integration, he came to believe that the cost of integration was too high for African Americans. In an essay published in 1966, he concluded, "This concept of integration had to be based on the assumption that there was nothing of value in the Negro community and that little of value could be created among Negroes" (in Pohlmann, 2003, p. 183). The goal of integration was not to preserve what was distinctive about Black culture and individuals, but rather to "blend into the white community" that provided the source of values and opportunity. "The civil rights movement," he said,

> saw its role as a kind of liaison between the powerful white community and the dependent Negro one. . . . We made no pretense of organizing and developing institutions of community power in the Negro community, but appealed to the conscience of white institutions of power. (p. 184)

Rather than challenging the power of White society by demanding equality, he thought that the Civil Rights Movement conceded to the values of the dominant society and willingly left the Black community behind. In a 1966 speech at Berkeley, Carmichael argued, following Albert Camus, Sartre, and Frantz Fanon, that Black Power emerged from the fact that people cannot condemn themselves. To work in alliance with Whites in order to condemn and reform White supremacy could only fail. Instead, Blacks needed to take power on their own behalf (Carmichael, 1966).

Although Ture is often credited with coining the phrase "Black Power," Richard Wright (1908–1960) published a book by that title in 1954. Wright proposed a vision of Africa as resistance to Western ideas and practices. The African character of Black Power, for Wright, emerged in the hypothetical biography of "a young boy . . . born in a tribe" on the Gold Coast (2008, p. 280). The boy, Wright imagined, was educated by missionaries, traveled to Europe or the United States and received a Western education and, in the process, learned the meaning of race and the place of Africans in the world. The young man resolved to "go back home and try to change things, to fight for freedom" (p. 283). At home, the young man found that the only ones who resisted the presence of Western imperialism were the traditional people, those who held to the ancient religious practices, told traditional stories, and spoke in the traditional tribal language. In short, the very people the young man had come to hate as "primitive" and "savage" necessarily became his allies.

So the imagined youth faced a dilemma of once rejecting the tribal tradition and, at the same time, finding that it is only in the embrace of the tribal legacy that he can find a means to resist the West.

> Feeling himself an outsider in his native land, watching the whites take the gold and the diamonds and the timber and the bauxite and the manganese, seeing his fellow blacks who were educated abroad siding with the whites, seeing his culture shattered and rendered abhorrent, . . . seeing that the black life is detribalized and left to rot, he finally lifts his voice in an agonized cry of . . . *black* nationalism. (2008, p. 288)

Rejecting both the democratic ideals of liberals and the economic appeals of the communists, Wright recommended instead that Africans develop their own distinctive ideals and communities. "You've got to find your *own* paths, your *own* values," he wrote, "the building of that bridge between tribal man and the twentieth century can be done in a score of ways" (p. 414). But Black Power is not only a matter of self-organizing, it must also confront imperialism on its own terms. Anticipating the later call of some Black Power thinkers, he concluded, "There is but one honorable course that assumes and answers the ideological, traditional, organizational, emotional, political, and productive needs of Africa at this time: AFRICAN LIFE MUST BE MILITARIZED!" (p. 415). In an open letter to Kwame Nkrumah, the prime minister of the Gold Coast (which became the nation of Ghana in 1957), Wright said, "if the choice is between traditional Western domination and this hard path, take the hard path!" (p. 418).

In 1957, Wright published another essay written after his travels in Africa, titled "White Man Listen!" Here he recognized, as had Du Bois before him, the imposition of a racial dualism in which Whites dominated the "other races" and in which resistance meant both fostering diverse traditions and critically challenging Whiteness. Importantly, for Wright, the system of racial difference established by the West led to a conception of the White race manifested in the experience of the oppressed. "The 'white man' is a distinct image in Asian-African minds," he wrote, that had nothing to do with a biological conception of race: "Scientifically speaking the leaders of Asia and Africa know that there is no such thing as race. It is, therefore, only from a historical or sociological point of view that the image of 'white man' means anything" (2008, p. 667). Resistance to white domination is a matter of unifying against the threat. In America, Marcus Garvey (1887–1940) served Wright as an example.

Garvey was born in Jamaica and, in 1914, founded the Universal Negro Improvement Association (UNIA). The UNIA was "an organization among Negroes that [was] seeking to improve the condition of the race" by founding a new nation in Africa "where Negroes will be given the opportunity to develop by themselves" (1992, vol. 2, p. 37). The UNIA was, Garvey said, committed to the rights of all people but was committed to fostering a "universal confraternity among the race" in order to promote "pride and love," to assist the needy, to promote "Spiritual worship among the native tribes of Africa," and establish schools and universities (p. 38). In 1917, Garvey traveled to New York and established the UNIA in the United States. Central to Garvey's plan was the need to establish economic ties between African-descended people around the world and this, he believed, required establishing a shipping company, the Black Star Steamship Line. With a subscription price of $5, members of the UNIA and others contributed sufficient resources to eventually purchase three steamships. In 1919, the UNIA also founded the Negro Factories Corporation that provided as many as 700 jobs in a variety of enterprises including grocery stores, a laundry, a dressmaking shop, and a doll factory. By 1920, the UNIA had four million members. Garvey's program was opposed by many African American leaders (including Du Bois), and in 1925, Garvey was convicted of mail fraud and then in 1927, he was deported to Jamaica. Wright's assessment of Garvey's program in 1957 was that it failed for two reasons: "it was premature, and the Negroes in America felt themselves more psychologically identified with America than with Africa" (2008, p. 685). In the end, Wright wrote, the rise of Black Power in Africa marked a revolution that the West could accept or reject. If the latter, he thought, the West would go to any length "to make the world safe for the 'white man's' conception of existence, to make the ideas of Mill and Hume and [John] Locke good for all people, at all times, everywhere" (p. 698).

Wright was born in Jackson, Mississippi, where he had attended segregated schools until he was forced to drop out of high school to earn money for his family. He moved to Chicago in 1927 and, while working at the US Post Office, became involved in the Communist Party. During this time, he began to write, and in 1936, he published a short story, "Big Boy Leaves Home," and became the chair of the South Side Writer's Group, which included a number of soon-to-be-famous African American writers. He moved to New York City the following year and worked for the Federal Writers' Project (FWP), a federally funded program created in 1935 under President Roosevelt's Works Progress Administration. The FWP initially employed writers to produce guidebooks describing the sights, history, culture, and economics of regions of the United States. The work of the project eventually included a series of oral histories that recorded the experience of former slaves, the lives of the poor in the Great Depression, and a large collection of urban and rural folklore.

In 1940, Wright published *Native Son*, and it was offered as a main selection of the widely popular Book-of-the-Month Club. *Native Son* is the story of Bigger Thomas, a poor Black man living in Chicago's South Side in the 1930s. Bigger is portrayed as a man made violent by his circumstances and—at least to many critics—portrayed the character of Blacks in America as angry and violent. Near the conclusion of the novel, as Bigger is being tried for murder, his lawyer presents a long address arguing that while Bigger did commit the crime, he had done so as a result of his poverty and anger brought about by his treatment by White society. He argued that Bigger Thomas was a product of a history of oppression and lived a "mode of life . . . stunted and distorted, but possessing its own laws and claims, an existence of men growing out of the soil prepared by the collective but blind will of a hundred million people" (1998, p. 388). As a result, "[h]emmed in, limited, circumscribed, he sees and feels no way of acting except to hate and kill that which he thinks is crushing him" (p. 390). Rather than pleading for Bigger's innocence, the lawyer concluded, his job was "to show how nonsensical it is to seek revenge on this boy under the pretense we are making a great fight for justice. If we do that, we shall be merely hypnotizing ourselves, and to our own ultimate disadvantage" (p. 395).

Wright's novel became a bestseller, and he joined the ranks of a generation of Black writers who used literature as a means of addressing the problems of violence, segregation, and poverty faced by African Americans. In addition to the ongoing work of Du Bois, these authors included Zora Neale Hurston, Ralph Ellison, James Weldon Johnson, and poets Jean Toomer, Margaret Walker, Claude McKay, Countee Cullen, and Langston Hughes. In 1952, Ellison published *Invisible Man*, which became one of the most visible novels of the twentieth century.

In 1949, James Baldwin (1924–1987), a young African American writer living in Paris, published a critical review of *Native Son*. Comparing Bigger Thomas with the character of Uncle Tom in Harriet Beecher Stowe's novel, *Uncle Tom's Cabin*, Baldwin argued that Bigger was the opposite of Uncle Tom, framed by the same logic but emphasizing the category of

Blackness as angry and violent rather than as passive and accepting. "Now as then," he wrote, "we find ourselves bound first without, and then within, by the nature of our categorization" (1998, p. 16). It does no good to rail "against this trap" since "We take our shape . . . within and against that cage of reality bequeathed us at our birth" (p. 16). Wright's characterization of Blackness as "the color of evil" (p. 17) reasserted the received categorizations that "were meant to define us," but they have "boomeranged us into chaos" (p. 15). He said, "It must be remembered that the oppressed and the oppressor are bound together within the same society; they accept the same criteria, they share the same beliefs, they both alike depend on the same reality" (p. 17). "In overlooking, denying, evading [human] complexity," he concluded about Wright's novel (and Stowe's before it), "we are diminished and we perish" (p. 13). In response to Bigger Thomas as "controlled, defined by his hatred and his fear" (p. 18), an alternative conception was needed that recognized the complexity of human oppression and liberation. Cooper had offered a similar call earlier with her observations about the complex intersections of race, class, and gender and the reality that some with racial privilege shared in oppression based on class or gender.

Baldwin grew up in Harlem with eight sisters and brothers. In middle school, he met the poet Countee Cullen (who was also his French teacher) and attended Dewitt Clinton High School, where he edited the school's literary magazine. While a student, Baldwin also became a Pentecostal preacher of some renown. He left preaching, and after completing high school, he took a job in construction. In his free time, he continued to read avidly and began to write short stories and novels. He met Richard Wright in 1944, who encouraged his writing and helped him receive a grant that allowed him to move to Paris in 1948 (Leeming, 1994). It was from here that he published his essay on Wright, and in 1955, he republished the essay and a number of others in a volume titled *Notes from a Native Son*. The volume included a second essay on Wright's book that argued again for the recognition of complexity in the context of American racism. "*Native Son* finds itself at length so trapped by the American image of Negro life and by the American necessity to find the ray of hope that it cannot pursue its own implications" (Baldwin, 1998, p. 31). Wright, he concluded, "can only proceed from the assumption . . . that Americans, who evade, so far as possible, all genuine experience, have therefore no way of assessing the experience of others and no way of establishing themselves in relation to any way of life which is not their own" (pp. 31–2).

At issue in Wright's work is the recognition that oppression in America is not reducible to any simple set of categories. Baldwin's own experience exemplified the issue. As a youth, Baldwin had a conversion experience at his church that led him to become a fourteen-year-old preacher. Even as he led worship and preached and tried to lead a life appropriate to his work, he also discovered that he was gay. The complex life of a teenager, at once a popular preacher in his neighborhood and at the same time a young man spending his free time with an older man who was also his lover, meant that simple divisions of Black and White, women and men, evil and good were not so clear. Baldwin himself became a kind of paradox in a country, he said, "devoted to the death of the paradox" (1998, p. 17).

In 1985 in an essay titled "Freaks and the Ideal of Manhood," he wrote, "it is not possible for the human being to be as simple as a stallion or a mare, because human imagination is perpetually required to examine, control and redefine reality" (1998, p. 814). Rather than understanding American life first in terms of race—as was common among those concerned with the increasing racial unrest in the 1950s—sexuality became his central framework. This is, in part, because "the idea of one's sexuality can only with great violence be divorced or distanced from the idea of self" (p. 815). In America, the "ideal of sexuality appears to be rooted in the American ideal of masculinity" (p. 815). This ideal, Baldwin wrote, "has created cowboys and Indians, good guys and bad guys, punks and studs, tough guys and softies, butch and faggot, black and white" (p. 815). Through these dualisms, Baldwin said, America made a "successful and glamorous . . . romance out of genocide and slavery" (p. 815). But Baldwin's own experience, he claimed, saved him from this "paralytically infantile ideal" (p. 815). As a result, "all of the American categories of male and female, straight or not, black or white, were shattered, thank heaven, very early in my life" (p. 819). The resulting perspective was one that lived with paradox and gained insight as a result.

While working at a bar called the Calypso in Greenwich Village, Baldwin came to see the alienation of the White patrons. Their disconnection had led them to seek therapy of all sorts. For Baldwin, such a pursuit of cures for their alienation actually amounted to "a desperate moral abdication" (1998, p. 826). The ideal of masculinity structured the White patrons' lives and drove them to seek the "relentlessly hetero (sexual?) keepers of the keys and seals, those who know what the world needs in the way of order and who are ready and willing to supply that order" (p. 827). The consequent "rage for order," he concluded, "can result in chaos and in this country chaos connects with color" (p. 827). Where Wright began with the division of race to explain the nature of Black and White, Baldwin began with the ideal of masculinity that served as a principle of order connecting oppositions and eliminating anomalies. Yet Baldwin himself marked the resistance. People who fall outside the ideal "are called freaks and are treated as they are treated—in the main, abominably—because they are human beings who cause to echo, deep within us, our most profound terrors and desires" (p. 828). His alternative account of human nature beyond the framework of masculinity reflected a plural world marked by the intersection of race, class, gender, and sexuality. Echoing Fuller's notion of a gender continuum, Baldwin said, "We are all androgynous, . . . because each of us, helplessly and forever, contains the other—male in female, female in male, white in black and black in white. We are part of each other" (p. 828).

When the civil rights protests began in 1955, Baldwin made a brief visit to the United States to watch rehearsals for his play, *The Amen Corner*, at Howard University. He returned to France in the summer as *Notes of a Native Son* was released. The following year, Baldwin published his second novel, *Giovanni's Room*, the story of an American expatriate living in Paris who falls in love with an Italian bartender, Giovanni. The novel was rejected by Baldwin's first publisher for its homoerotic content but was published by another press and quickly sold out. In the summer of 1957, Baldwin returned to the United States again, this time on an assignment from the American quarterly, *The Partisan Review*, to report on integration after the Brown decision. During his investigation, he met a wide range of civil rights activists including King. Over the next ten years, Baldwin participated in protests, gave speeches, and wrote essays on issues of race and desegregation, including two essays published together as the often-cited *The Fire Next Time* (1963). Writing in the first essay, a letter to his nephew, Baldwin raised the central issue of the Civil Rights Movement. "Please be clear," he wrote, "about the reality which lies behind the words *acceptance* and *integration*" (1998, p. 293). The implication was not that one should "try to become like white people" or that "*they* must accept *you*." Instead, African Americans must accept Whites because "they are still trapped in a history which they do not understand. . . .They have had to believe for many years, and for innumerable reasons, that black men are inferior to white men." Even though many "know better," to acknowledge what they know would be a danger to their identity as Whites. "And if the word *integration* means anything," he concluded, it means "that we, with love, shall force our brothers to see themselves as they are, to cease from fleeing from reality and begin to change it" (p. 294). Later that year, he joined King and Farmer and other union and civil rights activists in the March on Washington.

The development of the Black Power movement coincided with the end of Baldwin's intense political activism. While he was, in a sense, sympathetic to the idea of African Americans becoming politically powerful even as they expected less and less from Whites, there remained a tension. In part, Baldwin was concerned about the simplicity of understanding racial conflict in terms of Black and White. In a 1965 essay, "White Man's Guilt," Baldwin argued that "the great force of history comes from the fact that we carry it within us, are unconsciously controlled by it in many ways, and history is literally present in all that we do" (1998, p. 723). Here, race is a "historical construction" to which "we owe our frames of reference, our identities, and our aspirations" (p. 723). Resistance to a history of oppression becomes a process of asserting one's own agency to "recreate oneself according to a principle more humane and more liberating: one begins the attempt to achieve a level of personal maturity and freedom which robs history of its tyrannical power, and also changes history" (p. 723). The historical construction of Whiteness leads "to a fearful, baffling place where [Whites] have begun to lose touch with reality—to lose touch, that is, with themselves" (p. 724).

In "The Price of the Ticket," Baldwin offered a double-edged critique of those committed to the separation of Black and White. To African Americans who hold such a view, he observed that "the price of the black ticket is involved—fatally—with the dream of becoming white" (1998, p. 835). The aspiration will necessarily fail because there is no category of White: "part of the price of the white ticket is to delude themselves into believing that they are" (p. 835). African Americans, he concluded, "must find a way to keep faith with, and to excavate, a reality much older than Europe. Europe has never been, and cannot be, a useful or valid touchstone for the American experience because America is not, and never can be, white" (p. 836).

When Kwame Ture and others from SNCC and CORE began to use the idea of Black Power to frame their political agendas, they also rejected the commitment to nonviolence advocated by King and argued that resistance to the dominant culture could only be achieved by separating Blacks and Whites—the position implied in Wright's work and critiqued by Baldwin. New activists emerged in the context of Black Power; Huey Newton, Bobby Seale, and Eldridge Cleaver helped to form the Black Panther Party, perhaps the most visible Black Power group. The Panthers announced that they were committed to the liberation of African American communities and adopted a ten-point platform that called for self-determination of separate Black communities, full employment, reparations for slavery, housing, education, health care, an end to police violence against Blacks, and the end of US wars. Early work by the Party included providing food for poor neighborhoods and organizing citizen groups to observe police behavior. The Party quickly became controversial for, among other things, openly carrying weapons and for calling for a separate Black nation. But the positions they took, framed by a demand for Black Power, became a starting point for another important strand of philosophical resistance. Among those grounding their developing theories of oppression and change in a notion of Black Power were Malcolm X, Amiri Baraka, and James Cone.

**American Philosophies**

**Primary Texts**

Baldwin, James, *Collected Essays*, New York: Library of America, 1998.
King, Martin Luther, Jr. (1986). *A Testament of Hope: The Essential Writings and Speeches of Martin Luther, King, Jr.*, ed. James M. Washington. New York: Harper Collins.
Wright, Richard (2008). *Black Power*, intro. Cornel West. New York: Harper Collins.

# CHAPTER 19
# BLACK POWER
## MALCOLM X, JAMES CONE, AUDRE LORDE, BELL HOOKS, ANGELA DAVIS, AND CORNEL WEST

When Stokely Carmichael introduced the idea of Black Power into the Civil Rights Movement, it came as a surprise to King. Carmichael—now Kwame Ture—had been a strong supporter and a very visible leader of SNCC and an ally of the SCLC. He had been an organizer of the March on Washington and an advocate of the 1964 and 1965 Civil Rights Acts. But after the passage of the Acts, things had not changed: the outspoken Malcolm X (El-Hajj Malik El-Shabazz) was assassinated in February 1965; four girls were killed in the bombing of the Sixteenth Street Baptist Church in Birmingham; and Black activist James Meredith, who began a solo walk across Mississippi that he called a "March Against Fear," was shot by a sniper in June 1966. Despite the passage of civil rights laws, the federal government seemed unwilling or unable to respond to ongoing violence against Blacks. Ture decided to reject King's strategies of nonviolence and cooperation (Carmichael, 1966). When King challenged Ture's use of the term "Black Power" at a protest march, Ture responded, "Martin, I deliberately decided to raise this issue on the march in order to give it a national forum, and force you to take a stand for Black Power" (King, 1968, p. 31).

While King was sympathetic to the idea of Black Power, he criticized its direction. The problem was that "Black Power is a nihilistic philosophy born out of the conviction that the Negro can't win" (p. 44). In contrast with Gandhi's revolution, which was founded on hope, love, and nonviolence, Black Power, King claimed, was founded on despair, and "revolution, though born of despair, cannot long be sustained by despair" (p. 45). "In a multiracial society no group can make it alone," King asserted; rather, "To succeed in a pluralistic society . . . the Negro obviously needs organized strength, but that strength will only be effective when it is consolidated through the constructive alliances with the majority group" (p. 50). King's nuanced objection to the Black Power movement is often juxtaposed with the radical sentiments of Black Power's most widely recognized spokesperson: Malcolm X. Like King, however, Malcolm X's ideas about race and class in America reflect a more complex and nuanced story of philosophical development than is commonly attributed to them.

Malcolm X was born Malcolm Little in Omaha, Nebraska, in 1925. His father, Earl Little, was a Baptist minister and vocal supporter of Marcus Garvey's UNIA. After Little received death threats from a White supremacist group, the family relocated to Lansing, Michigan, where, in 1929, their house was destroyed by fire. Two years later, Reverend Little was found dead along the trolley tracks. Both the fire and Little's death were ruled "accidental" by the local police, although many suspected that they were responses to Little's activism. Even though he was a good student, Malcolm dropped out and went east to New York City where, in 1946, he was arrested and convicted of armed robbery. He served six years of his eight-to-ten-year sentence in a Massachusetts prison. During his time in prison, he read the works of Elijah Muhammad, leader of the Nation of Islam. When he was released from prison in 1952, Malcolm joined the Nation of Islam and became a minister and visible spokesperson. He also rejected his "slave name" "Little" and adopted the new surname, X, to mark the lost tribal name of his family (Marable, 2011).

The Nation of Islam was founded in 1930, committed to the central practices and beliefs of Islam—the Five Pillars—framed by the context of the particular historical circumstances faced by Africans in America. Laying the groundwork for the Black Power movement later, the Nation of Islam demanded freedom and justice and rejected integration as a means of achieving it. The policy of integration as developed in America they held to be "hypocritical," deceptive, and "intended to prevent black people from realizing that the time in history [had] arrived for the separation from whites" (Nation of Islam, 2014).

Malcolm X embraced both Islam and the particular commitments of the Nation of Islam and was credited with increasing its membership dramatically. In 1963, however, Malcolm learned that Elijah Muhammad, whom Malcolm admired and respected, had been violating his own principles of behavior by having sexual relations with at least six women who were members of the Nation and had conceived children with some of these women (and reportedly punished the women for becoming pregnant). Shortly after Malcolm confronted Elijah Muhammad, President Kennedy was assassinated, and Malcolm was asked to talk about the situation on behalf of the Nation. In his remarks, he said that the murdered president "was a clear case of 'the chickens coming home to roost'" (Malcolm X, 1965, p. 301). Citing the controversy over Malcolm's remark, Elijah Muhammad ordered Malcolm to remain publicly silent for ninety days. He complied, but in March 1964, Malcolm decided to resign from the Nation of Islam.

While Malcolm had been a charismatic advocate of the Nation of Islam program, following his resignation he began to modify his own commitments. He became more aware of and open to the ideals of the ongoing civil rights struggle he had previously rejected. He also made a pilgrimage to Mecca—the Hajj, one of the Pillars of Islam, which is the requirement that each believer travels once in their life to Mecca, the religious center of the Muslim world. What Malcolm found on his visit was contrary to the Nation of Islam's doctrine that Islam was a Black religion. "There were tens of thousands of pilgrims from all over the world," he wrote in a letter from Saudi Arabia. "They were of *all colors*, from blue-eyed blonds to black-skinned Africans, but were all participating in the same ritual, displaying a spirit of unity and brotherhood that my experiences in America had led me to believe could never exist between white and non-white" (1965, p. 59). His pilgrimage transformed his conception of Black Nationalism and refigured the revolution he sought. In one of his last speeches on behalf of the Nation of Islam before he was silenced, Malcolm addressed the idea of revolution sometimes claimed by the Civil Rights Movement. He argued that advocating for desegregation of lunch counters, theaters, parks, and toilets did not constitute a revolution. Like the resistance philosophies of Fortune, Pokagon, and Standing Bear, Malcolm explained that "[r]evolution is based on land. Land is the basis of all independence. Land is the basis of freedom, justice, and equality" (p. 9). The heart of Black Nationalism—the demand for a nation—was a demand for land, but as a result, he continued, it would also be "bloody," "hostile," and would know "no compromise" because a revolution "destroys everything that gets in its way" (p. 9).

After his return from Mecca and a trip to several African nations, he said in an interview, "I used to define Black Nationalism as the idea that the black man should control the economy of his community, the politics of his community, and so forth." But in a conversation with an Algerian ambassador—who was African but not Black—the ambassador "showed me where I was alienating people who were true revolutionaries dedicated to overturning the system of exploitation that exists on this earth by any means necessary" (1992, p. 159). To emphasize the shift in his thinking, he observed to the interviewer that he had not used the term "Black Nationalism" for several months. Despite his doubts about a specific formulation of nationalism, when he founded the Organization of Afro-American Unity (OAAU), he nevertheless continued to hold to the idea that the end of Black oppression would depend upon establishing communities that would "control our own destiny." While he sought the "unification of all people of African descent in [the Western Hemisphere]" (p. 39), he also recognized that security, economy, and even politics did not depend solely on a single unity but on the promotion of unified local communities. Such communities would be able to defend and sustain themselves even as they cooperated with other communities. They should, he argued, seek allies, though doing so would be "a drag" (p. 41). "We must take pride in the Afro-American community," he said, "for it is our home and it is our power" (p. 53).

On one hand, Malcolm X argued for the idea of a revolution to establish independence in a way that would afford both individual freedom and equality across the community. This commitment was reinforced by his reframing of the idea of civil rights in an April 1964 speech on "The Black Revolution." In light of his travels to Mecca and Africa, he observed that "America's strategy [for oppressing African Americans] is the same strategy as that which was used in the past by the colonial powers: divide and conquer" (1965, p. 51). In response, Blacks needed to recognize that, despite their own differences, they nevertheless shared larger common objectives: "freedom, justice, equality." If these goals determined the program, then "[w]e don't want to be integrationists. Nor do we want to be separationists. We want to be human beings" (p. 51). The goal of civil rights was an obstacle to change because it took up the issues in the context of US law and politics. Instead, the appeal "for recognition as human beings" is a matter of human rights and the court of appeal is the "world court." Once the struggle is so expanded, "it opens the door for all of our brothers and sisters in Africa and Asia, who have independence, to come to our rescue" (p. 53).

On the other hand, even as Malcolm argued for the importance of individual agency, he also claimed that races had agency to be valued as well. "A race of people is like an individual man; until it uses its own talent, takes pride in its own history, expresses its own culture, affirms its own selfhood, it can never fulfill itself" (1992, p. 53). In order to strengthen the agency of the race, the revolution that demands land and individual freedom must also be a cultural revolution. "We must recapture our heritage and our identity if we are ever to liberate ourselves from the bonds of white supremacy. We must launch a cultural revolution to unbrainwash an entire people" (p. 54). Such a revolution "must begin in the community and be based on community participation" (p. 55). Rather than Black Nationalism as a simple demand for separation, its revised form involved a complex development of distinct communities and individuals bound by a common culture and willing by degrees to engage in shared efforts across established boundaries.

On February 21, 1965, at the Audubon Ballroom in New York City, where he had led the first meetings of the OAAU, Malcolm X was assassinated. Three members of the Nation of Islam were convicted of his murder. Two of the men convicted of Malcolm's assassination were exonerated in 2021, and the third continued to claim his innocence of the crime and was eventually paroled.

In 1966, Amiri Baraka (1924–2014), then known as LeRoi Jones, an essayist, playwright, and poet, published a short essay on Malcolm X's legacy. For Baraka, what was central to Malcolm's conception of race and liberation were the interconnected ideas of land, culture, nation, and sovereignty. The result was a concrete demand for separate, landed communities that could foster a "national consciousness" (1966, pp. 239–40). "Malcolm's legacy was his life: what he rose to be and through what channels" (p. 239). He effectively drew together the religious convictions of the Nation of Islam, the practices of political engagement that framed the Civil Rights Movement, and a vision of national sovereignty drawn from his encounters with newly independent African nations. Malcolm's innovation was to set aside demands for nationhood and replace them with the recognition that Blacks already "are a nation" (p. 239). But where Malcolm seemed less clear on how best to understand the boundaries between Blacks and Whites, Baraka saw a clear line: Blacks must be understood as ontologically distinct—distinct in their "being"—from Whites (p. 241).

At the heart of Baraka's work was the idea that Black experience is shared but unique. It conditions both the identity and the consciousness of those who share it, and its products—music, literature, and art—are the distinct possessions of the people whose experience it is. What made for such an experience is not some genetic code but rather the concrete conditions of experience, the shared experience of slavery and Reconstruction, Jim Crow segregation, violence, limited access to education, and so on. In his 1963 book, *Blues People*, Baraka summarized: "the ugly fact that the Africans were forced into an alien world where none of the references or cultural shapes of any familiar human attitudes were available is the determinant of the *kind* of existence they had to eke out here" (Jones, 1963, p. 7).

Like Alain Locke, Baraka concluded that despite such hardships (or rather because of them) Blacks—the Black community, or more accurately the Black race—produced a great and distinctive art. But the very distinctiveness of the art and its continuing within the Black community and Black experience also reinforces the boundaries between Black and White. While Whites may perform Black music, their performance lacks authenticity, lacks a connection with the experience that made it possible. "The idea of a white blues singer," he wrote in 1968 in *Black Music*, "seems an even more violent contradiction of terms than the idea of a middle-class blues singer. The material of blues was not available to the white American" (2000, p. 37). Baraka set aside his central commitment to Black Nationalism in favor of Marxism in 1974. He wrote later that his change of view was "based on being involved in struggle—seeing for instance, the whole nationalist thing turn into its opposite. A lot of people were talking about black liberation, national liberation, then actually being in charge of exploitation." It became "clear," he concluded, "that skin color was not determinant of political content" (p. 249).

The adoption of the Marxist framework of economic analysis did not shift Baraka's commitment to the Black politics of Malcolm X's later work. In 1995, for the thirty-year anniversary of Malcolm's assassination (and in response to the release of Spike Lee's film *Malcolm X*, 1992), Baraka wrote, "In the 60s we summed up Malcolm as calling for Self Determination, Self Respect, and Self Defense" (2000, p. 514). The struggle was "an act of Self Determination" that also expressed "Self Respect," "the 'true Self Consciousness' Du Bois called for" (p. 514). "Self Defense," he explained, though often taken as a call for violence, was "a call for a force that will stop the wanton violence against the Afro American people" (p. 514). When Malcolm rejected the ideology of the Nation of Islam, he realized that "it was

Black revolution that was needed, which was political, not metaphysical and religious" (p. 514). Reacting against attempts to tame and distort Malcolm's message, Baraka called for a cultural politics that carried "our struggle into the schools, into the movie theaters, the concert halls, and the night clubs." To support the struggle, Baraka further called for Blacks to "build cultural and educational and arts institutions to provide an alternative to the poisonous fruits of the American superstructure" (p. 521). The Marxist analysis provided a resource for Baraka to generate a criticism within the Black community of those who sought to become part of the capitalist West and those committed to a different vision of human coexistence. Race continued to define the boundaries of community, even as Baraka decided that race alone was an insufficient critical tool.

Despite his criticism of the Black Power movement, King had also formed an expanded vision of civil rights that included recognition of economic injustice toward Blacks and Whites, both in the United States and beyond its borders. In this context, echoing his analysis in the "Letter from Birmingham Jail," King argued that "[w]e must rapidly begin the shift from a 'thing'-oriented society to a 'person'-oriented society" (1968, p. 186). The result was a vision of a community that fosters "a socially conscious democracy which reconciles the truths of individualism and collectivism" (p. 187). Recalling Royce and Locke, King concluded that a "genuine revolution of values means ... that our loyalties must become ecumenical rather than sectional. Every nation must now develop an overriding loyalty to mankind as a whole in order to preserve the best in their individual societies" (p. 190).

On April 4, 1968, King was assassinated on the balcony of a motel in Memphis, Tennessee, where he had come to support a strike by Memphis sanitation workers, as part of what he called the Poor People's Campaign. King presented the strike as an element in the effort to begin a new march on Washington by poor people of all races to demand an economic bill of rights. After the assassination, riots broke out in cities across the country, including Washington, D.C., Chicago, Pittsburgh, Detroit, Baltimore, and Louisville. The Poor People's Campaign continued, and on May 12, when King's widow, Coretta Scott King, joined with several thousand to establish a camp they called "Resurrection City" that would occupy the National Mall in Washington until Congress addressed their demands. For nearly a month, 3,000 people set up kitchens, clinics, police to keep order, a university, a chapel, and barber shops. For a time, Resurrection City was even given its own ZIP code. While they occupied the National Mall, residents organized marches to demand economic justice, lobbied congressional representatives, and gained much media attention. On June 20, police fired tear gas into the camp, and four days later, one thousand police cleared the camp. No economic bill of rights was passed by Congress.

While the Black Nationalist movement was committed to resistance and liberation, it adopted a view that often set aside concerns about other forms of oppression besides those overtly related to race. In Eldridge Cleaver's book, *Soul on Ice* (1967), Cleaver exemplified this sort of narrowness both in his discussions of women and his homophobic treatment of the work of Baldwin. Within the Black Panther Party, women and women's issues were set aside in favor of activism in support of Black masculinity. When Huey Newton fled to Cuba in 1974 to avoid being put on trial for the murder of Kathleen Smith, Elaine Brown was appointed the first woman to serve as the chair of the party. "A woman in the Black Power movement was considered, at best, irrelevant," Brown said in her autobiography. "A woman asserting herself was a pariah. A woman attempting the role of leadership was, to my proud black Brothers, making an alliance with the 'counter-revolutionary, man-hating, lesbian, feminist white bitches'" (1992, p. 357). From the perspective of the movement, Brown's appointment was "a violation of some Black Power principle that was left undefined. . . . [S]he was said to be eroding black manhood, to be hindering the process of the black race. She was an enemy of black people" (p. 357). Brown continued to lead the Party until Newton returned from Cuba in 1977 (he was eventually tried for murder but released after two hung juries). When Brown learned that Newton had sanctioned the beating of a female administrative assistant at the Panther Liberation School, Brown quit the Party and she and her daughter left the United States.

Against the narrowness of Black Nationalism (and the narrowness of both the Civil Rights Movement and the Feminist Movement), a new generation of women philosophers emerged, including Audre Lorde (1934–92), Angela Davis, and bell hooks (1952–2021).

Audre Lorde was a poet and essayist who grew up in New York City and graduated from Hunter College and Columbia University with a degree in library science. She eventually served as a professor at John Jay College and at Hunter. While Brown challenged the sexism of the Black Nationalist movement as a leader of the Black Panthers, Lorde identified as a Black lesbian within a society marked by racism and homophobia. For Lorde, the central problem faced by her, women, people of color, the poor, and the elderly was a systematic "blindness." While William James identified a "blindness" that marked impassable boundaries dividing people from each other, Lorde identified racism, sexism, heterosexism, and homophobia as "blindnesses" that "stem from the same root—an inability to recognize the notion of difference as a dynamic human force, one which is enriching rather than threatening to the defined self, when there are shared goals" (1984, p. 45). The inability to recognize the value of differences is in part a consequence of a lack of self-understanding, that is, the ability to recognize oneself as a "self-actualized individual." The "blindness" occurs not only among Whites in the dominant culture but also in the Black community itself.

When Black women assert themselves as having different experiences and concerns, Black men respond as if to a threat. "This is no threat," she declared. "It is only seen as one by those Black men who choose to embody within themselves those same manifestations of female oppression" (p. 46). This system of "blindness," she thought, was reinforced by threats against lesbians in particular. Such threats were a "code-warning" to Black women that they needed to show allegiance only to Black men and "any woman who wished to retain his friendship and/or support had better not be 'tainted' by women-identified interests" (p. 47). These same threats also reinforced the received view that people exist only in single categories. The threats were part of the demand that Black women should recognize race as essential—not being women—and so ally themselves with the cause of Black Nationalism, understood in the masculinist terms set out by leaders such as Cleaver and Newton. Lorde argued that such narrow conceptions of self were an inheritance from the dominant society. Instead of accepting imposed categories, she concluded, "Black women . . . have the right and responsibility to define ourselves and to seek our allies in common causes: with Black men against racism, and with each other and white women against sexism. But most of all," she concluded, "as Black women we have the right and responsibility to recognize each other without fear and to love where we choose" (p. 52).

The process of self-determination is not a private process, however. In a 1978 paper, "Uses of the Erotic: The Erotic as Power," Lorde argued that "[i]n order to perpetuate itself, every oppression must corrupt or distort those various sources of power within the culture of the oppressed that can provide energy for change." For women, "this has meant a suppression of the erotic as a considered source of power and information within our lives" (1984, p. 53). Lorde defined the erotic "as assertion of the lifeforce of women; of that creative energy empowered" (p. 55). "For the erotic," she wrote, "it is not a question of what we do it is a question of how acutely and fully we can feel in the doing." In Western culture, the erotic had been "vilified, abused and devalued" and identified as "a sign of female inferiority" so that to be "truly strong" in the dominant society, a woman must suppress and deny it. When it is not suppressed, the erotic is not only a means of enhancing one's own experience but connects one with others. It provides "the power which comes from sharing deeply in any pursuit with another person" (p. 56).

Isolating women in singular categories and narrowing the erotic to heterosexuality blocks the potential for creative action of all sorts and for diverse loves and alliances. Unlike many other lesbian activists at the time, she was not a separatist and so she was asked to justify her existence and her work as a woman and as a lesbian. "Because some piece of 'her' was not acceptable," Lorde had "to learn to hold on to all the parts of me that served me, in spite of the pressure to express only one to the exclusion of all others" (p. 143). The erotic—including the felt experience of connection—also serves as the foundation for the formation of communities that "[do] not mean shedding of our differences," or "the pathetic pretense that these differences do not exist." Communities founded on the erotic are, she held, a necessary condition for liberation (p. 112). As Cooper before her and Patricia Hill Collins after her, Lorde argued for a redefinition of oppression and resistance that is intersectional, that recognizes multiple dimensions of power and hope.

Central to Lorde's conception of intersectional resistance was the recognition of the dominance of a "*mythical* norm, which each of us within our hearts knows 'that is not me'" (p. 116). The norm, she held, is "defined as white, thin, male, young, heterosexual, Christian, and financially secure" (p. 116). Bound by the demand for homogenous selves against a background of an either/or logic, White feminists challenged the norms in terms of "their oppression as women," Black Nationalists in terms of race, gays and lesbians in terms of sexuality. Such demands overlook the complexity of power and force those whose identities are complex into new oppressions. In a 1979 address, Lorde identified the central logic of "an either/or model of nurturing" as framing the exclusion of difference and the failure to recognize interdependency or the reality of borderlands—regions, people, ideas between categories. "Interdependency between women is the way to a freedom which allows *I to be*, not in order to be used but in order to be creative" (p. 111). To carry on resistance by demanding a kind of purity of race or gender or sexuality fails to learn "how to take our differences and make them strengths. *For the master's tools will never dismantle the master's house.* They may allow us temporarily to beat him at his own game, but they will never enable us to bring about genuine change" (p. 112).

Even as she rejected the model of purity central to the dominant culture, Lorde also rejected the idea that it is the responsibility of the oppressed to "teach men as to our existence and our needs." To engage in such conversations is, she thought, to allow dominant society to evade its responsibilities and to reinforce its hierarchies. "This is an old and primary tool

> The future of our earth may depend upon the ability of all women to identify and develop new definitions of power and new patterns of relating across difference. The old definitions have not served us, not the earth that supports us. The old patterns, no matter how cleverly arranged to imitate progress, still condemn us to cosmetically altered repetitions of the same old exchanges, the same old guilt, hatred, recrimination, lamentation, and suspicion. (p. 123)

In 1981, bell hooks joined the response to both Black Nationalism and feminism. Born Gloria Watkins in Kentucky in 1952, she adopted the name "bell hooks" to honor her grandmother and to give her a way to have a voice that was not tied to her own limited biography. She received a BA from Stanford University, an MA from the University of Wisconsin, and, in 1983, a PhD from the University of California, Santa Cruz. The title of her 1981 book, *Ain't I a Woman: Black Women and Feminism*, was taken from an 1851 speech by Sojourner Truth when Truth stood to speak at a feminist convention in Akron, Ohio (Truth, 1851). A man had just argued that women did not deserve equal rights because they needed help in such simple tasks as getting into carriages and crossing ditches and mud puddles. Truth replied: "Nobody ever helps me into carriages, or over mud-puddles, or gives me any best place! And ain't I a woman?" She had plowed and planted, worked as hard as a man, been whipped by a man and still bore thirteen children, most sold into slavery. To reject women's rights because women were weak and so unable to bear the rights and duties of men made little sense in the face of Truth's life. For hooks, the point made by Truth had been lost in the century that followed. White feminists had abandoned Black women in their struggle for their own rights. hooks's goal in her book was to consider the impact of sexism during slavery, the resulting devaluation of Black womanhood, and its consequences for the antiracist and feminist movements of the 1960s and 1970s.

The present circumstances of Black women, she argued, are grounded in the experience, practices, and institutions of slavery. "A devaluation of black womanhood occurred as the result of the sexual exploitation of black women during slavery that has not altered in the course of hundreds of years" (1981, p. 53). After the Civil War, the devaluation continued and was promoted through anti-miscegenation laws aimed at barring marriages and childbearing across races, as well as by "lynching, castration, and other brutal punishments to prevent black men from initiating relationships with white women" (p. 61). At the same time, White society perpetuated "the myth that all black men were eager to rape white women so that white females would not seek friendships with black men for fear of brutal assault" (p. 61). The myth of the Black rapist was paralleled by the myth that "all black women were incapable of fidelity and sexually loose," so that Black women would be devalued and "no white man would marry a black woman" (p. 61). Taken together, the resulting systematic devaluation of Black women both outside and within Black communities set the stage for the continued exclusion of Black women from active leadership in the Civil Rights and Black Power movements and in the Feminist Movement.

hooks argued that the Civil Rights Movement inherited the sexism constructed over the previous century and used it to exclude women from leadership. In the Black Power movement, however, the treatment of women became an essential component in the effort to resist White supremacy. According to hooks, "[m]any black men who express the greatest hostility toward the white male power structure are often eager to gain access to that power" (p. 94). To do so, they needed to gain "public recognition of their 'manhood' by demonstrating that they were the dominant figure in the black family" (p. 94). hooks selected Baraka as an example of the attitudes cultivated in the Black Power movements. "Although Baraka presented [his] 'new' black nation . . . as a world that will have distinctly different values from those of the white world he is rejecting," she wrote, "the social structure he conceived was based on the same patriarchal foundation as that of white American society" (p. 95). The commitment to violence advocated by some leaders was, for hooks, another manifestation of the same patriarchy. "Sexism fosters, condones, and supports male violence against women, as well as encouraging violence between males. In a patriarchal society, men are encouraged to channel frustrated aggression in the direction of those without power—women and children" (p. 105). She concluded, "There can be no freedom for black men as long as they advocate subjugation of black women." Instead, "Freedom . . . as positive social equality that grants all humans the opportunity to shape their destinies in the most healthy and communally productive way can only be a complete reality when our world is no longer racist or sexist" (p. 117).

Transforming American society is not simply a matter of changing laws and hoping that institutions will reform. According to hooks, prejudice is a product of history and can only be reformed by first transforming education. "American women," she said, "have been socialized, even brainwashed, to accept a version of American history that was created to uphold and maintain racial imperialism in the form of white supremacy and sexual imperialism in the form of patriarchy" (p. 120). By changing how the history is understood, women could see how their dispositions were historical developments in service of oppression and then seek change. To understand the exclusion of Black women, women needed to understand how slavery transformed the status of women in White society, allowing them to "vacate their despised position and assume the role of a superior." As a result, "even though white men institutionalized slavery, white women were its most immediate beneficiaries" (p. 153).

As slaves came to take over domestic tasks, especially in the South, a new status was created for White women, establishing an ideal of leisure and privilege (an ideal even for women who did not directly benefit from the work of slaves). In the resulting system, the power of White women could be demonstrated only in relation to Black female slaves, often "by treating the slave in a brutal and cruel manner" (p. 153). At the same time, White men were able to "[flaunt] their sexual lust for the bodies of black women" and so "successfully pitted white women and enslaved black women against one another" (pp. 153–4). The advent of the feminist movement of the 1960s and 1970s operated within the same structure, and the result was the ongoing exclusion of Black women from both the women's movement and the movement to establish Black self-determination. This history, hooks argued, called for political solidarity and assuming the "responsibility for eliminating all the forces that divide women," including racism. Rather than setting feminism aside, hooks proposed to "re-appropriate the term 'feminism,' to focus on the fact that to be 'feminist' in any authentic sense of the term is to want for all people, female and male, liberation from sexist role patterns, domination, and oppression" (p. 195).

In the same year hooks published her challenge to feminism, Angela Davis, already a veteran in the Civil Rights and Black Power movements, added her voice to the demand for an antiracist struggle that also challenged sexism. While Lorde offered an intersectional analysis that took up heterosexism and homophobia, and hooks offered an analysis of the structure of patriarchy as a historical process grounded in the institution of slavery, Davis offered an analysis of Black liberation that considered the role of industrial capitalism. In her book, *Women, Race, and Class*, Davis argued that abolition and post-Civil War politics were dominated by the efforts of Northern industrial capitalists to control the Southern economy. The demands for civil rights from African Americans and women provided further opportunities for the interests of the dominant society to be advanced. After Reconstruction ended in 1876, Davis argued, "a serious ideological marriage had linked racism and sexism in a new way" (1981, p. 121). "White supremacy and male supremacy, which had always had an easy courtship," connected their programs through a renewed emphasis on "people of color—at home and abroad—. . . . portrayed as incompetent barbarians." At the same time, White women were "depicted as mother-figures" who "bore a very special responsibility in the struggle to safeguard white supremacy" (p. 121). This tension became a resource for reinforcing racial solidarity among Whites. The racial struggle that followed, however, was not inevitable. It was rather a resource that benefited the interests of the "new monopoly capitalist class" whose "apologists" sought "to provoke racist divisions" (pp. 123–4). "[R]acial conflict did not emerge spontaneously," Davis said, "but rather was consciously planned by the representatives of the economically ascendant class" to "impede class unity" (p. 124). Overlooked in assessments of resistance to these efforts was the willingness of Black women "to contribute . . . [to] the creation of a multiracial movement for women's political rights" that was "at every turn . . . betrayed, spurned and rejected by the leaders of the lily-white suffrage movement" (p. 148).

Crucial to the program of the capitalist class was the promotion of "the myth of the black rapist," also used in hooks's analysis, that evolved after the Civil War and was used to justify lynching African American men. Agreeing with hooks and Lorde, Davis also saw the "black rapist" image as one that unified White anger against African Americans, effectively keeping White women from engaging in resistance to racism. It also reinforced White women's dependent status and the exclusion of Black women from efforts to address both racism and sexism. Davis's analysis extended the examination of the myth to the economics of labor. Through the lurid press accounts and public lynchings in response to allegations of the rape of White women, White workers were convinced to exclude Blacks from their efforts to organize for better wages and working conditions. The result, consistent with the larger economic program Davis described, was to ensure a division among workers and a significantly less effective resistance to industrial capitalism. "The class structure of capitalism," that emerged in the twentieth century, "encourages men who would wield power in the economic and political realm to become routine agents of sexual exploitation" (p. 200). For Davis, the antirape movement was a key element in the attempt to achieve economic justice for workers regardless of race. "As the violent face of sexism, the threat of rape will continue to exist as long as the overall oppression of women remains an essential crutch for capitalism" (p. 201).

Davis placed the development of birth control—the "voluntary motherhood" movement of the early twentieth century—in the same context. She challenged earlier advocates, such as Sanger, for tying birth control to eugenics. Davis argued that eugenics was another means of controlling Black women and families in a way that reinforced racial hierarchies and aimed to limit the growth of Puerto Rican, African American, and American Indian communities. Although Davis acknowledged the importance of Sanger's work in the birth control movement, she also argued that once Sanger separated from the Socialist Party, she was heavily influenced by racist eugenicists such as Lothrop Stoddard, author of *The Rising Tide of Color Against White World Supremacy* (1920).

One of the most significant effects of the early birth control movement was the development of public policies of forced sterilization of women and men of color that continued into the 1970s. When abortion rights became linked with the birth control movement in the 1970s, many activists were surprised that few African American women joined the cause. According to Davis, the activists did not understand the history of their movement. "Had they done so, they might have understood . . . how important it was to undo the racist deeds of their predecessors, who had advocated birth control as well as compulsory sterilization as a means of eliminating the 'unfit' sections of the population" (p. 215). What Davis sought was "a revolutionary, multiracial women's movement that seriously addresses the main issues affecting poor and working class women" (1989, p. 7). Like Cooper, Lorde, and hooks, the key to such a movement was the recognition of the intersectional nature of oppression. They also agree that a unified movement will be one in which history plays a mediating role by allowing diverse women to find common ground in a "common foe," the intersection of economic injustice, sexism, and racism.

The plethora of philosophical innovations to subvert racism, classism, civil and economic injustices, and sexism built upon the tradition of resistance we have traced from Fortune to Davis. But, as the philosophies of resistance of the late nineteenth and early twentieth centuries were significantly informed by the Social Gospel movement, these new philosophies of resistance were influenced by the Christian traditions that had come to be a part of Black and White America. Black Theology, which is considered to have emerged as a distinctive school of Christian thought in the 1960s, began from the work of nineteenth-century Black religious thinkers who responded to Christianity as it developed in the context of Black experience. Disconnected from their religious roots in Africa and presented by slave masters with Christianity as the only option, Blacks made it a key component in understanding both their circumstances and their future estate. In the aftermath of slavery, the Black church became a central institution for the development of post-slavery African American culture and, in the period of legal segregation, took on the role of sanctuary and community center. When Blacks began to organize political action after the Brown Supreme Court decision, they did so with clergy leadership (e.g., the SCLC) and often used church facilities for education, training, and organizing. Many writers, including Du Bois, argued that the Black church was a distinctive invention of enslaved Africans and held that the Black church took the religious sources of imposed Christianity and transformed them into a new cultural infrastructure.

In 1949, a Black preacher, Howard Thurman (1899–1981), provided resources for the transformation in his book *Jesus and the Disinherited*. According to Thurman, "[t]oo often the price exacted by society for security and respectability is that the Christian movement in its formal expression must be on the side of the strong against the weak" (1949, p. 12). This is a mistake born of the central impulse of Christianity: "the human *will to share* with others what one has found meaningful to oneself elevated to the height of a moral imperative" (p. 12). Rather than recognizing that the impulse is first a desire to help others, it can also take the form of contempt for those who need help. In America, the benign impulse to share becomes contempt that establishes an oppressive social hierarchy that was then accepted as "normal" and "if normal correct; if correct, then moral; if moral, then religious. Religion is thus made a defender and guarantor of the presumptions" (p. 43). In order to transform the church, Thurman argued that the origins of Christianity needed to be considered in their own light. Given the circumstances of the first century, Jesus should not be understood as an advocate of the dominant system but rather someone who ministered to the disinherited Jews oppressed by the Roman Empire. If Christianity is first a religion of the excluded and oppressed, then, in the present world, the African American community—its oppression and material circumstances—should be the central concern of Christians.

Thurman grew up in segregated Florida. He completed his BA at Morehouse College in Atlanta and his divinity degree at Colgate Rochester Crozier Seminary in New York. Rather than pursuing a doctoral degree (as many encouraged him to do), Thurman served as a pastor in Ohio, then as the Dean of the Howard University Chapel in Washington, D.C. He studied for a time with Rufus Jones, a Quaker mystic, and traveled internationally, meeting Mahatma Gandhi in India. In 1944, Thurman moved to San Francisco where he served as copastor of one of the first racially integrated, explicitly multicultural churches in the United States. As the civil rights protests began in 1955, Thurman strongly advocated for nonviolence and regularly advised King and other movement leaders. He remained committed to integration even as many of the leaders began to advocate Black Power, and in 1971, he challenged the Black Power movement for its rejection of integration in favor of sharply separated communities. The problem, Thurman concluded, was that such separation gave anti-Black racists the very result they sought—segregation. "[T]o undertake to build community as a closed entity within the larger society is not only suicidal, but the sheerest stupidity" (1998, p. 294). At the same time, Thurman recognized the appeal of Black Power as a means of fostering identity and purpose among people long excluded from opportunities and resources. "White society has not only shut [Blacks] out of such involvements . . . but also it has robbed them of any sense of belonging in the present or in any imaginable future" (p. 293). From this perspective, "the new sense of community within self-determined boundaries seems the most realistic and immediately practical solution to a cruel and otherwise seemingly insoluble problem" (p. 293). In the end, the moral commitment to the disinherited that informed Thurman's critique of American society had helped to shift the orientation of traditional Christian theology toward a conception grounded in the experience of the poor, oppressed, and excluded.

James Cone (1938–2018) further developed the idea of Black Christianity as a theology of the liberation of the poor and oppressed. Cone grew up in segregated Arkansas and attended Philander Smith College in Little Rock, where he received his BA. He received a bachelor of divinity degree at Garrett Theological Seminary in Evanston, Illinois, and then completed an MA and PhD at Northwestern University in 1965. "The struggle," he wrote in his 2011 book, *The Cross and the Lynching Tree*, was "to make sense of being black and Christian." That struggle took shape in June 1968, two months after King was assassinated, as Cone wrote *Black Theology and Black Power* (1969). "While writing that book in my brother's church . . ., a place of worship where blacks regularly 'caught the spirit,' something happened" that he could not explain. "It seemed as if a transcendent voice were speaking to me through the scriptures and the medium of African American history and culture, reminding me that God's liberation of the poor is the primary theme of Jesus' gospel" (2011, p. 154). Unlike theologies that began from fixed texts or universal principles alone, Cone joined the long tradition of American thinkers who began reflection in the context of daily experience and suffering—the problems of people.

Cone concluded in *Black Theology and Black Power* that "[t]here is . . . a desperate need for a black theology . . . whose sole purpose is to apply the freeing power of the gospel to black people under white oppression" (1969, p. 31). Such a theology would show the relevance of Christianity to the "powerless black man whose existence is threatened daily by the insidious tentacles of white power" and at the same time "emancipate the gospel from its 'whiteness' so that blacks may be capable of making an honest self-affirmation through Jesus Christ" (p. 32).

Black theology begins from two concrete experiences: the ultimate reality of God and the particular reality of being Black in America. "The fact that I am Black is my ultimate reality" (p. 32). If this identity as Black is real, then it is "impossible to surrender [this] basic social reality" for some "higher, more universal reality." To do so would destroy oneself, one's identity. Therefore, if there is a higher reality, "it must be the very essence of blackness" (p. 33). To be otherwise, to be White or somehow beyond race would mean that God would not share in the experience of the particular oppression of Blacks. The way in which God shares the experience of Blackness, however, is in the active struggle against oppression here and now. "In Christ, God enters human affairs and takes sides with the oppressed. Their suffering becomes his; their despair, divine despair. Through Christ the poor man is offered freedom now to rebel against that which makes him other than human" (p. 36).

At the same time, Black Power "means *complete emancipation of black people from white oppression by whatever means black people deem necessary*" (p. 6). The idea of a liberatory Black Power, then, also shows the connection between Christianity and the Black Power movement: "Christianity is not alien to Black Power; it is Black Power" (p. 38). Cone asked whether Black Power—given its focus on Blacks and excluding Whites—is racist. He concluded, following Ture, that White racism seeks to deny opportunity and value to Blacks—to keep them down—while Black Power seeks to give Blacks "full participation in the decision making process affecting the lives of black people" (Ture, quoted in Cone, 1969, p. 16). Black Power, Cone claimed, was "an affirmation of the humanity of blacks in spite of white racism" (p. 16). White churches, he observed, believed that God was on their side without noticing who was being oppressed. "Genocide is the logical conclusion of racism. It happened to the American Indian, and there are ample reasons to believe that America is prepared to do the same to blacks" (p. 75). As resistance to racism and genocide, Black Power is to be understood as "God's new way of acting in America. It is [God's] way of saying to whites: 'Get used to it'" (p. 61).

In *A Black Theology of Liberation* (1970), Cone proposed six sources for Black theology and a single norm. The sources include Black experience, Black history, Black culture, revelation, scripture, and tradition. The foundation in Black experience also proves to be an insurmountable barrier for others. "The black experience," he wrote, "is possible only for black people" (1970, p. 57). Black identity comes "from the totality of black experience, the experience of carving out an existence in a society that says you don't belong" (p. 57). Black history becomes a process of individuation, of marking individuals and racial differences. Since "divine activity" is "inseparable from the history of black people" (p. 59), so God also shares in Black experience. Black culture combines the history of oppression with the affirmation of individual and collective power. These features of Black experience, with aspects of a dynamic (changing) religion, link oppressions with traditional sources of Christianity. The norm of Black theology that guides not only biblical interpretation, but moral judgment as well, is that Christ "is those very black men whom white society shoots and kills" (p. 80). If Christianity means caring about the experience of the oppressed, and such care involves the crucifixion and resurrection of Christ, and Christ is embodied in Black suffering, then Christianity itself is the process of suffering, death, and resurrection of the oppressed Blacks in America.

By starting with the experience of real suffering, Cone's focus on the oppressed also led to criticisms of his work. In his zeal to transform the circumstances of Blacks, some accused him of demonizing Whites and violating the central Christian principle of loving one's enemies. In doing so, Cone appeared to conclude that reconciliation with Whites was impossible. His response in *God of the Oppressed* (1975) was to argue that reconciliation was possible, but it was something that could only happen in response to liberation. The relation of Blacks and Whites will only change when "whites die to whiteness and are reborn anew in order to struggle *against* white oppression and *for* the liberation of the oppressed"; only then "there is a place for them in the black struggle of freedom." Finding a place in the struggle is reconciliation: "Here reconciliation becomes God's gift of blackness through the oppressed of the land" (1975, p. 242). Significantly, however, it is the Black community that will decide the "*authenticity* of white conversion" and "the place these converts will play in the black struggle." Why such a condition? In *Risks of Faith*, Cone said, "[t]here can be no reconciliation without honest and frank conversation" (1999, p. 136). The demand that only members of the Black community can decide when conversion is "authentic" is a consequence of the history of White supremacy that frames the perspectives of White people. What may look like genuine conversion from the perspective of Whites may be recognized as a failed attempt by those whose experience is at stake.[1]

The combined inheritance of Black theology and the intersecting philosophical analyses of the Black Power movement are embodied in the person and work of Cornel West, born in 1953 in Tulsa, Oklahoma, the grandson of a Baptist preacher. West's heroes, he reported, were singer James Brown, baseball player Willie Mays, his pastor Rev. Willie P. Cooke, and his grandfather. In the 1960s, as a teenager, West "resonated" with "the sincere black militancy of Malcolm X, the defiant rage of the Black Panthers, and the livid black theology of James Cone," though he did not fully agree with them (1999, p. 3). The approach to revolutionary change that West would come to be identified with was also derived from King, who served as "*the* touchstone for personal inspiration, moral wisdom and existential insight" for West (p. 4).

*Prophesy Deliverance! An Afro-American Revolutionary Christianity* (1982) in many ways brought together the diverse perspectives of the Civil Rights and Black Power movements of the 1950s, 1960s, and 1970s. For West, revolutionary Christianity provides a means to "enact the Afro-American humanist tradition in the post-modern period" (p. 133). This tradition, one of the four strategies adopted by African Americans to respond to the post-Civil War "challenges of self-image and self-determination," is "*promotion of an individuality strengthened by an honest encounter with the Afro-American past and the expansion of democratic control over the major institutions that regulate lives in America and abroad*" (p. 90). Such a view, he argued, was shared by Du Bois in his later work, Malcolm X after his Hajj, Newton, Davis, and Baraka in his later work. All five shared a "certain common value: the necessity for the democratic control over institutions in the productive and political processes" (p. 89).

Revolutionary Christianity, he argued, contains four elements. The first is the philosophical method of dialectical historicism involving the processes of negation of the dominant ideology, preserving truths about Black history and experience, and then using this preserved past to generate new ways of thought and action (pp. 108–9). The second element is "the theological worldview of prophetic Christianity," which is committed to the idea that "every individual regardless of class, country, caste, race, or sex should have the opportunity to fulfill his or her potentialities" (p. 16). The third element is accepting "the cultural outlook of Afro-American humanism," and the fourth element, "the social theory and political praxis of progressive Marxism," is the view that human liberation "occurs only when people participate substantively in the decision-making processes in the major institutions that regulate their lives" (p. 112). By emphasizing the necessity of participation, progressive Marxism requires individualization (as each person enters the process as an individual) and the operation of democratic wholes (institutions and means of production that make liberation sustainable).

In an address published in 1993, West reflected on the recent history of Black/White relations in the United States. "American culture seems to lack two elements basic to race relations," he said, "a deep sense of the tragic and a genuine grasp of the unadulterated rage directed at American society." The problem is not simply a matter of defending "white-skin privilege," but rather a "reluctance to look squarely at the brutal side and tragic dimension of the American past and present" (1993, p. 235). The 1960s, he wrote, was "a watershed period because black rage came out of the closet [as] white institutional terrorism was challenged" (p. 236). The response by those in power was to "reduce black persons into pathetic black victims" and "to redirect . . . black rage in and to black working class and poor communities." The "revolutions" proclaimed by King and Malcolm X did not lead to fundamental change in American society. West concluded with an unmistakable reference to Malcolm X's controversial declaration: "[T]he chickens now coming home to roost are not the ones we expected." The response to the demands of the Civil Rights and Black Power movements to address "the fundamental causes of black social misery—the maldistribution of wealth and power filtered through our corporate, financial and political elites," redirected Black rage against "racist individuals and communities, small players in the larger game of power in the city, state, and country" (p. 237). Yet after the effort spent and the lives lost, there remains one "truth about black rage: it must neither be ignited nor ignored" but rather be the source of power to continue the struggle.

## Note

1 Some other examples of work in this vein include Eddie Glaude Jr.'s *Exodus! Religion, Race, and Nation in Early Nineteenth-Century Black America* (2000) which took up pragmatic themes and thinkers to better understand Black identity and its relation to religion in America. Most recently, Dwayne Tunstall's *Doing Philosophy Personally: Thinking About Metaphysics, Theism, and Antiblack Racism* (2013) used the work of Gabriel Marcel and Lewis Gordon to address the threat of dehumanization present in anti-Black racism and developed a "phenomenologically nuanced religious existentialism" (p. xiii).

## Primary Texts

Cone, James H. (1998). *A Black Theology of Liberation*, Twentieth Anniversary Edition. New York: Orbis.
Davis, Angela (1981). *Women, Race, & Class.* New York: Random House.
hooks, bell (1981). *Ain't I a Woman.* Boston: South End Press.
Lorde, Audre (1984). *Sister Outsider.* Berkeley: Crossing Press.
Malcolm, X. (1992). *By Any Means Necessary.* New York: Pathfinder.
West, Cornel (1982). *Prophesy Deliverance! An Afro-American Revolutionary Christianity.* Philadelphia: Westminster Press.

# CHAPTER 20
# LATIN AMERICA

In July 1926, at a rally on the Plaza de las Armas in San Juan, Puerto Rico, the stage was dressed with American flags, and a crowd assembled to celebrate the eighth anniversary of the death of José de Diego, a leader of the Puerto Rican independence movement. José Coll y Cuchí (1877–1960), founder of the Puerto Rican Nationalist Party, addressed the waving flags: "American Flag, I salute you because you represent liberty and the first American republic." Coll y Cuchí echoed the proclamation, in 1898, by General Nelson Miles that the army of the United States will "bring you the fostering arm of a nation of free people, whose greatest power is in its Justice and Humanity to all those living within the fold." Miles's proclamation came just eight years after he led the US troops who carried out the massacre of Lakota people at Wounded Knee and just four years after he commanded the troops that put down the Pullman rail strike. Responding to Coll y Cuchí, and indirectly to Miles, a Harvard-trained lawyer, Pedro Albizu Campos (1893–1965), closed the rally by removing the flags that surrounded the podium and addressed them thus: "Flag of the United States! I do not salute because while you are the symbol of a free and sovereign nation, in Puerto Rico you represent piracy and pillage!" (MacMullan, 2022, pp. 77–8).

Albizu Campos was born in 1891 in Ponce, Puerto Rico. He excelled in school and was awarded a scholarship to study at the University of Vermont. After two years there, he transferred to Harvard College and, in 1916, completed a degree in Philosophy and Letters with a major in chemical engineering. He entered Harvard Law School the following fall. Responding to President Wilson's call for the United States to enter the war in Europe, Albizu Campos enlisted in the US Army as an officer. His assignment was delayed while he continued his studies. In 1918, he was assigned to organize a Puerto Rican volunteer corps just before the end of the war and was discharged in 1919.

While in law school, Albizu Campos developed a distinctive conception of Puerto Rican nationalism informed by the nineteenth-century Catholic theologian, Jaime Balmes, and through the influence of James Connolly, a leader of the Irish Republican Army and author of numerous articles and books that were widely circulated in the Northeast (Stevens-Arroyo, 2002).

Albizu Campos returned to Puerto Rico in 1921 and opened a legal practice. His speech at the Plaza de las Armas was only the beginning of his anti-colonial campaign based on the idea that Puerto Rico was first a land and community distinct from the United States and valuable in its own right. In a 1933 speech for El Día de la Raza (The Day of the Race), Albizu Campos summarized his conception of nationalism.

> It is the duty of every man and woman who own anything to share even with the enemy, for the enemy is his brother. Nationalism is the seat of world brotherhood and an

affirmation of our own dignity. Nationalism is based on the principle that our enemies have rights even when we are in battle. (Ferri, 1988, p. 155)

For Albizu Campos, nationalism was not only to benefit the people of Puerto Rico but also to contribute to other societies as well. "We have something good to instill in America. Let us begin by guaranteeing our civilization to our descendants in Puerto Rico and by bringing, in conjunction with Antillean nations, our civilization to North America so that it covers the world from pole to pole and endures on this planet forever" (p. 155).

Albizu Campos's program was framed by four principles: "the independence of Puerto Rico, the [formation of the] Antillean Confederation [a confederation of Caribbean Spanish-speaking states], the Pan American Union, and the supremacy of Latin American countries for the honor of all of us before posterity" (1988, p. 156). Puerto Rico, despite its colonialization (or because of it), he concludes, "has to play its part in history and has to be free in order to look posterity in the eye" (p. 156).

In 1935, the Chief of the Puerto Rican Police, E. Francis Riggs, was assassinated shortly after police killed four students at the University of Puerto Rico. Almost immediately, two young nationalists were accused of the murder and killed, and Albizu Campos was arrested and charged with sedition and plotting to overthrow the US government in Puerto Rico. He was convicted and sent to prison in Georgia. He was released and returned to Puerto Rico in 1947, where he resumed his political activism. During this time, he was under surveillance by the FBI. His declassified file includes transcripts of several speeches where Albizu Campos demands the end of US rule over Puerto Rico. He challenges the US system of English-language education and criticizes the claims of American democracy. "We are confronted," he says, "by a despotism that has elevated lynching to the category of democracy. To lynch a human being is an act of democracy in the United States." In response,

> We have to revert to the attitude of those people in the hills who have a machete handy to kill anyone who does not respect his wife or his son. Thus should Puerto Ricans defend their country irrespective of sacrifice. One can be very cultured but very much a slave; it isn't necessary to revert to history to prove it, the painful present condition of our people is sufficient. (FBI, 23)

In 1950, Albizu Campos was involved in a plot to assassinate US president Harry Truman. When the plot was discovered, he was arrested, convicted, and sentenced to eighty years in prison. He was pardoned in 1953 by the governor of Puerto Rico but was arrested again the following year when other followers attacked congressional representatives from the balcony of the House of Representatives while Congress was in session. Five Congressmen were wounded. Albizu Campos was finally released from prison in 1965, six months before his death. Despite criticism of his philosophy for its conservative Catholicism and allegedly antidemocratic commitments, Albizu Campos was viewed as a central leader in American liberation movements from the 1930s to the 1970s. He is also seen as making an original contribution to understanding nationalism not as racial but, echoing Du Bois, as cultural and that resistance to colonization should not stop at compromise (MacMullan, 2019 and 2023).

In 1968, Albizu Campos's conception of nationalism inspired José "Cha Cha" Jimenez, a member of a Puerto Rican street gang called the Young Lords in Chicago, while he served a ninety-day sentence in the Cook County jail. Jimenez, following the efforts of the recently formed Black Panthers, sought to transform the gang, renamed the Young Lords Organization and later the Young Lords Party (YLP), into a group committed to social activism and addressing the circumstances and injustices faced by members of the Puerto Rican community, first in Chicago and then in New York City and in other cities across the United States.

The YLP newspaper summarized the group's doctrine: "We in the Young Lords Party follow the teachings of Don Pedro [Albizu Campos]. We know that since the amerikkkan invasion of Puerto Rico in 1898, the united states has controlled the press, radio, television. They control the schools. Every day, our people are bombarded with more and more amerikkkan propaganda." In response, the YLP held that "Only the road of a mass revolutionary movement that participates in a protracted struggle against the . . . yankees [and their allies], can win our liberation and end the oppression by the rich of the poor" (Young Lords, 2010, 162), The Young Lords' 1970 "13 Point Program" declared its support for the liberation of not just Puerto Rico but also all Latino and "third world" peoples. In addition to calling for a socialist economy and echoing the program developed by Albizu Campos in the 1930s, the platform specifically demanded "control of our institutions and our land." Land, they declared, "BELONGS TO ALL THE PEOPLE" (p. 12).

The philosophies of resistance of Albizu Campos and the Young Lords suggest the larger point, mostly implicit in our discussion until now, that American philosophies of resistance are not just responses to the history of oppression and removal in the United States but respond also to broader processes of colonization. From the wider perspective of the American hemisphere, it is clear that some philosophies of resistance emerge from the experience of those within communities whose histories are bound up with Spanish and Portuguese language and colonization. These responses, when they connect with communities in North America, have become known as Latinx philosophy.

The term Latinx, which continues to be subject to debate, recalls the same definitional challenges faced by claims that there is an American philosophical tradition. In one sense, it marks the philosophy of a shared experience. In another, it marks a geographical category—places with ties to "Latin" America. Like "American", "Latinx" remains unstable and subject to change. Claudia Milian, in her analysis of the term "LatinX" writes,

> I find LatinX's fundamental and capricious arbitrariness an invitation to further inquiry that remains open to possibilities. LatinX anticipates deployment. There is no orderly or intelligible inside or outside. Xs are endless and so are the flows of Latins. . . . LatinX's ascendency allows us to think about X not merely as a trend or as something to be for or against, but as a point of orientation that allows us to start charting the realm of LatinX inquiry. (2019, p. 6)

LatinX (or Latinx) philosophy is another key strand of American philosophies of resistance.

On March 10, 1968, labor organizer Cesar Chavez (1927–1993) accepted a piece of bread from Senator Robert Kennedy, who would soon become a candidate for president of the United States. The bread marked the end of Chavez's 25-day fast and symbolically linked his sacrifice to demands for social justice across the nation and what many took to be the changing character of US politics. Kennedy's presence recognized Chavez and the three-year struggle of the farm workers of the Central Valley of California. While many press reports presented Chavez's fast as a hunger strike to protest the treatment of farm workers, José-Antonio Orosco (2008) argued that it was instead part of a larger vision of resistance. Rather than protest, Chavez's fast marked a penitential sacrifice, in which Chavez "hoped to clear his mind and gain better focus" on how best to lead the striking workers. At the same time, the fast provided an instance of self-sacrifice for the cause of others in a way that promoted nonviolence.

The fast had come at a time when many members of the striking United Farm Workers (UFW) union had grown frustrated. The strike had begun in September 1965 over the wages and working conditions of the thousands of workers who harvested California's grapes. The strike was first called by the Agricultural Workers Organizing Committee (AWOC), a union of primarily Filipino workers, whose efforts to negotiate contracts with the growers had been ignored. A few days after the AWOC declared its strike, the National Farm Workers Association (NFWA), which included primarily Chicanx workers (and later formally merged with the AWOC to form the UFW), joined the strike on September 16, Mexican Independence Day.

Cesar Chavez and Dolores Huerta founded the NFWA in 1962 after resigning earlier that year from the Community Service Organization (CSO) when the leadership of the CSO decided not to actively organize farm workers. The CSO, by then a well-known grassroots organization with increasing political visibility, was founded in 1947 in response to police violence against Latinx people and their systematic exclusion from educational and economic opportunities in California cities, especially Los Angeles. The CSO was founded by Antonio Rios, Edward Roybal, and Fred Ross, Sr., with support from Saul Alinsky, a community organizer from Chicago whose book *Rules for Radicals* (1971) remains a standard text for organizers. The CSO became a primary tool in obtaining a political voice for Mexican Americans in the cities of the Southwest.

Born in Arizona, Chavez moved with his family to California in search of work during the Great Depression. His family followed the farm work, and after attending dozens of different schools, he graduated from eighth grade and ended his formal education. In 1946, he enlisted in the navy and was discharged two years later, moving to Delano, a town in California's Central Valley, where he worked in the fields and began to read theology and political theory. Despite his limited formal education, Chavez was a voracious reader, and in conversations with a local priest and his fellow workers, he developed a distinctive approach to bringing about social change.

Huerta joined the staff of the CSO in 1955, the same year Chavez became a paid organizer. Huerta was born in New Mexico in 1930. She moved with her family to Stockton, California where she attended Stockton High School, completed a degree at what is now San Joaquin Delta Community College, and shortly afterward received a teaching certificate. She taught elementary school until she joined the CSO by founding the Stockton branch. With Chavez, Huerta found that the interests that dominated the CSO left out concern for the growing population of poorly paid farm workers who faced impossible working conditions and were deprived of educational opportunity. As the Civil Rights Movement gained visibility and community activism showed increasing promise as an instrument for change, Chavez and Huerta agreed that it was time to organize the farm workers. In 1960, Huerta founded the Agricultural Workers Association to lobby local government and register voters.

The movement Chavez and Huerta began in 1962 as they organized the NFWA came to be called *La Causa*—The Cause—and it took on broad significance. While its immediate goal was to form a union to represent the needs and interests of farm workers, it also sought a cultural revolution informed by the Mexican traditions that framed the lives of the workers. While Chavez affirmed the nonviolent methods practiced by King and the Civil Rights Movement, he reconceived the idea of nonviolence in the context of Mexican culture. The protests of the NFWA and later the UFW, according to José-Antonio Orosco, were framed by three ideas: pilgrimage, penitence, and revolution (2008).

In the spring of 1966, the striking workers took part in a 340-mile march from Delano to Sacramento. While the Civil Rights Movement had held a "march" on Washington, Chavez called the UFW action a *pilgrimage*, that is, he said, "a trip made with sacrifice and hardship as an expression of penance and of commitment." Such trips in Mexico—"to major shrines . . . especially to the Basilica of Our Lady of Guadalupe in Mexico City"—often involved "a petition to the patron of the pilgrimage for some sincerely sought benefit of body or soul" (quoted in Orosco, 2008, p. 25). The protest action was in part about reaffirming Mexican cultural practices in order to transform the circumstances of the people of the Central Valley. The march to Sacramento also recalled "the image of the Lenten penitential procession that takes place in many Mexican and Mexican American communities in the period before Easter" (Orosco, 2008, p. 26). As in his later fasts (he engaged in three public fasts in his career), the pilgrimage provided for a collective reflection on the circumstances of the workers and what they sought. Most importantly, the pilgrimage was meant "to purify themselves of any feelings of anger, resentment, or revenge" (p. 27). Huerta explained, "I know it's hard for people who are not Mexican to understand, but this is part of Mexican culture—the penance, the whole idea of suffering for something, of self-inflicted punishment. It's a tradition of very long standing" (quoted in Orosco, 2008, p. 28).

As striking workers prepared for the March, Chavez helped to draft a manifesto called *El Plan de Delano*. The declaration explicitly frames the walk as a pilgrimage of penance to acknowledge "the failings of Farm Workers as free and sovereign men" and to show their dedication to "the propositions we have formulated to end the injustice that oppresses us" (Chavez, 2002, p. 16). Significantly, the manifesto invoked the particular history of the Central Valley and the place of Mexican Americans in it: "our path travels through a valley well known to all Mexican farm workers . . . because . . . in this very same valley, the Mexican race has sacrificed itself for the last hundred years. Our sweat and our blood have fallen on this land to make other men rich" (p. 16). The pilgrimage served at once as a "witness" to the suffering of Mexican people and the beginning of a movement to seek "our basic God-given rights" without violence (p. 16). The manifesto then placed the pilgrimage and the movement in a larger perspective by echoing the title of Emiliano Zapata's revolutionary manifesto, "El Plan de Ayala."

Zapata (1879–1919), whose ancestors were both Indigenous Nahua people and Spanish, was a leader of the 1910 Revolution in Mexico. The "Plan of Ayala" opposed the reestablishment of a landowner's aristocracy after the Revolution and called for land redistribution and reform. "El Plan de Delano" likewise challenged the system of land ownership that impoverished migrant workers. "We shall strike," the Plan declared, "We shall pursue the REVOLUTION we have proposed" (2002, p. 18), that is, a revolution committed to nonviolence. The manifesto also invoked Benito Juarez (1806–1872), the president of Mexico who resisted the French occupation of Mexico and helped to restore the Mexican Republic in 1867. With Juarez, Chavez's Plan announced "EL RESPETO AL DERECHO AJENO ES LA PAZ"—respect for the rights of others is peace. The manifesto concluded with a call to revolution: "We are sons of the Mexican Revolution, a revolution of the poor seeking bread and justice. Our revolution will not be armed, but we want the existing social order to dissolve, we want a new social order" (p. 18).

Despite the visibility of the strike, the growers showed little interest in negotiating with the workers. In 1967, Chavez and the leadership of the UFW decided to expand the strike beyond the Central Valley to include the largest grape grower in the state, Giumarra Vineyards Corporation. When other growers allowed Giumarra to use their labels to avoid a boycott of Giumarra grapes, the UFW called for a nationwide boycott on all California grapes. The strike lasted until 1970, when most of the California grape growers signed contracts with the UFW covering more than 10,000 workers.

Chavez and Huerta put Chicanx activism and cultural demands in front of the dominant society alongside movements demanding civil rights, the recognition of Black Power, and the demand for American Indian sovereignty. In the wake of the activism of *La Causa*, a new literature emerged in the United States that marked the coming transformation of philosophy as a discipline. Latinx philosophy, visible by degrees since the end of the Second World War, became another key strand of the burgeoning "American" tradition. It also called into question the "American" tradition as it had been taken up in the discipline of philosophy, consisting primarily of pragmatism and its classical manifestations in Peirce, James, and Dewey. By the late 1980s, the literature labeled "Latin American" had come to include authors from the United States as well as Mexico, Brazil, Argentina, Peru, Chile, and the Caribbean. Rather than being seen as separate from the history and intellectual development of the United States, "Latin" America was increasingly seen as American "*sin mas.*" As philosopher Anibal Quijano observed in 2000, "Even though for the imperialist vision of the United States of America the term 'America' is just another name for that country, today it is the name of the territory that extends from Alaska in the North to Cape Horn in the South, including the Caribbean archipelago" (2000, p. 574n2).

Broadly defined by the intellectual response to the intersection of European, African, and Indigenous American peoples, the resulting heterogeneous philosophical tradition is one that extends and deepens the story that, in this book, we have confined to the United States. Seen this way, not only is American philosophy broader than classical pragmatism, but American philosophy as an account of philosophical resistance across the hemisphere is broader still. It remains bound to a common history marked by the coming of Europeans, the forced arrival of Africans, and the struggle, first by Indigenous peoples and then by others, to resist and transform the ways of thinking imposed by and inherited from Europe.

What the work of Chavez and Huerta contributed to philosophy was not only a conception of nonviolent resistance framed by Mexican culture, but it also demanded that the dominant society recognize that philosophy in the Americas was never really bounded by political borders but was a system of intellectual and material exchange that spanned the continents North and South. *La Causa*, and related movements, including the Puerto Rican independence movement beginning in the 1930s, marked a turning point in the philosophical discourse of the United States—one whose consequences are still unfolding.

Despite a long tradition of philosophy among academics in Central and South America, there was apparently little academic exchange with the United States before the 1930s. During the

Spanish-American War in 1898, some philosophers such as James acknowledged the need to think about the United States in relation to Latin America as an object of the United States' imperial aspirations. That interest was short-lived, however, despite ongoing US military and economic involvement across the Caribbean and Central and South America: in addition to the permanent occupation of Puerto Rico, the United States occupied Cuba from 1906 to 1909 and again from 1917 to 1922, the Dominican Republic from 1916 to 1924, Haiti from 1915 to 1934, Panama from 1904 to 1999 with the construction and management of the Panama Canal, and Nicaragua, invaded by the United States in 1912 and occupied until 1933. The military action across the region, sometimes called the "Banana Wars," was most often a part of efforts by the US government to defend the interests of US corporations, including the United Fruit Company and others. Visibility in the press and the significant questions raised by the use of American power registered little in the philosophical discourse of the time.

In part, this lack of attention was consistent with the continuing lack of attention by the academic mainstream at the beginning of the twentieth century to US colonialism in the Americas, Eastern Asia, and the Pacific, where the United States also occupied economically beneficial territories including the Philippines, Guam, and Hawaii. In part, the lack of attention was the consequence of a set of expectations about the philosophical "potential" of the people of the Americas. In 1927, Argentinean philosopher Coriolano Alberini (1886–1960) published a representative paper in the journal *The Monist*. While Alberini argued that there was a new philosophical movement in Argentina, the paper, "Contemporary Philosophic Tendencies in South America with a special emphasis on Argentina," began by rehearsing a common conception of philosophy in Latin America. Philosophy in the region, he observed, "has generally been the result of the adoption and application of European philosophic speculation rather than the fruit of a preoccupation with the subject matter of philosophy proper" (1927, p. 328). The result, he argued, was a series of philosophical phases framed by European sources: scholastic philosophy brought by the Catholic Church was replaced by French thought as independence movements began in the early nineteenth century, only to be replaced by European romantic movements as newly independent nations drafted constitutions. Once independence was achieved, the positivism of Auguste Comte and related European thinkers (especially Herbert Spencer) was accepted as the dominant philosophy.

Positivism imported a rigid notion of causation and progress that at first was imagined to be helpful to new governments in honestly assessing the circumstances of their people and for devising means of fostering progress. But these more or less mechanical models of control and economic development turned out to serve the leadership better than the people. Positivism became an instrument of dictatorship rather than a means of liberation. As Jorge J. E. Gracia and Elizabeth Millán-Zaibert observed, "[t]he indiscriminate application of the principle of causality to everything led positivism to deny freedom to human beings" (2004. p. 17). The resulting view set aside agency in favor of systems of power without accountability and so, as Gracia and Millán-Zaibert concluded, "[p]ositivism seemed to lead to an ethical dead end" (p. 17). Alberini agreed: "Positivism, it may be said bluntly, did not produce anything valuable in philosophy proper in South America" (1927, p. 330). While Alberini admitted that positivism had not been replaced in 1927, it was being challenged by "a hasty shift from the positivistic creed to the idealistic doctrine by virtue of contagion from philosophic reactions in Europe" (p. 332). Even as philosophy in the United States abandoned idealism as the dominant view, Latin

## American Philosophies

American thought, led by philosophers in Mexico and Argentina, took up the work of Henri-Louis Bergson (1859–1941), Benedetto Croce (1866–1952), and Ortega y Gasset (1883–1955).

In the late 1930s, Thomas Vernor Smith (1890–1964), born in Blanket, Texas, and a student and then colleague of Mead at Chicago, began planning for what became the First Inter-American Congress of Philosophy. The conference was to be held at Columbia University in December 1942, but the attack on Pearl Harbor and the US entry into the war led to delaying the conference until the following year at Yale University.

Brand Blanshard chaired the meeting, and in his opening remarks, he observed that philosophers in the United States knew "almost nothing" of "the Latin American mind, of its dominant interests, even of its leading exponents in literature and science and philosophy" (1943, p. 179). "This cannot go on," he continued. "For our own sakes, if for no other, we cannot afford to let it go on." The war, Blanshard thought, had made establishing strong connections between the Americas essential. Roosevelt's "Good Neighbor" policy, Blanshard suggested, which stressed the need for peaceful relations among the nations of the Americas, should serve as a model. The conference included eighteen scholars from Latin American countries, including the ministers of education in Colombia and El Salvador, philosophers Risieri Frondizi (1910–1983) and Francisco Romero (1891–1962), and historian Edmundo O'Gorman (1906–1995). The conference also included a number of prominent philosophers from the United States, including Edgar Brightman, Marvin Farber, William Ernest Hocking, and William Pepperell Montague. Herbert Schneider (1892–1984), who would later publish *A History of American Philosophy* (1946) (which ironically contained no mention of Latin American philosophy), was also present, as was F. S. C. Northrop (1893–1992), a graduate of Beloit College and Harvard, who cofounded the journal *Philosophy East and West* and helped to establish a place for Asian thought in academic philosophy.

The years following the conference saw a variety of works by Latin American and North American philosophers that sought to bring philosophy across the Americas into conversation. Patrick Romanell (1912–2002), who was born in Italy, received his PhD from Columbia University and taught at universities in Panama, Ecuador, Italy, and the United States. In 1947, he published "The Background of Contemporary Mexican Thought" in *Philosophy and Phenomenological Research*. Mexican philosophy, he declared, "no longer cares to be handmaiden to an extraneous master, be it church, state, or industry" (p. 256). The key to this change and its rejection of the dominant positivist philosophy was the 1910 Mexican Revolution and its origins in the work of a few young philosophers who founded the *Ateneo de la Juventud*, the "Athenaeum of Youth." By 1909, when the *Ateneo* was founded, the Mexican President Porfirio Díaz (1830–1915) had been in office for thirty-two years. Díaz, who had led the rebellion against the government of Benito Juarez and his successor in 1877, had ruled as the absolute leader of Mexico where the philosophy of positivism had served as a framework for establishing the policies and practices that kept him in office. The *Ateneo* provided a forum to question the authority of positivism. Members of the group included Pedro Henriquez Ureña (1884–1946), Alfonso Reyes (1889–1959), Antonio Caso (1883–1946), and José Vasconcelos (1882–1959). According to Ureña,

> We felt the intellectual oppression together with the political and economic oppression which a large part of the country was aware of already. We saw that the official philosophy

was too systematic, too definitive not to be mistaken. Then we embarked on reading all the philosophers whom positivism used to condemn as useless, from Plato, who was our greatest teacher, up to Kant and Schopenhauer. (Quoted in Romanell, 1947, p. 257)

The engagement with European philosophy outside positivism became a means of resistance, establishing (or reestablishing) philosophical questions that had been set aside in Mexican philosophy. Romanell's paper and his book, *Making of the Mexican Mind* (1952) introduced the North American academy to central Mexican philosophers, especially Caso and Vasconcelos.

Vasconcelos, who served in a variety of education posts, including Secretary of Education of Mexico, gave a series of lectures at the University of Chicago in 1926 titled "The Latin American Basis of Mexican Civilization." His conclusion in these lectures echoed his work published in 1922 titled *La Raza Cósmica*, "The Cosmic Race." According to Vasconcelos, every nation must be organized by "some high ideal." For the "great American nation"—the United States—the high ideal was "democracy and equal opportunities for every man." For Latin America, Vasconcelos concluded, "[b]roadness, universality of sentiment and thought" would "fulfill the mission of bringing together all the races of earth and with the purpose of creating a new type of civilization" (1926, p. 93). This unified "race," the cosmic race, was the product of the unification through procreation of the diverse "world races" that had come to live together in the Americas. The "dispersion of races," he wrote, would "come to an end on American soil," where humanity would be united "by the triumph of fecund love and the improvement of all the human races" in the production of "a fifth race into which all nations will fuse with each other" and so "gather all the treasures of History" (Gracia and Millán-Zaibert, 2004, p. 274). The racist dimensions of Vasconcelos's vision marked another strand of the eugenicist views held by many of his North American contemporaries. Vasconcelos argued for the inevitability of "race mixing"—*mestizaje*—that would lead to distinctive art and cultural forms thanks to the particular history of the Americas. This notion of *mestizaje* became a central component of later Latinx philosophy, especially in the work of Gloria Anzaldúa.

In 1949, Elizabeth Flower (1915–95) also published an account of the development of Mexican philosophy. Flower coauthored *A History of Philosophy in America* (1977) with Murray Murphey (which, like Schneider's earlier book, did not include a discussion of Latin American thought) and taught at the University of Pennsylvania. Martin Luther King, Jr. audited the first graduate seminar she taught there. She also routinely lectured at universities in Mexico, Chile, Colombia, Guatemala, and Peru. Her account of Mexican philosophy emphasized the philosophical vision of Caso, as opposed to Vasconcelos. For Flower, "Caso does not glorify the future for Mexico, as does Vasconcelos; rather he insists that she shake free from the inhibiting factors of the past. 'Let us show our aptitude for civilization. Enough of the crimes in the history of America!'" (1977, p. 129). Caso argued that it is not procreation that will produce a new "more civilized" society, but conscience as "an enthusiasm that draws people away from being the exclusive products of the fundamental drives of nourishment, procreation, and prestige; it molds them into corporate bodies" (1949, p. 129).

Northrop also joined the conversation in 1949 in his paper "The Philosophy of Culture and Its Bearing on the Philosophy of History." For Northrop, cultural difference rests finally on philosophical differences manifested in practices as routine as what counts as news in daily newspapers. Mexican culture "in its totality is not a simple culture giving expression to one ideology but a complex of at least five cultures with their independent unique ideologies each one competing for control" (1949, p. 569). The philosophy of culture—or perhaps the philosophy of cross-cultural interaction—"must bring out into the open the specific economic theory, political doctrine, religious beliefs (if any), and art forms of each ideology or attendant culture," as Northrop suggested in his book *The Meeting of East and West* (1946). The recognition of Latin American and Asian philosophy reinforced the conclusion that "The philosophy of culture is inescapable in the contemporary world with its ideological conflicts in both domestic politics and international relations" (p. 574).

At the same time, however, the direction of North American academic philosophy was moving against the vision of philosophy advocated by Northrop, Romanell, and Flower, and illustrated in the antipositivistic philosophies of Latin America. In 1949, Brazilian philosopher Euryalo Cannabrava (1906–1981) published "Present Tendencies in Latin American Philosophy" in the *Journal of Philosophy*. The paper was unsparing in its criticism of the very new developments that were praised by Romanell and Flower. Referring to the Second Inter-American Conference of Philosophy, he wrote, "[a]ll the irrational ingredients of idealistic metaphysics and existentialist humanism appeared with their bold effort to substitute emotional outbursts for methodical inquiry" (1949, p. 113). Thanks to a "superstitious attitude toward the 'inner' life," reason was presented as "useless and burdensome" and "was put in the awkward situation of a servant dismissed for incompetence and inability to carry out the master's orders" (p. 113). For Cannabrava, philosophers in Latin America were failing to keep up with philosophers in the United States who had shifted their focus from metaphysics to the philosophy of science. Although he granted that these philosophers of science "go too far, enthralling themselves with the cult or religion of scientific achievements," they nevertheless avoided the "[e]motional outbursts, dramatic vicissitudes, such as anguish, despair, and contempt of what spoils our existence" (p. 118) characteristic of Latin American philosophy. Placed in the context of the work of Neurath, Carnap, Bergmann, and analytic philosophy, Latin American philosophy—like pragmatism and phenomenology—found it hard to get a hearing.

The relative obscurity of Latin American thought did not mean that it was absent from philosophy in the United States. Risieri Frondizi, from Argentina, helped make a case for the place of Latin American philosophy in relation to North America and Europe. He began his philosophical education in Buenos Aires. He then completed an MA degree at the University of Michigan and his doctoral degree at the National Autonomous University of Mexico in Mexico City in 1950. While a student in the United States, he also took graduate courses at Harvard with Whitehead, Royce's student C. I. Lewis, and James's student, Ralph Barton Perry. He was a founding member of the philosophy department at the National University of Tucumán in Argentina, helped to found the department of philosophy at the University of Puerto Rico, and served as dean and then president of the University of Buenos Aires. He also taught at Yale, the University of Texas at Austin, UCLA, the University of Pennsylvania, Baylor, and for nine years at Southern Illinois University, Carbondale.

In 1951, Frondizi published an indirect rebuttal to Cannabrava and argued that there was a sharp divide between Latin American and North American philosophy. The difference he marked mirrored the divide present between continental philosophy, which is framed by phenomenology and existentialism, and the increasingly dominant analytic philosophy of the North American academy of the time. "The two Americas," he wrote, "are separated by dissimilar concerns; they are interested in different problems" (1951, p. 619). The central problem for Latin American philosophy was "man and his creatures" while the central interest in North American philosophy was "symbolic logic, methodology, philosophical analysis and semantics" (p. 620). Latin American philosophy, he argued, was "emotional and deeply rooted in a living experience" while the dominant philosophy made every effort to set aside the emotive aspect as "non-scientific" (p. 620). Rather than accepting the division (and marginalization of Latin American philosophy), Frondizi concluded that the contribution of Latin American philosophy was a distinctive philosophical "attitude": "the North American philosopher will realize that it is not necessary to cease being in order to become a philosopher" (p. 622).

Frondizi's own philosophical position focused on the nature of the self and the emergence of values. Recalling James's conception, Frondizi held that "the self is revealed in action; it reveals and constitutes itself by acting. It is nothing before acting and nothing remains of it if experience cease completely" (Gracia and Millán-Zaibert, 2004, p. 113). The resulting self is "an organized whole, an integrated structure, and experience . . . related to one another not through but within the whole" (p. 119). The whole is then a complex of experiences and commitments, past and future, which "cannot exist in separation." "Its multiplicity does not exclude its unity or vice versa." Also reminiscent of Follett's conception of the self, Frondizi concluded that "diversity underlies the structure but is in turn lost within it, for the elements uphold each other mutually in an intimate sort of interweaving in which it is impossible to distinguish warp from woof" (p. 120).

Even as North American philosophy moved away from philosophies grounded in humanism, Latin American philosophy intersected with a new movement that emerged from within the Catholic Church of South and Central America. This new theology responded, in part, to the work of Catholic philosophers Jacques Maritain (1882–1973) and Pierre Teilhard de Chardin (1881–1955) and to the efforts to transform the church by the Second Vatican Council (1962–1965). Priests in Brazil, Peru, Argentina, and Mexico sought ways of addressing the circumstances of the poor. By borrowing Marxist class analysis and combining it with a Christian theology of social justice, these activists established the basic commitments of what they called "liberation theology." Developed independently of Black liberation theology in the United States, Latin American liberation theology nevertheless began with the claim that Christianity must address the needs of the poor and oppressed. In 1971, Gustavo Gutierrez, a Peruvian priest who studied philosophy at the University of Leuven and received degrees from the Université Catholique de Lyon, published *Teología de la Liberación: Perspectivas* (*A Theology of Liberation: Perspectives*). Gutierrez described the approach of liberation theology as arising in response to the "sign of the times" (a phrase borrowed from the Second Vatican Council) and the rampant poverty of Latin America.

A theology of liberation would combine the philosophical methodology of Marxist analysis with the eschatological vision of Christianity and the "preferential option for the poor." Gutierrez further emphasized the need for these theoretical elements to be embedded in a wider "praxis," which would focus on the pastoral care of the poor across Latin America. "This kind of theology," Gutierrez asserted, "arising from concern with a particular set of issues, will perhaps give us the solid and permanent albeit modest foundation for, the *theology in the Latin American perspective* which is both desired and needed" (1988, p. 11). Despite efforts by the church to condemn Gutierrez's work, it came to inform many of the revolutions in South and

Central America over the following decades, including the Sandinista Revolution in Nicaragua in 1979 and the resistance movement in El Salvador that began in 1979 and was supported by Archbishop Oscar Romero, who was assassinated in 1980. The Salvadoran War continued until 1992, thanks in part to military support from the United States, which was aimed at preventing the rebels from establishing a communist government.

The same year Gutierrez published his seminal work, Paulo Freire (1921–1997) published *Pedagogia do Oprimido*, translated into English and published as *Pedagogy of the Oppressed* (1970). Freire was born to a middle-class family in Recife, Brazil, but his father fell ill as the Great Depression reached Brazil in 1929. The family was forced to move into a poor neighborhood where Paulo saw how unemployment, poverty, and illiteracy kept the poor from escaping. Eventually, Freire received a scholarship to attend a private high school. He completed college and graduate school and became a teacher. In the early 1960s, Freire became involved in conversations about liberation theology and soon began to apply elements of this view to his practice of teaching literacy in the favelas of Recife. The resulting "pedagogy of the oppressed" adopted the humanism of liberation theology, and its principal concern of recognizing and helping the poor, but set aside its explicit religious framework. In short, Freire advocated education that would respond to the dehumanizing conditions of poverty by providing support for students to recognize their own oppression and providing the means to undermine the categories and structures that held them in place. The process of liberation, *conscientizaçao*, that is, "conscientization," or the development of critical consciousness, was the central means of becoming humanized.

Liberatory education stood in contrast to what he called the "banking concept of education" in which the teacher "talks about reality as if it were motionless, static, compartmentalized, and predictable" and whose task is "to 'fill' the students with the contents of his narration" (1970, p. 71). The task of the oppressed, however, is the "great humanistic and historical task . . . to liberate themselves and their oppressors as well" (p. 44). Yet the oppressed are "submerged" in a world they cannot escape, reinforced by the banking model of teaching and learning. Liberation then requires the assistance of another class, "those who are truly solidary with" the oppressed (p. 45). These allies are "members of the oppressor class" who "take on a new form of existence through comradeship with the oppressed" (p. 61). These allies, as "teacher-students," support a process of learning determined by the students and their circumstances. As in the case of liberation theology, where priests provide resources to resist local oppression, for Freire, teachers have this "fundamental role" (p. 61). "A revolutionary leadership must accordingly practice *co-intentional* education" that will "unveil" the relation of the oppressed and will "re-create that knowledge" as a means of becoming human. With the help of teachers, Freire concluded, the oppressed can learn to be humans, to create "culture and history" and to *be* praxis, "the reflection and action which truly transforms reality" (p. 100).

Freire's work became enormously influential in North America in the 1980s and 1990s. Through the work of Henry Giroux, Peter McLaren, and others, *Pedagogy of the Oppressed* provided the starting point for a range of new educational theories called "critical pedagogy." The approach combined the long-standing vision of progressive education developed in significant part from Dewey's work, and the resources of critical theory (developed in the work of the Institute for Social Research—the Frankfurt School that included Max Horkheimer, Theodor Adorno, and Herbert Marcuse). The resulting educational philosophy challenged prevailing approaches to education that had, according to the critical pedagogy theorists, created a public school system that reinforced the advantages of the dominant class while producing a class of docile workers and consumers. The criticism of schooling led in the 1980s to the "Culture Wars" (discussed in Chapter 25) in which the critics faced a counter-challenge from philosophers including Allan Bloom in *Closing of the American Mind* (1987), John Searle in a series of essays including "The Storm over the University" (1990), and William Bennett in *The De-valuing of America: The Fight for Our Culture and Our Children* (1992). The philosophers were joined by literary theorist E. D. Hirsch, Jr., who published *Cultural Literacy: What Every American Needs to Know* (1987), and conservative pundit Dinesh D'Souza, whose book *Illiberal Education* (1991) argued against critical pedagogy's central commitments to pluralism and multiculturalism. Freire's work continues to have a wide influence and opened the way for further philosophical engagement with liberation philosophers in South and Central America.

Like Freire, Enrique Dussel (1934–2023) also began his work in the context of the emerging liberation theology movement. Dussel was born in La Paz, Argentina, and after completing a degree at Universidad Nacional de Cuyo, he studied in Spain. From 1959 until 1961, he lived on a kibbutz in Israel and began work on his first three books. In 1967, he returned to Argentina to teach at his alma mater. In 1975, after right-wing military forces took over the government from Juan Peron and Dussel's home was bombed, he left Argentina to teach at the National Autonomous University of Mexico. His contact with liberation theology began in the 1960s and led to a series of works that expanded the discussion of liberation from one framed largely by Catholic doctrine to one—like Freire's humanism—that was grounded in a broad conception of human nature and culture. In 1975, Dussel published *Filosofía de la Liberación* (published as *Philosophy of Liberation* in English in 1985).

For Dussel, the development of European philosophy had the effect of organizing global cultures in a system that placed Europe and its peoples, cultures, politics, and economic systems at the center and placed all others at the periphery to serve and support the center with their labor. "European philosophy . . . situated all men and all cultures—and with them their women and children—within its own boundaries as manipulable tools, instruments" (1985, p. 3). The philosophy of liberation challenges this order by "rising from the periphery, from the oppressed, from the shadow that the light of Being has not been able to illumine. Our thought sets out from non-Being, nothingness, otherness, exteriority, the mystery of no-sense. It is, then, a 'barbarian' philosophy" (p. 14). Dussel's corpus became widely available in English in the 1980s and began to influence philosophers working in North American philosophy as well. The emphasis on addressing the lived circumstances of the poor and marginalized made it a resource for a new generation of philosophers who saw the characteristic treatment of the poor and marginalized in Latin America as a consequence of the same fundamental constraints imposed by European colonization throughout the Americas.

By the late 1980s, Latin American philosophy in North America had gained new ground. The most audible voices in this period were those of Leopoldo Zea and Jorge J. E. Gracia. Zea (1912–2004) was born in Mexico City, and after briefly studying law, he completed a degree in philosophy at El Colegio de México, where he studied with José Gaos (1900–1969), a Spanish philosopher who had fled Spain when the fascist government of Francisco Franco took over in 1936. When Zea proposed a thesis on Greek philosophy, Gaos recommended that he choose a Mexican or Latin American subject matter instead. The result was a two-volume study of the rise and fall of positivism in Mexico. In 1949, Zea (along with Frondizi and others) participated in the second Inter-American Conference of Philosophy, where he gave a paper on the relation of Latin American and North American cultures, "two half-worlds, two Americas" that emerged from a "series of historical circumstances" (1949, p. 538).

Philosophy, Zea held, aspires to universality, but here universality had the character of a process that, "rightly understood, makes it possible for men and peoples to live together," which "exists when one man understands another, or one country understands another" (1949, p. 538). Such understanding had not yet been achieved between the "half-worlds." While Latin America, through leading thinkers, had spent more than a century attempting to understand the North, "North America has not been able to feel for South America any interest beyond a purely material one" (p. 542). The conference, he proposed, marked a turning point where "the effort" to find "universality"—or a common philosophical ground—might be possible. Such a philosophical perspective would begin in lived experience North and South: "The universal . . . must be achieved starting, as does all authentic philosophy, from our reality" (p. 543). The result might be a new American philosophy. "Why not go on," Zea asked, "to question ourselves about the possibilities of an American philosophy . . . a philosophy which respects what is private to each one of the Americas and can at the same time be valid for both?" (p. 543)

In 1963, Zea published an English translation of his book, *The Latin American Mind*, and in 1969, *Latin America and the World*. Both books broadly engaged his early project of attempting to shape the understanding of the two Americas by recognizing that philosophy arises from concrete experience and that its products shape the understanding and identity of the people whose experience is formative. Philosophy, from this perspective, he wrote in a 1968 article, provides "for the needs of the people, . . . direct[ing] attention to their problems and attempt[ing] to solve them" (p. 5). Authentic philosophy thus leads first to recognition of particularity and limitation and then to action. Latin Americans, Zea claimed, have experienced this shift of perspective: "Alone and limited, they are united with others" (p. 15). The result, he concluded, was not Latin American philosophy—a peculiar new kind of thinking—but "Simply philosophy, the traces of whose origins would be undeniable" (p. 15). That is, the experience of Latin American life would produce philosophy just as European life produced philosophy. The difference was in the origin, which in Latin America was in *mestizaje*, the mixing of European peoples and cultures with Indigenous American peoples and cultures in a distinctive place apart from Europe.

In 1989, Zea joined seven other philosophers as part of a special issue of the *Philosophical Forum* on "Latin American Philosophy Today." The volume was edited by Jorge J. E. Gracia (1942–2021), who was born in Cuba, completed high school in 1960, and immigrated to the United States, where he completed his undergraduate degree at Wheaton College and his PhD in philosophy at the University of Toronto. Drawing together key philosophers in this volume, Gracia helped to foster new interest in the work done in the United States and in Central and South America. He was "optimistic about the future of philosophy in Latin America" (p. 26) that was marked by two extremes. The first, associated with Marxism, sought to bring about social change, but also tended to set aside arguments in favor of developing "a general picture that makes sense or proves enlightening" and, in so doing, serves "to convince others of the value of their ideas" (pp. 23–4). At the other extreme were "philosophies whose primary interest was in arguments" (p. 24). The resulting tension seemed to mirror the tension that had developed in North American philosophy since the Second World War. Against the North American model for philosophy, however, Gracia urged Latin American philosophers "to listen to each other and take each other seriously" (p. 26). Recalling Frondizi's discussion four decades earlier of the relation between North and South, Gracia made a case for the need for a philosophical practice that could address a world of sharp differences against a background of shared history.

The 1989 volume included a paper by Ofelia Schutte, also Cuban, who completed her doctoral degree at Yale. Schutte's article began to address the apparent lack of women philosophers in the developing field of Latin American philosophy. The feminist response to such a gap, she suggested, was twofold: historical, and attentive to women's actual circumstances. Philosophers need to reconsider the history of Latin America and recognize the presence of women in that history. For example, Sor Juana Inez de la Cruz (1651–1695), a Mexican nun who, despite exclusion from intellectual circles, resisted attempts to silence her in order to give a philosophical account of her situation. Such historical analysis combined with attention to the actual circumstances faced by women in Latin America provided a framework to take up a distinctive Latin American feminism. Such a view, Schutte argued, would recognize the diversity of women's experiences and the diverse forms of their oppression, including violence against them, the lack of control over their own bodies, and the ways in which policies of economic development were destructive to their identity as women and to their place in their families. In short, "should women reject and give up their 'private' (domestic) identity so as to take on a 'public' identity on an equal level with men or should they enter the public arena to demand social changes and join in the work force without discarding their domestic identity as homemakers and mothers?" (1989, p. 80).

The resulting feminist standpoint was in many ways distinct from the feminism of North American philosophy, which Schutte claimed was "pervaded" by "the ideology of the individual" (1989, p. 81). Latin Americans, she concluded, "are trying to seek equality without losing community" (p. 81). Schutte's work set the stage for new conversations about the place of women in Latin America and helped to make a place for Latin American feminist philosophy. In 1993, Schutte published *Cultural Identity and Social Liberation in Latin American Thought*. The book connected questions of identity with the process of liberation central to liberation theology and the work of Gutierrez, Dussel, and Zea.

The issue of identity was addressed as well by Linda Martín Alcoff. Alcoff, Panamanian by birth but of mixed racial and ethnic origins, received her PhD from Brown University, where she worked with Martha Nussbaum. In her 2000 article, "Is Latina/o Identity a Racial Identity?" published in another collection edited by Gracia, she took up what Gracia saw as the central issue of the developing field of Latin American philosophy. Alcoff's response to the question challenged the "racial" model of difference structured around physical differences and biological inheritance by arguing in part that such ideas, rather than presenting stable categories, were themselves a product of context. At the same time, she challenged the "ethnic" model of difference that framed ethnic groups as social productions alone. The reality of Latinx experience, she argued, is a matter of both models. One's "look" and cultural practices adopted or enforced to mark differences among groups give one a "visible" identity and also an experienced identity that is equally real.

In "Latinos Beyond the Binary," Alcoff argued that the usual binary of Black and White racial differences, even if multiplied to include a category of Latinx, misses the realities of Latinx identity. The relevant binary is not Black/White, but the binary of "threat and promise that exists not only in the Anglo cultural imaginary but also in the policies and practices of the neo-liberal state" (2009, p. 112). The threat posed by Latinx people in the United States, she claimed, is uniquely economic and cultural. "[S]ituated as we all are in the Americas, where Spain is dominant throughout the hemisphere and no border is unnavigable" (p. 113), the economic and cultural character of Latin America will inevitably be transformative. She concluded, "[n]o other minority can realistically pose the threat of ballooning numbers we can" (p. 113). At the same time, what makes for a threat also makes for promise. "*Latinidad*," the process of fostering a unified Latinx identity, "is a highly marketable commodity," according to Schutte, which has helped to form new markets, sources of labor, and, in recent years, political power.

Framed by the binary of threat and promise, Latinx identity makes a case for a conception of difference that is bound to both race and ethnicity. Alcoff borrowed David Theo Goldberg's idea of "ethnorace," which affirms both the physical markers that organize difference and the ways that complex social and historical relations shape experience. As a result, the boundaries of difference are not fixed and defined by binaries but rather are relative to circumstances, subject to change, and subject to multiplication. Individuals freed from strict categories are able to acknowledge diverse identities and to foster them. Citing the idea of "communities of solidarity"—an idea common in union organizing—Alcoff argued that ethnorace supports the recognition of communities that "emerge organically from real and not only imagined shared experience and shared interests" (2009, p. 124). Combined with recognition of anti-Latinx racism as different from anti-Black racism and the practical consequences of "identity proliferation," ethnorace provides "a check on relatively useless generalizations so as to achieve more descriptive accuracy and predictive capacity and thus political efficacy" (p. 125).

Alcoff's analysis of identity emerged from her broad interests in epistemology, feminist philosophy, and the development of identity presented in her 2006 book, *Visible Identities: Race, Gender and Self*. She also argued for the importance of understanding the particular question of Latinx identity in the larger context of colonialism. Walter Mignolo, an Argentinean who received his doctorate from École des Hautes Études in Paris, and taught at Duke University beginning in 1993, asserted along with Alcoff that "modernity emerged from colonialism." He went on to explain that "Colonialism is constitutive of modernity, of its teleological macro-narratives of human progress, and of the material base necessary to provide both the surplus and self-representation required to imagine Europe as the vanguard of the human race" (Alcoff, 2007, p. 83).

With Dussel and Quijano, Mignolo argued for the centrality of a critique of colonialism both as a project to understand Latin American thought and as a transformative project of decolonization. The process at the center of the critique turns on what he calls "border thinking." Beginning with the work of Moroccan philosopher Abdelkébir Khatibi (1938–2009), Mignolo observed that the critique of colonialism is not a universal critique—challenging all of colonialism all at once as if its character and implications are always and everywhere the same. Rather, the critique ought to begin from local histories. The result is not a one-sided critique, but one that, in Khatibi's case, involves a critique of both Christianity and Islam, the competing powers whose intersection generated the subalterns—the oppressed and marginalized—of Morocco. "A double critique becomes at this intersection a border thinking," he wrote, "since to be critical of both . . . implies to think from both traditions, and, at the same time, from neither of them" (2000, p. 67). Border thinking is then a means of resistance to the powers of colonization and a means of reconstruction through the recovery of local knowledge that can become part of a new, liberatory experience.

The result is both epistemic and ethical because it ties together the intellectual critique of the dominant culture and a disposition to act. Border thinking is "a way of thinking that . . . is not intended to dominate and to humiliate; a way of thinking that is universally marginal, fragmentary, and unachieved" (2000, p. 68). It is not totalizing, but rather remains fragmentary and pluralistic. The resulting view is in many ways a familiar one in the American philosophical tradition of resistance: Mignolo mentions antecedents in the notion of "double consciousness" developed by Du Bois, the idea of "double vision" proposed by Wright, and Anzaldúa's idea of "mestiza consciousness" (p. 84). All these ways of thinking, Mignolo concluded, bring "to the foreground the irreducible epistemological difference, and the forms of knowledge that, being critical of modernity, colonization and capitalism still remain 'within' the territory, 'in custody' of the 'abstract universals'" (p. 88).

Like Mignolo, who argued for the connections between Latin America and Africa as a part of philosophical analysis of colonization and decolonization, Paget Henry, an Antiguan who received his doctorate in sociology from Cornell University, also argued that Caribbean philosophy could only be understood in relation to transatlantic traditions. His book, *Caliban's Reason: Introducing Afro-Caribbean Philosophy* (2000), helped to further define the scope and concerns of Latin American philosophy and open the way toward a broader hemispheric American philosophy. Central figures in this tradition are C. L. R. James (1901–1989), Aimé Césaire (1913–2008), Frantz Fanon (1925–1961), and Pedro Albizu Campos (1893–1965). Unlike Central and South American philosophy, the Afro-Caribbean philosophical tradition emerged from the intersection of French, Spanish, African, and African American philosophies. Henry argued that Caribbean philosophy developed in a context of plural cultural systems held together by colonization and imperial conquest. In this context, cultural elites are at once members of diverse colonial cultures and so struggle for legitimacy.

The result is philosophical reflection bound at once to resistance and to the work of cultivating identities, while at the same time developing "totalizations" as means of unifying differences and making a particular cultural system legitimate. Drawing on Shakespeare's *The Tempest* as one of "the most enduring accounts of the refiguring of Caribbean identities produced" by Europe, Henry proposed to understand Afro-Caribbean thought as a consequence of a process of "Calibanization." In service of Shakespeare's King Prospero in *The Tempest*, Caliban is "a cannibal, a child, a monster without language and hence a slave to be subdued and domesticated along with nature and history" (2000, p. 4). In exchange for this service, the King was prepared to give the cannibal language and so a limited degree of humanization. In this context, "the works of Caliban's reason are Afro-Caribbean philosophy's contributions to the cultural articulation of the problem of this particular existence—and how to respond to them" (p. 5).[1]

On July 3, 1987, eighteen young Mexican men were discovered suffocated in a boxcar that had just arrived in the train yard of Sierra Blanca, Texas. The men, traveling with a smuggler, had crossed the Rio Grande a few days earlier and waited for a way to go North to take advantage of summer hiring in Dallas. The smuggler eventually identified a train leaving near sunset for the North. Nineteen men entered the boxcar and the smuggler closed and locked the door to avoid attracting attention from the border patrol officers checking the train. The train was delayed in the South Texas heat. When it finally arrived in Sierra Blanca, the temperature in the car had reached 120 degrees and the sealed car provided little air circulation. One man survived. The tragedy led to headlines across the country: "Tragedy in boxcar underscores alien problem" (*Chicago Tribune*), "18 Suspected Aliens Die in Locked Boxcar" (*L.A. Times*), "Aliens Die Aboard Railroad Boxcar" (AP News). For the newspapers, it appeared that the men who died had no business in the North; they were alien to the place, outsiders, illegal. The deaths came just seven months after the 1986 Immigration Reform and Control Act was signed into law by President Ronald Reagan. The Act had been widely praised because it granted immunity to undocumented people who had been living in the United States since 1982 and because it began to hold employers responsible for ensuring that their workers could legally work in the United States. The newspapers expressed surprise that, despite the Immigration Reform Act, people continued to come North.

That same year, Gloria Anzaldúa (1942–2004) published *Borderlands/La Frontera: The New Mestiza*. Anzaldúa was born in South Texas and received degrees in education from Pan-American University (now the University of Texas Rio Grande Valley) and the University of Texas at Austin. The book is composed of essays and poetry and is written in a combination of English, Spanish, and Nahuatl, the language of the Aztec people. *Borderlands/La Frontera* spoke directly to the issues reflected in the Sierra Blanco tragedy and its treatment in the press. What the press—and those who produced the Immigration Act—failed to notice was that the border was not a clear line that could or should be enforced. Rather than a simple division between the United States and Mexico, Anzaldúa called the line "*una herida abierta*," an open wound. It did not mark the point where one nation ended and another began; it divided "a *pueblo*, a culture / running down the length of my body / staking fence rods in my flesh" (1999, p. 24). Borders, she said, "are set up to define places that are safe and unsafe, to distinguish *us* from *them*." The boundary between South and North was instead a borderland, "a vague and undetermined place created by the emotional residue of an unnatural boundary" (p. 25). From Anzaldúa's perspective, borderlands were not confined to the "narrow strip" marked by a fence or a river but extended North and South wherever people found themselves between cultures, communities, or economies. And wherever "the lifeblood of two worlds" merged, there formed a "third country—a border culture" (p. 25).

Anzaldúa identified herself as a person of the borderlands—a part of the United States and a part of Mexico, a woman in worlds dominated by men, an Indigenous American in worlds dominated by Europeans, a lesbian in homophobic worlds. Recalling Vasconcelos, she described the borderlands as a place of *mestizaje*, of mixing, where its inhabitants possess the possibility for a new consciousness she called "mestiza." "Because I, a *mestiza*," she wrote, "continually walk out of one culture/and into another,/because I am in all cultures at the same time, *alma entre dos mundos, tres, cuatro,/me zumba la cabeza con lo contradictorio./Estoy norteada por todas las voces que me hablan / simultáneamente* [Soul between two worlds, three, four, my head buzzes with contradictions. I am disoriented by all of the voices that speak to me at once]" (1999, p. 99). The *mestiza* identity is one of pain and one of promise. Like Du Bois's notion of double consciousness, Anzaldúa asserted that this position is at once part of both cultures and part of neither. "At some point, on our way to a new consciousness, we will have to leave the opposite bank." When this happens, "we are on both shores at once" or perhaps, she wrote, "we will decide to disengage from the dominant culture, write it off altogether as a lost cause, and cross the border into a wholly new and separate territory." Faced with the indeterminacy of a borderland, the future is open and *mestizas* have the power to choose their own direction. "*The possibilities are numerous once we decide to act and not react*" (pp. 100–1).

Mestiza consciousness has at least three aspects as Anzaldúa presented it. She is first of all a plural personality who "operates in a pluralistic mode—nothing is thrust out, the good, the bad and the ugly, nothing rejected, nothing abandoned" (1999, p. 101). At the same time, she makes unification a possibility. "That focal point or fulcrum, that juncture where the *mestiza* stands, is where phenomena tend to collide. It is where the possibility of uniting all that is separate occurs." And finally, "[i]n attempting to work out a synthesis the self has added a third element which is greater than the sum of its severed parts" (pp. 101–2). The mestiza, in short, is something new, like the product of abduction in Peirce's theory of inquiry, the source of originality and change. As a result, she concluded, "*Su cuerpo una bocacalle* [Her body is an intersection]. *La mestiza* has gone from being the sacrificial goat to becoming the officiating priestess at the crossroads" (p. 102). Rather than accepting boundaries as impassible barriers, the mestiza embodies the formative resistance of the borderlands' perspective. Anzaldúa's work marked intersectional resistance and a model of race theory, feminism, queer theory, and the practical politics of understanding borders. In the end, the new mestiza was both a means of challenging oppression and a necessity for survival, both for those in the borderlands and for those the borderlands connect. "To survive in the borderlands/you must live *sin fronteras* [*without borders*]/be a crossroads" (p. 212).

The tragedy at Sierra Blanco was not the last border tragedy. In May 2018, the US Department of Justice under President Donald Trump announced a "zero tolerance" policy that required the arrest and prosecution of anyone crossing the Southern border without authorization, including those seeking asylum under US law. Children who crossed the border with their parents were to be separated from their parents and held in shelters operated by the Office of Refugee Resettlement until their parents' cases were resolved. By the end of the year, according to the US Department of Health and Human Services, 2,737 children had been taken from their parents under the Trump policy (Southern Poverty Law Center). In total, more than 5,000 children were separated from their parents before the policy ended—a number difficult to confirm since systematic records of the children and their families were not kept by US Immigration and Customs Enforcement (ICE) (PBS). At least seven children died while in custody. The policy of family separation, though more limited in its use, continued despite the change in presidential administrations.

The concerns of Pedro Albizu Campos, Caesar Chavez, Gloria Anzaldúa, and philosophers like Risieri Frondizi about the character of Latin America and the division enforced by the history of colonialism and racism remain critical questions for North American society. The resistance philosophies of Latinx people remain a resource for addressing the conception of a border, of national identity, of the role of land and place, and the need to seek new shared futures. The call to survive in the borderlands recalls the thirteenth point of the Young Lords' platform that demands a socialist society that spans differences: "We want liberation, clothing, free food, education, health care, transportation, full employment and peace. We want a society where the needs of the people come first, and where we give solidarity and aid to the people of the world, not oppression and racism" (Young Lords, p. 13).

## Note

1. The works of Mignolo, Gracia, Dussel, and Quijano, as well as Henry's seminal work in Caribbean philosophy, have given rise to a new generation of Latin American philosophers including Eduardo Mendieta, Nelson Maldonado-Torres, and Alejandro Vallega among others. Some, such as Mendieta, made explicit use of the North American philosophical tradition, including the work of the classical pragmatists (Mendieta has written on Royce and Peirce, for example) and on more recent neopragmatism, especially the work of Rorty. José-Antonio Orosco's *Cesar Chavez and the Common Sense of Nonviolence* (2008) takes up the social criticism and thought of Chavez in the frame of his commitment to a deeply democratic society. Gregory Fernando Pappas edited *Pragmatism in the Americas* (2011), which included essays addressing the reception of pragmatism in the Hispanic world, arguing for the inclusion of Hispanic figures in the history of pragmatism, and using pragmatism to deal with present problems experienced in the Americas.

## Primary Texts

Alcoff, Linda Martín (2006). *Visible Identities: Race, Gender, and the Self.* New York: Oxford University Press.
Anzaldúa, Gloria (2007). *Borderlands/La Frontera*, 3rd edn. San Francisco: Aunt Lute Books.
Dussel, Enrique (1985). *Philosophy of Liberation.* Eugene, Oregon: Wipf and Stock.
Freire, Paulo (2000). *The Pedagogy of the Oppressed*, 13th Anniversary edn. New York: Bloomsbury Academics.
Schutte, Ofelia (1993). *Cultural Identity and Social Liberation in Latin American Thought.* Albany, NY: State University of New York Press.
Zea, Leopoldo (1963). *The Latin American Mind.* Norman, OK: University of Oklahoma Press.

# CHAPTER 21
# RED POWER, INDIGENOUS PHILOSOPHY
## VINE DELORIA, JR., AND CONTEMPORARY AMERICAN INDIAN THOUGHT

On February 27, 1973, the village of Wounded Knee, South Dakota (near the site of the 1890 massacre with which our story began) was occupied by a group of about 200 Native Americans, mostly from the Oglala Nation. The occupation was led by the American Indian Movement (AIM), a group founded in 1968 in Minneapolis to address the living conditions of Native people who had been relocated to urban centers by the US government. Though AIM was often seen as being at odds with Indians who lived on rural reservations in the West, the people of the Pine Ridge Reservation had invited the group to intervene on their behalf in an ongoing conflict with the Bureau of Indian Affairs (BIA) and the BIA-supported tribal council leaders. Pine Ridge, like most reservations, had reorganized its governmental system in the 1930s by adopting a formal constitution at the direction of the BIA, following the Indian Reorganization Act (IRA) passed in 1934 as part of Roosevelt's New Deal. Many of the practices and forms of Native self-government had been lost or had become dormant during the forced removal of most Native people from their homelands. The IRA imposed a form of government that "was almost a carbon copy of the structured, legalistic European form of government" (Deloria and Lytle, 1983, p. 101). The resulting mandated elections, often influenced by the BIA and by non-Native interests who wanted to acquire Native lands, led to situations in which elected leadership did not always represent the interests of the community.

In 1972, Dick Wilson, a member of the Oglala Nation at Pine Ridge, was elected tribal chairperson. He quickly placed relatives in many of the paid governmental positions funded by the BIA. He also decided to accept cash payments from the government in exchange for releasing claims to tribal lands in Paha Sapa (the Black Hills), long recognized as sacred land by Native peoples of the region, and 133,000 acres of the Badlands, which had been converted into a firing range by the US Army during the Second World War. In response to challenges to his authority, Wilson also established a security force named the Guardians of the Oglala Nation (often called the "GOON squad"), which became known for its violence against Pine Ridge residents who objected to Wilson's decisions. By February 1973, after protests to the BIA had no effect, tribal members gathered and decided to invite AIM to assist them in halting Wilson's "reign of terror." Word traveled quickly and Wilson reinforced the tribal headquarters in Pine Ridge. At a meeting of tribal members and AIM leaders, after much discussion about proper steps, a tribal elder suggested that AIM bypass the BIA office and tribal headquarters and occupy the village of Wounded Knee. The assembled members agreed, and on February 27, about 200 AIM supporters, led by Russell Means (Oglala) and Carter Camp (Ponca), took over the Catholic Church, a few houses, and the trading post (which contained supplies and a variety of weapons), and established roadblocks and barricades around the town. The next day, members of the GOON squad, federal marshals, and the FBI armed with large-caliber machine guns and armored vehicles surrounded the town. The two sides periodically exchanged fire over the next two months, eventually killing two Native people in the village and wounding others on both sides of the conflict.

The standoff attracted international attention, and prominent supporters of the occupiers included Jane Fonda (known as "Hanoi Jane" for her antiwar activism) and Marlon Brando (who declined his Academy Award for *The Godfather* to bring attention to the situation faced by Native Americans). Angela Davis attempted to visit Wounded Knee but was turned away at a roadblock by the FBI because she was "an undesirable person." The chief spokespeople for AIM, Means and Dennis Banks, presented a short list of demands calling for a congressional investigation into the enforcement of treaties signed with American Indian nations, an investigation of the administrative practices of the BIA, and another investigation into the conditions at Pine Ridge. Hank Adams (Assiniboine-Sioux), who had helped lead the Trail of Broken Treaties March the previous year and drafted its Twenty Point Proposal, was called in to negotiate an end to the standoff. AIM and the government agreed to end the occupation on May 8 and turn in their weapons. Most of the occupiers slipped out of the village on the night of May 7 (with their weapons), and the siege ended the next day.

In the agreement with AIM, the BIA, and the Nixon administration agreed to consider Oglala concerns about their treatment at Pine Ridge and to review the Twenty Point Proposal written by Adams that called for reestablishing tribal sovereignty, respecting treaties, restoring land taken after treaties were signed, protecting Indigenous freedom and culture, restoring rights to tribes that had been "terminated," eliminating the BIA, and establishing a federal commission reporting to the US president and responsible for "preserving equality between the Indians and the federal government." The Nixon administration did as promised but concluded that they could take no action since American Indian policy was a matter for Congress. Little concrete action followed. Wounded Knee II—as some called the occupation of Wounded Knee—identified and raised the visibility of Indigenous issues: unratified treaties for land already taken by the government and by White settlers, long-standing efforts to interfere with Indigenous cultures, and a program of genocide that few would acknowledge.

During the 1960s, while the Civil Rights and Black Power Movements gained worldwide attention for the plight of African Americans and the need for civil rights protections, American Indians were mostly silent. When the March on Washington was organized in 1963, various Indian advocacy groups including the National Council of American Indians (NCAI) declined to participate. In 1968, when King organized the Poor People's Campaign and occupied the National Mall with Resurrection City, only a few Native people joined the protest, and they illustrated their distrust of the movement by camping separately. At issue in their willingness to participate in the protests was the reality of sharply different histories. As Vine Deloria, Jr. (1933–2005), wrote in his 1969 *Custer Died for Your Sins: An American Indian Manifesto*, "when King began to indiscriminately lump together as one all minority communities on the basis of their economic status, Indians became extremely suspicious" (1969, p. 183). Deloria identified two issues. First, the Civil Rights Movement wanted, he said, to obliterate differences. Second, it demanded a new legal instrument—established through civil rights legislation—to bring about social change. Deloria dissented on both counts. First, Native peoples wanted differences to be recognized in order that their particular histories and circumstances were acknowledged. And second, Native peoples already had a legal system in place based on the treaties the tribes had signed preserving their land, fishing, mineral rights, and status as independent nations. What American Indians called for was "mutual respect with economic and political independence" (p. 185).

For Deloria, the Black Power Movement showed some signs of taking what American Indians thought was the right path. They began, he said, to consider "peoplehood." "Peoplehood is impossible without cultural independence, which is, in turn, impossible without a land base" (p. 180). Land, he argued, was the key. "No movement can sustain itself, no people can continue, no government can function, no religion can become a reality except it be bound to a land area of its own" (p. 179). The Civil Rights Movement involved selling "black, white, red, and yellow" people "a bill of goods which said that *equality* was the eventual goal" (p. 179). In practice, Deloria argued, "equality became sameness" and respect for differences was left to the side. The Black Power Movement recognized this and sought the recognition of differences and demanded respect.

"Red Power" entered the political lexicon in 1966 when Deloria and others at the NCAI convention that year used the term "as a means of putting the establishment on." Instead of taking it as a joke, Deloria was "greatly surprised when newspapermen began to take us seriously and even more so when liberals who had previously been cool and unreceptive began to smile at us in conferences" (1970, p. 114). Deloria remained skeptical of the phrase and its implications. "Many of us," he said, "fell into the trap of thinking that power movements . . . were new attempts to revitalize communities. We shortly realized our error. 'Power' became synonymous with demagoguery, and it became more important to scare people than to communicate with them" (p. 104). And though the name stuck, the real lesson was that "power . . . was creating and educating the local community so that it can move forward as a people fully cognizant of themselves" (p. 104).

The differences in how African and Native American peoples were treated were in part the result of particular policies and practices of White culture. "The white man," Deloria said, "forbade the black man to enter his own social and economic system and at the same time force-fed the Indian what he was denying the black" (1969, p. 173). While Blacks were excluded from White culture, denied access to education framed by the dominant culture, and kept primarily apart, American Indians were forcibly assimilated through land redistribution, boarding schools, US citizenship, and finally a systematic effort to terminate Native tribes (as discussed in Chapter 3). At the same time, the dispositions of the dominant culture were contradictory because they both imposed dominant cultural standards on Black communities and affirmed the images of American Indians as "noble savages," demanding that "the Indian don feathers and beads periodically to perform" (p. 172). The result was confusion on the part of the oppressed that manifested in disparate and mostly ineffective protests.

What was needed, Deloria proposed, was a critical understanding of "white culture." "For many Indians," he wrote, "the whites had no culture other than the one of continued exploitation" (p. 189). He explained that "*white* itself is an abstraction of an attitude of mind, not a racial or group reality" (p. 189). As an abstraction, Whiteness lacks a history and a relation to particular places. By giving up ties to their homelands, their languages, stories, and culture knowledge, Europeans in America have no roots. Echoing Du Bois's assessment in "Souls of White Folk," Deloria concluded, "*white culture* destroys other cultures because of its abstractness . . . it is not a culture but a cancer" (p. 188). The solution to racism was not equality but the ability to foster distinct communities on particular lands. European-descended people "are inevitably torn because they have no roots, they do not understand the past, and they have already mortgaged their future" (p. 194).

Deloria was born near the Pine Ridge Reservation, the son of Barbara Sloat and Vine Deloria, Sr., an Episcopal missionary, grandson of Philip Joseph Deloria, cofounder of the Society of American Indians (with Eastman, Parker, Boṇin, Du Bois, and others), and great grandson of *Tipi Sapa* (Great Lodge, who was also called Philip Joseph Deloria), one of the first Native American Episcopal priests. Deloria's aunt, Ella Deloria, was an anthropologist and student of Boas at Columbia University where she completed a PhD. After Vine, Jr. was born, his father transferred the family's tribal affiliation to the Standing Rock Reservation, where he served as a missionary. Vine, Jr., grew up fluent in English and both Lakota and Dakota dialects. He attended reservation schools as a boy but was later sent to an Episcopal boarding school in Minnesota. On graduation, he joined the Marines and served until 1956. He completed a Bachelor of Science degree at Iowa State University and received a degree in theology from Augustana Lutheran Theological Seminary in Illinois in 1963.

In 1964, Deloria became the executive director of the NCAI and effectively increased its membership and visibility among American Indians. He left his position to attend the University of Colorado Law School and completed his law degree in 1970. While a student at Colorado, frustrated by the lack of attention to Indian issues in the social reform movement and by the ongoing efforts of the federal government to eliminate tribes and gain access to tribal lands, Deloria wrote *Custer Died for Your Sins* (1969). The book was widely read and helped set the stage for the protests by Native Americans that began over the next few years. The book challenged the dominant culture and reform movements and called for "a cultural leave-us-alone agreement, in spirit and in fact" (1969, p. 27).

In the years after the publication of *Custer*, Deloria began a long academic career, first at Western Washington University, where he wrote his second book, *We Talk, You Listen: New Tribes, New Turf* (1970), which continued his critiques of the Civil Rights Movement and liberal individualism. He taught at the University of Arizona from 1978–90, where he helped to establish the first graduate degree in Native American Studies, and then taught for a decade at the University of Colorado at Boulder. He published seventeen books, including *God Is Red: A Native View of Religion* (1994), *The Metaphysics of Modern Existence* (1979), and two critiques of Western science and epistemology, *Red Earth, White Lies* (1995), and *Evolutionism, Creationism, and Other Modern Myths* (2002), as well as several books on American Indian law.

While Deloria is often viewed as a religious thinker and not a philosopher, the distinction between religion, philosophy, and practical matters is one that Deloria rejected. At the center of Indigenous life is a formative relationship with the land. Religion, for Deloria, incorporates philosophy and practice and so is not simply abstract reflection on spiritual matters or a moral code, but a concrete way of living-in-relation. "Religions," he wrote in *God Is Red*, "must be more complicated manifestations of the living earth itself and this aspect of religion is something that American Indians of all the peoples on earth represented" (1994, p. 148). While some would choose to focus on economics or politics as the fundamental terms for responding to present problems, Deloria argued that such a starting point misses what is necessary for a truly transformative result. What is necessary is "a radical shift in outlook from our present naïve conception of this world as a testing ground of abstract morality to a more mature view of the universe as a comprehensive matrix of life forms." Such a shift, Deloria said, is "essentially religious" (p. 284). For Deloria, the connection between lands, people, and culture means that "certain lands will create divergent beliefs and practices" (p. 289), a pluralism of "religions" but also a pluralism of "worlds." The ability to set aside abstract notions of religion and philosophy inherited from the West "is not a matter of learning new facts about life, the world, human history, or adopting new symbols and garments." It is rather a matter of adopting a way of life that involves "living on the land, living within a specific community, and having religious people with special powers within that community" (p. 291).

Deloria's claim that in most Native American traditions, land is an active participant in the life of the community connects with his general claim that Indigenous philosophies begin with what has been called "agent ontology," the idea that all things are or are parts of agents, things that act with a purpose. Such agents or persons are the intersection of what Deloria called "power and place," where power is a kind of motivating force that orders activities and place is the complex network of relations that make individuals and groups who and what they are. "Power and place," Deloria concluded, "produce personality." This formula "simply means that the universe is alive, but it also contains within it the very important suggestion that the universe is personal" (Deloria and Wildcat, 2001, p. 23). This ontological starting point then leads to an alternative epistemology as well. If things to be known are themselves agents, then knowing involves not only noting their behavior but also learning their purposes and interests. In the case of knowing other human agents, the process involves observing behavior but also asking questions, listening to answers, and allowing others to make suggestions and ask questions of their own.

In this context, some methods of knowing are viewed as appropriate, others are viewed as problematic, and some are even forbidden. Torture and vivisection of human beings are seen by most as unacceptable methods of gaining knowledge because they involve mistreating the subject of the inquiry. Knowing others, then, is not simply a process of acquiring facts but is a moral activity, guided by values that in turn guide the acquisition and interpretation of facts. There is, in effect, no sharp distinction between facts and values. When personhood is extended to the other-than-human parts of the universe, Deloria continued, the world is recognized as a moral universe: "[t]hat is to say, there is a proper way to live in the universe: There is [moral] content to every action, behavior, and belief" (1999b, p. 46). From this perspective, "all activities, events, and entities are related, and consequently it does not matter what kind of existence an entity enjoys, for the responsibility is always there for it to participate in the continuing creation of reality" (1999b, p. 47).

Knowledge, on this account, is acquired through long experience and cooperation. It is a fallible and open process, ready to engage anomalous experience—experience that does not fit our expectations or current knowledge. An Indigenous philosophy, according to Deloria, recognizes that universal claims are at best limited guides, subject to revision and failure considering the situation—the place—at hand. Such a view does not deny the value of science, but it refuses to grant science the final word over against experience framed by a particular culture and place. While Western experimental science works to extract knowledge from the world, Indigenous ways of knowledge emphasize observation and interaction grounded in a principle of presence and relatedness. In Native "religion," this principle is expressed in the phrase "all my relatives," which is used in ceremonies to invoke all agents including humans, other animals, plants, and the land. Deloria observed, "few people understood that the phrase also describes the epistemology of the Indian worldview, providing the methodological basis for the gathering of information about the world" (p. 52). The principle, he held, encompasses a distinctive metaphysics, ethics, and epistemology and produces a view shared by many American Indian cultures. The agent ontology that grounds this view can be seen as a philosophical position of resistance, undermining claims that demand universal authority but emerge from particular places and peoples. It also demands the accountability of knowers—scientists, politicians, and teachers, among others—and seeks strategies to promote the agency of others. If colonialism marks the social order of dispossession, genocide, and the rise of industrial capitalism, then agent ontology represents a form of decolonizing philosophy that recognizes both a history of oppression and a future of liberation framed by place.

The issues faced by Native Americans in the 1960s and 1970s were, as Deloria said, a consequence of a long history of confused federal policy balanced by ongoing racism framed by changing conceptions of personhood and agency emerging after the Civil War. The "Modern" era of American Indian policy began with the passage of the Indian Reorganization Act in 1934. The bill, largely developed by President Roosevelt's Commissioner of the Bureau of Indian Affairs, John Collier, officially ended the policy of allotment that began with the 1887 General Allotment (or Dawes) Act. The IRA also prevented transferring Indian lands or shares of tribal corporations to anyone but the tribe itself. "The major thrust of the [IRA]," wrote Deloria and his coauthor, Clifford Lytle, "was to minimize the enormous distinction and power exercised by the Department of the Interior and the Office of Indian Affairs" (1983, p. 14). With less interference from Washington, "tribal government was expected to become the rule rather than the exception" (p. 14). The resulting governments, however, were often the product of constitutions that had little to do with the traditions of the people expected to follow them. "Familiar culture groupings and methods of choosing leadership gave way to the more abstract principles of American democracy, which viewed people as interchangeable and communities as geographical marks on a map" (p. 15). One of the results of this policy was the rise of Dick Wilson and the GOON squad at Pine Ridge.

The Second World War ended most of the IRA policies of "experimentation in Indian regeneration" (p. 15) that began in 1934 and, in response to tighter budgets, many of the services designed to alleviate the hardships faced on reservations were eliminated or significantly reduced. Collier, attacked by many critics "who charged him with attempting to institute socialism on the reservations" (p. 16), left the BIA. In 1947, a commission headed by former president Herbert Hoover was charged with reducing the costs of the federal government. The report called for, among other things, giving American Indians "full citizenship by eliminating much of the discriminating legislation that bound them to the federal government" (p. 16), especially legislation that established the reservation system. In 1953, a coalition of budget-cutting conservatives, who believed that government programs undercut Indian success, and liberals, "now ashamed to realize that some of America's laws were reminiscent of the racial restrictions imposed on minorities by [Nazi Germany and its allies]," joined forces to pass House Concurrent Resolution 108. The resolution was not a bill but a statement that indicated the "sense" of Congress that tribes "should be freed from federal supervision and control" (Deloria and Lytle, 1983, pp. 17–18). Tribes who had signed treaties with the US government and so were recognized as nations in the past were "terminated" through an agreement between a voting majority of the tribe and the government. These tribes were no longer "recognized" and could no longer make claims for rights granted in the treaties, including land claims, fishing rights, and hunting rights. Once the tribes were legally disbanded, lands still held by the tribes were sold off and former tribal members each received cash settlements. Also, any support services promised in the treaties were officially eliminated.

The Klamath Tribe of Oregon and the Menominee Tribe of Wisconsin were among the largest tribes terminated. In August 1953, another bill, Public Law 280, was passed permitting "state governments to assume both civil and criminal jurisdiction over Indian reservations" in six Western states (Deloria and Lytle, p. 19). Prior to the law, tribal courts and the federal government shared jurisdiction. The law passed without consultation with the affected tribes and was seen as undermining principles of self-government established by treaties and the IRA. The law was modified in 1968 to include tribal consent, and it still applies only to certain states. In the end, although many tribes escaped the policy, 109 tribes were terminated under Concurrent Resolution 108, most of their lands sold, and more than 13,000 people lost their tribal membership. The policy was not used after President Kennedy took office, though it was not officially set aside until after President Nixon called for its end in 1970.

Philosophical resistance to termination emerged after the Second World War. D'Arcy McNickle (1904–1977) was part of Collier's staff as the IRA was developed and implemented. McNickle, a member of the Salish-Kootenai people raised on the Flathead Indian Reservation in Montana, attended the Chemawa Indian Boarding School in Oregon and, after selling his allotment land on the reservation, attended the University of Montana and Oxford University. After running short of funds in England, McNickle returned to the United States and lived in New York City where he began work on a semiautobiographical novel, *The Surrounded*, published in 1936. While in New York, McNickle attended classes at Columbia University and the New School for Social Research. In 1935, he was hired by the Federal Writers Project and assigned as a writer to the Bureau of Indian Affairs where he helped to implement the IRA and, in 1944, organized the first meeting of the NCAI. In 1954, with the program of termination in full swing, McNickle resigned from the BIA and moved to Colorado where he worked on projects to improve healthcare at the Diné (Navajo) reservation. Finally, in 1965, though he held no academic degree, McNickle became the chair of the anthropology department at the University of Saskatchewan where he completed *Native American Tribalism: Indian Survivals and Renewals* (1973) as well as his posthumously published novel, *Wind from an Enemy Sky* (1978).

In *Native American Tribalism*, McNickle offered a conception of Native American identity that helped to show why the program of the Civil Rights Movement was problematic for Indigenous people. He acknowledged that American Indian identity is "what persists" through change across significantly different tribes and despite cultural and environmental pressure to destroy such identities. Such an identity, he argued, is a particular way in which individuals and groups interact. "As a minority group within the general society, Indians take their cues from their group; they do not regard themselves as deprived members of an affluent society and they do not feel impelled to acquire status in that society" (1973, p. 13). Native individuals may seek particular advantages, he admitted, but "they pursue these ends in order that their own societies may endure" (p. 13). As McNickle noted, these "are the observable facts"; what sustains identity is "a common characteristic of Indian people": "they call themselves Indians, or more precisely, they refer to themselves by their own linguistic designation" (p. 13).

The act of self-naming also establishes boundaries that allow individuals "to retain a sense of who they are" (p. 13). McNickle quoted Fredrick Barth, a social anthropologist, who wrote, "[t]he nature of continuity of ethnic units' [identities] is clear: it depends on the maintenance of a boundary" (quoted in McNickle, 1973, p. 14). McNickle continued, "While scholars dispute among themselves over the question of cultural survival, the people who are the subjects of the dispute continue to think of themselves as Indians, to act like Indians" (p. 14). Despite efforts to assimilate Native peoples, McNickle observed, tribal identities kept "intact the invisible boundary which permitted them to recognize who they were and how to respond to each other" (p. 115). When the call for desegregation became central to social reform in the 1960s, Native people stood by the side. "Segregation . . . was not seen as denial of social status by Indians. They had never aspired to a place in the white man's society, except as individuals might make that choice for themselves" (p. 122). McNickle's view of identity, drawn from the Native American tradition that included Pokagon, Eastman, and Standing Bear, provided a foundation for thinking about self-determination. It is the preservation of lands and culture that is the key to Indigenous survival.

The potential for the reception of Native philosophy by non-Native philosophers was well demonstrated by Felix Cohen in his 1953 essay, "Americanizing the White Man." Cohen (1907–1953) was the son of Morris Cohen, a philosopher at City College of New York, and received his PhD in philosophy from Harvard in 1929 and his law degree from Columbia University Law School in 1931. From 1933 to 1947, Cohen worked for the US Department of the Interior, where he helped to develop the laws that laid the groundwork for the New Deal social programs. He also helped to draft the Indian Reorganization Act and, thanks to a growing interest in American Indian law, he led the Indian Law Survey and produced *The Handbook of Federal Indian Law* (1941), which still serves as a primary resource for lawyers, judges, and tribes. When federal policies began to shift from the IRA to Termination, Cohen resigned from the Interior Department and began a private practice where he successfully argued for voting rights for Native Americans living in Arizona and New Mexico. In his 1952 essay, he declared, "The real epic of America is the yet unfinished story of the Americanization of the White Man, the transformation of the hungry, fear ridden, intolerant men that came to these shores with Columbus and John Smith" (1960, p. 318).

For Cohen, Indigenous people were Americanizing the European immigrants and had already contributed on every level to the development of their lives and culture. By providing new food sources and agricultural techniques, Native Americans provided a means of survival that supported a growing population and economic expansion for the immigrants. Anthropologist Jack Weatherford has documented this line of material influence in *Indian Givers: How the Indians of the Americas Transformed the World* (1988). Native culture also provided models for self-governance. "Politically," Cohen wrote, "there was nothing in the kingdoms and empires of Europe in the fifteenth and sixteenth centuries to parallel the democratic constitution of the Iroquois Confederacy, with its provisions for initiative, referendum, and recall, and its suffrage for women as well as men" (1952, p. 319). He asked, "Is it any wonder that the greatest teachers of American democracy have gone to school with the Indian?" (p. 320).[1]

Native historian Donald Grinde and his coauthor, Bruce Johansen, have documented the likely influence of Native people on the development of the US government in *Exemplar of Liberty: Native America and the Evolution of Democracy* (1991) and Scott L. Pratt has considered the influence of Native American thought on the development of European American philosophy in *Native Pragmatism* (2002). Cohen concluded that "[a]s yet, few Americans and fewer Europeans realize that America is not just a pale reflection of Europe—that what is distinctive about America is Indian, through and through" (1952, p. 316). Historians and philosophers trained in European traditions "have not seen that American Indians today... are still teaching America to solve perplexing problems of land-use, education, government, and human relations, problems to which Europe never did find adequate answers" (p. 318).[2]

As Native issues became more visible, philosophers began to seek ways of engaging Native thought. One of the first Native thinkers to be taken up was Black Elk (1863–1950). Black Elk was a well-respected Oglala *wicasta wakan* (holy man) who, in 1930, dictated his autobiography to poet John Neihardt, who translated, edited, and published it in 1932. *Black Elk Speaks* tells his story from childhood until the beginning of the twentieth century, giving the perspective of someone who witnessed the defeat of Custer's Seventh Cavalry, the coming of the railroad to the West, and the aftermath of the Wounded Knee Massacre. As part of his story, he told Neihardt about the "spiritual" character of his people and his own spiritual journey as a boy and young man. The combination of narrative and reflections on larger meaning provided some philosophers a point of entry into one interpretation of Native thought.

Bruce Wilshire, in *The Primal Roots of American Philosophy: Pragmatism, Phenomenology and Native American Thought* (2000), argued for a "convergence" in the work of central figures in the European American tradition such as Thoreau, Emerson, James, Dewey, and others, with the implicit philosophical outlook presented in Black Elk's translated writings. "None of them," wrote Wilshire, "is caught up in modernism's dualisms, its divisions, such as mind versus body, spirit versus matter, scientific or real knowledge of this-here physical world versus superstitious belief in a nonphysical world off-there" (2000, p. 4). As a result, these philosophers, including Black Elk, "agree that fullness of life cannot derive from what's disclosed by the ever-growing class of scientific experts" (p. 4); rather, "the spiritual" is physical, found in experience, and leads to a better and different understanding of nature, human and otherwise.

Neihardt's work and Black Elk himself have been subjected to particular scrutiny because, though he was a holy man in an Indigenous tradition, Black Elk was also a Catholic convert and served as a deacon. Some have decided, in this light that *Black Elk Speaks* (which also suffers from inaccurate translations and additions by Neihardt) ought to be set aside as an example of Native philosophy. Despite the controversy, however, many have offered ways to understand Black Elk's apparent dual commitment to both Indigenous and European religions. In his introduction to an edition of *Black Elk Speaks*, Deloria argued that the book (both in spite of and because of its history) is a religious classic. What is most significant about the book, however, is not its reception by non-Natives but rather its influence "upon the contemporary generation of young Indians who have been aggressively searching for roots of their own in the structure of universal reality" (1999a, p. 233). Black Elk, he said, "shared his visions with John Neihardt because he wished to pass along to future generations some of the reality of Oglala life and... to share the burden of visions that remained unfulfilled" (p. 233).

Part of the Termination program included the passage of the Indian Relocation Act of 1956. The policy provided federal support for Indians to leave their reservations and find work in cities. The result was that large numbers of Native Americans left the impoverished conditions of rural reservations to live in cramped urban housing projects with few job opportunities. Problems quickly emerged as racism against American Indians combined with the experience of displacement, unemployment, and limited access to education. In Minneapolis, a group of young Native leaders, including Dennis Banks and Clyde Bellecourt, started AIM in 1968 to actively address the problems faced by urban Indians. Like other protest movements at the time, AIM sought to bring public attention to the plight of the oppressed. Among its early activities, AIM established a center dedicated to providing legal assistance to American Indians, and "survival schools" that offered a culture-based curriculum for Native children and youth. AIM also became involved in very visible protests, including the 1969 occupation of Alcatraz Island and the 1970 occupations of Mount Rushmore and a replica Mayflower, built as part of the three hundred and fiftieth anniversary of the Pilgrims' landing at Plymouth. In 1974, women who had been involved in the work of AIM established their own organization, Women of All Red Nations (WARN), as a response to growing "awareness of the distinctive gendered experiences of Indian men and women at the hands of the U.S. government" (Josephy et al., 1999, p. 51). AIM, WARN, and other organizations took the lead in a variety of protests in the 1970s.

The year before the Wounded Knee occupation, AIM and WARN helped to lead the Trail of Broken Treaties, a caravan of protesters in cars and trucks that began in California and was set to end in Washington, D.C., on the eve of the 1972 presidential election. On the way, Hank Adams, with input from the protesters, crafted the Twenty Point Proposal that Deloria described as "the best summary document of reforms put forth in this century" (Josephy et al., 1999, p. 50). In particular, it sought to repeal the 1871 Indian Appropriations Act that ended treaty-making with American Indian tribes. The protest arrived in Washington on time but found that arrangements had not been made to house the protesters. Instead, they went to the headquarters of the BIA and demanded a place to stay. When the BIA refused, the protesters stayed, occupying the headquarters for a week, destroying many of the offices and a significant number of documents related to carrying out treaty agreements.

The Trail was followed in 1978 by the Longest Walk, which also began in San Francisco and ended in Washington, D.C., and was intended to symbolize "the forced removal of Indians from their homelands and to draw attention to a growing backlash in government and in the country against Indian treaty rights" (Josephy et al., 1999, p. 53). The Nixon administration dismissed the central issues of the Twenty Points Proposal by concluding that, thanks to the 1924 Citizenship Act, the federal government was prohibited from relating to American Indians by treaties. "The citizenship relationship with one's government and the treaty relationship are mutually exclusive; a government makes treaties with foreign nations, not with its own citizens" (Deloria, 1974, p. xii).

The protests by American Indians, however, appeared to have some impact. When President Nixon declared the end of the Termination policies of the 1950s, he also declared the beginning of a new era that came to be called "self-determination." Congress passed, with much support from Native and non-Native advocacy groups, the central legislation of the new policy in 1975, the Indian Self-Determination and Education Assistance Act. The new law required that tribes have the right to contract for basic services, including education and health care, rather than having those services provided more or less by the BIA. As a result, individual tribes were able—many for the first time since they were forced onto reservations—to decide on their own priorities and programs.

Even as Congress was reforming Indian policy, the US courts were responding to more and more frequent legal cases begun by tribes and individual American Indians. For example, in 1973 the United States Justice Department filed suit against the State of Washington for Washington's infringement on Native fishing rights. The suit followed several years of active lobbying by Northwest tribes and a long series of protests against fishing restrictions imposed on members of tribes whose treaties with the United States guaranteed access to traditional fishing waters. Judge George H. Boldt heard the case and decided in favor of the tribes, granting fishing rights and the ability to take half of the fish harvest each year. The decision also reinforced the status of tribes as self-governing nations as well as the general principles of self-determination. As Charles Wilkinson concluded, "By the mid 1970s . . . tribal action on many different fronts had fundamentally reshaped the circumstances that held sway just a generation before" (2005, p. 205). Congress had replaced termination with self-determination, the federal government had responded to Native activism, and judges "took the trouble to plumb the historical roots and true meanings of treaties and other laws that at first blush seemed to contradict American notions of equality" (p. 205).

In 1984, Robert Bunge (1930–1996), a philosopher and head of American Indian Studies at the University of South Dakota, published *An American Urphilosophie: An American Philosophy BP (Before Pragmatism)*. Bunge was born and raised on the Rosebud Reservation in South Dakota, and his first language was Lakota. He received a PhD in philosophy from De Paul University and taught in the Department of Modern Languages at South Dakota. *An American Urphilosophie* was written "to demonstrate that a fully developed, if unwritten, philosophy—or, rather, philosophies—flourished on American soil long ages before the Europeans came here and continues to exert influence even today over the minds and hearts of thousands of American aborigines" (1984, p. 1). Using divisions drawn from Western philosophy, Bunge presented an interpretation of the philosophy of the Teton Sioux, discussing cosmology, epistemology, metaphysics, ethics, logic, and language.

What is most distinctive about Bunge's approach is that he examined Indigenous philosophy in light of its original language. The central principles of Lakota philosophy are called "*wakan$_t$*"—the name for "what is not understandable" and for "power" or action (pp. 72, 74)—and "*Wakantan$_t$ka*"—the "Great Mystery" (p. 25) and great power. The principles, like Deloria's "agent ontology," are both epistemic and ontological and require continuity between what a thing is and what it is known as. "The Lakota, and this writer also," he wrote, "have always had trouble accepting the 'either-or,' 'neither-nor,' propositions of the European two-valued logical orientation" (p. 51). To assert sharp distinctions (this is a tree and nothing else) ignores the limits of knowledge claims marked by *wakan$_t$*. And to suppose that a particular thing is what it is independent of its other relations ignores the ontological implications of *wakan$_t$*, the "mysterious" reality of being. At the same time, the principles also demand recognition of real boundaries and limits for knowledge. The power of something distinguishes it from other things and establishes its limits. The resulting view is one in which contradiction flourishes and where the activities of agents or persons organize and stabilize "areas of lived experience" (p. 51). "[T]he universe of the tribe," he concluded, "was personally upheld by the participation of every member in recreating and sustaining this universe. . . . Collectively and individually [the members] maintained the universe in working order" (p. 53).

## American Philosophies

In relation to the limits and possibilities of knowledge, the Lakota held that there were multiple forms of knowledge that, from a Western perspective, could be divided roughly along a continuum from mundane knowledge to supernatural thought, though the distinction "is made here to make Lakota philosophical assumptions intelligible to minds accustomed to thinking in categories of traditional European philosophy." In fact, "[t]he natural and supernatural worlds impinge and interpenetrate each other to a degree such that no real separation can be made" (p. 61). "All knowledge has its source ultimately with and in *Wakantan ka* and is transmitted to man in various ways" (p. 61).

Bunge concluded by observing that while some would see Lakota society as "backward regarding science and technology," they nevertheless developed "some very advanced ideas about how to live in harmony with the universe and its people, both animals and human. The time may not be far off when the Lakota and Native Americans generally become the teachers instead of the taught" (p. 179). From the Lakota perspective, philosophy is central to such harmony because it is "a life-style that continues despite all vicissitude and genocide, singularly strong and pervasive despite social and economic hardship" (p. 179). In order to attain such a lifestyle, Bunge argued, philosophers must take seriously what he calls the problem of language. Agreeing in many ways with Neurath and Carnap (discussed in Chapters 16 and 17), he wrote, the "real problem . . . is that language unconsciously or subconsciously forces down a grid upon the understanding and perceptions of the speaker of any particular language to a degree largely unsuspected and unappreciated" (p. 182). "There are," Bunge concluded, "multiverses of languages; although these multiverses are similar insofar as they are all human, nevertheless important differences do exist regarding how these multiverses are perceived through the filter of language" (p. 182). Native American philosophy provides both examples of such diversity and a philosophical means of engaging that diversity.

The federal Indian Relocation program also set the stage for another developing branch of Native American philosophy. Gerald Vizenor (Anishinaabeg and a member of the Chippewa of the White Earth Reservation) was born in Minneapolis where his father had been moved as part of the Indian Relocation Program. His father was murdered in 1936, and young Vizenor lived with various family members until he was eighteen when he enlisted in the army in time to serve in the Korean War. He was then stationed in Japan, where he began to write. Upon his return, he attended New York University, finished his BA, and did graduate work at the University of Minnesota. From 1964 until 1968, Vizenor served as director of the American Indian Employment and Guidance Center in Minneapolis, where he found the work of AIM to be less about the needs of Native people and more about the visibility of AIM's leaders. He worked as a journalist for the *Minneapolis Tribune* for two years and, after additional study at Harvard, became the director of the Native Studies program at Bemidji State University and later a professor at UC Santa Cruz and then UC Berkeley. He self-published his first poetry collection, *Two Wings and the Butterfly: Haiku Poems in English* (1962), and followed with his first novel, *Darkness in Saint Louis Bearheart* (1978). As a poet and novelist with a background in Western literature, Vizenor brought a sharply different perspective to the issues faced by Native Americans.

In his 1994 volume, *Manifest Manners: Postindian Warriors of Survivance*, Vizenor proposed a framework to understand the circumstances of Native people. Calling on the work of contemporary European theorists, especially Jean Baudrillard, he argued that Indians, as

Native and non-Natives alike experienced them, were "simulations." He called such simulations "manifest manners," a play on the idea of Manifest Destiny, the idea that Anglo-Saxons were destined to inherit the American continents. Manifest manners were the practices and ways of talking and thinking about the history of America and its Indigenous residents. Because these manners come to frame not only how the history unfolded but also how it is understood, "simulations of manifest manners are treacherous and elusive in histories . . . the most secure simulations are unreal sensations, and become the real without a referent to an actual tribal remembrance" (1994, p. 8). "Tribal realities," he said, "are superseded by simulations of the unreal, and tribal wisdom is weakened by those imitations, however sincere" (p. 8). Simulations, he said quoting Baudrillard, are "not simply to feign"; to feign is to make believe or pretend, as when one "feigns an illness." Rather, "Someone who simulates an illness produces in himself some of the symptoms." Feigning "leaves the principle of reality intact: the difference is always clear, it is only masked." Simulation, on the other hand, "threatens the difference between 'true' and 'false'; between 'real' and 'imaginary'" (p. 13).

In response to the effort to obscure and eliminate tribal realities, Vizenor posited the work of Native survivance; that is, "more than survival, more than endurance or mere response," survivance is "an active presence" (1998, p. 15). Survivance takes the form of stories that remember the tribal past and instruct present generations in what Vizenor called "sovenance," "that sense of presence in remembrance, that trace of creation and natural reason in native stories . . . native presence . . . not a romance of an aesthetic absence of victimry" (p. 15). From this perspective, "postindian" warriors are those who operated in the realm of simulations and whose activism was only a simulation of survivance. As simulations—not fakes—postindians take on the "symptoms" of the "real" as manifested in the history of dominance and oppression. Their resistance is "real" resistance, but not resistance to the system of domination; it is rather part of the system. The result is that postindians and the simulations of Native people he calls "*indian*" do not present the real situation faced by Native people, but the absence of Native people and their circumstances. The simulations, when recognized as such, show that Native people have been forgotten. In response to such forgetting, Vizenor argued for "transmotion," "that sense of native motion and an active presence, [that is] sui generis sovereignty . . . survivance, a reciprocal use of nature, not a monotheistic, territorial sovereignty" (p. 15). Sovereignty on this account is "in the visions of transformation: the humor of motion as survivance over dominance; the communal movement to traditional food sources; dreams and memories as sources of shared consciousness," stories, myths, memories of migration, "the spiritual and herbal powers to heal and locate lost souls" (p. 184). In short, though obscured by simulations of manifest manners, a distinctive Indigenous reality persists that should contravene postindian activism and make possible the restoration or perhaps the reemergence of Native America.

Vizenor's concern about the contrary movements of *Indian* simulations and the active pursuit of sovereignty is framed differently in the work of Dale Turner in *This Is Not a Peace Pipe: Towards a Critical Indigenous Philosophy* (2006). Turner argued that despite the separation between the images of Native people in the context of the dominant culture, Native peoples want to assert their differences and their sovereignty in their necessary political relations with Western governments in Canada and the United States. That is, "*If* Aboriginal peoples want to assert that they possess different world views," they will have to engage the legal and political discourses of the state effectively (2006, p. 5). While Turner, a member of the Temagami First

Nation in Ontario, wrote primarily about the situation faced by Indigenous people in Canada, his general argument has been taken up by others concerned with Indigenous sovereignty in the United States as well. Developing his view as a means of fostering pluralism among Native and settler peoples, Turner's work emerged out of the Canadian philosophical context framed both by First Nations rights and the ongoing independence movement of French-speaking Quebec. Philosophers including Charles Taylor, James Tully, and Will Kymlicka argued for a conception of individual identity that could be compatible with both liberal individualism and the recognition of the rights of groups. Turner argued that such liberal theories fail to address the problems of First Nations peoples because they "do not adequately address the legacy of colonialism," they "do not respect the sui generis nature of indigenous rights," they do not question the state's "unilateral claim of sovereignty," and they do not recognize that "a meaningful theory" is "impossible without Aboriginal participation" (p. 7). This last reason, Turner concluded, is the fundamental problem. Participation is blocked because "most Aboriginal peoples still believe that their ways of understanding the world are, de facto, radically different from Western European ways of understanding the world" (p. 7).

In response to the problem of participation, Turner argued for the need for "a group of indigenous intellectuals" who can "reconcile the forms of knowledge rooted in the indigenous communities with the legal and political discourses of the state" (p. 7). Using a phrase coined by Vizenor, Turner called these Indigenous intellectuals "word warriors." These intellectuals operate as interpreters—"thirds" of the sort suggested by Peirce and Royce—who "listen to their 'indigenous philosophers' while engaging the intellectual and political practices of the dominant culture" (p. 8).

The work of word warriors involves at least three philosophical projects. The first is the effort to understand Indigenous philosophies—"the normative source of indigenous difference"—as they are "articulated in indigenous languages (usually oral) by those who are recognized in their communities as keepers of these distinct ways of knowing the world" (p. 9). At the same time, the project of word warriors must include Indigenous intellectuals who "are educated in Western European philosophy and who engage its ideas on its own terms" (p. 9). The work also requires Indigenous intellectuals who will take up the history of Western thought as both "philosophy and political activity." These histories are necessary to reveal "Western European philosophy as a colonial activity" and so make a "critical space for indigenous voices in mainstream academia" (p. 9). The project, Turner concluded, requires a "division of intellectual labor that essentially delineates two kinds of intellectual leaders" (p. 119). The first group consists of "Indigenous philosophers" whose work preserves Indigenous communities "*as distinct peoples.*" The result, he concluded, is a kind of "indigenous essentialism" (2006, p. 119). The second group of intellectuals is the word warriors who are "intimately familiar with the legal and political discourses of the state while remaining citizens of indigenous nations" (p. 119).

As Turner himself serves as a word warrior, other recent thinkers also appear to take up similar work. Lee Thurman Hester (Choctaw) argued in *Political Principles and Indian Sovereignty* (2001) that theory needs to be set aside in favor of direct engagement with the inconsistencies between the established principles accepted by the US government and the treatment of American Indians. This sort of engagement will not be philosophical in the disciplinary sense, he said, because the discipline of philosophy has become overspecialized and technical and so inaccessible to the very people for whom it might make a difference.

Instead, Hester offered philosophical reflection framed by a set of overt practical goals in response to the concrete problems faced by Indigenous peoples.

Sandy Grande, a Quechua woman whose people are from the central Andes in South America, argued in *Red Pedagogy: Native American Social and Political Thought* (2004) for a conception of sovereignty and self-determination that, like Turner's, begins with "the tribe, the people, the community; the perseverance of these entities and their connection to indigenous land and sacred places" (p. 57). Just as Deloria made the process of sovereignty one that is necessarily bound to a land, Grande concluded "the vision of tribal stability—of community stability—rests in the desire and ability of indigenous peoples not only to listen to each other but also to listen to the land" (p. 57). Grande's particular project developed in response to educational theories informed by Marxism and the work of Michel Foucault. These critical theories, while they challenged the oppressive subjectivities produced by industrial capitalism and modernism, produced a theory of education that fell short of producing a way of teaching and learning that would address the circumstances of Native life in the Americas. By leaving out indigeneity, the role of Indigenous people as grounded, bound to a land and a more-than-human community, critical theories are unable to account for Indigenous identity, its value, and the means of fostering it.

Rather than adopt theories developed only in Western thought and culture, Grande argued for an "indigenous theory of subjectivity . . . that addresses the political quest for sovereignty, the socioeconomic urgency to build transnational coalitions, and creates the intellectual space for social change" (p. 118). Such a theory will occupy a "fourth space" that stands outside the space framed by Western nations and their borderlands. "Indigenous communities preceded the nation-state," but unlike those who occupy borderlands as a consequence of colonization—Grande cited Anzaldúa as an example—Indigenous people only appear to be border-crossers. When their original relation to the land is recognized, they emerge as outside both nations and borderlands. Decolonization, for Grande, is a process of realizing that "fourth space."

> The proposed construct of *indígena* is intended to guide the search for a theory of subjectivity in a direction that embraces the location of Native peoples in the "constitutive outside." Specifically, it claims a distinctively indigenous space shaped by and through a matrix of legacy, power, and ceremony. In so doing the fourth space of *indígena* stands outside the polarizing debates of essentialism and postmodernism. (p. 171)

Grande defines sovereignty as a "project organized to defend and sustain the basic right of indigenous peoples to exist in 'wholeness' and to thrive in their relations with other peoples" (p. 171). The definition is suggested by Taiaiake Alfred, Kahnawake Mohawk, in *Peace, Power, Righteousness* (1999/2009). For Alfred, sovereignty is a process that emphasizes distinct communities taken as wholes marked by a shared culture that fosters open communication, respect, and trust. From such a position of strength and unity, Indigenous peoples would also develop connections—social, political, and economic—with other communities. Indigenism, Alfred concluded, "is not a politically expedient kind of pan-Indianism, or the assimilative ideology . . . common in Latin American countries." Indigenism is rather a view that "brings together words, ideas, and symbols from different indigenous cultures to serve as tools for those involved in asserting nationhood." The view does not "supplant the local cultures of individual communities" but fosters them by providing a shared means of resistance that makes room for positive and pluralistic practices of decolonization (2009, p. 112).

Along with Turner and Hester, Viola Cordova (1937–2002) and a few others are Indigenous North Americans who are also philosophers within the academic discipline of philosophy. Cordova (Apache) was born in New Mexico and raised in Taos. She completed a BA at Idaho State and eventually attended the University of New Mexico, where she became one of the first Native American women to receive a PhD in the field. Her posthumously published volume of essays, *How It Is* (2007), provides examples of the sort of intellectual work sought by Turner. In answer to the question "Why Native American philosophy?" Cordova argued that Native American culture, like every other cultural group, "provides three definitions around which they build all subsequent determinations about the world they live in" (2007, p. 1). These definitions frame the world, what it is to be human, and the "role of a human in that world" (p. 1). To think that a single philosophical tradition has all the answers is a mistake, she said. "The challenge to find a way to live on the earth without wrecking it is so great, that we cannot afford to limit ourselves to only one way of thinking" (p. 2). For Cordova, "philosophy is a methodological endeavor," a particular kind of doing, so the processes of "analyzing Native American thought will be no different than those used to analyze other forms of human thought" (p. 3).

In 1996–7, Cordova became a Rockefeller Visiting Research Fellow at Lakehead University in Ontario, where Dennis McPherson and J. Douglas Rabb helped to begin the first graduate degree in Indigenous philosophy. The program began in response to a call by First Nations students for a program in which they could more formally study their own philosophical traditions. According to McPherson, the call for the program was not an effort to avoid studying Western philosophy, but rather a chance to study Indigenous traditions and to use the resources of these traditions for examining Western philosophy. The program was closed in 2001 for reasons of enrollment and cost, according to the institution. According to others, it closed for reasons related to the University's lack of interest in engaging Native people on any but the University's own terms.

Despite the fate of the graduate program, McPherson and Rabb were instrumental in making Native philosophy accessible to Native and non-Native students in both Canada and the United States. In 1993, they published *Indian from the Inside: Native American Philosophy and Cultural Renewal*, as a collaborative project coauthored by McPherson, an Ojibwa and member of the Couchiching First Nation, and Rabb, a non-Native person. McPherson and Rabb argued from what they called a "polycentric perspective," affirming the principle that "every view is a view from somewhere." They argued that the "fact that different cultures can have radically different worldviews reveals something very interesting not just about culture, not just about language, but about reality itself and the way in which we can come to know it" (2011, p. 20). Such a view rejects the idea that one can encounter the world "objectively," free of operating prejudices and stereotypes, but instead holds that experience is necessarily framed by prejudgments and categories that give it meaning. Such "relativism" is objective, according to McPherson and Rabb, because experience in a particular culture is framed by shared norms even as the experience also stands alongside the experience within another culture that is also objective. McPherson and Rabb offer evidence for the acceptability of polycentrism as a philosophical starting point by citing Western philosophers such as Mark Johnson. They also cite the "traditional Native American value closely related to interventive-noninterference"—a means of providing guidance without coercion—"and respect for difference" (p. 121). Like Bunge's work, *Indian from the Inside* represented an attempt to bring together the resources of Western philosophy and those of Indigenous philosophy, not just to affect what one knows, but to transform how one is and how one engages others and the wider world.

In the evening hours of November 20, 2016, law enforcement officers from the Morton County Sheriff's Department in South Dakota clashed with 400 protesters in below-freezing temperatures at a construction site along the Dakota Access Pipeline (DAPL). DAPL is a 1,172-mile-long pipeline that carries crude oil from the Bakken oil fields of North Dakota to a shipping terminal in Illinois. The initial protesters were members of the Standing Rock Sioux Nation, whose reservation stands just downstream from the pipeline. In April, they had set up a camp across the planned route of the pipeline to protest the project and block construction. The Native protesters were quickly joined by Indigenous people from other tribes and environmental activists from across the country and beyond. Despite the protest and the camp, the Army Corps of Engineers (responsible for issuing construction permits for projects of this sort) gave permission to allow the pipeline to cross a number of bodies of water, including the Mississippi River and the Missouri River just upstream from the Standing Rock reservation. In September, a US District Court judge rejected a lawsuit by the tribe to stop the pipeline. On the night of November 20, police arrived to remove the protesters from their encampment using tear gas, rubber bullets, and fire hoses. Over 300 protesters were injured and 26 people required hospitalization. In December, the Army Corps reversed its position and refused the permit for the pipeline to cross the Missouri. The next month, however, President Donald Trump, in one of his first acts as president, ordered the Army Corps to reverse its position again and allow the pipeline to be completed. The protesters left the camp in February.

The protest marked ongoing Native resistance to colonialism in North America—"a struggle over land and water in which a people were fighting for their lives," as Nick Estes (Lower Brule Sioux) described it. But "it was also a struggle over the meaning of land." In his book, *Our History is the Future* (2019), Estes continues, "For the Octei Sakowin," that is, for the Seven Council Fires of the union of Sioux nations, "the earth cradles the bones of our ancestors." Settler colonialism seeks to remove from the land not only the living tribes and their culture, but also their ties to the land: "their bodies needed to be removed—both from *beneath* and *atop* the soil therefore eliminating their rightful relationship *with* the land" (p. 47).

For Estes, the protests continued the resistance movement of the Ghost Dance prophets who challenged the colonial rule of the United States in the days before the massacre at Wounded Knee in 1890. "The Ghost Dance, in the revolutionary sense, was about life, not death; it was about imagining and enacting an anticolonial Indigenous future free from the death world brought on by settler invasion" (p. 16). The protest against the pipeline was framed by the sort of conception of being presented by Deloria, who echoed the conclusions of his Indigenous philosophical predecessors including Pokagon and Standing Bear. Dina Gilio-Whitaker (Colville Confederated Tribes) summarizes: "As the #NoDAPL [no Dakota Access Pipeline] movement made clear through the slogan 'Water is life,' Native resistance is inextricably bound to worldviews that center not only the obvious life-sustaining forces of the natural world but also the respect accorded the natural world in relationships of reciprocity based on responsibility toward those life forms" (Gilio-Whitaker, 2019, p. 13).

Estes and Gilio-Whitaker are part of a group of Indigenous thinkers committed to the idea of Native resurgence. For many, the history of settler colonialism in North America can only be addressed by demanding the recognition of the dominant culture of Indigenous peoples and their histories. In Canada, this recognition has taken the form of a Truth and Reconciliation Commission (modeled on the TRC formed in South Africa at the end of apartheid). The aim of the Canadian TRC was to provide "those directly or indirectly affected by the legacy of Indian Residential Schools with an opportunity to share their stories and experiences." Such "truth-telling," it was hoped, would provide the chance for Indigenous peoples and the dominant culture to become reconciled, that is, to coexist in harmony. Glen Coulthard (Yellowknives Dene), in *Red Skin, White Masks* (2014), argues that reconciliation converges with the need for recognition as the means to achieve the desired harmony. However, Coulthard holds that recognition—where the dominant culture is made aware of the unfortunate past—does not promote harmonious coexistence but rather is a means to cement the gains of the dominant culture and obscure claims by Indigenous people to their traditional lands.

For Coulthard, the process of recognition reaffirms the established conception of liberalism and its focus on individuals by seeking to free Indigenous people from their collective past in order to achieve individual freedom and success in Canadian society—that is, to reconcile with the dominant culture. Rather than seeking recognition within the dominant culture, Coulthard argues that Indigenous communities ought to reclaim their collective past and seek *self*-recognition (2014, p. 48). The result, according to Coulthard, is a resistance born out of resurgence that aims to set aside the demand for recognition by the dominant society and rebuild Indigenous communities in terms of their shared past and toward a shared, decolonized future.

Coulthard introduces the concept of grounded normativity to capture the alternative moral framework, literally grounded in particular places through revitalized relations with the land and the more-than-human agents that share the place. For Coulthard, Indigenous resurgence seeks to restore the ethical relations of Indigenous communities.

> Ethically, this meant that humans held certain obligations to the land, animals, plants, and lakes in much the same way that we hold obligations to other people. And if these obligations were met, then the land, animals, plants, and lakes would reciprocate and meet their obligations to humans, ensuring the survival and well-being of all over time. (p. 61)

While Coulthard uses the resources of Frantz Fanon and Karl Marx to make a case for resurgence, Leanne Simpson (Michi Saagiig Nishnaabeg) argues that the "intellectual and theoretical home of resurgence had to come from within Indigenous thought systems, intelligence systems that are continually generated in relationship to place" (Simpson, 2017, p. 16). Like Coulthard, Simpson rejects the conceptual framing of Western liberalism as a means of resurgence. Instead, recognition focuses on the history of "*dispossession* as a foundational force in [Indigenous] lives, [an] *expansive dispossession* as a gendered removal of our bodies and minds from our nation and place-based grounded normativities" (p. 43). For Simpson, colonization is a gendered process beginning with the imposition of a binary and hierarchical conception of gender difference. Removal then is not only removal from a place but also the elimination—the dispossession—of one's identity and place in the community.

Heteropatriarchy, for example, forcibly restructures communities, removing women from traditional leadership roles and forcing people who identify with neither men nor women (or identify with both) into one or the other of the acceptable categories, eliminating their traditional roles in the community. Resurgence is the process of reattachment: "Radical resurgence means nonhierarchical relationships between land and bodies, bodies meaning the recognition of our physicality as political orders, and our intellectual practices, emotions, spirituality, and hubs of networked relationships" (p. 44).

In some sense, the occupation of Wounded Knee in 1970 marked the effort of one group of Indigenous people in North America to reestablish relations outside the imposed colonial edifice constructed over centuries. As shown in the protest against the Dakota Access Pipeline and in ongoing Indigenous efforts to reclaim cultures and lands, the settler colonial project continues, and Indigenous philosophies of resistance continue to seek ways to refuse it. The vision of Kicking Bear (Prologue and Chapter 3), a leader of the Ghost Dance movement, predicted the end of settler colonialism and the return of Indigenous peoples, human and more-than-human, to the lands of America. This vision is recalled in the 2021 book, *Red Nation Rising: From Bordertown Violence to Native Liberation*. Nick Estes and his co-authors declare that "the future is Native." They continue:

> We are locked in a fight with settlers whose viciousness and savagery compensate for the precarity their presence makes in lands that do not claim them. This is their kinship. We have burned their villages to the ground before to protect our lands and nations. We will do it again to liberate our relatives. These will not be fires of destruction but of creation and reclamation. Only in the ashes ... will we find the raw material for our liberation. In the name of Native kinship, we will redistribute stolen land and stolen wealth boarded in their bordertowns, and this will create an abundance and equality for all life. Settler colonialism and capitalism interrupted Native kinship. When settlers are gone, we will resume this kinship as a practice and a place. (p. 129)

## Notes

1. Horace Kallen, who was a friend of Morris and Felix Cohen, published "On 'Americanizing' the Indian" in 1958, a harsh criticism of US Indian policy, especially termination, and a case for self-determination based on "anthropological understanding and the American ideal" (p. 472). A self-determination policy, he said, "calls for recognizing and respecting the right of the tribal cultures—and the faiths and the works that express, embody, and fulfill them—to live on" (p. 472).

2. Thomas Alexander, grandson of Hartley Burr Alexander, continued the study of Indigenous philosophies begun by his grandfather (and his father, philosopher Hubert Alexander). In his paper, "The Fourth World of American Philosophy: The Philosophical Significance of Native American Philosophy," Thomas Alexander argued that "American philosophy" must be understood as a narrative, not an account of an "essence." The narrative would include Indigenous origin stories alongside the founding tales and philosophical treatises of European America. When asked by students "What is so American about American philosophy?" he responded that "it is the story of how we got here, who we are, where we are going." He continued: "I give a natural history, a family genealogy, filled with characters, oddballs, geniuses, romantics, cynics, and reformers. I tell a story of emergence, how a people came to inhabit a land" (1996, p. 378). Central to this "family genealogy" are the stories of Native American peoples. These stories reflect a philosophical view

that emphasizes "a range of... themes, such as emergence, community, pluralism, naturalism, the nature of reason as social deliberation rather than individual consciousness, [and] the importance of chance and the precarious in the world" (p. 387).

## Primary Texts

Deloria, Vine, Jr (1999). *Spirit and Reason: The Vine Deloria, Jr., Reader.* Golden, CO: Fulcrum Press.

Coulthard, Glen Sean (2014). *Red Skin, White Masks : Rejecting the Colonial Politics of Recognition.* Minneapolis: University of Minnesota Press.

Simpson, Leanne Betasamosake (2017). *As We Have Always Done : Indigenous Freedom through Radical Resistance.* Minneapolis, MN: University of Minnesota Press.

Estes, Nick et al. (2021). *Red Nation Rising : From Bordertown Violence to Native Liberation.* Oakland, CA: PM Press.

Vizenor, Gerald (1998). *Fugitive Poses: Native American Indian Scenes of Absence and Presence.* Lincoln: University of Nebraska Press.

# CHAPTER 22
# FEMINIST PHILOSOPHY AND PRACTICE

As we have seen in the last few chapters, women participated in and led a variety of resistance movements for civil rights, Indigenous sovereignty, Black and Latinx identity, and farm workers' rights. They began to be aware of related concerns faced by women as women (despite differences among them). Together, the resistance movements of the 1960s ignited a renewed Feminist Movement that added new dimensions. Many women of color saw the struggle for racial equality as their primary struggle and argued that these issues of equality were both a matter of economics and gender.

Angela Davis, already noted in Chapter 19 for her activism in the 1960s, was one of three Black students in her freshman class at Brandeis University. A student of the Frankfurt School philosopher Herbert Marcuse, she eventually earned her PhD in philosophy from Humboldt University in Germany. Davis began teaching philosophy in 1969 at UCLA even as then-Governor Ronald Reagan asked the University system to ban her from teaching in California. She was fired that year for her membership in the Communist Party and then rehired by order of the California Supreme Court. She was fired again a year later. The Regents of the university cited as cause her declaration that her task as a professor was "to unveil the predominant, oppressive ideas and acts of this country [and] to begin to develop not only criticism but positive solutions and to carry out these paths in the universities. Otherwise academic freedom is a real farce" (Davis, quoted in Moore, Jr., 2016, p. 204). Shortly thereafter, she became a fugitive from the law, wanted for purchasing firearms that were used in a courtroom escape attempt that ended in the deaths of three people, including a Superior Court judge. J. Edgar Hoover made Davis the third woman named to the FBI's Ten Most Wanted Fugitive List. She was arrested, served eighteen months in jail, and then was acquitted of all charges.

In *Women, Race, and Class*, published in 1981, Davis provided an analysis of how women's experiences under slavery differed from men's—something that had been overlooked by most scholars. Not included in the prevailing notions of "femininity," given their role as laborers, Black women's female gender was specifically exploited as the shutting down of the slave trade required slave holders to "breed slaves" at a greater rate. Enslaved women were breeders, not mothers. Their distorted lives caused Black women (unlike most White women) to value domestic work and family as important and freeing. In "The Black Woman's Role in the Community of Slaves" (1972), an essay Davis wrote while in jail in 1971, she argued that domestic labor was the only meaningful labor available to slaves. According to Davis, because men and women shared in this labor, it gave rise to greater gender equality in the Black community. The ever-present sexual abuse and assault by White owners, however, added an extra element to the oppression Black women faced. Though this was largely ignored at the time, Davis pointed out that oppression by sexual abuse and assault continued as she noted that rape had also been used by the United States as a weapon of war in Vietnam. Such violence continues to be used by military forces in present-day conflicts.

Davis (as had Cooper before her) went on to point out the complex ways in which the fights to end slavery, reform labor, and gain women's equality were interconnected, even as there was racism present in both the labor and suffrage movements. The end of legal slavery did not change much for the lives of Black women. They either toiled in the fields under debt that kept them virtual slaves, or they entered work in the domestic sphere where they remained cut off from their own families and vulnerable to the sexual advances of the men in the households where they worked. Davis discussed the positive and negative ways in which the prominent figures in the three related movements dealt with the complex ways race, class, and sex intersected in the lives of individuals and groups of people.

While women of color were, and remain, particularly vulnerable to sexual assault, for Black men, the "myth of the black man as rapist" identified by bell hooks and Davis (and discussed in Chapter 19) continued to be perpetuated. Davis criticized some of her White feminist peers for both their "blindness" and their complicity. Similarly, the idea of "birth control," which many feminists thought would unite all women, carried different meanings depending on one's class and race. For Davis, in addition to their role in programs of racial purity in the eugenics movement, birth control and abortion played distinct roles for enslaved women. Rather than bring a child into life as a slave, it was common for enslaved women to end their pregnancies. In light of this history, it was far from obvious that access to abortion was a step toward freedom. For enslaved women, abortion was seen as an act of desperation, not something freely chosen. Similarly, birth control was often presented as a way for women to control reproduction and make sexual freedom possible. Many women saw this as an attack on the family, including many Black women who found strength and community in the family sphere. Birth control also promised to free women for careers and political activism—goals to which few women of color could realistically aspire in the early days of the Feminist Movement. Further, continuing programs of forced sterilization faced by the poor and women of color, past and present, showed the complex ways gender intersects with race and class. These complexities of "women's" experience, however, were not evident to many White feminists in the 1960s.

Similarly, although feminist philosophy identified and critiqued patriarchal social and political structures, and the patriarchal structure of philosophy itself, it took specific challenges to get mainstream feminist theory to name and critique the heteronormative patriarchal structures. We discussed the work of Audre Lorde in Chapter 19. Lorde was an early voice pointing to the need to consider the erotic as a form of knowledge and to take seriously a pluralistic take on sex and sexuality. In a 1985 interview, Lorde talked about the importance of Greenwich Village in the 1950s and 1960s as a space that allowed people to freely express their sex and sexuality and to build community that supported countercultural resistance. Before Lorde, Greenwich Village was an important space for Emma Goldman (see Chapter 10) in the early 1900s and James Baldwin in the 1940s (see Chapter 18). It also gave rise to the Beat generation and the counterculture of the 1960s and early 1970s. Lorde found a safe space in the Village to be out as a lesbian, though she felt she had to keep that part of herself hidden as a student and employee. The gay bars and clubs helped to create a sense of acceptance and provided a place for exploration, though she still experienced racism in the Village.

While Lorde notes that the ideal of the Village was more egalitarian than the reality, it still served to bolster her sense of the possibility of change in the face of the regular raids on gay bars that were prompted by the McCarthyism of the time. Lorde found that many in the gay and lesbian communities in which she found personal support were not interested in politics. While she was busy working in both the Civil Rights and Women's movements, she said many friends were puzzled by these efforts. When asked about the Stonewall Riots that occurred in the Village in 1969, she said it was all of a piece for her. She thought that the Black revolutionary work set the path for other movements; the courage and militancy of the Black movements, both Civil Rights and Black Power, showed that change was a real possibility if action was taken. Lorde saw the Stonewall Riots and the movements that followed (e.g., Pride parades, AIDS activism, marriage equality) as an extension of the possibilities sought by Black activism to the gay, lesbian, and transgender communities (which she also sees as largely rooted in Black culture) (Lorde, 1985).

Stonewall did create change. Sparked by the unrelenting police raids on gay and lesbian bars in the Village, in the summer of 1969 some people chose to fight back. In addition to the illegality of homosexual acts, masquerading as the opposite sex was also a crime. The police raided the popular gay bar the Stonewall Inn and focused on arresting cross-dressers and drag queens. Violence broke out and the police barricaded themselves inside. Riot police arrived and things quieted down until the next night when the Stonewall Inn opened again with the presence of protesters promoting "gay power." This time the police used tear gas and violence, but protesters were undeterred. Over the next few nights, protests continued and the police response abated.

The community formed out of this experience helped to organize the already existing Gay Rights Movement and sparked the first Gay Pride Parade, which began at the site of the Stonewall Inn a year later in June 1970. Other cities followed suit (https://www.history.com/news/stonewall-riots-timeline), and social and political practices slowly changed. For instance, seen by some as a step toward greater acceptance of gay and lesbian service members, Don't Ask Don't Tell (DADT) became official policy in 1994 under President Bill Clinton. Prohibiting discrimination or harassment of closeted homosexuals in the military, it banned openly gay, lesbian, or bisexual persons from serving. This ban was repealed in 2011 under President Obama. Civil Unions began to be legal in 1984, as the AIDS crisis spurred the need for same-sex couples to have hospital visitation rights and spousal benefits. Same-sex marriage then became legal in thirty-five states before it became legal nationwide in 2015. Philosophy also started to change. Journals, articles, and books addressing gender and sexuality began to appear. Some examples include Mary Daly's *Gyn/ecology: The Metaethics of Radical Feminism* (1978); Janice Raymond's *The Transsexual Empire: The Making of the She/Male* (1979); Adrienne Rich's "Compulsory Heterosexuality and Lesbian Existence" (1980); Marilyn Frye's *The Politics of Reality: Essays in Feminist Philosophy* (1983); Audre Lorde's *Sister Outsider* (1984); Jeffner Allen's *Lesbian Philosophy: Explorations* (1986); Janice Raymond's *Toward a Philosophy of Female Affection* (1986); Gloria Anzaldúa's *Borderlands/La Frontera: The New Mestiza* (1986); Sarah Lucia Hoagland's *Lesbian Ethics: Toward New Value* (1988); Eve Sedgwick's *Epistemology of the Closet* (1990); and Monique Wittig's *The Straight Mind and Other Essays* (1992). Much of this work fueled, and was fueled by, the ongoing Women's movement and the growth of feminist philosophy as a legitimate form of philosophy, though there were also tensions.

Not long after Stonewall, in 1973, the life-changing *Our Bodies, Ourselves* was published, giving women a greater sense of ownership over their bodies and their health. This same year was probably the height of the Consciousness Raising Group Movement, with estimates of 100,000 women in the United States participating in such groups. In the wake of this movement, 1974–1979 saw the publication of, among others, Susan Brownmiller's *Against Our Will* (1975), where she identified rape as a masculine ideology; Joanna Russ's (1937–2011) *The Female Man* (1975), which challenged notions of gender; Adrienne Rich's (1929–2012) *Of Woman Born* (1976), in which she argued that women need to reclaim childbearing and child-rearing from male "experts"; and Michelle Wallace's *Black Macho and the Myth of the Superwoman* (1979), in which she described how women remained marginalized in the patriarchal Black Power Movement.

The more mainstream Feminist Movement of the 1960s and 1970s is often referred to as second-wave feminism (the suffrage movement being seen as the first "wave"). It is acknowledged to have been largely a response to the 1963 publication of *The Feminine Mystique* by Betty Friedan (1921–2006). Friedan attended Smith College in 1938 with a major in psychology and did some graduate work in that field. In 1949, she was fired from her job as a journalist because she was pregnant. In *The Feminine Mystique*, Friedan noted that while women had increasing opportunities for education, society still focused on their roles as wives and mothers. Like Addams before her, she identified "the problem that has no name" as the growing dissatisfaction of college-educated women confined to these roles. A wave of consciousness-raising groups for women helped people to rethink the gender roles and expectations of US society. Friedan went on to found the National Organization for Women (NOW) in 1966. From the beginning, NOW worked to fight discrimination based on sex, worked for the enforcement of equal opportunity laws, and was instrumental in passing Title IX of the 1972 congressional Education Amendments meant to guarantee equal educational opportunities (including sports).

Women who were influenced by this work (and the work of French philosopher Simone de Beauvoir) were among the first to break into male-dominated professions, including philosophy. They also established Women's Studies Programs at a variety of colleges and universities. It can be argued that these early accomplishments did much to change the landscape for women, especially in the workplace. Intentionally or not, however, most of the work done by NOW focused on the concerns of White middle-class women. Commonly known as "liberal feminism," this approach to women's equality accepted the classical liberal idea of the individual as a rational, self-interested, autonomous bearer of rights. Liberal feminists did not try to fundamentally change the system, but argued for equal access and opportunities for women within the existing system.

First proposed in 1923, the Equal Rights Amendment (ERA), framed by liberal feminism, was presented to the US Congress by Representatives Martha Griffiths and Shirley Chisholm (later the first Black woman candidate for US president) in 1970. The language of the amendment was simple and straightforward: "Equality of rights under the law shall not be denied or abridged by the United States or by any state on account of sex." The amendment passed both houses of Congress in March 1972 with significant bipartisan support. To become law, the amendment required the approval (ratification) of thirty-eight states. By 1977, only thirty-five of the necessary thirty-eight states had ratified the amendment. It had been actively opposed by Phyllis Schlafly and the campaign she named STOP ["Stop Taking our Privileges"] ERA. She argued that the ERA would take away the exemption of women from military service and preference in child custody cases, among other things, and lead to gender-neutral bathrooms and gay rights. Her group famously delivered freshly baked bread to lawmakers to reinforce the idea that women should be at home (presumably baking bread). Eventually (in 2020), a total of thirty-eight states voted to ratify the ERA despite the congressional deadline of 1982, but in the meantime, six of those states voted to revoke their ratification. The ERA has never been fully ratified.

In 1973, the year following Congress's approval of the ERA ratification process, the Supreme Court established in a seven to two decision a constitutional right to abortion before fetal viability based on the Constitution's Fourteenth Amendment protecting individual privacy. The ruling in Roe v. Wade forced the end of abortion prohibitions that had been established in most states. Feminists saw the ruling as establishing the right of women to control their own bodies in response to a long history of restrictions imposed on women by men in power. The decision in Roe, and legal efforts to require equal rights, also reaffirmed the liberal conception of rights that inspired "first wave" feminism. The resulting changes realized at least some of the reforms long sought by philosophers including Charlotte Perkins Gilman, Jane Addams, and Margaret Sanger, though Gilman and Addams challenged the liberal conception of the self on which some of these reforms rested. Since Roe, there have been continual challenges to, and limitations placed on, the right to abortion, and in 2022, the Supreme Court eliminated the constitutional right to abortion in the six to three decision in Dobbs v. Jackson Women's Health Organization. In the wake of the decision, a majority of states reestablished prohibitions on most abortions, and access to birth control has once again become disputed.

In the midst of work on the ERA and the Roe decision, Gloria Steinem founded *Ms. Magazine* in 1972, in part to advocate for the ERA. A graduate of Smith College, Steinem was first noticed for her publication of "After Black Power: Women's Liberation" (1969). As an author and activist, she worked both within the system in order to make it more inclusive and offered challenges to the dominant White middle-class feminism that tended to accept much of the framework of the heteropatriarchy even as it tried to move (White) women into some traditionally male roles. Steinem also advocated for reproductive rights, gay rights, animal rights, and opposed the Vietnam and Gulf wars.

In *Outrageous Acts and Everyday Rebellions* (1983 with a third edition in 2019), Steinem published a range of her essays taking on body image, pornography, animal ethics, politics, and thinkers such as Alice Walker. Some of her best-known work is recounted: "If Men Could Menstruate," her time undercover as a Playboy bunny, and her early concerns about transexualism (a position she has since revised, signing an open letter in 2021 in support of trans rights). She repeatedly rejected dichotomies: "trying to divide human nature into masculine and feminine, comes from yin-yang, up-down, subject-object, winner-loser, this kind of notion which is in and of itself false. It kills complexity, it kills subtlety, it kills the opportunity to find other solutions" (Friedling, 1996). She also regularly critiqued the notion of power over others that she saw fueling a culture of fear: "We have patriotism, nationalism, capitalism all driving towards fundamentalism to serve these imagined enemies and to get power over the mind, spirit, and body. This power in order to fulfill itself must be void of these things—complexity, ambiguity, and mystery" (Steinem, 2004). In Steinem, we again see the complexity and diversity of the interconnected social concerns within the Feminist Movement.

Just as the Civil Rights Movement, environmental activism, and antiwar protests began to influence the academy, and philosophy in particular, so too did the feminist movements—liberal feminisms, socialist feminisms, radical feminisms, difference/sameness feminisms, women of color feminisms, transfeminisms, and more. Feminist philosophers not only identify with different kinds of feminist theory, they also come out of all the different schools/traditions—analytic, continental, American, Marxist, socialist—and the subdisciplines of philosophy with feminist ethics, feminist political theory, feminist philosophy of science, feminist epistemology, and ecofeminism as the biggest subject areas. Few women pursued PhDs in philosophy until the second half of the twentieth century. Since then, more women have begun to enter the field, though never in great numbers. Today, less than a third of the PhDs in philosophy are earned by women. Women philosophers work in all areas of philosophy now, but some bring a feminist perspective to their work. Much of the work opening philosophy to feminism was done by women who came of age during the feminist movement of the 1960s and 1970s. Because of this, feminist philosophy is still a relatively new field: the first journal of feminist philosophy, *Hypatia: A Journal of Feminist Philosophy*, was not established until the early 1980s.

Feminist philosophers built on the work of the feminist movement and began to raise questions about the historical figures of Western philosophy and their views on women. The inclusion of women and women's perspectives gave rise to both a critique of philosophy and the development of feminist philosophy. For example, Carol Gould edited *Beyond Domination: New Perspectives on Women and Philosophy* (1989), presenting a variety of feminist approaches to issues of value, ontology, science, theology, and oppression. Just a year later, Genevieve Lloyd published *The Man of Reason* (1984), in which she argued that philosophy presented a special problem for women and feminists. The rationalist ideals of philosophy, she argued, called for the transcendence of the feminine and took the model of proper rationality to be masculine.

In 1987, Mary Ellen Waithe began the publication of the four-volume *History of Women Philosophers*, extending the story of European philosophy from early women Pythagoreans in 600 BC to twentieth-century philosophers such as Beauvoir. In addition to recovering the writings of many of these women, Waithe's project also called into question the dominant understanding of Western philosophy. She asked: "Might we come to a different understanding of the nature of philosophy itself as a result of our acquaintance with the ideas of women?" (p. xviii). Elizabeth Spelman published *Inessential Woman: Problems of Exclusion in Feminist Theory* in 1988, highlighting the difficulties of giving a feminist account and critique of the history of Western philosophy, without falling into the trap of universalizing the experience of White middle-class women as if they account for the experiences of all women.

Nancy Tuana's *Women and the History of Philosophy* (1992) continued this discussion, as did the publication of Karen Warren's *An Unconventional History of Western Philosophy: Conversations between Men and Women Philosophers* (2009). While Tuana sought to "expose the ways in which . . . gender biases are woven into the very categories of philosophy" (1998, p. xiv), Warren's project sought to dissolve the "add-women-and-stir" dilemma faced by those who tried to include women philosophers in their teaching. She noted that the problem was misnamed. The project was not to *add* women thinkers but to *include* them. They had been there all along. Her approach paired female and male thinkers based on their common times and topics and framed these with commentary by contemporary women philosophers. Taken together, these works recovered a range of women philosophers who had been part of the Western philosophical tradition but excluded from its history, and provided new feminist interpretations of the received history. This work of historical recovery was a starting point from which many other areas of feminist study were developed.

Some early feminist philosophers challenged dominant approaches to political theory (e.g., Jean Bethke Elshtain's *Public Man, Private Woman* (1981), Davis's *Women, Race, and Class* (1981), Marilyn Frye's *The Politics of Reality* (1983), Alison Jaggar's *Feminist Politics and Human Nature* (1983), Marilyn French's *Beyond Power: On Women, Men, and Morals* (1985), Paula Gunn Allen's *The Sacred Hoop* (1992); Carole Pateman's *The Sexual Contract* (1988), Susan Moller Okin's *Justice, Gender, and the Family* (1989), Iris Marion Young's *Justice and the Politics of Difference* (1990)). As Gilman and Addams had done before, these works critiqued the rational, autonomous, atomistic concept of the individual connected with social contract theory and put forward new notions of a social individual and relational autonomy. They challenged the public/private divide and offered alternative conceptions of family and community.

In 1982, Carol Gilligan's *In a Different Voice*, gave rise to the field of the ethics (and politics) of care. Gilligan challenged the long-standing Kantian model of moral development and contended that humans needed to learn to think more in terms of relationships. This was followed by many feminist philosophers raising similar concerns but more specifically addressing ethics (e.g., Sara Ruddick's *Maternal Thinking: Toward a Politics of Peace* (1989), Sara Lucia Hoagland's *Lesbian Ethics* (1988), Claudia Card's *Feminist Ethics* (1991), Virginia Held's *Feminist Morality* (1993)). These are just a few examples of the work in these fields.

Taking a somewhat different focus, Judith Butler published *Gender Trouble* in 1990. Butler, born in Cleveland, attended Bennington College and Yale University, where she completed a PhD. Drawing on her early essay, "Performative Acts and Gender Constitution: An Essay in Phenomenology and Feminist Theory," Butler sought to raise questions about "what will and will not constitute an intelligible life, and how do presumptions about normative gender and sexuality determine in advance what will qualify as the 'human' and the 'livable'" (1999, p. xxii). She also raised political questions related to power and autonomy. She noted that male autonomy is actually based on female dependence. "[T]hat process of meaning-constitution," she wrote, "requires that women reflect that masculine power and everywhere reassure that power of the reality of its illusory autonomy" (p. 57). She stressed the notion of gender as, at least in part, a learned performance and also discussed ideas of agency. From this perspective, gender is not something that exists in advance as an essence, but is something that is routinely performed and can change as the performance of it changes. "[G]ender," she wrote, "is an act which has been rehearsed, much as a script survives the particular actors who make use of it, but which requires individual actors in order to be actualized and reproduced as reality once again" (1990, p. 227). Butler credited the work of people like Kate Bornstein, who wrote *Gender Outlaw* in 1994 and *Gender Outlaws* in 2010, for further complicating notions of gender with the inclusion of transgender and transsexual persons. Butler continued to write on these issues, and some of her work includes *Bodies That Matter* (1993), *The Psychic Life of Power* (1997a), and *Excitable Speech* (1997b).

Though Butler's work is deeply influenced by philosophy in the continental tradition, her work—like other American continental thinkers—nevertheless responds to lived circumstances, especially those grounded in American experiences. The 9/11 attacks and their aftermath provided both a disruption of the community and a demand to reconsider how to understand the United States in a new, demandingly pluralistic world. In her book *Precarious Life: The Power of Mourning and Violence* (2003), Butler said explicitly that she was writing in the aftermath of 9/11 as a "response to the conditions of heightened vulnerability and aggression that followed from these events" (2003, p. xi). Instead of taking the opportunity to rethink the United States's role in the global community, "heightened nationalist discourse, extended surveillance mechanisms, suspended constitutional rights, and developed forms of explicit and implicit censorship" were the response. She further noted that "These events led public intellectuals to waver in their public commitment to principles of justice and prompted journalists to take leave of the time-honored tradition of investigative journalism" (p. xi). Instead of pushing back, they were largely compliant in the use of fear, racism, and sexism to justify dehumanization and the silencing of the discourse necessary for democracy.

In *Undoing Gender* (2003), Butler again pointed to the tendency in the United States to respond to human vulnerability to violence by making even stronger appeals to sovereignty in the name of security. She suggested that an alternative would be to acknowledge that vulnerability and use it as a way to understand human interconnectedness. She argued that when "we commit violence, we are acting upon another," and that "we all live with this particular vulnerability. . . . The fact that our lives are dependent on others can become the basis of claims for nonmilitaristic political solutions" (p. 22). The response she had in mind is one that is incomplete and provisional rather than final and complete.

> [P]erhaps there is some other way to live in such a way that one is neither fearing death, becoming socially dead from fear of being killed, or becoming violent, and killing others, or subjecting them to live a life of social death predicated upon the fear of literal death. Perhaps this other way to live requires a world in which collective means are found to protect bodily vulnerability without precisely eradicating it. (p. 231)

Butler's *Frames of War: When is Life Grievable?* (2009) extended the analysis of these earlier works to take a deeper look at torture by focusing on the interdependency of persons. In this context, despite noting in *Undoing Gender* the importance of Cornel West's work and "the continuing relevance of the tradition of American pragmatism for contemporary struggles for racial equality and dignity" (2005, p. 245), in *Frames of War* she rejects pragmatism and progressivism (2009, p. 148) as affirming a "dyadic" framework. Pragmatism, she claimed, attempts to respond to divisions by positing a more inclusive framework; progressivism relativizes difference to a place in the development of the *sine qua non* of liberal democracy. While her latter assessment may echo our earlier discussions of progressivism (in contrast to the "lateral progress" of Jane Addams), her account of pragmatism seems to miss the point of the tradition—West's version in particular.

Butler's conclusion, in fact, seems very much in line with pragmatism as a philosophy of resistance. For Butler, the shared dependency and vulnerability of all humans make an us/them, either/or way of thinking incoherent. She concluded that the academic discipline of the humanities has a large role to play in shaping a new kind of discourse. Humanists need to

> reinvigorate the intellectual projects of critique, of questioning, of coming to understand the difficulties and demands of cultural translation and dissent, and to create a sense of

the public in which oppositional voices are not feared, degraded or dismissed, but valued for the instigation to a sensate democracy they occasionally perform. (2009, p. 151)

This conclusion is clearly in line with much of the pluralist and pragmatist strains of American philosophy. One reason for Butler's failure to see this connection is the limited understanding of the thinkers in the American tradition available in the mainstream of philosophy. Without these resources available, her work was instead based largely on the writings of theorists in French philosophy. Butler couched much of this work in terms of questioning epistemic and ontological regimes instead of working out of lived experience. The approach nevertheless shared its epistemic interests with ongoing work in feminist epistemology.

The 1970s efforts to pass the Equal Rights constitutional amendment and the dramatic transformation in women's lives made by the Supreme Court decision in Roe v. Wade in 1973 brought attention to the place of women in the professions in general and in the work of science in particular. The resulting concerns were framed by Sandra Harding as the "woman question in science," that is, the question of the status and presence of women in the fields of science. For Harding, this practical question gave way to the more serious critical question of whether science itself was irredeemably masculinist in its structure and practice. Efforts to respond to the second question—"the feminist question in science"—gave rise to a range of philosophical investigations of the idea of scientific knowledge and the conditions of its creation (Harding, 1986). Could science, for example, be objective if it corrected for its masculinist history and took up questions of concern primarily for women? Given the presence of bias in the process of knowing, is objectivity in science even possible, or does the idea of objectivity need to be reconceived?

Such focused questions for feminist theory, framed in terms of the concerns and methods developed in analytic philosophy over the previous two decades, became known as feminist epistemology and looked at how gender influences what we know and how we know things. There is great variety in the field, but there is a commitment to examining the ways women and other oppressed groups are systematically disadvantaged by the dominant paradigms of knowledge. This can result from a distrust or denigration of the feminine, denial of entry to the conversation, lack of credibility as knowers, or failure to take their situated experience into account. Much of feminist epistemology argued that one's situatedness matters to how and what one knows. The clearest form of this approach is known as feminist standpoint theory. Influenced by Black, Latina, and lesbian philosophy, this theory rejected the idea of a single feminist standpoint and instead acknowledged the multiplicity of standpoints among peoples, and even within one individual. Recalling the work of Addams, Cooper, Du Bois, and Follett, standpoint theorists held that it is particularly important to listen to accounts from persons on the margins as they can often provide a clearer lens through which to examine the dominant paradigm.

In 1983, Sandra Harding and Merill B. Hintikka published the collection titled *Discovering Reality: Feminist Perspectives on Epistemology, Metaphysics, Methodology, and Philosophy of Science*; Alison Jaggar and Susan Bordo edited *Gender/Body/Knowledge* (1989); Sandra Harding took up the questions of philosophy of science in *The Science Question in Feminism* (1986), and Evelyn Fox Keller challenged received concepts of objectivity in *Reflections on Gender and Science* (1985). In *The Flight to Objectivity: Essays on Cartesianism and Culture* (1987)

Bordo rethought the meaning of Cartesian doubt using the insights of feminist epistemology, feminist psychoanalysis, and Rorty's naturalism.

There have been others working in this area with figures in the American tradition other than Rorty. Kory Sorrell's *Representative Practices: Peirce, Pragmatism, and Feminist Epistemology* (2004) discussed how a community can represent itself and transform the world by representation. He calls on feminist theory as he takes up the issue of how authority operates within communities of inquirers and explores the role of narrative in knowing. He argues that there is not only a compatibility between Peirce and feminist epistemology but that Peirce would be a good resource for feminist epistemology. Peirce's fallibilism, and the pluralism and inclusiveness found in James and Dewey, are especially noted. Relatedly, Lara Trout's *The Politics of Survival: Peirce, Affectivity, and Social Criticism* (2010) took up issues of unintentional discrimination based on race, sex, sexuality, and class by focusing on the body, emotion, instinct, and habit. She argues that Peirce's philosophy can be a resource for feminist and race theorists in part because Peirce argues for the need for an inclusive community of inquirers (one way to mitigate against any particular bias becoming dominant) and argues against the imposition of views and structures by means of the method of authority.

*Beyond Epistemology: A Pragmatist Approach to Feminist Science Studies* (2003) by Sharyn Clough relies on the work of Donald Davidson and Richard Rorty to argue that feminist philosophers of science should not focus on epistemology but rather take a more empirical approach to actual lived harms. Relatedly, Alexandra Shuford's *Feminist Epistemology and American Pragmatism: Dewey and Quine* (2010) examined issues of physical embodiment (specifically the high rate of Caesarean sections) to create a naturalized epistemology rooted in the work of Dewey. She argues that Dewey makes room for embodiment as part of knowing in ways that feminist philosophers such as Louise Antony and Lynn Hankinson Nelson (using Quine) cannot.

Despite some inclusion of thinkers from the American tradition, the epistemological strand of feminist philosophy largely reflected the mainstream focus of analytic philosophy and had a tendency to dominate the subfield of feminist philosophy. But it brought a political and ethical slant. In 1991, Jane Duran published *Toward a Feminist Epistemology*, in which she examined androcentric assumptions in most theories of knowledge and argued for a naturalized and gynocentric view, which she called a contextualist and communicative principle that is always in process. She saw recognition of differences as a precondition of participatory decision-making. In the same year, Lorraine Code published *What Can She Know: Feminist Theory and the Construction of Knowledge* in which she argued that epistemology's claims to neutrality and objectivity mask the ways knowledge is always embedded in contexts and power relations. This affected who is seen as an authority and who can have or produce credible knowledge. She followed this up in numerous publications, including *Ecological Thinking: The Politics of Epistemic Location* (2006), in which she argued that ecological thinking can decenter humans in ways that will revise our engagement with knowledge. Such thinking begins in the "ecological situations and interconnections of knowers and knowing" (p. 6) that "interrogates and endeavors to unsettle the self-certainties of western capitalism and the epistemologies of mastery it underwrites" (p. 4).

As feminist epistemology developed in the 1980s and early 1990s, women philosophers of color challenged what they saw as the narrowness of feminist work in the field. Some of these figures were discussed earlier in this book: for example, hooks published *Ain't I a Woman*

(1981) taking on the racism of the White Women's Rights Movement. In her *Feminist Theory: From Margin to Center* (1989), she critiqued Friedan's liberal feminism for missing how gender, race, and class connect. Angela Davis sought to expand feminist theory in *Women, Race, and Class* (1981), and Audre Lorde, in her collection *Sister/Outsider* (1984) addressed issues of age, class, race, and sexuality from the perspective of being a Black lesbian. Gloria Anzaldúa collected essays by women of color to provide a challenge to White feminism's claims to a universal sisterhood in *This Bridge Called My Back* (1981). A few years later she published *Borderlands/La Frontera: The New Mestiza* (1999) in which she complicated notions of gender, race, and identity. In *Black Feminist Thought: Knowledge, Consciousness, and the Politics of Empowerment* (1990), Patricia Hill Collins presented a framework within which to understand the diverse thought of Black feminist intellectuals. She argued that Black women are reliable agents of knowledge whose standpoint offers avenues for empowerment. Responding to the lack of women of color in the field of philosophy, Naomi Zack published *Women of Color and Philosophy: A Critical Reader* (2000). She estimated that only 30 out of 10,000 in the field identified as women of color. In response, she selected an array of thinkers to write on the ways women of color relate to philosophy through critique, activism, and application, and proposed new directions of thought.

With the publication in 1989 of *The American Evasion of Philosophy*, Cornel West established a framework for rethinking who counted as an American philosopher. However, none of the philosophers West introduced in his retelling of the genealogy of pragmatism were women. Two years later, Charlene Haddock Seigfried called the gap in West's account into question in her paper, "Where are All the Pragmatist Feminists?" published in the leading feminist philosophy journal, *Hypatia*. "Pragmatists might be predisposed to be sympathetic to feminism, but too often do not engage in feminist analysis." West's book shows the same limitation: "West, unfortunately, exhibits a widespread pragmatist ignorance of feminist analyses of the pervasiveness of sex" and accepts the idea that race is more formative of American identity than is sex, missing the idea that race and sex are both central and implicated in each other (1991, p. 16). However, Seigfried took seriously the fallibilism that West saw as central to pragmatist philosophy. Even though his work had failed to take feminist pragmatism into account, there was nevertheless room for it to become a visible part of the tradition. She concludes that even though West leaves out the impact of American women, he recognizes that "pragmatism's openness to revision, its recognition of cultural specificity, and its refusal to speak for those who can more authentically speak for themselves" makes it open to a new, more inclusive, story (p. 16). Seigfried demonstrates this potential by introducing her readers to many of the thinkers we have discussed here including Addams, Calkins, and Goldman, and others not discussed here including Ellen Gates Starr, Melusina Fay Peirce, Christine Ladd Franklin, and Louise M. Rosenblatt.

Seigfried followed her 1991 paper with her 1996 book, *Pragmatism and Feminism: Reweaving the Social Fabric*. This book and her later work opened a new field for exploration and introduced forgotten or largely overlooked women in the history of American philosophy. Her work helped transform American philosophy from a narrow field focused largely on the work of Peirce, James, and Dewey into a wide engagement with philosophers—professional and otherwise—who took on the problems faced by people in their daily lives as they struggled against systems of oppression inherited from Europe and developed in the context of industrial capitalism.

Seigfried's reconstruction of American philosophy recognized women who influenced and challenged the development of philosophical resistance. In her work, Charlotte Perkins Gilman, Ella Flagg Young, Jessie Taft, Florence Kelley, Ethel Puffer Howes, Elsie Ripley Clapp, Mary Whiton Calkins, and Jane Addams join Patricia Hill Collins, bell hooks, Donna Haraway, Sandra Harding, and Lorraine Code to shape a framework for feminist pragmatism. The resulting perspective brings together the pragmatist commitments of the continuity of theory and practice, experience and nature, organism and environment, and knowledge and value with the feminist commitments to taking up the problems of women, their place in society, and their distinctive potential for transforming it. Seigfried pointed to common concerns shared by many feminists and pragmatists. Some of these include a dismantling of dichotomies, an understanding of our social interdependence, the importance of context, the need for philosophy to engage pressing issues of the day, a focus on pluralism, and the need to include diverse and marginalized communities in dialogue and action.

While she took up the pragmatist focus on cooperative intelligence, she also critiqued the patriarchal elements of the pragmatist tradition. Despite these critiques, Seigfried was at pains to encourage feminist philosophers to realize there was a long and strong feminist tradition rooted in thinkers and experiences in the Americas and distinct in many ways from their European counterparts (who tended to dominate feminist philosophy in the academy). Arguing that pragmatism and feminism should inform each other, she notes that pragmatism

> provides strong resources for feminist thinking since many of its positions address current feminist interests and debates. Among these are a pluralism and perpectivism that go beyond theory to advocate the actual inclusiveness of appropriately diverse viewpoints, including those of class, color, ethnicity, and gender, as a precondition of resolving problematic situations, whether these involve political, economic, epistemological, or ethical issues. (2001, 48)

Further, both pragmatism and feminism hold central roles for feelings as part of knowledge.

For Seigfried, a figure such as Jane Addams provides a good example of a thinker who rejected the idea of a static and fixed world, and static and fixed knowledge, in both theory and practice. Addams stands as an example of many key points of pragmatist feminism, such as creating inclusive places and procedures that are palpably open to differences and disagreements. For Seigfried, Addams "demonstrates the radical consequences of taking the pluralism, perspectivism, and finite limitations of human understanding seriously" (p. 222). When read as part of the tradition we are examining here, Addams (and Seigfried) address the problems faced by women as pragmatists with a philosophical approach

> that stresses the relation of theory to praxis, takes the continuity of experience and nature as revealed through the outcome of directed action as the starting point for reflection. Experience is the ongoing transaction of organism and environment; in other words, both subject and object are constituted in the process. When intelligently ordered, initial conditions are deliberately transformed according to ends-in-view, that is, intentionally, into a subsequent state of affairs thought to be more desirable. (Seigfried, 1996, pp. 6–7)

It is noteworthy that Addams remained influential in the fields of sociology and social work while she was largely ignored by philosophers until the late 1990s. In 2002, the University of Illinois Press reissued all of her major books, making it easier to teach her work. Several devoted biographers, including Louise W. Knight and Jean Bethke Elshtain, have also raised her profile, and through the work of Charlene Haddock Seigfried, Marilyn Fischer, and Maurice Hamington, she is better known among philosophers.[1]

Seigfried also edited a special edition of *Hypatia* on pragmatist feminism (1993), and *Feminist Interpretations of John Dewey* (2001), and wrote a very important introduction to Addams's *Democracy and Social Ethics* for Illinois University Press (2002). Her numerous paper presentations, journal articles, and book chapters opened up a new understanding of feminism, a new understanding of pragmatism, and introduced a whole host of figures who had been overlooked by the profession. She is still writing on Addams, Gilman, Dewey, and others. Her work complicates our understanding of the history of American philosophy as she uncovers evidence of the women originating ideas for which the "central" male figures have come to be known.

The recent publication of *Pragmatist Feminism and the Work of Charlene Haddock Seigfried* (2022) speaks to both her influence and the importance of pragmatism for feminist philosophy in general. Essays in this volume explore the many ways feminism and pragmatism can and should inform one another, in theory and practice. Following Seigfried's lead, the volume argues for the distinctive feminist contributions of Addams, Anzaldúa, Calkins, Cooper, Dewey, Gilman, and James, as well as more contemporary thinkers such as Boggs, Collins, Rorty, and West. Black feminist visionary pragmatism and feminist new materialism are also shown to be parts of the developing pragmatist feminism. These feminists, the volume argues, illustrate the importance of pragmatist feminism for publicly engaged philosophy and philosophical activism. They also point to a pragmatist feminist method of inquiry, developed by Seigfried, which relies on perplexity, sympathy, cooperative action, radical empiricism, and experimental logic. This volume, framed by Seigfried's work, demonstrates the depth of pragmatist feminism as a subfield in philosophy and its importance as a challenge to mainstream philosophy as well as pragmatist and feminist philosophy in particular.

Seigfried's *Pragmatism and Feminism: Reweaving the Social Fabric* impacted contemporary discussions about gender and feminism. Her work opened the field for other works on feminism coming out of the American tradition, including Shannon Sullivan's *Living Across and Through Skins: Transactional Bodies, Pragmatism, and Feminism* (2001), which brought Dewey's thought together with the work of some continental and feminist philosophers (Nietzsche, Merleau-Ponty, Butler, and Harding) to examine (among other things) habit, communication, and the personal and cultural structures of gender. Sullivan highlights contributions pragmatism can make to phenomenology, critical race theory, and feminism by providing a different approach to ideas such as experience, truth, and reality, and to actual lived bodily habits. Rooted in an approach that is pluralistic, fallible, flexible, and future-oriented, Sullivan argues that pragmatism has much to offer to improve human experiences of the world.

Picking up on the importance of the future, Erin McKenna's *The Task of Utopia: A Pragmatist and Feminist Perspective* (2001) also used the work of Dewey in combination with key feminist philosophers (e.g., Elshtain, Gilman, Goldman, Jaggar, Okin, Seigfried, and Iris Marion Young) to examine how conceiving of possible futures through a pragmatist feminist lens works to improve social and political conditions in the present. Rather than seeking static end-states or relying on violent revolutions, she develops a process model of utopia that grows out of democratic experimentation to create possible futures-in-process that can guide further inquiry, point to some present action, and sustain critical hope.

Still, most feminist philosophy, at least as it is found in the academy, disregards most of the feminist strands of the American tradition. *Contemporary Feminist Pragmatism* (2012), edited by Maurice Hamington and Celia Bardwell-Jones, presents an interesting array of essays addressing topics such as race, exclusion, democracy, education, ethics, hospitality, gardening, and animals. Seeking to move beyond the recovery of women and feminism within the history of pragmatist philosophy, the editors sought to examine the contemporary significance of pragmatist feminism for contemporary problems and purposes.

The editors of *Contemporary Feminist Pragmatism* argue for the potential value of connecting pragmatism and the feminist philosophy that has long disregarded it.

> On the most basic level, pragmatism values the primacy of practice, the importance of experience, and an acceptance of fallibilism. Similarly, feminism views women's lives as important sites of knowledge and seeks to transform society toward social justice. The mixing of these two traditions generates a more robust framework that can creatively address the intimate connections between theory and practice. (2012, pp. 1–2)

Similarly, Elizabeth Anderson, a philosopher trained in the analytic tradition, in her 2014 APA Dewey Lecture titled "Journeys of a Pragmatist Feminist," describes her "discovery" of pragmatism as she sought to take up problems that were not confined to the discipline of philosophy. "Little did I know that I was retracing the path for philosophy urged by Dewey in *Reconstruction in Philosophy*!" As a result, she "found pragmatist methodology most fruitful for addressing philosophical problems. Start by exploring the problem as it emerges in practice, in the experiences of the people who confront it." This methodology, though, requires pluralism as it understands "that insight comes from diverse sources, that different people, due to their social roles and identities, diverse cognitive styles and developed skills, and varied values and interests, are positioned to notice different phenomena, to draw different connections, and use different tools to address their problems" (p. 83). She goes on to argue that "Feminists and pragmatists are joined in holding that unjust social relations, such as those that constitute institutionalized race and gender inequality, distort inquiry by suppressing insights from the less advantaged, reinforcing stereotypes and other prejudices, and granting epistemic authority to ignorant views due to the social power of those who assert them" (p. 84).

Seigfried, too, had argued for the value of connecting pragmatism and feminism for many of the same reasons. Lorraine Code, though, challenged her on this claim. Code argues that pragmatism's emphasis on "instrumental reasoning" undermines its ability to challenge established ways of thinking. "[A]ppeals to instrumental outcomes," Code writes, "have to be reinterpreted with a large measure of feminist skepticism in view of the alignments of 'instrumental reason' with specific readings of affluent masculinity, amply documented by Nancy Hartsock and Genevieve Lloyd" (1998, p. 29). Given such limits, Code claims that "perhaps the most significant conclusion that emerges from *Feminism and Pragmatism* is that pragmatism needs feminism even more than feminism needs pragmatism" (p. 29). Seigfried replies: "The problem, I think, is that pragmatism is such a radical reconstruction of philosophy that it takes some time to grasp that, as a result of its paradigm shift, conventional terms like 'instrumental reasoning' have been subverted and have to be understood in a new context" (1998, p. 27). What Code missed—and feminist pragmatists recognize according to Seigfried—is that feminism is or should be instrumental in taking action to change the circumstances of women. By accepting the binary of means and ends, as Seigfried claims Code has, Code is encouraging feminists to "perpetuate rather than undermine the pernicious dualisms they have inherited" (p. 27).

An example of challenging the binary of means and ends can be found in Grace E. Lavery's *Pleasure and Ecstasy: Of Pen Names, Cover Versions, and Other Trans Techniques* (2023). This book provides an example of bringing pragmatism together with trans theory in the section titled "How to Change Sex Like a Pragmatist." While the main point of the book is to bring Freud into conversation with literary examples of transition, this is done within a pragmatist framework. Lavery points out that they do not "study" pragmatism but they find a pragmatist notion of realism (where real is "what works in amelioration" (p. xix)) important in order to sidestep "the ontological problematization of transsexuality." "(R)ather than asking what the transsexual is," trans pragmatism focuses on

> developing techniques by which transitions might be more fully effectuated. This trans pragmatism affirms in all places that transition works, that despite expectations, it is possible, and that it happens. . . . As an essentially pragmatic philosophy, the trans cultivation of technique has been neither "essentialist" nor "anti-essentialist," insofar as those terms have organized much of the political content of feminist thought since the 1970s. (pp. x–xi)

Lavery specifically calls on the work of Peirce to support their position.

> I tend to follow the classical formulation of Charles Sanders Peirce: "Consider what effects, which might conceivably have practical bearings, we conceive the object of our conception to have. Then, our conception of these effects is the whole of our conception of the object." The truth-value of a proposition is equal to its necessary effects. . . . I would suggest that Peirce's maxim might clear up much of the fogginess around the metaphysical definitions of "woman" that have become contentious: a trans woman is a woman if and only if she is referred to as a woman; likewise an absolutist definition of women deriving from gamete size (or chromosome, etc.). . . . Since plenty of people do use the word "woman" to refer to trans women, for whom many of those reductive characteristics do not apply, the latter definition is of limited use. (p. xviii)

Lavery's work demonstrates once again, the importance of pragmatism for feminist theory and opens up a new avenue for pragmatist feminists to explore.

Patricia Hill Collins credits Seigfried for challenging the long-accepted genealogy of pragmatism, bringing in a number of women to join Peirce, James, and Dewey. Collins asks what would happen if Alain Locke was also considered a peer of these thinkers. She writes:

> Themes such as how social inequalities of race, class and gender shape experiences, the centrality of power to participatory democracy, and ethical issues raised by social justice agendas might have been more centrally located within the pragmatist canon had the

works by "members of the historically recognized movement of American pragmatism" not been defined as coterminous with pragmatism itself. Thus had Alain Locke's "critical pragmatism" and Black women's "visionary pragmatism" been incorporated earlier, American pragmatism itself might have been quite different. (2011, p. 14)

Collins herself has done much to bring the work of Anna Julia Cooper and Ida Wells-Barnett into the pragmatist circle (both were contemporaries of Addams, Gilman, and the "founding fathers"). She thinks this is important for understanding that intersectionality has a longer history than many feminist thinkers seem to understand. She also describes Black feminism of the late nineteenth and early twentieth centuries as a "visionary pragmatism" that grew out of embodied experience, was informed by the relationality of complex worldviews, and sought to reconstruct systems of power with an eye to social justice. Both Black feminism and pragmatism arose as alternatives to positivist, deterministic views connected with eugenics thinking of the time. In her book *Intersectionality as Critical Social Theory* (2019), Collins notes that there is a renewed interest in social inequality within pragmatist philosophy, and she hopes that more engagement with Locke's critical pragmatism and Black feminist visionary pragmatism will result in greater engagement with issues of power and with social action.

An important example of wrestling with issues of power and putting pragmatist feminism to use in connection with pressing contemporary issues is *Reckoning: Black Lives Matter and the Democratic Necessity of Social Movements* (2021), by Deva R. Woodly. In this book, Woodly explores the Movement for Black Lives through the lens of radical Black feminist pragmatism (RBFP). She understands RBFP as "a set of practices for understanding and working against domination and oppression rather than a doctrine" (p. 49). Radical denotes a way of questioning, Black feminism an ethical system, and pragmatism a form of judgment that shapes action. She references the importance of the "Deweyan concept of social intelligence, a fundamental investment in pragmatic imagination, a commitment to democratic experimentation, and an aim toward liberatory ends" (p. 51). The pragmatist imagination, in particular, is both speculative and practical, is concerned with the "not yet here" (p. 50) and is informed by "the *lived experience* of the most marginalized in the direction of what we all deserve" (p. 51).

The Movement for Black Lives is committed to the idea that other worlds are possible. While Woodly contrasts this with a utopian imagination that is not comfortable with uncertainty, what she has in mind is clearly consonant with what McKenna argued for in *The Task of Utopia* and, like McKenna, Woodly shares an interest in Deweyan inquiry. Drawing on the work of Melvin Rogers, Woodly understands Deweyan inquiry and the method of intelligence as a critical orientation, a theory of action, and as democratic experimental action in the world (2021, p. 57). Woodly also draws on Du Bois, Cooper, and hooks to highlight the contributions of those living at the margins (and often seen as not mattering) to this theory of action and to democratic experimental action in the world, with the Movement for Black Lives as an example. Woodly argues that radical Black feminist pragmatism informs the movement, and she argues that the movement offers challenges for feminism and pragmatism themselves if they seek to remain relevant to the battle against despair.

Feminist philosophy in the American tradition, in general, has sought to battle against despair and to help construct a better world. Feminist philosophers did much to change how women viewed themselves and their roles in society. They changed the Women's movement and feminist theory (including the development of queer and trans philosophy). They also helped to change thinking and laws. In addition to the ERA, feminist philosophers have written works that influenced debates and laws on equal education, equal pay, pornography, pregnancy leave, child care, surrogacy, disability rights, sexual harassment, rape, gay/lesbian rights, trans rights, domestic violence laws, same-sex marriage, and more. One recent, very public example can be seen in the 2015 Supreme Court ruling in Obergefell v. Hodges, which legalized same-sex marriage in the United States. Following the Dobbs ruling that overturned Roe, concerns emerged about the legalization of interracial marriages, which had been secured in Loving v. Virginia in 1967. So, in 2022, the Respect for Marriage Act, which included protections for same-sex and interracial marriages, was approved in the US Congress and signed into law.

Feminist philosophers also changed philosophy as an academic discipline—what counts as philosophy and who counts as a philosopher. One can see the tension between these aspects of philosophical work in the lives of the feminist philosophers themselves. There was a perceived conflict between doing good philosophy and doing good as a philosopher. *Singing in the Fire: Stories of Women in Philosophy* (2003), edited by Alcoff, presented narratives of many founding feminist philosophers, some of whom tell of a desire to make philosophy meaningful and relevant. They discussed the importance of the founding of the Society of Women in Philosophy (SWIP), even as some cautioned against it becoming exclusionary. Others discussed the impossibility of meeting the standard of being a professional philosopher. One was seen either as an overachiever and so threatening, or as "smiling too much" to make others comfortable with their unexpected (and sometimes unwelcome) presence. Overt sexism and sexual harassment marked many of the stories and often serve to connect their philosophical work with various forms of social domination. While many of these women wanted to make philosophy relevant to life and so grew disillusioned with mainstream analytic philosophy, to do so came with the cost of not being seen as doing "real philosophy." Since many philosophers already assumed that women were not up to the task of doing "real philosophy," this complicated the efforts of women to be taken seriously in the profession.

As a consequence of these assumptions, within the academy today, there is a tendency for feminist philosophers to address other academics rather than the problems of the day faced by those outside. This may be due to the desire to gain credibility within the profession and be seen as doing "real philosophy." Yet, even when women philosophers do take on contemporary issues, it is often done using highly technical language and by referencing the history of feminist philosophy more than the experiences of people. Many have returned to talking about knowledge rather than putting philosophy to use in the world, though the two projects are clearly connected. One place where talking about knowledge results in putting philosophy to use in the world is in the contributions of ecofeminism and ecowomanism to environmental philosophy. Ecofeminism combines insights from feminist epistemology, feminist philosophy of science, feminist ethics, and feminist political theory, while ecowomanism combines insights from the lived experiences of Black women, the land, and other-than-human animals in ways that critique, complicate, and enrich ecofeminism.

Alice Walker coined the term womanism in 1983 in her book *In Search of Our Mothers' Gardens: Womanist Prose*. Her original definition has four parts: The first part includes these ideas: "A black feminist or feminist of color;" "Usually referring to outrageous, audacious, courageous or *willful* behavior"; being responsible, grown-up, or serious. The second part notes that a womanist "Prefers women's culture, women's emotional flexibility, . . . and women's strength"; and "A woman who loves other women, sexually and/or nonsexually." The third part notes a love of music, dance, the moon, Spirit, food, and roundness and who "Loves herself." And finally, the most quoted part of the definition: "Womanist is to feminist as purple is to lavender" (p. xi). Walker's own work always includes a concern for the planet and other animals. The term ecowomanist emerged to identify work that focused on how the oppressions faced by land, other-than-human animals, and by people of color—especially African American women—are linked. Ecowomanism entails a focus on social justice issues such as environmental racism and maintains space for spiritual connections to be taken seriously. Walker argues that we need a female-reverencing spirituality that is earth-centered if we hope to stop the extractive use and exploitation of peoples and the planet.

Ecofeminism emerged in the United States with Susan Griffin's *Woman and Nature: The Roaring Inside Her* (1978). Carolyn Merchant's book *The Death of Nature* (1980) solidified ecofeminism as an important part of feminist philosophy generally. Merchant argued that the scientific and industrial revolutions had promoted a mechanized view of nature that she found dangerous. Building on the work of earlier feminists, Merchant argued that the positivist epistemology that had come to control science and philosophy was what caused the "death of nature." Rather than seeing the environment as a living organism, it had become separated into inert parts to be controlled and dominated. Further, women were linked to nature by language and conceptual schemes and so, too, were a force to be controlled and dominated.

Not surprisingly, women had made up the majority of the early conservationist movement of the late 1800s and early 1900s, putting their support largely behind the vision promoted by John Muir. Rachel Carson's (see Chapter 23) work in the mid-1950s and early 1960s resulted in the contemporary environmental movement, and women continue to make up the bulk of the environmental and animal activists. Most local activists and grassroots movements are the work of women concerned about their homes and communities. Merchant provided a new ethic to guide such work—what she calls a Partnership Ethic. This ethic included seeing equality among human and nonhuman communities; moral consideration for humans and nonhumans alike; respect for cultural and biodiversity; inclusiveness of women, minorities, and nonhumans; and ecologically sound management of ecosystems that contribute to the health of all.

Coming from the postmodern perspective, Donna Haraway also addressed some of these issues in her works: *Primate Visions: Gender, Race, and Nature in the World of Modern Science* (1989); *Simians, Cyborgs, and Women: The Reinvention of Nature* (1991); *The Companion Species Manifesto* (2003); and *When Species Meet* (2008). Haraway emphasized the ways in which masculine bias influenced science and pointed to the limits of objectivity. Her work also pointed to the dangers of essentialism and called for feminists to get beyond the kind of naturalism that sometimes resulted in views that reduced women to their bodies. She also wrote about the ways in which human and other animal beings co-constitute each other.

Going in a different direction, Karen Warren became a leading figure in ecofeminism with her 1987 and 1990 articles in *Environmental Ethics* and her book *Ecofeminist Philosophy*, published in 2000. Warren presented the logic of domination as the underlying problem that linked issues of race, class, gender, and species. While many feminists had identified dualistic and hierarchical thinking as a main problem with Western philosophy, Warren argued that, on their own, dualisms could be descriptively accurate. Dualism without a value hierarchy attached could be merely descriptive of something found in the world. Humans, however, tended to attach value to one side of a dualism, and this led to value hierarchies. The real problem emerged, though, when such a system of valuation took place within the logic of domination, which assumed that the more valued have the right to dominate and use the less valued. According to Warren, this was the mechanism that underlies all forms of oppression and was what connected various forms of social domination among humans and human domination of the rest of nature.

By 1990, there were a number of people writing on ecofeminism, and so Irene Diamond and Gloria Feman Orenstein edited *Reweaving the World: The Emergence of Ecofeminism*, a collection of essays that made clear the connection between environmental degradation and the poverty and vulnerability of women in the developing world. Concerns about the environment were linked with social justice concerns within ecofeminism and ecowomanism from the start. There was also a recognition of different positionalities (which included other than humans) and the importance of understanding intersectionality in a way that included race, class, gender, age, and species (among other considerations). Carol J. Adams and Lori Gruen note that "Ecofeminism addresses the various ways that sexism, heteronormativity, racism, colonialism, and ableism are informed by and support speciesism and how analyzing the ways these forces intersect can produce less violent, more just practices" (2014, p. 1).

While there was a reliance on earlier work within feminist philosophy that critiqued science, expanded ethics, and rethought political and economic structures, ecofeminism and ecowomanism also challenged individuals to change their thinking and habits and to reform social structures to support a more livable future. For example, Maria Mies and Vandana Shiva's *Ecofeminism* (2010, 2014) looks at the everyday needs and environmental grassroots activism of women around the world. Linking patriarchy and militarism with ecological degradation, they argue for an ethic that requires resisting the commodification of natural resources and women's labor. They reject the "myth of catching up" that drives so much of economic development and insist that humans need to learn to live within limits and to respect the rest of nature rather than exploit it. Shiva has also written *Staying Alive: Women, Ecology, and Development* (1988, 2016) and *Earth Democracy: Justice, Sustainability, and Peace* (2005, 2015). For Shiva, taking the perspectives of women of color seriously is paramount to such efforts, returning us to the importance of ecowomanism as part of these conversations.

Taking on a different focus, many ecofeminists and ecowomanists directed particular attention to human relationships with other animals and raised ethical and environmental concerns about living with and eating other animal beings. Greta Gaard edited *Ecofeminism: Women, Animals, and Nature* (1993); Carol Adams and Josephine Donovan edited *Beyond Animal Rights* (1996) and *The Feminist Care Tradition in Animal Ethics* (2007); and Adams and Lori Gruen edited *Ecofeminism: Feminist Intersections With Other Animals and the Earth* (2014). Adams's work in *The Sexual Politics of Meat* (1990), *Neither Beast Nor Man* (1994), and *The Pornography of Meat* (2003 & 2020) did much to show the theoretical and practical links among our views of, and treatment of, women, minorities, the poor, animals, and nature. She points to the many ways both language and images commonly link women and other animal beings in ways that make them passive and consumable. Nature and other animals are feminized and often sexualized (virgin timber, "sexy" cows in commercials for milk), while human women are naturalized and women of color in particular are often portrayed as exotic wild animals. Adams argues that women and other animals are understood to be for the use and pleasure of another—usually seen from a White male gaze and understood as existing for their pleasure. Reducing other living beings to objects of consumption (be that sexual or literal consumption) does violence and perpetuates injustices as it supports the logic of domination. Given these historical and conceptual connections, Adams argues that all those concerned with social justice should work to undermine the logic of domination and should adopt a vegan diet. Most contemporary ecofeminists follow this line of thinking.

Lori Gruen's *Entangled Empathy: An Alternative Ethic for our Relationship with Animals* (2015) calls for a kind of caring attentiveness to the lives of others with whom we can empathize, rather than a focus on rights. For her this involves a blend of emotion and cognition that helps us respond to the needs, desires, and vulnerabilities of those with whom we are entangled. In her view it is never ethical to engage in relationships of exploitative instrumentalism, and she believes that killing animals for food is exploitative instrumentalism. She does not believe other animals should be understood as edible, as doing so fails to respect them as subjects.

In contrast, Val Plumwood argues that humans cannot live without using and eating others. While she thinks it is wrong to reduce any other living being to merely being edible, she does not believe all consumption of other animals is a form of exploitative instrumentalism. In 1993, Plumwood published *Feminism and the Mastery of Nature* and, in 2001, *Environmental Culture: The Ecological Crisis of Reason*. Plumwood's work uncovers the details of the logic of domination (which she also calls the logic of colonization) and points to centrism (e.g., androcentrism, anthropocentrism, eurocentrism), backgrounding (ignoring that on which one depends—e.g., men's dependence on women's labor, humans' dependence on healthy ecosystems), and remoteness (e.g., technological, epistemological, communicative, spatial, temporal, consequential) as key elements of maintaining the logic of domination. Her work included a specific focus on how humans treat other animal beings—domesticated and "wild." Her critiques of factory farming are powerful and share much in common with the work of Adams and Gruen, but Plumwood does not (unlike most contemporary ecofeminists) call for veganism as the only ethical diet as that just moves the line of moral considerability from a human/animal dualism to a human/plant dualism. Instead, she calls for a contextual semi-vegetarianism that opposes industrialized agriculture and respects animals, plants, and humans and the myriad relationships among them. Plumwood's work is influenced by thinkers in the American tradition—Peirce and Dewey in particular. As a consequence, she is more contextual, more pluralist, and less absolutistic in her approach.

More directly influenced by the American tradition, Erin McKenna has published several books on animal issues using a pragmatist ecofeminist framework: *Pets, People, and Pragmatism* (2013); *Livestock: Food, Fiber, and Friends* (2018); and *Living with Animals: Rights, Responsibility, and Respect* (2021). Together, these works offer contextualized examinations of a wide array of animal issues, arguing that humans can't opt out of relationships with other animal beings (we can't just leave them alone), but we should seek to ameliorate these relationships. In *Livestock*, she notes,

> Human relationships with other animal beings are always in process. At any given time . . . some of these relationships are respectful of the needs and desires of the various animal beings and others are not. *At no time, however is there an option to just stop being in relation with one another.* Even the cessation of all livestock production . . . would not

end humans' connectedness to these creatures. Given this, the focus should be on how to improve the relationships humans have with various other animal beings. This requires an openness to new understandings and real change in how we live together and relate. (p. 19)

Such amelioration can take many forms, though. Moral absolutism (such as mandating veganism) unnecessarily limits the possibilities and fixes people's thinking in rigid positions that aren't useful when examining how actual human and other animal beings are situated in the world. For a pragmatist ecofeminist, the complexity and plurality of lived experiences require a more nuanced and flexible approach, and this is the key difference between the positions presented by thinkers such as Adams and Gruen and those presented by Plumwood and McKenna. In most other respects, all these thinkers share much in common, including a feminist commitment to dismantling binaries such as male/female and reason/emotion, as well as working to fight the logic of domination/colonization in its myriad forms.

It should be evident from this discussion that feminist philosophy is a diverse field, encompassing many traditions, subject areas, and subfields of philosophy. It is often, but not always, politically motivated and/or focused. What is generally shared, though, is a concern for how the exclusion of women and other minorities from the field of philosophy has impacted the very nature of philosophy, be that philosophy of science, epistemology, metaphysics, ethics, or social and political philosophy. We have highlighted the important addition of pragmatist feminism as a long-present but recently named school of feminist thought that is an important resource for all feminist thinkers and activists. The pragmatist feminists' attention to real-world amelioration is important to keep in mind as they wrestle with epistemological, metaphysical, political, and ethical concerns. Their focus is usually on the results and applications of rethinking the epistemologies, metaphysics, political theory, and ethics, rather than the more technical internal debates that often absorb philosophy. This approach to philosophy is one found in many of the fields of applied philosophy. Next, we turn to environmental philosophy and the pragmatist environmentalism that has emerged as one such example.

## Note

1 Fischer's works, *On Addams* (2003), *Jane Addams and the Practice of Democracy* (2009), and *Jane Addams's Evolutionary Theorizing: Constructing "Democracy and Social Ethics"* (2019) provide an important historical understanding of Addams's work and place in philosophy, as well as noting the ways Addams's philosophy could be an important asset for current issues. Hamington co-edited the *Oxford Handbook on Jane Addams* (2023). In his own works, Hamington examined Addams's contributions to epistemology, ethics, and feminist theory in *The Social Philosophy of Jane Addams* (2009), and in *Embodied Care: Jane Addams, Maurice Merleau-Ponty and Feminist Ethics* (2004), he used her work to ground an emerging area in feminist care ethics. Hamington also edited *Feminist Interpretations of Jane Addams* (2010) in the *Re-reading the Canon* series. This collection examined Addams's feminist analysis of a variety of issues and pointed out that she provides radical and pluralist roots to the American and pragmatist traditions.

# American Philosophies

## Primary Texts

Hill-Collins, P. (2019). *Intersectionality as Critical Social Theory*. Durham: Duke University Press.
Seigfried, C. H. (1996). *Pragmatism and Feminism: Reweaving the Social Fabric*. Chicago: University of Chicago Press.
Woodly, D. R. (2021). *Reckoning: Black Lives Matter and the Democratic Necessity of Social Movements*. Oxford: Oxford University Press.

# CHAPTER 23
# ENGAGED PHILOSOPHY AND THE ENVIRONMENT
## JOHN MUIR, ALDO LEOPOLD, JOSEPH WOOD KRUTCH, RACHEL CARSON, AND CONTEMPORARY ENVIRONMENTAL PRAGMATISM

In the second half of the twentieth century, academic philosophy largely retreated from addressing the major problems of the day, in part in response to loyalty oath requirements started by President Truman in 1947 and the rise of McCarthyism in 1950 (see Chapter 16), and in part to separate academic philosophy from philosophy viewed as ideological and connected to the wars of the first half of the twentieth century. Other philosophy in the American tradition done outside of the academy nevertheless continued to address ongoing and growing problems of war and peace, poverty, and the environment. The environmental themes raised by earlier American philosophers like Emerson and Thoreau had been taken up by John Muir (1838–1914) and Aldo Leopold (1887–1948) in the late 1800s and early 1900s. This tradition continued in the 1950s and 1960s with the publication of major environmental works by Joseph Wood Krutch (1893–1970) and Rachel Carson (1907–1963). This occurred despite academic philosophy's shift to focus on language and science (not politics) and despite pressure from outside the academy to stay out of the way of the unbounded development of natural resources. Philosophy, as a whole, increasingly engaged with environment and animal-related issues in the 1970s, and both areas remain central concerns for those working within the American tradition.

The work of John Muir was essential to the creation of the contemporary environmental movement, as well as to the creation of the National Parks and National Forests in the United States. He was not only influenced by reading the works of Emerson and Thoreau, but he also managed to influence Emerson and other intellectuals and politicians with his own work. Muir hosted Emerson (discussed in Chapter 5) on a visit to Yosemite in 1871. He also hosted President Theodore Roosevelt in 1903. In his book *A Passion for Nature: The Life of John Muir* (2011), Donald Worster argued that Muir shared the outlook presented by the pragmatists of the time, whom he named as Chauncey Wright (1830–1875), known for his concept of "cosmic weather" as a way to understand the mixture of chance and regularity in nature, Peirce (Chapter 8), James (Chapter 7), and Oliver Wendell Holmes, Jr. (1841–1935), an associate justice of the US Supreme Court known as a "legal pragmatist." Specifically, Muir noted their common interest in science, their acknowledgment that all knowledge is partial, and the idea that human society is part of nature. He also argued that they share a propensity to seek practical solutions rather than develop and promote an absolute dogma (pp. 306–9). Muir's desire to find ways humans could continue to use nature while doing less damage was spurred on by his visit to the Chicago Columbian Exposition (discussed in Chapters 2–4). Visiting in the first month of the fair in 1893, Muir noted that while the fair promoted agriculture, manufacturing, mines, and machinery with the names of the buildings, nowhere did it note the ecological toll such "progress" had taken. Water and air were more polluted, soils were being depleted, and many species were in decline. Muir's concern mirrored Pokagon's at the Chicago Fair: "The cyclone of civilization rolled westward, the forests of untold centuries were wiped away, streams dried up, lakes fell back from ancient bounds, and all our fathers once loved to gaze upon was destroyed, defaced, or marred" (Pokagon, 2001, p. 33—discussed in Chapter 2). Muir continued to wrestle with how to balance the human use of natural resources with a love and respect for nature. Despite what might have been common cause, Muir not only overlooked Native Americans as allies in his work, but he also actively critiqued them as a people and sought their removal from lands he wished to "preserve."

Aldo Leopold followed in the wake of Muir's work, though his concerns were more directed toward finding ways for the continuation of human use of natural resources rather than setting them aside to be "wild." Leopold identified the causes of human overuse of nature as an impoverished individualism, a get-rich-quick mentality, and the commodification of nature. Caught up in the "progress" of the time, Leopold joined the US Forest Service to help ensure that resources would be available for future development. The time he spent in the Southwest, though, introduced him to the environmental damage—soil erosion, flooding, and the introduction of invasive species—that resulted from human development. His concerns about the supposed growing efficiency of farming proved to be prophetic when from 1934 to 1941 the "Dust Bowl" drought resulted in a mass exodus from the Midwest. The government tried to temper the problems of individualism (farming without concern for the land of others) and the desire to use land for immediate economic gain with the 1934 Taylor Grazing Act and the 1935 Soil Conservation and Domestic Allotment Act. Despite the new laws, the tendency to see and treat land as a commodity continued.

Leopold introduced a view that understood land as a biotic community that includes humans within a complex and dynamic system. The "scientific" approach to agriculture was, in fact, disruptive to the biotic community, and Leopold worked to convince farmers and hunters to use the science of ecology. Rather than seeing various plants and animals as pests that could be controlled with poisons and hunting, he argued that humans need to understand the complex and interactive nature of the various relations in a system. He saw that "solutions" such as DDT and killing wolves were worse than the "problems" they were introduced to solve. These attempts at control were based on a philosophy of competition and violence rather than cooperation and community.

Against the idea that land was just a commodity, Leopold conceived it as a complex system including soil, water, plants, insects, and animals. "Land, then, is not merely soil," he said, "it is a fountain of energy flowing through [an open] circuit" in which "some energy is dissipated in decay, some is added by absorption from the air, some is stored in soils, peats, and forests; but it is a sustained circuit, like a slowly augmented revolving fund of life" (1949, p. 253). He called on humans to understand themselves as part of this community and to extend ethics to the land. To do this wisely, though, humans need to try to understand the land and their impact on the system. He noted that while change is a part of the dynamic circuit, humans make changes at a speed, and on a scale, that makes adjustment of the system difficult. Consequently, humans need to think carefully about the impact of their actions. This requires a different approach to science, one that includes love and respect.

The dominant conception of land, he thought, derived from the biblical command in the Old Testament that humans should be fruitful and multiply, subdue the earth, and have dominion over it (Gen. 1.28). Such a conception of the use of nature was, Leopold concluded in his book *A Sand County Almanac* (1949), incompatible with conservation.

> We abuse land because we regard it as a commodity belonging to us. When we see land as a community to which we belong, we may begin to use it with love and respect. There is no other way for land to survive the impact of mechanized man, nor for us to reap from it the esthetic harvest it is capable, under science, of contributing to culture. (pp. xviii–xix)

To make this change in attitude a reality, Leopold, like Dewey (Chapter 11) and Addams (Chapter 6), was committed to a ground-up democratic approach. Leopold was even involved in Dewey's work in the League for Independent Political Action (LIPA) in the late 1920s and early 1930s. The LIPA sought a radical overhaul of current government agencies in favor of more progressive policies on issues of production, labor rights, and farming (among others), and also pushed for the creation of a progressive third party.

There were several reasons for Leopold's commitment to democracy: first, people need to be invested in the land in order to effectively change their habits and attitudes. "This face-about in land philosophy cannot," he claimed, "be imposed on landowners from without, either by authority or by pressure groups. It can develop only from within, by self-persuasion, and by disillusionment with previous concepts." Second, national policies cannot understand and respect the needs of local ecosystems. There is no general solution to particular problems. For example, "A wildlife plan," Leopold explained, "is a constantly shifting array of small moves, infinitely repeated, to give wildlife due representation in shaping the future minds and future landscapes of America" (1999, p. 198). People must see themselves as part of the community so that they realize they are acting on their own behalf when they act to sustain the health of local lands. In an echo of Addams, Leopold described this as "the difference between vertical and horizontal planning" (quoted in Newton, 2008, p. 173), where "horizontal planning" is local and aims to distribute goods and responsibility throughout the community.

He hoped that people, once they understood the nature of their interdependence with other living things, could learn to limit their appetites: "Now we must face the question whether a still higher 'standard of living' is worth its cost in things natural" (1949, p. xvii). He also hoped people would come to see the value of other life in more than simply economic terms (though he never completely dismissed this way of valuing). He noted that, "[it] is increasingly clear that there is a basic antagonism between the philosophy of the industrial age and the philosophy of the conservationist" (quoted in Newton, 2008, p. 251). Like many of the thinkers discussed in earlier chapters (including Gilman, Addams, Royce, Dewey, Du Bois, Kallen, Follett, and Alain Locke), Leopold called for the development of socially attuned individuals. He rejected what he called the "bogus individualism" of extreme capitalism (Newton, 2008, p. 259).

Joseph Wood Krutch took up Leopold's land ethic in his nature writings, and by the late 1940s and early 1950s, Krutch was known for finding in nature the remedy for the over-mechanized modern life. But that is not where he started. Krutch was a graduate student and then professor of literature at Columbia while Dewey was teaching there. Krutch's best-known "philosophical" work was *The Modern Temper*, which he published in 1929—the same year Dewey published *The Quest for Certainty*. Dewey recognized the industrial, economic, and political pressures that threatened to eclipse individuality and liberty and offered a hopeful, melioristic response based on democracy and education. While Krutch largely shared Dewey's concerns, his book ended in despair.

We know that Krutch sent Dewey an inscribed copy of his book, but other details of their relationship are unknown. However, some of the differences between them are clear. Krutch could not let go of the desire for absolutes. He thought that philosophy had become a slave to science and, in his view, science left no room for human values. Dewey saw science as just one way that humans understand and interact with the environment and as continuous, not separate from, values. While many read Dewey as endorsing the very kind of surrender to science that worried Krutch, Krutch recognized in Dewey (and James) a more hopeful humanistic approach. All three thinkers shared a concern for the impoverished approach of behaviorism and other mechanistic views of human psychology and society. Krutch elaborated on this in *The Measure of Man* (1952a) when he pointed to the danger of developing dogmatic approaches to understanding humans and human society, since all such views are based on fallible knowledge. He argued that the behaviorism of B. F. Skinner (1904–1990) was a favorite tool of totalitarian regimes, as were the simplified, mechanized understandings he found in the work of Marx and Freud. He noted James and Whitehead as exceptions to this tendency, as they did not accept simple deterministic or mechanistic views. While other philosophies were beginning to restrict philosophy to the subject and methods of science, Krutch noted that pragmatism went beyond science to include religion, aesthetics, and ethics. But back in 1929, he was unable to join in their melioristic approach. He also could not accept the continuity of humans with the rest of nature. He ended *The Modern Temper* resigned to the loss of humanism but said that "we prefer to fail as humans than live as animals" (1929, p. 249).

Krutch's position began to change when, at the age of fifty, he spent a sabbatical year in the Arizona desert. *The Desert Year* (1952b) marked a shift in his thinking based on a transformative experience. In this book, and many others, including *The Voice of the Desert* (1955), *The Great Chain of Life* (1956), *Grand Canyon* (1958), *The Forgotten Peninsula* (1961), and *And Even If You Do* (1967), to name a few, Krutch developed an understanding of humans as a part of nature and elaborated an ethic for guiding human interactions with each other and the rest of nature. Much of this was built on the work of Leopold's land ethic and Albert Schweitzer's (1875–1965) concept of a reverence for life. At the start of *The Great Chain of Life*, Krutch reversed his conclusion to *The Modern Temper*. He noted that humans are animal-like and suggested that this fact might be just the thing to combat the mechanized view of humans that worried him. He again challenged the behaviorist models of animal and human life and argued that evolution suggests that there is intelligence and feeling throughout all life. Beasts are not beastly and humans should explore the "privilege of being animal" (1956, p. viii) and become sympathetic observers. He critiqued the laboratory sciences for impoverishing human understanding of other beings and instead joined ethologists of the time, such as Konrad Lorenz (1903–89), in trying to understand other beings within their various environments. According to Krutch, trying to reduce all behavior to instinct or conditioning did not make sense on this account, because social adjustment and individual variation also play a demonstrable role (p. 137).

Throughout his work, Krutch continued to reject the Cartesian dualism of mind and body, blaming it for the mechanized view of life that was beginning to dominate science and philosophy. Also, while he accepted the theory of evolution, he challenged what he saw as an overly simplistic reliance on survival value to explain all change. Like Peirce, Krutch explored the role of chance in the universe and suggested that evolution need not be purposeless. "Could it be that the 'purpose' of evolution is not survival, but awareness?" (1956, p. 127). He believed all life had a psychic aspect that is rooted in the individual. He noted that many dismissed this kind of view thanks to its apparent similarities with Lamarckian evolution (that acquired traits could be inherited) and vitalism (the view that living things were motivated by a life force). But he challenged this rejection by pointing to the inadequacies of the behaviorist and mechanized "survival of the fittest" views. He accepted that natural selection operated in evolution, but he asked why natural selection should be the only explanatory factor. The trouble with relying on natural selection alone was that it gave humans the idea that they could know and control life and its future development. This view resulted in a wasteful and dangerous approach to life. Krutch believed that while humans cannot conquer nature, they could destroy it.

At the same time that Krutch was using the desert to educate humans about their fragile connections with the rest of life, Rachel Carson began her literary career educating the public about the ocean. While she is best remembered for *Silent Spring*, published in 1962 (and often credited with starting the contemporary environmental movement), her first books were *Under the Sea Wind* in 1941, *The Sea Around Us* in 1951, and *The Edge of the Sea* in 1955.

Born outside an increasingly industrial and polluted Pittsburgh, she attended the Pennsylvania College for Women (now Chatham College). She received a master's degree in zoology at Johns Hopkins at a time when few women entered scientific fields. She had to withdraw from the doctoral program to begin work at the US Bureau of Fisheries to support her recently widowed mother and orphaned nieces.

Carson was always a writer. Early in her life, people noticed and encouraged her talent and ability to bring emerging scientific understanding to the public in an entertaining way. For instance, *Under the Sea Wind* was written from the point of view of the fish. Published one month before the bombing of Pearl Harbor, it did not receive the attention it might have. Importantly, in that first book, she noted that humans are just one of many predators in the world and that they should be careful about being too destructive. This warning was amplified in 1945 in an article she sent to *Reader's Digest*, warning that the use of DDT was part of a strategy of a "total war" against nature that unnecessarily threatened to upset the balance of nature on which all life depends. In *The Gentle Subversive*, Mark Hamilton Lytle writes:

> Carson properly imagined herself in the role of those rare writers, such as the early ecologist Aldo Leopold, whose capacity for broad synthesis and clear exposition shaped their world's understanding of nature in ways most scientists seldom could. In an era of narrowly focused research, scientists had less capacity for grand theory. As Carson explained, . . . she hoped to provide "an imaginative searching out of what is significant

in the life history of the earth's ocean," while at the same time addressing "questions thus raised in the light of the best scientific knowledge." (2007, pp. 70–1)

In her second book, *The Sea Around Us*, she took a clearly biocentric view inspired by Leopold and warned about the fragility of island ecosystems. This book won a National Book Award and freed her to earn her living by writing.

*The Edge of the Sea* was less popular but did much to develop her view of the complex interdependence of various life forms with each other and with their environments. She noted how environments alter creatures and creatures alter environments in complex, dynamic relationships. "The life of the shore," she wrote, "by the very fact of its existence there, gives evidence that it has dealt successfully with the realities of its world—the towering physical realities of the sea itself, and the subtle life relationships that bind each living thing to its own community" (1955, p. 19). The connections and dependencies among the creatures and conditions at the "edge of the sea" led Carson to reinforce a larger principle of connection. "[I]n the sea nothing lives to itself." With the presence of life, she continued, "[t]he very water is altered, in its chemical nature and in its capacity for influencing life processes," leading to the recognition of a unified conception of nature. "So the present is linked with past and future, and each living thing with all that surrounds it" (p. 39). She also emphasized that while it is important to *know about* the relationships as much as possible in order to sustain healthy ecosystems, it is equally important to *feel with* the rest of life. If humans do not develop this feeling with the rest of life, they are likely to continue to think they can control and conquer the rest of nature.

For Carson, the development of the atomic bomb and chemicals like DDT (eventually banned in the United States in 1972) were just two examples of this danger. This desire to conquer seemed to be based on fear that was connected directly to the widespread fear of foreign invaders that flourished in the 1950s. Interestingly, the McCarthy era climate of fear was transferred to parts of nature. For instance, in 1957 the "war on fire ants" talked about the ants as "red foreign invaders" that required an all-out assault rather than targeted control. When Carson began to point to the dangers of the chemical assault that was emerging, she was accused of (among other things) being an agent of communist aggressors. The United States of the 1950s was not open to ideas that challenged the powers of business and government.

And chemicals were big business. DDT, one of the biggest, was credited with controlling diseases transmitted by mosquitoes and lice during the Second World War, and after the war, a new market needed to be found. Along with other chemicals developed as part of the Cold War, DDT was turned loose to battle the perceived enemies of agriculture—the hordes of insects. Data began to emerge that this use of chemicals was killing fish, birds, and domesticated animals. Given that humans did not immediately die upon exposure, such chemicals were deemed to be safe. The idea of the dangers of accumulated chemical exposure was hard to prove. Carson wrote *Silent Spring* to warn the public of the possible dangers to which they were being exposed, without their knowledge or permission. She concluded her book by asserting that "The 'control of nature' is a phrase conceived in arrogance, born of the Neanderthal age of biology and philosophy, when it was supposed that nature exists for the convenience of man." She described the use of "the most modern and terrible weapons" against insects and thereby the entire ecosystem as "our alarming misfortune" (1962, p. 297). In place of this mentality of control, she continued to develop the idea that humans need to see their interdependence with the rest of nature and work to maintain a healthy environment if they hope to be healthy themselves. People need to study the complex interactions of various life forms and learn to work *with* these rather than try to obliterate a perceived enemy. As Leopold had noted, heavy-handed human interventions usually make things worse, not better.

The root of the problem was the arrogance of thinking that humans know everything *and* the desire to control nature and other people. In discussing various examples of chemical interventions that were done without the knowledge or permission of affected people, she raised these related concerns.

> Who has made the decision that sets in motion these chains of poisonings, this ever-widening wave of death that spreads out, like ripples when a pebble is dropped into a still pond? Who has placed in one pan of the scales the leaves that might have been eaten by the beetles and in the other the pitiful heaps of many-hued feathers, the lifeless remains of the birds that fell before the unselective bludgeon of insecticidal poisons? Who has decided—who has the *right* to decide—for the countless legions of people who were not consulted that the supreme value is a world without insects, even though it be also a sterile world ungraced by the curving wing of a bird in flight? The decision is that of the authoritarian temporarily entrusted with power; . . . .(1962, p. 127)

Much of what concerned Carson was the undemocratic nature of the widespread use of chemicals. Profit was trumping democracy and liberty. She was not against the use of chemicals in every case. "It is not my contention," she wrote, "that chemical insecticides must never be used. I do contend that we have put poisonous and biologically potent chemicals indiscriminately into the hands of persons largely or wholly ignorant of their potentials for harm" (p. 12). She instead argued for the informed, intelligent, and targeted use of chemicals, noting that nature fights back, and that without more selective use of the chemicals humans had developed, these chemicals would become increasingly ineffective. As she observed, "To have risked so much in our efforts to mold nature to our satisfaction" through the use of chemical pesticides, "yet to have failed in achieving our goal would indeed be the final irony. Yet this, it seems, is our situation" (p. 245). By 1969, the World Health Organization (WHO) ended its Global Malaria Eradication Program that used DDT to eliminate malaria-transmitting mosquitoes. While some credited Carson's critique in *Silent Spring* for the end of the program, it was primarily the consequence of something Carson predicted: the mosquitoes WHO sought to control developed resistance to DDT and its use no longer controlled malaria (Kinkela, 2011).

Carson's work ignited a storm. Chemical companies demonized her, but the public response to the book forced the administration of President John F. Kennedy to respond. Among other things, the Environmental Protection Agency was created. At the same time, the chemical industry fought back. The president of Montrose Chemical Corporation (a DDT manufacturer) said that Carson did not write as a scientist "but rather as a fanatic defender of the cult of the balance of nature" (quoted in Kinkela, 2011, p. 119). Another critic, Frederick Stare at the Harvard School of Public Health, concluded that Carson wrote "with passion and beauty but with very little scientific detachment." Echoing the consensus among analytic philosophers at the time, Stare continued, "Dispassionate scientific evidence and passionate propaganda are two buckets of water that simply can't be carried on one person's shoulders.... Miss Carson flounders as a scientist in this book" (quoted in Kinkela, 2011, p. 119).

The secretary and general counsel of Velsicol Corporation, Louis A. McLean, connected Carson's work directly to the dangers of the Cold War. "[I]n addition to the sincere expressions of opinions by natural food faddists, Audubon groups and others," the chemical industry also had to deal with "sinister influences" who attacked the industry with two purposes. The first purpose was "to create the false impression that all business is grasping and immoral," and the second was to "reduce the use of agricultural chemicals ... so that our food supply will be reduced" to the impoverished levels of the Eastern bloc (quoted in Kinkela, 2011, p. 126). In short, the opponents of the chemical industry, including Carson, sought to undermine capitalism and harness food production as a weapon against the West. Despite the charges from the interests put at risk by Carson's critique, her work nevertheless set the stage for change, both in national policy and in philosophy as well.

In addition to the emergence of environmental philosophy (and eventually work on ethics and animals), those concerned with the Vietnam War began to note the widespread use of chemicals in that war. The effects of Agent Orange and napalm, an incendiary gel that was used to burn fields, forests, villages, and people in Vietnam, are still with us today. The use of chemicals in agriculture was part of what fueled the growing agricultural labor movement under the leadership of Cesar Chavez (1927–1993) (see Chapter 21). A less commonly noted consequence was the contribution of this work to feminism and the eventual development of ecofeminism and animal-focused philosophy (see Chapter 22). The recognition of environmental racism also became part of the Civil Rights Movement (see Chapter 19).

Even as most academic philosophers stood by, the work of philosophy continued in the context of the environmental and social revolutions that began in the 1950s. The Civil Rights Movement, Black Nationalism, *La Causa*, and labor issues, alongside demands for Native American sovereignty and women's liberation, were joined by protests against the Vietnam War and growing concern about the changes in the physical landscape of America and the prospects of its human and nonhuman inhabitants. In response, the Antiwar Movement and the Environmental Movement emerged and were intertwined.

In 1964, the activist and folk singer Joan Baez led a large demonstration that kicked off years of protests across the country, involving a wide range of people. Martin Luther King, Jr., and the Black Panthers, despite their support for President Johnson for passing the Civil Rights Act, joined in protesting US involvement in Vietnam. King wrote that the people of Vietnam "must see the Americans as strange liberators.... Our government felt then that the Vietnamese people weren't ready for independence, and we again fell victim to the deadly Western arrogance that has poisoned the international atmosphere for so long" (1986, pp. 636–7). SNCC moved from civil rights activism to antiwar work. Bobby Seale, a prominent member of the Black Panthers, was arrested in the wake of the antiwar riots surrounding the 1968 Democratic National Convention. Arrested along with seven other activists, including Abbie Hoffman, for crossing state lines to start a riot—ironically a charge issuing out of the recently passed Civil Rights Act—Seale was sentenced to four years in prison. Women Striking for Peace (WSP) emerged in 1967 to join with Addams's long-existing Women's International League for Peace and Freedom. Environmental issues entered in when students at the University of Wisconsin protested Dow Chemical Company's participation in a campus job fair due to its production of napalm. The increasing awareness of the environmental destruction caused by the use of chemicals in warfare added to the protests centered on the loss of human life.

The environment, the war, and Native sovereignty were connected in the fishing protests—the "fish-in" movement—by tribes in the Pacific Northwest. As Sidney Mills, a Cherokee and Yakima man and wounded Vietnam veteran, declared in 1968: "I have given enough to the US Army—I choose now to serve my people" (Josephy et al., 1999, p. 23). Even as the United States committed vast resources to Vietnam, it allowed commercial overfishing and destruction of ecosystems and species while ignoring the environmental concerns and treaty rights of Indigenous people. For Deloria, the Vietnam War was "merely another symptom of the basic lack of integrity of the government, a side issue in comparison with the great domestic issues which must be faced . . . before this society destroys itself" (1969, pp. 52–3).

Given the draft, college students found themselves highly involved in these issues through activist organizations such as Students for a Democratic Society and in response to efforts by federal, state, and local governments to stop student protests against the war. On May 4, 1970, troops from the Ohio National Guard opened fire on an unsanctioned student protest at Kent State University. The students were protesting the invasion of Cambodia by the US military. Four students were killed, and nine others were wounded. The protest was a direct response to the announcement by President Richard Nixon on April 30, 1970, that the United States had begun an invasion (he called it an "incursion") into Cambodia to reach military bases occupied by North Vietnamese troops. While the United States had been at war in Vietnam since the Gulf of Tonkin Resolution in 1964 (and unofficially since 1954), the war appeared to be winding down in 1969. Nixon had been elected in part on his promise to end the war. His announcement marked a new escalation of US involvement and an inevitable increase in US casualties. Since most soldiers on the ground in Vietnam were college-aged men involuntarily drafted into service, it was not surprising that the announcement led to protests at campuses across the country. Some protesters opposed the military action, others the draft, and still others opposed a government they believed was bent on imperialism.

Eleven days later, on May 15, as students across the country joined in a general student strike to protest the killings at Kent State and the Cambodian invasion, students at Jackson State College, a historically Black college in Jackson, Mississippi, joined the protest. Although the details remain unclear, after a mostly peaceful march, some marchers began to throw rocks and light fires. In response, local and state police assembled near a large group of students who had gathered in front of a residence hall. The police officers fired into the crowd and the building behind. Though the officers said later that they had been fired on from the residence hall, no evidence was ever found to confirm the story. Joseph Rhodes, Jr., a member of the Commission on Campus Unrest established by President Nixon, described what happened next: "When the sound of gunfire stopped two young black men lay dead on the ground and a dozen other young black kids writhed from their wounds in front of the police officers, who calmly reloaded their weapons, not one of them attempting to render aid" (1974, p. 309). The protests at Kent State and Jackson State were only two of dozens of antiwar protests that faced violent responses that spring. While the killings at Kent State led to an investigation and the indictment of eight members of the National Guard, no indictments were filed in the aftermath of the killings at Jackson State.

Campus unrest was not new in 1970. Beginning in the mid-1960s, protests on campuses became increasingly common. In part, the protests echoed protests off-campus to bring about civil rights legislation. They were also part of the growing Antiwar Movement and took up larger issues of social and economic injustice. In 1960, a long-standing group called the Student League for Industrial Democracy changed its name to Students for a Democratic Society (SDS), and in 1962 held its first convention at the University of Michigan. The founding document of the SDS was the Port Huron Statement, a manifesto that advocated for participatory democracy, the elimination of nuclear weapons, and a goal of "creating a world where hunger, poverty, disease, ignorance, violence, and exploitation are replaced as central features by abundance, reason, love, and international cooperation" (Port Huron, 1962). The SDS quickly began to organize chapters at campuses throughout the United States and organized protests over the next decade in opposition to the Vietnam War and in favor of civil rights. Another group, the SNCC, was founded at a meeting in 1960 at the historically Black college, Shaw University, in Raleigh, North Carolina. SNCC, begun with a small grant from the SCLC, focused on civil rights activism and was instrumental in organizing the 1963 March on Washington led by Martin Luther King, Jr. Together, SNCC and the SDS (and other less visible groups) helped to organize many protests on campuses and off in the 1960s and 1970s (see Chapters 18 and 19).

The 1970 shootings at Kent State University resulted in a national student strike. Many faculty members across the country found themselves sympathetic with the students and were able to use the issues surrounding the war to teach the importance of thinking for oneself. Many philosophy professors were likely involved too, though, at this point in time, it is not possible to give an accurate list of who they were. What we can say is that only a few philosophers took up the issues surrounding the war directly in their philosophical work. Those who did risked not being taken seriously as philosophers given the state of professional philosophy at the time, both in terms of the questions academic philosophy asked and as a result of the atmosphere produced by the anti-communist surveillance and loyalty oaths of the 1950s.

Government surveillance did not end with the conclusion of formal anti-communist hearings. We now know that similar surveillance was occurring in the 1960s and 1970s. President Johnson used the CIA to investigate those involved in domestic protests. President Nixon continued this surveillance, and the CIA's Operation CHAOS watched those involved in antiwar efforts, civil rights activities, women's liberation, and environmental causes. Those involved in the counterculture movement of the 1960s and 1970s were all under suspicion. Operation CHAOS ended during the Watergate affair, and there was a backlash against this kind of government surveillance of US citizens. Despite the professional risks, philosophers formed the Radical Philosophy Association (1982), Concerned Philosophers for Peace (1983), and the North American Society for Social Philosophy (1984). Since these groups were focused on doing something with philosophy rather than working only within the academic discipline, they were open to a wide range of philosophical approaches—Marxism, feminism, critical race theory, postcolonial theory, phenomenology, anarchism, post-structuralism, and environmentalism. Although not declared "American" philosophers, their work emerged from the problems faced in the wider American community and sought to resist dominant ways of thinking both in the academy and the world.

While protests over Vietnam resulted in a nationwide student movement, some of this energy spilled over to create the Women's movement of the time (discussed in Chapter 22) and the Environmental Movement. The first Earth Day in the United States was held on April 22, 1970. Around twenty million people participated, and separate environmentally focused groups began to coordinate their efforts. After seeing the consequences of a large oil spill in Southern California, Democratic Senator Gaylord Nelson (later to win the Presidential Medal of Freedom for this work), Republican Congressman Pete McCloskey, and Harvard graduate student Denis Hayes worked to coordinate a national teach-in on the environment. The political energy around environmental issues that followed from the increasing awareness about these issues crystallized in the Clean Air, Clean Water, and Endangered Species Acts, as well as the creation of the Environmental Protection Agency. Until the era of those pieces of federal legislation, most environmental concerns were considered fringe concerns of "granola-eating hippies." Most people drove large cars, fueled by cheap leaded gas, and because of this, air pollution (smog) was starting to get some people's attention. At the same time, the use and misuse of dangerous pesticides gained some prominence. Thanks to the more coordinated political and social effort of the burgeoning environmental movement, many issues began to get serious public attention: pollution, garbage disposal (recycling), species conservation, and population issues.

The work outside the academy by thinkers like Muir, Leopold, Krutch, and Carson made possible another major shift in the landscape of American philosophy. Carson was a bridge person—a pioneering woman as well as an early ecologist—who did much to change how many Americans understood the relationship of humans with the rest of nature. As we've already discussed, her publication of *Silent Spring* in 1962 is credited with starting the contemporary environmental movement, and this, in turn, gave rise to the emergence of environmental philosophy, and environmental ethics in particular. While only a few of the seminal works in environmental philosophy were published in the late 1960s (Lynn White's, "Historical Roots of Our Ecological Crisis" in 1967 and Garrett Hardin's "The Tragedy of the Commons" in 1968), the 1970s saw an explosion of philosophers engaging environmental issues.

The first US conference on environmental philosophy was held in 1971 at the University of Georgia. Many of those papers were published in *Philosophy and Environmental Crisis* (Blackstone, 1974). The papers addressed issues of obligations to animals, obligations to future generations, the role of technology, the need to change ideologies and outlooks (atomism vs. holism), and the need to change lifestyles and consumption. In 1973, Australian philosopher and logician Richard Routley (later known as Richard Sylvan) published "Is There a Need for a New, an Environmental, Ethic?" and Norwegian philosopher Arne Naess (1912–2009) published "The Shallow and the Deep, Long-Range Ecology Movement: A Summary," setting up what would become an ongoing discussion about how to understand the value of nature.

By 1979, environmental philosophy was a clearly emerging field, and Eugene Hargrove began publishing the journal *Environmental Ethics*. It is important to note that not all philosophers saw this kind of work as "real philosophy." Colleagues, for instance, told Hargrove that what he was doing was not philosophy but just "being a good citizen" (2012 interview with McKenna). This attitude contributed to his struggle to get tenure. Applied ethics in general, including environmental and medical ethics, made many philosophers uncomfortable because such a focus bypassed the internal struggle in philosophy departments between analytic philosophy and nonanalytic approaches and instead focused on problems and questions. It also made questions of value and ethics central again. As academic philosophy had tried to drop questions of ethics and politics in order to strive to be more scientific, many philosophers saw the move to applied ethics as a backward turn.

This tension caused philosophy to become caught up in larger political struggles once again. With Ronald Reagan's election as president in 1981, William Bennett, who earned a PhD in philosophy from the University of Texas at Austin, came to head the National Endowment for the Humanities (NEH). One of his first moves was to rule out "value research." When proposals for programs on environmental ethics were put forward, they were judged either as relativistic, and so not rigorous enough, or as aimed to indoctrinate participants in a particular position. During the presidency of George H. W. Bush (from 1989 until 1993), Hargrove reported being asked by officials at the NEH to include a section on how he could run an NEH Institute on environmental issues without embarrassing the president. He chose not to pursue the application under such conditions. With William Jefferson Clinton as president (from 1993 until 2001), the NEH once again took up programs related to environmental ethics, but this ended in 2001 with the presidency of George W. Bush. Hargrove contended that this pattern of contesting the place of values in research was just another move in "the culture wars" that have gone on in the United States since the late nineteenth century (see Chapter 24). These contests about the place of values in education, in particular, have a long history, not to mention efforts to answer questions about kinds of value (instrumental, intrinsic, aesthetic) and the status and nature of values (universal or contextual, one or many, unchanging or changing).

When questions of value are entertained, some see the value of the environment in instrumental terms. This means that nature is seen as a resource for human use, and the value of nature is judged by the value of that use. This view has guided much of conservation in the United States. When Gifford Pinchot (1865–1946) argued for the system of national forests in the early twentieth century, it was on the grounds of preserving resources for use by future generations. He argued that the use of natural resources, which required wisdom and planning, was a necessary and good thing—leading to human prosperity. The same kind of argument can be seen today in many environmental debates. Some believe that practically speaking, it is better to appeal to the self-interest of humans by pointing to the use value of nature. These are anthropocentric (human-centered) arguments. Contemporary anthropocentric arguments point to how, for example, preserving an ecosystem can save people money by allowing the ecosystem to filter water, control flooding, or limit "pests." These are called "ecosystem services"—clearly pointing to the focus on how environmentally sound policies are a matter of human benefit.

The focus on use or instrumental value worries those who find intrinsic and aesthetic value in nature to be most important. The call to focus on intrinsic value in nature rests on the idea that nature has value in its own right, apart from any use humans may have for it. As was mentioned earlier, Muir took this approach in countering Pinchot. Muir found God's temples in nature and saw much more than resources to be developed when he encountered the beauty of the West. This approach was famously taken up by Naess, who developed the idea of "deep" ecology to counter what he saw as the "shallow" ecology based on use value. Naess noted the influence of Carson's work on his own and argued that humans should see themselves as part of an ecosystem rather than its master or manager.

In the United States, a well-known advocate of the intrinsic value of nature is Holmes Rolston III. Rolston's essay "Is There an Ecological Ethic?" was published in 1975 and is seen as the first article in a mainstream philosophy journal (*Ethics*) to challenge the idea that the value of nature was to be found in the value it had for humans. Instead, he argued for the intrinsic value of nature. Furthermore, he found value in the whole of an ecosystem and argued that the value of an ecosystem or species trumped the needs and interests of individuals. This ecological holism is to be understood, however, within the context of a biocentrism that respects all living organisms, with humans being just one organism among many in an ecosystem. Rolston argued for a nonanthropocentric approach to the environment and appealed to the aesthetic value of nature.

Those who focus on the aesthetic value of nature combine the other two value arguments in an interesting way (though often unrecognized). The value of the aesthetic pleasure humans may derive from nature is a particular kind of use value, but it usually rests on the idea of respecting the integrity and value of natural systems in their own right. Muir also appealed to the aesthetic value of nature in his defense of the national park system and thought nature was an important source of spiritual renewal. Today we find arguments that the aesthetic experience comes from direct contact with nature, and so humans need to preserve spaces for such experiences. There is also ongoing debate about whether increased scientific knowledge about a natural object improves or detracts from the quality of an aesthetic experience of it.

Worried that environmental philosophy had become too exclusively about ethics, and too influenced by science and analytic philosophy, continental philosophers began to enter the field. In 1997, the International Association for Environmental Philosophy was established to foster conversation among continental philosophers and provide another voice in the field. The Association began to publish the journal *Environmental Philosophy* in 2004. *Rethinking Nature: Essays in Environmental Philosophy* (edited by Bruce V. Foltz and Robert Frodeman) was published in 2004 to further these efforts. Similar efforts can be seen in the publication of *Animal Philosophy* (edited by Matthew Calarco and Peter Atterton), also published in 2004, which brings continental views to animal issues.

Viewed within the context of American pragmatism, though, no one of these approaches captures the complex and changing nature of what it means to be a live creature (human or other being) living in and through a mutually transformative relationship with the rest of one's environment (natural and social). Nor does any single approach to ethics: deontological ethics, utilitarian ethics, virtue ethics, or care ethics. As Dewey notes, however, while each of these can capture some aspects of the complex relationships and ethical claims, no one of these theories can be responsive to the complexity of lived conditions.

Moral extensionist approaches have sparked a more general debate about whether *one* moral theory (monism) could handle the various environmental issues, or whether multiple approaches (pluralism) would be better. The monist approach has a tendency to replicate the internal debates among philosophers, though applied to a new set of issues. This has resulted in some deep divides among environmental and animal-focused philosophers. The pluralist approach has resulted in some interesting blended positions, as well as philosophers working with practitioners and academics in other fields. Much of this work is done by people working in, or influenced by, the American tradition of philosophy we have been discussing.

One prominent example can be found in the work of ecofeminist theorist Val Plumwood. Richard Routley, who was mentioned earlier in this chapter, along with Val Routley (who later became Val Plumwood), argued against anthropocentric approaches to environmental ethics by positing the "last man" scenario. They suggested that the logical conclusion of anthropocentric positions is that if there was just one human left and that person destroyed an ecosystem or a sentient creature, no harm would be done. Since there are no interests of other humans at stake, there is no harm. They argued that this counterintuitive conclusion should prompt a reevaluation of environmental ethics.

Plumwood, who was well known for her work in logic, wrote *Feminism and the Mastery of Nature* in 1993 and became a well-known ecofeminist (see Chapter 22). She argued that the logic of colonialism rests on the domination of nature as well as the interlocking systems of oppression based on race, class, and gender. *Environmental Culture: The Ecological Crisis of Reason* (2001) took up the concern that much of the contemporary world is run by a "hubristic and sado-dispassionate form of economic and scientific reason" that is exclusionary and dangerous (p. 2). She argued that we need to develop an "environmental culture that values and fully acknowledges the non-human sphere and our dependency on it" (p. 3). The American strand of philosophy directly influenced Plumwood as she referenced the work of Dewey when discussing the problematic effects of remoteness. She was concerned that people are "blind" to their environmental impact as they are separated in time and space from the impact of their actions on the environment and other people. This remoteness allowed people to take actions that harm the earth, other animals, and human communities. More indirectly, she took up many of the ideas and themes found in this tradition—an emphasis on experience, community, and democracy. Though she did not overtly identify herself as a pragmatist, the argument could be made.

The distinctive American tradition of pragmatism has also entered discussions of the environment more directly and forms a valuable model of engaged philosophy. Such efforts were collected in *Environmental Pragmatism* edited by Andrew Light and Eric Katz and published in 1996. The goal of the book was to bring environmental philosophy to bear on policy. The editors said that environmental pragmatism is the "open-ended inquiry into the specific real-life problems of humanity's relationship with the environment" (p. 2). Some of the authors grounded their work in the classical pragmatists, while others in a pragmatist methodology. The standpoint of environmental pragmatism embraced a metatheoretical pluralism and sought to address actual problems.

The work of Bryan G. Norton, Andrew Light, Eric Katz, Ben A. Minteer, Shane Ralston, and Anthony Weston, in particular have had a sustained impact on the field of environmental philosophy. Norton's work put pragmatism on the map in the field by arguing against monistic nonanthropocentrist positions in favor of the need for weak anthropocentrism within environmental philosophy. Further, he suggests that most of the time, those taking a nonanthropocentric stance and those taking an anthropocentric stance arrive at similar policies and practices. Rather than spend philosophical energy on the anthropocentric vs. nonanthropocentric debate, he thinks we should work with a broad or weak anthropocentrism that allows for critique of destructive and consumptive views of nature without requiring the embrace of nonanthropocentrism. This allows groups with differing understandings of how to value nature to converge on similar policy and action plans—what Norton called the convergence hypothesis. Andrew Light not only championed the convergence hypothesis as he developed his own methodological pragmatism, but he also carried it into practice when he worked on policy for the US Department of State (2013–16) and the US Department of Energy (2021–present).

In contrast to Norton and Light, many prominent environmental philosophers (e.g., Holmes Rolston III, Laura Westra, J. Baird Callicott) take issue with Norton's defense of a role for anthropocentric values within environmental philosophy, ethics, and policy. Eric Katz, for example, in his *Nature as Subject: Human Obligation and Natural Community* (1997) challenges American pragmatism as too anthropocentric to be useful for developing an environmental ethic. Such an ethic, for Katz, must have "direct moral consideration and respect for the evolutionary processes of nature" (p. xvi). While pragmatism may respect the evolutionary processes of nature, Katz argues that it does not respect nature's autonomy and instead supports human interventions within nature. For Katz, once there is a human intervention (even if on behalf of some part of nature such as species conservation), nature is lost and an artifact is all that remains.

For Katz, all domesticated animals are artifacts and not part of the natural community. They are "no more natural than a wooden table" (p. 85). They are at best irrelevant, and at worst damaging, to nature and to his vision of an environmental ethic (p. 28). He puts forward a modified holism that starts with a first principle of respect for an ecosystem or natural community (holism) but which is guided by a secondary principle that aims to protect natural individuals (p. 23). He thinks this guards against the dangers of holism disregarding individual beings (e.g., animals and plants) and entities (e.g., rivers and mountains) within a natural community and still allows for the sacrifice of some individuals for the health of the natural community (pp. 25, 28). He argues that this approach must rest on some notion of nonanthropogenic value in natural beings and entities (though this need not be intrinsic value). In his view, though pragmatism has the strengths of a pluralist and relational approach and understands the need to evaluate specific situations rather than search for a universal, it understands value only in anthropocentric terms and results in subjective relativism (pp. 71–3). According to him, pragmatism also fails to understand that human intervention within nature is a problem. Any imposition of a human plan seeks to control otherness (domination) and turns nature into a human artifact (pp. 93, 110). This kind of understanding of pragmatism is what those working within environmental pragmatism are up against as they seek to show that pragmatism is rooted in "humility and [a] sense of human dependency on natural conditions" and calls on humans to "respect and cooperate with nature rather than dominate it" (Minteer, 2012, p. 84).

Ben A. Minteer's *Refounding Environmental Ethics: Pragmatism, Principle, and Practice* (2012) argues that we need to choose "policy pragmatism over philosophical purity, democracy over dogma, and impact over ideology" (p. 3). He argues that environmental philosophy needs to stop being a discussion among philosophers and engage other disciplines in a collaborative style that makes philosophy practical. He thinks that a "philosophically sound and policy-relevant environmental ethics will necessarily be a pluralistic, naturalistic, and collaborative environmental ethics" (p. 3). This also entails a fallibilistic approach that does not seek "fixed and immutable beliefs" or "certainty and moral purity" (p. 9). This does not mean a surrender to skepticism, though. While pragmatist fallibilism results in pluralism, open-mindedness, and tolerance, it does not rule out identifying "factual error and distorting forces" (p. 9). In response to worries such as Katz's that pragmatism results in subjective relativism, Minteer argues that pragmatism's moral pluralism "does not commit us to any unprincipled moral promiscuity" (p. 118) and is more realistic since "individuals are differently situated and are shaped . . . by dissimilar traditions and experiences, as well as the fact that novel ethical situations and problem contexts are always emerging." Peirce, James, and Dewey argue for understanding human experience as "contingent, dynamic, and multifaceted" (p. 117). This results in a challenge to the dominant monistic, nonanthropocentric environmental ethics which relies on a metaphysical and epistemological foundation of intrinsic value (pp. 10, 68).

Minteer argues that pragmatism has room for noninstrumental values as long as they are understood in a nonfoundational, contextual manner and are evaluated in terms of their effectiveness for practice, policy, and human welfare. They, like all other values, need to be "entirely open to public criticism and revision" and not operate in a universalistic fashion (2012, pp. 67–8, 72). Further, environmental pragmatists embrace experimental methods, tolerance, and inclusivity as necessary to good environmental deliberation, decision-making, and policy (p. 12). They embrace the virtues of "tolerance; openness; free communication; nondogmatic, fallibilistic attitude toward held beliefs" (p. 28). The realities of "contingency, change, and unpredictability reinforce these virtues" (p. 31) and help us deal with conflicting values (p. 35) without falling into "unprincipled moral promiscuity" (p. 118). This approach moves us beyond "hard-and-fast ontological polarities" and "can accommodate noninstrumental elements into a problem-oriented and pluralistic model of environmental ethics" (p. 74) that supports the natural piety Dewey calls for. Dewey understands "nature as the whole of which we are parts" and sees humans as parts "marked by intelligence and purpose" but always "dependent upon the cooperation of nature" (LW 9, p. 18). Dewey calls for a "reverence toward nature, which in his antidualistic understanding comprises both human social relations and the nonhuman environment" (Minteer, 2012. p. 81).

Shane J. Ralston's *Pragmatic Environmentalism: Toward a Rhetoric of Eco-Justice* (2013) uses the work of John Dewey and Aldo Leopold to develop a pragmatic form of environmental communication that can help move action in the direction of eco-justice. He argues that we need both a rhetoric of control and a rhetoric of restraint in order to navigate the complex ways human desires interact with the well-being of the rest of nature. While Dewey is more commonly seen among environmental philosophers as espousing a view of control, Ralston points to Dewey's calls for natural piety, harmony with nature, and leaving a sustainable environment for future generations as evidence that Dewey combines the rhetorics of control and restraint. Ralston argues that it is important to understand Dewey more fully because environmental philosophy loses key philosophical resources when it dismisses pragmatism as brute utilitarianism or instrumentalism (p. 10). For instance, pragmatism seeks to overcome dualisms and resists both absolutism and relativism as it understands human experience as tied to the rest of nature and understands inquiry and experience as beginning already in the middle of things, which requires adjustment to circumstances (p. xvi). Such adjustment entails both accommodation (acquiescing to the environment) and adaptation (manipulating the environment to one's needs) (p. 62). A pragmatist approach to environmental philosophy looks both backwards and forwards in order to inform present inquiry and suggest possible solutions that respect the integrity and dynamic stability of nature and call for restraint on the part of humans without dismissing all human valuing as irrelevant. In short, it makes room for the kind of modified anthropocentrism Norton calls for in his work.

Norton's *Sustainability: A Philosophy of Adaptive Ecosystem Management* (2005) uses pragmatism to rethink the environmental problems with which we are presented by rethinking the language we use and how that may limit or open up our options. He aimed at a multidisciplinary and publicly engaged environmental philosophy that rests on experience and experimentation. He argues that environmental pragmatism is more than a problem-oriented approach; it is a habit of mind and inquiry that eschews appeals to a priori or essentialist categories and instead embraces experimentation and situational intelligence. Being contextual and pluralistic, he argues, is not the same as being relativistic. Pragmatist inquiry is tied to the natural and cultural communities that are part of the situation being examined and acted upon, so it is not an "anything goes" pluralism. What ties pragmatism together for Norton is that it is

> a stubborn attempt to see knowledge and evaluation as contextual and conditioned by the agreements and disagreements existent in real situations with real people, real stakes, real dialogue, and real attempts at cooperative behavior. In this context, shared agreements provide the platform, and disagreements inspire the group to rest their hypotheses and find new possible solutions. (p. 505)

While many approaches to environmental ethics are at odds with animal ethics, pragmatism provides one way to bridge that gap. In *Back to Earth: Tomorrow's Environmentalism* (1994), Anthony Weston stresses that "even the most elementary politeness requires at least thinking about how other creatures might care to live with us (or not), rather than taking it upon ourselves to define and thereby limit them too." (p. 13). This move relies on understanding humans as part of nature, not as some kind of external caretaker. We need to understand "that we are part of this system—that it is not somehow 'ours,' that it has a coherence of its own, depths of order and possibility that we may not even suspect. Most of the action has nothing to do with us. . . . Nature conserves us, as the Naskapi Indians say, not we it" (p. 3).

Tracing the long history of human connections with other animal beings that result in companionship and wonder, he argues that

> learning to live with other animals is not a matter of somehow crossing centuries-old barriers into a new world. It is instead, to recognize—in the literal sense, to "re-cognize," to re-acknowledge—that we already exist within them, that we can hardly even utter two sentences or spend a night dreaming without invoking them. Our cultural history as well as our evolutionary history is thoroughly shared with other animals. (p. 33)

Weston argues that this connection is created by shared sociality, perception, sensation, and communication, even as these very traits also point to important differences among the vast variety of life. But many humans have lost a sense of what is shared with other animal beings and have overemphasized differences, even denying any shared nature. "We already live in social relations with any number of other creatures: yes. . . . All of this is only a shadow of what it once was." Focused on other humans and our built environments, many humans have lost any sense of other worlds. Weston continues, "This loss, this turning inward, I shall call 'desolation.' *Desolation*: literally, driving ourselves into loneliness. Every species lost or driven to the corners, every natural place remade for our purposes, leaves us and our places a little closer to dominating the stage" (p. 85). This then allows for what Weston terms self-validating reduction. With little to no experience with other animal beings, we believe whatever we are told about them, such as that they are stupid, aggressive, or unfeeling. Other animals and land continue to be reduced because many humans hold a reduced view of what they are and can be. To end the cycle of reduction, we need to find space for respectful interaction rather than continue down the road of separateness. "Precisely the maintenance of something like 'margins' emerges as part of the answer," and wild and wilderness should not be understood as the absence of humans (p. 130). This will require that humans develop what Weston calls transhuman etiquettes that begin with recognition and acknowledgment of others and take them seriously on their own terms (pp. 146, 153).

Work to develop a transhuman etiquette and ethic in a pragmatist vein can be seen in *Animal Pragmatism: Rethinking Human-Nonhuman Relations*, edited by Erin McKenna and Andrew Light in 2004. This book sought to focus the growing interest in pragmatism among environmental philosophers on issues more specifically focused on other-than-human animal beings. The editors call on pragmatism as an approach to inquiry that starts with where we are and with how we understand things. We should use our experiences as we examine any particular ethical issue, but "pragmatism challenges received experience and inherited wisdom and impels people to be critical of their habits. Rather than just providing principles to guide practice it focuses on developing a critical approach to life in which all people can engage" (p. 9). The recognition that philosophical theories are tools of inquiry means that pragmatism is a genuinely pluralistic approach. Following Dewey's recognition of the need for diverse modes of inquiry, one can see that all of the ethical theories are useful tools but none alone help guide ethical deliberations in all circumstances.

Minteer and McKenna have continued with this focus on pragmatism and animals. McKenna first focused on animals commonly understood as pets and livestock. In *Pets, People, and Pragmatism* (2013) she argues that in order to have respectful relationships with animal beings commonly viewed as pets (horses, dogs, and cats in particular), it is important to understand these animal beings as species, breeds, and individuals. This means that generalized conclusions, such as the claim that horse racing is abusive or that it is always wrong to declaw a cat, are not possible. Varying contexts and individualized beings require more complex approaches. Using a pragmatist and evolutionary framework, she argues (unlike Katz) that there is nothing unnatural about domestication but that there are many ethical concerns about how humans treat domesticated animal beings. This argument continues in *Livestock: Food, Fiber, and Friends* (2018).

In *Livestock*, McKenna and some of her students interviewed farmers and ranchers about how they viewed the human relationship with the rest of nature and the impact of those views on how they raised and killed animals for agricultural purposes. Drawing primarily on pragmatism and ecofeminism, these views and practices are examined on environmental, animal welfare, and social justice grounds. Drawing on the work of Dewey, she argues that "openness to seeing other animals as having personalities and individuality and being creatures with 'developing careers' that need to be respected is an important insight" (p. 24). These books were followed by a general, introductory book explicitly using a pragmatist ecofeminist/ecowomanist approach to a variety of concerns related to human relationships with other animal beings—*Living With Animals: Rights, Responsibility, and Respect* (2021). In this book, McKenna addresses topics such as biomedical research, entertainment, farming, hunting, and zoos. She focuses on how to avoid absolutistic moral thinking that results in singular solutions or tries to end human relationships with other animal beings altogether. Instead, she argues that "Humans need to remember that their lives and deaths are intertwined with the rest of nature; they need to remember that to be human is to be related to the rest of life, not separate from or superior to it" (p. 158). What is needed is to find respectful ways to build relationships (Weston's transhuman etiquette). This book also begins to take up questions of how humans should relate to those animal beings commonly considered wild, the topic of a later work (coauthored with Mary Trachsel and Tess Varner).

Minteer has already focused on wildlife concerns. In *The Fall of the Wild* (2019), he argues from a pragmatic preservationist perspective that acknowledges both the need for some human interventions to save ecosystems and species and values a sense of the wild and respect for nature (p. 119). While not disavowing technological interventions, he warns that humans need to exercise humility and restraint. Given that human actions have endangered species through direct killing and indirect harm through climate change, there "is a real need for action." But "this interventionist impulse should be checked when it poses a moral hazard by threatening to undermine concern for those environmental goods and relationships it is also our responsibility to maintain as a commitment both to wild nature for its own sake and to the intergenerational community of which we are just a part" (p. 127). He develops this position by drawing on classical pragmatism (Peirce, James, and Dewey), especially Dewey's call to adapt to, and cooperate with, natural forces. But unlike some who call themselves environmental pragmatists in order to justify any kind of intervention, Minteer stresses pragmatism's sense of contingency, fallibilism, restraint, and moral limits (p. 11).

Not only are environmental and animal pragmatism examples of a newly invigorated and increasingly visible American philosophy, but the entire field of applied philosophy and ethics owes much to the American tradition and spirit of philosophy as it seeks to bring philosophy to bear on the problems the world faces. This impetus can be found in the classical American thinkers. Dewey and Tufts had an "applied" section in their *Ethics* text—1908 and 1932—in which they took up issues of labor, business, and changing gender roles. They worried about separating theory and practice. We see this in more contemporary philosophers doing applied philosophy (biomedical ethics, food ethics, and business ethics, for example), many of whom had some exposure to the American tradition or work directly out of the tradition.[1]

In this part, Social Revolutions, we have tried to show some of the ways philosophy was and is an important part of ongoing social struggles. We have looked at the philosophical sources from the past that helped shape our understanding of these problems and provided a sampling of some of the ways philosophers remain engaged with these issues in the twenty-first century. We have also pointed out some ways that the understanding of philosophy itself was transformed by engaging with these struggles. This new understanding made more room for the tradition of American philosophy within the discipline. It has become an important resource for those working within philosophy on traditional philosophical problems, for philosophers working to use philosophy to better understand and analyze problems of the world, and for those who work more directly on such problems of the world as practitioners in education, law, politics, and social activism.

To see how it is that the largely hidden, if not seemingly eclipsed, American philosophical tradition remained strong and vibrant, we next turn to its revitalization and its role in the present world. To accomplish this in Part VI, "Democratic Futures?" the contemporary nature of the material requires us to shift our approach a bit. We can no longer provide the kind of historical context we have so far tried to provide. It is not yet clear what historical events will drive the future of American philosophy and we cannot, of course, identify in advance what work will turn out to be most influential. Instead, we continue the story of American philosophy, focusing on a set of philosophers who seem to well represent the ongoing strands of philosophical resistance that emerge from the tradition we have charted, and who respond to disruptions and crises of the twenty-first century.

For the most part, however, while Carson and others worried about human and ecosystem health, academic philosophy remained safely ensconced within the walls of the university. Nevertheless, US society was undergoing a cultural shift as it dealt with a series of conflicts. While people were challenging the Vietnam War, long-standing conventions of race relations, women's rights, labor relations, and the draft, most philosophers focused on technical problems within the field of philosophy. Some of those doing "technical" philosophy in the academy were engaged politically in their personal lives, though the field itself had only a few who engaged with the issues of the day *as* philosophers. While the work of these few would eventually do much to change the landscape of American philosophy, the more public voices were found among other intellectuals.

## Note

1 There are many others working in the fields of animal and environmental pragmatism. For example, contra Norton, Hugh McDonald's *John Dewey and Environmental Philosophy* (2004) argued for pragmatism as a resource for the development of a nonanthropocentric ethic. *Pragmatism and Environmentalism* (2012), edited by McDonald, addresses issues of environmental aesthetics, environmental justice, environmental ethics, and environmental pedagogy. *The Agrarian Vision: Sustainability and Environmental Ethics* (2010), by Paul B. Thompson, provides a pragmatic approach that is rooted in community and moves to policy. More recently, Brian Henning's *Value, Beauty, and Nature: The Philosophy of Organism and Metaphysical Foundation of Environmental Ethics* (2023) argues against what he sees as flaws with environmental pragmatism and argues for a Whiteheadian process approach instead. He worries about what he sees as a too-exclusive focus on policy among environmental pragmatists and an anti-philosophical bent that results from not wanting to take up metaphysical issues, which are important to changing people's worldviews. He argues that there are resources for doing such worldview transformation work in Whitehead, Peirce, James, and Dewey but that most environmental pragmatists don't do this work. He then defends the fallibilistic pluralism and anti-reductionist empiricism found in these thinkers.

## Primary Texts

Carson, Rachel (2002). *Silent Spring*. Boston: Houghton Mifflin.
Krutch, Joseph Wood (1956). *The Great Chain of Life*. Boston: Houghton Mifflin.
Leopold, Aldo (1949). *Sand County Almanac*. Oxford: Oxford University Press.
Minteer, B. A. (2012). *Refounding Environmental Ethics: Pragmatism, Principle, and Practice*. Philadelphia: Temple University Press.
Norton, B. G. (2005). *Sustainability: A Philosophy of Adaptive Ecosystem Management*. Chicago: University of Chicago Press.
Plumwood, V. (2001). *Environmental Culture: The Ecological Crisis of Reason*. New York: Routledge.

# PART IV
## DEMOCRATIC FUTURES?

# CHAPTER 24
# RECOVERY AND REVITALIZATION OF THE AMERICAN TRADITION

The most pressing problem of America's communities has almost always been how to sustain communities in the face of deep differences: historical, cultural, linguistic, economic, religious, gendered, racial, and in relation to the very land on which communities live. As we noted at the end of the previous chapter, from the perspective of the present day, it becomes increasingly difficult to look at the near past and know what will matter most as American futures develop. Abstract commitments to democracy and equity, to freedom and opportunity, become harder to imagine in the concrete, daily living, especially when the abstract principles have not changed the circumstances of many in the community. The story of American philosophy is perhaps best told in this near-term context through the work of philosophers who at least see themselves resisting the structures that seem to limit futures committed to the flourishing of individuals in community.

It is useful to take the counsel of Melvin Rogers in *The Darkened Light of Faith* (2023), "The question of what American *is* or *can be* may defy articulation, but we cannot get on with figuring out where we should go and who we ought to be without narrating the past to which we belong" (p. 6). This commitment to narrating the past is apparent throughout our story of American philosophies of resistance. The point is not to worry about "the *True* or *Final* description of the past" but rather to "aid us in making decisions about who we are and what we should become." Rogers sees this as the "aspirational character of the American imagination." Speaking of the African American tradition in particular, he observes that imagining futures "forms the foundation on which African Americans have often relied to make sense of their appeals to the nation. In this, they have placed their faith" (p. 6). We would argue that this same framework—narrating the past in order to find futures to believe in—is part of the broad American tradition we have charted and, in these last chapters, emerges in the work of many who have sought to find a way forward in a darkening world.

In order to imagine what "we should become," American philosophers have often turned to developments in other disciplines as they sought resources for helping philosophy engage with real-world problems. American philosophy also influenced these other disciplines—economics, psychology, biology, sociology, physics, and education. Richard Bernstein (1932–2022) has argued that the influence of pragmatism, in particular, was so pervasive that it was (and often remains) invisible. At other times, however, such influence has been quite visible. For instance, the work of C. Wright Mills (1916–62), an influential and controversial sociologist, was rooted in the work of Peirce, Dewey, and Mead. Following the work of Thorstein Veblen (1857–1929) and his *Theory of the Leisure Class* (1899), Mills's critiques of the "power elite" and his diagnosis of the increasingly disempowered and disappointed middle class remain relevant today.

Born in Waco, Texas in 1916, Mills began his studies at the University of Texas at Austin in 1935. There he earned an MA in philosophy under the guidance of a department deeply influenced by the American tradition, thanks in part to their graduate training at the University of Chicago. The work of Mead was especially influential. Clarence Ayres (1891–1972), who completed his PhD at Chicago in 1917 and taught economics at Texas, did much to introduce Mills to Dewey and Veblen, while George V. Gentry, who studied with Mead and completed his PhD in 1931, brought out the importance of the work of Peirce. Mills was greatly influenced by David Miller's interpretation of Mead and by Miller's readings of James and Royce. After Miller completed his undergraduate degree at Emporia State University in Kansas, he began his graduate program at the University of Chicago, where he took classes from Mead. After Mead's death in 1931, Miller completed his work with Charles Morris and, over the next decade, became known as one of the leading scholars of Mead's work. When Mills went on to the University of Wisconsin for a PhD in sociology, his studies of these thinkers went with him. His dissertation, posthumously published as *Sociology and Pragmatism* (1964), demonstrated the enduring influence of this tradition on all his work.

While his dissertation included what many would see as misreadings of Dewey's work consistent with some of the "instrumentalist" readings of pragmatism, Mills's work could be seen as an important use of philosophy to create social change. He also accepted something like Dewey's conception of "critical intelligence," that critical intelligence was part of the process of social change, and that its use called for the work of public intellectuals. At the same time, Mills also identified what he took as an important omission in Dewey's work. Mills argued in *Sociology and Pragmatism* that Dewey saw "reality," "technologically or socially," on the model of "a small town of artisans or a farming community" (1964, p. 392). The result was a conception of action as "of an individual" outside of the context regulated by a state or other more or less inflexible rules. Dewey's conception of action is instead "conduct at the edge of social structures, such as frontier types of society that are edging out into places not hampered by social organization" (p. 393). In the context of politics, this conception of action seems to defer to the method of inquiry, and so pragmatists find themselves unable to make principled stands in advance of careful inquiry. "Politically," Mills wrote, "pragmatism is less expediency than it is a kind of perennial mugwump" (p. 394).

Mills granted that in the context of technology and biology, where problems are identified and resolved through ongoing inquiry, this approach might work. But "[w]hen such a category [of action] is generalized . . . into the fields of political movements, it faces power problems. . . or it ignores power issues, doesn't see them, defines issues around them" (1964, p. 394). The latter position "is the Deweyan slant" (p. 394). Mills's work, even as it affirmed aspects of pragmatism, also attempted, as Follett had two decades earlier, to add an explicit analysis of power as central to the process of critical intelligence. Unfortunately, Mills found few intellectuals willing to take up the critical and constructive task. He criticized his own discipline of sociology for its part in this failure, and he further criticized sociologists for their myopic concern with computing statistics that would allow them to be hired by corporations and the government.

Paralleling the changes in philosophy, sociology took a positivistic turn in the mid-twentieth century. This concerned Mills. In addition to being based on an inadequate and reductionist understanding of knowledge, Mills found that this approach turned sociologists into hired technocrats, rather than free-thinking intellectuals who could critique and challenge the economic and political conditions of their times. This betrayed Dewey's hope that the social sciences could be an important tool in bringing critical intelligence to bear on social problems.

While critical of what he saw as Dewey's reformist approach to social change, Mills nonetheless embraced Dewey's larger hope and worked to make sociology a discipline that could help expose and counter what he saw as the increasing centralization of power and the growing indifference of the larger public.

Mills argued that US democracy was indeed under threat from domination, but that threat was not an external one. It was rather the increasing corporatization and use of mass media that brought the danger of reducing individuality even as the political, economic, and military power in the country was increasingly in the hands of a small "power elite." "As the means of information and of power are centralized," he wrote in 1956, "some men come to occupy positions in American society from which they can look down upon, so to speak, and by their decisions mightily affect, the everyday worlds of ordinary men and women" (p. 3). Such an "elite," he thought, enabled its members "to transcend the ordinary environments of ordinary men and women." The elite, he continued, "are in positions to make decisions having major consequences" whether they act or not (pp. 3–4). The power elite "command the major hierarchies and organizations of modern society"—big corporations, "the machinery of the state," the military, education, and so on. "Advisers and consultants, spokesmen and opinion-makers," professional politicians, lobbyists, members of the "upper classes," and celebrities, in turn, support the elites. Taken together, these servants of power carry out the decisions of the elite and so manage the lives of the rest of society. At the same time, he saw an increasing imperialistic temper among that power elite and wrote critically of US involvement in Latin America. He contended that the United States was using Latin America as a source for resources and labor, citing Puerto Rico as a prime example (*Puerto Rican Journey*, 1950). He saw Cuba as attempting to break this relationship of use and the US response to this resistance as an attempt to coerce compliance (*Listen Yankee: The Revolution in Cuba*, 1960).

These studies are examples of his lifelong focus on issues of economic inequality and the growing inequality of power in US society. Two of his most influential books are *White Collar: The American Middle Classes* (1951) and *The Power Elite* (1956), both of which exhibit the influence of Veblen. Veblen studied with Peirce at Johns Hopkins and went on to earn his PhD in philosophy and economics at Yale in 1884, where he worked with Noah Porter, president of Yale and a Congregational minister-turned-moral-philosopher who authored several texts including *The Human Intellect with an Introduction upon Psychology and the Human Soul* (1868). Veblen also studied with William Graham Sumner, who advocated for *laissez-faire* economics and a philosophy of social Darwinism. After Veblen was unable to secure a professorial job upon graduation, he spent six years educating himself on his family farm in Minnesota, until he received a fellowship to study economics at Cornell in 1891. In 1892, he took a teaching position at the University of Chicago, where he and Dewey got to know one another. His magnum opus, *A Theory of the Leisure Class*, was published in 1899 and remains an important text today.

Among other things, Veblen emphasized the influence of institutions and technology on the economy, the strength of habit on decision-making, and the importance of state regulations in understanding capitalism as a power system that tended to limit choice and freedom. These emphases were important in the work of both Dewey and Mills. Dewey's interpretation of the history of philosophy owes much to Veblen's account of the development of civilization as defined by a quest for leisure. Mills credits Veblen with Americanizing the work of Marx by understanding that status and prestige may mean more than class in the US context. Veblen and

Mills shared a broad understanding of "technology" to include the tools (knives, guns, bombs) *and* the skills needed to use the tools. They also recognized that science and technological development are social, not individual, endeavors. Mills was more cautious than Veblen regarding the hope that often accompanies technological development, however, emphasizing the ways social institutions can constrain and co-opt technology. Critical intelligence must be applied to the development and use of technology as well as to the structures of power that govern their use if it is to serve a common interest rather than private and state power alone. Some of this concern with technology was paralleled in the work of Lewis Mumford (1895–1990).

Mumford, an award-winning writer, wrote over thirty books and 1,000 essays. He never received a college degree, nor did he hold a university appointment. He did not try to write "objective history," but instead focused on "usable history" that helped to expose the sources of contemporary problems. His interests were wide-ranging, and he lived out his ideas: he was an active advocate for nuclear disarmament, spoke out against McCarthy, and opposed various highway projects that would harm neighborhoods, to name just a few. Here we focus on his understanding and critique of technology.

Born in Flushing, New York, Mumford attended both City College of New York and the newly opened New School for Social Research but fell ill with tuberculosis and did not complete a degree. After his recovery—and the mobilization of the US Army in the First World War—Mumford enlisted and served as a radio operator. He was discharged in 1919 and found work as an editor at the literary journal, *The Dial*, whose first editor was Margaret Fuller (see Chapter 5). He published his first book in 1922, *The Story of Utopias*.

In 1926, he published *The Golden Day: A Study in American Experience and Culture*. In the concluding chapter, he directly challenged pragmatism and especially Dewey. "Mr. Dewey's pages," Mumford wrote, "are as depressing as a subway ride; they take one to one's destination, but a little the worse for wear" (p. 256). Writing style aside, Mumford sought to challenge what he saw as Dewey's willingness to accept the status quo as the framework for reform. "[W]ho does not feel in back of [Dewey's philosophy]," he said,

> the shapelessness, the faith in the current go of things, and the general utilitarian idealism of Chicago, the spirit which produced the best of the early skyscrapers, the Chicago exposition, Burnham's grandiose city plan, the great park and playground system, the clotted disorder of interminable slums, and the vitality of a handful of experimental schools. (p. 256)

He concluded, "The deficiencies of Mr. Dewey's philosophy are the deficiencies of the American scene itself" (p. 261).

Despite the challenge, Mumford nevertheless found in Dewey's work a key central principle that would frame his own work in the future. "According to Dewey, thought is not mature until it has passed into action" (1926, p. 259). Dewey's criticism of philosophers seemed to Mumford to be correct:

> the falsity of philosophy is that it has frequently dealt with ideas which have no such issue, while the weakness of the practical world is that its actions are unintelligent

routine, the issue of an unreflective procedure. Action is not opposed to ideas: the means are not one thing, and the final result of attending to them quite another: they are not kitchen maids and parlor guests, connected only by being in the same house. Means which do not lead to significant issues are illiberal and brutal; issues which do not take account of the means necessary to fulfill them are empty and merely "well-meaning." (pp. 259–60)

In light of this demand that intellectual work have relevance, Mumford himself engaged in an ongoing program of social critique informed in a significant measure by his interpretation of First World War. As he described it in *The Myth of the Machine: The Pentagon of Power* (1970), the war marked the creation of a "megamachine," an organization of human life and capacity in service of power.

Writing *The Condition of Man* in 1944 in the face of the efficient violence of the Second World War, Mumford noted that the machine had come to push persons aside and the capacity of organization had become destructive. For Mumford, "all that the Nazis have done is to bring to a more rapid climax a process that was more slowly, more insidiously, undermining our whole civilization" (p. 396). He argued that the old drama of expansion and conquest needed to be replaced; humanity needed to simplify and evaluate. Although he had attacked Deweyan pragmatism in *The Golden Day*, in *The Condition of Man* Mumford drew on Dewey's notion of growth to call for critical assessment of the new and the possible. "Do our life-plans make for the fulfillment and renewal of the human person, so that they will bear fruit in a life abundant: ever more significant, ever more valuable, ever more deeply experienced and more widely shared?" (p. 423). To make this kind of evaluation possible, Mumford claimed, we must get beyond a blind faith in technological improvement and make sure that persons remain central. If we do not do this, we will continue on the path of an increasing scale of corruption and terrorism.

Mumford had even more cause for concern when he published *The Myth of the Machine: The Pentagon of Power* in 1970. He noted that, from the start, the United States faced a contradiction of freedom and fraud. Never quite living up to the obligations left by the legacies of slavery and genocide, Americans continued on the path of ongoing expansion and conquest. As the values of increasing mechanical uniformity and using nature for power and financial gain took over, the importance of human variety was lost. In light of his long discussion of the history of science and technology, Mumford suggested that the main lesson is that "*Man cannot be trusted with absolutes*" (p. 74). According to Mumford, absolutism repeatedly results in destruction and extermination, and the pretense of scientific neutrality or aloofness is dangerous and irresponsible. The shift from science focused on knowledge to science focused on usable products should also come with a coinciding responsibility for the uses to which those products are put. In the 1960s, he was already concerned about the environmental impacts of industrializing food production and even argued that the US focus on industrial capacity resulted in a failed approach to the war in Vietnam. Even as the United States bombed roads, cities, and production plants in order to cripple munitions production and the transport of troops, the North Vietnamese government responded by using human power instead of machines to repair the damage, advancing to the South despite US bombing (p. 144).

The military's dependence on technology, evinced in this strategy, was problematic for Mumford.

[the]more dependent the military machine became on technical inventions and mass production of weapons, the greater the immediate profits to the national economic system—even though in the long run succeeding generations would find these putative gains offset by the cost of reparations, repairs, and replacements, to say nothing of human wretchedness. (1970, p. 242)

In this way, economic prosperity and political power are seen as directly tied to war. Since the creation of atomic weapons, the United States has found itself in a permanent state of war, which has helped political, economic, and military powers convince the public of the need for an unfettered corporate culture in order to maintain national security. For Mumford, this combination of powers was the *megamachine,* and one of its primary objectives was to create a docile public conditioned to an increasingly technological environment. Such a machine, he argued in *Technics and Human Development* (1967), operated with "two devices": "a reliable organization of knowledge, natural and supernatural; and an elaborate structure for giving orders, carrying them out, and following them through" (p. 199). For such a system, pointless production was a necessary component. In response, Mumford argued for the rejection of the claim that "newer and bigger must be better." Interestingly, he gave the New York World Trade Center as an example of "purposeless giantism and technological exhibitionism that are now eviscerating the living tissue of every great city." According to Mumford, while the building drove up real estate values, it also increased traffic congestion and decreased the quality of life for city inhabitants (1970, caption text, picture 20). It was an example of how moneyed interests often trump public ones.

Mumford drew on the work of Veblen to discuss the ways in which we have replaced the value of work with the value of consumption, and he pointed to the work of Rachel Carson to note the dangers of the irresponsible use of the products of science once they are primarily seen as a source of profit. Mumford thought that the worldwide student movements of the 1960s demonstrated an awareness that the problem was "the power System itself, in its present technologically expansive and compulsive form. In short, this is nothing less than a revolt against a power-centered 'civilization'" (1970, p. 372). If humans are not to become completely subservient to a machine-driven power structure, Mumford argued, drawing on James, then human persons ought to be taken as the starting point of a profound re-orientation and change of habits.

Mills also worried that some technology reduced workers to tools and servants rather than providing them with the opportunity to develop into craftsmen. He argued that this resulted in a separation of work from the rest of an individual's life and had the effect of creating a separate sphere of leisure that itself had become the object of commodification and planning. He found this most evident in the emergence of a new middle class and described the phenomenon in *White Collar.*

In this work, he noted that the new middle class is not based on property ownership, but rather on service roles within corporations. The rhetoric of the independent, entrepreneurial spirit no longer applies (if it ever did), even as large businesses try to use it to keep the masses from placing regulations on their industries. Mills believed that, with the illusion of independence still alive, the middle class had fought regulation and taxation on the one hand and the efforts of the labor movement on the other. "Small business's attitude toward government, as toward labor, plays into the hands of big business ideology. In both connections, small businessmen are shock troops in the battle against labor unions and government controls" (1951, p. 53). Neither a part of the power elite, nor seeing themselves as part of labor, those in this middle class are behind a "veil of indifference." "[W]hite-collar people are scattered along the rims of all the wheels of power: . . . they themselves are without potency and without enthusiasm for the urgent political clash" (p. xviii). The notion of free competition is used to maintain the status quo, but, Mills concluded, the nature of competition had changed. While some small businesses succeed, they do so by surrendering their independence. The small business owner serves corporate interests and serves the customer: "During business hours at least he must allow the customer always to be right" (p. 32). Within the corporation, white-collar workers faced not just alienation from the work and the larger social context, but alienation from their own selves. They sold their services and sold their smiles.

Professionals had become salaried and so lost their independence as well. This included academics: "The professor is, after all, an employee," Mills wrote, "subject to what this fact involves, and institutional factors select men and have some influence upon how, when, and upon what they will work" (1951, p. 151). Academics were supposed to have more freedom than other professionals to generate independent and critical thought, but they rarely used this freedom and, according to Mills, began to surrender it.

The deepest problem of freedom for teachers is not the occasional ousting of a professor, but a vague general fear—sometimes called "discretion" and "good judgment"—which leads to self-intimidation and finally becomes so habitual that the scholar is unaware of it. The real restraints are not so much external prohibitions as manipulative control of the insurgent by the agreements of academic gentlemen. (p. 151)

In addition to financial factors, Mills was thinking of the political climate constraining academics at the time. "Such control is, of course, furthered by hatch acts, [and] by political and business attacks upon professors" (1951, p. 152). Originally seen as "people who live *for* and not *off* ideas," professors generally sought prestige more than money (p. 143), but as the prestige of academia suffered in a society focused on monetary wealth, many instead saw the path to success leading them to less creative but safer jobs as administrators and consultants. This yielded monetary rewards and enabled some to build a career based on connections with those in power. Intellectuals hoping for research money or higher academic positions thus came to censor themselves by refraining from taking up controversial topics or theses in their writing and teaching. "Tacitly, by his silence, or explicitly in his work, the academic intellectual often sanctions illusions that uphold authority, rather than speak against them" (p. 152).

This kind of acquiescence gave even more power to those few who had come to wield it— the power elite. For Mills, the increasing centralization of power in economic, political, and military affairs had created a power elite that made the idea of government by the consent of the governed outdated. The military had gained political and economic influence, and the corporation, often with ties to the military, had increasingly gained political influence. The reach of economic, political, and military interests extended to the realms of religion, education, and family, and it operated (with the help of the media) to manufacture consent. Mills saw this trend as parallel to what had happened in Nazi Germany. He saw the Western democracies as increasingly vulnerable to the same "totalitarian monopolistic capitalism" that drove the German economy and reduced human labor to just one more depersonalized input (1967, p. 171). Similarly, he saw little difference between the United States and the

Soviet Union, claiming that neither is a "properly developing society" (p. 155). A "properly developing society" was, for Mills, one in which decisions are made as the result of public debate, and industry is an instrument that supports the public's choices, rather than driving the choices themselves. When a society is characterized "by the frenzied pursuit and maintenance of commodities," it is an "overdeveloped nation." In these societies, "life, labor and leisure are increasingly organized. Focused upon these [commodities], the struggle for status supplements the struggle for survival; a panic for status replaces the proddings of poverty" (p. 240).

The hope Mills held for changing the social situation was not found in the tradition of liberalism. This tradition is too individualistic, too focused on competition yielding a balance of power and equitable economic distribution, and too trusting in the idea of government obeying an independent will of the people. As Cornel West and others have since noted, Mills unfairly identified Dewey with this liberal tradition and Mills argued that it was time to get beyond pragmatism's failure to provide a structural analysis of society. Mills saw Dewey as too focused on particular problems and situations and so unable to go beyond piecemeal reform in his recommendations. West called this a "creative misreading of Dewey" that allowed Mills to go on to formulate his own critique and recommendations (1989, p. 126). Be that as it may, it also had the effect of hiding Mills's debt to Dewey and the American tradition more broadly.

In *C. Wright Mills: A Native Radical and His American Intellectual Roots* (1984), Rick Tilman argued that Mills was an important link between the radical tradition of Veblen and Dewey and the New Left that emerged in the 1960s. Not understanding this heritage resulted in limited options for the new radicals. Tilman went on to characterize the American radical tradition as one that stresses the capacity of the individual and the importance of individual participation, promotes class and racial equality, is antiauthoritarian, anti-statist, and "intellectually eclectic" in drawing on insights from multiple perspectives and traditions (p. 187). This American tradition is different from both liberalism and Marxism and offers an important challenge to the power elite and the growing political apathy that so concerned Mills and others.

One of those others was John Kenneth Galbraith (1908–2006). An economist and public intellectual, he published widely on topics of economics and power. Born in Canada, he received his PhD in agricultural economics from the University of California, Berkeley, in 1934 and soon after became a US citizen. He taught at Harvard, though he was often at odds with the department of economics and the administration over issues of academic freedom and his support of student protests in the 1960s. He served several US presidents, was the ambassador to India, and for five years served as an editor of *Fortune* magazine. He also published more than four dozen books, countless articles, and wrote and hosted a series on economics for BBC television—*The Age of Uncertainty* (1977). He has also received many awards, including the Medal of Freedom in 1946 from President Truman, the Lomonosov Award (given by the Russian Academy of Sciences) in 1993, the Order of Canada in 1997, and the Presidential Medal of Freedom in 2000 given by President Clinton, as well as honorary degrees from nineteen colleges and universities.

Galbraith's highly productive and extensive career spanned the time from McCarthyism to 9/11, and throughout, he was a vocal participant and critic. He began his work in the administration of Franklin Delano Roosevelt and concluded his active career during the administration of George H. W. Bush. During that time, he worked as a scholar, bureaucrat, and governmental adviser to try to stabilize economic and political conditions during the Second

World War, the Cold War, the Korean War, the Vietnam War, the bombing of Cambodia, the Iran hostage crisis, the fall of the Berlin Wall, and the first war in Iraq. Following several years of racial violence, in 1968 he lived through a cascade of world-changing events: the Tet Offensive in Vietnam, the assassinations of Martin Luther King Jr. and Robert Kennedy, the violence of the Democratic National Convention in Chicago, and the election of Richard Nixon. He would go on to watch and comment on events such as Watergate (1972–74), the 1980s Savings and Loan crisis, and the Iran/Contra affair (1986). In all his work, he attempted to convince people of the importance of thinking for themselves and fighting the undue economic influence of the rich and of corporations. This focus on the capacity for free and critical intelligence punctuated his concerns about the effects of excessive military spending and a reliance on technology.

But the seeds of these concerns had been planted many years before. His first book, *American Capitalism: The Concept of Countervailing Power* (1952), became influential for the insight that the market economy did not increase human freedom and for acknowledging the role of power in economic outcomes. These themes would be developed over the course of his lifetime. In *The Affluent Society* (1958), Galbraith went on to coin the term "the conventional wisdom" and make the point that such "wisdom" always eventually loses its relevance to the world. He said that all ideas must yield to circumstances, and he encouraged people not to be swept into dogmas—especially those that protect power and money. The unwillingness of the fortunate to pay their share for public goods is evidence of thinking more about short-term individual benefit than long-term good. He gave examples of people's tendency to value their cars over the public roads they drive on, or the diminishment of the postal service in an age when affluent people can afford telephones. "We set great store by the increase in private wealth but regret the added outlays for the police force by which it is protected" (1958a, p. 133). This contradiction in values leads to contradictions about what the government should and should not support. Though to question the nature of production and demand is to question the system as a whole.

We know that today we produce too much and much that is not good for us. Yet already in 1958, Galbraith pointed out the growing problems of obesity, cancer, and heart disease that were all the result of the way food and goods are produced for human consumption. One of his early pieces, an essay titled "How Much Should a Country Consume?" (1958b), "identified human appetite as the source of the problem of economic growth for its own sake." He cautioned against the planned obsolescence of products given the use of nonrenewable resources, and in addition to discussing the polluting effects of gasoline, he also recognized the growing dependence on foreign energy sources and the impact this had on foreign policy. Galbraith argued that all of this has the effect of increasing consumer debt, depleting natural resources, harming human health, and polluting the environment.

To keep consumption up and growing, Galbraith noted the necessity for advertising to manufacture new demand even when people's needs and desires have been met. The system must reject the idea of satisfaction. With this focus on consumption, combined with the business-friendly attitude that the government is nothing but a hindrance, we get a logic that "makes education unproductive and the manufacturer of the school toilet seats productive" (1958b, 184). Galbraith argued that public decisions should not be made by businessmen and emphasized the need to invest in education if we want people capable of thinking through problems we have yet to imagine.

The launch of Sputnik by the Soviet Union just as *The Affluent Society* went to press simply underscored Galbraith's argument about a society's need to balance public and private pursuits and secured Galbraith an opportunity to influence world events more directly. During the 1960s, Galbraith was very much involved with the political events of the time, advising President Kennedy on a host of issues from pricing and growth to poverty, civil rights, and Vietnam. His advice had to contend with that of other advisors, and there is still dispute about the workings and consequences of the Kennedy administration. No matter one's assessment, however, it is clear that Galbraith was an academic working in the world—putting theory into practice and developing theory based on experience.

In *Economics and the Public Purpose* (1973), Galbraith continued his earlier arguments but emphasized the way economics had been used to cloak the growing power of the corporation. Instead of a market based on competition that allowed the consumer some role in fixing prices and determining demand, there is an oligopoly at work, in which the industry fixes prices and determines what will be produced. But this change remained hidden to many, so the corporations that were polluting the environment could blame those who consumed their products instead of taking responsibility themselves. Galbraith thought people were beginning to see the situation for what it was and that the public's blind faith in technology was beginning to end. The economic ruse that shielded corporations from culpability could only function "so long as the exercise of its power does not threaten public existence." However, when people's lives are genuinely at stake, "persuasion is less successful." "[W]hen houses and health care are unavailable and male deodorants are abundant, the notion of a [corporation's] benign response to public wants begins to buckle under the strain" (p. 9). Galbraith was not against technology, but he argued that we should consider the uses to which it is put and responsibly account for its costs. These costs could be seen in labor displacement (often disproportionately affecting minorities), environmental pollution (which we now know also often disproportionately affects minorities), and the oppression of women. As we have seen, these are the same issues that some academic philosophers were beginning to take up as well. While Galbraith made specific proposals for addressing many issues that were and remain debatable, his main "solution" was the "emancipation of belief." The difficulty of this task lies in the fact that "power that is based on belief is uniquely authoritarian; when fully effective, it excludes by its nature the thought that would weaken its grasp." Galbraith went on to say that "The present task is to win freedom from the doctrines that, if accepted, put people in the service not of themselves but of the planning system" (p. 223). He thought this was most likely to happen as the pain of the inequality produced by the current system becomes increasingly evident. He saw the protests of the youth at the time as a good sign, as was the activism of the Civil Rights and Women's Rights Movements.

It should be obvious that much of what Galbraith said echoes the work of the American philosophers discussed in parts I and II. In fact, when discussing the issues facing women, Galbraith seemed to borrow heavily from the work of Gilman, though he did not mention her explicitly. He noted that the emancipation of women will change life in general, exposing the high costs of living in the suburbs along with the cost of consumption connected to cars, houses, pets, food, and children. This will in turn make these norms of consumption subject to change. He argued that women should be admitted to all levels of education and all professions, and so he expected a growing need for childcare, laundries, professional housecleaning, prepared foods, and public transportation. He thought this would further affect how the work week was constructed and wages determined.

A prime target for Galbraith was the growing disparity between the pay of top executives and workers in a corporation. This was taken up most directly in *The Culture of Contentment* (1992), where he returned to the idea that those who are contented do not want to support those in need. With the growth of the middle class, there are now more in the contented class who will defend the very rich in their right not to be taxed because they too want their incomes protected. What gets missed, though, is the many ways the government spends money to protect the contented. For instance, those with power call on the government to insure banks against failure but resist spending on food stamps. Even as poverty grows and the split between the top and bottom incomes increases, many still focus on their own short-term benefit. Contentment goes with the idea that the government should leave things alone, and this laissez-faire approach resulted in the deregulation of a number of industries that contributed to the culture of mergers and acquisitions during the 1980s. The Savings and Loan (S&L) crisis of the late 1980s and early 1990s also illustrated Galbraith's point: after the deregulation of S&Ls in 1980 and the passage of the Tax Reform Act of 1986, the value of small loans (S&Ls' principal means of income) dropped precipitously. In addition, the real estate boom of the 1980s had caused many S&Ls to lend recklessly, and these factors (along with many others) resulted in nearly one quarter of the savings and loan associations in the United States becoming insolvent during the next few years. In response, the federal government moved to bail the banks out, at a cost of around $87 billion, incurring large budget deficits throughout the early part of the 1990s.

Galbraith accused economists (and some philosophers) of accommodating this culture of contentment by defending limited government, justifying the uninhibited pursuit of wealth, and reducing the sense of responsibility for the poor. He thought they also aided in the continued support for increased military spending, even in the absence of an identifiable threat or enemy. The collapse of the Soviet Union might have enabled a shift in public priorities from defense to domestic needs, but the fear and habits remained in place.

Galbraith had predicted the economic crisis of 1987 based on the growing focus on contentment and faith in continued economic growth. In his introduction to *The Great Crash of 1929*, which he published in 1954, Galbraith looked back in time to help examine present circumstances. Ironically, the biggest difference between 1929 and 1987 was that in 1987, there were more safety nets in place and the very people who caused the crash were better protected. One reason for this is that those with power find ways to protect that power. He examined this in his 1983 book *The Anatomy of Power*. One aspect of his analysis in that book was that power often operates by social conditioning and acceptance. "The acceptance of authority, the submission to the will of others, becomes the higher preference of those submitting. This preference can be deliberately cultivated—by persuasion or education" (p. 24). Some welcome this submission, as mentioned above, so they do not have to think for themselves. Galbraith reiterated the need to cultivate the "emancipation of belief" in order to avoid the dangers of accepting the conventional wisdom and present contentment.

His concern about the use of power extended to all dogmatic and extreme views across the political spectrum. This points to an important place for the work of academics—perhaps philosophers in particular. On the occasion of his retirement from Harvard, he took the opportunity to praise those academics who worked within the university structure but also suggested the need for academics to engage the world outside the campus walls. He differentiated between what he called "inside people" and "outside people." "The insiders make their lives within the university community; the outsiders are only associated with it. The outside men—

most of us, alas, have been men—are the best known; the insiders are the most useful" (1983, p. 134). He goes on to caution, though, that "they are also subject to a temptation, which is . . . to see preoccupation with public affairs, involvement with public issues, participation in heated debate or occasional descent into acrimony, as somehow beneath their academic dignity" (p. 135). In fact, what was needed from academic philosophers was an active reengagement with the problems of people.

The kind of engaged and applied philosophy discussed in Part III, "Social Revolutions," was enabled and extended by the work done to revitalize American philosophy. The renewed attention to pragmatism and other related American thinkers is usually credited to the response to Rorty's publication of *Philosophy and the Mirror of Nature* (1979). While this did much to bring the American tradition to the attention of the philosophical community as a whole, there had been many others who had worked on and out of this tradition all along. Nonetheless, after the publication of this popular work, Rorty became the public face of American philosophy in general, and pragmatism in particular.

In "Fighting Terrorism with Democracy," written for *The Nation* a year after the terrorist attacks of September 11, 2001, Rorty sounded very much like Dewey (and Mumford, Mills, and Galbraith). He noted the use of fear to distract people from the real questions and to motivate them to surrender their own freedoms in return for the hope of security. The violence was used as an excuse to conduct attacks on unrelated parties and to grow the military and military spending. "It is in the interest of the Republican Party both to have a blanket war-powers resolution passed, and to make sure that the country thinks of itself as 'at war' for as long as possible." Rorty claimed that the party was run by "an amazingly greedy and cynical oligarchy, with no interest whatever in either the rights of the citizen or the welfare of the poor," which created a dangerous state of mind (2002, p. 11). He suggested that nothing we can do can actually make us secure (an assertion of fallibilism) and that there is much to be lost in the surrender of civil liberties and in the perpetual focus on war.

By the time Rorty wrote this, he was one of America's best-known philosophers, even as he saw himself moving beyond what he took to be the limits of philosophy to work as a professor of Humanities. His work defined decades of debate within philosophy and influenced a wide array of fields such as education, psychotherapy, social theory, law, historiography, and literary theory. He saw philosophy as being about epistemology—truth and knowledge claims. In his view, since truth claims are about sentences, and sentences are the product of a language, and languages are human creations, truth is a human creation. He concluded that since truth is so contingent, we should stop worrying about it and move into a postphilosophical world where we abandon argument for narrative and persuasion and replace the philosopher with the poet and the bourgeois liberal ironist. He saw the problems of philosophy (as defined by epistemology) as uninteresting and not relevant to the problems of the world. This was reflected in his view of professional philosophy, which Rorty saw as increasingly technical, boring, and unhelpful. For these views, he garnered much criticism but also much interest (both within and outside of academic philosophy).

Born in 1931, Rorty was the son of leftist New York intellectuals who supported the views of Trotsky and opposed Lenin. Growing up in a politically active home in which much attention was given to his education, his parents worried that the technical philosophy he first came to do was not of much use in changing the world. His first work in philosophy was done at the

University of Chicago during a time when there was a struggle over the pragmatist heritage of that department. At a time when logical positivism was dominant in many departments, Rorty did his master's thesis on Whitehead under the direction of Hartshorne in 1952 and continued to work on pragmatism at Yale, where he went for his PhD. His dissertation pointed to some shortcomings in analytic philosophy, including its narrowness, and offered a more pluralistic approach than was in fashion. He considered himself a therapeutic positivist who tried to link the work of analytic philosophy with other traditions.

After receiving his PhD in 1956, he served two years in the military (during peacetime) before taking an appointment at Wellesley College. In his early work, he became a well-known analytic philosopher. His growing reputation resulted in a job offer, and in 1961, he moved to Princeton, where he spent much of his philosophical career, despite being regularly recruited by other universities. In 1967, he published a collection of essays titled *The Linguistic Turn: Recent Essays in Philosophical Method*, in which he gathered work from prominent analytic philosophers and noted the many accomplishments of this school of philosophy while also encouraging analytic and nonanalytic philosophers to listen to each other.

In 1979, when he was elected to be the president of the Eastern Division of the APA (due at least in part to his positive reputation among analytic philosophers), his philosophical work took a critical and public turn with the publication of *Philosophy and the Mirror of Nature*. Rorty had hinted at this shift in his essay "The World Well Lost" (1972) (which later appeared in *Consequences of Pragmatism* (1982)) and his 1961 article "Recent Metaphilosophy" in which he turned to the likes of James, Dewey, and Wittgenstein to critique analytic philosophy. "The analytic movement in philosophy served us well in making us self-conscious about metaphilosophical issues. But analytic philosophers have too often been "reductionist" metaphilosophers: they have used metaphilosophical analyses to reduce their opponents to absurdity, but they have lacked the courage to apply these analyses to themselves" (p. 317). But it was *Philosophy and the Mirror of Nature* that would remake his reputation. In this book, Rorty questioned the role of philosophy as understanding knowledge and providing the method for grounding knowledge claims. He put forward Dewey, Heidegger, and the later Wittgenstein as important philosophers who had broken free of the search for foundational knowledge and systems. While written in an analytic style, this book marked a break in his focus and approach to philosophy. This public shift coincided with a more general push by others to open up philosophy again to nonanalytic approaches and issues.

As mentioned in Chapter 17, Rorty presided over the 1979 business meeting in which members of the American Philosophical Association (APA) protested what they saw as an analytic stranglehold over the programs and offices of the APA. Rorty agreed that the APA suffered from a kind of tyranny of the majority and tried to change the composition of the program committee. He would later call for "pragmatic tolerance" so that "both sides see the other as honest, if misguided, colleagues, doing their best to bring light to a dark time." He said "that although there are relations between academic politics and real politics, they are not tight enough to justify carrying the passions of the latter over into the former" (1982, p. 229).

Then Rorty gave his presidential address titled "Pragmatism, Relativism, and Irrationalism." In this address (later published in *Consequences of Pragmatism*), Rorty called on the assembly to give up the analytic project of achieving clarity and certainty and urged philosophers to stop modeling themselves on scientists. He also championed Dewey and James, more clearly aligning himself with the pragmatist tradition: Pragmatism, he said, "names the chief glory of our country's intellectual tradition. No other American writers have offered so radical a suggestion for making our future different from our past, as have James and Dewey" (1982, p. 160). Rorty would go on to argue elsewhere that Dewey stood at a crossroads, blending nineteenth-century metaphysics with twentieth-century postmodern critique of enlightenment philosophy. For Rorty, the former (metaphysics) ought to be set aside in order that the latter (postmodern critique) could join with Wittgenstein and Heidegger in generating a philosophical perspective not bound to unverifiable (and problematic) notions of reality. When he published *The Consequences of Pragmatism*, he set a new direction for American philosophy.

However, not all agree with his understanding of Dewey or pragmatism more generally. While the analytic philosophers worried about Rorty's turn away from truth and knowledge, some pragmatists worried that he replaced the pragmatist focus on experience with a focus on language. He received praise and critique from all quarters. In light of Rorty's siding with the pluralist rebellion at the APA, it seemed to many analytic philosophers that Rorty had betrayed them. To many working in the traditions of continental and American philosophy, it seemed that he played fast and loose with major figures and texts of those traditions. Even as criticism mounted, others saw Rorty as a breath of fresh air.

Increasingly unhappy at Princeton, Rorty was also increasingly unhappy in philosophy. As he called for what he saw as a postphilosophic world, he was frustrated by the limits of the institutional disciplines. His work was often more popular outside of philosophy departments. In 1982, Rorty received a MacArthur "genius grant" and moved out of philosophy to take a position as University Professor of Humanities at the University of Virginia. Despite his own move out of professional philosophy, some claim that he was nevertheless "a legitimate heir to the pragmatic tradition by virtue of his implicit focus upon a problematic deeply embedded in the American experience: the fact and consequences of *plurality* in its psychological, social, and political forms" (Hall, 1994, p. 66). This claim comes from David Hall in *Richard Rorty: Prophet and Poet of the New Pragmatism*, in which he argued that while Rorty embraced the pluralism that emerged when he abandoned the foundational project, many others failed to take the consequence of pluralism seriously. "Rorty is a good illustration of a thinker who has taken very seriously a very serious problem. [P]luralism (if not the relativism that threatens to come along with it) is a fundamental, intransigent aspect of our intellectual culture" (p. 79).

After having made his case to deconstruct the project of analytic philosophy, Rorty tried to work out the positive case for what philosophy could look like in a postphilosophic world. In 1989, he published *Contingency, Irony, and Solidarity*, in which he argued that the work of self-creation is a private activity and does not share a language with the public activity that seeks justice. He thought we needed to give up on the hope of a single vision or theory and instead rely on narrative accounts to get agreement about how we should behave. For Rorty, the liberal was one who thinks cruelty is the worst thing we do to each other, while the "ironist" understood that all beliefs are contingent and emerge in a cultural, historical, and linguistic context. He again dismissed philosophy's focus on truth and argument and suggested that the most we can do is persuade others that "our" vocabulary is attractive and useful. *Objectivity, Relativism and Truth* (1991) followed this line of thought in going beyond various forms of realism and working out the implications of his view of pragmatism as antirepresentationalism. The essays in this book are largely focused on the work of Donald Davidson.

Rorty's writing on pragmatism intersected with ongoing historical studies of the classical pragmatists, stirring controversy among scholars of the tradition over what many saw as Rorty's cavalier readings of texts. That controversy, and the opening made by *Philosophy and the Mirror of Nature*, produced what many called a pragmatist revival.

The revival, in fact, had begun at least a decade before Rorty's book drew the attention of pragmatists and analytic philosophers, and continues today. In 1963, John E. Smith (1921–2009) published *The Spirit of American Philosophy*, which began to recover the history of American philosophy from narratives like the one presented by Brodbeck in 1950. He also published *Purpose and Thought: The Meaning of Pragmatism* (1978). In 1968, H. S. Thayer (1923–2008) published *Meaning and Action: A Critical History of Pragmatism*, while from the more mainstream analytic side A. J. Ayer (1910–89) published *The Origins of Pragmatism* and Morton White (1917–2016) published *Pragmatism and the American Mind* (1975). John J. McDermott (1932–2018), who had cofounded SAAP and was a leader in the pluralist rebellion at the APA in 1979, published in 1969 the two-volume *Basic Writings of Josiah Royce* that made much of Royce's work (most of it out of print since the 1910s) available to new audiences of scholars and students. Nine years later, in 1978, McDermott followed with a single-volume collection of James's work, *The Writings of William James*. While Ralph Barton Perry had published a two-volume set titled *The Thought and Character of William James* in 1935, McDermott's collection once again made it easy to teach James's work and, since it included most of his principal work (much, again, previously out of print), it made the philosophy of James accessible to a wider public. In 1969, the first volume of Dewey's collected works was published, edited by Jo Ann Boydston. The thirty-seventh and final volume of the collected works was published in 1991. The collected works made Dewey's entire corpus available for study and debate. Given all of this activity within the field of American philosophy, Rorty's *Consequences of Pragmatism* (1982) should be seen as an important addition to scholarship in the American tradition (perhaps aided in its visibility by Rorty's credentials as a leading analytic philosopher), but continuous with the work of many others.

By the late 1990s, Rorty was looking beyond philosophy, though, and turned to political theory in *Achieving Our Country* (1998) and *Philosophy and Social Hope* (1999). In these books, he called for a return to a version of Dewey's pragmatism in social and political matters, and the reform approach of the twentieth-century progressive era. He tried to work out the implications of this for education, law, religion, and ethics, although he remained critical of multiculturalism and gender and sexuality studies for focusing on issues of identity rather than economics. For instance, in an article defending universities against the charge that they were run by a liberal left-leaning faculty (made by authors such as Allan Bloom), he wrote that multiculturalism started

> as one more attempt to get white middle-class males to behave better toward the people they enjoy shoving around—black and brown people, women, poor people, recent immigrants, homosexuals. It hoped to encourage these groups to take pride in themselves rather than accept the derogatory descriptions that the white males had invented for them. By now, however, it has turned into an attempt to get jobs and grants for psychobabbling busybodies. (1995, p. 74)

He worried this made left-leaning academics an easy target for the likes of the Republican Speaker of the US House of Representatives, Newt Gingrich, who could dismiss the academics as eccentric and perverse and so ignore their critiques of the growing gap between the rich and the poor.

Focused primarily on economic inequality, Rorty's project of reform did not include much attention to some important contemporary debates, nor did his pluralism and liberalism always seem to mesh with his own thinking. In *Achieving Our Country*, he wrote about the social revolutions of the 1960s: "America will always owe an enormous amount to the rage which rumbled through the country between 1964 and 1972. We do not know what our country would be like today, had that rage not been felt. But we can be pretty certain that it would be a much worse place than it is" (1998, p. 68). Here he acknowledged that the old reformist left probably could not have ended the war in Vietnam but worried that the new left was too focused on revolution and was not well positioned to create actual reforms aimed at improving the lives of those who were economically and politically disenfranchised. Given increasing globalization, he thought, "The world economy will soon be owned by a cosmopolitan upper class which has no more sense of community with any workers anywhere than the great American capitalist of the year 1900 had with the immigrants who manned their enterprises" (p. 85). He predicted that this would cause the public to seek a strongman to vote for: "someone willing to assure them that, once he is elected, the smug bureaucrats, tricky lawyers, overpaid bond salesmen, and postmodernist professors will no longer be calling the shots." Any gains made by Black and brown Americans and homosexuals will be wiped out, and overt racism and misogyny will reappear. "All the resentment which badly educated Americans feel about having their manners dictated to them by college graduates will find an outlet" (p. 90).

For Rorty, this was a self-inflicted wound of the new left. He argued that the loss of hope and pride brought on by academics who pushed a narrative of an unredeemable US focused on world domination (Mills being one of Rorty's examples) was crippling and resulted in increased theoretical critique and decreased on-the-ground reforms (1998, pp. 7, 55–57). As already mentioned, he thought the focus on things like multiculturalism and feminism was to blame.

> To take pride in being black or gay is an entirely reasonable response to the sadistic humiliation to which one has been subjected. But insofar as this pride prevents someone from also taking pride in being an American citizen, from thinking of his or her country as capable of reform, or from being able to join with straights or whites in reformist initiatives, it is a political disaster. (p. 100)

He thought that while "many things should chasten and temper such pride . . . nothing a nation has done should make it impossible for a constitutional democracy to regain self-respect" (p. 32).

His critique of the new left went further. In *Richard Rorty: The Making of an American Philosopher* (2008), Neil Gross noted that after a 1968 student sit-in at Stanford, Rorty wrote to fellow philosopher Gregory Vlastos to say that, while he thought he was glad the students had been granted amnesty, he was conflicted.

> When the question came up when Nassau Hall (at Princeton) was threatened with a sit-in, I agreed with [Princeton President] Goheen's view that they be given 24 hours worth

of persuasion and then cleared out by the cops. I still think this is right, but every once in a while I begin to wonder whether I'm turning into a fascist. (In Gross, 2008, p. 326)

Again, in 1970, Rorty wrote to his father to complain about the cost of the damage done by demonstrators at Stanford. He wrote, "I am really afraid that the little brats will bring on a wave of fascist repression if they keep going," and that he was worried that more riots would make it possible for the government "to organize a secret police with no trouble at all" (in Gross, 2008, p. 326). He remained committed to slower approaches, claiming that

> This standard bourgeois liberal view of mine has the same cynicism of all bourgeois liberal views—it says to the people on whose necks one trods that it will be better for their children's children if they keep on getting trodden upon while we educate the more intelligent of their children to understand how society works. But I believe it anyway. I honestly think that we—the parasitic priestly class which confers sacraments like BAs and Ph.D.s—are the best agency for social change on the scene. I don't trust the aroused workers and peasants to do themselves or anybody any good. (In Gross, 2008, p. 327)

Further, while Rorty opposed the Vietnam War, he was equally worried about the anti-American views expressed by many protesters. Despite the atrocious actions of the United States in Vietnam, Rorty remained committed to the cultural heritage of this country. Patriotism can be radical in its own right, and Rorty worried that the more militant movements harmed the potential of the "leftist patriot." In *Achieving Our Country*, Rorty worried that the loss of a critical patriotism brought about by the new left resulted in "a spectatorial, disgusted, mocking left" (1998, p. 35) that steps back from life (rejecting liberal reformist initiatives as discredited humanism) to theorize and prioritize knowledge over hope (pp. 36–37). In its place, he argues for something akin to a "Deweyan pragmatic, participatory Left" (p. 38), which he saw exemplified in figures such as Galbraith.

Bernstein noted that Rorty was very tied to his identity as a leftist. Rooted in his (Rorty's) parents' form of Trotskyist intellectual political critique, Bernstein highlights Rorty's worries about what he called the "cultural left" (which emerged in the 1960s and 1970s) not understanding class issues and focusing too much on difference and identity. Rorty worried they had given up on programs of reform to focus on which texts to teach. Ironically, Bernstein noted that Rorty's own work stopped well short of providing actual programs of reform. He provided lofty rhetoric but not much by way of suggestions for concrete action. Further, Rorty's dismissal of political theory concerned Bernstein. "[T]heory informs concrete programs for action," Bernstein said. "Without a modicum of theoretical analysis and debate, liberal reform can too easily degenerate into mindless activism and the search for quick fixes" (2003, p. 136). Just as Rorty worried about mindless rhetoric on the right, Bernstein worried about the same on the left. He said that while there is much to admire in Rorty's "inspirational liberalism," there is also much that causes concern. "[W]ithout pragmatic toughness and a concrete program for reform, patriotic inspirational liberalism too easily degenerates into an empty rhetorical hand waving" (p. 138).

Another prominent philosopher who critiqued Rorty's take on pragmatism was Hilary Putnam (1926–2016). Putnam found the American tradition useful for developing a new engaged philosophy. Like Rorty, Putnam presents an interesting bridge figure in the story of American philosophy. A prominent voice in the areas of the philosophy of mind, the philosophy of language, the philosophy of mathematics, and the philosophy of science, he was firmly part of the story of analytic philosophy in America. Later, however, Putnam (as did Rorty) turned to Dewey and pragmatism to release philosophy from the narrowness of the analytic tradition.

Putnam did his graduate work at Harvard and UCLA, where he received his PhD in 1951. He wrote on probability under Reichenbach and began teaching at Harvard in 1965. While his philosophical work focused on technical issues in philosophy, he (unlike Rorty) was politically active by supporting civil rights and opposing the war in Vietnam. He organized campus protests, was the faculty advisor for the Students for a Democratic Society, and taught courses on Marx. In 1968, he became a member of the Progressive Labor Party (PLP). These activities were noticed, and Harvard tried to censure Putnam. Putnam left the PLP in 1972. In 1976, he was elected president of the APA, and in 1980 the president of the Association of Symbolic Logic.

His early work, mostly publications of his papers such as *Reason, Truth, and History* (1981), focused on the nature of truth, knowledge, and rationality. *Realism and Reason* (1983), *Representation and Reality* (1988), and *Mind, Language, and Reality* (1975) all dealt with the philosophy of mathematics and science, as well as philosophy of language and the philosophy of mind. The turn in his thought can be seen in later books like *Pragmatism: An Open Question* (1995), in which he came to take seriously the pragmatist tradition. He was specifically interested in the ideas of pluralism, holism, and the interpenetration of facts and values. He worried about how pluralism and tolerance could be embraced without the possible difficulties of epistemological skepticism. "It is an open question," he wrote, "whether an enlightened society can avoid a corrosive moral skepticism without tumbling back into moral authoritarianism" (p. 2). This question led him back to the work of Peirce, James, Dewey, and Wittgenstein. He was joined in this work by Ruth Anna Putnam (1927–2019), who became interested in the work of William James. (It is important to note that Ruth Anna Putnam shared this interest in pragmatism and wrote numerous journal articles and edited the *Cambridge Companion to William James*.) He was not introduced to these thinkers directly in his academic work, but outside the classroom by a retired, visiting professor (A. E. Singer, Jr.) at the University of Pennsylvania, where Putnam had done his undergraduate work. Eventually, Putnam came to embrace some of the ideas he had been exposed to by Singer: the idea that the fact/value divide was a false divide, the strength of a fallibilistic rather than skeptical approach, and the idea that philosophy was not all about argument but was also about how to live.

This shift was motivated by a growing disenchantment with mainstream analytic philosophy, which Putnam thought was too enamored of science. In the preface to *Renewing Philosophy* (the published version of his 1990 Gifford lectures), he said: "Analytic philosophy has become increasingly dominated by the idea that science, and only science, describes the world as it is in itself, independent of perspective" (1992, pp. ix–x). He also worried about the alternative offered by the likes of Derrida, Nelson Goodman (1906–98), and Rorty, as they denied "that we have a cognitive relation to extralinguistic reality." He turned to Wittgenstein and Dewey to find a way to "see our various forms of life differently without being either scientistic or irresponsibly metaphysical" (p. xi). He argued that while Dewey was largely ignored, Rawls's popular political theory was like Dewey's project, and so Dewey could be used to get an "epistemological justification of democracy" which Putnam saw as "the precondition for the full application of intelligence to the solution of social problems" (p. 180).

He emphasized that he was not against technical argument, nor was he opposed to more literary approaches to philosophy. "I fully grant that the positivists, for example, did a great service to philosophy," he asserts, "by showing how the methods of modern mathematical logic could be used to carry the investigation of a great many philosophical arguments and issues much further than it had been carried before; and the deconstructionists, for all their faults, have called attention to aspects of literature—in particular, to aspects of philosophical literature—which the tradition has neglected." Putnam concludes, however, that "philosophy cannot be either para-science or para-politics" (1992, p. 197). He found in James a good balance for philosophers to emulate. "In James, a sympathetic understanding of the need for commitment is always tempered by a healthy awareness of the horror of fanaticism" (p. 196). This is why he appreciates the pragmatist focus on holism, pluralism, and fallibilism. In *Pragmatism: An Open Question* (1995), he rejected Rorty's version of pragmatism as too dichotomous and offered his own which he saw as more holistic. He rejected Rorty's relativism and instead focused on pluralism and fallibilism as ways to move us to concrete action. He argued that Peirce, James, and Dewey all saw "democratically conducted inquiry" as trustworthy "not because it is infallible," but because inquiry is a self-revising process. "At the same time," he goes on to say, "James and Wittgenstein would have asked us to remember that what is publicly verified (or even what is intersubjectively 'warrantedly assertable') is not all of what any human being or any culture can live by" (p. 75). He further noted that there are many needs in society—including the need for tolerance—and that philosophy is important in examining these needs: "But telling us again and again that 'there is nothing outside the text,' or that all our thought is simply 'marks and noises' which we are 'caused' to produce by a blind material world to which we cannot so much as refer, is not an exploration of any of them." Putnam concludes that this is rather "a fruitless oscillation between a linguistic idealism which is largely a fashionable 'put on' and a self-refuting scientism" (p. 75). He tried to offer an alternative. While some analytic philosophers thought Putnam had lost his way, others began to be more open to work rooted in this American tradition. For some, he provided a level of credibility for the American tradition within the philosophical world.

Both Bernstein (addressed more fully in the next chapter) and Putnam shaped their work in the wake of Rorty, but Rorty's work is just one take on the importance and use of this American tradition. Rather than seeing Rorty as recovering or reviving a dead tradition, he may better be seen as finding resources in an ongoing line of writing that helped him patch the holes he found in the analytic tradition. Rather than seeing American philosophy as a tradition that had been eclipsed and needed Rorty to revive it, Bernstein argued that American pragmatism was not so much eclipsed as too successful in its project. Connecting philosophy to the problems people face in their lives, many students of those philosophers who first took up the task of doing philosophy in an American spirit inspired their students to get to work addressing the problems rather than addressing the profession of philosophy. Many of these students became sociologists, psychologists, and educators. Bernstein argued that pragmatism was alive and well in such work, though it was not named. Be that as it may, without being named, its success was masked to many teaching and writing philosophy in the 1960s and 1970s. In the meantime, most philosophers ignored or derided the work of these early American philosophers. As mentioned earlier, though, there were exceptions.

One important exception was John E. Smith. While he did not often teach classes specifically on these figures, he did include them in the discussion and ran book groups focused on their work. He taught Rorty, though their differences remained strong (Smith notes that his 1992 *America's Philosophical Vision* is written to address what Rorty's over-emphasis on epistemology leaves out of this vision). Smith had a stronger influence on Bernstein and shared much more in common with him. Bernstein credited a 1954 reading group on Dewey, organized by Smith, with opening up the vitality of the pragmatic tradition to him. By 1957, Smith was writing on the importance of this tradition in his paper "The Course of American Philosophy." In *The Spirit of American Philosophy* (1963), Smith took up the work of Peirce, James, Royce, Dewey, and Whitehead. He said the "spirit" was more than a set of doctrines. Rather, he thought it was about beliefs, style, and a particular stance toward life (p. 187). Unlike the analytic tradition that dominated when he was writing, Smith described the philosophy developed in America as committed to the notion that ideas make a difference and that thinking emerges from life situations. He said that American philosophers have not "been satisfied merely to praise ideas or to expound on them; they have been animated rather by the desire to see them embodied and provided with whatever power it is within the capacity of the human self to bestow" (pp. viii–ix).

Smith later listed what he took to be some of the other hallmarks of American philosophy in *American Philosophical Vision* (1992): an openness of mind and experimental spirit; an approach that could do justice to the reality of change and development; and the acknowledgment that ideas themselves are important and can be evaluated by their relevance to life. He believed that when this spirit was lost, philosophy also lost the ability to connect to the public at large. Smith saw this as a problem since the pressing problems of the day would gain from the careful thinking philosophy can bring to an issue. In *Purpose and Thought: The Meaning of Pragmatism* (1978), he argued for the recovery of the resources of these past philosophies in order to find out what they had to say and so be in a position to put them to use.

In addition to his crucial editorial work, John J. McDermott wrote from within the American tradition, doing both the work of recovering sources and putting them to use. In 1965, he published *The American Angle of Vision* (Parts 1 and 2) reframing the history of American philosophy as a history of American experience. He developed the resulting conception of experience in three books: *The Culture of Experience: Philosophical Essays in the American Grain* (1976), *Streams of Experience: Reflections on the History and Philosophy of American Culture* (1986), and *The Drama of Possibility: John J. McDermott's Philosophy of Experience* (2007), a collection of essays. He wrote about figures such as James, Dewey, and Royce in connection with existential philosophers such as Camus. He used them all to write about life. Also influenced by the work of Emerson, Peirce, Whitehead, Santayana, and Mead, some of the central ideas McDermott took up include a focus on embodiment, relationality, and our ongoing attempts to make meaning in a changing world.

A gifted and passionate teacher, McDermott's ability to convince his students that the questions and problems raised in his work really do matter to them resulted in a powerful pedagogy committed to meliorism. John Ryder noted McDermott's "faith in the capacity of people to examine their circumstances, explore possible alternatives, and take the action . . . to recreate their lives." He went on to say that such faith "is an important antidote in a world too easily seduced by simple and totalizing approaches that can engender a passivity of mind and body" (in Campbell and Hart, 2006, p. 212).

McDermott explored the problem of being an individual who lives with commitment and purpose in a world that may have no purpose of its own. He addressed the very important question of how to live as a self-consciously terminal creature. For McDermott, the question is, "Can we experience ourselves as terminal and yet live creative, probing, building lives...?" He said, "I for one, believe that we can live this way; nay, I believe that it is *only* in this way that we live a distinctively human life" (in Campbell and Hart, 2006, p. 285). Death is not the problem for McDermott: isolation from experience and lack of growth in life are.

In addition to a call to focus on relationships and pluralism, McDermott said that if "reality is evolutionary, developmental, and processive rather than static or complete in any way, then it is imperative to realize that positions taken by human diagnosis and human intervention are significantly, although partially, constitutive of the future course of events" (2007, p. 151). McDermott called people to thoughtful action and said that if we believe in "our capacity to effect human healing of unnecessary suffering and in our responsibility to do so, then we shall, in time create a human community worthy of the rich human tradition of hope, aspiration, and wisdom" (p. 155). This is to be done in the face of our impermanence and so day by day. He tried to use the approach of meliorism to avoid the extremes of pessimism and optimism. He wrote that meliorism

> takes no captives, makes no excessive claims, nor bows out in frustration at the opposition. Dewey evokes the deepest sentiments of human life, too often unsung and too often derided: that the nectar is in the journey, that ultimate goals may be illusory, nay, most likely are but a gossamer wing... Day by day, however, human life triumphs in its ineluctable capacity to hang in and make things better: not perfect, simply better. (pp. 157–8)

For McDermott, philosophy helps us ask questions and avoid living second-hand lives. When it is well done, it helps us shake off our "ontological lethargy" (p. 375), and becomes an activity aimed at improving life.

At some points in his work, McDermott (like Rorty) worried that we may have "lost the capacity to rework and reconstitute the viability of a pluralistic and mosaic communal fabric which, in truth, is simply quintessential if we are to survive as a nation" (2007, p. 266). At others, though, he identified the resources of a pluralistic, experiential, and experimental approach to amelioration. Pluralistic communities can help us stay open to various and mediated interpretations that aim at amelioration.

Smith and McDermott are examples of philosophers who kept the American tradition alive by introducing students to the central figures of the tradition and by embedding their own writing within that tradition. They worked both to keep the tradition alive and to put the tradition to work and called on others to do the same. They backed this up by encouraging and supporting the work of younger scholars who took them up on the challenge. The work of recovery and application has been done (and continues to be done) by many different individuals who have answered this call.

The work of a broad range of philosophers and historians since the 1970s has ensured that the American tradition is alive and well. Sustained work on figures such as Peirce, James, Dewey,

Royce, Alain Locke, and Addams provided the starting place for a broader development of the tradition, both in pragmatism and in conceptions of the tradition like the one represented in our account of American philosophy. It also made possible the use of the tradition in addressing issues of the day—in philosophy and in society. Some philosophers working in the analytic tradition, like Philip Kitcher, also began to call for philosophy to return to real problems and found pragmatism to be an important tradition to recover in order to do this work. His *Preludes to Pragmatism: Toward a Reconstruction of Philosophy* (2012) consciously sets aside those like Brandom and Putnam whom he finds working too hard to link pragmatism to analytic philosophy. "Pragmatism should not be domesticated and brought into the precincts of 'normal philosophy,' so that James and Dewey can join the pantheon of respectable philosophers. To paraphrase Marx, the point is not to continue philosophy-as-usual, but to change it" (p. xiv).

Others continue to try to domesticate pragmatism, though. For instance, *Pragmatism: An Introduction* (2012) by Michael Bacon gives little space to Peirce, James, and Dewey (and none to figures such as Alain Locke and Addams), and then focuses on the likes of Quine, Sellars, Davidson, Rorty, Putnam, Habermas, Bernstein, Haack, Misak, and Brandom. Cheryl Misak's *The American Pragmatists* (2013) makes the pragmatists in her image. Limiting the tradition to a theory of truth and taking Rorty as the only alternative to her analytic version of pragmatism are two errors that result from her limited take on the figures and concerns present in the tradition. Such "domestication" results in misunderstandings and narrow interpretations. One of the consequences of such approaches to the tradition is that it diminishes the possible insights for approaching contemporary issues. It limits the ways philosophers can take up a public role. This is especially important as we live in a time filled with opposing absolutist views. One consequence of such views is a struggle between more open and pluralistic approaches and more narrow and monistic approaches. This struggle is represented in the field of philosophy itself and in the world at large.

One example can be found in the view that expressed the idea that the United States was postracial (see Daniel and Williams, 2014). This resulted in moves to end integration policies and to end attention to voter discrimination while simultaneously adding new voter restrictions. These moves are tied to calls for proof of citizenship and the debates over immigration policy. For example, beginning in the 1980s, the courts began to make decisions that resulted in the erosion of the progress made in desegregating schools. This was accompanied by other actions that pushed for parental choice in schools and removed incentives for schools to voluntarily work to improve integration. The Supreme Court decision in Brown v. Board of Education in 1954 declared that the idea of separate but equal education was unconstitutional and required school districts to move to integrate schools. Since 1990, various court decisions made the case that the desegregation orders were meant to be temporary, and now nearly half the schools that were under court orders to desegregate are no longer under judicial oversight. This has begun a slow process of resegregation in the schools that does not violate the Brown decision that only applied to state-sponsored segregation. It does not apply to segregation that occurs based on where people choose to live or where they choose to send their children to school. This, of course, assumes that such choices are made freely in a state of equal opportunity. But housing policies in the United States have not created equal opportunity. George W. Romney was appointed the Secretary of Housing and Urban Development under Nixon and began the work of increasing the availability of housing for the poor and of desegregating neighborhoods (and thereby schools). Such attempts have had limited effect, however, on the complex housing markets where even today race is a determining factor in where one lives and one's access to education, employment, and wealth (Loh et.al., 2020).

On another front, in 2013 the Supreme Court struck down a key element of the 1965 Voting Rights Act. Arguing that the country has changed significantly with regard to race, this decision allowed states with historical records of racial discrimination to change voting procedures and districting without federal approval. After the Supreme Court decision, Texas immediately announced plans for a voter identification law (enacted in 2021) that had previously been blocked. Texas is just one of nineteen states to now have such laws. These efforts have been coupled with attempts to end access to early voting (especially on weekends), curtail polling times and places, and end same-day voter registration. These debates are part of, or are grounded in, what was labeled the "culture wars" in the 1980s and 1990s. In the next chapter, we turn to those debates and the importance of philosophers engaging more directly with issues of culture as public intellectuals.

# CHAPTER 25
# AMERICAN PHILOSOPHY AND "THE CULTURE WARS"

We have shown a number of ways in which the American philosophical tradition has been public and socially active—from the late 1800s to today. While today one can find many scholars engaging with the American tradition of philosophy, there is still work to be done in the realm of historical recovery and analysis, as well as in the use of this tradition to explore contemporary issues. It is also important to examine some examples of philosophers engaged in the public philosophical project of promoting critical thought and action in a tradition of pluralism and resistance. Without the presence of this voice, we are unlikely to escape the kind of "culture wars" that were spawned in the United States in the 1960s and continue in various forms to this day.

> There is a religious war going on in our country for the soul of America. It is a cultural war, as critical to the kind of nation we will one day be as was the Cold War itself. And in that struggle for the soul of America, Clinton & Clinton are on the other side, and George Bush is on our side.

This comes from Pat Buchanan's speech at the 1992 Republican convention. He blamed what he took to be the liberal positions on abortion, drugs, homosexuality, the environment, gun rights, privacy, censorship, the separation of church and state, and popular culture for the loss of what it really means to be American. "My friends, this election is about much more than who gets what. It is about who we are. It is about what we believe. It is about what we stand for as Americans" (1992).

This war for the soul of America had been going on for some time. In his article "The Cultural Wars: American Intellectual Life, 1965–1992," Harvard sociologist Daniel Bell presented his take on the conflict in US intellectual life that resulted in attacks on the canon by feminism and multiculturalism. Known primarily as the author of *The End of Ideology*, published in 1960, Bell argued in this article that since 1965, there has been an increasing polarization of views among radicals, conservatives, and liberals. The result has been the loss of any intellectual center in the United States and an increasingly permissive society. He argued that the Vietnam War and the resulting draft resulted in "the eruption of a large youth cohort" and that this "was tied to a music-drug culture and ... to a sexual revolution. The movement was not revolutionary, in the sense of having a programmatic alternative to capitalist society, but rebellious." (2000, p. 81). He thought there was a distinct shift in a different direction with the election of Ronald Reagan in 1980. This shift built on the work of conservatives such as William F. Buckley Jr., and neoconservatives who were immersed in the work of Leo Strauss (1899–1973).

An example of the early roots of this tension from the 1960s can be found in an interview with Gore Vidal and Buckley at the 1968 Democratic National Convention in Chicago. Buckley and Vidal disagreed about the police actions being taken against the protesters outside the convention and about the protesters' right to assemble and speak. Vidal, who had been out with the protesters, said they were peaceful, but the police were not. Buckley, who had watched the protesters from his hotel window, said the protesters were deliberately provoking the police. When asked if the raising of the Viet Cong flag had been meant to provoke a reaction that could be compared to the raising of the Nazi flag, the two became visibly agitated. In the ensuing discussion, Vidal called Buckley a "pro-crypto-Nazi," and Buckley responded: "Now listen, you queer, stop calling me a crypto-Nazi or I'll sock you in your goddamn face and you'll stay plastered" (Vidal and Buckley, 1968).

Buckley was a well-known conservative who served in the CIA for two years. In 1951, he authored *God and Man at Yale: The Superstitions of Academic Freedom* in which he critiqued the university for forcing liberal beliefs on the students, and in 1954, he published *McCarthy and His Enemies* in which he defended McCarthy as a patriot. These put him on the political map, and in 1955, he established the conservative paper the *National Review*. In 1959, he published *Up from Liberalism* in which he attacked liberalism for having no orthodoxy, even as he also critiqued particular stances being offered by conservative politicians. In *Nearer My God* (1997), he criticized what he saw as the Supreme Court's attack on religion in schools. He saw religion being replaced with multiculturalism (a tenet of liberalism), and this worried him. He continued to have differences with other conservatives, though. For instance, he critiqued Ayn Rand as too dogmatic and antireligious, and he came to be critical of White supremacists and anti-Semites. He was an independent thinker and worried other conservatives when he argued for the legalization of marijuana. In 1965, Buckley debated James Baldwin on the issue of race and the American dream at an event sponsored by the Cambridge Union, England. From 1966–99, he hosted *Firing Line* on the Public Broadcasting Service (PBS), where he engaged in debate with many leading figures about contemporary issues, including his 1969 debate with Noam Chomsky on issues of military intervention and terrorism. Buckley's work contributed to a growing conservative movement that emerged after the passage of the 1964 Civil Rights Act and helped elect Ronald Reagan as president of the United States in 1980.

The election of Reagan represented an important point in what has come to be seen as a longer battle for the soul of America. One key moment in this war was the publication of *A Nation at Risk*, the 1983 report from Reagan's National Commission on Excellence in Education. While a report on education was not out of the ordinary and fell in line with similar reports written under Truman, Eisenhower, and Kennedy, this report came at a time when William J. Bennett was a rising critic of education who claimed that the humanities had been hijacked by the "fads" of feminism and multiculturalism. Bennett served as head of the National Endowment for the Humanities (NEH) under Reagan from 1981 until he was appointed to serve as Secretary of Education from 1985–88. In response to *A Nation at Risk*, he supported competency-based testing for teachers rather than degrees, performance pay for teachers, national test standards for students, parental choice in schools, and holding teachers accountable for what and how much their students know. Much of this was at odds with recommendations in the report itself, but he used the growing concern that US students were falling behind to fuel support for his views. At the university level, he supported a classical education, discouraged multiculturalism, and asked colleges to enforce drug laws. Worried that the more accepting attitude toward some drugs that arose in the 1960s was harming youth, he took over as the Director of the National Office of Drug Control in 1989.

Bennett's books include: *The De-Valuing of America: The Fight for Our Culture and Our Children* (1992) in which he sought to focus education on content, character, and choice, and *Body Count: Moral Poverty... and How to Win America's War Against Crime and Drugs* (1996) in which he focused on youth who, due to the use of drugs and alcohol, kill, rob, and rape with relative impunity (interestingly, he did endorse gun control here). A decade later, he published *America: The Last Best Hope*, Vols I and II (2006, 2007), in which he provided a patriotic history of the United States. In 2013, he added to debates about the value of college degrees in *Is College Worth It?* (with David Wilezol, 2013). Here, he questions the continuing value of higher education for the general populace and instead suggests that it "should be a choice for some, depending on educational prowess, opportunity, and financial considerations" (p. xiv).

During Bennett's time as Secretary of Education, two books were published that caught the public's attention and are still being debated today. In 1987, the culture wars were evident in public and political discourse in the United States. Philosopher Allan Bloom's *Closing of the American Mind* was published in 1987. It was number one on the New York Times Non-fiction Best Seller list for four months. Bloom (1930–92) was critical of the focus on language and logical positivism in philosophy departments at the expense of addressing political and ethical issues. "Positivism and ordinary language analysis... repel students who come with humanizing questions" (p. 378). At the same time, though, he found the focus on deconstruction in literature departments to result in an erosion of reason and an increase in relativism (p. 379). In response to this crisis, he focused on a "great books" approach to higher education.

Bloom identified the Black Power movement, feminism, rock music, fast food, and left-leaning intellectuals for failing to sustain the rational and critical discourse expected of citizens of a democracy. He worried that the university's role as a conservator of values and dialogue was threatened by an uncritical embrace of pluralism and an appreciation of difference. He was particularly worried about the displacement of philosophy by the culture at large. As mentioned, this included a critique of both the embrace of continental philosophy and a critique of logical positivism. Like May Brodbeck in her challenge to Deweyan philosophy in the 1950s (Chapter 16), Bennett had special blame for pragmatism and Dewey in particular. Dewey was blamed for an unhealthy focus on openness to the new (1987, p. 29), a rejection of the past (p. 56), and too much reliance on science (p. 195). This openness resulted in immigrants and minorities laying claim to respect for their differences rather than conforming to majority expectations; they were seen as having no concern for the common good. According to Bloom, "All such teachers of openness had either no interest in or were actively hostile to the Declaration of Independence and the Constitution" (p. 33). For Bloom, such openness leads to relativism, and relativism leads to indifference and conformity (p. 34).

Bloom's response was to suggest a return to the "great books." This was in many ways inspired by his work with his mentor, Leo Strauss, who was a political philosopher and classicist at the University of Chicago when Bloom studied there. That the books Bloom listed happened to be all by White men, he suggested, was just how it was and in no way made his list vulnerable to critique. He rejected the openness of indifference that he thought was "promoted with the twin purposes of humbling our intellectual pride and letting us be whatever we want to be, just as long as we don't want to be knowers." He embraced the openness "that invites us to the quest for knowledge and certitude, for which history and the various cultures provide a brilliant array of examples for examination" (1987, p. 41). Lamenting the loss of requirements to learn languages, philosophy, and science, he noted that

> [t]o be open to knowing, there are certain kinds of things one must know which most people don't want to bother to learn and which appear boring and irrelevant. If openness means to "go with the flow," it is necessarily an accommodation to the present. (pp. 41–2)

Blaming the openness of the counterculture of the 1960s, Bloom found the university and the culture at large subject to the pressure and passions of the masses. "Whether it be Nuremberg or Woodstock, the principle is the same" (p. 314). Both represent for Bloom the unthinking and the irrational.

While Bloom's book sat at number one, E. D. Hirsch's *Cultural Literacy: What Every American Needs to Know*, also published in 1987, sat at number two on the Best Seller list. Hirsch lamented the state of primary and secondary education in the United States. In this book, he took care not to blame teachers or television for what he saw as the declining performance of US students. What he blamed was an approach to teaching that focused on the process of learning rather than the content of what is learned. This resulted in a loss of the basic knowledge that everyone needs to have in order to do well socially and economically. He lamented the fact that Bennett had given his book an endorsement since this resulted in many missing what he saw as the revolutionary message of his work.

Hirsch argued that Martin Luther King Jr.'s dream rested on "mature literacy." "No modern society can hope to become a just society without a high level of universal literacy" (1987, p. 12). Without a basic common knowledge, he argued, the privileged will remain privileged and the powerless will remain powerless.

> Illiterate and semiliterate Americans do not feel themselves to be active participants in our republic, The civic importance of cultural literacy lies in the fact that true enfranchisement depends upon knowledge, knowledge upon literacy, and literacy upon cultural literacy. (p. 12)

He noted that this call for literacy comes from radicals and conservatives alike. *The Black Panther* newspaper, for instance, not only displayed a high level of cultural literacy in its appeals to cultural symbols of equality and freedom to make the case for racial equality, it also ran articles calling for the improved education of Black children (pp. 22–3).

Hirsch traced the roots of this struggle back to an 1893 report that endorsed a broad humanist education that focused on the same skills and content for all and a 1918 report that rejected a content approach and instead focused on contentless skills that would help prepare citizens for different jobs based on their interests and skills. In *Cultural Literacy*, Hirsch blamed the work of John Dewey for this shift. He did, however, acknowledge that both reports were concerned with promoting the democratic ideals of the country. He also noted that while by 1918 immigration was quickly increasing the number and diversity of students in school, the country was graduating a higher percentage of its citizens from high school. What he lamented was that while the 1918 report expressed a laudable desire to put everyone through high school, it assumed that many students would be constitutionally unable to assimilate the knowledge necessary for literate culture. The stress on individual differences and on vocational training implicitly accepted a permanent stratification of economic and social positions. (1987, p. 121)

Rather than argue about which report had more democratic intentions, he argued that we can see that "[c]ertainly the 1893 idea that everyone can and should start out from the same educational foundation was an admirable democratic ideal that needs to be renewed" (p. 121).

While many equated the work of Bloom and Hirsch, they are in fact quite different in many respects. While they both believe that their view of education is what is needed in order to promote democracy, Bloom's view is rooted in a "great books" approach that resists the pluralism that comes from the inclusion of feminist and multicultural perspectives. Hirsch, on the other hand, thinks this pluralism is an important catalyst for growth in knowledge but that it needs to be undergirded with a common education that holds the culture together. He argued that disagreements about diversity were really just disagreements about the degree of diversity that was desirable. Interestingly, he argued that while we might disagree about how to handle immigration, there was agreement that linguistic pluralism was undesirable. He writes:

> The great American apostles of pluralism—William James and Horace Kallen chief among them—assumed that our diversity would develop in a context of a common language. They assumed that although we might act and think very differently, we would talk and argue with each other as members of a single language community, peacefully and in literate English. Our diversity has been represented by the motto on all our coins—E PLURIBUS UNUM, "out of many one." Our debate has been over whether to stress the many or the one. (1987, p. 96)

He went on to note that even Kallen had a list of sacred texts and topics, not too unlike what Hirsch himself proposed. Hirsch argued that, of course, any such list requires regular updating as cultures change and grow. In fact, he says, "Cultural revision is one of our best traditions" (p. 101). For this reason, he argued, his approach was very different from Bloom's "great books" approach. Nonetheless, Hirsch's basic call was for a more traditional focus on the content of education and a return to the skills of reading, memorizing, and testing. While theorists like Dewey might be "right to say the 'higher values' traditionalists invoke are not the special property of Western culture" and that "human values can be taught through many sorts of materials, traditional or untraditional," they were too focused on individuality. Hirsch argued that a child needs a sense of tradition before any kind of meaningful individuality can emerge. "[I]n the end, given our newly gained understanding of literacy, we must be traditionalist about content. For we have learned the paradox that traditional education, which alone yields the flexible skill of mature literacy," is what makes real equality possible (p. 126).

The use of the word "culture" made it easier for many to misread Hirsch and equate him with cultural conservatives like Bennett and Bloom and religious conservatives like Buchanan. To distance his approach from those like Bennett, Bloom, and Buchanan, in later works, Hirsch moved to using the term "core knowledge" instead of culture. This resulted in the Common Core movement in education. But even in this move to embrace Hirsch's ideas, there remained much philosophical confusion. "When 'Cultural Literacy' was published, it was a cannon shot in the long war between progressives and essentialists, or traditionalists, over how American children ought to be taught." This is from a 2013 article (September 27) in the *New York Times* titled "Culture Warrior, Gaining Ground: E. D. Hirsch Sees His Education Theories Taking Hold" by Al Baker. He describes the success of Hirsch as combating a failed approach to education rooted in the work of John Dewey. "From Dewey's teachings, for example, came the idea of 'learning by doing': going to a forest, say, in addition to just learning about it in class" (2013). The space race with the Soviet Union caused many to lament what they saw as the loss of content and facts in education and blame Dewey for what they saw as a failed education system.

Hirsch himself supported this view of Dewey's work in his 1987 book when he blamed Dewey (and others) for "intellectual inconsistencies" that had "disastrous consequences" (p. 122). While he did acknowledge that Dewey was critical of some of what was done in his name, Hirsch remained critical of Dewey. However, by the time he wrote *The Schools We Need and Why We Don't Have Them* (1996), Hirsch was clearer in distinguishing Dewey's work from the child-centered approach. In fact, in this book he refers to himself as a pragmatist and argues that "[t]he pragmatist tries to avoid simplifications and facile oppositions" (p. 7). As a result, he situates Dewey between the extremes of those who focus on the process of education (rather than content) to allow the natural unfolding of the child, and those who demand rigid and rote learning of content (p. 51). He noted that as early as 1902, Dewey tried to overcome the "polarity between child-centered and subject-centered education" (p. 58), but that this polarity is still with us today. He lauds Dewey and William C. Bagley (Dewey's colleague at Columbia University) for their understanding of the role of common knowledge in the successful functioning of democracy (p. 18). He writes that "The integrationist traditions represented by Dewey, Bagley, and others was the finest and soundest tradition of pedagogical thinking in the United States" (p. 124) and hopes that "American pragmatism and independent thinking can make inroads against progressivist orthodoxy" (p. 132).

This correction about Dewey, and the shift in Hirsch's work, has been overlooked by many—supporters and detractors. For some, like Henry A. Giroux, Professor of English and Cultural Studies, Hirsch "is normalizing a view of teaching and content which, in the current moment, enshrines the standardization of knowledge and assessment, which I believe is very deadly for what it means for students to learn and think creatively and critically" (quoted in Baker, 2013). Giroux continues: "There is a corporate-driven, pedagogical machine out there that would reduce classroom learning to rote memorization, embraces high-stakes testing and derides any kind of critical pedagogy as a pathology" (quoted in Baker, 2013). Hirsch's work is indeed used by those who (unlike Hirsch himself) seek a certain kind of uniformity in the content and values being taught. These figures blame teachers, television, and the loss of particular cultural values for what they see as a decline in American values and ability. They, like Buchanan and Bloom, blame feminists, multiculturalists, and environmentalists for what they see as the loss of those very traditions that made the United States great.

One example of this attempt to blame feminists and others for the problems of education can be found in the works of Dinesh D'Souza. His books over the years illustrate the persistence of the issues that were at stake in the battle for the soul of America in the 1980s and 1990s. His *Illiberal Education: The Politics of Race and Sex on Campus* (1991) revisits Buckley's theme that liberal activists have hijacked the university. *The End of Racism: Principles for a*

*Multiracial Society* was published in 1995. In this book, D'Souza argued that racism was not the main explanation for racial inequality but rather a dysfunctional Black culture and the failed remedies of multiculturalism and proportional representation. In 2007, he published *The Enemy at Home: The Cultural Left and Its Responsibility for 9/11*, in which he makes the claim that the "cultural left" is to blame for the rage that led Muslims to the events of 9/11. By cultural left, he means many of the same people and organizations that worried Buchanan back in 1992 when he addressed the Republican National Convention: Hillary Clinton, Ted Kennedy, Noam Chomsky, the ACLU, NOW, Planned Parenthood, and Human Rights Watch. In 2011, he published *The Roots of Obama's Rage* and in 2012, *Obama's America: Unmaking the American Dream*. He argued in both books that President Obama is responsible for what D'Souza sees as the declining power of the United States.

It is clear that the issues being fought over during these culture wars are the very issues that have been at stake since the beginning of this story of American philosophy: monism or pluralism (unity or diversity), status quo or change, exclusion or inclusion. Most of the same topics are also still being disputed: the understanding of the family, of race, of gender, of the environment. Some of the figures discussed in this story of American philosophy appear as disputed figures in these culture wars—James, Kallen, and Dewey. Others have entered into the debates themselves.

Philosophers such as Chomsky, Baldwin, Rorty, and West all debated with Buckley and D'Souza and commented on the issues of the day in writing and on the air. Interestingly, Buchanan has written on Chomsky, defending him against charges of "hating America" and recognizing that despite their vast differences, they shared some views and concerns. At the same time though, fellow conservative Buckley found he could not defend Buchanan against charges of anti-Semitism. As already mentioned, D'Souza singled out leading intellectuals whom he thought were responsible for the negative view of America held by many Muslims. Rorty wrote a review of D'Souza's book *The End of Racism* in which he criticized D'Souza (and most conservatives) for a lack of argument and genuine debate. Rorty and Hirsch taught together and wrote in praise and critique of each other's work. They considered themselves part of the old left that was universalistic and not the new left that focused on inclusion via multiculturalism and feminism (see Chapter 22). This can stand in opposition to thinkers like West, but Rorty often praised West's work, as he did in the review of D'Souza's book just mentioned. The lines of convergence and divergence among these public figures are not always clear.

Chomsky received his PhD from the University of Pennsylvania in 1955 and spent his career at MIT in the Department of Linguistics and Philosophy. As a leading opponent of the war in Vietnam, Chomsky published *The Responsibility of Intellectuals* in 1967, an essay in the *New York Review of Books*, and *American Power and the New Mandarins* in 1969. Echoing Kallen's critique of the unity of the science movement, Chomsky challenged people working in science and government for uncritically providing the technologies and organization that make modern warfare possible and called on all intellectuals to take responsibility for the actions of their country. Following Bourne's critique of Dewey, Chomsky also argued that pragmatism embraced the growing tendency to use "science" to manipulate behavior and thinking. In *Intellectuals and the State* (1977), he again blamed Dewey for supporting the First World War and critiquing pacifism (though his assessment was based on a presentation that was arguably not fair to Dewey's position). His main point was that intellectuals need to be publicly involved in challenging the propaganda of business and government. In a totalitarian state, he argued, thought control is not a secret, whereas in a democracy, it is more complicated. "The democratic system of thought control is seductive and compelling. The more vigorous the debate, the better the system of propaganda is served, since the tacit, unspoken assumptions are more forcefully implanted" (1982, p. 81).

Democratic education can be a way to resist the propaganda and create free minds, but education as it is practiced generally is a tool of the powerful. Praising Dewey in *Chomsky on Miseducation* (2000a), Chomsky thought that few have followed Dewey's model for education, and as a result, American society was only more vulnerable to corporate and governmental control of education. Schools had become a place where students learn to conform and not question official versions of historical events. Chomsky wanted a critical citizenry.

Chomsky was also a regular critic of US foreign policy. For example, he opposed US support of the Contras in Nicaragua in the 1980s and the killing of Osama bin Laden in 2011. "We might ask ourselves how we would be reacting if Iraqi commandos landed at George W. Bush's compound, assassinated him, and dumped his body in the Atlantic" (2011). Also, a regular critic of US domestic policy, he opposed the death penalty and the "war on drugs." US domestic drug policy does not carry out its stated goals, and policymakers are well aware of that. If it isn't about reducing substance abuse, what is it about? "It is reasonably clear, both from current actions and the historical record, that substances tend to be criminalized when they are associated with the so-called dangerous classes and that the criminalization of certain substances is a technique of social control" (2002).

In both foreign and domestic affairs, Chomsky emphasized the importance of an independent press and worried about the effects of government and corporate "ownership" of the press today. In *Necessary Illusions: Thought Control in Democratic Societies* (1989), he noted Dewey's criticism of the press as controlled by economic interests and actively working to create apathy and indifference in the general public. For Chomsky, the public awakening of the 1960s posed a real challenge to business interests and the government. In *Hegemony or Survival: America's Quest for Global Dominance* (2003), Chomsky asserted that those with power do not want to be challenged, and they make it unpatriotic to question or challenge the dominant discourse.

> [Those in power] declare that it is unpatriotic and disruptive to question the workings of authority—but patriotic to institute harsh and regressive policies that benefit the wealthy, undermine social programs that serve the needs of the great majority, and subordinate a frightened population to increased state control. (p. 217)

He believed this is what happened in the wake of 9/11. In his discussion of the terrorist attack in his book *9-11* (2001), he reiterated a point he made in much of his writing, and especially in *The Culture of Terrorism* from 1988, that the United States is a leading terrorist state. He recited a list of conflicts in which he believed the United States had directly and indirectly killed and terrorized the civilians of other countries. The use of bombing, the arming of combatants, the refusal of food and medical aid, and the use of economic sabotage are just some of the ways Chomsky thought the United States enforces its will. Much of the death toll is silent and invisible.

Chomsky also charged the government and the press with an effort to demonize the enemy. He did not think the response to 9/11 was unique or new in this, but rather that it was part of a long history of manipulating consent for violent interventions—including the controversial use of preemptive and preventative attacks. "It is much easier to personalize the enemy, identified as the symbol of ultimate evil, than to seek to understand what lies behind major atrocities" (2001, p. 37). Chomsky argued that the roots of the 2001 attack could be found in the history of US imperialism and terrorism. He pointed specifically to the acts of violence done in the name of fighting Soviet aggression and saw Reagan's "war on terror" as both a precursor and a cause for the later attack and response. The immediate response to the attacks on the United States, to starve the people of Afghanistan, exemplified for Chomsky the kind of "silent death toll" the United States often inflicts. He hoped people would wake up to this and protest, as many did in the 1980s in response to Reagan's involvement in Central America. But he was still cautious: "[We] should not underestimate the capacity of well-run propaganda systems to drive people to irrational, murderous, and suicidal behavior" (p. 69).

At the center of Chomsky's political work was a commitment to raise the level of public awareness, concern, and action with regard to important social issues. Referencing Dewey's analysis of the role of big business in social and political issues, Chomsky joined Dewey in calling for critical engagement with the issues of the day. Whether it was civil rights, labor unions, or the Environmental Movement, he thought improvement only comes with struggle and must be maintained with struggle. Business interests work to roll back change by distracting the public. He wrote, "Lacking any support in a depoliticized society in which popular organizations that might sustain a functioning democracy have largely eroded, individuals are in a difficult position, often unable to come to understand what they think, believe, and want" (1997, pp. 192–3). People might even react irrationally, but this is no problem from the perspective of business interests so long as their irrational actions do not challenge those with privilege. Chomsky thought that what was needed was a public that was capable of thinking for itself and challenging privilege.

When Bloom published *The Closing of the American Mind*, critical of the Left's effort to undermine a canonical approach to education and the consequent erosion of confidence in the truth, Chomsky dismissed the book as representative of the effort to use education to serve the interests of power. "[T]he main point," he said in an interview, "is that the entire school curriculum, from kindergarten through graduate school, will be tolerated only so long as it continues to perform its institutional role" (2003b, p. 25). Bloom's book was part of an effort to force education to do what it was expected to do. "Take all this business about Allan Bloom and that book everybody's been talking about, *The Closing of the American Mind*," Chomsky said. "I don't know if you've bothered looking at it—it's mind-bogglingly stupid" (p. 26). The problem is that Bloom assumes that there is "some array of 'the deep thoughts,' and we smart people will pick them out and you dumb guys will learn them—or memorize them at least, because you don't really learn them if they're just forced on you." Instead, he concludes, "The point is, it doesn't matter what you read, what matters is how you read it" (p. 27).

Rorty also reviewed the book, accusing Bloom of having clear doubts about the efficacy of democracy and a pluralistic society. Instead, Rorty (who had been a classmate of Bloom's at Chicago) thought that Bloom followed the lead of other Straussians who "reject Emerson's and Dewey's attempt to find one's moral identity in membership in a democratic community.

They consider such an attempt—the attempt to pretend that a pluralistic democratic society can be more than an incoherent 'simulacrum of community'—to be . . . childish" (1998, p. 28). In his own piece on Bloom, Sidney Hook praised Rorty's review of the book. While Hook disagreed with Bloom on his understanding of philosophy and his recommendations for curriculum (he preferred those he had offered himself), he did agree with Bloom that the real source of the problems in education could be found in the radical and rebellious actions of students and faculty in the 1960s. He wrote: "Secondary education . . . is afflicted by increasing violence, drug addiction, and sexual promiscuity" (Hook, 1989, p. 123). He praised Bloom for noting the "parallel between the riotous American students in the sixties and the behavior of the Nazi-infected students in German universities after Hitler came to power" (p. 126). He criticized Martha Nussbaum for denying "the truth about the rampaging students of the sixties" in her review of the book (p. 126). Just this sampling demonstrates the diversity within the philosophical community and the importance of having philosophers engaging with such popular works.

Richard Bernstein and Cornel West (discussed in the next chapter) also took up the role of public philosophers in the American tradition. Bernstein was a classmate and longtime friend and defender of Rorty. He was born in Brooklyn in 1932 to the children of immigrants who were not highly educated. In 1945, when Bernstein was twelve, his older brother was killed in action as a navigator in the US Air Force. Despite this loss, his parents encouraged his educational goals, and like Rorty, Bernstein attended the University of Chicago as an undergraduate. In 1951, he was just nineteen when he received his BA in philosophy. Too young to enter graduate school, he went to Columbia University, graduated summa cum laude in 1953 in General Studies, and then went on to Yale and received his PhD in 1958.

He remained at Yale as a faculty member, but the university denied him tenure, even while he was granted promotion. His case remains one of the most famous tenure cases and is sometimes referred to as the "Bernstein Affair." It resulted in student protests and was written about in the *New York Times*, *Time Magazine*, and *Newsweek*. While the *New York Times* hypothesized that the decision was the result of Bernstein's critique of some of Yale's policies, students surmised that Yale did not appreciate his creative teaching style. Other philosophers from around the country suggested it was due to an internal split between analytic and speculative philosophy. The department had gone through a change with the departure of four philosophers for the University of Pittsburgh—Wilfred Sellars among them—and so Bernstein faced a conflicted department. Some department members did suggest that Bernstein's scholarly work was not original, was primarily exegesis, and not up to the level required. Further, they did not want to give into student preferences. While his case eventually resulted in tenure reform at Yale, he moved on to teach at Haverford College for twenty-three years and then at the New School for Social Research from 1989 until his death in 2022. The New School's mission is to "foster the highest standards of scholarly inquiry while addressing issues of major political, cultural, and economic concern." Dewey had helped found the New School and Kallen was one of the first philosophy professors to teach there. Bernstein carried on in this tradition.

Given their long history, Bernstein and Rorty frequently shared drafts of essays and books and were longtime conversational partners. Bernstein wrote that early on they differed in that he *started* philosophy with an eye to the fallibilism and pluralism of the pragmatic tradition, while Rorty was initially convinced that the analytic approach to philosophy was the right way. As that changed for Rorty, Bernstein frequently defended Rorty against his critics, even though he also had critiques of his own. Despite some of their differences, Bernstein provided the decisive review that resulted in the publication of *Philosophy and the Mirror of Nature*. "I explained just why the book would delight some readers and infuriate others," Bernstein recalls in an essay in *The Pragmatic Century* (Davaney et al., 2006). He predicted that it "would prove to be one of the most discussed books during the next decade—and told the editor that he would be crazy not to publish it!" (p. 100). Bernstein found Rorty to be a thought-provoking and challenging conversation partner. He said, "I am outraged when I hear those caricatures of him as superficial, flip, and morally callous." Rorty, he continued, was part of "that great tradition of ironic moralists who are deeply concerned about the abuses of humiliation and the degradation of poverty" (p. 100).

Bernstein did much to secure Rorty's reputation as he took up Rorty's work in his own books and put him on par with the likes of Heidegger, Husserl, Foucault, Derrida, Habermas, Gadamer, and Arendt. In his most widely read books—*Beyond Objectivism and Relativism* (1983) and *The New Constellation* (1992)—Bernstein took Rorty very seriously, even as he took him to task. In *Beyond Objectivism and Relativism*, Bernstein was concerned to address the growing divide between the extreme position of objectivism (the position that there is and must be some ahistorical and permanent framework for knowledge and understanding), and relativism (the position that all we encounter and can know is a nonreducible plurality, that is, always relative to social and historical circumstances). Using James's term, he thought neither position was a "live option." The spirit of fallibilism that permeates the history of natural science no longer allows absolutism to be a live option, while the extreme versions of relativism as a thoroughgoing subjectivism have also been countered.

For Bernstein, we are left with a more interesting choice between "fallibilistic objectivism" and "non-subjective relativism." Addressing work going on in the natural and social sciences, he points to what he saw as a growing interest to move beyond this debate to focus on the understanding and interpretations made possible if we recover hermeneutics. While he appeals to the work of Gadamer, Habermas, Arendt, and Rorty to make his case, the voices of Peirce, James, and Dewey were also involved in the conversation. Bernstein was concerned with how communities come to shared understandings because such understandings have "practical and political consequences" and so can "draw us toward the goal of cultivating the types of dialogical communities in which *phronesis*, judgment, and practical discourse become concretely embodied in our everyday practices" (1983, p. 223). He goes on to note that plurality does not need to divide people but is an opportunity to arrive at temporary resolutions through debate and conversation. We need to address how communities break down, and how and why some people are excluded from the conversation, but in between those problems he maintains that there are moments of solidarity on which we can build. For this reason, "the movement beyond objectivism and relativism is not just a theoretical problem but a practical task" (p. 230), one he calls on us to begin "furthering the types of solidarity, participation, and mutual recognition that is founded in dialogical communities" (p. 231).

In *The New Constellation*, a book he saw as a sequel to *Beyond Objectivism and Relativism* and its "non-foundational pragmatic humanism" (1992, p. 2), he took up some new conversation partners: Heidegger, Foucault, and Derrida. Habermas and Rorty also remained. Rather than try to reconcile or integrate the variety of positions and traditions represented, he saw them as part of a juxtaposed cluster of ideas that make up a constellation. He argues that we need to learn to listen to each other when there are common concerns, despite our differences. There is much to be learned if we maintain a pluralistic and fallibilistic approach. This was most forcefully put in the appendix to the book, his 1988 presidential address to the Eastern Division of the APA, "Pragmatism, Pluralism, and the Healing of Wounds." Here he notes that philosophy in America is, and always has been heterogeneous and that this is its strength. The pragmatic tradition arose out of this pluralism and the less "professional" climate in philosophy at the time. It is a tradition that had, and continues to have, a deep influence on philosophy and other disciplines even as few acknowledge that history. It is a theme he again took up in *The Pragmatic Century* and *The Pragmatic Turn* (2010).

Bernstein argued that the pragmatists were ahead of their time and that both analytic and continental thought were just starting to catch up. For him, pragmatism was not a method or set of doctrines but an ethos that included antifoundationalism, fallibilism rather than relativism, an acknowledgment of the social character of the self, an awareness of contingency and chance, and owning up to the inescapable plurality we face. This was contrasted with the arrogant ideology that Bernstein sees in the analytic tradition. He was careful to distinguish the content and approach of analytic philosophy—which can share much in common with some of the pragmatists—from the attitude of those who hold it as the *only* way to do *real* philosophy. He pointed to people like Rorty, McIntyre, and Putnam as philosophers well-versed in the methods and subjects of analytic philosophy who moved on to open conversations with other approaches. He found this a hopeful sign of an emerging engaged, fallibilistic pluralism that will allow us to respond to conflict with dialogue and help us seek understanding. He was careful to distinguish this from "flabby" pluralism in which we superficially borrow from other traditions to make our own case, "polemical" pluralism that fails to listen and only tries to advance one's own position, and "defensive" pluralism in which we acknowledge the work of others but assert in advance that it is unimportant.

Interestingly, when he pointed to contemporary pragmatists, they were almost all philosophers who follow the analytic line. In *The Pragmatic Turn*, the philosophers Bernstein referenced and praised included some figures we have already discussed: Rorty, Putnam, Quine, Davidson, and Sellars. More contemporary figures fall into the categories of neo- and new pragmatists: Robert Brandom (a student of Rorty's who tried to argue that there is room for truth), John McDowell (who argued for more certainty than Rorty), Cheryl Misak (whose work on Peirce focused on truth), Jeffrey Stout (whose work also challenged Rorty and argued for a more robust conception of truth and nature), Christopher Hookway (whose work on Peirce focused on sentiment, inquiry, and truth), and Bjorn Ramberg (whose work focused on issues of truth). This approach as a whole, despite internal diversity, remained focused on problems of truth, objectivity, representation, and reality, despite the call by Rorty (their founding figure) for philosophy to get beyond such a focus. These figures focused on trying to legitimate some ideas found in the pragmatists to an analytically trained audience. For instance, in his opening to the chapter on Putnam in *The Pragmatic Turn*, Bernstein writes that Putnam was involved in the "most important and exciting philosophical debates of the past half century." He went on to list the topics of these debates: "philosophy of science, logic, mathematics, language, mind, perception, epistemology, and metaphysics" (2010, p. 153). This kind of move seems designed to link pragmatism to the analytic tradition and the more limited focus of what counts as legitimate philosophy. This is at odds with Bernstein's larger project to open up conversational bridges across approaches and concerns. While Putnam may have been broader, the more narrowly focused neopragmatists do not generally represent the engaged, fallibilistic pluralism Bernstein so often wrote about.

This concern with engaged, fallibilistic pluralism was central to Bernstein's more political work. In *John Dewey: On Experience, Nature, and Freedom* (1960), *Praxis and Action* (1971), and *The Restructuring of Social and Political Theory* (1976), Bernstein tried to show that philosophy needs to be more responsive to the times. "There is a felt need for reunion in philosophy," he wrote, "for new perspective and vision that is informed by the lessons of careful analysis." To take this direction, philosophers could learn from Dewey, "who sought to unite speculative imagination with a sensitive concern for the variety of human experience and the specific 'problems of men'" (2006, p. 13). Bernstein saw in the activism of the 1960s and 1970s a growing unrest with the limits of the dominant analytic tradition in philosophy and the social sciences and offered an array of thinkers to help address what he saw as an "emerging new sensibility." Appeals to value neutrality and metaethics were not enough to address the growing unrest and protest.

Bernstein did not just write about this; he lived it as well. In *The Pragmatic Century*, he gives a sense of his times as he describes the conservative nature of Yale. "These were the days of McCarthyism. The great hero was a recent graduate, William Buckley . . . I was the faculty advisor for the John Dewey Society—a group committed to participatory democracy and opposed to the pernicious influence of McCarthyism" (2006, p. 112). Bernstein also joined other Yale faculty and students in Mississippi in the summer of 1964 to help with voter registration and the organization of "Freedom Schools." His concern with improving social and political life also came out in *Praxis and Action* (1971).

In this book, Bernstein worked through Marxism, existentialism, pragmatism, and analytic philosophy to examine how we can free individuals and groups to work within the polis and create the possibility of living well. For Bernstein, all these schools of thought have strengths and weaknesses. His goal was to bring them into conversation with each other, and his readers into conversation with multiple approaches to pressing problems. For instance, Marxists may be justified in worrying that a Deweyan approach to reform has real limits, but Deweyan concerns about the risk of totalitarianism emerging from the radicalism of Marxism also deserve attention. Analytic philosophy can help us get clear on concepts and ideas, but it is too isolated from life. Existentialism engages the problems of the day but comes with a risk of nihilism. What Bernstein wanted was for philosophers to take off their blinders and be open enough to learn from each other. We need to learn to approach philosophies as orientations rather than dogmas. He thought this was the key strength of pragmatism. "The essential fallibility of all inquiry is no cause for despair, but rather an incentive for openness and for testing as rigorously and critically as we can all hypotheses and theories." Since meaning is social, he said, "[we] must not only countenance, but seek out intersubjective criticisms of all hypotheses." The ideal to be sought was the "establishment of a free, open, self-critical community of inquirers" (1971, p. 199).

Bernstein followed through on this by arguing for a pluralistic approach in other disciplines as well. In *The Restructuring of Social and Political Theory*, he asserted that "An adequate, comprehensive political and social theory must be at once empirical, interpretative, and critical" (1976, p. xiv). This was just another example of how his open and dialogical approach worked to build on the strengths he found in a myriad of disciplines and schools of thought and created the possibility of a stronger and more open democratic society. This is the central concern of his 2003 book *The Abuse of Evil* that we discussed in the prologue as a response to the response to 9/11. His assessment was rooted in a concern with the future of democracy and the importance of the "establishment of a free, open, self-critical community of inquirers" (p. 199).

# CHAPTER 26
# AMERICAN PHILOSOPHY FOR THE FUTURE

Cornel West, like Bernstein and most of the philosophers in the tradition we've been discussing, shares concerns about the future of democracy. West's story emerges in the recovery of philosophical pragmatism in the work of Richard Rorty. West was a student of Rorty's when he was at Princeton as a graduate student. West recalls that "My eye-opening and horizon-broadening encounter with Richard Rorty made me an even stronger Wittgensteinian, although with gestures toward Dewey." He goes on to note that "Rorty's historicist turn was like music to my ears—nearly as sweet as the Dramatics, the Spinners, or the Main Ingredient, whom I then listened to daily for sanity" (1999, p. 7). These words point to some of the intellectual roots of West's philosophical approach. They also point to his understanding of philosophy as music and his hope to create a "danceable philosophy." He argued that the role of the philosopher (or intellectual) was like that of the artist—to critique the powerful and provide hope for the disadvantaged and oppressed. The intellectual should be "a critical organic catalyst" (1993a/2009, p. 102). For West, philosophy was not an objective or dispassionate activity. In one of his earliest and best-known books, *Prophecy Deliverance! An Afro-American Revolutionary Christianity* (1982), he said:

> I understand philosophy to be a social activity of intellectual pursuit always already infused with cultural concerns and political choices often unbeknown to its participants. As an active Afro-American participant in the philosophical enterprise, I merely try to make my cultural concerns and political choices crystal clear. (p. 12)

His concerns include the critique and promotion of individuality and democracy in the pursuit of broader social freedom for all. To do this, he uses the resources of his prophetic Christianity, the tragic sensibility of the existentialist philosophy of Russian playwright Anton Chekhov, and the "reforming orientation" of pragmatism.

West found in pragmatism a questioning, open-ended, antifoundationalist philosophy that is committed to inquiry, democracy, and amelioration. In *The American Evasion of Philosophy: A Genealogy of Pragmatism* (1989), he traced a story of pragmatism from Emerson to Rorty and ended with his own version of prophetic pragmatism that included resources from the work of Roberto Unger, Michel Foucault, and Gayatri Spivak. While his is a contested account, it is also an influential account. West argued that pragmatism "evaded" the epistemology-centered philosophy that dominated the field and so was able to provide a powerful form of cultural criticism that is an important resource. His own prophetic pragmatism requires a rich intellectual tradition and the empowerment of the disadvantaged. "Prophetic pragmatism," he writes, "rests upon the conviction that the American evasion of philosophy is not an evasion of serious thought and moral action. Rather such evasion is a rich and revisable tradition that serves as the occasion for cultural criticism and political engagement" (p. 239). This criticism and engagement are the sources of the hope that West blends with the death and despair which the oppressed face.

West believed that most of the thinkers in the American tradition discussed in this book failed to deal adequately with the tragic element of life. He found Royce and Hook to be exceptions to this, but he addressed the lack, as John McDermott did, by adding a heavy dose of existentialism to his diagnosis of America's social ills and to his prescription for hope. West was also concerned that neopragmatism, rooted in the work of Rorty, would fail to adequately take up issues of power and would ultimately prove to be inadequate as a philosophy of actual reform. Instead, West wrote in *Keeping Faith: Philosophy and Race in America* (1993a/2009) that Rorty's work was confined to "departmental internecine struggles" that "have yet to spill over into serious cultural and political debates regarding the larger issues of public concern" (p. 128). He further asserts that "Rorty's work gives us mappings and descriptions with no explanatory accounts for change and conflict." What West seeks instead is "prophetic criticism," which is "partisan, partial, engaged and crisis-centered, yet always keeps open a skeptical eye to avoid dogmatic traps, premature closures, formulaic formulations or rigid conclusions" (p. 23). The pragmatism of James and Dewey are resources for such prophetic criticism. West rejected Bourne-inspired critiques of pragmatism that argued pragmatism was aimless, yet at the same time, he was aware of its potential blind spots. Discussing pragmatism and politics, he said that "At its worst, it became a mere ideological cloak for corporate liberalism and managerial social engineering" in America; on the other hand, "at its best, it survived as a form of cultural critique and social reform at the service of expanding the scope of democratic process and broadening the arena of individual self-development here and abroad" (p. 103). To help promote pragmatism at its best, West used the work of thinkers like Dewey and Du Bois in combination with theorists such as Marx, Antonio Gramsci (1891–1937), and Foucault.

West also complicated the pragmatist focus on dialogue and education as the way to mediate conflicts. While fully committed to dialogue and education as tools of reform, West believed they can work this way only when embedded in a society that honestly confronts racism, sexism, classism, and heterosexism. He argues that "unattended racial and sexual polarizations, and untheorized cultural and personal conflicts that permeate and pervade our past and present" (1993a/2009, p. 137) have made liberal intellectuals impotent. This is why West put forward his version of prophetic pragmatism. Facing up to how White supremacy and male dominance infect the very structure of US democracy is the only basis for moving forward. "Prophetic pragmatism gave courageous resistance and relentless critique a self-critical character and democratic content," he writes. "It analyzes the social causes of unnecessary forms of social misery, promotes moral outrage against them, organizes different constituencies to alleviate them, yet does so with an openness to its own blindnesses and shortcomings" (p. 139).

Unlike Rorty's neopragmatism, West's prophetic pragmatism seeks to avoid "making criticism a fetish or democracy an idol." Fetishizing criticism, he says, "yields a sophisticated ironic consciousness of parody and paralysis" while "idolizing democracy produces mob rule." Prophetic pragmatism is a way to fight "despair, dogmatism and oppression" (1993a/2009, pp. 139–40). For West, it is a way to fight the lethargy often induced by the dominance of the business mentality, consumerist culture, and the impact of cultural conservatism. He had described these in the introduction to *The Ethical Dimensions of Marxist Thought* (1991). "Consumer culture—a way of life that spawns addictive personalities and passive citizens—promotes a profound spiritual impoverishment and moral shallowness" (1991, pp. xi–xii). This kind of culture results in decay and what West calls "civic terrorism": "the sheer avalanche of mindless and calculated violence in our social fabric [which] haunts many urban, suburban, and rural streets." He lists deteriorating physical infrastructure, growing class inequality, xenophobia, and ecological destruction as facts that "frighten most Americans." It is hard to see how to address problems at a time when "money-driven elections and packaged politicians (turned fundraisers) have made the political system virtually an ugly joke—whose punchline is on the American people" (p. xi).[1] Ironically, perhaps, West was a declared candidate for the US presidency as an independent in the 2024 elections, though his candidacy was distinct from those of candidates in the major parties in his call for people to think independently as they pursue justice and equality. His campaign website declared, "His unwavering commitment to independent thought and his unapologetic pursuit of truth have made him a revered figure, inspiring others to follow their path, think critically, and never back down from the pursuit of a more just and enlightened world" (West, 2024).

West's books *Race Matters* (1993b) and *Democracy Matters: Winning the Fight Against Imperialism* (2004) both continued to take up these concerns and promote his version of prophetic pragmatism. *Race Matters* begins with an analysis of the 1992 beating of Rodney King as a "multiracial, trans-class, and largely male display of justified social rage" (1993b, p. 1). West argues that it was not so much about race, but instead about the combination of economic decline, a sense of powerlessness, and political lethargy. The growing gap between the rich and poor is more centrally West's concern. This inequality leads to cynicism and pessimism. When combined with political and cultural disenfranchisement, the result can be a paralyzing nihilism. Without hope, there is no struggle to make new meanings and make things better.

West called for new leaders and criticized the academy for failing to produce the leaders needed. He pointed to the failure of Black leaders to critique Clarence Thomas when he was nominated for the Supreme Court. "The very fact that no black leader could utter publicly that a black appointee for the Supreme Court was unqualified shows how captive they are to white racist stereotypes about black intellectual talent" (1993b, p. 23). West saw himself as standing alone in questioning the racial reasoning that required the Black community to close ranks in support of Thomas. West further noted that historically this closing of ranks was usually done at the expense of Black women—in this case Anita Hill. West suggested that self-critique is a necessary process for a healthy community and argued that a coalition of the oppressed would be more effective at promoting the humanity of all people. This shift in thinking is frustrated by the fact that contemporary Black scholars, unlike Du Bois, are concerned primarily with narrow discipline-based problems rather than problems of communities. This is, according to West, a not too surprising consequence of an academic world that rewards specialized jargon over political engagement. Any scholar who challenges this model may feel pressure from colleagues and administrators to return to mainstream academic topics. This is especially true for women and people of color.

West's personal journey is as important to this story as his philosophy. He did good mainstream scholarly work, but he never divorced this from his social and political concerns. The son of parents born in Louisiana in the era of Jim Crow, he marched with them in civil rights demonstrations. His commitment to action was evident when in high school he and several other Black student body presidents organized to get more classes in Black studies. West went to Harvard in 1970 as an undergraduate and "became part of the first generation of young black people to attend prestigious lily-white institutions of higher learning in significant numbers" (1991, p. xvii). Studying philosophy there, he was taught by (among others) Hilary Putnam and John Rawls. He also was influenced by various Marxists, Trotskyites, and the work of theologian Reinhold Niebuhr while he wrestled with the distinct approaches of Malcolm X and Martin Luther King, Jr. He then went off to Princeton and encountered (among others) Rorty. After two years he returned to Harvard as a Du Bois fellow and produced his dissertation (which would become the book *The Ethical Dimensions of Marxist Thought*) while still in his mid-twenties.

He was a professor at Union Theological Seminary in 1977. It was there that he published *Prophecy Deliverance!* and became involved with the Democratic Socialists of America (DSA). He moved to Yale Divinity School in 1984, where he produced *The American Evasion of Philosophy* (1989). West was arrested for his support of the attempts by the clerical workers at Yale to unionize. His next major move was to go to Princeton as a member of the religion department and director of the Afro-American Studies program. He returned to Harvard in 1994. He discussed his time at Harvard in *Democracy Matters* as an example of the importance and difficulty of combating the plutocratic elites.

Written after 9/11, in 2004, *Democracy Matters* pointed to the need to combat three dogmas: the free market mentality, aggressive militarism, and growing authoritarianism. As with Bernstein, West was disturbed by the response to 9/11 and the consequences of growing fear and distrust. In addition to justifying preemptive strikes against potential enemies, the growing militarism also required the sacrifice of soldiers who were largely working class and people of color. It justified violence against "others" and fomented a fear that was made concrete in the Patriot Act passed by the US Congress in October 2001. The Act created "new tools" to combat terrorism that included making it easier to spy on US citizens and non-citizens within the United States. "The cowardly terrorist attacks of 9/11 have been cannon fodder for the tightening of surveillance," West wrote. "The loosening of legal protection and slow closing of meaningful access to the oversight of governmental activities . . . are justified by the notion that safety trumps liberty and security dictates the parameters of freedom" (2004, pp. 6–7). As with Bernstein, West noted how this kind of response shut down the possibility of dialogue on which democracy depends. He concluded that "This is the classic triumph of authoritarianism over the kind of questioning, compassion, and hope requisite for any democratic experiment" (p. 7).

West argued that in order to address these antidemocratic dogmas, the United States needed to face up to its own history of oppression and critique. "America has a long tradition of excoriating, painful, and powerful critiques of the arrested development of our democracy," he writes, among which are the "imperial expansionist genocide of the Native Americans," the violent opposition to unionization and labor laws, the subjugation of women and homosexuals, and "most especially and centrally of the deeply antidemocratic and dehumanizing hypocrisies of white supremacy" (2004, pp. 13–14). The Socratic questioning philosophers engage in is critical to this work of national self-examination and confession. But philosophers need to take this questioning outside of the academy, and the public has to stop seeing such questioning as unpatriotic. This is the best hope for a democratic awakening:

> This is what happened in the 1860s, 1890s, 1930s, and 1960s in American history. Just as it looked as if we were about to lose the American democratic experiment—in the face

of civil war, imperial greed, economic depression, and racial upheaval—in each of these periods a democratic awakening and activist energy emerged to keep our democratic project afloat. (p. 23)

We opened this study by trying to make clear what an American philosophy of resistance is. West stands as a prominent example of an academic and public intellectual who is both a philosopher and an activist. Other public intellectuals, whom we mentioned as we framed our discussion in the first chapter, include Grace Lee Boggs and her husband James. For Boggs and Boggs, philosophy is an essential part of change—revolution and evolution—because it critically engages the concepts that are used to solve problems and imagines new ones. But philosophy does not stop with speculative work. It is continuous with the activism required to challenge the established systems and use new ideas to transform indeterminate or disrupted situations of the community into stable new ones.

In the Boggses' work, real change in a society that begins in criticism of established ideas, and ends in the transformation of daily life, has at least two features: it is local and has a potentially wider impact by changing how similar circumstances are thought about. Recalling Dewey's theory of inquiry where inquiries emerge in an unsettled situation and resolve when that situation is transformed, inquiries also leave a remainder—guidelines for how one can respond to similar situations in the future. These "leading principles," as Peirce and Dewey called them, are fallible if only because their further application is to new circumstances that will inevitably differ by degrees from the original situation. It is a failure to take this fallibility seriously that leads philosophers to what Dewey called the philosopher's fallacy, where the results of inquiry (in a particular situation) are accepted as universally true for every situation (Boydston, 1967–1990, LW 1, pp. 351–2).

When Grace Lee (1915–2015) and James Boggs (1919–93) began their work in Detroit, it was first to respond to the deep poverty, miseducation, lack of opportunity, and failure of imagination in the neighborhoods of that city. As they sought answers to present problems, they shared those answers with others, promoting community organizing across the nation. Grace Lee was born in Providence, Rhode Island, to Chinese immigrant parents who ran a restaurant. She received a bachelor's degree from Barnard College in 1935 and received her PhD from Bryn Mawr College in New York City in 1940. At Bryn Mawr, Boggs studied with Paul Weiss, who had studied with Alfred North Whitehead at Harvard and had, with Charles Hartshorne, edited the *Collected Papers of Charles S. Peirce*—making significant parts of Peirce's unpublished work available for the first time. Boggs wrote her dissertation on George Herbert Mead (1863–1931) who received his PhD in 1888 from Harvard where he studied with Josiah Royce (and where he served as tutor for the children of William James). In 1891, Mead joined John Dewey at the University of Michigan and they became close friends. When Dewey moved to the University of Chicago, Mead moved with him and stayed at Chicago until his early death.

While Boggs studied Dewey and took seriously his theory of experience and education, Mead was a revelation for her. His theory of communication and concept of the "generalized other" provided Boggs with a conceptual framework to think about communities. Even more important, she writes, "Although I didn't know it at the time, Mead prepared me for the next stage in my own development by providing me with (1) a way to look at great ideas in their connection with great leaps forward in history, and (2) an analysis of how the self and society develop in relation to each other" (Boggs, 1998, p. 33). Change, on her developing account, was driven by "great ideas"—ideas that provided new ways to think about problems and to imagine possible futures—and that these ideas could spur dramatic transformation of human societies.

Following her graduation, with little idea of what to do, she "recalled that although both George Herbert Mead and John Dewey had been born in New England, they developed their distinctively American philosophy of pragmatism in Chicago" (1998, p. 35). So, in the fall of 1940, she moved to Chicago. Charles Morris, then chair of philosophy at the University of Chicago, offered her a low-paying job in the philosophy library. The pay led her to find free housing in a basement room infested with rats. Soon after, she became part of a tenants' association founded by the Socialist Workers Party (a communist organization and followers of Leon Trotsky) that sought ways of forcing landlords to address the rat problems in that part of the city. The activism of the South Side Tenants Organization inspired Boggs to focus on political activism and political theory. "Having been born female and Chinese American," she wrote, "I had known from early on that changes were needed in our society, but not until I left the university in 1940 with a PhD in philosophy did it occur to me that I might be involved in making those changes" (2012, p. 56).

In 1941, Boggs met the Trinidadian historian and political theorist C. L. R. James (1901–89) who was on a lecture tour for the Socialist Workers Party. The following year, she moved to New York City to work for James. She served as an editor for publications by the party's Correspondence Committee and prepared the first English translations of Karl Marx's *Economic and Philosophic Manuscripts of 1844*. In 1952, she met James Boggs, also a member of the Workers Party, when he visited New York for meetings with the party. Born in Alabama, when he turned eighteen, James moved to Detroit to find work. In 1938, as part of the New Deal's Works Progress Administration (WPA) program, he completed a trade school and in 1940 was hired as an autoworker at Chrysler. In 1953, he and Grace Lee were married, and over the next forty years, they collaborated on books and articles, community organizing, and political activism.

In their 1974 book, *Revolution and Evolution in the Twentieth Century*, Boggs and Boggs diagnosed the disruptions of American society since the Second World War as a consequence of "the contradiction between economic and technological overdevelopment and political and human underdevelopment" (2008, xix). To bring about change, they argued, would require something more than incremental adjustments to the dominant system. For some, the key to change is disruption in the form of rebellion or insurrection. For example, the Occupy Movement of 2011, the Black Lives Matter protests of 2020, and the January 6 "Insurrection" of 2021 are cases that seem committed to change. For Boggs and Boggs, an insurrection is "a concentrated attack upon existing authority by members of an oppressed group . . . during the course of a revolutionary struggle." Insurrections are a stage of revolution. With rebellions, they disrupt "the society, but [they do] not provide what is necessary to establish a new social order" (p. 17).

For the Boggses, rebellions, insurrections, revolts, and even coups are only surface changes—efforts to take power but potentially without a vision of the future or the conceptual changes needed to foster new growth. Rebellion and insurrection are natural responses to a people's oppression. When Detroit erupted in riots following MLK's assassination, the community was disrupted. Reliable structures of oppression were broken. City and state authorities worked to quickly reestablish the structures that ensured the system of employment and capital wealth would continue unchanged. But the riots by themselves provided little support for real change because they were primarily reactions against the establishment and expressions of frustration. They were important because they represented people "standing up," asserting their humanity. What was needed in their wake was a larger vision, a sense of direction, so that the insurrections of a given day anticipated further action. Such action was not to be more insurrection, more destruction, but action that established new structures that changed the circumstances that gave rise to the initial actions. "A revolution," they write, "is not just for the purpose of correcting past injustices. A revolution involves a projection of [human beings] into the future.... [It] is a specific way in which the evolution of [humanity] is advanced" (p. 19). Revolutionary thinking, they continue, "has as its purpose to discover where [humanity] should be tomorrow so that we can struggle systematically and programmatically to arouse the great masses of the people to want to go there" (pp. 18–19).

James Boggs summarizes what he took to be standard responses to the dominant system in his essay "Liberation or Revolution?" as a matter of choosing from two alternatives: Either the American people

> can continue to drift . . . hoping against hope that the politicians will solve the problems of our society for us or that somehow things will get better for us even if they get worse for somebody else. Or we can realize that . . . we are entering a new era—the era when human beings will derive their happiness *not from* moving onward and upward but from realizing a new concept of citizenship based on social and political responsibilities we assume for our communities, our nation, and our planet. (2011, pp. 303–04)

Solutions, in this case, are not "progressive" in the sense of moving "onward and upward," but something like lateral progress, to recall Jane Addams's term, to share goods and foster the communities at hand. For example, in response to a proposal to add gambling in Detroit to solve its financial problems, Boggs and Boggs proposed an alternative vision of the future:

> the vision of a new kind of city whose foundation would be people living in communities and citizens who take responsibility for decisions about their city instead of leaving these to politicians or to the marketplace, and who also create small enterprises that emphasize the preservation of skills and produce goods and services for the local community. (2008, p. xix)

To Cornel West's hope for the future, Grace Lee and James Boggs add the expectation that such hope will not be fulfilled without the kind of transformation that comes with revolutions as they understand them. Like prophetic pragmatism, revolution "requires a paradigm shift in how we address the three main questions of philosophy: What does it mean to be a human being? How do we know? How shall we live?" The shift requires "rejecting the scientific rationalism . . . which recognizes as real only that which can be measured." It means instead "that we must be willing to see with our hearts and not only with our eyes" (2008, p. xvi).

While classical pragmatism and its subsequent iterations through the twentieth and twenty-first centuries are rightly seen as philosophies of resistance (and most versions of neopragmatism are rightly seen as counter resistance), pragmatism has also been criticized for its limits.

Randolph Bourne and May Brodbeck have raised versions of the same concern. For Bourne, pragmatism was too easily reduced to instrumentalism and so could be a valuable tool to be directed by whatever values its user brought to the work. That Italian pragmatism of the 1920s (and the pragmatism of William James) was embraced by Benito Mussolini, the dictator of Italy and ally of Nazi Germany, can be seen as a case in point.[2] When May Brodbeck criticized John Dewey's philosophy as dangerous because it made possible the harnessing of "facts" by values, undermining truth and making authoritarianism possible, she echoed the earlier criticisms and helped to rationalize the emergence of analytic philosophy as the dominant strand in the American academy. For Brodbeck, pragmatism provides a case study in a philosophy that fails to stay clear of the value questions that frame possible futures and drive resistance and revolution. The program of Boggs and Boggs clearly fails in the same way as it unapologetically calls for philosophy to establish values and lead change.

Leonard Harris, writing from the tradition of African American thought, raised a challenge to pragmatism that was similar in some ways to those of Bourne and Brodbeck but with a conclusion along the lines of Boggs and Boggs. For Harris, pragmatism alone is insufficient for most resistance. At the center of his concern is the response (historical and theoretical) that pragmatism provided to enslavement and immiseration. The classical pragmatists, despite their commitments to growth and community, nevertheless mostly ignored the plight of Black Americans who lived under Jim Crow laws, Indigenous Americans whose land was taken and whose culture was targeted for destruction, and other immiserated peoples around the colonial world.

In 1983, Harris published *Philosophy Born of Struggle: An Anthology of Afro American Philosophy from 1917*, the first anthology of African American philosophers. In 1989, he published *The Philosophy of Alain Locke* that made many of Locke's important essays available for teaching and study for the first time. In 1999, he edited *The Critical Pragmatism of Alain Locke* and argued that the term "critical pragmatism" best described the radical nature of Locke's pragmatism and his own. The importance he gives to Locke's works can be seen in his coauthored (with Charles Molesworth) biography of Locke in 2008—*Alain L. Locke: The Biography of a Philosopher.* Harris also established the annual Philosophy Born of Struggle conference in 1993, bringing together an impressive array of theorists, including Anthony Appiah, Lucius Outlaw, Cornel West, and Lewis Gordon (among others). In addition, his original work on insurrectionist ethics has been taken up by a generation of younger scholars who are looking for resources to bring philosophy to bear on issues of inequality and oppression.

In this work on insurrection, Harris suggested that the character traits most often praised by society may not fit what is needed in the context of inequality and oppression. Instead of submissiveness, self-effacement, and complacency, what is called for is rather audacity, tenacity, boldness, anger, aggressiveness, irreverence, and guile. "A radical transformation of misery, exploitation, starvation, and hopelessness . . . may well depend on . . . adversarial, insurrectional, and revolutionary struggle" (1999, p. 456).

*A Philosophy of Struggle: The Leonard Harris Reader* (2020), edited by Lee A. McBride III, brings together a number of Harris's essays. As McBride notes, philosophy born of struggle "begins with the full range of human experiences (including genocide, slavery, exploitation, misery, degradation, cognitive dissonance, cynicism, etc.)" and should "help people assess their situation and facilitate the mitigation of struggles and misery, the actual experiences of surviving human populations" (p. 1). Harris's notion of philosophy "supports an ethics of insurrection" which has four main tenets: 1) "a willingness to defy accepted norms and authority figures when they cause or maintain immiseration"; 2) "a marshalling of the social and political forces of porous and variegated social collectives on behalf of the subjugated"; 3) "a conception of humanity or personhood that recognizes all human beings as members of the moral community or potential bearers of honor"; 4) "a valorizing of insurrectionist character traits (e.g., indignation, enmity, tenacity, or irreverence)" (p. 6).

Lee McBride takes up Harris's work in his book *Ethics and Insurrection: A Pragmatism for the Oppressed* (2021). Here, he argues that it is important for pragmatism to take up Harris's challenge in "Can a Pragmatist Recite a Preface to a Twenty Volume Suicide Note? Or Insurrectionist Challenges to Pragmatism—Walker, Child, and Locke" (p. 46). Does classical pragmatism retain racist valuations, support patriarchal structures, and/or rely on structures rooted in economic exploitation? McBride argues that much goes unscrutinized in pragmatism.

> (I)f the episteme in which we live influences our moral reasoning far more than we typically realize, if conceptual monsters abound and concrete misery and necro-being are left unpictured, then this would seem to suggest that pointed change is needed. It seems to suggest that we may need to rebel against norms and institutions that condition subjection, misery, and loss of corporeal well-being. . . . It seems to suggest that we may need to leave our inherited categories and habitual modes of conduct—to walk away from the *customary* pragmatic values and methods of cooperative intelligence. (p. 60)

Pragmatism notes that traditions, norms, cultures, and institutions are always changing and changeable, though. "Resistance traditions can codify and perpetuate uplifting stories, norms, and teloi, helping said traditions to orient their struggles and shape their futures to the extent possible" (p. 120). This requires all of us to be active agents of change (p. 121). While McBride supports Harris's insurrectionist character traits, he thinks love and empathy are also needed. "Thus, I want to leave space within philosophical discourse for empathy, anger, love, and logical experimentation. I want to wield both positive affects and negative affects, particularly for oppressed groups" (p. 87). Using Harris, McBride brings together the experimental, ameliorative aspects of pragmatism with the insurrectionist or revolutionary values that require opposition to oppression.

For Harris, though, there is a problem with pragmatism's commitment to amelioration and to settling unsettled situations. Harris sees pragmatism as committed to finding ways to moderate disruption and dampen conflict even if this means compromise. The response to slavery that led to the Missouri Compromise of 1820, which prevented the spread of slavery in the US by strengthening it where it already existed, marks a response meant to ameliorate a conflict. The Compromise of 1850 that established the Fugitive Slave Law requiring all escaped enslaved persons to be returned to their "owners," even from free states, was a similar response. The circumstances faced by the poor and unemployed in the midst of the growing wealth of the US during the Great Depression of 1929–39 was ameliorated by the policies of the New Deal. While the poor received some support, the wealth of the rich was protected and expanded. Escape from the ranks of the immiserated was possible but only by affirming the system of poverty and wealth that framed it.

Dewey, as we have discussed, actually challenged New Deal policies for failing to address the conditions that sustained poverty in the US. Like Addams before him, he favored the wider distribution of goods and opportunity, not the reinforcement of the structures of wealth and power that had been in place before the Depression began. Harris recognizes this aspect of the work of Dewey and Addams (and others), but he argues that their pragmatism does not provide the framework for their commitment to the poor and to fostering a democratic community.

For Harris, Dewey's values are not necessary consequences of pragmatism but the product of other commitments to prevent suffering and promote the dignity of all human beings. Dewey even gives reason to think that this may be the case. Dewey's faith in democracy is not a requirement for inquiry. One can inquire even while oppressed or oppressing. Yet, if one needs to choose a ground for making judgments, democratic arrangements are the right choice for Dewey as they offer the possibility of ongoing change and self-correction. He asks, "Can we find any reason that does not ultimately come down to the belief that democratic social arrangements promote a better quality of human experience, one which is more widely accessible and enjoyed, than do non-democratic and anti-democratic forms of social life?" (LW 13, p. 18). The structure of inquiry sets up the need to make choices. Democratic values are not derived from this structure by necessity; rather, they are selected as grounds that lead to a certain sort of future.[3]

To see the limits of pragmatism, Harris proposes a test of a philosophy's ability to have an impact on experience. He declares: "A philosophy that fails at speaking to miseries such as necro-being, that is, that which makes living a kind of death . . . is a failed philosophy" (2020 p. 198). For Harris, a philosophy that passes the test speaks to miseries by encouraging attitudes and practices that stand against the systems that establish and perpetuate such lives. In response to slavery, for example, a philosophy that is worth its salt is one that establishes a duty to oppose the system actively, even violently. It establishes a duty to insurrect. Harris argues that pragmatism as traditionally conceived fails the insurrectionist test. Its commitment to the standard of successful inquiry—that is, to an inquiry's ability to settle an unsettled situation—lacks significant normative resources to reject systemic injustices and those political movements that seek to preserve them (e.g., the populism of the early twentieth century and the nationalism of Trump). For Harris, there are no compelling standards within the philosophical toolbox of pragmatism (or most other moral theories) that would, in all cases, demand standing on the side of peoples harmed by imperialism, slavery, starvation, and necro-being.

Pragmatism, and its case for pluralism and fallibilism, is a philosophy of resistance. Harris argues, however, that the vision of a democratic future does not follow directly from the critical grounds pragmatism offers. Instead, one must look to experience more directly. Even as Dewey undermines established systems and unmoors them from given foundations, he, like Richard Rorty after him, nevertheless asserts that we can see and feel human suffering and we can, as a result, value the amelioration of it. An enslaved person, to use Harris's example, has a moral duty to insurrect because the conditions of enslavement enforce suffering. While not foundations in the sense of Western philosophical foundations, such commitments are grounds for judgment for both the philosophers themselves and—given their appeal to their readers—ought to be grounds for others as well. There is no necessity for such grounds, but there are reasons that emerge in human experience in relation to hoped-for futures. Empathy with suffering leads to, but does not necessitate, the purpose of a future in which suffering is alleviated.

For Harris, pragmatism, as a method that adopts the success of its efforts as its primary value, must reject insurrection because it is likely to fail. Instead—more after the everyday sense of "pragmatic" than the philosophical school of thought—pragmatism would favor some compromised alternative that achieves "success" while nevertheless prolonging suffering in hopes that circumstances will eventually change. Harris makes a case for what he calls "critical" pragmatism that offers the possibility of adopting an unshakable value without recourse to necessity. Here, Harris follows Alain Locke (Chapter 15) in thinking that there are values humans hold in common—"functional universals." As Locke said, "For if once this broader relativistic approach could discover beneath the expected culture differentials of time and place such functional 'universals' as actually may be there, these common-denominator values would stand out as pragmatically confirmed by common human experience" (1989 p. 56). To act as an agent involves purpose; in this case, one can accept given purposes that cause suffering and immiseration or one can choose another foundation that responds to experience with hope for a future without suffering and immiseration. Such foundations are revisable and fallible, but nevertheless, they ground judgment across different situations.

Harris attributes the idea of "critical" pragmatism to Alain Locke. For Harris, Locke's critical pragmatism can be read as confronting "a world of paradoxes and dilemmas." Harris continues:

> Locke believed that we should accept moral imperatives. He recognized that the promotion of moral imperatives was often occasioned or warranted dogmatism and absolutism. We should certainly try to avoid uncritical attitudes associated with dogmatism and absolutism, as well as intolerance, However, I interpret Locke as warranting a degree of self-certainty, uncompromising attitudes, and belief in otherwise unwanted behavior that accompany actualizing moral imperatives. (2020, 193)

Locke put it this way:

> All philosophies, it seems to me, are in ultimate derivation philosophies of life and not of abstract, disembodied "objective" reality; products of time, place, and situations ... But no conception of philosophy, however relativist, however opposed to absolutism, can afford to ignore the question of ultimates or abandon what has been so aptly though skeptically termed the "quest for certainty." (Quoted in Harris, 2020, p. 193)

Value ultimates are important in Locke's view in order to have the evaluation of values, but while the functions are common across humanity, value ultimates—the way these functions are carried out—differ by culture and are subject to revision.

When "insurrection" became a common term in discussions of the present and future of the United States, the "insurrection" of January 6, 2021, came to be compared with the "insurrections" associated with the Black Lives Matter Movement that happened the previous summer. More insurrections were expected, and more have happened. In a world where alternate facts can justify alternate futures—some pluralistic, some populist, some committed to the status quo—simple appeals to fallibilism are not sufficient. Simple fallibilism, after all, holds that the "facts" may turn out to be false. Critical fallibilism, however, goes further and finds responses that stifle thinking to be dangerous given the uncertain nature of the world.

How one holds their insurrectionist commitments matters. Bernstein argued that critical fallibilism is open to correction but is not indecisive. In his view critical fallibilism and engaged pluralism require the courage to test ideas in public and to listen to others rather than hide behind simplistic and rigid responses.

When we think about American philosophy for the future, West affirms the expectation that American philosophy will continue to be committed to fallibilism and pluralism. Grace Lee and James Boggs agree with West that real change will not come by Socratic questioning alone but will require action. Rather than gradual action and slow evolution, they argue that change is punctuated by disruption—by insurrections and revolutions—in order to bring about futures where human values provide guidance in the face of technology and a system of economic power and hierarchical wealth. But all insurrections are not equal. Those that do not have a vision of the future or have visions that are narrow and exclusive are more likely to be destructive and serve to reinforce rather than undermine the system they hoped to challenge. What Harris proposes—and we think West and the Boggses would agree—is that insurrection be framed by a commitment to human dignity, reciprocity, and the value of flourishing communities. "Communities," Harris concludes, "rather than simple ubiquitous entities, are groups whose future is contingent on variables that shape their character. Rather than disjointed aggregates, there are ties that bind but not invariably" (2020, p. 232). Ties, in this case, refer to "social locations," to what Harris calls "platforms of identity," that constitute "our deepest moral commitments to mates, children, relatives, lovers, friends, coworkers, and physical surroundings" (p. 232). In this context, "Incommensurability [the lack of a common ground] is an inescapable variable" (2020, p. 242). Here commitments to reciprocity and dignity can provide the resources to both maintain the differences and find local points of contact where ideas can be shared and mutual growth fostered. Such a vision, for Harris, is distant at best, even impossible for our present world. Nevertheless, commitment to such a world grounds a duty to insurrect that is widespread. For Harris, "Some insurrectionists are terrorists, and others are absolute pacifists . . . Some are poets, taxicab drivers, hairdressers, owners of publishing companies, or novelists" (p. 202). A duty to insurrect is, Grace Lee Boggs would say, not in order to gain power or disrupt for the sake of disruption, but in order to bring about a revolution whose "purpose [is] to discover where [humanity] should be tomorrow so that we can struggle systematically and programmatically to arouse the great masses of the people to want to go there" (2008, pp. 18–19).

In this book, we have traced philosophy's role in the democratic project. As West says, and many of the examples presented in this volume show, it takes courage to be such an intellectual activist. It requires the rejection of simplistic black-and-white thinking; it means engaging in unpopular critique. "To talk about race and empire in America," he asserts, "is to talk about how one musters the courage to think, care, and fight for democracy matters in the face of a monumental eclipse of hope, an unprecedented collapse of meaning, and a flagrant disregard for the viewpoints and aspirations of others" (2004, p. 60). For West (as for Bernstein), this required that inquiry also include the religious. West rejected the fundamentalist, dogmatic, and authoritarian approaches to religion that eschew real public debate and discourse. He also eschewed the dogmatism and authoritarianism that he found in the secular visions of Rawls and Rorty. He argues instead for a "new democratic Christian identity" (2004, p. 165) that can combat the growing nihilism *and* the Christian Right.

Further, intellectuals must return to the task of nurturing minds. This requires that academics broaden their focus beyond theoretical problems within their discipline and engage in public discourse. West himself regularly taught in prisons, appears frequently on various television and radio shows, played the role of "Counselor West" in two of the three *Matrix* films, has given numerous talks all across the nation, and produced music. Not all have seen this work as "real philosophy" or even as acceptable academic work.

While at Harvard, West taught very popular courses in Afro-American studies, kept up his writing and lecturing, and supported a campaign for living wages. Soon after President Lawrence Summers arrived at Harvard, West was called to his office. This meeting seems to have occurred just a month after the events of 9/11. West's department head, Henry Louis Gates, Jr., supported West by sending Summers a long letter detailing West's professional work. But Summers did not value West's work and questioned his political affiliations. Summers found West's recent rap CD to be an embarrassment to Harvard and told him he "needed to write a major book on a philosophical tradition to establish [him]self" (2004, p. 193). As West writes, "he was apparently unaware that I had written just such a book twelve years earlier, and that I was in fact quite well established, having earlier held tenured positions at both Yale and Princeton" (p. 193). There were other charges, and Summers said they would meet bimonthly so that Summers could monitor West's work. West responded by pointing to his record and soon accepted a long-standing offer to return to Princeton.

According to West, as public support for Summers faltered, they met again, and Summers apologized. However, in the press, Summers said he had not apologized and never would. After that, West referred to Summers as the "Ariel Sharon of American higher education"—a bully and an ineffective leader. This sparked charges of anti-Semitism, and as West said, "The whole ugly incident reflects the crass level to which the university world has sunk; it has become a competitive, market-driven, backbiting microcosm of the troubles with American business and society at large" (2004, p. 197).

The failure of others in academia and the public to respond by defending academic freedom troubled West. For him, it represented "a spinelessness in the academy that is antithetical to the important role universities should be playing in holding up standards of truth and integrity and working to impart faith in those standards to our youth" (2004, p. 198). Academics need the freedom and courage to engage with pressing problems and to do so in ways that motivate young people.

This kind of engagement is important as a means to overcome the increasing polarization that resulted from the response to 9/11. It represents hope grounded in concrete action and pushes us to fight both dogmatism and nihilism. "It only requires that we be true to ourselves," West explains, "by choosing to be certain kinds of human beings and democratic citizens indebted to a deep democratic tradition and committed to keeping it vital and vibrant" (2004, p. 218). While there are no guarantees of success, such engagement is better than nihilism and is the best hope we have. "And if we lose our precious democratic experiment, let it be said that we went down swinging . . . with style, grace, and a smile that signifies that the seeds of democracy matters will flower and flourish somewhere and somehow" (p. 218).

West also has pointed out that although his PhD is in philosophy, he has never held a position in a philosophy department. He turned down such offers in order to preserve his freedom to write about the wide array of topics he found important. It says something about philosophy that this was the choice he faced. Unlike Rorty, who left philosophy departments because he thought we were in a postphilosophic era, West remained committed to the importance of philosophy for our troubled world. He does say, however, in an essay titled "On My Intellectual Vocation," that he "never aspired to be a professional academic or scholar." Rather, he sought "to be a man of letters in love with ideas in order to be a wiser and more loving person, hoping to leave the world just a little better than I found it." But to make the world better is not only a matter of action, for West. He concluded, "I take great delight in the free play of the mind and I believe intellectual work is indispensable for social change" (1999, p. 19). In the story we have been telling here, West is an example of a philosopher of resistance. While he challenges the dominant system both by challenging the concepts that frame domination and by actions intended to unsettle the system and make space for new futures, his is not a life to copy directly—one has to find their own way. However, his example is one to emulate if philosophy is to have a viable future in America.

What is the future of American philosophies of resistance? We now need to think about how the tradition moves forward and how you, the reader, can become engaged as an academic philosopher or by living out a philosophical way of life developed in the rich American tradition of resistance. We believe that there are at least eight broad thematic conceptions that continue the work of the tradition and deserve more attention. What follows is not an exhaustive list but rather a list of those that come readily to mind in the wake of this study. These themes are expressed as commitments to conceptions of power and resistance, boundary and place, pluralism and agency, and fallibilism and hope.

## Power and Resistance

The idea of power is one that critics say American philosophy avoids. While it is true that many of the central figures say little directly about power, the concept is developed in the tradition in a variety of ways. Mary Follett (Chapter 14), for example, identified the central problem of social relations—power—and declared that "our task is . . . to learn . . . how to develop power" (1924, p. xii). For Follett, "genuine power is not coercive control, but coactive control. Coercive power ['power over'] is the curse of the universe; coactive power ['power with'], the enrichment and advancement of every human soul" (p. xiii). Decades earlier in his 1860 *The Conduct of Life*, Emerson wrote, "Life is the search after power," a stark claim anticipating Nietzsche (whose work began with his reading of Emerson). But Emerson continued, "and this is an element with which the world is so saturated—there is no chink or crevice in which it is not lodged—that no honest seeking goes unanswered" (1860, p. 47). Power, in this case, is that which fills the gaps, lies between things such that the search for power is also the search for connections.

Although often set outside philosophical conversation, the question of power nevertheless fills the chinks and crevices of the tradition. Power in its ordinary sense typically implies a kind of active force that can be harnessed to accomplish tasks. Louis Mumford (Chapter 24), in the second volume of *Myth of the Machine* (1974), sees in this idea and its successive definitions the framework for a structure of power that defined American life. Tracing the meaning of power in the *New English Dictionary*, Mumford noted that the first definition, dating from 1297, "possession or command over others" was succeeded by a new definition, the "legal ability, capacity, or authority to act," in 1486. In 1727, "power" took on a "technological role as 'any form of energy or force available for application to work'" (p. 240). Finally, as "horsepower, waterpower, windpower, woodpower, coalpower, electricpower, oilpower, and . . . nuclear power," diverse systems became what he called "the Pentagon of Power," a "megamachine": "a machine in the orthodox technical sense, as a 'combination of resistant bodies' so organized as to perform standardized motions and repetitive work" (p. 240). "Power" in this sense—"power over" as Follett called it—marked the forced unification of systems where its resistant parts were essential to its success.

C. Wright Mills (Chapter 24), writing in 1958, described another dimension of power as focused on "whatever decisions men make about the arrangements under which they live." The "basic problem of power," for Mills, asked "who is involved in making [these decisions] (or not making them)" (1958, p. 29). Decision-making systems by mid-century eliminated the assumption that people must be "governed by their own consent" because "[a]mong the means of power that now prevail is the power to manage and manipulate . . . consent" so that "much power today is successfully employed without the sanction of the reason or the conscience of the obedient" (p. 29). Power, again as power over, marked the harnessing of agency in service of unifying economic, political and military systems in what Mills called "the permanent war economy," a system that "rests upon great secrecy of plan and intent" (1956, pp. 293–94). The purposes of individuals and groups are put in service of the purposes of the system. "It is just," he said, "that people are of necessity confused and must, like trusting children, place all" decisions—economic, political and military—"in the hands of experts." After all, he concluded, "everyone knows that somebody has got to run the show" (p. 294).

Martin Luther King, Jr. (Chapter 18) challenged what he took to be the dominant conception of power in his 1963 presidential address to the SCLC. "[S]ome of our philosophers," he declared, "[have gotten] off base" by viewing power and love as "opposites—polar opposites—so that love is identified with a resignation of power, and power with a denial of love" (1986, p. 247). For King, as for Follett, power is genuine only when it is accompanied by a sense of connection and the need to work things out together. "What is needed," King continued, "is a realization that power without love is reckless and abusive, and love without power is sentimental and anemic" (p. 247). In contrast to power in the analyses of Mumford and Mills, "Power at its best is love implementing the demands of justice, and justice at its best is power correcting everything that stands against love" (p. 247).

A few years later, Cone (Chapter 19) echoed Follett's claim that power with is finally a matter of self-determination, the self-determination of communities that reinforced differences while seeking common purposes in the face of experienced problems. "Black power," he said in *Black Theology and Black Power*, "means black freedom, black self-determination, wherein black people no longer view themselves as without human dignity but as men, human beings with the ability to carve out their own destiny" (1969, p. 6). The idea is not unlike the conception of power central to the Indigenous American traditions we have considered (Chapter 21). Power is a motive force that distinguishes agents from each other even as it motivates the distinctive relations that make someone—human or not—the person or agent they are. Power is not an imposition but a condition for the possibility of purposes that can prove to promote both a sense of self and a sense of connection across the boundaries that divide.

## American Philosophies

The conception of power as it developed in the American philosophies we consider here is fundamentally a matter of resistance to dominant systems that overdetermine the lives of its parts. The "megamachine" of Mumford is manifested again and again in America and the globalizing economy as it strives to order its parts, narrow its diverse habits and ideals, and reinforce its hierarchies even as it offers, on one hand, freedom to those who are willing to conform, and oppression to those who become essentially "resistant parts." In either case, action is determined from the outside through domination, submission, or compromise. Real resistance, as Follett suggested, is found in self-determination, in cultivating histories, habits, and ideals that begin outside the "Pentagon of Power" and flourish in their connections with others.

Power and resistance in the American tradition mark the drive for pluralism instead of assimilation and for unifying instead of separating. When Du Bois (Chapter 13) declared that the goal of racial groups in the United States was to embrace the "unifying ideal of race," he (like Cone after him) proposed a kind of power that both separated and united America along the edges of its parts. Such power—power with—would not seek a final unity but a process of uniting with others here and there where the boundaries encountered would be the source of new life and experience. Rather than a resistance essential to the megamachine, American philosophies of resistance, by attending to the situation at hand, become obstacles to the system, wrenches in the works rather than the friction that guarantees an efficient system. Power and resistance give rise to boundaries and place, mark the importance of pluralism and agency, and make fallibilism and hope possible.

## Boundary and Place

It is not a surprise that some people from South and Central America refer to themselves as Americans, especially in light of their shared colonial past. Given globalization, or at least North/South economic, labor, and cultural interactions, it is becoming apparent that peoples throughout the Western Hemisphere face related problems of economic depression, racism, sexism, and environmental destruction. It is also apparent that the shared history of the hemisphere is one framed by the dual tragedies of genocide and slavery, both of which are part of the legacy of the European invasions of the past 500 years. Indigenous people North and South were displaced, died of disease, and were killed by Europeans through slavery, rape, and war. In 1491, about one-hundred million people lived in the Western Hemisphere. By 1691, the population of Indigenous Americans had declined by 90–95 percent.[4] Slavery began almost immediately following the arrival of Europeans, first by enslaving Native Americans in South and Central America. It continued with the arrival of African-born slaves in Cuba in 1501 and in Virginia in 1619. Lands obtained from America's Indigenous peoples and slave labor from African peoples provided the economic foundation for the "new" European world. In philosophy, a greater awareness of this shared history of place will demand greater attention to the shared problems and the shared conceptual frameworks that seek decolonization and the construction of new ways of life in the Americas.

Recalling the conception of boundaries offered by Anzaldúa (Chapter 20), as well as earlier philosophers including Peirce, James, Dewey, Calkins, Kallen, and Locke (Chapters 7, 8, 9, 11, 12 and 15), boundaries define individuals and groups and at the same time are porous and provide the possibility of new ideas, resources, and ways of life. Boundaries are not abstract, and they are not simply the meeting of one thing with another. A boundary creates a new space, "a vague and undetermined place" in a state of constant transition. The boundaries in and between North and South America mark distinct cultures, histories, lands, and ecosystems. At the same time, they mark "border *lands*," concrete places where people live and work, love and die. Across these borderlands, through the efforts of the people of the place, Alain Locke observed, "cultural exchange passes in reciprocal streams from the conquerors to the conquered and from the conquered to the dominant groups" (1946, p. 10). The special character of boundaries affords such exchanges. As Peirce pointed out, boundaries are logically indeterminate spaces. They mark the meeting of two sides but cannot be reduced to either or both. They are, as Anzaldúa says, "neither one nor the other but a strange doubling" (1999, p. 41).

The resistance tradition of American philosophy placed the issue of boundaries at the center of questions of identity and community. These spaces served as a means for understanding the pluralism of experience and the possibility of border-crossing as a tool for cultural advancement and cultural stability. Boundaries and borders should not only be understood, as they commonly are in discussions of immigration, as obstacles and walls, but as ever-changing places that constitute who we are as individuals and members of communities, nations, and the world. These borderlands are a means of understanding difference and sameness and the possibilities of the future. The future of American philosophy must involve the affirmation of this complex understanding of borders and boundaries.

Theories of place that recognize boundaries and address the problems of plurality through a notion of community mirror, in key ways, King's vision of the "world house" and Royce's idea of "Beloved Community." The fluidity of boundaries and borders demonstrates the importance and complexity of community but do not undermine the importance of place. Once framed by a historically rooted conception of place, notions of boundaries and borders take on new meaning and become resources for addressing problems in new ways. Place is more than a location on a map; it is where and when experience happens. As a result, places are formative of one's sense of self and one's sense of community. Places include the land on which one depends, the built environment, and systems of education, politics, and economy. In our world today, this can include virtual locations and identities. Places also include people and other forms of life and the languages they speak and understand.

As the bounded contexts of experience, places also lead to an alternative conception of knowledge consistent with the epistemic theories of the classical pragmatists and their successors. Universal claims, whether of philosophy or biology or practical matters, are themselves of a place, and their reach is always less than universal. Such claims can, again, never be certain for all time, but nevertheless are useful, relevant, leading principles that guide the inhabitants of a place. As the guiding ideas change, the place changes as well, altering values and borders, even as the guiding ideas themselves remain limited in their reach. As addressed in the Indigenous philosophical tradition by Standing Bear and Deloria, places (and their framing boundaries) are first principles of philosophical reflection requiring both recognition and respect. Ontologically, places are necessarily bounded (even virtual places, though they may be more fluid) and so the ideas and ways of life that emerge from them are necessarily limited as well. Even though much of the American tradition leaves the notion of place in the background, its presence is nevertheless implied in the fallibilist conception of knowledge and the resistance to universal claims. The concept of "grounded normativity" proposed by Indigenous philosophers Glen Coulthard and Leanne Simpson (Chapter 21) argues that places are also the literal ground of values. The activity of the people of a place—human and other-than-human—and the activity of the land, the water, the sun, and air together set the standards for what is good and what must be resisted. The lessons of one place may help other places, but values are local and the product of living communities.

When American philosophical thought affirms the idea that experience is always placed somewhere and somewhen, it can consider again ideas received from the dominant tradition and reconceive them. As Du Bois proposed in *Dusk of Dawn* (1970), for example, capitalism and its universal economic motivations, when seen from the place of Black communities in the mid-twentieth century, can be reconstructed around the need for economically self-sufficient communities connected by larger reciprocal exchanges with other small communities. Rather than requiring uniform economies, such a view calls for diverse economies that are balanced in their work and needs with other places. Recent examples of other place-based revisions to capitalist economies include the "buy local" movement (especially in food production and distribution), barter economies (the online marketplace "Craigslist," for instance), and "free" economies that rely on the refuse of modern urban life (organizations that collect and redistribute excess food from restaurants and grocery stores, for instance). On a global scale, systems of "fair trade" production provide alternative modes of exchange that begin with a respect for economic differences rather than the sameness of global capitalism. Microlending systems established throughout the Americas and other parts of the world provide money to businesses too small for support from global banks. The resulting small loans can transform local communities and, through repayment, can pass such support to other places. Practices that at once reaffirm differences and support interaction function as boundaries that foster places as sites of resistance and growth.

## Pluralism and Agency

The affirmation of place also implies new methods of thinking and new understandings of pluralism and agency. Just as Addams, Dewey, Follett, Carson, and Galbraith (Chapters 6, 11, 14, 23, and 24) sought cooperation with scholars outside philosophy in order to address the problems of their times and places, new philosophical efforts emerging from the tradition are likely to be interdisciplinary efforts interested in addressing the lived problems of present communities. For example, while some combine philosophy with animal studies and anthropology, others use a pragmatist-informed method to bring together neuroscience and cognitive science to understand long-standing philosophical problems.

Philosophy must resist isolation both in the theories it discusses and the actions to which it leads. Just as this pluralism of disciplines will be important to the future of philosophy, pluralism of both theories and experiences will be important as well. For example, gender and sexuality have exploded into a vast array of ways to understand the character of human life. One can encounter heterosexual monogamous and polyamorous sexuality, bisexuality, and homosexual monogamous and polyamorous sexuality all in the space of a single community. Multiple genders are increasingly accepted in various communities. The scientific community has come to acknowledge a variety of transgender individuals, and technology makes it possible for people to physically change the sex they were assigned at birth.

Pluralism of experience makes it clear that there are also different conceptions of agency (of *who* acts). Different notions of gender, for example, imply different ways of acting, different interests, and different consequences. Cultural differences provide alternative means for understanding who agents are and where they come from. Conceptions of agency in Christianity and Islam often hold that selves—agents—are a divine gift. Contemporary naturalists often hold that agents are a biological product of evolution. Some confine recognized agents to a certain range of beings, human beings, or beings of a particular race or gender. At the center of concern in all these understandings of agency is the recognition that theories of who agents are intersect with the experience of agency to define individuals and their communities. The received account from much of Western philosophy recognizes human beings alone as agents, individual and autonomous. At the same time, Indigenous philosophy recognizes human beings and other nonhuman beings as agents. Within the American tradition, philosophers including Peirce, Royce, Addams, and Deloria (among others) recognize both individuals and communities as agents. For Peirce and some Indigenous philosophers, even ideas, stories, and "futures" are agents.

The centrality of agency has long been part of American philosophies of resistance. Agency is what was transformed in the mainstream in the wake of the Civil War and redefined—or reasserted practically—as part of the work of philosophers as well as activists. Philosophers such as Pokegon, Gilman, Addams, Cooper, Follett, Kallen, and Locke sought to assert a new conception of who acts as a means of transforming their communities. For example, the reemergence of Indigenous sovereignty reasserted the agency of communities and their places and reframed the idea of recognition in the present world.

The notion of agency that emerges as part of the resistance to colonialism and empire is one that recasts the character of experience as the interaction of many different agents. The result, as Deloria concluded, is a "moral universe" in which other relations—epistemic, ethical, social, aesthetic—are relations between agents or persons. Agency—the ability to act with a purpose—demands the recognition of porous boundaries so that agents are neither cut off from others nor indistinguishable from them. Agents require a locus of action, a place, and they are necessarily diverse. At the same time, agents are temporal beings able at once to be partly determined by their past and able to act in terms of a future that is indeterminate.

This emergent conception of agency is at risk on at least two fronts. Ontologically, agency is under the long-standing threat of being reduced to the action of discrete beings, isolated except for their materiality. This takes the form of modern individualism, which risks reducing values and what matters to materiality (i.e., ontological reductionism). The second threat is that, politically, agency excludes communities and the other-than-human. The risk here is that in the setting of policies, the only things that can be taken into account are human-centered and often individually centered. Human desires and interests become all that count. On this view, Indigenous tribes and communities have no agency. Nor do other species, individual animals, or ecosystems.

For some in the American tradition, agency is widely shared and applies as much to human society as to everything else, animate and inanimate. For others, agency is narrowed to human society alone, and for still others, it is limited to individual human beings. The lesson of the tradition of resistance is that the narrowing of agency to humans has been bound up with the rise of industry, the desire for control, and the fear of what is to come. Widening the conception of who counts as an agent has been instrumental in the resistance and essential to the reconstruction of life in America. Freedom, as even recent analytic philosophy has claimed, is tied to the autonomy of agents. The meaning of autonomy and the nature of agents, however, is greater than such theories have imagined. The future of American philosophy—as an extension of the resources and commitments of the past century of resistance—seems directed toward the affirmation of diverse agencies as a resource for resistance, but also as a ground from which new opportunities can arise. Attention to agents—individual and collective—refocuses consideration on boundaries and places and raises the question of the possibilities of failure and of hope. The failure of agents—their limitations and errors—seems at first to undercut a philosophical method aimed at amelioration. Yet, as we have seen, the American tradition has a long-standing recognition of the importance of integrating fallibilism with hope in moments of conflict and struggle.

## Fallibilism and Hope

In addition to grappling with how to understand and respond to various other forms of agency, humans also need to continue to grapple with their fallibilism. Being finite and limited, no known creature has access to all ways of knowing. As a consequence, all limited creatures are subject to "blindness" and error. Ontology cannot be ignored—the ground of difference exceeds our ability to explain and compare, from a single perspective, the things that count. For example, animal studies that go beyond understanding how other animal beings are and are not like human beings open up the possibility of discovering new things about the world we share. The study of birds reveals new understandings of the earth's magnetic field; new discoveries about how dolphins process their sonar signals provide new approaches for humans to consider; studying the wing structure of owls is leading to quieter and more efficient wind turbines. Pluralism thus becomes even more important as an antidote to our potential individual and group inability to see. It is by encountering other perspectives that new things can be seen and known.

While a pluralistic approach helps address what James called "a certain blindness," as limited creatures, humans remain inexorably subject to error. This is why Peirce (Chapter 8) insisted that inquiry, when properly done, is self-correcting. Unlike inquiry grounded in tenacity, authority, or imagined a priori principles, inquiry as the "method of science" recognizes the necessity of making and testing hypotheses and adopting practices that are "error sensitive." Inquiry, in whatever form, always begins with a fund of ideas and practices already established and so must be ready to question not only possible solutions but also the received ideas that set the problem in the first place. This is why a method of inquiry developed within the pluralist American tradition should be a self-correcting method based on experimentation and revision of ideas and actions.

The study of American philosophy requires this same method of inquiry. While some philosophers write without any apparent understanding of the history of the tradition, others write in a celebratory tone and seek to persuade others that American philosophers have important insights. In order to have a more critical engagement, it is necessary to find, name, and address limitations in the work and thought of these attempts to recover and use the tradition. On one hand, failure to engage the broad history of the tradition is misleading and undermines the tradition and its potential as a transformative resource in the face of present problems. On the other hand, it is not surprising that some scholars focus on historical recovery alone. As a largely ignored and unfairly criticized philosophical approach, it is important to "set the record straight." However, there is also work to be done in confronting the "blindness" and limitations of these thinkers. We are all complicit in various prejudices and social habits that are only revealed when a community of inquirers challenges us to think beyond such limitations. Some contemporary thinkers are engaged in just this kind of work, but, as always, more needs to be done.

The work of the earlier thinkers in the tradition, strengthened by such critique, makes valuable resources as philosophers try to address contemporary problems. In addition to needing the assistance of other disciplines, as mentioned above, it is important to approach contemporary problems with an attitude of humility rather than an attitude of mastery that expects problems can be solved once and for all. Philosophers need to be *partners* with other academics, practitioners, and activists and need to be open to having their positions "corrected" by the experience and knowledge of the practitioners and activists with whom they engage. For example, Addams learned much from her engagement with workers, labor activists, and politicians. Contemporary philosophers need to open themselves to such experiences in order to address contemporary problems such as poverty, pollution, and power.

This is where hope for the present and future lies. It is important to remember that in this tradition, hope is not understood in terms of unfounded dreams. Rather, hope must be grounded in the realities of the present situation and a critical consideration of the possibilities for the future. This requires that we face up to the limitations, blind spots, and prejudices in the cumulative history of the United States and the American philosophical tradition. It means we must acknowledge the ways in which the present and future possibilities are grounded in place and built upon an oppressive and genocidal past, and not just the more progressive story of increasing inclusivity and equality. Bernstein, McDermott, and West are some examples of thinkers who embody this kind of challenging hope. It is hope with a tragic sensibility.

As Bernstein noted, "The essential fallibility of all inquiry is no cause for despair, but rather an incentive for openness and for testing as rigorously and critically as we can all hypotheses and theories." Since meaning is social, he said, "[we] must not only countenance, but seek out intersubjective criticisms of all hypotheses." The ideal to be sought was "the establishment of a free, open, self-critical community of inquirers" (1971, p. 199). West echoes both the caution and the hope when he points to the risks and possibilities of the American tradition of philosophy. "At its worst, it became a mere ideological cloak for corporate liberalism and managerial social engineering which served the long-term interests of American capital." But at its best, West said, "it survived as a form of cultural critique and social reform" that sought to bring about a more pluralistic democratic process (1993a, p. 103). As West concluded, hope is justifiable only if there is critical attention paid to the divisions, inequities, and violence of the past and the present.

For Harris,

> Adversarial traditions, that is, traditions of resistance that emanate from oppressed social entities, are voices that often perceive community as becoming. That is, the immiserated members of social entities—women, African Americans, Hispanics, workers, and so

on—can only pursue liberation by engaging in resistance struggles intended to create new traditions and alternative communities. (2020, p. 221)

Harris's critique of pragmatism also reminds us that while hope is framed by the past and present—understanding the history of oppression and what must be challenged for new communities to emerge—it is not the case that all futures must be attainable or workable to inspire hope. When Malcolm X and Martin Luther King, Jr. called for change, the futures they sought were far from likely. That a future is "right," worthy of commitment, and worthy of hope does not mean that it is achievable. This is the point of an ethics of insurrection. It is important to cultivate both a method of inquiry that can address the present indeterminate situation and to envision a future in which growth and the flourishing of a place are realized, even if the likelihood of such a result does not at present exist. This, for Harris, is the duty to insurrect— the duty to destroy oppressive institutions, to feed the hungry, to care for the sick, to stand with the oppressed—regardless of the potential for these efforts to be successful.

American philosophies of resistance do not uniformly embrace this sort of commitment (though some do), but this diverse tradition of philosophers and activists knows that this is the question at stake. How can we bring about futures that expand connections while maintaining differences and promoting the growth of diverse individuals and communities? Commitments made to bring about change may turn out to be mistaken, but commitments are nevertheless required. As Woodly argues about the Black Lives Matter Movement in *Reckoning* (see Chapter 22), the "pragmatic orientation toward transformation means that movement organizers are keenly aware, as Dewey was, that their knowledge is contingent and that experience may cause them to change their minds, revise their vision, or alter their tactics" (2021, p. 58). Nonetheless, she finds the movement leaders to be committed to democratic experimentation and pragmatic imagination. Echoing Harris, West, and the Boggs, she writes,

> pragmatic imagination is rooted in inquiry about current conditions and oriented toward actions given those conditions. This kind of imagination does not rely on any single ideology to show the path from the world as it is to the desired one that might be. Instead, it demands that those who desire the change make the way. This includes not only imagining what could be, but also, crucially, plotting a course and designing the process and means that those involved will use to make strides toward their goals. (p. 53)

This story has tried to trace some examples of the divisions, inequities, and violence to which attention must be paid. These include genocide, imperialism, class exploitation, gender inequality, environmental devastation, and war. We have tried to present the story of American philosophy as a struggle to address these issues. It is itself a conflicted story with moments of humor, courage, cowardice, and tragedy. For hope to remain a real possibility, it is important to take up the story in as complete a way as possible and use all the philosophical resources made available by the ongoing conversations of American philosophy. When we do, it becomes clear that there is a valuable tension among the many threads of American philosophies of resistance.

On one hand, the tradition calls for philosophers and activists to work to ameliorate present problematic situations. It is important to avoid the temptation to think one has the final or complete answer, as this often results in closing down inquiry and limiting community in the hope of "fixing" a problem or providing a "final solution." This is the absolutistic mentality Bernstein (and others) worried about. Rather, an approach that seeks amelioration grounded in thoughtful inquiry and pluralistic discourse is presently the best hope.

McDermott amplifies this message when he points to the resources of a pluralistic, experiential, and experimental approach to amelioration. His essays on Emerson and Royce argue that imagination helps us deal with risk and instability; it can help us construct possibility. Further, pluralistic communities can help us stay open to various and mediated interpretations that aim at amelioration. McDermott calls people to thoughtful action and says that if we believe in "our capacity to effect human healing of unnecessary suffering and in our responsibility to do so, then we shall, in time create a human community worthy of the rich human tradition of hope, aspiration, and wisdom" (2007, p. 155).

On the other hand, parts of the tradition recognize that sometimes amelioration by degrees is not an acceptable future. Among the American philosophies of resistance, the work of Harris, Grace Lee and James Boggs, Emma Goldman, Mary Follett, James Cone, Kwame Ture, Audre Lorde, Pedro Albizu Campos, Vine Deloria Jr., Glen Coulthard, Leanne Simpson, and Nick Estes, among many others, argue that amelioration by compromise is sometimes not the answer. Agreeing with Follett when she argues that compromise is another form of domination, these philosophers demand that resistance find new futures that can organize change in the present whether they are likely futures or not. Such futures are found not among those in power with privilege and opportunity but in the lives of those oppressed. Harris observes: "the immiserated members of social entities . . . can only pursue liberation by engaging in resistance struggle intended to create new traditions and alternative communities" (2020, p. 221). If the futures we hope for are to include "the communities of the downtrodden, wretched, degraded, raped, victims of cruelty, the objects of viciousness, then they are subjects integral to a conceptualized community that is to become" (p. 221). When a philosophy agrees that our hope is in the long run, then the aspirations of the present are futures—ends-in-view—where some immiseration, some rape, some cruelty is expected. In the American philosophical tradition, the hope that seeks amelioration "in time" is always balanced against the hope that stands with the oppressed and seeks no compromise.

So, this is a story that is still in the telling. That means we do not provide an ending here, but an opening to the future. We hope this account can help ground such an opening and guide the future of American philosophy by the lights and shadows of its past, even as the tradition is embodied by a new generation of philosophers, scholars, and social activists engaged in addressing the pressing problems of the present and future. We hope that the story presented here provides an opportunity for those students who read it to not only consider their own roles in creating lives of meaning and purpose for themselves, but also the social and political conditions that make such lives of meaning and purpose a possibility for all.

## Notes

1   The 2010 decision by the Supreme Court in Citizens United v Federal Elections Commission made the money-driven nature of elections worse by removing restrictions on election spending by corporations and other outside groups.

2  See Colapietro 2007, Elliot 1926 and Diggins 2015. Also, see Maddalena 2019 who criticized the connection.
3  This paragraph and the next two are taken from (Absolute Pragmatism. Invited lecture. Central European Pragmatist Forum, University of Vienna, June 2024) Pratt 2024.
4  Population of the Americas before Columbus landed is controversial. See Stannard, 1992; Shoemaker, 1999; and Dunbar-Ortiz, 2015.

# EPILOGUE

On a stage in Chicago, the Republican candidate shouted, "America first, last and always!" to an enthusiastic crowd. He had held the office before, but scandals and court cases had made the race to return to office after four years heated. Recent campaign ads had focused on his pledge to "drive the crooks and thieves and lawbreakers out . . . so that the people, their homes and their property" would be safe again. The ads also declared that he would restore America's ideals that had come to be "sneered at" and seen in a false light so that "your children may blush with shame when studying the history of their country." Under the new administration, children would be "taught to love their country." Commentators declared that the candidate was a "red-blooded American" and "the champion of true Americanism" (Nichols, 2017). He won the election, taking leadership away from the Democrats. Within the first year, he fired government employees who had worked under the previous administration, attempted to transform education by limiting what university faculty could say, and began systematically removing unacceptable books from libraries while his supporters advocated for book burning to speed up the process. Within two years of returning to office, the nation fell into a deep economic depression and the opposing party won the next election.

There is much to learn from history about where we are and what might follow. The candidate, here, was William "Big Bill" Thompson, the last elected Republican mayor of Chicago, who rode the third "America First" wave into an election victory despite being chased from office four years earlier in 1923. Thompson's 1927 election to a third term as mayor also channeled the passions and policies of the nationwide America First movement into action that included attacks on education, book burning, and efforts to remove people painted as political enemies from posts in government. (See Bukowski (2013) and Schottenhamel (1952).)

The America First slogan had a long history by 1927. It was first used by the American Party in the 1850s. Like populists of the later nineteenth century, the American Party was a "Nativist" political organization that had begun as a secret society committed to opposing immigration and attacking Catholics, who they believed were conspiring to take over the country. The party's popular name, The Know-Nothing Party, came from its early days when members were told that if anyone asked about their party, members should say that they "know nothing." In the years before the Civil War, the Know-Nothings claimed as members at least one-hundred congressmen, eight governors, and the majority of representatives in at least six state legislatures.

The America First movement that gave Big Bill Thompson the resources for his reelection began when Senator Warren G. Harding, a Republican, used the phrase in his 1920 presidential campaign as the name for his nationalist and isolationist platform. Harding won the election. Soon after, the Ku Klux Klan adopted the phrase and even claimed they owned its copyright. By the 1930s, the phrase was primarily used by far-right groups and in 1940 was used to name the nationalist group, the America First Committee, that actively opposed US involvement in the Second World War and was viewed by many as anti-Semitic and pro-fascist. Charles Lindbergh, the famous pilot who was the first to cross the Atlantic flying solo in 1927, was one of the leading voices (see Diamond, 2018). Lindbergh, already known as a nationalist and eugenicist, was welcomed to Chicago after his return from Europe by Thompson at a campaign rally in 1927.

Jane Addams responded to the America First movement when she challenged the Immigration Act that was signed into law in 1924 by Republican President Calvin Coolidge (who succeeded Harding when Harding died in office in 1923). The law restricted immigration beyond the limits placed by the 1921 Emergency Quota Act and included a provision barring any immigration from Asia. The law had been a legislative priority of those committed to the America First platform. In her article, "Immigration under the Quota," Addams called out candidate Big Bill Thompson, described the claims of his campaign and argued that they were cases of what she called "vital lies." Vital lies, described first by British expatriate philosopher and writer Violet Paget (writing under the name Vernon Lee), were claims that could motivate a crowd without regard to truth, as long as the ends sought were never achieved. Vital lies "work" so long as the results are still to come. When they are fulfilled—with the election of some politician or the adoption of some other (or old) way of doing things—and the promises are not fulfilled, the "lie" becomes clear. Thompson's followers responded to his unfounded claims about education and immigration, and his ad hominem attacks on his political enemies, by joining in support of such "vital lies." When the problems these lies were meant to address were not solved, the lie was clear. The best vital lie is one that can never be fulfilled.

Addams writes, "Everyone wants to be like his neighbors, which is doubtless an amiable quality, but leading to one of the chief dangers of democracy—the tyranny of the herd mind" (1930, p. 289). After Thompson's successful campaign, he failed to fulfill his promise to realize at the local level the demands of America First and lost his bid for reelection in 1931. This illustrated for Addams that vital lies can only work until they encounter an end, either one of fulfillment or of failure. Thompson may have had more time in power, but the Great Depression began in October 1929, destroying the city's economy and any chance of meeting the expectations he set in his campaign (see Pratt, 2022).

The America First movement, the populists before them, and the rising "Make America Great Again" movement of the 2010s and 20s demonstrated a commitment to antipluralism and simple fallibilism. They demonized immigrants and framed non-White people as outsiders. To justify these commitments, often in the face of counterevidence, the movements adopted a view that called into question claims of truth in ways familiar to the American philosophical tradition. For example, the "Great Replacement" theory, used to justify calls for severe restrictions on immigration, was held by many America First adherents and their successors. The "theory" claimed that immigrants and others (people of color, Jews, Catholics) were aiming to replace "native-born" White Americans in jobs, education, and leadership positions. These views were called into question by facts that showed that the claims of the theory were simply not true. One sort of response by advocates of the theory—beyond the loud reaffirmation of the theory—was to hold that claims that challenged the theory, like all claims, could be false. Some new evidence could be discovered, and one could find that the replacement theory was true all along. In light of this possibility, one should be willing to entertain the contrary claims—that immigrants were, in fact, replacing native-born Americans. That claim too could be mistaken, but lacking certainty, one is able to claim the "alternate facts" as correct until final evidence settled the matter.

The selection of the "alternate facts" over the "facts" is then a matter of choice based on one's other convictions. The view is a limited fallibilism because once one has chosen to embrace the "alternate facts," the believer feels no further obligation to consider the evidence. Given the status of "facts," when the press reports facts that challenge nationalist beliefs like this, especially if offered without the "other side," they are seen by advocates of America First and their successors as "fake news." Much of the mainstream press adopted the practice of "both-sides-ing" to address these sorts of objections by making sure to give "equal time" to both sides of a debate, even if the facts rest solely on one side. This framework for knowledge, when it emerged in the political environment of the first Trump campaign, was named by the Oxford English Dictionary in 2016 as "post-truth."

"Post-truth" is a term used to describe a situation where claims about the world are made true, not by "facts" of one sort or another, but by political interests and emotions, especially anger and fear. In a world of post-truth, "facts" become resources to use in support of the outcome already decided and are not part of the process of deciding which outcome to seek. Lee McIntyre, in his book *Post-Truth*, concludes that "post-truth amounts to a form of ideological supremacy, whereby its practitioners are trying to compel someone to believe in something whether there is good evidence for it or not. And this," he adds, "is a recipe for political domination" (2018, p. 13).

Philosophies of resistance, after more than a century of challenging the dominant view that there is only one set of truths and one set of foundations, came face to face with a new situation: a world where the claims of those suffering under the dominant system appear no more truer than the claims of those who dominate. In this post-truth world, philosophies of resistance not only need to challenge oppression and exclusion, but need to continue to assert grounds from which to demand inclusion and opportunity. As Corey Barnes shows us in his 2022 book *Alain Locke on the Theoretical Foundations for a Just and Successful Peace*, Locke provides an example of just such work.

For Locke, human values are rooted in places and histories. If they are, he argued, the idea of absolute values must be dethroned. This does not mean a kind of anarchic relativism in which peace and genocide are somehow equivalent values. Values, for Locke, can be evaluated by how they function and how they stand up to interrogation and inquiry (pp. 32–33). Arbitrary assertion of values—or their assertion in support of some antidemocratic or oppressive purpose—along with the refusal to interrogate those values, is a form of absolutism that leads to arbitrary dogmatism. Absolutism, according to Locke, is the belief that values can be justified and enacted independently of social and historical conditions (p. 27). This affirmation of values—or "truths" in a post-truth world—independent of circumstances leads to value commitments without exploring their possible justifications or those for competing values. The resulting value commitments, Barnes argues, are "immune to disputation. Many of the absolutes that agents attempt to impose on others are considered beyond critique and are not amenable to debate. And because they are ahistorical, they require no justification by, and cannot be revised in light of, practical considerations and evidence" (p. 28).

Like "vital lies," absolutist values "are true, beyond critique, debate, or suspicion, and justified without (and therefore not susceptible to changes in) evidence" (Barnes, p. 28). Leonard Harris anticipates this line of thinking when he writes those American philosophies "are like jazz sessions because we select from past compositions, reliving them in the selection, even as we create a new picture that captures our own modernity, sense of mission, and portrayal of a living past" (2002, p. 6). "Foundations"—the grounds for truth and value—if there are any in this American tradition, are not fixed but emergent, growing out of the present in light of the past toward a vision of an expansive future.

*American Philosophy from Wounded Knee to the Present* was first written in response to the 9/11 terror attacks and the new challenges to established ways of thinking that followed. In the years before the first edition, America and the world were disrupted by wars in Afghanistan and Iraq; the Great Recession of 2007–09; and the election of the first Black US President in 2008 and the backlash to changes brought by Obama's eight-year term. Since the first edition, America and the world have faced new wars in Ukraine, Syria, and Israel; the first election of Donald Trump as president and the politics of division and civil war that ensued; the COVID pandemic of 2020–23; the murder of George Floyd (and many other Black Americans) by law enforcement in 2020 and the protests that followed; the "insurrection" of January 2021; the attempted assassinations of then-candidate Donald Trump; and Trump's reelection as President of the United States.

As we write, disruption and resistance continue. For the philosophers of the American academy in the 1950s, the turmoil of their day helped to make a case for philosophy to focus its attention on questions that they imagined transcending the messy and dangerous world in which they lived. We have argued that while this was perhaps effective for a time as a means of protecting some philosophers from censure and from feeling responsible for bringing about change, philosophy as a practice of criticism and activism for change persisted. While not always successful, philosophies of resistance nevertheless challenged the dominant patterns of American society and fought against allowing these patterns to become a "block universe"—an unchallenged block of doctrine and practice that ensures the suffering of many, often for the comfort of a few. There are, we insist, lessons to be learned from those philosophical efforts that should not be set aside in the present day—or rather in *your* day.

As we have seen throughout this story, American philosophies of resistance have been active and publicly engaged even as they considered new and better ways to think about the problems they and their communities faced and as they imagined futures to be sought through their actions. As expected of a tradition committed to pluralism, there have also always been disagreements about the best way for philosophy to play out its role. The tradition we have traced here is one that is generally committed to expanding and opening discourse in order to sustain possibilities for individuals, capable of thoughtful participation, to shape their individual and social lives. As the previous chapters have shown, this spirit of American philosophy is alive and well and engaged with the problems people face.

Such engagement, however, cannot be sustained without the constant attention and efforts of those working in this tradition. As we noted in the Prologue, Bernstein worried that in the wake of 9/11 the United States was in danger of slipping into a kind of antipluralism that could endanger the discourse needed to sustain an open democracy. Having finished his book *Radical Evil: A Philosophical Interrogation* (2002) just days before the attack on 9/11, Bernstein considered revising it. He then realized that what concerned him about the response to 9/11 was not the concept of evil, but the use (or abuse in this case) of the concept. Reflecting on Radical Evil in the introduction to his later book, *The Abuse of Evil* (2005), Bernstein explains that "Interrogating evil is an ongoing, open-ended process . . . because we cannot anticipate what new forms of evil or vicissitudes of evil will appear" (2005, p. vii). Generally, talk of evil has spurred critical argument and debate among religious and philosophical thinkers. The abuse of evil is when people talk about evil in order to shut down discourse and block critical thought about complex issues.

For Bernstein, the responses to 9/11 represented a "clash of mentalities." One mentality "is drawn to absolutes, alleged moral certainties, and simplistic dichotomies." The other, which he called "pragmatic fallibilism," "argues that we must not confuse subjective moral certitude with objective moral certainty" and is "skeptical of an uncritical rigid dichotomy between the forces of evil and the forces of good" (2005, p. viii). Responses that stifle thinking are dangerous given the uncertain nature of the world. But some see complex and subtle thinking as indecisive and therefore dangerous in the face of concrete problems. Bernstein argued that pragmatic fallibilism is open to correction but is not indecisive. Critical fallibilism and engaged pluralism require the courage to test ideas in public and to listen to others rather than hiding behind simplistic and rigid responses.

Although one might worry that this approach falls into relativism, Bernstein argued that it does not. There are limits to tolerance; echoing the work of Alain Locke and Kallen (among others), he says, "[w]e cannot tolerate those who are actively intolerant—those who seek to undermine the very possibility of discourse, dialogue, and rational persuasion. But how are we to decide when these limits have been reached?" (2005, p. 60). The curtailing of civil liberties often appears to be an attractive immediate response, but such action is dangerous. More openness, not less, is the better response—whether to the "cold war" or the "war on terror." The same goes for listening to dissent: Bernstein asserts that labeling dissenters as "unpatriotic" hurts discourse.

Further, when one is so certain about being right, there is no need for questioning or further analysis. Whether it is McCarthy, Nixon, George W. Bush, or Donald J. Trump, as David Susskind observed, there is "a disdain for contemplation or deliberation, an embrace of decisiveness, a retreat from empiricism, a sometimes bullying impatience with doubters and even friendly questioners" (quoted in Bernstein, 2005, p. 84). How decisions are reached and how they are held (tentatively or absolutely) is as important as the decisions themselves. Bernstein notes that after 9/11 there were responsible defenders of military intervention, but they did not appeal to absolutes, certainty, or a crusade against evil. They did not use the fear of an enemy to manipulate people and curtail liberties; such actions corrupt politics. There is no grand solution, Bernstein concludes, only the call for all to oppose the abuse of evil.

So, what is to be done? For Bernstein, ordinary citizens must stand up to and oppose the political abuse of evil, challenge the misuse of absolutes, expose false and misleading claims to moral certainty, and argue that we cannot deal with the complexity of the issues we confront by appealing to—or imposing—simplistic dichotomies (2005, p. 121). He goes on to say that "There is a role for public intellectuals, educators, journalists, and artists to help guide the way—just as Holmes, James, Peirce, and Dewey did at a different time under radically different historical circumstances" (p. 121). Bernstein concludes that democracy is fragile and requires critical fallibilism and engaged pluralism at all levels of society.

An example of what Bernstein had in mind could be seen in the 2012 re-election of Barack Obama. This election illustrated the "clash of mentalities" in a way that earlier elections, even the election of Obama in 2008, did not. In the wake of the 2010 Citizens United Supreme Court decision, corporate interests and Tea Party conservatives asserted a vision of government in which compromise was viewed as a failure of commitment. Policies advocated by this mentality and carried forward in the Make America Great Again movement included the elimination of abortion rights, the prohibition of gay marriage, increasingly restrictive immigration laws, the devaluation of non-Western religions, and the view of poverty as a personal failing.

In contrast, the other mentality offered a vision of government framed by pragmatic fallibilism and pluralism. President Obama, as the most visible advocate of this vision at the time, argued for a government guided by principles that are open to discussion, debate, experimentation, revision, and gradual reform. In policy discussions, this vision led to efforts to address widely shared problems that affect immigrants, women, the poor, and other disadvantaged populations. Such an approach does not guarantee or even suggest that those committed to pragmatic fallibilism and engaged pluralism will always get things right. It only allows for the possibility of open discussion and self-correction.

In a sense, Obama represented a practical application of elements of the American philosophical tradition. According to James T. Kloppenberg's *Reading Obama: Dreams, Hope, and the American Tradition* (2012), Obama was introduced to the work of James, Dewey, Du Bois, and Alain Locke as an undergraduate student. Through these thinkers, he learned about the need to build community in order to make justice real. His work as a community organizer in Chicago followed the work of Addams and Hull House and was where he learned the importance of listening—listening to those in need and to those with opposing viewpoints. As Seigfried notes in "The Courage of One's Convictions or the Conviction of One's Courage? Jane Addams's Principled Compromise," Addams's activism did not appeal to dogmatic stances or moral certainty, and she was willing to make compromises in order to achieve concrete improvements in people's lived experience. Seigfried argues that this is itself a principled decision and not "an expression of indecisiveness or moral relativism" (2008, p. 41). Understanding compromise as the "recognition of multiple perspectives that need to be respected and examined," Addams's commitment to compromise is seen as radical because it embodies "a profound respect for the individuality and dignity of all human beings that obliged her to see their point of view and work with them toward a mutually satisfactory resolution of whatever issue set them apart" (p. 44). In Obama's words, the call is to see "our democracy not as a house to be built, but as a conversation to be had" (quoted in Kloppenberg, 2012, p. 161).

Critics see this emphasis on deliberation, investigation, and revision of outmoded claims as a weakness and a lack of commitment. But this is a misunderstanding; it is rather a different kind of commitment. Kloppenberg writes that Obama "evinces a particular kind of conviction, the conviction of a democrat committed to forging agreement rather than deepening disagreements." "Whereas many radicals as well as many conservatives believe that they possess the truth and that their opponents are evil as well as misguided," Kloppenberg concludes, "Obama accepts different political perspectives as a normal and healthy sign of a vibrant culture" (2012, p. 222). Following Bernstein, Kloppenberg asserts that the mindset that amplifies conflict and creates fear disables democracy. "Only when we affirm the process of continuous and open-ended experimentation do we affirm the principle of democracy" (p. 265).

In his December 2024 remarks to the Obama Foundation's Democracy Forum in Chicago, Obama reaffirmed the vision of a pluralistic democracy even in the face of opposition in the wake of the 2024 elections. The ideal of such a democracy, he observed, involves the commitment "to a system of rules and habits that help us peacefully resolve our disputes; we try to cultivate habits—those practices that encourage us not just to tolerate each other but also—

every so often—join together in collective action." That this vision worked smoothly through much of the twentieth century was largely due to those it left out. "The fact is," he continued, "for most of our history, our democracy was built on top of a deeply entrenched caste system— formal and informal, based on race and gender and class and sexual orientation." Resistance to that system—much of which we have discussed here—brought real change in access to power, education, and economic resources. These changes brought backlash and resentment, leading eventually to new versions of old populist and nationalist politics.

In the wake of the 2024 elections in the United States and other democracies around the world, Obama asked: "Can the idea of pluralism work in the current moment? And, for that matter, is the concept even worth saving?" In response, he offered three points to explain his concept of democratic pluralism. First, echoing the likes of Addams, Dewey, and Alain Locke, pluralism is about "recognizing that in a democracy, power comes from forging alliances, and building coalitions, and making room in those coalitions" for those who may disagree with you but also have shared concerns. Second, recalling Follett's idea of *power-with*, Obama said that "Pluralism does not require us to deny our unique identities or experiences, but it does require that we try to understand the identities and experiences of others and to look for common ground." And third, echoing the activists of the American philosophical tradition, "Pluralism works better when it is about action and not just words." In its hopeful tone and its recommitment to a democratic vision, the speech recalled much of the rhetoric from his terms as president.

But the speech was given eight years after he left office. He asks, "What happens when the other side has repeatedly and abundantly made clear they're not interested in playing by the rules?" "It's a problem," he says,

> And when that happens, we fight for what we believe in. There are going to be times, potentially, when one side tries to stack the deck and lock in a permanent grip on power, either by actively suppressing votes, or politicizing the armed forces, or using the judiciary or criminal justice system to go after their opponents. And in those circumstances, pluralism does not call for us to just stand back and say "well, I'm not sure, that's okay". In those circumstances, a line has been crossed and we have to stand firm and speak out and organize and mobilize as forcefully as we can.

While perhaps unsatisfying to those seeking a final answer, his response is almost a summary of the message one can take from the story of American philosophies of resistance.

It has arguably never been the case that a vision of democratic pluralism of the sort proposed by Addams, Bernstein, or Obama was a foregone commitment on the part of most Americans. The election of 2016 and the ensuing years of crisis have taught us that there are diverse visions of the future and that the process of engaging others in open discussion and encouraging them to let go of their framing dichotomies and moral certainty may not work. As new versions of old aspirations to domination emerge, its advocates may not be willing to listen to claims that their failure to be open, or the narrowness of their desires for the future, are problematic— especially across a table from a group of educators and intellectuals.

What American philosophies of resistance teach is that careful discussion and fallibilism are themselves not always enough to resist dominance and bring about change. As Leonard Harris recognized, resistance is also about taking a stand or rather having a duty to take a stand.

There was, it is likely, no vision of the future that Bernstein would have approved that was not fundamentally committed to democratic processes. There was no vision of America that Ida B. Wells Barnett would accept that approved of occasional lynching (instead of its absolute prohibition), or Jane Addams of a future in which only a few children died of starvation or abuse (though there were multiple approaches to preventing such starvation and abuse). Rachel Carson would not have settled for a world in which any chemicals were used indiscriminately or in service of corporate profits over the safety of humans and their environments. Any system that left decisions about chemical use in the hands of "the authoritarian temporarily entrusted with power" (1962, p. 127) was unacceptable.

American philosophers of resistance may grant different ways of proceeding, by debate, by nonviolent protest, by violence, or even by guile. But all of them envisioned a future that was, by everything they could consider, better than the present, more fruitful of new experiences, and richer in connections. In the face of new crises, philosophers of resistance are prepared to adjust their approaches, even the details of their visions, but they are morally certain that their task is to make a better future, even if there isn't just one such possible future. They also recognize that their commitments, what they value, and how they seek change grow from where they live, its grounds, its history, and its peoples. Its impact and scope grow, as James and McDermott said, by the edges. The vision expands through contact with others and itself grows and changes if one maintains what John E. Smith called the spirit of American philosophy: an openness of mind and experimental spirit; an approach that could do justice to the reality of change and development; and the acknowledgment that ideas themselves are important and can be evaluated by their relevance to life (Smith, 1963).

The 2016 election of Donald Trump, his 2020 campaign, and his 2024 campaign and reelection embodied "the mindset that amplifies conflict and creates fear," disabling democracy. Even more disabling were the events of January 6, 2021. These events amplify Bernstein's worry that the United States is in danger of slipping into a kind of antipluralism that could endanger the discourse needed to sustain an open democracy. Central to the election rhetoric in the last presidential elections of 2012, 2016, 2020, and 2024 and to the events of January 6 has been the use and abuse of fear and division. The presumption is that the antidote to fear is certainty and claims by one vision or another that are speculative or experimental are necessarily less certain and so are to be rejected. Like the fear that led to the militarization of South Dakota and the massacre that followed at Wounded Knee Creek, the fear that emerged from 9/11 became a fear of others and a willingness to set some principles aside in order to avoid imagined future harm. Those habits continue to have force within US political and cultural discourse. The alternative presented by the tradition examined here is to approach such conflicts, or perceived conflicts, with inquiry and openness and an ongoing commitment to Deweyan democratic experimentation, Roycean commitment to community, Peircean fallibilism, Jamesian pluralism, Lockean reciprocity, Addams's idea of "lateral progress," and Pokagon's commitment to the land itself. Even with these alternatives, though, fear is not unfounded. We live in a precarious world that is made more precarious by human technology, greed, and inattentiveness. It is not a mistake to be afraid, but it is important to decide how to respond to the fear. The American tradition we have charted has advocated a response of openness and tolerance that leads to the possibility of amelioration and hope—but there are no guarantees.

# BIBLIOGRAPHY

## Prologue

Bahm, L. Frank. (1891). "Wounded Knee Editorial." *Saturday Review*, January 3. Available online: https://warwick.ac.uk/fac/arts/english/currentstudents/undergraduate/modules/fulllist/second/en213/term1/l_frank_baum.pdf (accessed July 18, 2024).
Bernstein, R. J. (2005). *The Abuse of Evil: The Corruption of Politics and Religion since 9/11*. Malden, MA: Polity Press.
Bush, G. W. (2001). *Address to a Joint Session of Congress and the American People*. Speech presented to the United States Congress, Washington, DC, September 20.
DeMallie, R. (1982). "The Lakota Ghost Dance: An Ethnohistorical Account." *Pacific Historical Review* 51: 385–406.
Eastman, C. A. (1916/1977). *From the Deep Woods to Civilization: Chapters in the Autobiography of an Indian*. Lincoln: University of Nebraska Press.
Kicking Bear (1890/1977). "I Bring You Word from Your Fathers the Ghosts." In W. C. Vanderwerth (ed.), *Indian Oratory*, 197–201. New York: Ballantine Books.
New York Times (1890). "It Looks Like War." *New York Times*, November 23. Available online: https://www.proquest.com/historical-newspapers/looks-more-like-war/docview/94782132/se-2 (accessed July 18, 2024).
Perez-Rivas, M. (2001). "Bush Vows to Rid the World of 'Evil-doers.'" *CNN*, September 16. Available online: http://edition.cnn.com/2001/US/09/16/gen.bush.terrorism (accessed February 25, 2014).
Porter, Robert P. (1892). *Compendium of the Eleventh Census: 1890, Part I.—Population*. Washington, DC: Government Printing Office.
United States Institute of Peace. (2023). "The Costs of War—Iraqi Civilians." Available online: https://watson.brown.edu/costsofwar/costs/human/civilians/iraqi (accessed July 18, 2024).
Watson Institute. (2022). "In Afghanistan, Was a Loss Better than Peace?" Available online: https://www.usip.org/publications/2022/11/afghanistan-was-loss-better-peace (accessed July 18, 2024).

## Chapter 1

Alfred, T. (2002). "Sovereignty." In P. J. Deloria and N. Salisbury (eds.), *A Companion to American Indian History*, 460–74. Malden, MA: Blackwell.
Boggs, J., and G. L. Boggs. (1974/2008). *Revolution and Evolution in the Twentieth Century*. New York: Monthly Review Press.
Boydston, J. A. (1967–1990). *John Dewey: Early Works 1882–1898; Middle Works 1899–1924; The Later Works: 1925–1953*. Carbondale: Southern Illinois University Press.
Kelley, Robin D. G. with Eve Tuck and K. Wayne Yang. (2013). In Tuck and Yang, *Youth Resistance Research and Theories of Change*. New York: Routledge.
Lysaker, J. (2012). "Essaying America: A Declaration of Independence." *The Journal of Speculative Philosophy* 26 (3): 531–3.
McDermott, J. (2007). *The Drama of Possibility: Experience as Philosophy of Culture*, ed. D. Anderson. New York: Fordham University Press.
Menand, L. (2001). *The Metaphysical Club: A Story of Ideas in America*. New York: Farrar, Straus and Giroux.

# Bibliography

Modrow, Sebastain, and Melissa Smith, trans. (n.d.). "The Papal Bull Inter Caetera of May 4, 1493." Available online: https://doctrineofdiscovery.org/assets/pdfs/Inter_Caetera_Modrow&Smith.pdf (accessed July 18, 2024).

Pratt, S. L. (2002). *Native Pragmatism: Rethinking the Roots of American Philosophy*. Bloomington, IN: Indiana University Press.

Rogers, Melvin L. (2023). *The Darkened Light of Faith : Race, Democracy, and Freedom in African American Political Thought*. Princeton: Princeton University Press.

Seigfried, C. H. (1996). *Pragmatism and Feminism: Reweaving the Social Fabric*. Chicago: University of Chicago Press.

Stuhr, J. (1997). *Genealogical Pragmatism: Philosophy, Experience, and Community*. New York: State University of New York Press.

Tuck, Eve, and K. Wayne Yang. (2014). *Youth Resistance Research and Theories of Change*. New York: Routledge.

West, C. (1989). *The American Evasion of Philosophy: A Genealogy of Pragmatism*. Madison: University of Wisconsin Press.

## Chapter 2

Curry, T. J. (2021). "The Fortune of Wells: Ida B. Wells-Barnett's Use of T. Thomas Fortune's Philosophy of Social Agitation as a Prolegomenon to Militant Civil Rights Activism." *Transactions of the Charles S. Peirce Society* 4: 456–82.

Douglass, Frederick. (1894). Chapter 1—Introduction. In Ida B. Wells-Barnett *The Reason Why the Colored American Is Not in the World's Columbian Exposition. The Afro-American's Contribution to Columbian Literature*. Accessed through University of Pennsylvania Digital Library. Available online: http://digital.library.upenn.edu/women/wells/exposition/exposition.html.

Flinn, J. J. (1893). *Official Guide to the World's Columbian Exhibition*. Chicago: Columbia Guide. Available online: http://archive.org/details/officialguidetow00flin (accessed May 22, 2024).

Fortune, T. T. (2007). *Black and White: Land, Labor and Politics in the South*. New York: Washington Square Press.

Fortune, T. T., and S. L. Alexander. (2008). *T. Thomas Fortune, the Afro-American Agitator : A Collection of Writings, 1880–1928*. Gainesville: University Press of Florida.

Hill Collins, P. (2002). Introduction. In Wells-Barnett, *On Lynching*. New York: Humanity Books, pp. 9–24

Kingsbury, G. W. (1915). *History of the Dakota Territory*. Vol. 3. Chicago: S. J. Clarke.

Pokagon, S. (1899). *O-Gî-Mäw-Kwe Mit-I-Gwä-Kî (Queen of the Woods)*. Hartford, MI: C. H. Engle.

Pokagon, S. (2001). "Simon Pokagon Offers *The Red Man's Greeting*." In F. E. Hoxie (ed.), *Talking Back to Civilization: Indian Voices from the Progressive Era*. Boston: Bedford/St. Martins.

US Census Bureau (1890). *Extra Census Bulletin*. Available online: http://archive.org/stream/extracensusbulle00unit/extracensusbulle00unit_djvu.txt (accessed May 22, 2024).

Wells-Barnett, I. (1894). *The Reason Why the Colored American Is Not in the World's Columbian Exposition. The Afro-American's Contribution to Columbian Literature*. Accessed through University of Pennsylvania Digital Library. Available online: http://digital.library.upenn.edu/women/wells/exposition/exposition.html

Wells-Barnett, I. (2002). *On Lynching*. New York: Humanity Books.

Wells, Ida B. (1970). *Crusade for Justice: The Autobiography of Ida B. Wells*, ed. Al. M. Duster. Chicago: University of Chicago Press.

White, T., and W. Igleheart. (1893). *The World's Columbian Exposition, Chicago, 1893*. Philadelphia: P.W. Ziegler & Co.

## Chapter 3

Commissioner of Indian Affairs. (1893). "Sixty-Second Annual Report," 448–56. Washington, DC: Government Printing Office. Available online: https://carlisleindian.dickinson.edu/sites/default/files/docs-publications/BIA-Annual-Report_1893_Narrative_OCR.pdf (accessed July 18, 2024).
Dodge, M. A. (1894). "The Beastliness of Modern Civilization—Evolution the Only Remedy." In John Wesley Hanson (ed.), *World Congress of Religions*. New York: Monarch Book.
Domosh, M. (2002). "A 'Civilized' Commerce: Gender, 'Race', and Empire at the 1893 Chicago Exposition." *Cultural Geographies* 9.2: 181–201.
Eastman, C. A. (1911). *The Soul of the Indian*. Boston: Houghton Mifflin.
Eastman, C. A. (1977). *From the Deep Woods to Civilization : Chapters in the Autobiography of an Indian*. Lincoln: University of Nebraska Press.
Hall, G. S. (1916). *Adolescence : Its Psychology and Its Relations to Physiology, Anthropology, Sociology, Sex, Crime, Religion and Education*. New York: D. Appleton.
Hofstadter, R. (1955). *Social Darwinism in American Thought*, Rev. edn. Boston: Beacon Press.
Kellogg, L. C. (1912). "Industrial Organization for the Indian." In *Proceedings of the First Conference of the Society of American Indians*, 43–56. Washington, DC.
Kellogg, L. C. (1920). *Our Democracy and the American Indian: A Comprehensive Presentation of the Indian Situation as it Is Today*. Kansas City, MO: Burton.
Parker, A. C. (1912). "The Philosophy of Indian Education." In *Proceedings of the First Conference of the Society of American Indians*, 68–76. Washington, DC.
Parker, A. C. (1916a). "The Social Elements of the Indian Problem." *The Journal of American Sociology* 22 (2): 252–67.
Parker, A. C. (1916b). "Problems of Race Assimilation in America." *The American Indian Magazine* 4 (4), October–December: 283–304.
Pearce, T. (2020). *Pragmatism's Evolution : Organism and Environment in American Philosophy*. Chicago: The University of Chicago Press.
Spencer, H. (1862). *First Principles*. New York: H. M. Caldwell.
Spencer, H. (1894). "Social Evolution and Social Duty." In John Wesley Hanson (ed.), *World Congress of Religions*. New York: Monarch Book.
Spencer, H. (1900–1901). *The Principles of Sociology*, vol. 1. New York: Appleton and Company.
Standing Bear, L. (1933/1978). *Land of the Spotted Eagle*. Lincoln: University of Nebraska Press.
White, T. l., and W. Igleheart. (1893). *The World's Columbian Exposition, Chicago, 1893*. Philadelphia ; P.W. Ziegler & Co.

## Chapter 4

Addams, J. (1990). *Twenty Years at Hull House*. Chicago: University of Illinois Press.
Addams, J. (2007). *Newer Ideals of Peace*, eds. B. A. Carroll, and C. F. Fink. Urbana: University of Illinois Press.
Cooper, A. J. (1894). *The World's Congress of Representative Women: A Historical Résumé for Popular Circulation of the World's Congress of Representative Women, Convened in Chicago on May 15, and Adjourned on May 22, 1893, under the Auspices of the Woman's Branch of the World's Congress Auxiliary*, ed. M. W. Sewall, 711–15. Chicago: Rand McNally.
Cooper, A. J. (1998). *The Voice of Anna Julia Cooper: Including a Voice from the South and Other Important Essays, Papers, and Letters*, eds. C. C. Lemert, and E. Bhan. Lanham, MD: Rowman & Littlefield.
Crunden, R. M. (1984). *Ministers of Reform: The Progressives' Achievement in American Civilization, 1889–1920*. Urbana and Chicago: University of Illinois Press.
Fuller, M. (1860). *Woman in the Nineteenth Century: And Kindred Papers Relating to the Sphere, Condition and Duties, of Woman*. Boston: J. P. Jewett.

# Bibliography

Fuller, M. (1994). *The Portable Margaret Fuller,* ed. M. Kelley. New York: Penguin.

Gilman, C. P. (1899). *Women and Economics: A Study of the Economic Relation between Men and Women as a Factor in Social Evolution.* Boston: G. P. Putnam's Sons.

Gilman, C. P., and L. S. Schwartz (1989). *The Yellow Wallpaper and Other Writings.* New York: Bantam Books.

Knight, L. W. (2005). *Citizen: Jane Addams and the Struggle for Democracy.* Chicago: University of Chicago Press.

Knight, L. W. (2010). *Jane Addams: Spirit in Action.* New York. W. W. Norton & Company.

"Margaret Fuller". Available online: https://www.womenofthehall.org/inductee/margaret-fuller/ (accessed July 19, 2024).

May, V. (2007). *Anna Julia Cooper, Visionary Black Feminist Routledge.* New York: Routledge.

Wagner, Sally Roesch. (1992). "The Iroquois Influence on Women's Rights." In Jos Barreiro (ed. with an introduction), 15–34. *Indian Roots of American Democracy.* Ithaca, NY: Akwekon Press, Cornell University.

Ward, L. (1907). *Pure Sociology,* 2nd edn. New York: Macmillan.

Zwarg, C. (1995). *Feminist Conversations: Fuller, Emerson, and the Play of Reading.* Ithaca: Cornell University Press.

## Chapter 5

Buell, L. (2003). *Emerson.* Cambridge, MA: Belknap Press of Harvard University Press.

Emerson, R. W. (1883). *Miscellanies,* ed. J. E. Cabot. Boston and New York: Houghton, Mifflin.

Emerson, R. W. (1939). *The Letters of Ralph Waldo Emerson in Six Volumes,* ed. R. L. Rusk. New York: Columbia University Press.

Emerson, R. W. (1983). *Selected Writings of Ralph Waldo Emerson,* ed. W. H. Gilman. New York: New American Library.

Emerson, R. W.. (2012). "Letter to Martin Van Buren President of the United States." In D. Mikics (ed.), *The Annotated Emerson.* Cambridge, MA: Belknap Press of Harvard University Press , 93–99.

Fredrickson, G. M. (1965). *The Inner Civil War : Northern Intellectuals and the Crisis of the Union.* 1st edn. New York: Harper & Row.

Holbrook, J. (1829). *American Lyceum, Or Society for the Improvement of Schools and Diffusion of Useful Knowledge.* Boston: Old South Works.

Howe, J. W. (1881). *Modern Society.* Boston: Roberts Brothers.

Kuklick, Bruce. (1979). *The Rise of American Philosophy : Cambridge, Massachusetts, 1860–1930.* New Haven ; Yale University Press.

Lowell, J. S. (1884). *Public Relief and Private Charity.* New York: G. P. Putnam's Sons.

Lysaker, J. T. (2008). *Emerson and Self-Culture.* Bloomington, IN: Indiana University Press.

Thoreau, H. D. (1975). *The Selected Works of Thoreau,* ed. W. Harding. Boston: Houghton Mifflin.

Thoreau, H. D. (1988). *The Maine Woods.* New York: Penguin Books.

Whitman, W. (1881). "By Blue Ontario's Shore." Available online: www.whitmanarchive.org/published/LG/1871/poems/160 (accessed May 22, 2014).

## Chapter 6

Addams, J. (2002a). *Democracy and Social Ethics,* ed. C. H. Seigfried. Urbana: University of Illinois Press.

Addams, J. (2002b). *The Long Road of Woman's Memory.* Urbana: University of Illinois Press.

# Bibliography

Addams, J. (2007). *Newer Ideals of Peace,* eds. B. A. Carroll, and C. F. Fink. Urbana: University of Illinois Press.

Bryan, W. J. (1925). *The Dawn of Humanity: The Menace of Darwinism, and the Bible and its Enemies.* Chicago, Ill., and Pasadena, Calif: Altruist Foundation.

Carlson, M. (2013). "The Panic of 1893." In R. E. Parker, and R. M. Whaples (eds.), *Routledge Handbook of Major Events in Economic H*istory, 40–9. New York: Taylor & Francis Group.

Dewey, J. (2005). *The Correspondence of John Dewey, 1871–1952,* vols. 3, ed. Larry Hickman, Electronic edn. Charlottesville, Virginia, USA: InteLex Corporation.

Du Bois, W. E. B. (1957). *The Ordeal of Mansart.* New York: Mainstream Publishers.

Gladden, W. (1894). *Tools and the Man: Property and Industry under Christian Law.* Cambridge: Riverside Press.

Gladden, W. (1898). *Our Nation and Her Neighbors.* Columbus, OH: Quinius & Ridenour.

James, W. (1890). *The Principles of Psychology.* New York: H. Holt.

James, W. (1977). *The Writings of William James,* ed. J. J. McDermott. Chicago: University of Chicago Press.

Lease, M. (1890). "A Woman's Work." Available online: https://historymatters.gmu.edu/d/5303/ (accessed July 18, 2024).

Lease, M. (1890b). *Wall Street Owns This Country.* Available online: https://www.historyisaweapon.com/defcon1/marylease.html (accessed July 18, 2024).

Lease, M. (1895). *The Problem of Civilization Solved.* Chicago: Laird and Lee. Available online: https://digital.lib.niu.edu/islandora/object/niu-gildedage%3A24027 (accessed July 18, 2024).

Lovett, L. L. (2007). *Conceiving the Future Pronatalism, Reproduction, and the Family in the United States, 1890–1938,* 1st edn. Chapel Hill: University of North Carolina Press.

Miles, N. A. (1911). *Serving the Republic: Memoirs of the Civil and Military Life of Nelson A. Miles, Lieutenant-General, United States Army.* New York: Harper & Bros.

Morolo, P. (2011). "Wars of Civilization: The US Army Contemplates Wounded Knee, the Pullman Strike, and the Philippine Insurrection." *International Labor and Working-Class History*, Fall 2011, No. 80 (Fall 2011): 77–102.

Maddux, K. (2013). "Fundamentalist Fool or Populist Paragon? William Jennings Bryan and the Campaign against Evolutionary Theory." *Rhetoric and Public Affairs* 16(3): 489–520.

Müller, J. (2016). *What Is Populism?* Philadelphia: University of Pennsylvania Press.

People's Party. (1892). "The "Omaha Platform" of the People's Party." Available online: https://www.americanyawp.com/reader/16-capital-and-labor/the-omaha-platform-of-the-peoples-party-1892/ (accessed July 18, 2024).

Postel, C. (2009). *The Populist Vision.* Oxford: Oxford University Press.

Presbyterian Church (USA). (2011). *The Constitution of the Presbyterian Church (USA.): Part II.* Louisville, KY: Published by the Office of the General Assembly.

Rauschenbusch, W. (1913). *Christianity and the Social Crisis.* London: Macmillan.

Riggs, T., ed. (2015). "Pullman Strike." *Gale Encyclopedia of U.S. Economic History*, 2nd edn., vol. 2, Gale, 1078–80. *Gale In Context: U.S. History.* Available online: link.gale.com/apps/doc/CX3611000739/UHIC?u=euge94201&sid=bookmark-UHIC&xid=ffb303f2 (accessed October 7, 2022).

Roosevelt, T. (1916). Fear God and Take Your Own Part. New York: George H. Doran Company.

Rose, W. J., and B. Trueblood (1904). *Official Report of the Thirteenth Universal Peace Congress.* Boston: Peace Congress Committee.

Sumner, W. G. (1918). *The Forgotten Man and Other Essays.* New Haven: Yale University Press.

Watson, T. (1892). *The People's Cause.* Boston: The Arena Publishing Co.

Watson, T. (1908). *The Life and Speeches of Thos. E. Watson.* Nashville, Tenn: N.p.,

Washington, B. T. (1895). "Booker T. Washington Delivers the 1895 Atlanta Compromise Speech." Available online: https://historymatters.gmu.edu/d/39/ (accessed July 21, 2024).

Washington, B. T. (1995). *Up from Slavery,* ed. W. L. Andrews. New York: Oxford University Press.

# Bibliography

## Chapter 7

Myers, G. (2001). *William James: His Life and Thought*. New Haven: Yale University Press.
James, W. (1879). "The Sentiment of Rationality." *Mind* 4: 317–46.
James, W. (1920). *The Letters of William James,* ed. H. James. Boston: Atlantic Monthly Press.
James, W. (1977). *The Writings of William James,* ed. J. J. McDermott. Chicago: University of Chicago Press.
James, W., F. Bowers, and K. Skrupskelis. (1975). *The Meaning of Truth*. Cambridge, MA: Harvard University Press.
Pratt, S. L. (2002). *Native Pragmatism: Rethinking the Roots of American Philosophy*. Bloomington: Indiana University Press.
Russell, B. (1910). *Philosophical Essays*. London: Longmans, Green, and Co.
Sumner, W. G. (1992). *On Liberty, Society, and Politics: The Essential Essays of William Graham Sumner,* ed. R. C. Bannister. Indianapolis: Liberty Fund.

## Chapter 8

James, W. (1907/1975). *Pragmatism: A New Name for Some Old Ways of Thinking*. Cambridge, MA: Harvard University Press.
Peirce, C. S. (1931–1958). *Collected Papers of Charles Sanders Peirce,* vol. 8, eds. C. Hartshorne, P. Weiss, and A. W. Burks. Cambridge, MA: The Belknap Press of Harvard University Press.
Peirce, C. S. (1992). *The Essential Peirce,* vol. 1, eds. N. Houser, and C. Kloesel. Bloomington, IN: Indiana University Press.
Peirce, C. S. (1998). *The Essential Peirce,* vol. 2. Bloomington, IN: Indiana University Press.
Saussure, F. (1916/1959). *Course in General Linguistics*. Translated by W. Baskin. New York: McGraw-Hill.
Sherriff, J. K. (1989). *The Fate of Meaning: Charles Peirce, Structuralism, and Literature*. Princeton: Princeton University Press.

## Chapter 9

Auxier, R., ed. (2000). *Critical Responses to Josiah Royce, 1885–1916*. Bristol, UK: Thoemmes Press.
Calkins, M. W. (1911). "The Idealist to the Realist." *The Journal of Philosophy, Psychology and Scientific Methods* 8 (17): 449–58.
Calkins, M. W. (1926). "On Certain Difficulties in the Modern Doctrine of Essence." *The Journal of Philosophy* 23 (26): 701–10.
Clendenning, J. (1999). *The Life and Thought of Josiah Royce*. Rev. and expanded ed. Nashville: Vanderbilt University Press.
Holt, E. B., Marvin, W. T., Montague, W. P., Perry, R. B., Pitkin, W., and Spaulding, E. G. (1912). *The New Realism: Cooperative Studies in Philosophy*. New York: Macmillan.
Royce, J. (1896). *The Spirit of Modern Philosophy*. Boston and New York: Houghton Mifflin.
Royce, J. (1900–1901). *The World and the Individual,* First and Second Series. New York: Macmillan.
Royce, J. (1903). *Three Papers Relating to the Philosophical Conference of October 19, 1903*. Harvard Archives Royce Papers, Box 73.
Royce, J. (1995). *The Philosophy of Loyalty,* ed. J. J. McDermott. Nashville, TN: Vanderbilt University Press.
Royce, J. (2001). *The Sources of Religious Insight,* ed. F. M. Oppenheim. Washington, DC: Catholic University Press of America.
Royce, J. (2005). *The Basic Writings of Josiah Royce,* ed. J. J. McDermott. New York: Fordham University Press.

Royce, J. (2009). *Race Questions, Provincialism, and Other American Problems: Expanded Edition*, eds. S. L. Pratt, and S. Sullivan. New York: Fordham University Press.

Werkmeister, W. H. (1949). *A History of Philosophical Ideas in America*. New York: Ronald Press.

## Chapter 10

Addams, J. (2002). *Peace and Bread in Time of War,* ed. K. Joslin. Urbana: University of Illinois Press.

Addams, J. (2005). *Writings on Peace*, eds. M. Fischer, and J. D. Whipps. London: Continuum International.

Baker, J. H. (2011). *Margaret Sanger: A Life of Passion*. New York: Hill and Wang.

Butler, N. M. (1922). *AAUP Bulletin*, 8. American Association of University Professors.

Campbell, J. (2006). *A Thoughtful Profession: The Early Years of the American Philosophical Association*. Chicago, IL: Open Court.

Chafee, Z. (1920). *Freedom of Speech*. New York: Harcourt, Brace and Howe.

Davis, A. (1973). *American Heroine: The Life and Legend of Jane Addams*. London: Oxford University Press.

Goldman, E. (1931). *Living My Life*. New York: Alfred Knopf.

Goldman, E. (1969). *Anarchism and Other Essays*. New York: Dover.

Goldman, E., and A. Berkman (1917). *Anarchism on Trial: Speeches of Alexander Berkman and Emma Goldman Before the United States District Court in the City of New York, July, 1917*. New York: Mother Earth Publishing Association.

Gornick, V. (2011). *Emma Goldman: Revolution as a Way of Life*. New Haven: Yale University Press.

Grant, M. (1922). *The Passing of the Great Race: Or, The Racial Basis of European History*. London: C. Scribner's sons.

Roosevelt, T. (1916). *Fear God and Take Your Own Part*. New York: George H. Doran Co.

Sanger, M. (1920). *Woman and the New Race*. New York: Brentano's.

Sanger, M. (1922). *The Pivot of Civilization*. New York: Brentano's.

Wilson, W. (1918). *President Wilson's State Papers and Addresses,* ed. A. Shaw. New York: George H. Doran Co.

## Chapter 11

Bourne, R. (2002). *In Search of a Democratic America: The Writings of Randolph S. Bourne*, ed. M. S. Sheffer. Lanham, MD: Lexington Books.

Boydston, J. A. (1967–1990). *John Dewey: Early Works 1882–1898; Middle Works 1899–1924; The Later Works: 1925–1953*. Carbondale: Southern Illinois University Press.

Dewey, J. (1998). *The Essential Dewey: Volume 1,* eds. L. A. Hickman, and T. M. Alexander. Bloomington, IN: Indiana University Press.

Dewey, J. (2009). *The Essential Dewey: Volume 2: Ethics, Logic, Psychology,* eds. L. A. Hickman, and T. M. Alexander. Bloomington, IN: Indiana University Press.

Peirce, C. S. . (1992). *The Essential Peirce*, vol. 1, eds. N. Houser, and C. Kloesel. Bloomington, IN: Indiana University Press.

## Chapter 12

Boas, F. (1938). *The Mind of Primitive Man*, Revised edn. New York: Macmillan Co.

Bowne, B. P. (1908). *Personalism*. Boston: Houghton Mifflin Co.

## Bibliography

Calkins, M. W. (1888). *Sharing the Profits*. Boston: Ginn.
Calkins, M. W. (1907/1925). *The Persistent Problems of Philosophy: An Introduction to Metaphysics Through the Study of Modern Systems*, 5th edn. New York: Macmillan.
Calkins, M. W. (1917). "Militant Pacifism." *International Journal of Ethics* 28 (1): 70–9.
Calkins, M. W. (1918). *The Good Man and the Good: An Introduction to Ethics*. New York: Macmillan.
Calkins, M. W. (1919a). *A First Book in Psychology*. New York: Macmillan.
Calkins, M. W. (1919b). "The Personalistic Conception of Nature." *The Philosophical Review* 28 (2): 115–46.
Calkins, M. W. (1930). "The Philosophic 'Credo' of an Absolutistic Personalist." In G. P. Adams, and W. P. Montague (eds.), *Contemporary American Philosophy: Personal Statements*, 197–218. New York: Macmillan.
Calkins, M. W., and J. M. Baldwin (1930). *A History of Psychology in Autobiography: Volume 1*. Worcester: Clark University Press.
Deacon, D. (1997). *Elsie Clews Parsons: Inventing Modern Life*. Chicago, IL: University of Chicago Press.
Drake, D. (1930). "The Philosophy of a Meliorist." In G. P. Adams, and W. P. Montague (eds.), *Contemporary American Philosophy: Personal Statements*, 275–97. New York: Macmillan.
Furumoto, L. (September 1, 1980). "Mary Whiton Calkins (1863–1930)." *Psychology of Women Quarterly* 5 (1): 55–68.
Krikorian, Y. H. (1944). *Naturalism and the Human Spirit*. New York: Columbia University Press.
Latour, B. (2005). *Reassembling the Social: An Introduction to Actor-Network-Theory*. Oxford: Oxford University Press.
Parsons, E. C. (1906). *The Family; An Ethnological and Historical Outline with Descriptive Notes: Planned as a Text-Book for the Use of College Lecturers and of Directors of Home-Reading Clubs*. New York and London: G. P. Putnam's Sons.
Parsons, E. C. (1914). *Fear and Conventionality*. New York: G. P. Putnam's sons.
Parsons, E. C. (1915). "The Aversion to Anomalies." *The Journal of Philosophy, Psychology and Scientific Methods* 12 (8): 212–19.
Parsons, E. C. (1917). *Notes on Zuñi*. Lancaster, PA: Published for the American Anthropological Association.
Parsons, E. C. (1994). *The Journal of a Feminist*. Bristol: Thoemmes.
Pearson, K. (1900). *The Grammar of Science*. London: Adam & Charles Black.
Pratt, S. L. (2005). Wounded Knee and the Prospect of Pluralism. *Journal of Speculative Philosophy* 19 (2): 150–66.
Sellars, R. W. (1932). *The Philosophy of Physical Realism*. New York: Macmillan.
Tarde, G. (1903). *The Laws of Imitation,* trans. E. W. C. Parsons. Gloucester, MA: P. Smith.

## Chapter 13

Du Bois, W. E. B. (1899). *The Philadelphia Negro: A Social Study*. Philadelphia: University of Pennsylvania.
Du Bois, W. E. B. (1903). *The Souls of Black Folk: Essays and Sketches*. Chicago: McClurg.
Du Bois, W. E. B. (1918). "Close Ranks." *The Crisis* 16 (3): 111.
Du Bois, W. E. B. (1920). *Darkwater: Voices from Within the Veil*. New York: Harcourt, Brace and Howe.
Du Bois, W. E. B. (1968). *The Autobiography of W. E. B. Du Bois: A Soliloquy on Viewing My Life from the Last Decade of Its First Century*. New York: International Publishers.
Du Bois, W. E. B. (1986). *Writings*. New York: Library of America.
Du Bois, W. E. B. (2007). "The Conservation of Races." *Penn State Electronic Classics*. Available online: http://www2.hn.psu.edu/faculty/jmanis/webdubois/DuBoisNegro-ConservationRaces6x9.pdf (accessed May 26, 2014).
Krugler, David F. (2015). *1919, the Year of Racial Violence : How African Americans Fought Back*. New York, NY: Cambridge University Press.

Sandburg, C. (1919). *The Chicago Race Riots, July. With an Introductory Note, by Walter Lippmann*. New York: Harcourt, Brace and Howe.

Wells-Barnett, I. B. (1920). *The Arkansas Race Riot*. Chicago: Hume Job Print.

## Chapter 14

Alexander, H. B. (1919). "Wrath and Ruth." *The Journal of Philosophy, Psychology and Scientific Methods* 16 (10): 253–8.

Alexander, H. B. (1999). *The World's Rim: Great Mysteries of the North American Indians*. Mineola, NY: Dover.

Cohen, M. R. (1919). "Communal Ghosts and Other Perils in Social Philosophy." *The Journal of Philosophy, Psychology and Scientific Methods* 16 (25): 673–90.

Cohen, M. R. (1927). "Concepts and Twilight Zones." *Journal of Philosophy* 24 (25): 673–83.

Cohen, M. R. (1929). "Vision and Technique in Philosophy." *The Philosophical Review* 3: 127–52.

Cohen, M. R. (1930). "The Faith of a Logician." In G. P. Adams and W. P. Montague (eds.), *Contemporary American Philosophy: Personal Statements*, 219–48. New York: Macmillan.

Cohen, M. R. (1931). *Reason and Nature: An Essay on the Meaning of Scientific Method*. Glencoe, IL: Free Press.

Cohen, M. R., and F. S. Cohen (1930). *Selected Readings in the Philosophy of Law*. New York: Prepared for the private use of the students of St. John's College School of Law.

Fisher, R., W. Ury, and B. Patton. (2012). *Getting to Yes: Negotiating an Agreement without Giving In*. Revised and updated edition. London: Random House Business.

Follett, M. P. (1924). *Creative Experience*. New York: Longmans, Green and Co.

Follett, M. P. (1942). *Dynamic Administration: The Collected Papers of Mary Parker Follett*, eds. H. C. Metcalf and L. Urwick. New York: Harper and Row Publishers.

Follett, M. P. (1998). *The New State: Group Organization the Solution of Popular Government*. University Park, PA: Pennsylvania State University Press.

Holt, E. B. (1915). *The Freudian Wish and Its Place in Ethics*. New York: H. Holt.

Tonn, J. C. (2003). *Mary P. Follett: Creating Democracy, Transforming Management*. New Haven: Yale University Press.

## Chapter 15

Carter, Jacoby Adeshei (2016). *African American Contributions to the Americas' Cultures: A Critical Edition of Lectures by Alain Locke*. New York: Palgrave Macmillan.

Harris, L., and C. Molesworth (2008). *Alain L. Locke: Biography of a Philosopher*. Chicago: University of Chicago Press.

Kallen, H. M. (1942). *Art and Freedom*. New York: Duell, Sloan and Pearce.

Kallen, H. M. (1956). *Cultural Pluralism and the American idea: An Essay in Social Philosophy*. Philadelphia: University of Pennsylvania Press.

Kallen, H. M. (1998). *Culture and Democracy in the United States*. New Brunswick, NJ: Transaction.

Locke, A. (1925). *The New Negro: An Interpretation*. New York: A. and C. Boni.

Locke, A. (1989). *The Philosophy of Alain Locke: Harlem Renaissance and Beyond*, ed. L. Harris. Philadelphia: Temple University Press.

Locke, A., and B. J. Stern (1946). *When Peoples Meet: A Study in Race and Culture Contacts*. New York: Hinds.

Lugones, M. (2003). *Pilgrimages/Peregrinajes: Theorizing Coalition against Multiple Oppressions*. Lanham, MD: Rowman & Littlefield.

Ross, E. A. (1914). *The Old World in the New: The Significance of Past and Present Immigration to the American People*. New York: Century.

# Bibliography

Toll, W. (1997). "Horace M. Kallen: Pluralism and American Jewish Identity." *American Jewish History* 85 (1): 57–74.

## Chapter 16

Boydston, J. A. (1967–1990). *John Dewey: Early Works 1882-1898; Middle Works 1899-1924; The Later Works: 1925-1953*. Carbondale: Southern Illinois University Press.

Brodbeck, M. (1950). "The Emergence of American Philosophy." *American Quarterly* 2 (1): 39–52.

Brodbeck, M. (1952). "Philosophy in America: 1900–1950." In M. Brodbeck, J. Gray, and W. Metzger (eds.), *American Non-fiction: 1900–1950*, 3–94. Chicago: Henry Regnery Company.

Brodbeck, M. (1963). "The Philosophy of John Dewey." In E. G. Allaire, M. Brodbeck, R. Grossman, H. Hochberg, and R. G. Turnbull (eds.), *Essays in Ontology, Iowa Publications in Philosophy*, Vol. 1, 188–215. The Hague: Martinus Nijhoff.

Du Bois, W. E. B. (1968). *The Autobiography of W. E. B. Du Bois: A Soliloquy on Viewing My Life from the Last Decade of its First Century*. New York: International Publishers.

Edmonds, David. (2020). *The Murder of Professor Schlick : The Rise and Fall of the Vienna Circle*. Princeton, NJ: Princeton University Press.

FBI File (2014). *Rudolf Carnap*. Available online: http://vault.fbi.gov/Rudolph%20Carnap/Rudolph%20Carnap%20Part%205%20of%206/view (accessed May 26, 2014).

Halberstam, D. (2007). *The Coldest Winter : America and the Korean War*, 1st edn. New York: Hyperion.

Hook, S. (1927). *The Metaphysics of Pragmatism*. Chicago, IL: Open Court.

Hook, S. (1933). *Towards the Understanding of Karl Marx: A Revolutionary Interpretation*. New York: John Day.

Hook, S. (1936). *From Hegel to Marx, Studies in the Intellectual Development of Karl Marx*. London: Victor Gollancz.

Hook, S. (1950). "Heresy, Yes—But Conspiracy, No." *New York Times*, July 9, pp. 154, 167. Available online: https://timesmachine.nytimes.com/timesmachine/1950/07/09/113165206.html?pageNumber=154 (accessed July 22, 2024).

Hook, S. (2002). *Sidney Hook on Pragmatism, Democracy, and Freedom: The Essential Essays*, eds. R. B. Talisse, and R. Tempio. Amherst, NY: Prometheus Books.

Jørgensen, J. (1951). *The Development of Logical Empiricism*. Chicago: University of Chicago Press.

Kallen, H. M. (1940). "The Meanings of 'Unity' Among the Sciences." *Educational Administration and Supervision* 26 (2): 91–7.

Kallen, H. M. (1946a). "The Meanings of 'Unity' among the Sciences, Once More." *Philosophy and Phenomenological Research* 6 (4): 493–6.

Kallen, H. M. (1946b). "The Significance of the Unity of Science Movement: Reply." *Philosophy and Phenomenological Research* 6 (4): 515–26.

Lewis, D. L. (2000). *W. E. B. Du Bois, 1919–1963: The Fight for Equality and the American Century*. New York: Henry Holt.

Loewenberg, J. (1930). "Problematic Realism." In G. P. Adams and W. P. Montague (eds.), *Contemporary American Philosophy: Personal Statements*, 55–84. New York: Macmillan.

Loewenberg, J. (1959). *Reason and the Nature of Things*. LaSalle, IL: Open Court.

McCumber, J. (2001). *Time in the Ditch : American Philosophy and the McCarthy Era*. Evanston, Ill: Northwestern University Press.

Murzi, R. (2001). "Rudolf Carnap." *The Internet Encyclopedia of Philosophy*. Available online: www.iep.utm.edu/carnap (accessed May 26, 2014).

Neurath, O. (1937). "Unified Science and Its Encyclopedia." *Philosophy of Science* 4 (2): 265–77.

Neurath, O. (1940). "Universal Jargon and Terminology." *Proceedings of the Aristotelian Society* 4: 127–48.

Neurath, O. (1946a). "After Six Years." *Synthese* 5 (1), 77–82.

Neurath, O. (1946b). "The Orchestration of the Sciences by the Encyclopedism of Logical Empiricism." *Philosophy and Phenomenological Research* 6 (4): 496–508.
Reisch, G. (2005). *How the Cold War Transformed Philosophy of Science: To the Icy Slopes of Logic*. London: Cambridge University Press.
Royce, J. (1919). *Lectures on Modern Idealism*. New Haven: Yale University Press.
Royce, J. (1925). *Fugitive Essays by Josiah Royce*. Cambridge: Harvard University Press.
Stewart, G. R. (1950). *The Year of the Oath : The Fight for Academic Freedom at the University of California*. Garden City, New York: Doubleday & Company, Inc.
Uebel, T. (2011). "Vienna Circle." *The Stanford Encyclopedia of Philosophy*. Available online: http://plato.stanford.edu/archives/spr2014/entries/vienna-circle (accessed May 26, 2014).
Wiggins, F. O. (1951). *"The Ideology of Interest." Conflict in the Social Order: Proceedings*. Minneapolis: Centennial Lecture Series.
Wise, S. (2014). Available online: www.worldjewishcongress.org/en/biography/51 (accessed May 26, 2014).

## Chapter 17

Brodbeck, M. (1963). "The Philosophy of John Dewey." In E. G. Allaire, M. Brodbeck, R. Grossman, H. Hochberg, and R. G. Turnbull (eds.), *Essays in Ontology, Iowa Publications in Philosophy*, Vol. 1, 188–215. The Hague: Martinus Nijhoff.
Brogan, W., and J. Risser, eds. (2000). *American Continental Philosophy*. Bloomington, IN: Indiana University Press.
Davidson, D. (1974). "On the Very Idea of a Conceptual Scheme." *Proceedings and Addresses of the American Philosophical Association* 47: 5–20.
De Laguna, G. (1951). "Main Trends in Recent Philosophy: Speculative Philosophy." *The Philosophical Review* 60 (1): 3–19.
Derrida, J. (1969). "The Ends of Man." *Philosophy and Phenomenological Research* 30 (1): 31–57.
Farber, M. (1928). *Phenomenology as a Method and as a Philosophical Discipline*. Buffalo, NY: University of Buffalo.
Farber, M. (1959). *Naturalism and Subjectivism*, Albany: SUNY Press.
Farber, M. (1966). *The Aims of Phenomenology: The Motives, Methods, and Impact of Husserl's Thought*. New York: Harper & Row.
Hartshorne, C. (1983). *Insights and Oversights of Great Thinkers*. Albany, NY: State University of New York Press.
Lachs, J. (2014). *Freedom and Limits*, ed. P. Shade. New York: Fordham University Press.
Lewis, C. I. (1929). *Mind and the World-Order; Outline of a Theory of Knowledge*. New York: C. Scribner's Sons.
Nelson, L. H. (1990). *Who Knows? From Quine to a Feminist Empiricism*. Philadelphia: Temple University Press.
Sellars, W. (1967). *Philosophical Perspectives: Metaphysics and Epistemology*. Atascadero, CA: Ridgeview.
Sellars, W. (1991). *Science, Perception and Reality*. Atascadero, CA: Ridgeview.
Quine, W. V. O. (1960). *Word and Object*. Boston: MIT Press.
Quine, W. V. O. 1969. Ontological relativity and other essays. New York: Columbia University Press.
Quine, W. V. O. (1980). "Two Dogmas of Empiricism." In *From a Logical Point of View: Nine Logico-philosophical Essays*, 20–46. Cambridge: Harvard University Press.
Quine, W. V. O. (1981). *Theories and Things*. Cambridge: Harvard University Press.
Rorty, R. (1970). *The Linguistic Turn: Recent Essays in Philosophical Method*. Chicago: University of Chicago Press.
Rorty, R. (1979). *Philosophy and the Mirror of Nature*. Princeton: Princeton University Press.
Russell, B. (1963). *An Inquiry into Meaning and Truth*. Baltimore: Penguin Books.
Standing Bear, L. (1933/1978). *Land of the Spotted Eagle*. Lincoln: University of Nebraska Press.

# Bibliography

Whitehead, A. N. (1925/1967). *Science and the Modern World*. New York: Free Press.

Whitehead, Alfred North, and Bertrand Russell. 1963. *Principia Mathematica*. 2d ed. Cambridge [Eng.]: University Press.

Whitehead, A. N. (1929/1978). *Process and Reality : An Essay in Cosmology,* Corrected edn, eds. D. R. Griffin, and D. W. Sherburne. New York: Free Press.

Wild, J. D. (1955). *The Challenge of Existentialism*. Bloomington, IN: Indiana University Press.

Wild, J. D. (1958). "Is There a World of Ordinary Language?" *The Philosophical Review* 67 (4): 460–76.

Wild, J. D. (1969). *The Radical Empiricism of William James*. Garden City, NY: Doubleday.

Wilshire, B. (2002). *Fashionable Nihilism: A Critique of Analytic Philosophy*. New York: State University of New York Press.


## Chapter 18

Baldwin, J. (1956/2001). *Giovanni's Room*. London: Penguin.

Baldwin, J. (1961). *The Amen Corner: A Drama in Three Acts*. New York: Samuel French.

Baldwin, J. (1963). *The Fire Next Time*. New York: Dial Press.

Baldwin, J. (1998). *Collected Essays*. New York: Library of America.

Carmichael, S. (1967). "Speech given at Garfield High School, Seattle, Washington April 19, 1967." Available online: www.aavw.org/special_features/speeches_speech_carmichael01.html (accessed May 28, 2014).

Carmichael, S. (29 October 1966). "Black Power." Available online: https://voicesofdemocracy.umd.edu/carmichael-black-power-speech-text/ (accessed July 22, 2024).

Carpenter, C. C. J., et al. (1963). "Statement by Alabama Clergymen." Available online: www.stanford.edu/group/King/frequentdocs/clergy.pdf (accessed May 28, 2014).

Du Bois, W. E. B. (1970). *Dusk of Dawn: An Essay Toward an Autobiography of a Race Concept*. New Brunswick, NJ: Transaction.

Garvey, M. (1992). *The Philosophy and Opinions of Marcus Garvey,* vol. 2, ed. A. Jacques-Garvey. New York: Athenaeum.

King, Jr, M. L. (1964). *Why We Can't Wait*. London: Harper & Row.

King, Jr, M. L. (1967). *Where Do We Go from Here: Chaos or Community*. Boston: Beacon.

King, Jr, M. L. (1986). *A Testament of Hope*. San Francisco: Harper & Row.

Leeming, D. A. (1994). *James Baldwin : A Biography,* 1st edn. New York: Knopf.

Lewis, J., and M. Orso (1998). *Walking with the Wind: A Memoir of the Movement*. New York: Simon and Schuster.

Pohlmann, M. D., ed. (2003). *African American Political Thought: Capitalism vs. Collectivism, 1945 to Present*. New York: Routledge.

Supreme Court (1954). "Opinion—Brown—347us483." Available online: http://brownvboard.org/content/opinion-brown-347us483?page=2 (accessed May 28, 2014).

Wright, R. (1998). *Native Son*. New York: Harper Perennial.

Wright, R. (2008). *Black Power: Three Books from Exile: Black Power, The Color Curtain, and White Man, Listen!*. New York: Harper Perennial Modern Classics.


## Chapter 19

Baraka, A. (Jones, L.) (1966). *Home: Social Essays*. New York: William Morrow.

Baraka, A. (Jones, L.) (1963). *Blues People: Negro Music in White America*. New York: Harper Collins.

Baraka, A. (Jones, L.) (2000). *The LeRoi Jones/Amiri Baraka Reader,* ed. W. J. Harris. Berkeley, CA: Thunder's Mouth Press.

Brown, E. (1992). *A Taste of Power: A Black Woman's Story*. New York: Pantheon Books.

Carmichael, S. (29 October 1966). "Black Power." Available online: https://voicesofdemocracy.umd.edu/carmichael-black-power-speech-text/ (accessed July 22, 2024).
Cleaver, E. (1967). *Soul on Ice*. New York: McGraw-Hill.
Cone, J. H. (1969). *Black Theology and Black Power*. New York: Seabury Press.
Cone, J. H. (1970). *A Black Theology of Liberation*. Philadelphia: Lippincott.
Cone, J. H. (1975). *God of the Oppressed*. New York: Seabury Press.
Cone, J. H. (1999). *Risks of Faith: The Emergence of a Black Theology of Liberation, 1968–1998*. Boston, MA: Beacon Press.
Cone, J. H. (2011). *The Cross and the Lynching Tree*. Maryknoll, NY: Orbis Books.
Davis, A. Y. (1981). *Women, Race, & Class*. New York: Random House.
Davis, Angela Y. 1989. *Women, Culture & Politics*. First edition. New York: Random House.
Glaude, E. S. (2000). *Exodus!: Religion, Race, and Nation in Early Nineteenth-Century Black America*. Chicago: University of Chicago Press.
hooks, b. (1981). *Ain't I a Woman: Black Women and Feminism*. Boston, MA: South End Press.
King, Jr, M. L. (1968). *The Trumpet of Conscience*. New York: Harper & Row.
Lee, S. (1992). *Malcolm X*. Directed by Spike Lee. Brooklyn: Forty Acres and a Mule Filmworks.
Lorde, A. (1984). *Sister Outsider: Essays and Speeches*. Trumansburg, NY: Crossing Press.
Malcolm X. (1965). *Malcolm X Speaks*. Edited with Prefatory Notes by G. Breitman. New York: Grove Press.
Malcolm X. (1992). *By Any Means Necessary*, 2nd edn. New York: Pathfinder.
Marable, M. (2011). *Malcolm X : A Life of Reinvention*. New York: Viking.
Nation of Islam (2014). "What the Muslims Want." Available online: www.noi.org/muslim_program.htm (accessed May 28, 2014).
Stoddard, L. (1920). *The Rising Tide of Color Against White World-Supremacy*. New York: Scribner.
Thurman, H. (1949). *Jesus and the Disinherited*. New York: Abingdon-Cokesbury Press.
Thurman, H. (1998). *A Strange Freedom: The Best of Howard Thurman on Religious Experience and Public Life,* eds. W. E. Fluker, and C. Tumber. Boston: Beacon Press.
Tunstall, D. A. (2013). *Doing Philosophy Personally : Thinking about Metaphysics, Theism, and Antiblack Racism,* 1st edn. New York: Fordham University Press.
Truth, S. (1851). "Speech Delivered at the Women's Convention, Akron, Ohio, 1851." Available online: www.fordham.edu/halsall/mod/sojtruth-woman.asp (accessed May 28, 2014).
West, C. (1982). *Prophesy Deliverance! An Afro-American Revolutionary Christianity*. Philadelphia: Westminster Press.
West, C. (1993). *Beyond Eurocentrism and Multiculturalism*. Monroe, ME: Common Courage Press.
West, Cornel. 1993. *Prophetic Thought in Postmodern Times*. Monroe, Me: Common Courage Press.
West, C. (1999). *The Cornel West Reader,* 1st edn. New York, NY: Basic Civitas Books.

## Chapter 20

Alberini, C. (1927). "Contemporary Philosophic Tendencies in South America, with Special Reference to Argentina." *The Monist* 37 (3): 328–34.
Alcoff, L. M. (2006). *Visible Identities: Race, Gender, and the Self*. New York: Oxford University Press.
Alcoff, L. M. (2007). "Mignolo's Epistemology of Coloniality." *The New Centennial Review* 7 (3): 79–101.
Alcoff, L. M. (2009). "Latinos Beyond the Binary." *The Southern Journal of Philosophy* 47 (S1): 112–28.
Alinsky, S. D. (1971). *Rules for Radicals; A Practical Primer for Realistic Radicals*. New York: Random House.
Anzaldúa, G. (1999). *Borderlands/La Frontera: The New Mestiza,* 2nd edn. San Francisco: Aunt Lute.
Bennett, W. J. (1992). *The De-valuing of America: The Fight for Our Culture and Our Children*. New York: Summit Books.

# Bibliography

Blanshard, B. (1943). "First Inter-American Conference: Opening Remarks by the Chairman." *Philosophy and Phenomenological Research*, 4 (2): 178–9.

Bloom, A. D. (1987). *The Closing of the American Mind: How Higher Education Has Failed Democracy and Impoverished the Souls of Today's Students*. New York: Simon and Schuster.

Cannabrava, E. (1949). "Present Tendencies in Latin American Philosophy." *The Journal of Philosophy* 46 (5): 113–19.

Chavez, C. (2002). *The Words of César Chávez*, eds. R. J. Jensen, and J. C. Hammerback. College Station: Texas A & M University Press.

D'Souza, D. (1991). *Illiberal Education: The Politics of Race and Sex on Campus*. New York: Free Press.

Dussel, E. D. (1985). *Philosophy of Liberation*. Maryknoll, NY: Orbis Books.

FBI, Federal Bureau of Investigation. (Nd). "Pedro Albizu Campos Part 01 of 01. FBI Records—The Vault." Available online: https://vault.fbi.gov/pedro-albizu-campos/pedro-albizu-campos-part-01-of-01/view (accessed July 21, 2024).

Ferri, J. M. (1988). Pedro Albizu Campos, "El Maestro": Translation and Rhetorical Analysis of Selected Speeches (Publication No. 89112426). Doctoral Dissertation, Temple University. Ann Arbor: UMI.

Flower, E., and M G. Murphey (1977). *A History of Philosophy in America*. New York: Capricorn Books.

Freire, P. (1970/2005). *Pedagogy of the Oppressed*, trans. Myra Bergman Ramos. New York: Continuum.

Frondizi, R. (1951). "On the Unity of the Philosophies of the Two Americas." *The Review of Metaphysics* 4 (4): 617–22.

Gracia, J. J. E., and E. Millán-Zaibert, eds. (2004). *Latin American Philosophy for the 21st Century: The Human Condition, Values, and the Search for Identity*. Amherst, NY: Prometheus Books.

Gutiérrez, G. (1988). *A Theology of Liberation: History, Politics and Salvation*, 15th Anniversary edn. Maryknoll, NY: Orbis.

Henry, P. (2000). *Caliban's Reason: Introducing Afro-Caribbean Philosophy*. New York: Routledge.

Hirsch, E. D. (1987). *Cultural Literacy: What Every American Needs to Know*. Boston: Houghton Mifflin.

MacMullan, T. (2019). ""We love and adore our fatherland like a goddess:" The Radical Catholic Nationalism of Pedro Albizu Campos." *Inter-American Journal of Philosophy* 10 (2): 1–24.

MacMullan, T. (2022). *From American Empire to América Cósmica through Philosophy: Prospero's Reflection*, 1st edn. Lanham, Maryland: The Rowman & Littlefield Publishing Group, Inc.

Mignolo, W. (2000). *Local Histories/Global Designs: Coloniality, Subaltern Knowledges, and Border Thinking*. Princeton, NJ: Princeton University Press.

Milian, Claudia (2019). *LatinX*. Minneapolis: University of Minnesota Press.

Northrop, F. S. C. (1946/1966). *The Meeting of East and West*. New York: Collier Books.

Northrop, F. S. C. (1949). "The Philosophy of Culture and Its Bearing on the Philosophy of History." *Philosophy and Phenomenological Research* 9 (3): 568–75.

Orosco, J. (2008). *Cesar Chavez and the Common Sense of Nonviolence*. Albuquerque: University of New Mexico Press.

PBS. (2022). "How a Trump-Era Policy that Separated Thousands of Migrant Families Came to Pass." Available online: https://www.pbs.org/newshour/show/how-a-trump-era-policy-that-separated-thousands-of-migrant-families-came-to-pass (accessed July 21, 2024).

Quijano, A. (2000). "Coloniality of Power, Eurocentrism, and Latin America." *Nepantla: Views from South* 1 (3): 533–80.

Romanell, P. (1947). "The Background of Contemporary Mexican Thought." *Philosophy and Phenomenological Research* 8 (2): 256–65.

Romanell, P. (1952). *The Making of the Mexican Mind*. Lincoln: Nebraska University Press.

Schneider, H. W. (1946). *A History of American Philosophy*. New York: Columbia University Press.

Schutte, O. (1989). "Philosophy and Feminism in Latin America: Perspectives on Gender Identity and Culture." *Philosophical Forum* 20: 62–84.

Schutte, O. (1993). *Cultural Identity and Social Liberation in Latin American Thought*. Albany, NY: State University of New York Press.

Searle, J. (1990). "The Storm over the University." *New York Review of Books* 37 (19): 34–42.

Southern Poverty Law Center. (2022). *Family Separation—A Timeline*. Available online: https://www.splcenter.org/news/2022/03/23/family-separation-timeline (accessed July 21, 2024).

Stevens-Arroyo, Anthony M. 2002. "The Catholic Worldview in the Political Philosophy of Pedro Albizu Campos: The Death Knoll of Puerto Rican Insularity." U.S. Catholic historian 20.4: 53–73.
Vasconcelos, J. (1922). *La Raza Cósmica*. Paris: Agencia mundial de libreria.
Vasconcelos, J., and M. Gamio (1926). *Aspects of Mexican Civilization*. Chicago: University of Chicago Press.
Young Lords (YLP). (2010). *The Young Lords A Reader*, eds. I. Morales, and D. Oliver-Velez. New York: NYU Press.
Zea, L. (1949). "The Interpenetration of the Ibero-American and North American Cultures." *Philosophy and Phenomenological Research* 9 (3): 538–44.
Zea, L. (1963). *The Latin-American Mind*. Norman, OK: University of Oklahoma Press.
Zea, L. (1968). "Philosophy and Thought in Latin America." *Latin American Research Review* 3 (2): 3–16.
Zea, L. (1969). *Latin America and the World*. Norman, OK: University of Oklahoma Press.
Zea, L. (1989). "Identity: A Latin American Philosophical Problem." *Philosophical Forum* 20: 33–42.

## Chapter 21

Alexander, T. M. (1996). "The Fourth World of American Philosophy: The Philosophical Significance of Native American Culture." *Transactions of the Charles S. Peirce Society* 32 (3): 375–402.
Alfred, G. R. (1999/2009). *Peace, Power, Righteousness: An Indigenous Manifesto*, 2nd edn. Don Mills, ON: Oxford University Press
Black, E., and J. G. Neihardt (1932). *Black Elk Speaks: Being the Life Story of a Holy Man of the Ogalala Sioux*. New York: W. Morrow.
Bunge, R. (1984). *An American Urphilosophie: An American Philosophy, BP (Before Pragmatism)*. Lanham, MD: University Press of America.
Cohen, F. S. (1941). *Handbook of Federal Indian Law*. Available online: http://thorpe.ou.edu/cohen.html (accessed May 28, 2014).
Cohen, Felix S. 1952. Americanizing the White Man. vol. 21. *The American Scholar* Vol. 21 (2): 177–191.
Cohen, F. S. (1960). *The Legal Conscience: Selected Papers of Felix S. Cohen*. New Haven: Yale University Press.
Cordova, V. F. (2007). *How It Is: The Native American Philosophy of V. F. Cordova*, eds. K. D. Moore, and K. Peters. Tucson: University of Arizona Press.
Coulthard, G. S. (2014). *Red Skin, White Masks : Rejecting the Colonial Politics of Recognition*. Minneapolis: University of Minnesota Press.
Deloria, V. (1969). *Custer Died for Your Sins: An Indian Manifesto*. New York: Macmillan.
Deloria, V. (1970). *We Talk, You Listen: New Tribes, New Turf*. New York: Dell Pub.
Deloria, V. (1994). *God Is Red: A Native View of Religion*, 2nd edn. Golden, CO: Fulcrum.
Deloria, V. (1974). *Behind the Trail of Broken Treaties: An Indian Declaration of Independence*. New York: Delacorte Press.
Deloria, V. (1979). *The Metaphysics of Modern Existence*. San Francisco: Harper & Row.
Deloria, V. (1995). *Red Earth, White Lies: Native Americans and the Myth of Scientific Fact*. New York: Scribner.
Deloria, V. (1999a). *For This Land: Writings on Religion in America*, ed. J. Treat. New York: Routledge.
Deloria, V. (1999b). *Spirit and Reason: The Vine Deloria, Jr., Reader*, eds. B. Deloria, K. Foehner, and S. Scinta. Golden, CO: Fulcrum.
Deloria, V. (2002). *Evolution, Creationism, and Other Modern Myths: A Critical Inquiry*. Golden, CO: Fulcrum.
Deloria, V., and C. M. Lytle (1983). *American Indians, American Justice*. Austin: University of Texas Press.
Deloria, V., and D. R. Wildcat (2001). *Power and Place: Indian Education in America*. Golden, CO: Fulcrum.

# Bibliography

Estes, N. (2019). *Our History Is the Future : Standing Rock versus the Dakota Access Pipeline, and the Long Tradition of Indigenous Resistance.* London: Verso.

Estes, N., et al. (2021). *Red Nation Rising : From Bordertown Violence to Native Liberation.* Oakland, CA: PM Press.

Gilio-Whitaker, D. (2019). *As Long as Grass Grows : The Indigenous Fight for Environmental Justice, from Colonization to Standing Rock.* Boston, MA: Beacon Press.

Grande, S. (2004). *Red Pedagogy: Native American Social and Political Thought.* Lanham, MD: Rowman & Littlefield.

Grinde, D. A., and B. E. Johansen (1991). *Exemplar of Liberty: Native America and the Evolution of Democracy.* Los Angeles, CA: American Indian Studies Center, University of California.

Hester, T. L. (2001). *Political Principles and Indian Sovereignty.* London: New York.

Josephy, A. M., J. Nagel, and T. R. Johnson (1999). *Red Power: The American Indians' Fight for Freedom*, 2nd edn. Lincoln: University of Nebraska Press.

Kallen, H. M. (1958). "On 'Americanizing' the American Indian." *Social Research* 25 (4): 469–73.

McNickle, D. A. (1936). *The Surrounded.* New York: Dodd, Mead & Co.

McNickle, D. A. (1973). *Native American Tribalism: Indian Survivals and Renewals.* New York: Published for the Institute of Race Relations by Oxford University Press.

McNickle, D. A. (1978). *Wind from an Enemy Sky.* San Francisco: Harper & Row.

McPherson, D. H., and J. D. Rabb (1993/2011). *Indian from the Inside: Native American Philosophy and Cultural Renewal*, 2nd edn. Jefferson, NC: McFarland.

Pratt, S. L. (2002). *Native Pragmatism: Rethinking the Roots of American Philosophy.* Bloomington, IN: Indiana University Press.

Simpson, L. B. (2017). *As We Have Always Done : Indigenous Freedom through Radical Resistance.* Minneapolis, MN: University of Minnesota Press.

Turner, D. A. (2006). *This Is Not a Peace Pipe: Towards a Critical Indigenous Philosophy.* Toronto: University of Toronto Press.

Vizenor, G. R. (1962). *Two Wings the Butterfly: Haiku Poems in English.* St. Cloud, MN: Priv. Printing.

Vizenor, G. R. (1978). *Darkness in Saint Louis Bearheart.* Saint Paul: Truck Press.

Vizenor, G. R. (1994). *Manifest Manners: Postindian Warriors of Survivance.* Hanover: Wesleyan University Press.

Vizenor, G. R. (1998). *Fugitive Poses: Native American Indian Scenes of Absence and Presence.* Lincoln, NE: University of Nebraska Press.

Weatherford, J. M. I. (1988). *Indian Givers: How the Indians of the Americas Transformed the World.* New York: Crown.

Wilkinson, C. F. (2005). *Blood Struggle: The Rise of Modern Indian Nations.* New York: Norton.

Wilshire, B. W. (2000). *The Primal Roots of American Philosophy: Pragmatism, Phenomenology, and Native American Thought.* University Park, PA: Pennsylvania State University Press.


## Chapter 22

Adams, C. J. (1990). *The Sexual Politics of Meat: A Feminist-Vegetarian Critical Theory.* New York: Continuum.

Adams, C. J. (1994). *Neither Man Nor Beast: Feminism and the Defense of Animals.* New York: Continuum.

Adams, Carol J. 2003. *The Pornography of Meat.* Continuum.

Adams, C., and Lori Gruen (2014). *Ecofeminism: Feminist Interactions with other Animals and the Earth.* New York: Bloomsbury.

Alcoff, L. M. (2003). *Singing in the Fire: Stories of Women in Philosophy.* Lanham, MD: Rowman & Littlefield.

Anderson, E. (2104). "Journeys of a Pragmatist Feminist." *Proceedings and Addresses of the American Philosophical Association* 88: 71–87.

Anzaldúa, G. (1999). *Borderlands/La Frontera: The New Mestiza*, 2nd edn. San Francisco: Aunt Lute.
Bordo, S. (1987). *The Flight to Objectivity: Essays on Cartesianism and Culture*. Albany, NY: State University of New York Press.
Bornstein, K. (1994).*Gender Outlaw: On Men, Women, and the Rest of Us*. New York: Routledge.
Bornstein, K., and S. B. Bergman (2010). *Gender Outlaws: The Next Generation*. Berkeley, CA: Seal Press.
Boston Women's Health Book Collective. (1973). *Our Bodies, Ourselves*. New York: Simon and Schuster.
Brownmiller, S. (1975). *Against Our Will: Men, Women and Rape*. New York: Simon and Schuster.
Butler, J. (1990/1999). *Gender Trouble: Feminism and the Subversion of Identity*. New York: Routledge.
Butler, J. (1993). *Bodies That Matter: On the Discursive Limits of "Sex."* New York: Routledge.
Butler, J. (1997a). *The Psychic Life of Power: Theories in Subjection*. Stanford, CA: Stanford University Press.
Butler, J. (1997b). *Excitable Speech: A Politics of the Performative*. New York: Routledge.
Butler, J. (2003). *Precarious Life: The Powers of Mourning and Violence*. London: Verso.
Butler, J. (2005). *Undoing Gender*. London: Routledge.
Butler, J. (2009). *Frames of War: When Is Life Grievable?* London: Verso.
Card, C. (1991). *Feminist Ethics*. Lawrence, KS: University Press of Kansas.
*Clough, S. (2003). Beyond Epistemology: A Pragmatist Approach to Feminist Science Studies.* New York: Rowman & Littlefield.
Code, L. (1991). *What Can She Know? Feminist Theory and the Construction of Knowledge*. Ithaca: Cornell University Press.
Code, L. (1998). "Feminists and Pragmatists: A Radical Future?" *Radical Philosophy* 87: 22–30.
Code, L. (2006). *Ecological Thinking: The Politics of Epistemic Location*. Oxford: Oxford University Press.
Daly, M. (1973). *Beyond God the Father: Toward a Philosophy of Women's Liberation*. Boston: Beacon Press.
Daly, M. (1978). *Gyn/ecology: The Metaethics of Radical Feminism*. Boston: Beacon Press.
Davis, A. Y. (1972). "The Black Woman's Role in the Community of Slaves." *The Massachusetts Review* 13 (1/2): 81–100.
Davis, A. Y. (1981). *Women, Race, & Class*. New York: Random House.
Diamond, I., and G. F. Orenstein (1990). *Reweaving the World: The Emergence of Ecofeminism*. San Francisco: Sierra Club Books.
Donovan, J., and C. J. Adams, eds. (1996). *Beyond Animal Rights: A Feminist Caring Ethic for the Treatment of Animals*. New York: Continuum.
Donovan, J., and C. J. Adams, eds. (2007). *The Feminist Care Tradition in Animal Ethics: A Reader*. New York: Columbia University Press.
Duran, J. (1991). *Toward a Feminist Epistemology*. Savage, MD: Rowman & Littlefield.
Elshtain, J. B. (1981). *Public Man, Private Woman: Women in Social and Political Thought*. Princeton, NJ: Princeton University Press.
French, M. (1985). *Beyond Power: On Women, Men, and Morals*. New York: Summit Books.
French, M. (1992). *The War Against Women*. New York: Summit Books.
Friedan, B. (1963). *The Feminine Mystique*. New York: W. W. Norton.
Friedling, Melissa, and Susan L. Trollinger (1996). "Reflections and Projections on American Feminism and Culture: An Interview with Gloria Steinem." Available online: https://ecommons.udayton.edu/cgi/viewcontent.cgi?article=1061&context=eng_fac_pub (accessed July 20, 2024).
Frye, M. (1983). *The Politics of Reality: Essays in Feminist Theory*. Trumansburg, NY: Crossing Press.
Gaard, G. C. (1993). *Ecofeminism: Women, Animals, Nature*. Philadelphia: Temple University Press.
Gilligan, C. (1982). *In a Different Voice: Psychological Theory and Women's Development*. Cambridge, MA: Harvard University Press.
Gould, C. C., ed. (1989). *Beyond Domination: New Perspectives on Women and Philosophy*. Totowa, NJ: Rowman & Littlefield.
Griffin, S. (1978). *Woman and Nature: The Roaring Inside Her*. New York: Harper & Row.

# Bibliography

Gruen, L. (2015). *Entangled Empathy: An Alternative Ethic for our Relationship with Animals.* Woodstock, NY: Lantern Publishing.

Gunn Allen, Paula. 1992. *The Sacred Hoop: Recovering the Feminine in American Indian Traditions.* Beacon Press.

Hamington, M., and C. Bardwell-Jones, eds. (2012). *Contemporary Feminist Pragmatism.* New York: Routledge.

Haraway, D. J. (1989). *Primate Visions: Gender, Race, and Nature in the World of Modern Science.* New York: Routledge.

Haraway, D. J. (1991). *Simians, Cyborgs, and Women: The Reinvention of Nature.* New York: Routledge.

Haraway, D. J. (2003). *The Companion Species Manifesto: Dogs, People, and Significant Otherness.* Chicago: Prickly Paradigm Press.

Haraway, D. J. (2008). *When Species Meet.* Minneapolis: University of Minnesota Press.

Harding, S. G. (1986). *The Science Question in Feminism.* Ithaca: Cornell University Press.

Harding, S. G., and M. B. Hintikka, eds. (1983). *Discovering Reality: Feminist Perspectives on Epistemology, Metaphysics, Methodology, and Philosophy of Science.* Dordrecht, Holland: D. Reidel.

Held, V. (1993). *Feminist Morality: Transforming Culture, Society, and Politics.* Chicago: University of Chicago Press.

Hill-Collins, P. (1990). *Black Feminist Thought: Knowledge, Consciousness, and the Politics of Empowerment.* New York: Routledge.

Hill-Collins, P. (2011). "Piecing Together a Genealogical Puzzle: Intersectionality and American Pragmatism." *European Journal of Pragmatism and American Philosophy* 3 (2): 1–27.

Hill-Collins, P. (2019). *Intersectionality as Critical Social Theory.* Durham: Duke University Press.

Hoagland, S. L. (1988). *Lesbian Ethics: Toward New Value.* Palo Alto, CA: Institute of Lesbian Studies.

hooks, b. (1981). *Ain't I a Woman: Black Women and Feminism.* Boston, MA: South End Press.

hooks, b. (1984). *Feminist Theory from Margin to Center.* Boston, MA: South End Press.

Jaggar, A. M. (1983). *Feminist Politics and Human Nature.* Totowa, NJ: Rowman & Allanheld.

Jaggar, A. M., and S. Bordo, eds. (1989). *Gender/Body/Knowledge: Feminist Reconstructions of Being and Knowing.* New Brunswick, NJ: Rutgers University Press.

Keller, E. F. (1985). *Reflections on Gender and Science.* New Haven: Yale University Press.

Lavery, G. E. (2023). *Pleasure and Ecstasy: Of Pen Names, Cover Versions, and Other Trans Techniques.* Princeton: Princeton University Press.

Lloyd, G. (1984). *The Man of Reason: "Male" and "Female" in Western Philosophy.* Minneapolis: University of Minnesota Press.

Lorde, A. (1984). *Sister Outsider: Essays and Speeches.* Trumansburg, NY: Crossing Press.

Lorde, A. (1985). "Neighbourhood Voices: Audrey Lorde Interview." Available online: http://herstories.prattinfoschool.nyc/omeka/items/show/972, http://herstories.prattinfoschool.nyc/omeka/items/show/973 (accessed July 20, 2024).

McBride, L., and E. McKenna, eds. (2022). *Pragmatist Feminism and the Work of Charlene Haddock Seigfried.* New York: Bloomsbury.

McKenna, E. (2001). *The Task of Utopia: A Pragmatist and Feminist Perspective.* New York: Rowman & Littlefield.

McKenna, E. (2013). *Pets, People, and Pragmatism.* New York: Fordham University Press.

McKenna, E. (2018). *Livestock: Food, Fiber, and Friends.* Athens GA: University of Georgia Press.

McKenna, E. (2021). *Living With Animals: Rights, Responsibilities, and Respect.* New York: Rowman & Littlefield.

Merchant, C. (1980). *The Death of Nature: Women, Ecology, and the Scientific Revolution.* San Francisco: Harper & Row.

McBride, Lee and Erin McKenna, eds. 2022. *Pragmatist Feminism and the Work of Charlene Haddock Seigfried.* Bloomsbury Press.

Mies, M., and V. Shiva (2010, 2014). *Ecofeminism.* London: Zed Books.

Moore, H. Jr. (2016). "Angela—Symbol of Resistance." In Angles Y. Davis (ed.), *If they Come in the Morning... Voices of Resistance*, 203–212 London: Verso.

# Bibliography

Moraga, C., and G. Anzaldúa, eds. (1981). *This Bridge Called My Back: Writings by Radical Women of Color*. Watertown, MA: Persephone.
Okin, S. M. (1989). *Justice, Gender, and the Family*. New York: Basic Books.
Pateman, C. (1988). *The Sexual Contract*. Stanford, CA: Stanford University Press.
Plumwood, V. (1993). *Feminism and the Mastery of Nature*. New York: Routledge.
Plumwood, V. (2001). *Environmental Culture: The Ecological Crisis of Reason*. New York: Routledge.
Rich, A. (1976). *Of Woman Born: Motherhood as Experience and Institution*. New York: Norton.
Ruddick, S. (1989). *Maternal Thinking: Toward a Politics of Peace*. Boston: Beacon Press.
Russ, J. (1975). *The Female Man*. New York: Bantam Books.
Seigfried, C. H. (1996). *Pragmatism and Feminism: Reweaving the Social Fabric*. Chicago: University of Chicago Press.
Seigfried, C. H. (2001). "John Dewey's Pragmatist Feminism." In Shannon Sullivan and Nancy Tuana *Feminist Interpretations of John Dewey*, 47–77. University Park: Penn State University Press.
Seigfried, Charlene Haddock. 1991. "Where are all the Pragmatist Feminists?" in *Hypatia*, Vol 6. No. 2, pp. 1-20.
Shiva, V. (1988, 2016). *Staying Alive: Women, Ecology, and Development*. Berkeley: North Atlantic Books.
Shiva, V. (2005, 2015). *Earth Democracy: Justice, Sustainability, and Peace*. Berkeley: North Atlantic Books.
Shuford, A. (2010). *Feminist Epistemology and American Pragmatism: Dewey and Quine*. New York Bloomsbury.
Sorrell K. (2004). *Representative Practices: Peirce, Pragmatism, and Feminist Epistemology*. New York: Fordham University Press.
Spelman, E. V. (1988). *Inessential Woman: Problems of Exclusion Feminist Thought*. Boston, MA: Beacon Press.
Steinem, G. (1969). "After Black Power, Women's Liberation." *New York Magazine,* April 7.
Steinem, G. (2004). "Leaps of Consciousness." Available online: https://www.feminist.com/resources/artspeech/genwom/evespeechwp.html (accessed July 20, 2024).
Steinem, Gloria (2019). *Outrageous Acts and Everyday Rebellions*, third edition. Picador.
Sullivan, S. (2001). *Living Across and Through Skins: Transactional Bodies, Pragmatism, and Feminism*. Bloomington: Indiana University Press.
Trout, L. (2010). *The Politics of Survival: Peirce, Affectivity, and Social Criticism*. New York: Fordham University Press.
Tuana, N. (1992). *Woman and the History of Philosophy*. New York: Paragon House.
Waithe, M. E. (1987). *A History of Women Philosophers*. Dordrecht: M. Nijhoff [puis] Kluwer Academic.
Walker, A. (1983). *In Search of Our Mothers Gardens: Womanist Prose*. Fort Washington, PA: Harvest Books.
Wallace, M. (1979). *Black Macho and the Myth of the Superwoman*. New York: Dial Press.
Warren, K. (2000). *Ecofeminist Philosophy: A Western Perspective on What it Is and Why it Matters*. Lanham, MD: Rowman & Littlefield.
Warren, K., ed. (2009). *An Unconventional History of Western Philosophy: Conversations between Men and Women Philosophers*. Lanham, MD: Rowman & Littlefield.
Woodly, D. R. (2021). *Reckoning: Black Lives Matter and the Democratic Necessity of Social Movements*. Oxford: Oxford University Press.
Young, I. M. (1990). *Justice and the Politics of Difference*. Princeton, NJ: Princeton University Press.
Zack, N., ed. (2000). *Women of Color and Philosophy: A Critical Reader*. Malden, MA: Blackwell.

## Chapter 23

Blackstone, W. T. (1974). *Philosophy & Environmental Crisis*. Athens, OH: University of Georgia Press.

# Bibliography

Calarco, M., and P. Atterton, eds. (2004). *Animal Philosophy: Essential Readings in Continental Thought: Ethics and Identity*. London: Continuum.
Carson, R. (1941). *Under the Sea Wind*. New York: Simon and Schuster.
Carson, R. (1951). *The Sea Around Us*. London: Oxford University Press.
Carson, R. (1955). *The Edge of the Sea*. Boston: Houghton Mifflin.
Carson, R. (1962). *Silent Spring*. Boston: Houghton Mifflin.
Deloria, V. (1969). *Custer Died for Your Sins: An Indian Manifesto*. New York: Macmillan.
Dewey, J., and J. H. Tufts (1932). *Ethics*. New York: H. Holt.
Dewey, J. (1989). *A Common Faith*, in *John Dewey, Later Works: Vol. 9: 1933–1934*, ed. Jo Ann Boydston. Carbondale: Southern Illinois University Press.
Foltz, B. V., and R. Frodeman, eds. (2004). *Rethinking Nature: Essays in Environmental Philosophy*. Bloomington, IN: Indiana University Press.
Hardin, G. (1968). "The Tragedy of the Commons." *Science* 162: 1243–8.
Hargrove, E. (2012). Personal interview with E. McKenna.
Josephy, A. M., J. Nagel, and T. R. Johnson (1999). *Red Power: The American Indians' Fight for Freedom*, 2nd edn. Lincoln: University of Nebraska Press.
Katz, E. (1997). *Nature as Subject: Human Obligation and Natural Community*. New York Rowman & Littlefield.
King, Jr, M. L. (1986). *A Testament of Hope*. San Francisco: Harper & Row.
Kinkela, D. (2011). *DDT and the American Century: Global Health, Environmental Politics, and the Pesticide That Changed the World*. Durham, NC: University of North Carolina Press.
Krutch, J. W. (1929). *The Modern Temper: A Study and Confession*. San Diego: Harcourt, Brace and Co.
Krutch, J. W. (1952a). *The Desert Year*. New York: Viking.
Krutch, J. W. (1952b/1978). *The Measure of Man: On Freedom, Human Values, Survival, and the Modern Temper*. Gloucester, MA: Peter Smith.
Krutch, J. W. (1955). *The Voice of the Desert*. New York: W. Sloane Associates.
Krutch, J. W. (1956). *The Great Chain of Life*. Boston: Houghton Mifflin.
Krutch, J. W. (1958). *Grand Canyon*. New York: W. Sloane Associates.
Krutch, J. W. (1961). *The Forgotten Peninsula: A Naturalist in Baja California*. New York: W. Sloane Associates.
Krutch, J. W. (1967). *And Even If You Do: Essays on Man, Manners, and Machines*. New York: William Morrow.
Leopold, A. (1949). *A Sand County Almanac, and Sketches Here and There*. New York: Oxford University Press.
Leopold, A. (1999). *For the Health of the Land: Previously Unpublished Essays and Other Writings*, eds. J. B. Callicott, and E. T. Freyfogle. Washington, DC: Island Press [for] Shearwater Books.
Light, A., and E. Katz, eds. (1996). *Environmental Pragmatism*. London: Routledge.
Lytle, M. H. (2007). *The Gentle Subversive: Rachel Carson, Silent Spring, and the Rise of the Environmental Movement*. New York: Oxford University Press.
McDonald, H. P. (2004). *John Dewey and Environmental Philosophy*. Albany, NY: State University of New York Press.
McKenna, E., and A. Light, eds. (2004). *Animal Pragmatism: Rethinking Human-Nonhuman Relationships*. Bloomington, IN: Indiana University Press.
McKenna, E. (2013). *Pets, People, and Pragmatism*. New York: Fordham University Press.
McKenna, E. (2018). *Livestock: Food, Fiber, and Friends*. Athens GA: University of Georgia Press.
McKenna, E. (2021). *Living With Animals: Rights, Responsibilities, and Respect*. New York: Rowman & Littlefield.
Minteer, B. A. (2012). *Refounding Environmental Ethics: Pragmatism, Principle, and Practice*. Philadelphia: Temple University Press.
Minteer, B. A. (2019) *The Fall of the Wild*. New York: Columbian University Press.
Mies, M. (1993). "The Myth of Catching-Up Development." In M. Mies, and V. Shiva (eds.), *Ecofeminism*, 55–69. Atlantic Highlands, NJ: Zed Books.

Naess, A. (1973). "The Shallow and the Deep, Long-range Ecology Movement. A Summary." *Inquiry* 16 (1–4): 95–100.
Newton, J. L. (2008). *Aldo Leopold's Odyssey*. Washington: Island Press/Shearwater Books.
Norton, B. G. (2005). *Sustainability: A Philosophy of Adaptive Ecosystem Management*. Chicago: University of Chicago Press.
Plumwood, V. (1993). *Feminism and the Mastery of Nature*. New York: Routledge.
Plumwood, V. (2001). *Environmental Culture: The Ecological Crisis of Reason*. New York: Routledge.
Pokagon, S. (2001). "Simon Pokagon Offers *The Red Man's Greeting*." In F. E. Hoxie (ed.), *Talking Back to Civilization: Indian Voices from the Progressive Era*. Boston: Bedford/St. Martins.
Ralston, S. (2013). *Pragmatic Environmentalism: Towards a Rhetoric of Eco-justice*. Kibworth, Leicester: Troubador.
Rolston, H. (1975). "Is There an Ecological Ethic?" *Ethics* 18 (2): 93–109.
Stone, C. D. (1972/2010). *Should Trees Have Standing? Law, Morality, and the Environment*. New York: Oxford University Press.
Sylvan, R. (1973). "Is There a Need for a New, an Environmental, Ethic?" In Andrew Light and Holmes Rolston III *Environmental Ethics: An Anthology*, 47–52.
Weston, A. (1994). *Back to Earth: Tomorrow's Environmentalism*. Philadelphia: Temple University Press.
White, L. (1967). "The Historical Roots of Our Ecological Crisis." *Science* 161: 1203–7.
Worster, D. (2008). *A Passion for Nature: The Life of John Muir*. New York: Oxford University Press.

## Chapter 24

Ayer, A. J. (1968). *The Origins of Pragmatism: Studies in the Philosophy of Charles Peirce and William James*. London: Macmillan.
Bacon, M. (2012). *Pragmatism: An Introduction*. Boston: Polity.
Bernstein, R. J. (1966). *John Dewey*. New York: Washington Square Press.
Bernstein, R. J. (2003). "Rorty's Inspirational Liberalism." In Charles Guignon and David R. Hiley *Richard Rorty*, 124–138. London: Cambridge University Press.
Campbell, J., and R. E. Hart, eds. (2006). *Experience as Philosophy: On the Work of John J. McDermott*. New York: Fordham University Press.
Daniel, G. R., and H. V. Williams (2014). *Race and the Obama Phenomenon*. Jackson, MS: University Press of Mississippi.
Galbraith, J. K. (1952). *American Capitalism: The Concept of Countervailing Power*. Boston: Houghton Mifflin.
Galbraith, J. K. (1954). *The Great Crash of 1929*. New York: Houghton Mifflin.
Galbraith, J. K. (1958a). *The Affluent Society*. New York: Houghton Mifflin.
Galbraith, J. K. (1958b). "How Much Should a Country Consume." In J. K. Galbraith, H. Jarrett, and R. F. T. Future (eds.), *Perspectives on Conservation: Essays on America's Natural Resources*, 89–99. Baltimore: Johns Hopkins Press.
Galbraith, J. K. (1973). *Economics and the Public Purpose*. Boston: Houghton Mifflin.
Galbraith, J. K. (1977). *The Age of Uncertainty*. Boston: Houghton Mifflin.
Galbraith, J. K. (1983). *The Anatomy of Power*. New York: Houghton Mifflin Harcourt.
Galbraith, J. K. (1992). *The Culture of Contentment*. New York: Houghton Mifflin.
Gross, N. (2008). *Richard Rorty: The Making of an American Philosopher*. Chicago: University of Chicago Press.
Hall, D. L. (1994). *Richard Rorty: Prophet and Poet of the New Pragmatism*. Albany, NY: State University of New York Press.
Kitcher, P. (2011). *The Ethical Project*. Cambridge, MA: Harvard University Press.
Kitcher, P. (2012). *Preludes to Pragmatism: Toward a Reconstruction of Philosophy*. New York: Oxford University Press.

# Bibliography

Loh, T. H., C. Coes, and B. Buthe (2020). "The Great Real Estate Reset." *Brookings Institution*. Available online: https://www.brookings.edu/articles/trend-1-separate-and-unequal-neighborhoods-are-sustaining-racial-and-economic-injustice-in-the-us/ (accessed 23 July 2024) .

McDermott, J. J. (1976). *The Culture of Experience: Philosophical Essays in the American Grain*. New York: New York University Press.

McDermott, J. J., ed. (1978.) *The Writings of William James: A Comprehensive Edition*. Chicago: University of Chicago Press.

McDermott, J. J. (1986). *Streams of Experience: Reflections on the History and Philosophy of American Culture*. Amherst: University of Massachusetts Press.

McDermott, J. J., ed. (2005). *The Basic Writings of Josiah Royce*, vols. I and II. New York: Fordham University Press.

McDermott, J. J. (2007). *The Drama of Possibility: Experience as Philosophy of Culture,* ed. D. Anderson. New York: Fordham University Press.

Mills, C. W. (1950). *The Puerto Rican Journey: New York's Newest Migrants*. New York: Harper.

Mills, C. W. (1951). *White Collar: The American Middle Classes*. New York: Oxford University Press.

Mills, C. W. (1956). *The Power Elite*. New York: Oxford University Press.

Mills, C. W. (1960). *Listen Yankee: The Revolution in Cuba*. New York: Ballantine Books.

Mills, C. W. (1964). *Sociology and Pragmatism*. New York: Oxford University Press.

Misak, C. J. (2013). *The American Pragmatists*. Oxford: Oxford University Press.

Mumford, L. (1922). *The Story of Utopias*. New York: Boni and Liveright.

Mumford, L. (1926). *The Golden Day: A Study in American Experience and Culture*. Boston: Beacon Press.

Mumford, L. (1944). *The Condition of Man*. London: Martin Secker & Warburg.

Mumford, L. (1967). *The Myth of the Machine: Technics and Human Development*. New York: Harcourt Brace Jovanovich.

Mumford, L. (1970). *The Myth of the Machine: The Pentagon of Power*. New York: Harcourt Brace Jovanovich.

Perry, R. B. (1948). *The Thought and Character of William James*. Cambridge: Harvard University Press.

Porter, N. (1868). *The Human Intellect with an Introduction upon Psychology and the Human Soul*. New York: C. Scribner.

Putnam, H. (1975). *Mind, Language, and Reality*. Cambridge [Eng.]: Cambridge University Press.

Putnam, H. (1981). *Reason, Truth, and History*. Cambridge [Cambridgeshire]: Cambridge University Press.

Putnam, H. (1983). *Realism and Reason*. Cambridge [Cambridgeshire]: Cambridge University Press.

Putnam, H. (1988). *Representation and Reality*. Cambridge, MA: MIT Press.

Putnam, H. (1992). *Renewing Philosophy*. Cambridge, MA: Harvard University Press.

Putnam, H. (1995). *Pragmatism: An Open Question*. Oxford, UK: Blackwell.

Putnam, R. A., ed. (1997). *The Cambridge Companion to William James*. Cambridge: Cambridge University Press.

Rogers, M. (2023). *The Darkened Light of Faith*. Princeton: Princeton University Press.

Rorty, R. (1961). "Recent Metaphilosophy." *The Review of Metaphysics* 15 (2): 299–318.

Rorty, R. (1967). *The Linguistic Turn: Recent Essays in Philosophical Method*. Chicago: University of Chicago Press.

Rorty, R. (1979). *Philosophy and the Mirror of Nature*. Princeton: Princeton University Press.

Rorty, R. (1982). *Consequences of Pragmatism: Essays, 1972–1980*. Minneapolis: University of Minnesota Press.

Rorty, R. (1989). *Contingency, Irony, and Solidarity*. Cambridge: Cambridge University Press.

Rorty, R. (1991). *Objectivity, Relativism, and Truth*. Cambridge: Cambridge University Press.

Rorty, R. (1995). "The Demonization of Multiculturalism." *The Journal of Blacks in Higher Education* 7: 74–75.

Rorty, R. (1998). *Achieving Our Country: Leftist Thought in Twentieth-Century America*. Cambridge, MA: Harvard University Press.

Rorty, R. (1999). *Philosophy and Social Hope*. New York: Penguin Books.

Rorty, R. (2002). "Fighting Terrorism with Democracy." *Nation* 275 (13): 11–13.
Smith, J. E. (1950). *Royce's Social Infinite: The Community of Interpretation*. New York: Liberal Arts Press.
Smith, J. E. (1963). *The Spirit of American Philosophy*. New York: Oxford University Press.
Smith, J. E. (1978). *Purpose and Thought: The Meaning of Pragmatism*. New Haven: Yale University Press.
Smith, J. E. (1992). *America's Philosophical Vision*. Chicago: University of Chicago Press.
Tillman, R. C. (1984). *C. Wright Mills: A Native Radical and His American Intellectual Roots*. University Park, PA: Pennsylvania State University Press.
Veblen, T. (1899/1994). *The Theory of the Leisure Class*. Introduction by R. Lekachman. New York: Penguin Books.
White, M. G. (1973). *Pragmatism and the American Mind: Essays and Reviews in Philosophy and Intellectual History*. New York: Oxford University Press.

## Chapter 25

Baker, A. (2013). "Culture Warrior, Gaining Ground: E. D. Hirsch Sees His Education Theories Taking Hold." *New York Times*, September 27.
Bell, D. (1992). "The Cultural Wars: American Intellectual Life, 1965–1992." *Wilson Quarterly* 16 (2): 74–107.
Bell, D. (2000). *The End of Ideology: On the Exhaustion of Political Ideas in the Fifties*. Cambridge, MA: Harvard University Press.
Bennett, W. J. (1992). *The De-valuing of America: The Fight for Our Culture and Our Children*. New York: Summit Books.
Bennett, W. J. (2006–2007). *America: The Last Best Hope*, vol. 2. Nashville, TN: Nelson Current.
Bennett, W. J., and D. Wilezol (2013). *Is College Worth It? A Former United States Secretary of Education and a Liberal Arts Graduate Expose the Broken Promise of Higher Education*. Nashville, TN: Nelson Current.
Bennett, W. J., J. J. DiIulio, and J. P. Walters (1996). *Body Count: Moral Poverty . . . and How to Win America's War Against Crime and Drugs*. New York: Simon & Schuster.
Bernstein, R. J. (1971). *Praxis and Action*. London: Duckworth.
Bernstein, R. J. (1976). *The Restructuring of Social and Political Theory*. New York: Harcourt Brace Jovanovich.
Bernstein, R. J. (1983). *Beyond Objectivism and Relativism: Science, Hermeneutics, and Praxis*. Philadelphia: University of Pennsylvania Press.
Bernstein, R. J. (1992). *The New Constellation: The Ethical-Political Horizons of Modernity/Postmodernity*. Cambridge, MA: MIT Press.
Bernstein, R. J. (2005). *The Abuse of Evil: The Corruption of Politics and Religion Since 9/11*. Malden, MA: Polity Press.
Bernstein, R. J. (2010). *The Pragmatic Turn*. Cambridge, UK: Polity Press.
Bloom, A. (1987). *The Closing of the American Mind*. New York: Simon and Schuster.
Buchanan, P. (1992). "Republican Convention Address." Available online: http://buchanan.org/blog/1992-republican-national-convention-speech-148 (accessed April 14, 2014).
Buckley, W. F. (1951). *God and Man at Yale: The Superstitions of Academic Freedom*. Chicago: Regnery.
Buckley, W. F. (1954). *McCarthy and His Enemies*. Chicago: Henry Regnery.
Buckley, W. F. (1997). *Nearer, My God: An Autobiography of Faith*. New York: Doubleday.
Buckley, W. F., and P. J. Dos (1959). *Up from Liberalism*. New York: McDowell, Obolensky.
Chomsky, N. (1967). The Responsibility of Intellectuals (Book Review). *The New York Review of Books*, February 23.
Chomsky, N. (1969). *American Power and the New Mandarins*. New York: Pantheon Books.

## Bibliography

Chomsky, N. (1977). *Intellectuals and the State*. Available online: https://www.ditext.com/chomsky/is.html (accessed July 23, 2024).
Chomsky, N. (1982). *Towards a New Cold War: Essays on the Current Crisis and How We Got There*. New York: Pantheon Books.
Chomsky, N. (1988). *The Culture of Terrorism*. Boston, MA: South End Press.
Chomsky, N. (1989). *Necessary Illusions: Thought Control in Democratic Societies*. Boston, MA: South End Press.
Chomsky, N. (1997). *The Cold War & the University: Toward an Intellectual History of the Postwar Years*. New York: New Press.
Chomsky, N. (2000a). *Chomsky on Miseducation*, ed. D. P. Macedo. Lanham, MD: Rowman & Littlefield.
Chomsky, N. (2001). *9-11*. New York: Seven Stories Press.
Chomsky, N. (2002). "On the War on Drugs." Available online: www.chomsky.info/interviews/20020208.htm (accessed October 22, 2012 and May 28, 2014.).
Chomsky, N. (2003). *Hegemony or Survival: America's Quest for Global Dominance*. New York: Metropolitan Books.
Chomsky, N. (2003b). "The Function of Schools." In K. J. Saltman, and D. Gabbard (eds.), *Education as Enforcement: The Militarization and Corporatization of Schools*, 26–35. New York ; Routledge Falmer.
Chomsky, N. (2011). "Noam Chomsky: My Reaction to Osama bin Laden's Death." Available online: www.guernicamag.com/daily/noam_chomsky_my_reaction_to_os/ (accessed October 22, 2012).
Davaney, S. G., and W. G. Frisina (2006). *The Pragmatic Century: Conversations with Richard J. Bernstein*. Albany: State University of New York Press.
Dewey, J. (1960). *John Dewey on Experience, Nature, and Freedom. Representative Selections*, ed. R. J. Bernstein. New York: Liberal Arts Press.
D'Souza, D. (1991). *Illiberal Education: The Politics of Race and Sex on Campus*. New York: Free Press.
D'Souza, D. (1995). *The End of Racism: Principles for a Multiracial Society*. New York: Free Press.
D'Souza, D. (2007). *The Enemy at Home: The Cultural Left and Its Responsibility for 9/11*. New York: Doubleday.
D'Souza, D. (2010). *The Roots of Obama's Rage*. Washington, DC: Regnery Pub.
D'Souza, D. (2012). *Obama's America: Unmaking the American Dream*. Washington, DC: Regnery Pub.
Hirsch, E. D. (1987). *Cultural Literacy: What Every American Needs to Know*. Boston: Houghton Mifflin.
Hirsch, E. D. (1996). *The Schools We Need and Why We Don't Have Them*. New York: Doubleday.
Hook, S. (1989). "*The Closing of the American Mind*: An Intellectual Best-seller Revisited." *American Scholar* 58 (1): 123–35.
Rorty, R. (1998). "That Old-Time Philosophy." *The New Republic* April 4: 28–33.
Vidal, G., and W. F. Buckley (1968). "ABC Television Debate." Available online: https://www.youtube.com/watch?v=ZY_nq4tfi24 (accessed April 14, 2014.)

## Chapter 26

Anzaldúa, G. (1999). *Borderlands/La Frontera: The New Mestiza*, 2nd edn. San Francisco: Spinsters, Aunt Lute.
Bernstein, R. J. (1971). *Praxis and Action*. London: Duckworth.
Boggs, G. L. (1998). *Living for Change an Autobiography*. Minneapolis: University of Minnesota Press.
Boggs, G. L., and S. Kurashige. (2012). *The next American Revolution : Sustainable Activism for the Twenty-First Century*. Updated & Expanded edn. Berkeley, CA: University of California Press.
Boggs, J., and G. L. Boggs. (1974/2008). *Revolution and Evolution in the Twentieth Century*. New York: Monthly Review Press.
Boggs, J., and S. M. Ward. (2011). *Pages from a Black Radical's Notebook : A James Boggs Reader*. Detroit: Wayne State University Press.

Colapeitro, V. (2007). "'Di al tuo amico Giuliano…' Gli entusiasmi di James e le riserve di Peirce," ["'Tell your friend Julian…' James's enthusiasms and Peirce's reservations]. In G. Maddalena, and G. Tuzet (eds.), *I pragmatisti italiani tra alleati e nemici* [The Italian pragmatists between allies and enemies], 97–114. Milano: AlboVersorio.

Cone, J. H. (1969). *Black Theology and Black Power*. New York: Seabury Press.

Boydston, J. A. (1967–1990). *John Dewey: Early Works 1882–1898; Middle Works 1899–1924; The Later Works: 1925–1953*. Carbondale: Southern Illinois University Press.

Diggins, J. P. (2015). *Mussolini and Fascism: The View from America,* 1st edn. Princeton: Princeton University Press

Du Bois, W. E. B. (1970). *Dusk of Dawn: An Essay Toward an Autobiography of a Race Concept*. New Brunswick, NJ: Transaction.

Dunbar-Ortiz, R. (2015). *An Indigenous Peoples' History of the United States*. Boston: Beacon Press.

Elliot, W. Y. (1926). "Mussolini, Prophet of the Pragmatic Era in Politics." *Political Science Quarterly* 41 (2): 161–92.

Emerson, R. W. (1860). *The Conduct of Life*. New York: Houghton, Mifflin, and Company.

Follett, M. P. (1924). *Creative Experience*. New York: Longmans, Green and Co.

Harris, L. (1983). *Philosophy Born of Struggle: An Anthology of Afro American Philosophy from 1917*. Dubuque, IA: Kendall/Hunt Publishing Co.

Harris, L., ed. (1999). *The Critical Pragmatism of Alain Locke*.Latham, MD: Rowman and Littlefield .

Harris, L., and C. Molesworth (2008). *Alain L. Locke: The Biography of a Philosopher*. Chicago: University of Chicago Press.

King, Jr, M. L. (1986). *A Testament of Hope*. San Francisco: Harper & Row.

Locke, A., and B. J. Stern (1946). *When Peoples Meet: A Study in Race and Culture Contacts*. New York: Hinds, Hayden & Eldredge.

Locke, A. (1989). *The Philosophy of Alain Locke: Harlem Renaissance and Beyond,* ed. L. Harris. Philadelphia: Temple University Press.

McBride, L. III, ed. (2020). *A Philosophy of Struggle: The Leonard Harris Rea*der. London: Bloomsbury.

McBride, L. III, ed. (2021). *Ethics and Insurrections: A Pragmatism for the Oppressed*. London; Bloomsbury.

McDermott, J. (2007). *The Drama of Possibility: Experience as Philosophy of Culture,* ed. D. Anderson. New York: Fordham University Press.

Maddalena, G. (2019). "Vailati, Papini, and the Synthetic Drive of Italian Pragmatism." *European Journal of Pragmatism and American Philosophy* 9: 1. Available online: https://journals.openedition.org/ejpap/1533 (accessed July 23, 2024).

Mills, C. W. (1956). *The Power Elite*. New York: Oxford University Press.

Mills, C. W. (1958). "The Structure of Power in American Society." *The British Journal of Sociology* 9 (1): 29–41.

Mumford, L. (1970). *The Myth of the Machine: The Pentagon of Power*. New York: Harcourt Brace Jovanovich.

Shoemaker, N. (1999). *American Indian Population Recovery in the Twentieth Century,* 1st edn. Albuquerque: University of New Mexico Press.

Stannard, D. E. (1992). *American Holocaust : Columbus and the Conquest of the New World*. New York: Oxford University Press.

West, C. (1982). *Prophesy Deliverance! An Afro-American Revolutionary Christianity*. Philadelphia: Westminster Press.

West, C. (1989). *The American Evasion of Philosophy: A Genealogy of Pragmatism*. Madison: University of Wisconsin Press.

West, C. (1991). *The Ethical Dimensions of Marxist Thought*. New York: Monthly Review Press.

West, C. (1993a/2009). *Keeping Faith: Philosophy and Race in America*, 2nd edn. New York: Routledge.

West, C. (1993b). *Race Matters*. Boston: Beacon Press.

West, C. (1999). *The Cornel West Reader*. New York: Basic Civitas Books.

West, C. (2004). *Democracy Matters: Winning the Fight Against Imperialism*. New York: Penguin Press.

# Bibliography

West, C. (2024). "Cornel West [for President]." Available online: https://www.cornelwest2024.com (accessed July 22, 2024).

Woodly, D. R. (2021). *Reckoning: Black Lives Matter and the Democratic Necessity of Social Movements.* Oxford: Oxford University Press.

# Epilogue

Addams, J. (1930). "Immigration under the Quota," *Second Twenty Years at Hull House.* New York: Macmillan, 263-303.

Barnes, C. L. (2023) *Alain Locke on the Theoretical Foundations for a Just and Successful Peace,* 1st edn. Cham, Switzerland: Palgrave Macmillan.

Bernstein, R. (2002). *Radical Evil: A Philosophical Interrogation.* Cambridge, UK: Polity Press.

Bernstein, R. (2005). *The Abuse of Evil: The Corruption of Politics and Religion since 9/11.* Malden, MA: Polity Press.

Bukowski, D. (2013). "Big Bill Thompson: The Model Politician." In P. M. Green and M. G. Holli (eds.), *The Mayors: The Chicago Political Tradition,* 4th edn, 61–81. Carbondale, IL: Southern Illinois University Press.

Carson, R. (1962). *Silent Spring.* Boston: Houghton Mifflin.

Diamond, A. (2018). "Who Put America First?" *Smithsonian Magazine,* vol. 49. Available online: https://www.smithsonianmag.com/history/behold-america-american-dream-slogan-book-sarah-churchwell-180970311/

Harris, L., S. L. Pratt, and A. Waters. (2002) *American Philosophies : An Anthology.* Malden, MA: Blackwell Publishers.

Kloppenberg, J. T. (2012). *The Education of Barack Obama.* Princeton: Princeton University Press.

McIntyre, L. C. (2018) *Post-Truth.* Cambridge, MA: The MIT Press.

Nichols, J. (2017). "Chicago mayor Big Bill Thompson used "America First" decades before Trump." *The Chicago Reader* (June 2). Available online: https://chicagoreader.com/blogs/chicago-mayor-big-bill-thompson-used-america-first-decades-before-trump/ (accessed July 24, 2024).

Obama, B. H. (2024) "My Remarks at the 2024 Obama Foundation Democracy Forum." *Medium.* Available online: https://barackobama.medium.com/my-remarks-at-the-2024-obama-foundation-democracy-forum-4043c5c7b2a2 (accessed December 9, 2024.

Pratt, S. L. (2022). "Vital Lies and the Fate of Democracy." In P. M. Shields, M. Hamington, and J. Soeters (eds.), *The Oxford Handbook of Jane Addams,* 55–74. Oxford University Press.

Schottenhamel, G. (1952). "How Big Bill Thompson won control of Chicago." *Journal of the Illinois State Historical Society (1908-1984)* 45 (1): 30–49.

Seigfried, C. H. (2008). "The Courage of One's Convictions or the Conviction of One's Courage? Jane Addams's Principled Compromise." In M. Fischer, C. Nacenoff, and W. Chmielewski (eds.), *Jane Addams and the Practice of Democracy,* 40–59. Champaign: University of Illinois Press.

Smith, J. E. (1963). *The Spirit of American Philosophy.* New York: Oxford University Press.

# INDEX

Abbott, Lyman   25
Absolute Idealism   177
Absolute Pragmatism   372
absolutism   148, 159–61, 174, 304, 315, 345, 359, 375
academia   176, 317, 361
activism   41, 64, 94, 100, 173, 211, 215, 232, 248, 259, 267, 271, 277, 279, 285, 320, 347, 353–4, 376, 378
Adams, Carol J.   285
Adams, Hank   248, 256
Addams, Jane   34–6, 39, 61–7, 99–104, 119–20, 145–6, 270–1, 277–9, 287, 332, 357–8, 366–7, 374, 378–80
Adjusted Compensation Payment Act   164
Afghanistan   xiii–xiv, 343, 376
agency   11, 18, 48, 153, 209, 213, 233, 252, 273, 362–4, 366–8
agent ontology   251–2, 257
agents   71, 74–5, 90–1, 108, 143–4, 150, 153, 175, 251, 277, 359, 363, 367–8; *see also* agent ontology; person
Agricultural Workers Organizing Committee (AWOC)   230
Alcoff, Linda Martín   241–2, 246, 283
Alexander, Hartley Burr   93, 141, 265
Alexander, Hubert   265
Alexander, Thomas M.   113, 151, 265
Algerian War   190
amelioration   107, 286–7, 331, 349, 357–8, 368, 370–1, 380; *see also* meliorism
amendment   33–4, 100, 132, 270
American Communist Party   172
American Indian; *see* Native American
American Indian Citizenship Act   24
American Indian Movement (AIM)   247–8, 256, 258
American Labor Party   175
American Philosophical Association (APA)   86, 93, 120, 141, 181, 192–4, 323–5, 328
American Woman Suffrage Association (AWSA)   33–4
anarchism   93–7, 99–100, 298
Anarchist Exclusion Act   94, 96, 161
animal studies   13, 80, 284–7, 289, 305–7, 366, 368
Anthony, Susan B.   34
anthropocentric   300, 302–3
anti-communism   174
Antilynching Act   16
anti-Semitism   123, 166, 341, 361
Anzaldúa, Gloria   10, 235, 243–6, 261, 277, 279, 364–5

Appiah, Anthony   356
Arendt, Hannah   345
Argentina   232–4, 236–7, 239
army, xii   44, 51, 94, 101, 163, 165, 227, 258
authenticity   214, 224
authoritarian   295, 320, 380
authoritarianism   161, 352, 356, 360
autonomy   24, 270, 273, 303, 368
Ayer, A. J.   182, 325
Ayres, Clarence   312
Aztec people   244

Bagley, William C.   340
Baldwin, James   188, 199, 206–10, 215, 268, 341
Baldwin, James Mark   124
Banks, Dennis   248, 256
Baraka, Amiri   209, 214–15, 219, 224
Bardwell-Jones, Celia   280
Barnard College   123–4, 353
Beard, Charles   100
Beauvoir, Simone de   270
Beecher, Henry Ward   33, 41
behaviorism   292
Belgian war   137
beliefs   5–6, 9–10, 80, 102, 112, 126–7, 136–7, 182–3, 185–6, 251, 320, 330, 358–9
Bellecourt, Clyde   256
beloved community   85, 87, 89, 91, 200, 365; *see also* Great Community
Bennett, William J.   239, 300, 336–9
Berkman, Alexander   96
Bernstein, Richard J.   xiv, 327, 329–30, 344–7, 352, 360, 369, 376–7, 379–80
birth control   34, 96–8, 128, 220–1, 268, 271
Black Elk   255
Black Lives Matter   xiv, 282, 288, 354, 359, 370
Black Nationalism   212–14, 216, 218, 296
Black Panthers   209, 215–16, 224, 229, 296, 338
Black Power   204–6, 209–13, 215–25, 232, 269, 271, 363
Black Theology   221, 223–4
blackness   207, 223–4
blood   45, 61, 136, 141, 144, 231
Bloom, Allan   239, 325, 337–40, 343–4
Boas, Franz   23, 125–8, 153, 250
Boas, George   118
Boggs, Grace Lee   7, 353–5, 360
Boggs, James   7, 353–5, 360, 371
borderlands   217, 244–5, 261, 365
*Borderlands/La Frontera*   244, 246, 277

# Index

borders   xii–xiii   4, 10–11, 47, 49, 81, 134, 215, 242, 244–5, 365
Bordo, Susan   275
Bornstein, Kate   273
boundaries   71, 134–5, 155, 184, 213–15, 239, 242, 244–5, 254, 257, 362–6, 368
bourgeois   327
Bourne, Randolph   99, 102–3, 105, 155, 356
Bowne, Borden Parker   121–2, 200
Boydston, Jo Ann   325
Bradley, Francis Herbert   177
Brandom, Robert   187, 332, 346
Brazil   232, 237–8
Brightman, Edgar Sheffield   122
British Empire   45–6, 85
Brodbeck, May   6, 176, 179, 194, 337, 356
brotherhood   56, 119, 146, 202, 212
Brown, James   224
Brown, John   46
Brown v. Board of Education (US Supreme Court Decision)   203, 332
Brownmiller, Susan   270
Buber, Martin   189, 200
Buchler, Justus   118
Buckley, William   336, 340–1, 347
Bunge, Robert   257–8, 263
Bureau of Indian Affairs (BIA)   28, 247, 252–3
Bush, George H. W.   300, 318
Bush, George W.   xiv, 300, 342
Butler, Judith   93–4, 191, 273–5, 279

Cabot, Ellen Lyman   87
Cabot, Richard   87
California   85, 174, 177, 230, 256, 267
Calkins, Mary Whiton   87, 117, 129, 200, 278
Cambodia   297, 319
Cambridge Union   336
Camp, Carter   247
Campbell, James   94
Camus, Albert   204
Canada   25, 259–60, 262, 264, 318
Cannabrava, Euryalo   236
capitalism   58, 60, 62, 78, 95, 174, 176, 220, 265, 271, 291, 296
capitalists   59, 119, 137, 168, 174, 215
Card, Claudia   273
care ethics   287
Caribbean   134, 232–3, 246
Carmichael, Stokely; see Ture, Kwame
Carnap, Rudolf   166–7, 170, 172–4, 182–3, 236, 258
Carnegie, Andrew   64, 96
Carson, Rachel   284, 289, 293, 308, 316, 380
Carter, Jacoby Adeshei   160, 162
Caso, Antonio   234–5
Catholic Church   233, 237, 247
census   xi, 14
certainty   xiii–xiv, 102, 107–8, 112–13, 178–9, 282, 318, 323, 359, 374, 377–80

chaos   91, 104, 208
Chardin, Teilhard de   237
charity   13, 51, 63, 71
Charles S. Peirce Society   353
Chavez, Cesar   230, 246, 296
Cherokee Nation   45
Chicago Fire   13
Chicago riots   132; see also Pullman Strike; Haymarket affair/riot
Chicago Tribune   244
Chicago World's Fair; see Columbian Exposition
Chicanx activism   230, 232
Child, Lydia Maria   31, 41
childbearing   218, 270
childcare   36, 38, 320
China   106, 171
Chomsky, Noam   336, 341–3
Christianity   xii, 21, 26, 30, 42, 59–60, 67, 90, 221–4, 237, 242
citizenship   57, 155, 252, 332, 355
Citizenship Act   256
Citizens United v. Federal election Commission (US Supreme Court decision)   110, 371
civil disobedience   49–50, 201
civility   45, 50
civil liberties   100, 110, 322, 377
civil rights   199–205, 213, 215, 218, 220, 224–5, 232, 248, 269, 298, 320
Civil Rights Movement   199, 201, 204, 208, 211–12, 214, 216, 219, 230–1, 248–50, 253, 296
Civil War   4, 8, 14–15, 17, 19, 33, 41, 46, 50–1, 53–4, 56, 69, 89, 117, 123, 135, 153, 155, 174, 177, 218, 220, 252, 353, 367, 373, 376
classical pragmatism; see pragmatism
classism   97, 221, 350
Cleaver, Eldridge   209, 215–16
Clendennning, John   85
Cleveland, Grover   54, 62, 273
Clews, Henry   123
Clinton, Hillary Rodham   341
Clinton, William Jefferson   300, 335
Clough, Sharyn   185, 276
coal   144, 163
Code, Lorraine   276, 278, 280
Cody, William "Buffalo Bill"   23
coercion   109, 263
coexistence   6, 19, 42, 133
cognition   82, 167, 286
Cohen, Felix   254, 265
Cohen, Morris   125, 141–5, 149, 151, 153, 254–5
Colapeitro, Vincent M.   372
cold war   171, 174, 177, 189, 294, 296, 319, 335, 377
Collier, John   252–3
Collins, Patricia Hill   16, 19, 217, 277–9, 281–2, 288
colonialism   242, 245, 260, 263, 285, 302, 367
colonization   29, 125, 137, 228–9, 243, 261, 264, 286
Columbia University   61, 93–4, 100, 125–7, 141–2, 153, 171, 174, 216, 234, 250, 253, 292, 340, 344

## Index

Columbian Exposition   13–14, 21–4, 29, 39, 53–4, 71, 78, 289
Columbus   254, 372
commodities   119, 290–1, 318
communism   60, 94, 96, 170–4
Communist Party   170, 173–5, 206, 267
community   xiii, 5, 7, 10, 16, 22, 25, 27, 30–1, 44–5, 49, 51, 58, 65, 73, 79, 81, 85, 90–1, 98, 108, 122, 132, 135, 138, 141, 143–5, 147, 149–51, 157, 169, 194, 199, 201, 204, 212, 215–16, 221–2, 224, 227, 229, 241, 247, 249, 264–6, 268–9, 273–4, 294, 298, 307–8, 311, 322, 326, 339, 343–4, 348, 354–8, 366, 371, 378, 380
  and Addams   36, 64
  and Bernstein   347, 369
  and Calkins   121
  and Cohen   142
  and Davis   267
  and Deloria   251, 261
  and Dewey   76
  and Du Bois   133–4, 203
  and Follett   146, 148
  and Gilman   36
  and Katz   303
  and Lee   353
  and Leopold   290–1
  and linguistic   188
  and Malcolm X   213
  and McDermott   331
  and Peirce   36, 80, 82, 276
  and Plumwood   302
  and Quine   182, 185
  and Royce   86–9, 200, 365
  and West   251, 351
community centers   147, 221
Community Service Organization (CSO)   230
complexity   21, 96, 113, 207, 217, 268, 271, 287, 301, 365, 377
compromise   98, 147, 150–1, 168, 177, 212, 228, 357, 359, 364, 377–8
Comstock Law   97
conduct   4, 22, 35, 44, 70, 78, 106, 312, 357
Cone, James H.   209, 211, 222–4, 226, 363–4, 371
Confederacy   89
Congress on Racial Equality (CORE)   202
Connor, Eugene "Bull"   199
conquest   42, 103, 315
conscience   204, 235, 363
consciousness   43, 73, 148, 214, 238, 266, 277
Conscription Act   100, 104
conservation   98, 136–7, 291, 300
conservatives   335–6, 338, 341, 378
constitution   82, 95, 110, 252, 337
*Contemporary American Philosophy*   122, 173
continental philosophy   188, 191–2, 236, 337
continuity   10–11, 78, 80–1, 117–18, 122, 178, 185, 254, 257, 278, 292
Cooke, Willie P.   224

Cooper, Anna Julia   29–31, 38–9, 70, 85, 217, 221, 275, 282
Cooper, James Fenimore   9, 41
cooperation   19, 22, 56, 60, 63, 81, 154, 161, 169, 211, 251
Cordova, Viola   262
Cornell University   181, 243
Coulthard, Glen Sean   264, 266
counter-resistance   143, 151, 170, 194
courage   58, 87, 269, 323, 360–1, 370, 377–8
creativity   149, 151, 182
crisis   44, 50, 53, 132–3, 141, 161, 308, 321, 379–80
critical pragmatism   282, 356, 359
critique   78, 99–100, 187–8, 242–3, 250, 272, 277–8, 311–12, 326, 337, 341, 344–5, 349, 352, 369–70, 375
cruelty   72–3, 324, 371
Cruz, Juana Inez de la, Sister   241
Cuba   53–4, 64, 165, 215–16, 233, 240, 313, 364
Cuban Revolution   313
Cullen, Countee   207
cultivation   46, 156, 281
cultural pluralism   138, 153–62, 179
culture   5–6, 10–11, 26–7, 32–4, 47, 105, 126–8, 136–7, 153–6, 158–61, 205–6, 213–14, 221–2, 239–40, 244–5, 248–9, 251–2, 261–3, 337–9, 356–7
Custer, George Armstrong   248, 250

Dakota Access Pipeline (DAPL)   263, 265
Dakota Indians   25, 55
Daly, Mary   269
Darwin, Charles   21, 37, 59, 78–9, 128
Davidson, Donald   118, 182, 186, 332, 346
Davis, Angela Y.   95, 211, 216, 220–1, 224, 226, 248, 267–8, 273, 277
Dawes Act; *see* General Allotment Act
DDT   290, 293–5
de Laguna, Grace Mead   181–2
Debs, Eugene   94, 119
debt   132, 268, 318
Declaration of Independence   5, 56, 337
decolonization   11, 242–3, 252, 261–2, 364
deconstruction   190–1, 337
dehumanization   225, 238, 274, 352
Delaney, Martin   29–30
Deloria, Ella   126, 250
Deloria, Jr., Vine   247–53, 255–7, 261, 263, 266, 297, 365, 367, 371
Deloria, Sr., Vine   250
democracy   xiii–xiv, 27–8, 50, 61–3, 99, 101–2, 105–6, 108, 132, 134, 138, 143–4, 146–7, 154, 157, 160–2, 170–1, 215, 228, 235, 280, 292, 302–3, 311, 337, 339–40, 342, 349–50, 352, 374, 377–8
  and Addams   63, 374
  and Bernstein   xiv, 377
  and Bloom   343
  and Butler   274

409

# Index

and Chomsky  343
and Dewey  61, 102, 105–6, 358
and Du Bois  134, 138
and Follett  144, 146
and Kallen  153
and King  215
and Leopold  291
and Locke  157, 160–1, 379
and Rorty  343
and West  349, 352
Democratic National Convention in Chicago  319, 336
Democratic Socialists of America (DSA)  352
demonstrations  101, 199, 296, 351
Dennett, Daniel  182
deontological ethics  301
deportation  57, 96, 98–9
depression  34, 36, 53, 69–70, 157, 163–4, 358
Derrida, Jacques  82, 190
desegregation  208, 212, 254
despair  71, 201, 211, 223, 236, 282, 292, 347, 350, 369
destruction  xiii, 91, 104, 131, 168, 265, 297, 315, 355–6
Detroit  44, 215, 353–5
Dewey, Alice Chipman  61, 106
Dewey, John  xiv, 5–8, 10, 63–4, 76–7, 96, 99, 102, 105, 108, 110, 112–13, 126, 145, 163–5, 170–1, 174, 176, 179, 181, 189–90, 232, 238, 276–7, 279–81, 291, 303–4, 307–8, 312, 323–5, 328–9, 331–2, 337, 339, 341, 344, 350, 353–4, 357, 364, 370, 377
  and Addams  39, 61–2, 101, 104, 133, 366
  and Bernstein  330, 345, 347
  and Boas  127
  and Bourne  103, 356
  and Brodbeck  177–8
  and Chomsky  342–3
  and Darwin  28
  and democracy  xiii, 106, 358
  and education  107, 109, 342
  and ethics  109
  and Hirsch  340
  and Krutch  292
  and Mills  312–13, 318
  and Mumford  314–15
  and naturalism  117
  and Peirce  107
  and Plumwood  286
  and Rorty  193, 322, 349, 358
  and Sellars  118
  and Trotsky  110, 172
  and war  101, 103–4, 106, 110–11
dialectic  62
dialectical historicism  225
dialogical  345, 347
dialogue  278, 305, 337, 346, 350, 352, 377
Diamond, Irene  285
direct action  16, 71, 199

discourse  191, 232–3, 274, 345, 357, 360–1, 371, 376–7, 380
disintegration  151
dispossession  25, 252, 264
disruption  10, 54, 151, 158, 273, 308, 354, 360, 376
diversity  72, 127, 137, 154, 237, 241, 258, 338–9, 341, 344, 346; *see also* cultural pluralism; multiculturalism
Dodge, Mary Abigail (aka Gail Hamilton)  23
dogmas  xiv, 9, 42–3, 73, 105–7, 112, 144, 183, 195, 347, 352
dogmatic  xiii, 72, 106–7, 112, 321, 336, 360
dogmatism  112, 144, 160–1, 359–61, 375
domination  4, 9, 15, 145, 147, 150–1, 272, 302–3, 364, 371, 379
Donovan, Josephine  285
Douglass, Frederick  15
Drinnon, Richard  100
drugs  99, 335, 337
D'Souza, Dinesh  341
Du Bois, W. E. B.  xiii, 6, 46, 58, 133–9, 143, 145, 158, 175–6, 203–6, 221, 243–4, 249–50, 350–2, 366, 378
dualisms  32, 109, 178, 183, 186, 193, 208, 255, 281, 284–5, 304
Duran, Jane  276
Dussel, Enrique  239, 241–2, 246

Earth Day  299
Eastman, Charles (Ohiyesa)  xiii, 25–6, 28, 49, 70, 85, 254
ecofeminism  272, 283–5, 296, 302, 306
ecosystems  284, 294, 297, 300–3, 307, 365, 367
Edie, James  190
education  13–14, 28–31, 59–62, 101–2, 104–5, 107–10, 125–6, 234–6, 238, 255–6, 319–22, 336, 338–40, 342–4, 350, 373–4
Ellison, Ralph  206
Elshtain, Bethke  273, 279
Emerson, Ralph Waldo  8, 31, 34, 41–52, 117, 255, 289, 330, 343, 349, 362, 371
empire  27, 53–67, 85, 254, 360, 367
empiricism  75, 186–8, 190, 377
empowerment  277, 349
engagement  48, 72, 74, 191, 239, 260, 276–7, 282, 343, 361, 368–9, 376
England  167, 181–2, 253, 336
enslavement  155, 356, 358
environmental  284, 297, 299
environmental philosophy  283, 287, 299, 301–4, 308
environmentalism  298, 305, 308
epistemology  9, 82, 242, 250–2, 257, 276, 287, 322, 330
equal rights  31, 33, 55, 96, 218, 271, 275
Equal Rights Amendment (ERA)  270
equality  46, 201, 203–4, 212–13, 241, 248–9, 257, 265, 267–8, 270, 338–9
erotic  217, 268

410

## Index

error  9, 74, 80, 88–9, 118, 160, 173, 249, 303, 332, 368
Espionage Act  94, 98, 100
essence  7, 9, 83, 185, 223, 265, 273
establishment  9, 139, 169, 249, 347–8, 355, 369
Estes, Nick  263–6, 371
ethics  63–4, 105, 109, 124, 273, 280–1, 284–5, 287, 292, 299–301, 303, 306–7, 356–7
ethnic groups  155, 160
ethnicity  98, 242, 278
ethnography  126–7
eugenics  79, 97–8, 125, 220–1, 235, 268, 282, 374
European philosophy  21, 28, 235, 239, 258, 272
evolution  21, 23, 27, 37–8, 54, 58–9, 78–80, 292–3, 353–5
evolutionary theory  21, 23, 28, 37, 48, 54, 59, 71, 78, 177, 293
existentialism  189–90, 236, 347, 350
experience  4–6, 72–5, 80–1, 87–8, 104–8, 145–9, 156, 167–70, 181–8, 192, 205–8, 214, 217–18, 222–5, 240, 251, 262, 304–6, 358–9, 364–7
experiment  9, 61, 107, 112, 184, 331, 357, 371
experimentation  304–5, 368, 378
explanation  123, 177, 194, 341
exploitation  4, 17, 21, 136–7, 139, 213–14, 218, 220, 249, 284, 298, 356

factories  53, 103, 156
faith  311, 314, 321, 330, 350, 358, 361
fallacy  106–7, 112, 353
fallibilism  xiv–xv, 276–7, 280, 322, 329, 344–6, 358–60, 362, 364, 368, 374, 379
fallibility  173, 347, 353, 369
Fanon, Frantz  63, 204, 243, 264
Farber, Marvin  188, 195, 234
Farmers' Alliance  57, 59
farming  xii, 59, 290–1, 306
fascism  104, 106, 109–10, 160, 239, 327
fear  62, 96, 102, 107, 111, 177, 218, 274, 294, 321–2, 368, 377–8, 380
Federal Bureau of Investigation (FBI)  94, 170, 172, 228, 247–8, 267
Federal Election Commission  110, 371
Federal Writers' Project (FWP)  206
federalism  148
Feigl, Herbert  166, 187
femininity  32, 37, 267
feminism  32, 127–8, 219–20, 241, 245, 271–2, 277–8, 280–1, 286, 288, 296, 298, 302, 326, 335–7, 341
  Black Nationalism  218
  epistemology  272, 275–6, 283
  ethics  272–3, 283, 287
  first-wave  279
  liberalism  270–1, 277
  material  122
  pragmatism  8, 279–80, 282
  pragmatism (*see also* pragmatism)
  second-wave  270
  socialist  271

feminist pragmatism  277–8; *see also* pragmatism
Fenton, William N.  28
Fifteenth Amendment (US Constitution)  33
Fifth International Congress  164, 166
First World War  91, 94–5, 99, 104, 106, 111, 117, 123, 131–3, 157, 163, 314–15, 341
Fischer, Marilyn  279, 287
Flathead Indian Reservation  253
Flowers, Elizabeth  235–6
Follett, Mary Parker  141, 144, 151, 362, 371
force  xiv, 7, 23, 25, 27, 32, 37, 54, 96, 103–4, 106–7, 117, 148, 155–6, 159, 164, 171, 199, 201, 209, 211, 214, 217, 219, 251–2, 258, 263–4, 284, 362–3, 377, 380
foreign policy  319, 342
Fortune, T. Thomas  6, 17
Foucault, Michel  151, 261, 345, 349–50
Frankena, William  181–2
Frankfurt School  238
Frankfurter, Felix  154
Franklin, Christine Ladd  77, 277
free love  96, 128; *see also* love
freedom  30–1, 46–7, 102, 106–9, 156, 191–2, 212–13, 219, 223–4, 267–8, 317–18, 361
Freire, Paulo  238–9, 246
Frelinghuysen University  29
French, Marilyn  273
Frick, Henry Clay  96
Friedan, Betty  270
Frondizi, Risieri  234, 236–7, 240–1
Fuller, Margaret  29, 31–3, 41, 43–4, 48, 208, 314
future  xv, 4, 6–7, 10–11, 28, 73, 83, 85, 89, 93, 104, 109, 113, 125, 128, 138–9, 154–5, 167, 191, 193, 218, 235, 237, 245, 250, 252, 263, 279, 294, 311, 314, 324, 331, 349–71, 379–80

Gaard, Greta  285
Gadamer, Hans-Georg  345
Gage, Matilda  33
Galbraith, John Kenneth  318–22, 327, 366
Gaos, José  239
Garrett Theological Seminary  222
Garvey, Marcus  205–6
gay  182, 207, 217, 269, 326
gender  16, 18, 128, 207–8, 242, 246, 273, 275, 277–9, 284–5, 366–7
genealogy of pragmatism  8, 277, 281, 349
General Allotment Act  24, 161, 290
genocide  24–5, 27, 155, 223, 248, 252, 258, 356, 364, 370, 375
Gentry, George V.  312
Ghost Dance  xi–xii, 14, 25, 55, 125–6, 263, 265
Giddings, Franklin  123
Gifford lectures  85–6, 181, 328
Gilligan, Carol  273
Gilman, Charlotte Perkins  36–9, 41, 70, 76–7, 143, 271, 273, 279, 282, 291, 367
Giroux, Henry A.  238, 340

411

# Index

Gladden, Washington  60–1, 67, 83
Glaude, Eddie  225
God  21, 43, 137, 141, 167, 177, 222–4, 250, 336
Gödel, Kurt  166
Goldenweiser, Alexander  125, 153
Goldman, Emma  93–5, 100, 268, 371
Gordon, Lewis  225, 356
Gould, Carol  272
Gracia, Jorge J. E.  233, 235, 237, 239–41, 246
Gramsci, Antonio  350
Grande, Sandy  261
Grant, Madison  98
Gray, James  179
Great Britain  91, 165–6, 170
Great Community  90; *see also* beloved community
Great Depression  109, 163–4, 206, 230, 238, 357, 374
Great Migration  132
Great War  141, 143, 145, 153
Griffin, Susan  284
growth  9, 14, 24, 26, 37–8, 51, 54, 62, 75, 78, 102–7, 113, 154–5, 164, 221, 315, 319–21, 331, 339, 354, 356, 360, 366, 370
Gruen, Lori  285–6
Guitierrez, Gustavo  237–8, 241

Haack, Susan  332
Habermas, Jürgen  332, 345
habit  6, 21, 26–7, 37, 65, 78, 80, 82, 96, 105–7, 109, 113, 121, 128, 153, 156, 158, 161, 172, 276, 279, 285, 291, 304, 306, 313, 316, 321, 364, 369, 378, 380
Haiti  159–60, 233
Hall, David  324
Hall, G. Stanley  24, 126
Hamington, Maurice  279–80, 287
Haraway, Donna J.  122, 278, 284
Hardin, Garrett  299
Harding, Sandra G.  185, 275, 278–9, 373–4
Harding, Warren G.  94
Hargrove, Eugene  299–300
harmony  32, 55, 78, 96, 146, 154–5, 165, 169, 258, 264, 304
Harper, William Rainey  61
Harris, Leonard  28, 157, 162, 356–60, 369–71, 375, 379
Hart, Albert Bushnell  135, 145, 331
Hartshorne, Charles  181, 189, 323, 353
Harvard Divinity School  43, 51
Harvard University  77, 86–7, 117–18, 120, 135, 145, 148, 153–4, 156–7, 164–6, 181–2, 187–90, 328, 351–3, 361
Hawaii  111, 233
Hayden, Sophie  29
Haymarket affair/riot  95
Hegel, G. W. F.  62, 95, 125, 172
Hegelian  106
Heidegger, Martin  189, 191, 193, 323–4, 345
Hekman, Susan  122, 185

Held, Virginia  273
Henry, Paget  243, 246
Hester, Lee Thurman  260–1
Hickman, Larry  113
Hill, Anita  351
Hintikka, Merill B.  275
Hirsch, E. D.  239, 338–41
Hitler, Adolf  110, 165, 344
Hoagland, Sara Lucia  273
Hocking, William Ernest  87, 188–9, 234
holism  182–6, 193, 299, 303, 328–9
Holland  166
Holmes, Jr., Oliver Wendell  8, 97, 289
Holt, Edwin B.  91, 148–9
homophobia  216, 220
homosexuality  96, 165, 167, 325–6, 335, 352, 366
Hook, Sidney  9, 117, 171, 179, 344
hooks, bell  211, 216, 218–20, 226, 268, 276, 278, 282
Hookway, Christopher  346
Hoover, Herbert C  163–4, 252
Hoover, J. Edgar  94–5, 100, 172, 267
hope  10–12, 112, 161, 210–11, 313–14, 326–7, 349–52, 355, 359–62, 368–71, 378
Horkheimer, Max  238
Howard University  17, 157, 208
Howe, Julia Ward  41, 46, 51
Howison, George  122
Huerta, Dolores  230–2
Hughes, Langston  206
Hull House  34–6, 39, 61–3, 101, 104, 119, 135, 378
humanism  237–9, 292, 327
humanitarians  xii, 71
humility  73, 206, 303, 369
Hunt, William Morris  69
Hurston, Zora Neale  126, 206
Husserl, Edmund  188–90, 345
*Hypatia*  272, 277, 279
hypotheses  7, 80, 106, 305, 347, 368–9

idealism  42, 44, 86, 90–1, 117–29, 168, 173, 177, 192, 233
identity  134–5, 213–14, 222–3, 225, 240–2, 244–6, 253–4, 260–1, 264, 267, 277, 325, 327, 360–1
ideology  9, 214, 235–6, 241, 299, 303, 335, 346, 370
imagination  43, 73, 107, 207, 282, 311, 347, 353, 370–1
imitation  87, 124–5, 127, 259
immigrants  54, 94, 97–8, 101, 153–4, 254, 325–6, 337, 344, 374, 378
immigration  154, 165, 172, 338–9, 365, 373–4
Immigration Act  244, 374
Immigration Reform Act  244
immiseration  356–7, 359, 371
imperialism  61, 64, 85, 104, 204–5, 219, 297, 343, 351, 358, 370
imposition  28, 150, 205, 264, 276, 303, 363
inclusive  168, 276, 278, 284, 304, 369
incommensurability  72, 360

412

# Index

independence 4–5, 24, 87, 96, 101, 166, 190, 212–13, 228, 233, 296, 316–17
India 222, 318
Indian Appropriations Act 256
Indian boarding schools 24, 249, 253
Indian Citizenship Act 24
Indian Philosophy 21
Indian Relocation Act 255
Indian Relocation Program 258
Indian Removal Act 44, 66
Indian Reorganization Act (IRA) 96, 247, 252–4
indictments 199, 297
Indigenous North American; *see* Native American
individual 7–9, 25, 36–9, 41–3, 48–52, 60–6, 78–83, 86–90, 105–9, 126–9, 143–4, 146–50, 153–5, 213, 223–5, 253–4, 260, 262, 264, 266, 268, 270, 290–3, 318–19, 363–8
individualism 27, 39, 60, 76, 78, 108–9, 215, 290, 367
individualistic 24, 38, 49, 63, 111, 318
industrial capitalism xiii, 4, 26, 83, 138, 164, 220, 252, 261
industrialization 14, 41, 60
inequality 46, 154, 172, 201, 313, 320, 351, 356
inquirers 6, 107, 276
inquiry 6–7, 61–3, 105–8, 112–13, 143, 164, 173, 178, 279–80, 304, 306, 312, 346–7, 353, 358, 368–71
instrumentalism 102, 105, 112, 304, 356
insurrect 133, 354–60, 370, 376
integration 21, 144–5, 147, 150–1, 161, 202–4, 208–9, 212, 222, 332
intelligence 18, 38, 46, 57, 78, 102–4, 106–9, 119, 156, 187, 304–5
Inter-American Journal of Philosophy 394
International Committee of Women for Permanent Peace (ICWPP) 99–100
intersectionality 282, 288
intolerance 73, 95, 107, 112, 128, 160–1, 359
invasion xiii–xiv, 9, 53, 165, 171, 297
Iraq xiii–xiv, 319, 376
Italy 234, 356

Jackson, Andrew 44, 66
Jackson State University 297
Jaggar, Alison M. 273, 275
James, C. L. R. 243, 354
James, Henry 69
James, William xiii, 6, 63–4, 66, 69–77, 80, 85, 88, 90, 96, 113, 120, 122, 124–5, 134–5, 144, 148–9, 153, 159, 174, 176, 188–90, 192, 227, 233, 236–7, 276, 279, 281, 289, 292, 308, 312, 316, 323–5, 328–32, 341, 345, 350, 353–4, 364, 368, 377, 380
Japan 106, 163, 170–1, 258
Jesus Christ xi, 221–4
Jim Crow 52, 59, 132, 203, 214, 351, 356
Johansen, Bruce 254
John Dewey Society 347
Johns Hopkins University 24, 61, 77, 85, 141

Johnson, James Weldon 206
Johnson, Lyndon B 201, 296, 298
Johnson, Mark 262
Jones, LeRoi; *see* Baraka, Amiri
Jørgensen, Jørgen 166
*Journal of Philosophy* 128, 236
judgment 7, 89, 101, 107–8, 112, 169, 282, 345, 358–9

Kallen, Horace M. 125, 153–7, 159, 162, 165–70, 176, 190, 291, 341, 344, 367
Kant, Immanuel 82, 193, 235
Katz, Eric 302–3, 306
Keller, Evelyn Fox 185, 275
Kellogg, Laura Cornelius 27–8
Kennedy, John F. 202, 212, 253, 295, 320
Kennedy, Robert 190, 201, 319
Kent State University 297–8
Khatibi, Abdelhebis 242
Kicking Bear xi–xii, 9, 11, 25, 28, 265
King, Jr, Martin Luther 190, 210, 319, 338
Kinkela, David 295–6
kinship 79, 265
Kitcher, Philip 332
Kloppenberg, James T. 378
Knight, Louise W. 279
knowledge 8–9, 11, 48–9, 64, 74–5, 105, 112, 118, 138, 165–8, 187–8, 251, 257–8, 275–8, 294–5, 315–16, 323–4, 327–8, 338–40, 369–70
Knudson, Albert C. 122
Korean War 174–5, 258, 319
Krikorian, Yervant H. 117
Krutch, Joseph Wood 289, 292–3, 299, 308
Ku Klux Klan 153–4, 202, 373
Kuklick, Bruce 41
Kymlicka, Will 260

labor 17–19, 36–9, 53–7, 65–7, 119–21, 132, 147, 163–4, 267–8, 285–6, 316–18
labor laws 60, 352
labor struggles 93, 120
labor unions 145, 317, 343
laborers 19, 56–8, 119, 137, 267
Lachs, John 5, 192–3
Lakota xi–xii, 28, 54, 250, 257–8
Lamarck, Jean-Baptiste 37, 78
land 13–14, 17–19, 23–4, 26–8, 44, 56–9, 66, 132, 137–8, 165, 212–14, 229, 231, 247–56, 261, 263–5, 283–4, 290–2, 364–6
land redistribution 23, 231, 249
language 22, 24, 81–2, 136, 164–5, 167–8, 177–8, 181–8, 190, 243–4, 257–8, 284–5, 322, 324, 337–8
Larrabee, Harold A. 117
Laski, Harold 143, 148
Latin American, philosophy 57, 227–46, 261, 313
Latinx experience 241
Latour, Bruno 124
Lavery, Grace E. 281

413

# Index

League for Independent Political Action (LIPA)   291
League of Nations   104, 111, 131, 141
Lee, Spike   214
Lenin, Vladimir   131, 322
Leopold, Aldo   289–92, 294–5, 299, 304, 308
Lewis, C. I.   175–6, 183, 187, 202, 236
Lewis, David   182
Lewis, John   202
Lewis, Perry   181–2
liberalism   45, 105–6, 110, 171–2, 264, 318, 326, 336
liberation   106, 203–4, 209, 214–15, 219, 222, 224–5, 229, 233, 237–9, 298, 370–1
Liberia College   135
Light, Andrew   302, 306
Lincoln, Abraham   23, 34, 50
linguistic turn   176, 178, 182, 184, 186, 188, 193, 323
Lippmann, Walter   9
literature   6, 12–13, 24, 34, 157, 159–60, 206, 214, 232, 234, 329
Lloyd, Genevieve   272, 280
Locke, Alain Leroy   xiii, 86, 153, 156, 214, 281–2, 291, 332, 356, 359, 365, 375, 377–9
Locke, John   206
Loewenberg, J.   173, 174, 176
Logic   xii–xiii, 77, 82, 87, 107–8, 177–8, 183, 237, 286–7, 302, 328
logical empiricism   167–8, 170, 195
logical positivism   163–83, 187, 323, 337
logicians   31, 77, 389
Lorde, Audre   211, 216–17, 220–1, 226, 268–9, 277, 371
Lorenz, Konrad   292
love   13, 25, 27, 31–2, 43, 50, 56–7, 59–60, 73, 78–9, 89, 96–7, 112–13, 121, 135, 142, 167, 205, 207–9, 211, 216–17, 235, 284, 290–1, 298, 357, 360, 362–3, 365, 373; *see also* free love
Lowell, Josephine Shaw   41, 46, 51
Lowie, Robert   125
Lugones, Maria   155
lynch laws   15–16, 161
lynching   15–16, 19, 123, 132, 136, 218, 220, 380
Lysaker, John   4–5, 10, 42

MacArthur, Douglas   163, 171
McBride, Lee   357
McCarran-Walter Act (Immigration and Nationality Act)   172
McCarthy, Joseph   171–2, 179, 314, 336, 377
McCarthyism   176, 189, 268, 289, 318, 347
McCumber, John   176
McDermott, John J.   4, 11, 91, 193, 325, 330–1, 350, 369, 371, 380
McDonald, McDonald   308
McDowell, John   187, 346
McKay, Claude   206
McKenna, Erin   279, 282, 286–7, 299, 306
McKinley, William   94, 96
McLaren, Peter   238

MacMullan, Terrance   394
McNickle, D. A.   253–4
McPherson, Dennis   262
Madison, James   123
Malcolm X   211, 214, 225
Maldonado-Torres, Nelson   246
management   96, 147, 233
manifest destiny   42, 259
Marcel, Gabriel   225
Marcus, Ruth   193–4
Marcuse, Herbert   238, 267
Maritain, Jacques   237
marriage   42, 45, 77, 95–6, 124, 127, 183, 218, 220, 269, 283
Marvin, Walter T.   91
Marx, Karl   142, 171–2, 264, 292, 313, 328, 350, 354
Marxism   171–2, 214–15, 237, 240, 261, 298, 318, 347
Marxists   272, 347, 352
masculinity   32, 37, 208
masses   18, 22, 30, 59, 97, 110, 139, 316, 338, 355, 360
mathematics   77, 142, 181, 183, 346
Mead, George Herbert   234, 311–12, 330, 353–4
meliorism; *see also* amelioration
melting pot   101, 154
Mendieta, Eduardo   246
mentalism   122
Merchant, Carolyn   284
mestiza consciousness   10, 243, 245
mestizaje   235, 240, 244
metaethics   181, 347
metaphor   66, 168–9
Metaphysical Club   8, 70
metaphysics   77, 122, 124, 177, 181, 250, 252, 287; *see also* ontology
methodology   237, 275, 280
Mexico   110, 172, 231–2, 234–5, 237, 240, 244
Michigan   32, 61, 176, 187, 211
Mies, Maria   285
Mignolo, Walter   242–3, 246
Miles, General Nelson   xi, 13, 53, 71, 125, 227
militarism   4, 121, 285, 352
militarization   123, 380
Miller, David   312
Mills, C. Wright   8, 206, 311–14, 316–18, 322, 326, 363
minorities   123, 147, 167, 200, 242, 252, 284–5, 287, 320, 337
Minteer, Ben A.   302–3
Misak, Cheryl J   332, 346
Modern Philosophy   85, 87
monism   72, 75, 301, 341
Montague, William Pepperell   90–1, 234
Moore, Addison   70
Moore, G. E.   187
moral theories   78, 120–1, 301, 358
Morrill Act   23
Morris, Charles   170, 312, 354
Morrow, William   392

## Index

motherhood 96
Mott, Lucrecia 31, 33
Muir, John 284, 289–90, 299–301
multiculturalism 156, 191, 239, 325–6, 335–6, 341
Mumford, Lewis 314–16, 322, 363–4
Murphey, Murray 235
music 45, 160, 167, 170, 214, 284, 349, 361
Mussolini 356
Myers, Gerald 69
myth 109, 183, 188, 218, 220, 259, 268, 270
Myth of the Machine 315, 362

Naess, Arne 299–300
Nagel, Ernest 117
National American Woman Suffrage Association 34
National Association for the Advancement of Colored People (NAACP) 25, 133–4, 165, 202
National Civil Liberties Bureau 100
National Civil Liberties Bureau (later ACLU) 100, 341
National Council of American Indians (NCAI) 248, 250, 253
National Endowment for the Humanities (NEH) 300, 336
National Farm Workers Association (NFWA) 230–1
National Organization for Women (NOW) 270
National Woman Suffrage Association (NWSA) 33–4
nationalism 7, 57, 102, 205, 213, 227–8, 271, 358
nationalist 373–4
nationhood 172, 214, 261
Nation of Islam 212–14, 242, 367
Native American xi, 10, 13–14, 23–9, 32–3, 48–9, 54, 70–1, 141, 155, 169, 184, 221, 223, 232, 244, 247–58, 261–3, 265–6, 290, 296, 352, 356, 364
native peoples xi–xiii, 13–14, 23, 27, 32, 48, 125, 155, 247–8, 254, 258–9, 261–2
*Native Pragmatism* 8, 255
natives 126, 184
naturalism 117–29, 195, 266, 276, 284
nature xii–xiii, 17–18, 26–7, 32, 37–8, 42–3, 47–9, 71–2, 118, 147–8, 150–1, 177–8, 207–8, 284–5, 289–95, 299–308, 319–20, 346–7
Navajo (Diné) Nation 23, 253
Nazi Germany 98, 165, 252, 317, 356
Nazis 165–6, 168, 315
Negro 15, 30, 45, 58, 133–5, 157, 160, 201, 204, 211
negro race 30, 64, 136, 157
Neihardt 255
Nelson, Lynn Hankinson 185, 195, 276
neopragmatism 143, 246, 347, 350, 355
Neurath, Otto 166–70, 179, 236, 258
neutrality 93, 143, 170, 194, 276, 315
New Deal 164, 254, 357
*New Mandarins* 341
new mestiza 244–5, 277
Newton, Huey 119, 209, 215–16, 224, 291
nihilism 193, 347, 351, 361
Nineteenth Amendment 34, 100

Nixon, Richard 253, 256, 297–8, 319, 332
non-citizens 56, 172, 352
nonviolence 202, 209, 211, 222, 230–1
North American Society for Social Philosophy (NASSP) 245, 298
Northrop, F. S. C. 234–6
Norton, Bryan G. 308
Nussbaum, Martha 155, 241, 344

Obama, Barack Hussein 341, 376–9
obligations 65, 173, 264, 299, 315, 375
Ohiyesa; *see* Eastman
Okin, Susan Moller 273, 279
Omaha Platform 56
ontology 6, 11, 72, 75, 108, 179, 184, 272, 368; *see also* metaphysics
oppression 4–5, 16, 18, 30–1, 33, 58, 83, 91, 98, 121, 123–4, 128, 134, 136–7, 157, 199–201, 203, 205, 207, 209, 215, 217–24, 229, 238–9, 241, 243, 245–6, 256, 259, 267, 272, 278, 282, 284–5, 302, 320, 350–1, 354, 356–7, 364, 370–1, 375
Orenstein, Gloria Feman 28
Organization of Afro-American Unity (OAAU) 213
Orosco, José-Antonio 230–1, 246
Outlaw, Lucius 356
outrage 17, 45

pacifism 65, 102, 104, 121, 341
pacifists 99, 102, 104
Panic of 1893 52–3
Pan-Indian Movement 261
Pappas, Gregory Fernando 246
paradox xv, 136–7, 207–8, 339, 359
Parker, Arthur C. 26–8, 70
Parsons, Elsie Clews 129
passage 33–4, 44, 46, 66, 98, 211, 252, 255, 321, 336
past xiii, 4, 7, 9–10, 42, 50, 58, 66, 78, 80, 89, 93, 98, 105, 108, 111, 113, 143, 147, 149, 165, 168, 177, 179, 183, 185, 191, 194, 213, 222, 224–5, 235, 237, 250, 252, 259, 264, 268, 294, 307, 311, 324, 330, 337, 346, 350, 355, 364, 367–71, 375–6
Pateman, Carole 273
patriarchy 219–20
Patriot Act 352
patriotism 18, 99–100, 104, 133, 161, 173, 271, 327, 342, 352
peace 50–1, 64–5, 99–100, 102, 104, 145, 172–3, 261, 285, 375
Peace Information Center (PIC) 175
Pearson, Karl 125, 127, 153
Peirce, Charles Sanders 69–70, 77–83, 86–7, 89, 107, 245–6, 276, 281, 329–31, 346, 353, 364–5, 367–8
Peirce, Juliette Pourtalai 77
Peirce, Melusina Fay 36, 277
People's Lobby 163
People's Party 55–6, 58
Perry, Ralph Barton 90–1, 236, 325

415

# Index

person   29, 35, 43, 47, 49, 51–2, 55, 60, 62, 71–5, 77, 79, 85, 87–8, 93, 96, 102, 105, 108, 121–2, 127, 129, 136, 143, 148, 150, 153–5, 157, 159, 163, 172, 175, 179, 187, 194, 200–1, 209, 211–12, 215, 217, 224–5, 244–5, 247–8, 251–2, 257, 262, 269, 273–5, 279, 295–6, 299, 302, 306, 308, 315–17, 343, 350–1, 357–8, 362–3, 367, 378
personalism   121–2, 200
personality   96, 200, 245, 251
personhood   251–2, 357
phenomenology   181, 188–90, 236, 255, 273, 279, 298
philosophy of science   167, 176, 179, 181, 236, 275, 287, 328, 346
Philosophy of Struggle   356
physics   72, 112, 125, 166, 183, 185, 311
Pinchot, Gifford   300
Pine Ridge Agency   xi–xii
Pine Ridge reservation   xi–xii, 13, 247–8, 252
Pitkin, Walter B.   9
place   xiii–xiv, 4–5, 10–11, 48–9, 54–5, 153–6, 188–9, 191–2, 203–4, 224, 231, 241, 244–5, 251–2, 264–5, 274–5, 278, 300, 358–9, 362–7
Planned Parenthood   97, 341
Plaza de las Armas   227
Plessy v. Ferguson   52, 203
Plumwood, Val   286–7, 301–2, 308
pluralism   xiii–xv, 9–11, 71–4, 105, 148, 153–5, 159–62, 167, 194, 251, 278, 301–3, 324, 328–9, 339, 346, 358, 360, 362, 364, 366, 368, 376–9
pluralistic   8, 72, 144, 211, 274, 306, 323, 331, 343, 347, 368, 371
Pokagon, Simon   13, 19, 24
polarization   xiv, 335, 350, 361
politics   xiv, 6, 17, 19, 50, 164, 166–7, 170–2, 185, 194, 212–13, 269, 273, 323
Poor People's Campaign   215, 248
Postel, Charles   55, 67
post-structuralism   188, 190–1, 298
post-truth   375
power   25, 33, 106, 144–6, 150–1, 164, 204, 217–20, 225, 251–2, 257, 261, 271, 273, 282, 312–21, 341–4, 362–4, 379–80; see also Black Power; Red Power
pragmatism   8–9, 70–2, 74–6, 112, 148, 176–7, 182–4, 194, 232, 246, 274, 276–7, 280–2, 292, 302–8, 311–12, 322–5, 327–30, 332, 337, 340–1, 346–7, 349–50, 354–9
    Absolute Pragmatism   90
    Deweyan pragmatism   103, 113, 179
    feminist pragmatism   278–9
    Jamesian pragmatism   125, 135
    prophetic pragmatism   349–50
    Radical Black Feminist Pragmatism   282
Pratt, Scott L.   8, 10, 28, 70, 125, 254, 372, 374
precarious   177, 265, 274
prejudice   82, 101, 136, 219, 262, 280, 369
present   4–8, 11–12, 32–4, 70–3, 89–91, 108–9, 135–8, 141–3, 147–8, 170–2, 183–5, 190–3, 218–22, 227–8, 267–8, 276–7, 338–41, 359–61, 369–71, 376–8
Presidential Medal of Freedom   172, 299, 318
prestige   235, 313, 317
pride   62, 136, 141, 213, 325–6
Principia Mathematica   181
prison   94, 103, 166, 211–12, 228, 296, 361
privilege   33, 71, 76, 89, 124, 219, 270, 343, 371
progress   9, 13–15, 22, 62–4, 79, 93, 98, 106, 233, 274, 290, 332
Progressive Labor Party (PLP)   328
progressives   110, 340
propaganda   142, 229, 342
prophetic pragmatism   349–51, 355; see also pragmatism
psychology   61, 72, 113, 120, 135, 166, 270, 311, 313
public goods   36, 319
Puerto Rico   54, 64, 227–9, 233, 313
Pullman, George M.   53
Pullman Strike   xi, 52–3, 61, 63, 78, 94–5, 105
purpose   5, 9, 11–13, 69–70, 86–8, 98–9, 107–8, 121–2, 147–8, 150, 222–3, 251, 296, 304–5, 330–1, 355, 358–60, 363, 371
Putnam, Frederick Ward   23, 126
Putnam, Hilary   327, 352
Putnam, Ruth Anna   328

quest   4, 6, 58, 90, 313, 338
Quijano, Anibal   232, 242, 246
Quine, W. V. O.   118, 182–7, 193–5, 276, 332, 346

Rabb, J. Douglas   262
race   15–19, 26–33, 44–6, 56–9, 64–5, 85–9, 97–8, 131–9, 156–60, 201–5, 207–9, 211–18, 235, 242, 276–7, 336–41, 353–6, 360–1; see also racism
race riots   131, 133, 135–7, 139, 157
racism   57, 123, 126, 133–4, 136, 216, 219–21, 223, 242, 245–6, 249, 252, 268, 274, 277; see also race
racists   172, 219, 223
Radical Black Feminist Pragmatism (RBFP)   282; see also pragmatism
radical empiricism   75, 190, 279
Radin, Paul   125
rage   326, 341
Ralston, Shane   302, 304
Ramberg, Bjorn   346
Randall, Jr., John Herman   117–18
Randolph, Philip A.   202
rape   16, 218, 220, 267, 270, 283, 337, 364, 371
rationalism   75, 82, 355
Rauschenbusch, Walter   53, 60, 67
Rawls, John   328, 352, 360
Reagan, Ronald   172, 244, 300, 335–6
realism   82–3, 91, 117–18, 177, 281, 324, 328
    critical   118, 177, 187
    new   91, 118
reality   75, 195, 219, 255, 257, 273, 275, 312, 328
reasoning   82–3, 122, 280

416

# Index

reciprocity   27, 159–61, 263, 360
reconciliation   62, 200, 224, 264
reconstruction (era)   14, 18, 105, 109, 113, 126, 214, 220, 278, 280, 368
*Red Pedagogy*   261
Red Power   247–65
reformation   34, 143
relationality   25, 151, 282, 330
relativism   73–4, 159, 161, 167, 262, 304, 323–4, 329, 337, 345–6, 377
reproduction   37, 97, 107, 268
Rescher, Nicolas   187
reservations (American Indian)   xi–xii, 247, 252–3, 255–6, 263
resistance   xiii–xv, 9–11, 27–8, 43–5, 90–1, 113, 151, 158, 204–5, 208–9, 220–1, 228–30, 259, 262–5, 355–7, 362, 364–9, 375–6, 379
Reyes, Alfonso   234
Rich, Adrienne   269–70
Ridge, John (Walker-on-the-Mountains)   44
Rios, Antonio   230
riots   131–3, 163–4, 215, 296, 327, 354–5
Rogers, Melvin   282, 311
Rolston III, Holmes   300, 302
Romanell, Patrick   234
Romero, Francisco   234
Romney, George W.   332
Roosevelt, Franklin D.   164–5, 202, 318
Roosevelt, Theodore   60, 99, 123, 125, 164, 234
Rorty, Richard   60, 178, 185, 193, 276, 324–6, 349, 358
Rosebud Reservation   257
Ross, Sr., Fred   230
Routley, Richard (also Richard Sylvan)   299, 301
Roybal, Edward   230
Royce, Josiah   85–91, 117–18, 120, 122, 124–5, 134–5, 142, 148–9, 153, 173, 176–7, 325
Ruddick, Sara   273
Russell, Bertrand   74–5, 166, 178, 181, 187, 247
Russia   109, 111, 131, 142, 173
Ryder, John   330

sacrifice   56, 63, 147, 165, 228–9, 231, 303, 352
sameness   11, 200, 365–6
San Francisco   85, 222, 246, 256
Sandburg, Carl   132–3
Sanger, Margaret   93, 96, 271
Santayana, George   5, 118, 135, 330
Saussure, Ferdinand   82
savagism   22, 24, 26, 28, 44, 48, 204
Schneider, Herbert   234–5
Schoolcraft, Jane   33
Schutte, Ofelia   241–2, 246
science   22–4, 59, 77–8, 125, 165–6, 168–70, 172–3, 178, 183, 185–6, 195, 272, 275–6, 283–4, 289–93, 314–16, 328, 341
Seale, Bobby   209, 296
Searle, John   239

Second World War   111, 117, 126, 160–4, 171–2, 176, 182, 187–8, 232, 247, 252–3
security   45, 63, 171–2, 213, 221, 274, 322, 352
Sedgwick, Henry   144
Sedition Act   94, 98, 161
segregation   27, 57, 123, 135, 200–3, 206, 222, 254, 332
Seigfried, Charlene Haddock   11, 277–81, 288, 378
self-determination   209, 217, 224, 254, 256–7, 261, 265, 363–4
selfish   128, 164
Sellars, Roy Wood   117–18, 187
Sellars, Wilfrid   118, 122, 187–8, 193, 195, 332, 344, 346
semantics   237
semiotics   77, 81
Seneca Falls   33
settlement movement/house   35–6, 51, 86, 146
sexism   15, 36, 194, 216, 218–21, 274, 285, 350, 364
Sheffer, Henry   176, 182, 187
Shiva, Vandana   285
sign   81–2
Simpson, Leanne   264, 366, 371
Singer, Jr. A. E.   328
skepticism   xiv, 303, 328
Skinner, B. F.   292
slavery   17–19, 31, 44–7, 49–50, 132, 160, 201, 208–9, 218–21, 267–8, 356–8, 364
Smith, John Edwin   5, 193, 254, 325, 330–1, 380
Smith, Thomas Vernon   234
social gospel movement   25, 51, 53–67, 71, 100, 199, 221
socialism   18, 60, 66, 73, 94–6, 142, 172, 221, 229, 245, 252, 272, 352
Socialist Workers Party   354
sociality   22, 200
Society for Phenomenology and Existential Philosophy (SPEP)   190–1, 193
Society for the Advancement of American Philosophy (SAAP)   193
Society of American Indians (SAI)   24–8, 250
Society of Women in Philosophy (SWIP)   283
sociologists   148, 150, 166, 311–12, 329
sociology   22, 123–4, 133, 243, 279, 311–13
soldiers   xi–xii, 61, 99, 102, 131–2, 297, 352
solidarity   60, 125, 141, 160, 203, 246, 324, 345
Sorrell, Kory   276
Southern Christian Leadership Conference (SCLC)   199, 201–2, 211, 221, 298, 363
Soviet Union   99, 110–12, 170–1, 175, 192, 318, 320–1, 340
Spanish Civil War   174
Spaulding, Edward Gleason   91
species   24, 37–8, 284–5, 290, 297, 301, 305–7, 367
Spelman, Elizabeth   272
Spencer, Herbert   21, 233
Stalin, Joseph   110, 170
Standing Bear, Henry   28

417

# Index

Standing Bear, Luther   xiii, 27–8, 49, 70, 137, 192, 212, 254, 263, 365
Standing Rock reservation   250, 263
starvation   356, 358, 380
Stein, Gertrude   146
Steinem, Gloria   271
Stone, Lucy   34
Stowe, Harriet Beecher   206
strikes   61–3, 96
Student Nonviolent Coordinating Committee (SNCC)   202, 204, 209, 296, 298
Students for a Democratic Society (SDS)   297–8, 328
Stuhr, John   5
suffrage movement   29–30, 33, 128, 201, 254, 268, 270
Sullivan, Shannon   279
Sumner, William Graham   9, 54, 64, 71, 313
suppression   xv, 54, 95, 109, 123, 165, 176, 194, 217
sympathy   30, 51, 57, 63, 73, 79, 81, 99, 159, 172, 175, 279

Talisse, Robert B.   179
Tarde, Gabriel de   124–5, 127
Tarski, Alfred   174, 182
Tax Reform Act   321
Taylor, Charles   260
technology   14, 22, 109, 111, 126, 258, 312–16, 319–20, 341, 360, 380
tenacity   80, 356–7, 368
Termination Acts (Indian)   24, 253–4
terrorism   xiii–xiv, 203, 315, 322, 336, 342–3, 352, 360
theology   117, 122, 154, 177, 189, 222–3, 230, 237, 250, 272
Thomas, Clarence   351
Thompson, Anna Boynton   145
Thompson, Paul B.   308
Thoreau, Henry David   31, 41, 47–50, 117, 255, 289
Thurman, Howard   221
Ticknor, Anna Eliot   145
Tillich, Paul   189
tolerance   54, 72–4, 123, 159–61, 168, 170, 303–4, 323, 328–9, 377, 380
Toomer, Jean   206
Toynbee Hall   34–5
tragedy   155–6, 244–5, 299, 370
transcendence   168, 272
treason   93, 103
Treaty of Versailles   104, 131
Trilling, Lionel   8
Trotsky, Leon   110, 322, 354
Trout, Lara   276
Truman, Harry S.   170, 289, 318
Trump, Donald   245, 263
truth   70, 72–4, 105, 112, 142, 158, 182–3, 189, 218, 225, 322, 324, 328, 343–4, 346, 374–5
Truth, Sojourner   33, 218
Tuana, Nancy   185, 272
Tuck, Eve   11
Tufts, James Hayden   109, 307

Tully, James   260
Tunstall, Dwayne   225
Ture, Kwame   204, 209, 211, 248, 371
Turner, Dale   259–62
Twain, Mark   64

U. S. S. R; *see* Soviet Union
uncertainty   72, 107–8, 156, 282
Unger, Roberto   349
unionization   35, 63, 352
unions   62, 119, 148
United Farm Workers (UFW)   230–2
United Nations   111, 164, 171
unity   43, 61–2, 71, 105, 146, 164–70, 199, 212–13, 341, 364
Unity of Science; *see* unity
Universal Negro Improvement Association (UNIA)   205
Universal Peace Congress   64
University of California, Los Angeles (UCLA)   70, 85, 166, 170, 173–4, 218, 236, 267, 318, 328
University of Chicago   61, 76, 166, 189, 235, 312–13, 323, 337, 344, 353–4
Ureña, Pedro Henríquez   234
US Congress   55, 58, 77, 123, 270, 283, 352
US Department of Justice   175, 245
US mail   53–4, 97
US Secretary of State   165, 175
utilitarian ethics   301, 314

Vallega, Alejandro   246
Van Buren, Martin   44–5
Vasconcelos, José   98, 234–5, 244
Veblen, Thorstein   312–14, 316, 318
veterans   8, 14, 163–4, 220
Vidal, Gore   336
Vienna Circle   125, 166–7, 182
Vietnam   191, 271, 296–8, 319–20, 327
Vietnam War   188, 296–8, 308, 319, 327, 335
Vizenor, Gerald   258–60, 266
vulnerability   274, 285–6

Waismann, Frederick   166
Waithe, Mary Ellen   272
*wakan˛, Wakantan˛ka*,   255, 257–8
Walker, Margaret   206
Wall Street   56–7, 79
Wallace, George   202
Wang, Hao   182
war on drugs   342
war on terror   343, 377
Ward, Lester F.   37
warranted assertions   112
Warren, Karen J.   203, 272, 284–5
Washington, Booker T.   29, 64, 67
Watson, Thomas E.   58–9
Wayne Yang, K.   11
weapons   xii, 52, 112, 131, 209, 247–8, 267, 296–7, 316

# Index

Weatherford, Jack   254
Weiss, Paul   189, 353
Wellesley College   119, 323
Wells-Barnett, Ida B.   15–19, 29, 36, 70, 132–3
Wendell, John   157
West, Cornel   8, 210–11, 224, 226, 274, 277, 318, 344, 349, 355–6
Weston, Anthony   302, 305–6
Westra, Laura   302
*White Collar*   313, 316
White Earth Reservation   258
Whitehead, Alfred North   166, 181–2, 189, 195, 236, 292, 308, 323, 330, 353
whiteness   17, 136–7, 205, 209, 223–4, 249
Whitman, Walt   52
Wiggins, Forrest O.   174
Wilshire, Bruce   193–4, 255
Wilson, Dick   247, 252
Wilson, Woodrow   93, 99–101, 104, 131, 134, 141, 153, 186, 227, 247
Wisconsin   32, 44, 56, 170, 253
wisdom   47, 55, 87, 138, 142, 185, 300, 306, 319, 321, 331
Wittgenstein, Ludwig   193, 323–4, 328–9, 349
Women of All Red Nations (WARN)   224

Women Striking for Peace (WSP)   296
Women's Peace Party (WPP)   99–100
Woodly, Deva R.   282
Works Progress Administration (WPA)   206, 354
World Columbian Exposition; *see* Columbian Exposition
World Health Organization (WHO)   295
World Trade Center   xiii, 316
Wounded Knee   xii–xiii, xv, 13, 53, 71, 248, 256, 263, 376
Wounded Knee Creek   xi, 6, 25, 380
Wounded Knee Massacre   13, 25, 255
Wright, Chauncey   289
Wright, Richard   204, 207, 210,

Yale Divinity School   117, 352
Young, Iris Marion   143, 273, 279
Young Lords Party (YLP)   229

Zack, Naomi   277
Zea, Leopoldo   239–41, 246
Zinn, Howard   164
Zionism   165
Zuni people   123